ENGLISH TO THE MAX

ENGLISH TO THE MAX

1,200 PRACTICE QUESTIONS TO MAXIMIZE YOUR ENGLISH POWER

LEARNINGEXPRESS®

NEW YORK

Copyright © 2008 LearningExpress, LLC.

All rights reserved under International and Pan-American Copyright Conventions. Published in the United States by LearningExpress, LLC, New York.

Library of Congress Cataloging-in-Publication Data:
English to the max: 1,200 practice questions to maximize your English power.
    p. cm.
ISBN 978-1-57685-704-5 (1-57685-704-2)
1. English language—Examinations, questions, etc.   I. LearningExpress (Organization)
PE1114.E645   2008
428.0076—dc22

2008012379

Printed in the United States of America

9 8 7 6 5 4 3 2 1

First Edition

For more information or to place an order, contact LearningExpress at:
  2 Rector Street
  26th Floor
  New York, NY 10006

Or visit us at:
  www.learnatest.com

Contents

ENGLISH
TO THE MAX

Introduction

THE PROLIFIC WRITER and inventor Benjamin Franklin once said: "Failing to prepare is preparing to fail." As Franklin astutely pointed out, preparation is the key to success. *English to the Max: 1,200 Practice Questions to Maximize Your English Power* prepares you for success by powering up your verbal, reading, writing, and critical thinking skills through intensive English review and practice. Mastering the assignments in this book will help you succeed on many levels: in your language arts classes, on assessment and entrance exams, in the data-driven multimedia college and workplace environment that you will be entering in the near future, and as a lifelong learner. To help you reach your goals, this handbook offers several features:

- a streamlined review of punctuation, modifiers, subject-verb agreement, tense agreement, and antecedent-pronoun agreement, with practice questions organized at increasing levels of difficulty
- lessons on sentence structure basics and pointers on identifying contextual clues in sentence-completion test questions
- paragraph development lessons with practice exercises targeted at different skill levels
- individualized mini-lessons and writing prompts for three common essay forms—persuasive, expository, and narrative—including essay models and detailed rubrics for scoring
- 77 literary response writing prompts for use in timed practice writing sessions
- a chapter on essay writing with guidelines for crafting first-rate introductory, supporting, and concluding paragraphs
- a revision checklist for use during essay writing practice
- critical reading passages featuring intensive targeted reading and critical analysis practice

- supplementary "Get a Grip" grammar, research, writing, and reading sidebars featuring useful information
- "Word Bite" definitions throughout the book
- a multimedia grammar resource list
- a vocabulary-building list of supplementary multimedia resources
- a literary devices crossword puzzle
- a multicultural enrichment reading list featuring titles geared to middle school to high school level
- detailed answer keys
- a glossary

How should you use this book? First, set a goal. What are you trying to achieve? By the time the middle school years roll around, most students are well aware of their grasp of grammar (or lack thereof) or their ability (or inability) to create a terrific lead sentence. Are you an English hater? Would you rather slurp curdled milk spiked with cayenne pepper than write an essay? Or are you a book fiend who burns through the reading list like a fire blazing through a parched forest? Are you good at grammar? Do you ace your essays? Now think about the areas where a little extra rehab is needed. Do you need help unblocking writer's block? Do you mangle your modifiers? Do you know what a modifier is?

Unless you are in dire danger of failing a class because of a particularly weak area, it is strongly recommended that you tackle the chapters in this book in chronological order. LearningExpress encourages you to highlight the tips and passages that are most essential to your particular area of focus. Don't be afraid to create graffiti around the borders of the pages by doodling notes and spotlighting important passages with gobs of neon highlighter. You might want to place a double underline under the words or sentences that you want to focus on or place your own personal notes

or symbols (such as +++▲♥$☺☻##!?//<>) by important words or sentences.

It's also suggested that you purchase a minute timer so that you can time your writing practices. Timed writing practices ranging from 15 to 30 minutes will accustom you to outlining, brainstorming, and writing under pressure.

English to the Max covers a lot of ground, but if you really want to excel in your studies, it's important to get into the habit of reading. Do you read the daily newspaper? Read the movie reviews and study the way the critic analyzes the movie failures and the movies that are destined for Oscar gold. Do you like to read people's opinions about the latest news and events? Head straight to the editorial section and dig right in! If you've had a bad day at school and you need a laugh, the comics section will cheer you up. And if you think that cartoons are just for kids, you might be interested to know that there are plenty of adults who enjoy reading or watching their favorite cartoons. Bart Simpson rules!

It is highly recommended that you supplement the lessons and practice sessions in this book with at least a half hour of supplementary reading per day. To help you achieve your reading goals, we've included an enrichment reading list in Chapter 9, "Critical Reading," to help you find appropriate reading selections. Enjoy!

Get a Grip Study Tip

While you are studying, it's okay to listen to soft classical music, but be sure to turn off your cell phone and other electronic devices until your study period is over.

1 ▶ Punctuation Power-Up

TODAY'S DATA-DRIVEN INFORMATION AGE demands stronger reading and writing skills. Being able to think clearly and to create interesting content is important. Having a good grasp of the rules of punctuation is equally essential. You don't have to *love* punctuation; you just have to respect it a little. The best way to master punctuation and sentence mechanics is to learn the basic rules and use those rules during daily writing practice. You might also consider taking passages from books and copying them into your notebooks to reinforce the patterns of proper punctuation and sentence structure.

Mastering the intricacies of the English language is a gradual process that will become easier and more rewarding as your proficiency increases, and as you grow more confident in your abilities. Because becoming an active reader and writer is crucial to achieving success in language arts, it is suggested that you make reading and writing important parts of your daily activities by reading a wide variety of media and by taking advantage of some of the supplementary material listed in the Chapter 3 resource list.

The following is a quick reference guide. We suggest you read the entire guide before moving on to other sections.

Period (.)

- Periods signal that a sentence has come to a complete stop. → *Sentences that do not require a question mark or exclamation point should end with a period.*
- A period is used to indicate a decimal. → *a GPA of 3.9*
- A period separates dollars and cents. → *The price of the loaf of bread is $2.89.*
- A period follows an initial in a name. → *Is Robert W. Smith here today?*
- A period indicates that a word is being used in abbreviated form. → *Diva Apparel & Accessory Co., Inc.*
- Use a period to end a command. → *Take this book to Mrs. Grundy's office.*
- Use a period to separate letters in abbreviations. → *C.E. [common era]*

Question Mark (?)

- Always place a question mark at the end of a direct question. → *What kind of maintenance schedule should I follow?*
- When a question includes a direct quote, the question mark of the overall sentence is placed outside (after) the end quotation mark. → *Did Mr. Keats say, "The reading assignment is due on the last Friday of November"?*
- If a direct quotation is itself a question, the question mark is placed inside (before) the end quotation mark. → *Mark asked, "Does anyone want more soda?"*

Exclamation Point (!)

- Place an exclamation point after a word, phrase, or sentence that requires extra emphasis or one that conveys an especially strong emotion. → *That car is speeding out of control!*
- Place an exclamation point after an interjection. → *Wow!*
- Exclamation marks are placed inside quotation marks only when they are part of the direct quote. → *Melissa screamed "Help!" when her bicycle's rain-soaked brakes unexpectedly failed.*

Quotation Marks (" ")

- When using a direct quote from an outside source, place double quotation marks around the speaker's words, and use a comma or colon directly before the quote. → *The local news anchor reported: "Retailers are responding to lackluster consumer spending by slashing prices on apparel, electronics, and household goods."*
- The titles of chapters, articles, poems, songs, and short stories require quotation marks. → *"The Road Not Taken"*
- The rules of American standard English dictate that periods and commas are always placed inside (before) end quotation marks, whereas sentence structure determines placement of other punctuation, such as question marks and colons. → *"I like to listen to hip-hop classics by Tupac Shakur, Ice Cube, and Eminem," said Lisa.*
- When punctuating dialogue—conversations between two or more speakers—enclose each speaker's words in quotation marks.
- Use single quotation marks when enclosing quoted material inside a direct quotation. → *When John and I discussed the writings of Henry David Thoreau, he remarked, "I especially appreciate Thoreau's sentiment: 'The bluebird carries the sky on his back.'"*

Semicolon (;)

- Use a semicolon to separate individual items or word groups in a series containing commas. → *Field trips are planned for Monday, May 5; Tuesday, May 6; and Wednesday, May 7.*
- Use a semicolon before adverbial connectives such as *however*, *nevertheless*, and *therefore* joining together two independent clauses. → *Cheryl tried out for cheerleading with her arm in a cast; nevertheless, her routine dazzled the judges.*

Colon (:)

- Use a colon directly in front of a listing of a series of items. → *While I was at the supermarket, I picked up the following: cheese, rolls, pie, and bottled water.*
- A colon separates hours and minutes. → *Let's meet for lunch at 1:30 P.M.*
- A colon can be substituted for a comma before a direct quote. → *Ms. Jones said: "Students who are missing more than five homework assignments will have points taken off their final grades."*
- To separate biblical chapter and verse, a colon is used after the chapter, with the verse appearing directly after the colon. → *Isaiah 61:3*
- A colon is placed at the end of the salutation line in a formal letter. → *Dear Mr. Smythe:*
- A colon separates the city and publisher in a bibliographical citation or note. → *New York: Alfred A. Knopf*
- Use a colon between titles and subtitles.

Apostrophe (')

- Use an apostrophe when letters have been deleted. → *It's [It is] time for a change.*
- An apostrophe is used with an *s* at the end of a word in order to indicate ownership. → *On the day she was absent, Ms. Carlson's homeroom class was very unruly.*
- Only an apostrophe is added to a plural word ending with an *s* to indicate ownership. → *The books' pages were scattered across the floor.*

Comma (,)

The best way to learn to use commas properly is to study and imitate proper comma usage in model sentences. Reinforce your comma punctuation skills by reading the specific rule for each situation and then practicing what you've learned by copying each model sentence five times in the spaces provided.

Rule: Place a comma before a coordinating conjunction (*and, or, but, nor, so, for, yet*) joining two or more independent clauses.

Model sentence:
I was going to go to the party, but I fell asleep while watching television.

Practice:

1. _____

2. _____

3. _____

4. _____

5. _____

Rule: Place a comma between all of the items in a list.

Model sentence:
She shopped for paper plates, napkins, cups, and plastic spoons.

Practice:

1. _____
2. _____
3. _____
4. _____
5. _____

Rule: Place a comma directly after tags or phrases preceding direct quotations.

Model sentence:
The author of the best-selling novel declared, "I can't wait to start working on my next book."

Practice:

1. _____
2. _____
3. _____
4. _____
5. _____

Rule: Place a comma between dates, addresses, and titles:

Model sentence:
Robert Smith, PhD, received his doctoral degree on May 14, 2007.

Practice:

1. _____
2. _____
3. _____
4. _____
5. _____

Rule: Set off nonrestrictive appositives and nonessential phrases and clauses by placing a comma on both sides. (Do not use commas with restrictive appositives such as *the poet Robert Frost*.)

Model sentence:
Will's girlfriend, Halle [nonrestrictive appositive], whom he has dated for two years [nonessential clause], doesn't know how to drive.

Practice:

1. _____
2. _____
3. _____
4. _____
5. _____

Rule: Place a comma directly after conjunctive adverbs and transitional phrases, such as *however, also, then, therefore, for instance, in conclusion, in fact,* and *for example.*

Model sentence:
In fact, the black shoes are handcrafted in Italy.

Practice:

1. _____
2. _____
3. _____
4. _____
5. _____

Rule: Use a comma after an introductory adverbial clause or a prepositional phrase.

Model sentence:
Under the decaying front porch, we discovered a box filled with books and old letters.

Practice:

1. _____
2. _____
3. _____
4. _____
5. _____

Rule: Place a comma within (before) the end quotation mark of a direct quote preceding a tag (unless the quote ends with a question mark or an exclamation point).

Model sentence:
"I'm going on vacation next week," said Tanya.

Practice:

1. _____
2. _____
3. _____
4. _____
5. _____

Hyphen (-)

- Use a hyphen whenever two or more words are joined together to serve as an adjective directly before a noun (unless the first word ends in *-ly*). → *The well-regarded teacher was honored for his exceptionally hard work and dedication.*
- Use a hyphen when writing out fractions and compound numbers. → *I spent one-third of my allowance on books and DVDs.*
- Use a hyphen with compound nouns. → *My sister-in-law works at the local mall.*

Grammar-Gram

If a word is not listed in the dictionary as a compound word (for example, *notebook* or *self-esteem*), write it as two separate words (for example, *test taker*).

Parentheses

- Place parentheses around letters or numbers that mark divisions in a series. → *The main rules of the class are the following: (1) don't speak when someone else is speaking, (2) act respectfully toward your teacher and your classmates, and (3) work hard and complete all of your assignments.*

- Use parentheses to enclose supplementary material. → *Dorothy (Mrs. Thomas) Walker, an animal welfare activist, recently adopted an elderly mixed-breed dog from the local animal shelter.*

Ellipses (. . .)

- Ellipses signify that material has been omitted from the middle of a quotation, but they are normally not placed at the beginning or end of a quotation. → *In his play* Uncle Vanya, *Anton Chekhov wrote: "Man has been endowed with reason, with the power to create . . . but up to now he hasn't been a creator, only a destroyer."*

Get a Grip on Punctuation

Help!! Writer Wigs Out on Exclamation Points!

Exclamation points are like cayenne pepper—use them to add a dash of excitement, but don't be heavy-handed or they will irritate the reader. If you have used more than one exclamation point on a page, focus instead on revising to make more precise word choices that will interject your writing with the same degree of enthusiasm that you are hoping to achieve by using exclamation points.

Comma Use and Abuse

Some writers sprinkle commas into their writing like Parmesan cheese over a plate of spaghetti or sprinkles onto a cake. Yikes! The best way to avoid this type of comma abuse is to ask yourself the following question before using a comma: What specific punctuation rule applies to this particular situation? If a rule doesn't fit the situation, you might be creating a dreaded comma splice by placing a comma between two independent clauses that are direly in need of a coordinating conjunction (there are seven of them: *and*, *but*, *for*, *or*, *nor*, *so*, and *yet*).

▶ Practice Questions

Choose the punctuation mark that is needed in each of the following sentences. If no additional punctuation is needed, choose **e**.

1. "It isn't fair!" shouted Martin. Coach Lewis never lets me start the game!"
   - **a.** .
   - **b.** ,
   - **c.** !
   - **d.** "
   - **e.** correct as is

2. Maureen's three sisters, Molly, Shannon, and Patricia are all spending the summer at their grandmother's beach house.
   - **a.** ;
   - **b.** –
   - **c.** !
   - **d.** ,
   - **e.** correct as is

3. For the centerpieces, the florist recommended the following flowers daisies, tulips, daffodils, and hyacinths.
   a. :
   b. ,
   c. .
   d. ;
   e. correct as is

4. Lily is an accomplished gymnast she won three medals in her last competition.
   a. ;
   b. ,
   c. ?
   d. :
   e. correct as is

5. Everyone was shocked when Max Smithfield— a studious, extremely bright high school senior decided that college was not for him.
   a. ;
   b. ,
   c. —
   d. :
   e. correct as is

6. Kims assistant, usually so reliable, has been late for work three times this week, without any excuse.
   a. '
   b. ,
   c. ;
   d. .
   e. correct as is

7. Before sending out invitations, Margo checked the party date with her mother-in-law.
   a. ,
   b. ;
   c. —
   d. .
   e. correct as is

8. "I remember" Luis recollected, "the first time I was allowed to walk home from school by myself."
   a. ?
   b. ,
   c. :
   d. ;
   e. correct as is

9. Madeline Larkin our office manager, is the most organized person I've ever known.
   a. :
   b. ;
   c. —
   d. ,
   e. correct as is

10. I spend most of my time at the gym on the treadmill walking is my favorite form of exercise.
    a. ,
    b. ?
    c. ;
    d. !
    e. correct as is

Choose the alternative that shows the best punctuation for the underlined part of the sentence. If the sentence is correct as is, choose **e**.

11. Simone bought three new pairs of <u>shoes even though she</u> had put herself on a tight budget just last week.
    a. shoes, even though, she
    b. shoes, even though she
    c. shoes. Even though she
    d. shoes; even though she
    e. correct as is

12. Most residents of the building have <u>air conditioners however I've</u> always found that a ceiling fan is sufficient.
    a. air conditioners however: I've
    b. air conditioners, however, I've
    c. air conditioners however, I've
    d. air conditioners; however, I've
    e. correct as is

13. "Are you <u>okay," asked Timothy, "Are</u> you sure you don't want to sit down and rest for a while?"
    a. okay?" asked Timothy. "Are
    b. okay?" asked Timothy, "Are
    c. okay," asked Timothy? "Are
    d. okay?" asked Timothy? "Are
    e. correct as is

14. The owners of the restaurant <u>maintain that only</u> organic ingredients are used in their kitchen.
    a. maintain, that only
    b. maintain that, only
    c. maintain: that only
    d. maintain—that only
    e. correct as is

15. Before the student could be hired by the <u>company, the students</u> adviser had to provide a letter of recommendation.
    a. company the students
    b. company, the student's
    c. company, the students'
    d. company the students'
    e. correct as is

16. The <u>volunteers who would like to work the morning shift</u> should sign their names on this sheet.
    a. volunteers, who would like to work the morning shift
    b. volunteers who would like to work the morning shift,
    c. volunteers, who would like to work the morning shift,
    d. volunteers who, would like to work the morning shift,
    e. correct as is

17. The employees asked whether the company would be offering tuition <u>reimbursement within the next three years?</u>
    a. reimbursement within the next three years!
    b. reimbursement, within the next three years.
    c. reimbursement within the next three years.
    d. reimbursement, within the next three years?
    e. correct as is

18. This is the new restaurant you've been talking <u>about, isn't it?</u>
    a. about isn't it?
    b. about, is'nt it?
    c. about, isn't it.
    d. about isn't it.
    e. correct as is

19. <u>Turnips a root vegetable</u> can be mashed, roasted, or used in casseroles.
  a. Turnips, a root vegetable,
  b. Turnips, a root vegetable
  c. Turnips, a root vegetable—
  d. Turnips a root vegetable,
  e. correct as is

20. They met for the first time on <u>August 27, 1972 in Seattle, WA.</u>
  a. August 27 1972 in Seattle, WA.
  b. August 27 1972, in Seattle WA.
  c. August 27, 1972 in Seattle, WA.
  d. August 27, 1972, in Seattle, WA.
  e. correct as is

▶ Capitalization

Don't Capitalize

- the seasons of the year → *spring, summer, fall, winter*
- written-out references to specific dates of the month → *the tenth day of February*
- geographical directions → *I told him to drive north.*
- the first word in a quotation that is written as a phrase instead of a complete sentence → *He said that he would prefer to "spend some time at the shore" during the summer months.*
- the names of academic subjects, unless they are languages such as English or titles of academic courses → *second-year calculus; Advanced Calculus II*
- the first letter(s) of words of an academic degree → *bachelor of arts*
- prepositions, conjunctions, and articles in a book or article title, unless they appear as the first or last word

Do Capitalize

- the first letter(s) of proper nouns referring to specific beings, places, and things such as the names of continents, countries, states, cities, races, nationalities, religions, and languages
- the first letter(s) of the names of months, weekdays, and holidays → *New Year's Day*
- the first word of a sentence → *School is in session today.*
- the first letter(s) of the name of a geographical location → *She left for a business trip out West.*
- the first letter of an individual's first, middle, and last names → *President John Quincy Adams*
- the first letter(s) in the name of an animal → *My cat is named Miss Kitty.*
- the first letter of the first word of a direct quotation that is written as a complete sentence → *Principal Roberts said, "Research indicates that an extended school day increases academic achievement."*
- all of the letters in an acronym → *ASPCA*
- the first letter in each word of an organization's name → *American Red Cross*
- the pronoun *I* → *I am going to school early today.*
- the first letter in the first, last, and major words in the title of a book, magazine, computer software program, poem, story, play, song title, film, or work of art (However, the titles of certain poems, magazines, and such are sometimes typed completely in lowercase letters for artistic effect.)
- the first letter(s) of a brand name → *Crest toothpaste*
- the first letter(s) of the name of a river, ocean, or other large body of water → *Mississippi River*
- the first letter in Mother, Father, Dad, Mom, Grandfather, Grandma, and so on if they are not preceded by a possessive noun or pronoun → *I met Dad in front of the diner.*
- the first letter(s) in a company name → *General Electric*

- the first letter(s) in the name of a school, college, or university → *Columbia University*
- the first letter(s) of the names of streets, buildings, and institutions when they are part of a proper noun → *Wall Street; White House*
- the first word of each item in an outline → *Introduction*
  1. *Chapter 1*
  2. *Chapter 2*

Examples of Capitalization in Titles

Amelia Rules! (comic book)

American Idol (television show)

"Casey at the Bat" (poem by Ernest Lawrence Thayer)

Girl with a Pearl Earring (work of art by Johannes Vermeer)

The Hitchhiker's Guide to the Galaxy (book by Douglas Adams)

March of the Penguins (film)

Paradise Lost (lengthy poem by John Milton)

Popular Science (periodical)

A Raisin in the Sun (play by Lorraine Hansberry)

"The Tell-Tale Heart" (short story by Edgar Allan Poe)

"What a Wonderful World" (song)

Zone Alarm Internet Security Suite 7 (software)

▶ Practice Questions

For the following questions, choose the lettered part of the sentence that contains a word that needs a capital letter. If no additional words should be capitalized, choose **e**. Refer to the preceding checklists if you want to be certain about your choice.

21. Last week, | dr. Tanya Miller received |
    a   b
    a special award from the | city of Atlanta. |
                               c   d
    Correct as is
    e

22. The new bakery | in the center of town |
    a   b
    sells a wide assortment | of italian pastries. |
                              c   d
    Correct as is
    e

23. Michael Blake, jr., |
    a
    is such an accomplished golfer |
                                b
    that he won three tournaments | in a row. |
                                c   d
    Correct as is
    e

24. Catherine complained loudly, |
    a
    "why can't you ever | pick me up on time |
              b   c
    in the morning?" | Correct as is
          d   e

25. The Declaration of Independence |
    a
    is one of the most important |
                            b
    documents in the history | of the United States.
                          c   d
    Correct as is
    e

26. Sally's Sweet shop, |
                    a

one of the oldest businesses in town, |
                                b

is located on one of the main streets |
                              c

of Millersville. | Correct as is
      d   **e**

27. My first childhood pet, | a gray cat named otis,
                    a   **b**

| was given to me as a gift | on my fifth birthday. |
                    c   **d**

Correct as is
      e

28. The local elementary school |
                            a

is organizing a screening |
                    b

of the movie *toy story* | as a fund-raiser. |
                    c   **d**

Correct as is
      e

For each question, find the sentence that has a mistake in capitalization or punctuation. If you find no mistakes, mark choice **d**.

29. **a.** My least favorite season is Winter.
 b. Next Friday, Uncle Jake is coming to visit.
 c. Maureen served as treasurer for the women's organization.
 d. no mistakes

30. **a.** "Can you attend next week's meeting?" she asked.
 b. His new car was damaged in the accident.
 c. The girls' giggled through the whole movie.
 d. no mistakes

31. **a.** Leo told her, to call the customer service department in the morning.
 b. She put up signs all over town, but she didn't get any response.
 c. Occasionally, her neighbors ask her to feed their cat.
 d. no mistakes

32. **a.** Did you see all three movies about Shrek?
 b. She was given an award by mayor Chambers.
 c. Math and science are my two best subjects.
 d. no mistakes

33. **a.** A major highway is being built on the outskirts of town.
 b. When you reach the traffic light on Berkshire Road, turn right onto Springfield Boulevard.
 c. We were staying at my sister's cape Cod vacation home.
 d. no mistakes

34. **a.** The instructor asked us if we needed more time?
 b. Carla's mother is a pediatric dentist.
 c. Every item in the store costs less than a dollar.
 d. no mistakes

35. **a.** Jane's family owned three Persian cats.
 b. My Uncle always takes the subway to Yankee Stadium.
 c. Everyone knows that Marisa's favorite book is *Pride and Prejudice*.
 d. no mistakes

36.
a. "I'll do the grocery shopping for you, grandma," Lucy said.
b. "Where can I find the best pizza in town?" he asked.
c. "Be sure to arrive two hours early," she warned.
d. no mistakes

37.
a. I always have a hard time getting up in the morning.
b. We took: a tent, a cooler, and a sleeping bag.
c. The fog was as thick as potato soup.
d. no mistakes

38.
a. This is someone elses coat.
b. Which of these songs was recorded by Bruce Springsteen?
c. That book must be yours.
d. no mistakes

39.
a. Don't stand in my way.
b. Cecilia and I fought our way through the crowd.
c. The vegetables were old rubbery and tasteless.
d. no mistakes

40.
a. Remember to walk the dog.
b. "Don't run"! Mr. Ellington shouted.
c. It's supposed to snow today and tomorrow.
d. no mistakes

41.
a. Charleen's parents worried whenever she drove the car.
b. Who designed the Brooklyn Bridge?
c. Diseases like Smallpox and Polio have been virtually eradicated.
d. no mistakes

42.
a. Can you find the Indian ocean on this map?
b. Which river, the Nile or the Amazon, is longer?
c. Lerner Avenue runs into the Thompson Parkway.
d. no mistakes

43.
a. He's the best dancer in the school.
b. We were planning to go, but the meeting was canceled.
c. "Okay," she said, I'll go with you."
d. no mistakes

44.
a. Does Judge Parker live on your street?
b. Twenty government officials met to deal with Wednesday's crisis.
c. The Mayor spoke at a news conference this morning.
d. no mistakes

45.
a. My brother Isaac is the best player on the team.
b. Because of the high cost; we decided not to go.
c. Where's your new puppy?
d. no mistakes

46.
a. I have learned to appreciate Mozart's music.
b. My cousin Veronica is studying to be a Veterinarian.
c. Mr. Shanahan is taller than Professor Martin.
d. no mistakes

47. a. "You look just like your mother," Ms. Jones told me.
b. "Please be careful," he said.
c. Tyler asked, "why do I have to go to bed so early?"
d. no mistakes

48. a. Do you prefer root beer or orange soda?
b. In which year did world war II end?
c. I like to study the geography of the Everglades.
d. no mistakes

49. a. Colds like many other viruses are highly contagious.
b. Call me when you feel better.
c. Did you wash your hands, Michael?
d. no mistakes

50. a. The industrial revolution began in Europe.
b. Is Labor Day a national holiday?
c. General Patton was a four-star general.
d. no mistakes

51. a. Carmen brought bread, and butter, and strawberry jam.
b. Let's look at the map.
c. Be sure to thank Aunt Helen for the gift.
d. no mistakes

52. a. My Aunt Georgia loves to read Eighteenth-Century novels.
b. Eli's sister's cousin lives in Alaska.
c. Is that a German shepherd?
d. no mistakes

53. a. Those shoes are too expensive.
b. Michael's best friend is Patrick.
c. Did you hear that Inez got a new puppy.
d. no mistakes

Questions 54–57 are based on the following passage. First, read the passage; then, choose the alternative that shows the best capitalization or punctuation for each underlined part.

Madam Helena P. <u>Blavatsky born</u> in Russia on May 8, 1831, claimed to have psychic powers and to be capable of performing feats of clairvoyance and telepathy. During her 60 years, she traveled to many <u>countries—including</u> the United States, England, India, and Egypt—in order to study the occult. Although many considered her a <u>fake throughout</u> her lifetime she was surrounded by faithful believers, including such influential persons as British statesman Allen O. Hume and Swedish countess Constance Wachtmeister. To this day, followers commemorate the date of her <u>death calling</u> May 8 "White Lotus Day."

54. a. Blavatsky: born
b. Blavatsky—born
c. Blavatsky, born
d. Blavatsky. Born
e. correct as is

55. a. countries, including
b. countries: including
c. countries. Including
d. countries including
e. correct as is

56. a. fake, throughout
  b. fake. Throughout
  c. fake: throughout
  d. fake; throughout
  e. correct as is

57. a. death. Calling
  b. death, calling
  c. death: calling
  d. death; calling
  e. correct as is

Questions 58–61 are based on the following passage. First, read the passage; then, choose the alternative that shows the best capitalization or punctuation for each underlined part.

312 Maple Avenue
Chicago, IL 60632
June 2, 2006

Mark <u>Franklin, general manager</u>
Wholesome Food Store
1245 Main Street
Chicago, IL 60627

<u>dear Mr. Franklin;</u>

I am writing to complain about the behavior of one of your sales clerks. On <u>Monday May 22nd I</u> visited your store to return a package of ground turkey that I had purchased the day before. When I explained to your sales clerk that the expiration date on the package was May 1st, she was <u>extremely rude and she</u> refused to refund my money. This is not the kind of

treatment I expect from your fine establishment. I hope you will make restitution and have a discussion with your staff about customer service. My receipt is enclosed.

Sincerely yours,

Melanie Jeffords

58. a. Franklin, general Manager
  b. franklin, General Manager
  c. Franklin, General Manager
  d. Franklin, General manager
  e. correct as is

59. a. Dear Mr. Franklin.
  b. Dear, Mr. franklin,
  c. dear Mr. Franklin:
  d. Dear Mr. Franklin:
  e. correct as is

60. a. Monday, May 22nd I
  b. Monday May 22nd; I
  c. Monday. May 22nd I
  d. Monday, May 22nd, I
  e. correct as is

61. a. extremely rude, and she
  b. extremely rude: and she
  c. extremely rude? And she
  d. extremely rude and, she
  e. correct as is

▶ Answers

1. d. There should be a quotation mark before the word *Coach* to set off the dialogue.

2. d. Commas set off nonrestrictive appositives, phrases that say the same thing as the previous phrase in different words. (A comma should be placed after *Patricia*.)

3. a. A colon can go before a list. (Place a colon after the word *flowers*.)

4. a. A semicolon can be used to separate two main clauses that could each stand alone as complete sentences.

5. c. Dashes can be used to set off a parenthetical element, for emphasis. (Place another em dash after the word *senior*.)

6. a. The possessive *Kim's* requires an apostrophe.

7. e. This sentence is punctuated correctly.

8. b. Commas set off parenthetical elements and always go inside the quotation marks in a line of dialogue. (Place a comma after the word *remember*.)

9. d. Commas set off a word or phrase that describes the subject but does not alter the meaning of the entire sentence. (Place a comma after the word *Larkin*.)

10. c. A semicolon can be used to separate two main clauses that could each stand alone as complete sentences. (Place the semicolon after the word *treadmill*.)

11. b. The comma separates the main clause from the long, descriptive subordinate clause.

12. d. The semicolon can be used to separate two main clauses that could each stand alone as complete sentences, and the comma follows the conjunctive adverb *however*.

13. a. The quotation is a question, and the tag *asked Timothy* ends the sentence.

14. e. The sentence is punctuated correctly.

15. b. The word *student's* is possessive and needs an apostrophe.

16. e. The sentence does not require any additional punctuation.

17. c. This is a declarative sentence; it asks an indirect question, so a question mark should not be used. Also, to add the comma is incorrect.

18. e. The sentence is punctuated correctly.

19. a. The phrase *a root vegetable* is a nonessential element in the sentence and needs to be set off with commas.

20. d. Commas separate dates and addresses.

21. b. A title, such as *Dr.*, requires a capital.

22. d. Nationalities and languages require capitals.

23. a. *Jr.* is a kind of title and therefore takes a capital.

24. b. The first letter of a direct quotation takes a capital.

25. e. Capitalization is correct.

26. a. All words in the proper name of a place or company require capitals.

27. b. Proper names require capitals.

28. c. Movie titles are capitalized.

29. a. *Winter* should not be capitalized.

30. c. There should not be an apostrophe after the word *girls*.

31. a. The comma is incorrect and should be deleted.

32. b. *Mayor* should be capitalized because it refers to a particular mayor.

33. c. *Cape Cod* is a proper noun, and both words should be capitalized.

34. a. This is a declarative sentence that asks an indirect question, so the question mark should be replaced with a period.

35. b. *Uncle* is not used as a proper noun and should not be capitalized.

36. a. *Grandma* is used as a proper name and should be capitalized.

37. b. A colon should not be used between a verb and its objects.

38. a. There should be an apostrophe in the word *else's*, which is possessive.

39. c. The commas are missing from this series of adjectives.

40. b. The quotation mark should appear on the outside of the exclamation point: *"Don't run!"*

41. c. The word *polio* and *smallpox* should not be capitalized. Diseases are not capitalized unless a proper noun is part of the name.

42. a. *Ocean* should be capitalized.

43. c. To set off the dialogue, there should be a quotation mark before the word *I'll*.

44. c. *Mayor* should not be capitalized, because it does not precede the name of a particular mayor.

45. b. A semicolon is not used between a dependent and an independent clause. Use a comma.

46. b. *Veterinarian* is not a proper noun and should not be capitalized.

47. c. The word *Why*, which begins the quotation, should be capitalized.

48. b. *World War* is a proper noun and should be capitalized.

49. a. The phrase *like many other viruses* should be set off by commas because it is a nonessential element in the sentence.

50. a. *Industrial Revolution* should be capitalized.

51. a. The commas in this sentence should be deleted. Commas are not used in a series when the series is already linked by conjunctions.

52. a. The names of centuries are not capitalized.

53. c. This sentence asks a question and should end with a question mark.

54. c. Commas are used to set off a word or phrase that describes the subject but does not alter the meaning of the entire sentence.

55. e. Dashes are used to set off parenthetical elements, for emphasis.

56. a. The comma is used after an introductory element.

57. b. The comma separates the main clause from the descriptive subordinate clause.

58. c. Titles require capitals.

59. d. First words of salutations, titles, and proper names all take capitals; a colon follows the salutation in a business letter.

60. d. Commas set off parenthetical elements.

61. a. A comma goes before *and* when *and* links two main clauses.

2 ▶ Agreement

THE SAYING "Birds of a feather flock together" definitely applies to present tense subject-verb agreement; **singular** subjects pair up with singular verb tenses and **plural** subjects pair with plural verbs. In other words, a singular person or thing requires a singular verb, while more than one person or thing requires a plural verb.

"The neighbor's dog [singular subject] is [singular verb] barking" is an example of singular subject-verb agreement, while "the neighbor's dogs [plural subject] are [plural verb] barking" is an example of plural subject-verb agreement. A verb must *always* agree with its subject, even if the subject appears after the verb.

The previous example of subject-verb agreement is relatively clear-cut; however, there are cases in which determining subject-verb agreement gets a lot trickier. The following are general guidelines that will keep your subjects and verbs in good standing.

Collective nouns are the nouns that refer to a group of people or things as a singular unit. For example, we use the collective noun *fish* to refer to a single filet or several pounds. We use the collective noun *rice* to refer to a single grain or an entire bowlful, and when we say *lettuce*, we could be referring to one leaf of lettuce or an entire head. Some frequently used collective nouns are *work, traffic, mail, news, furniture, equipment, plastic, rain, silver, air, gasoline, sugar, water, wine, tea,* and *coffee.*

- Since collective nouns are perceived as one lone unit, they usually require a singular verb. → *The staff [collective noun] is [singular verb] participating in a fund-raising marathon.*
- **Compound subjects** (subject words separated by the word *and*) are plural and require plural verbs. → *Beans and rice [compound subject] were [plural verb] on sale at the market last week.* Exception: When beans and rice are viewed as a single dish (single subject), the verb is singular. → *Beans and rice is my favorite dish.*
- **Indefinite pronouns** such as *much, each, anybody, anyone, no one, someone,* and *everyone* require a singular verb.
- When money or time is the subject, use a singular verb if you are writing about a total amount of time or money and a plural verb when you are writing about individual units. → Singular: *I thought that a million dollars [singular unit total amount] was an outrageous price to pay for that painting.* Plural: *Thousands of dollars [individual units] were wasted on repairs for the archaic building.*
- When the subject of a sentence is uncountable, such as the number of tea leaves or coffee grains in a container of tea or coffee, the verb is singular. → *The tea [uncountable subject] has mysteriously vanished from the pantry.*

The most important thing that you must remember about tense agreement is that past and present events can't be occurring at the same time, so be sure to use either all past tense or all present tense for events occurring in the same time frame.

Get a Grip Grammar Tips

Forever-Single Pronouns

The following pronouns are always singular: *one, someone, somebody, anyone, anybody, no one, nobody, everyone, everybody, each, either,* and *neither.*

Birds of a Feather Flock Together

Since repetition is essential to memorization, post this list in a place where you will see it at least a dozen times in the next month.

- The plural pronouns *many, both, few,* and *several* must be matched with plural verbs.
- When two subjects are joined by *and,* use a plural verb.

▶ Practice Questions

For the following questions, choose the underlined part of the sentence that contains a grammatical error. If there are no errors, choose **e**.

62. Every year, <u>a few committed</u> citizens <u>exceeds</u>
    a   (b)

our <u>expectations and</u> work tirelessly
    c

<u>to improve</u> our community programs in
    d

significant ways. No error
                        e

63. <u>Each of</u> the employees <u>have had</u> a <u>half-hour</u>
    a   (b)   c

evaluation meeting <u>with</u> his or her supervisor.
                    d

No error
    e

64. Here <u>are</u> one of the three <u>keys</u> you <u>will need</u> to
        (a)   b   c

unlock the office door <u>tomorrow</u>. No error
                        d   e

65. Soon after Donovan left <u>to walk</u> to <u>work, he</u>
                            a   b

realized <u>that</u> he <u>would forget</u> his umbrella.
        c   (d)

No error
    e

66. <u>Someone from</u> the garage phoned <u>to say</u> <u>that</u>
    a   b   c

the car had been fixed and <u>asking</u> if we would
                            (d)

pick it up by 5:00. No error
                    e

67. In 1963, Betty <u>Friedan's</u> exposé of domesticity,
        a   b

The Feminine Mystique, became <u>an immediate</u>
                                c

best-seller <u>and creating</u> a national sensation.
            (d)

No error
    e

68. The staff at the <u>university</u> library <u>deserve</u>
        a   b

recognition for <u>helping to locate</u> the
                c

<u>many sources needed</u> for the successful
    d

completion of my doctoral dissertation.

No error
    (e)

69. <u>Homesteaders</u> on the <u>Great Plains</u> had to build
    a   b

homes, find water <u>in a semiarid</u> land,
                    c

<u>and to learn</u> to understand the blessings of the
    (d)

environment. No error
                e

70. <u>During</u> the winter season, homeowners should
    a

change <u>their</u> disposable furnace filters at least
        b

once <u>a month; a</u> dirty filter <u>reduce</u> furnace
        c   (d)

efficiency. No error
            e

71. <u>Watching</u> the film, I <u>begun</u> to ask <u>myself</u> why I
    a   (b)   c

cared about <u>these characters</u> when I felt such
                d

an intense unease. No error
                    e

Fill in the blank with the correct verb form.

72. On March 15, 2006, the Maywood Recreation Department requested a grant from the state to rebuild the community center that _____ in the recent fire.
a. destroys
b. will be destroyed
c. had been destroyed
d. is being destroyed

73. We have _____ more sweets since that wonderful bakery opened down the block.
a. ate
b. been eating
c. been eat
d. eat

74. While attempting to _____ his broken bicycle, Leo Donner realized that he didn't have the proper tools.
a. be repairing
b. have repaired
c. repair
d. repaired

75. _____ the police immediately.
a. Call
b. Called
c. Been calling
d. To call

76. The biggest problem with Martha's garden _____ too many weeds.
a. will have been
b. were
c. will have
d. was

77. Last week, Tracy and Shane were honored at a luncheon for their part in rescuing a child who _____ into an icy pond.
a. falls
b. would fall
c. had fallen
d. has fallen

78. The woman who confronted the owner of the unleashed dog _____ angry.
a. were
b. was
c. are
d. have been

79. The boy _____ the bat and ran to first base as fast as he could.
a. swings
b. swinged
c. swung
d. swing

80. There _____ four excellent restaurants in the center of town.
a. is
b. are
c. was
d. being

81. The noise from the lawn mowers _____ louder as the morning progresses.
a. gets
b. get
c. have gotten
d. are getting

Replace the underlined words with the phrase that best completes the sentence. If the sentence is correct as is, choose **a**.

82. The words *Equal Justice Under Law* <u>is carved</u> above the main entrance to the Supreme Court.
   a. correct as is
   b. carved
   c. has been carved
   d. are carved
   e. been carved

83. A corporation created by the federal government during the Great Depression, the Tennessee Valley Authority (TVA) is responsible for <u>flood control, must generate electric power, and soil conservation.</u>
   a. correct as is
   b. flood control, generating electric power, and for soil conservation.
   c. controlling floods, generating electric power, and soil conservation.
   d. flood control, the generation of electric power, and soil conservation.
   e. flood control, for the generation of electric power, and conserving the soil.

84. According to traditional Chinese medicine, people with healthy livers <u>are said to be calm and that they possess</u> unerring judgment.
   a. correct as is
   b. are said to be calm and to possess
   c. said to be calm and possessing
   d. have said to be calm and to possess
   e. are said to be calm and possessive of

85. When the phone <u>is ringing, Jacoby had been writing</u> in his journal.
   a. correct as is
   b. rings, Jacoby was writing
   c. rang, Jacoby was writing
   d. had rung, Jacoby was writing
   e. rang, Jacoby will be writing

86. <u>To determine the speed of automobiles, radar is often used by the state police.</u>
   a. correct as is
   b. To determine the speed of automobiles, it is often necessary for the state police to use radar.
   c. In determining the speed of automobiles, the use of radar by state police is often employed.
   d. To determine the speed of automobiles, the state police often use radar.
   e. Radar by state police in determining the speed of automobiles is often used.

87. I have a cross-training exercise program: <u>I swim laps, play tennis, the weight machines, and bicycle riding.</u>
   a. correct as is
   b. I swim laps, play tennis, lift weights, and ride a bicycle.
   c. I swim laps, play tennis, I lift weights, and bicycle riding is a change.
   d. swimming laps, tennis, lifting weights, and the bicycle.
   e. swim laps, play tennis, lifting weights, and riding a bicycle.

88. We all arrived at the theater on time, but before we bought our tickets, Candace <u>says that she's changed her mind and doesn't</u> want to see the movie after all.

a. correct as is

b. said that she had changed her mind and didn't

c. is saying that she'd changed her mind and doesn't

d. told us that she is changing her mind and didn't

e. tells us that she had changed her mind and doesn't

89. Because he was given a local anesthetic, <u>Josh was conscience throughout the operation.</u>

a. correct as is

b. Josh had a conscience during the operation.

c. the operation was completed with Josh consciousness.

d. the operation was done while Josh held consciousness.

e. Josh remained conscious throughout the operation.

Find the sentence that has a mistake in grammar or usage. If you find no mistakes, mark choice **d**.

90. a. No, it's not true.

b. The curtain closed, and the people will applaud.

c. My sister is a nurse practitioner.

d. no mistakes

91. a. They talked through the entire movie.

b. The plants in this garden does not require much water.

c. She always brings turkey sandwiches for lunch.

d. no mistakes

92. a. Where are Gianna's art supplies?

b. Darren should of been given a chance to audition.

c. It's going to take all day.

d. no mistakes

93. a. Olivia took her older sister out for lunch.

b. Nicholas is learning to speak German.

c. Franklin drunk three bottles of water after the game.

d. no mistakes

94. a. She showed us five different shades of blue paint.

b. The liveliest one of the three puppies are not adopted yet.

c. This is the best birthday party I have ever had.

d. no mistakes

95. a. When I go the museum, I wore comfortable shoes.

b. She was approached, but she declined the offer.

c. There are seven floors in this building.

d. no mistakes

96. a. David and Mickey danced in the street.

b. Here is the photographs I wanted to show you.

c. My grandfather owns a 1967 Mustang.

d. no mistakes

97. a. It has not rained since last April.

b. The jurors walked solemnly into the room.

c. Had we known, we would not have come.

d. no mistakes

98. a. The dog's barking woke us.
　　b. Ursula has broke one of your plates.
　　c. The sun rose from behind the mountain.
　　d. no mistakes

99. a. After we sat down to eat dinner, the phone rung.
　　b. "Keep a positive attitude," he always says.
　　c. Sign here.
　　d. no mistakes

100. a. The children's books are over there.
　　b. She missed the bus and arrives late.
　　c. There is hardly enough food for a mouse.
　　d. no mistakes

101. a. The winners were announced yesterday.
　　b. Liam was the only one of the boys who were chosen.
　　c. Although Nick was not selected, he was happy for the others.
　　d. no mistakes

102. a. He shook the crumbs from the tablecloth.
　　b. We will strive to do our best.
　　c. I see that Fred has wore his old shoes.
　　d. no mistakes

103. a. When I heard the alarm, I jump out of bed.
　　b. Mr. Fox is the president of his own company.
　　c. At night, I listen to jazz on the radio.
　　d. no mistakes

Choose the sentence that is the most clearly written and has the best construction.

104. a. All the children got out their rugs and took a nap.
　　b. All the children have gotten out their rugs and took a nap.
　　c. All the children got out their rugs and have taken a nap.
　　d. All the children gotten out their rugs and taken a nap.

105. a. At first I was liking the sound of the wind, but later it got on my nerves.
　　b. At first I liked the sound of the wind, but later it has gotten on my nerves.
　　c. At first I like the sound of the wind, but later it got on my nerves.
　　d. At first I liked the sound of the wind, but later it got on my nerves.

106. a. As the old saying goes, a cat may look at a king.
　　b. A cat looking at a king, according to the old saying.
　　c. The old saying being, a cat may look at a king.
　　d. A cat looking at a king, in the old saying.

107. a. A longer happier life, caused by one's owning a pet.
　　b. Owning a pet, for one to live a longer, happier life.
　　c. To live a longer, happier life by one's owning a pet.
　　d. Owning a pet can help one live a longer, happier life.

108.   **a.** One of the first modern detectives in literature were created by Edgar Allan Poe.

   b. One of the first modern detectives in literature was created by Edgar Allan Poe.

   c. Edgar Allan Poe having created one of the first modern detectives in literature.

   d. In literature, one of the first modern detectives, created by Edgar Allan Poe.

109.   **a.** My brother and I going to see the ball game.

   b. My brother and I are going to see the ball game.

   c. My brother and I seeing the ball game.

   d. My brother and I to the ball game.

110.   **a.** I don't like fish as much as my sister does.

   b. I don't like fish as much as my sister.

   c. Fish isn't liked by me as much as my sister.

   d. My sister likes it, but I don't like fish as much.

111.   **a.** We ate the popcorn and watch the movie.

   b. While watching the movie, the popcorn was eaten.

   c. Popcorn, while watching the movie, was eaten.

   d. We ate the popcorn while we watched the movie.

For the following questions, choose the underlined part of the sentence that contains a grammatical error. If there are no errors, choose answer **e**.

112. All <u>employees</u> with two <u>years'</u> experience
        a   b

<u>are entitled</u> to full <u>benefits</u>, including health
        c   d

insurance, life insurance, a retirement plan,

and stock options. No error
                     e

113. <u>To find</u> the perimeter of a <u>polygon, add</u> the
        a   b

<u>lengths</u> of <u>it's</u> sides. No error
   c   d   e

114. After the <u>director and assistant</u> director both
                   a

<u>resigned, we</u> all wondered <u>who would</u> be
        b   c

appointed <u>to fill</u> their positions. No error
           d   e

115. Last spring, my <u>cousin and I</u> packed <u>the tent, the</u>
                        a   b

sleeping <u>bags, and</u> a cooler filled with food
              c

and headed <u>west.</u> No error
              d   e

116. Although <u>mollusks</u> usually have soft
                  a

<u>bodies and</u> muscular feet, <u>it</u> may also <u>have</u> hard
        b   c   d

shells. No error
        e

117. For all of those people <u>who have vowed</u> to give
  a

up fatty foods, video games, and shopping for

the new year, <u>here's</u> an incentive to keep <u>him</u>
  b (c)

on the <u>straight and</u> narrow path. No error
  d e

118. <u>Even as</u> the mainstream music industry pushes
  a

<u>further into</u> the digital world of solid state
  b

circuitry, <u>there is</u> a renewed interest in old-style
  c

<u>amplifiers and</u> speakers. No error
  d (e)

119. <u>To formalize</u> and commit <u>themselves</u> to <u>there</u>
  a b (c)

new government, the Pilgrims <u>signed</u> the
  d

Mayflower Pact. No error
  e

120. Last summer around the <u>end of July,</u> my
  a

<u>brother,</u> Aunt Clarissa, and <u>me</u> jumped
  b (c)

into the Ford <u>station wagon and</u> headed out of
  d

the city. No error
  e

121. The term *blood type* <u>refers to</u> one of the many
  a

groups <u>into which</u> a <u>person's</u> blood
  b c

<u>can be categorized,</u> based on the presence or
  d

absence of specific antigens. No error
  (e)

122. Although the chances of <u>being victimized</u> are
  a

slim, if <u>your</u> not careful, airport thieves—<u>who</u>
  (b) c

look like <u>ordinary travelers</u>—can make off
  d

with your purse, your wallet, your phone card,

and all your credit cards. No error
  e

123. <u>Although</u> this <u>was</u> an <u>unusually dry</u> summer,
  a b c

the corn crop was not <u>seriously</u> damaged.
  d

No error
  (e)

Fill in the blank with the correct pronoun.

(124.) That fine circus elephant now belongs to my
sister and _____.
  - **(a.)** I
  - **b.** me
  - **c.** mine
  - **d.** myself

125. If you don't stop playing _____
video games, you will miss the bus.
  - **a.** that
  - **(b.)** those
  - **c.** them
  - **d.** this

126. George and Michael left _____
backpacks at school.
  - **a.** his
  - **(b.)** their
  - **c.** there
  - **d.** its

127. If you steal _____ artichoke from Petra's garden, you'll be sorry.
- **a.** them
- **b.** those
- **c.** that
- **d.** these

128. We arranged the flowers and placed _____ in the center of the table.
- **a.** it
- **b.** this
- **c.** them
- **d.** that

129. _____ met more than ten years ago at a mutual friend's birthday party.
- **a.** Her and I
- **b.** Her and me
- **c.** She and me
- **d.** She and I

130. My parents approved of _____ taking guitar lessons.
- **a.** my
- **b.** me
- **c.** I
- **d.** mine

Replace the underlined words with the phrase that best completes the sentence. If the sentence is correct as is, choose **a**.

131. It was either Kendra or Zoë who <u>brought their</u> volleyball to the picnic.
- **a.** correct as is
- **b.** brought her
- **c.** brought there
- **d.** brang their
- **e.** brang her

132. <u>Whose car will you take when you drive to their</u> house?
- **a.** correct as is
- **b.** Whose car will you take when you drive to there
- **c.** Who's car will you take when you drive to their
- **d.** Who's car will take when you drive to there
- **e.** Which car will you take when you drive to there

133. <u>If someone is looking</u> for the best car loan, you should compare interest rates at several banks.
- **a.** correct as is
- **b.** When one is looking
- **c.** If you are looking
- **d.** To have a person look
- **e.** When someone is about to look

134. The friendship between Andre and Robert <u>began when he and his</u> family moved to Ohio.
- **a.** correct as is
- **b.** Andre and Robert's friendship began when he and his
- **c.** The friendship among the two boys began when he and his
- **d.** The friendship between Andre and Robert began when Robert and his
- **e.** Andre and Robert's friendship began when their

Find the sentence that has a mistake in grammar or usage. If you find no mistakes, mark choice **d**.

135. a. Of the four of us, I am the tallest.
  b. Wilson's brother is a chemical engineer.
  c. That fine circus elephant now belongs to my sister and I.
  d. no mistakes

136. a. His family has lived in this town for 35 years.
  b. You're the only one who can remember that song.
  c. That's the quickest way to get to Sylvia's house.
  d. no mistakes

137. a. "Meet me at six o'clock," she said.
  b. Tired of running, she slowed her pace to a fast walk.
  c. Gabriel and me will attend the geography bee.
  d. no mistakes

138. a. Sheila's sister wanted to accompany us to the party.
  b. Who's scarf is this?
  c. "Be sure to wear something comfortable," she said.
  d. no mistakes

139. a. The main problem Jim had was too many parking tickets.
  b. As the bears ran toward us, it was growling.
  c. Try using less butter next time.
  d. no mistakes

140. a. Kamala was the most intelligent person in the group.
  b. The Eiffel Tower is in Paris, France.
  c. Nick Carraway is a character in *The Great Gatsby.*
  d. no mistakes

141. a. They weren't the only ones who didn't like the movie.
  b. "Please come back another time," Aunt Julie begged.
  c. "Threes a crowd," he always says.
  d. no mistakes

142. a. The first house on the street is there's.
  b. I love the fireworks on the Fourth of July.
  c. My grandparents live in San Juan, Puerto Rico.
  d. no mistakes

143. a. Either Cassie nor I heard the door open.
  b. How many people signed the Declaration of Independence?
  c. Draw up a plan before you make your decision.
  d. no mistakes

144. a. It's not my fault that you and him got caught.
  b. "Do you brush twice a day?" Dr. Evans asked.
  c. What's the weather report?
  d. no mistakes

145. a. Couldn't you arrive fashionably late?
  b. You're assumption is correct.
  c. I know that Bowser will be well treated.
  d. no mistakes

146.
  a. We invited Mayor Chen to speak at our school.
  b. The alarm sounded, and the firefighters jumped into the truck.
  c. The committee members should work as hard as one can.
  d. no mistakes

147.
  a. He wore two different-colored socks to class.
  b. Rhonda's sister bought a new Pontiac.
  c. Lake Superior is the largest of the Great Lakes.
  d. no mistakes

148.
  a. She and I have been friends for more than ten years.
  b. Is that one of the O'Farrell children?
  c. They took too much time to answer.
  d. no mistakes

Choose the sentence that is the most clearly written and has the best construction.

149.
  a. Melanie wrote to her sister once a week while she was living abroad.
  b. While her sister was living abroad, Melanie wrote to her once a week.
  c. When traveling abroad, a letter was written once a week by Melanie to her sister.
  d. Her sister received a letter once a week from Melanie while she was living abroad.

150.
  a. Some of the instructions I have to follow are very detailed, but that doesn't bother one as long as they are clear.
  b. Some of the instructions I have to follow are very detailed, but that doesn't bother you as long as they are clear.
  c. Some of the instructions I have to follow are very detailed, but it doesn't bother a person as long as they are clear.
  d. Some of the instructions I have to follow are very detailed, but that doesn't bother me as long as they are clear.

151.
  a. In search of the missing teenagers, who still had not been found through snake-ridden underbrush all day, the exhausted volunteers had struggled.
  b. All day the exhausted volunteers had struggled through snake-ridden underbrush in search of the missing teenagers, who still had not been found.
  c. All day the exhausted volunteers had struggled through snake-ridden underbrush who still had not been found in searching for the missing teenagers.
  d. The exhausted volunteers who still had not found in search of the missing teenagers when they had struggled through snake-ridden underbrush.

152. a. One New York publisher have estimated
that 50,000 to 60,000 people in the United
States want an anthology that includes the
complete works of William Shakespeare.

b. One New York publisher has estimated that
50,000 to 60,000 people in the United
States want a anthology that includes the
complete works of William Shakespeare.

c. One New York publisher has estimated that
50,000 to 60,000 people in the United
States want an anthology that includes the
complete works of William Shakespeare.

d. One New York publisher has estimated that
50,000 to 60,000 people in the United
States want an anthology that included the
complete works of William Shakespeare.

▶ **Answers**

62. b. This is an error in subject-verb agreement.
The subject, *committed citizens*, is plural
and requires a plural verb form. In this
case, the correct form is *exceed*, not the
singular form, *exceeds*.

63. b. The error is grammatical; there is no
subject-verb agreement in this sentence.
The subject *each* is singular and requires a
singular verb form. In this situation, the
correct form is *has had*.

64. a. This is an error in agreement. The singular
noun *one* requires the singular verb *is*.
When the subject (in this case *one*) follows
the verb, as in a sentence beginning with
here or *there*, be careful to determine the
subject. In this sentence, the subject is not
the plural noun *keys*.

65. d. This sentence has an illogical shift in verb
tense. The sentence should read: *He realized
that he had forgotten his umbrella.*

66. d. In this sentence, there is faulty parallelism.
The word *asking* should be replaced by the
verb *asked*. This sentence is in the past
tense, so the two verbs *asked* and *phoned*
should be parallel.

67. d. The use of the present participle *creating*
results in a sentence with faulty parallelism.
A form of the verb *create* should be parallel
with the preceding verb *became*, which is in
the past tense. The word *creating* should be
replaced by *created*.

68. b. There is no subject-verb agreement in this
sentence. The singular collective noun *staff*
requires a singular verb form. Therefore,
the plural form *deserve* should be replaced
with the singular *deserves*.

69. d. This sentence has faulty parallelism. There
are three items in a series in this sentence:
build homes, *find water*, and *learn to understand the blessings*. To make these three
items parallel, the word *to* should be
deleted in the underlined portion represented by choice **d**.

70. d. There is no subject-verb agreement in the
sentence. The subject of the second independent clause is *filter*, a singular noun.
Therefore, the singular form of the verb
should be used. The verb *reduce* should be
replaced by the verb *reduces*.

71. b. The error is in verb formation. The sentence requires the past tense of the verb
begin. To correct this error, the past participle *begun* should be replaced with the past
tense *began*.

72. c. The sentence requires a verb in the past perfect tense.

73. b. The verbal form *been eating* fits with the verb *have*.

74. c. The infinitive form of the verb *repair* goes with *to* in the sentence.

75. a. This is a command; the subject of the sentence is understood (*You call*).

76. d. The verb *was* agrees with its subject, *problem*, and is in the past tense.

77. c. Because the action took place before the past *honored*, the only correct choice is the past perfect *had fallen*.

78. b. This is the only choice that is in agreement with the singular subject *woman*.

79. c. The correct verb form is the past tense *swung*.

80. b. The verb *are* agrees with the plural noun *restaurants*.

81. a. The singular verb *gets* agrees with the singular noun *noise*.

82. d. A plural subject takes a plural verb; because the subject *words* is plural, the verb *are carved* must also be plural.

83. d. The three underlined elements make a coordinated series; to clearly express their relationship to each other, they need to abide by one consistent grammatical construction. In choice **a**, the verb *must generate* breaks the parallelism. In choice **b**, the word *for* breaks the parallelism. In choice **c**, the series changes construction, adopting a different type of parallel construction; however, the third element, *soil conservation*, does not use a present participle verb before it and therefore breaks the parallelism. In choice **e**, none of the three elements are parallel.

84. b. The two underlined elements make a coordinated pair; they need to abide by one grammatical construction. Only in choice **b** are both verbs in their infinitive form.

85. c. In choice **c**, the tenses of *rang* and *was writing* agree; there is no shift in tense.

86. d. Choice **d** is best because it is written in the active voice.

87. b. The second clause of this sentence requires a parallel construction. Choice **b** is the only one in which all four elements use the same grammatical construction, a verb in the present tense followed by a noun.

88. b. This is the best answer because no verb shifts into present tense. For the sentence to be logical, all the verbs should remain in the past and past perfect tenses.

89. e. *Conscience* is a moral awareness; *conscious* is a physical awareness. Josh was awake and physically aware of his environment. Choice **b**, like the original sentence, uses the wrong word to describe Josh's condition.

90. b. The correct verb form is *applauded*.

91. b. There is no subject-verb agreement. The verb should be plural because the subject, *plants*, is plural.

92. b. The verb is incorrect. The correct form is *should have been*.

93. c. The verb in this sentence has been incorrectly formed; it should be *drank*, not *drunk*.

94. b. There is no subject-verb agreement. The verb should be singular because the subject, *the liveliest one*, is singular.

95. a. The sentence makes an illogical shift in tense from the present to the past tense.

96. b. There is no subject-verb agreement. The verb should be plural because the subject, *photographs*, is plural.

97. d. There are no errors.

98. b. The correct verb form is *broke* or *has broken*.

99. a. The correct verb form is *rang*.

100. b. The sentence makes an illogical shift in tense from the past to the present tense.

101. b. There is no subject-verb agreement. The verb should be singular because the subject, *one* (not *boys*), is singular.

102. c. The correct verb form is *has worn*.

103. a. This sentence makes an illogical shift in tense from the past to the present tense.

104. a. The verbs *got* and *took* agree in tense.

105. d. The verbs *liked* and *got* agree in tense.

106. a. This is a complete sentence; the others are fragments.

107. d. This is a complete sentence; the others are fragments.

108. b. This is a complete sentence; **c** and **d** are fragments; in choice **a**, the verb does not agree in number with its subject, *one*.

109. b. This is a complete sentence; the others are fragments.

110. a. The comparison between the speaker's and his or her sister's taste for fish is clearest in this sentence. In choice **b**, the speaker likes his or her sister better than fish. Choice **c** does not make sense. Choice **d** has an ambiguous pronoun; *it* probably refers to fish, but who can tell?

111. d. In this sentence, the verb tense between the independent clause and the subordinating clause agree. In choice **a**, the lack of agreement in tense makes the sentence unclear as to time; choice **b** doesn't make it clear who ate the popcorn; choice **c** implies that the popcorn watched the movie.

112. e. Because there are no grammatical, idiomatic, logical, or structural errors in this sentence, **e** is the best answer.

113. d. This is a grammatical error. The contraction *it's* (meaning *it is*) should be replaced by the possessive pronoun *its*.

114. e. Because there are no grammatical errors in this sentence, the best answer is choice **e**.

115. e. Because there are no grammatical errors in this sentence, choice **e** is the best answer.

116. c. This is an error of agreement. The singular pronoun *it* does not agree with the plural noun *mollusks*. In this sentence, *it* should be replaced by the plural pronoun *they*.

117. c. This is an error in agreement. The singular pronoun *him* does not agree with its antecedent, the plural noun *people*. The word *him* should be replaced with the plural pronoun *them*.

118. e. Because there are no grammatical errors in this sentence, choice **e** is the best answer.

119. c. The word *there* should be replaced by the possessive pronoun *their*.

120. c. The pronoun *me* should be replaced by the pronoun *I*. In this sentence, *my brother, Aunt Clarissa, and I* is the subject, and the nominative (subjective) case is required. *Me* should be used only as an object pronoun.

121. e. Because there are no grammatical errors in this sentence, choice **e** is the best answer.

122. b. *Your* should be replaced by *you're*. Because these two words are pronounced alike, they are often confused. *Your* indicates possession, whereas *you're* is the contraction of *you are*.

123. e. Because there are no grammatical, idiomatic, logical, or structural errors in this sentence, **e** is the best answer.

124. b. The correct form of the pronoun is *me* (objective case).

125. b. The pronoun agrees in number with the noun to which it refers, and *them* should not be used as an adjective.

126. b. The antecedent, *George and Michael*, is plural, so the plural pronoun *their* is the correct choice.

127. c. The pronoun *that* agrees in number with the noun to which it refers, *artichoke*.

128. c. The pronoun *them* agrees with the plural noun *flowers*.

129. d. *She and I* is the subject of the sentence, so the subjective case is needed.

130. a. The possessive case is used before the word *taking*, because *taking* functions as a noun in this sentence.

131. b. There are two potential problems in this sentence: (1) the grammatical agreement between the nouns *Kendra or Zoë* and the pronoun *her* and (2) the formation of the verb *to bring*. In choice **b**, both of these are correct. Because the sentence reads *Kendra or Zoë*, the pronoun must be singular; only one of them brought the volleyball. *Brought* is the past tense of *bring*. The original sentence is wrong because the pronoun *their* is plural. Choice **c** is wrong because *there* is not a correct pronoun. Choices **d** and **e** are incorrect because *brang* is not the past tense of *bring*.

132. a. This choice is the only one that uses the proper form of possessive pronouns.

133. c. This choice is best because it is the only one in which there is no shift in person: *If you are looking . . . , you should compare. . . .* All of the other choices shift from third person (*someone, one, a person*) to second person (*you*).

134. d. When the relationship between a pronoun and its antecedent is unclear, as it is in this sentence, it should be changed to avoid ambiguity. There are two boys, Andre and Robert, and choice **d** makes the relationship clear: Robert's family moved, and not Andre's family.

135. c. The word *I* should be replaced with the word *me*, because the pronoun is the object, not the subject.

136. d. There are no errors.

137. c. The correct pronoun is *I*, not *me*.

138. b. The contraction *who's* is incorrect. The correct usage is the possessive *whose*.

139. b. This sentence contains a shift in number. *Bears* is a plural noun, so the clause should be *they were growling*.

140. d. There are no errors.

141. c. The contraction *three's*, which means *three is*, is the correct usage.

142. a. The correct usage is the possessive *theirs*, not *there's*.

143. a. *Either* is incorrect. Use *either* with *or* and *neither* with *nor*.

144. a. The pronoun *him* is incorrect. *He* should be used because *you* and *he* are the subjects of the dependent clause.

145. b. The contraction *You're* should be replaced with the possessive *Your*.

146. c. This sentence makes a shift in person. It should read: *The committee members should work as hard as they can.*

147. d. There are no errors.

148. d. There are no errors.

149. b. In the other choices, the pronoun reference is ambiguous; it is unclear who is traveling abroad.

150. d. The other answers contain unnecessary shifts in person from *I* to *one*, *you*, and *a person*.

151. b. This is the only choice that is clear and unambiguous. All the other choices contain misplaced modifiers, resulting in unclear and illogical statements.

152. c. This is the only choice that is grammatically correct. Choices **a** and **d** use the verbs incorrectly. Choice **b** uses *a* instead of *an* before *anthology*.

3 ▶ Modifiers—Are Yours Misplaced or Dangling?

WHAT WRITERS DO when they alter a word is a lot like what tailors do when they modify a piece of fabric or an article of clothing. A tailor takes a needle to a hem to adjust its length or width just as a writer uses a **modifier** to limit and define a word. In both cases, customization is being performed. Just as there are different ways to modify a garment, there are also different ways to modify a word. There are four different types of modifiers:

1. **prepositional phrase:** a phrase beginning with a preposition and ending with a noun or pronoun. When prepositions such as *about, across, above, along,* and *before* precede a noun or pronoun, the preposition and its object combine together to form a prepositional phrase.
2. **adjective:** a part of speech that modifies a noun or pronoun by describing it. You can usually find an adjective in front of the word it is describing, but adjectives have also been known to follow a word if they are being used as a complement: *The school is superb. We did nothing important.*

3. **adverb:** a part of speech that modifies a verb, an adjective, or another adverb. Adverbs help the reader to understand the *Where? When? How?* about the verb, adjective, or other adverb. Adverbs can often be spotted by their *-ly* endings, but there are exceptions.

4. **appositive:** a noun phrase that is used to fill in the blanks and provide additional information about a noun: *Miley Cyrus, a popular singer and actress, is working on a new movie about her character Hannah Montana.*

Have you ever **misplaced** your modifier? Hmmm, if you've misplaced your modifier, the best place to find it is far away from its rightful home. Here is an example of a modifier that was lost and then found.

Misplaced: Please discuss the classroom rule sheet that is enclosed with your child.

Found: Please discuss the enclosed classroom rule sheet with your child.

Have you ever **dangled** your modifier? A dangling modifier can best be described as a homeless vagabond, because it has lost its way and there's no place for it to go. More formally, a dangling modifier can be defined as a word or phrase that is intended to modify a specific part of a sentence that is missing, so the modifier has not been placed next to the word or phrase that it was meant to modify. Let's look at an example of a dangling modifier in action: *Desiring good teaching jobs, private schools are swamped with teaching resumes.* Because it's pretty obvious that it's not the private schools that are desiring good teaching jobs, the verbal phrase modifier *desiring good teaching jobs* is dangling—it doesn't have an appropriate word to modify.

Get a Grip

The Mega Super-Important Adjective Modifier Rule

Adjectives almost always modify the noun that they are closest to. There are very few exceptions!

What you need to do in this case is ask who, or what, is "desiring good teaching jobs"? To help the verbal phrase modifier find a home, the sentence is corrected by adding a word or group of words for the dangling modifier to modify. Let's look at the revised version of the sentence: *Desiring good teaching jobs, teachers are swamping private schools with resumes.* The modifier has found a purposeful new home, because it is now modifying the word *teachers*.

Don't you just love a happy ending?

Get a Grip on Adverbs

If you have trouble remembering their function, just remember this: **Adverbs** "add" information about where, when, how, or to what extent.

Example
When the meal was served, Laura ate quickly. (The adverb *quickly* modifies the word *ate* by describing how fast Laura ate her meal.)

Resources

Immel, Constance, and Florence Sacks. *Better Grammar in 30 Minutes a Day* (New York: Career Press, 1995).

Merriam-Webster's Collegiate Dictionary, 11th ed. (Springfield, MA: Merriam-Webster, 2003).

O'Conner, Patricia T. *Woe Is I Jr.: The Younger Grammarphobe's Guide to Better English in Plain English*. Drawings by Tom Stiglich (New York: Putnam Juvenile, 2007).

Rogers, James, ed. *The Dictionary of Clichés* (New York: Facts on File, 1985; Ballantine Books, 1987).

Webster's New World Speller/Divider (New York: John Wiley & Sons, 1992). Poor spellers will love this quick-reference spelling guide!

Grammar-Building Games for Middle School/ High School Students

Grammar Mania!

Language Detective

Parts of Speech Challenge

Writing Skills Success in 20 Minutes a Day, 3rd ed. (LearningExpress).

▶ Practice Questions

For the following questions, choose the underlined part of the sentence that contains a grammatical error. If there are no errors, choose **e**.

153. <u>Frightened,</u> the little boy screamed <u>loud</u> as his
    a   **b**

<u>neighbor's</u> friendly <u>80-pound dog</u> bounded up
  c   **d**

the sidewalk. No error
        e

154. Gwen's friend Luke—<u>once the star</u> quarterback
               a

of his college football team and now a

<u>successful restaurateur</u>—<u>owns</u> ten restaurants
  b   **c**

and <u>has published</u> three award-winning
    d

cookbooks. No error
        (e)

155. At 3,434 miles long, the Yangtze, a <u>major</u>
               a

east-west trade and <u>transportation route</u>, is
          b

<u>easily</u> the <u>longest</u> river in Asia. No error
  c   **d**   **(e)**

156. Despite its daunting <u>three-hour</u> length, the
            (a)

<u>movie's</u> popularity <u>continues to grow;</u> last
  b   **c**

week, <u>it took</u> in $12.7 million. No error
    d   **e**

157. The love seat is now <u>being installed</u> in some
            a

New York movie theaters, <u>giving</u> couples the
          b

option of lifting the arm <u>between</u> the seats to
          c

create a <u>more cozier</u> viewing experience.
      d

No error
(e)

158. Some buildings, <u>such as</u> the White House,
　　　　　　　　　　　a

Saint Paul's <u>Cathedral,</u> and the Taj Mahal,
　　　　　　　b

deserve to be preserved not only because

of <u>their</u> artistic excellence <u>but also</u> because of
　　c　　　　　　　　　　　**d**

their symbolic associations. No <u>error</u>
　　　　　　　　　　　　　　　(**e**)

159. Because they <u>close</u> resemble sound arguments,
　　　　　　　　(**a**)　　　　　　　　　　　**b**

fallacious arguments can sound convincing, so

be sure to <u>carefully organize</u> your thoughts
　　　　　　　c

when <u>you're</u> writing an opinion paper.
　　　　d

No error
e

160. <u>When</u> the professor called out Pete's name,
　　a

<u>he walked</u> rather <u>hesitant</u> to the front of the
　　b　　　　　(**c**)

room and stood <u>there</u> shaking. No error
　　　　　　d　　　　　　　**e**

161. The puppy had been treated <u>bad</u> by <u>its</u>
　　　　　　　　　　　　　　(**a**)　　**b**

previous <u>owner, but</u> the people at the animal
　　　　　c

shelter <u>worked hard</u> to find a loving home for
　　　　d

little Scotty. No error
　　　　　e

Fill in the blank with the correct adjective or adverb.

162. In many popular movies today, the heroes are
_____ armed than the villains.
(**a.**) more heavily
b. more heavy
c. heavier
d. more heavier

163. The cake I made last week tasted _____
than the one I made today.
a. best
b. more better
(**c.**) better
d. more good

164. Of the three brothers, Andre is the _____.
a. taller
(**b.**) tallest
c. more tall
d. most tallest

165. Riding the Tornado at the amusement park
was _____ than the boy thought it would
be.
(**a.**) more terrifying
b. more terrifyingly
c. terrifying
d. most terrifying

166. This year, our company sold _____
magazine subscriptions than ever before.
a. less
b. lesser
c. few
(**d.**) fewer

Replace the underlined word(s) with the word or phrase that is grammatically correct. If the sentence is correct as is, choose **a**.

167. The book had <u>a frighteningly and unhappy ending.</u>
   a. correct as is
   b. a frighteningly and unhappily ending.
   c. an ending that was frightening and unhappily.
   d. a frightening and unhappy ending.
   e. an ending that was frightening and it was also an unhappy one.

168. Since her graduation from business school last spring, Adela has become known <u>as the more important</u> member of her graduating class.
   a. correct as is
   b. as the most important
   c. as the most importantly
   d. as the more importantly
   e. like the most important

169. <u>There wasn't nothing that could have been easier.</u>
   a. correct as is
   b. There was nothing that could have been more easier.
   c. Nothing could have been more easier.
   d. Nothing couldn't have been more easy.
   e. Nothing could have been easier.

170. <u>I was clearly the happiest person in the crowd.</u>
   a. correct as is
   b. It was clear that I was the happier person in the crowd.
   c. Of all the people in the crowd, I was clearly the happier.
   d. In the crowd, clearly, I was the happier person.
   e. Of all the people in the crowd, clearly, I being the happiest.

171. Strip mining, the <u>cheaper</u> method of mining, is controversial because it jeopardizes the environment.
   a. correct as is
   b. more cheap
   c. most cheapest
   d. cheapest
   e. more cheaply

Find the sentence that has a mistake in grammar or usage. If you find no mistakes, mark choice **d**.

172. **a.** The steam rose up from the hot pavement.
   b. She put the kitten down carefully beside its mom.
   c. Neither of us is going to the party.
   d. no mistakes

173. **a.** The lost dog wandered sad through the streets.
   b. Frustrated, Boris threw his pencil across the room.
   c. We'll stop at their house first.
   d. no mistakes

174. **a.** Have you ever read the book *Little House on the Prairie*?
    b. She urged me not to go.
    c. Stop, look, and listen.
    d. no mistakes

175. **a.** Anne will head out first, and Nick will follow her.
    b. Maya Angelou, a famous writer, directed the movie *Down in the Delta* in 1998.
    c. The clerk asked for my address and phone number.
    d. no mistakes

176. **a.** We sold less cookies this year than we did last year.
    b. That parrot doesn't talk.
    c. Don't spend too much money.
    d. no mistakes

177. **a.** She spread the frosting too thickly.
    b. "What is your answer?" she asked.
    c. We waited while he stopped to make a phone call.
    d. no mistakes

178. **a.** The Adirondacks are mountains in New York.
    b. President Carter led negotiations to transfer control of the Panama Canal back to Panama.
    c. That river is terribly polluted.
    d. no mistakes

179. **a.** *Trading Spaces* is one of the most popular shows on television.
    b. Which color do you like better, the teal or the flamingo pink?
    c. Mango-peach berry juice is the most awfulest drink.
    d. no mistakes

▶ Answers

153. **b.** In this sentence, *loud* modifies the verb *screamed*. The adverb *loudly* should be used instead of *loud*.

154. **e.** Because there are no errors in this sentence, **e** is the correct choice.

155. **e.** Because there are no errors in this sentence, **e** is the correct choice.

156. **e.** Because there are no errors in this sentence, **e** is the correct choice.

157. **d.** The double comparative *more cozier* is redundant; just the comparative word *cozier* is sufficient to convey the idea that New York movie theaters will become more comfortable with the addition of love seats.

158. **e.** Because there are no errors in this sentence, **e** is the correct choice.

159. **a.** In this sentence, *close* attempts to modify the verb *resemble*. The adverb *closely* should be used instead of *close*.

160. **c.** In this sentence, *hesitant* attempts to modify the verb *walked*. The adverb *hesitantly* should be used instead of *hesitant*.

161. **a.** Use *bad* when modifying a noun; use *badly* when modifying a verb. The verb *treated* should be modified by the adverb *badly*, not the adjective *bad*.

162. **a.** The missing phrase modifies the verb *are armed* and creates a comparison between two types of people, heroes and villains. Therefore, you need a comparative form of the adverb *heavily*.

163. **c.** The comparison is between two things, a cake made last week and a cake made today; choices **a** and **d** can be ruled out. Choice **b**, *more better*, is redundant. Choice **c**, *better*, is the best choice to make the comparison.

164. b. The comparison is being made among three brothers; therefore, this sentence requires a superlative. Choices **a** and **c** compare only two things, and choice **d** is redundant.

165. a. The missing phrase modifies a noun, *riding*, and makes a comparison between two things, what he thought and what it was; therefore, the sentence requires a comparative adjective. Choice **b** is a comparative adverb. Choice **c** does not make a comparison, and choice **d** is a superlative, a comparison of three or more things. Choice **a**, *more terrifying*, is the correct choice.

166. d. Use *fewer* with nouns that can be counted.

167. d. Adjectives modify nouns, and adverbs modify verbs. In choice **d**, the adjectives *frightening* and *unhappy* correctly modify the noun *ending*. In the original sentence and in choice **b**, the adverb *frighteningly* incorrectly attempts to modify a noun. In choice **c**, the adverb *unhappily* incorrectly attempts to modify a noun. Choice **e** is unnecessarily wordy.

168. b. The sentence makes a comparison between Adela and all other members of the graduating class; therefore, the superlative form *most* should be used. The original sentence and choice **d** are wrong because they use the comparative *more*. Choice **c** is wrong because the word *importantly* is an adverb and cannot modify the noun *member*. Choice **e** is wrong because it uses the word *like* incorrectly.

169. e. This is the correct choice because the sentence uses *easier* correctly and does not contain a double negative. The other choices either use two negative words within a single sentence or use an incorrect comparative form of *easy*.

170. a. The sentence compares an individual and an entire crowd of individuals; therefore, it requires a superlative. Only choice **a** coherently uses the superlative *happiest* to make the comparison among all the many people in the crowd.

171. d. This sentence makes a comparison between strip mining and all other types of mining; therefore, it requires a superlative. The original sentence and choice **b** compare only two things, while choice **e** inappropriately uses an adverb. Choice **c** uses a double superlative and is redundant.

172. d. There are no errors.

173. a. The adjective *sad* should be replaced with the adverb *sadly*, which correctly modifies the verb *wandered*.

174. d. There are no errors.

175. d. There are no errors.

176. a. This sentence has a usage error: *fewer* cookies, not *less* cookies.

177. d. There are no errors.

178. d. There are no errors.

179. c. *Most awfulest* is a double superlative, and therefore redundant.

Sentence Sense

> "When I use a word," Humpty Dumpty said in a rather scornful tone, "it means just what I choose it to mean—neither more nor less."
>
> "The question is," said Alice, "whether you can make words mean so many different things."
>
> "The question is," said Humpty Dumpty, "which is to be master— that's all."
>
> —Lewis Carroll, *Through the Looking Glass*

THIS CHAPTER IS designed to provide targeted practice in the area of sentence structure, sentence completion, and vocabulary building.

▶ Sentence Structure

Tape this rule to your wrist if you must, but do not forget it: In order to be complete, a sentence must contain a subject and a predicate (verb). **Phrases** do not contain both a subject and a predicate, but they are part of a sentence that does contain a subject and a predicate. Sentences that do not contain both a subject and a predicate are called **sentence fragments**, because they are not complete. Repeat after me: *A complete sentence requires a subject and a predicate.* If either element is missing, a complete sentence does not exist.

Word Bite: *Phrase*

A **phrase** is a group of words that does not have a subject and a predicate (verb) and can't stand alone as a sentence.

In other words, you must always tell the reader the subject of each sentence and what that subject is doing or being. Because the subject-predicate rule is so important, we've set it off here so that you can highlight it with the brightest and boldest highlighter that you have.

Get a Grip

The Mega Super-Important Subject-Predicate Rule

In order to be complete, a sentence *must* contain *a subject and a predicate.*

Now, what are those pesky things called clauses? Do we really need them? Yes! Trying to build a sentence without a clause is like trying to build a house without a frame. There are several forms of clauses that you really must get to know. An **independent clause** is a free agent containing the subject and predicate that it needs to function independently—it is complete and expresses an idea or concept entirely on its own. A **dependent (subordinate) clause** is a different story—it is incomplete and is classified as either essential or nonessential. In an **essential dependent clause**, the information that the clause contains is indispensable to the meaning of the sentence. If a clause is a **nonessential clause**, the information in it is supplementary. Thankfully, sentences don't have feelings, because if they did, the nonessential clause would likely develop an inferiority com-

plex. Nonessential clauses add depth and interesting detail to a sentence, but they're not necessary.

There are the four classifications of sentences:

1. **Simple sentence:** a sentence that contains one subject and one verb (one main idea)

   Example
   Rachel cooked dinner.

   Rachel is the only subject in the sentence. *Cooked* is the only verb in the sentence.

2. **Compound sentence:** a sentence in which clauses are linked together with a coordinating conjunction: *and, but, for, or, nor, so, yet*

   Example
   Rachel cooked dinner, and Jack set the table.

   Two clauses are linked together using the coordinating conjunction *and.*

3. **Complex sentence:** a sentence that is made up of an independent clause and a subordinate (dependent) clause

   Example
   Rachel cooked dinner *because she was expecting company.*

   The italic portion is the subordinate clause, because it can't stand alone.

4. **Compound-complex sentence:** a sentence that is made up of more than one independent clause and at least one subordinate clause

   Example
   Jumping rope at the top of the driveway, Pamela pretended to ignore her brothers playing football, but <u>she laughed out loud when one of them almost ran into a tree.</u>

Get a Grip on Sentence Structure

Snag Those Frags

If a friend came up to you and said, "After walking my dog," you'd probably ask: "What happens after you walk your dog?" *After walking my dog* is a sentence fragment; it is a subordinate clause that cannot stand alone. You can identify subordinate clauses by becoming familiar with the most commonly used subordinating conjunctions that are used to construct these clauses:

after	although	and	as
because	before	if	since
so	that	though	unless
until	when	whenever	where
wherever	which	while	who
why			

▶ Practice Questions

Choose the sentence that best combines the original two sentences.

180. The airport is called the Glynco Jetport. The airline reservations and travel systems refer to its location as Brunswick, Georgia.

   a. Where the airport is called the Glynco Jetport, the airline reservations and travel systems refer to the location as Brunswick, Georgia.

   b. But the airport is called the Glynco Jetport, the airline reservations and travel systems refer to the location as Brunswick, Georgia.

   c. Even though the airline reservations and travel systems refer to the location as Brunswick, Georgia, the airport is called the Glynco Jetport.

   d. When the airport is called the Glynco Jetport, the airline reservations refer to the location as Brunswick, Georgia, and the travel systems.

181. Recently there have been government cutbacks in funds. Experts foresee steady hiring in the government's future.

   a. Despite recent government cutbacks in funds, experts foresee steady hiring in the government's future.

   b. Whereupon recent government cutbacks in funds, experts foresee steady hiring in the government's future.

   c. So that there have been recent government cutbacks in funds, experts foresee steady hiring in the government's future.

   d. Nonetheless, there have been recent government cutbacks in funds, experts foresee steady hiring in the government's future.

182. The federal government has diversity of jobs and geographic locations. The federal government offers flexibility in job opportunities that is unmatched in the private sector.

a. In spite of its diversity of jobs and geographic locations, the federal government offers flexibility in job opportunities that is unmatched in the private sector.

b. No matter its diversity of jobs and geographic locations, the federal government offers flexibility in job opportunities that is unmatched in the private sector.

c. Because of its diversity of jobs and geographic locations, the federal government offers flexibility in job opportunities that is unmatched in the private sector.

d. The federal government has diversity of jobs and geographic locations, it offers flexibility in job opportunities that is unmatched in the private sector.

183. The Greeks thought that the halcyon, or kingfisher, nested on the sea. All birds nest on land.

a. Whereupon all birds nest on land, the Greeks thought that the halcyon, or kingfisher, nested on the sea.

b. The Greeks thought that the halcyon, or kingfisher, nested on the sea, whereas all birds nest on land.

c. Whenever all birds nest on land, the Greeks thought that the halcyon, or kingfisher, nested on the sea.

d. The Greeks thought that the halcyon, or kingfisher, nested on the sea, as all birds nest on land.

184. There have been great strides in the practical application of quantum physics in the past decade. We are no closer to actually understanding it than were the physicists of the 1920s.

a. Unless there have been great strides in the practical application of quantum physics in the past few decades, we are no closer to actually understanding it than were the physicists of the 1920s.

b. In the past few decades, we are no closer to actually understanding it than were the physicists of the 1920s, until there have been great strides in the practical application of quantum physics.

c. Although there have been great strides in the practical application of quantum physics in the past few decades, we are no closer to actually understanding it than were the physicists of the 1920s.

d. In the past few decades, if there have been great strides in the practical application of quantum physics we are no closer to actually understanding it than were the physicists of the 1920s.

185. The wisdom of the hedgehog is applauded in medieval bestiaries. The hedgehog makes a burrow with two exits and, when in danger, rolls itself into a prickly ball.

a. The wisdom of the hedgehog is applauded in medieval bestiaries, while the hedgehog makes a burrow with two exits and, when in danger, rolls itself into a prickly ball.

b. The hedgehog makes a burrow with two exits and, when in danger, rolls itself into a prickly ball, so its wisdom is applauded in medieval bestiaries.

c. The hedgehog makes a burrow with two exits and, when in danger, rolls itself into a prickly ball, but its wisdom is applauded in medieval bestiaries.

d. Its wisdom applauded in medieval bestiaries, the hedgehog makes a burrow with two exits and, when in danger, rolls itself into a prickly ball.

186. Some people believe fairy tales are merely children's stories. Some people believe fairy tales carry important psychological truths for adults.

a. When some believe they carry important psychological truths for adults, some people believe fairy tales are merely children's stories.

b. Some people believe fairy tales are merely children's stories, whereupon some believe they carry important psychological truths for adults.

c. Because some believe fairy tales carry important psychological truths for adults, some people believe fairy tales are merely children's stories.

d. Some people believe fairy tales are merely children's stories, yet some believe they carry important psychological truths for adults.

187. Most species of the bacterium Streptococcus are harmless. Some species of Streptococcus are dangerous pathogens.

a. Whereas most species of the bacterium Streptococcus are harmless, some are dangerous pathogens.

b. Since most species of the bacterium Streptococcus are harmless, some are dangerous pathogens.

c. As most species of the bacterium Streptococcus are harmless, some are dangerous pathogens.

d. Because most species of the bacterium Streptococcus are harmless, some are dangerous pathogens.

188. The man nodded politely. His expression was bewildered.

a. Nodding politely, the man's expression was bewildered.

b. The man nodded politely his expression was bewildered.

c. The man nodded politely, his expression bewildered.

d. The man nodded politely, since his expression was bewildered.

189. Watching a TV show is a passive behavior. Playing a computer game is an interactive one.

a. Watching a TV show is a passive behavior, or playing a computer game is an interactive one.

b. Watching a TV show is a passive behavior, for playing a computer game is an interactive one.

c. Watching a TV show is a passive behavior, but playing a computer game is an interactive one.

d. Being that playing a computer game is an interactive one, watching a TV show is a passive behavior.

190. Socrates taught that we should question everything, even the law. He was both greatly loved and profoundly hated.

a. That he was both greatly loved and profoundly hated, Socrates taught that we should question everything, even the law.

b. Socrates taught that we should question everything, even the law, so he was both greatly loved and profoundly hated.

c. Socrates taught that we should question everything, even the law, which he was both greatly loved and profoundly hated.

d. Socrates taught that we should question everything, even the law, for he was both greatly loved and profoundly hated.

191. Sailors were said to catch albatross with baited hooks let down into the ship's wake. To kill the albatross was thought to be bad luck, so they were released immediately.

a. Sailors were said to catch albatross with baited hooks let down into the ship's wake, then release them again, for to kill the albatross was thought to be bad luck.

b. With baited hooks let down into the ship's wake, sailors were said to catch albatross then release them again, so to kill the albatross was thought to be bad luck.

c. Sailors were said to catch albatross with baited hooks let down into the ship's wake, then release them again, or to kill the albatross was thought to be bad luck.

d. To kill the albatross was thought to be bad luck, sailors were said to catch albatross with baited hooks let down into the ship's wake, only to release them immediately.

192. The symptoms of diabetes often develop gradually and are hard to identify at first. Nearly half of all people with diabetes do not know they have it.

a. The symptoms of diabetes often develop gradually and are hard to identify at first, so nearly half of all people with diabetes do not know they have it.

b. The symptoms of diabetes often develop gradually and are hard to identify at first, yet nearly half of all people with diabetes do not know they have it.

c. Nearly half of all people with diabetes do not know they have it, and the symptoms of diabetes often develop gradually and are hard to identify at first.

d. The symptoms of diabetes often develop gradually for nearly half of all people with diabetes do not know they have it and are hard to identify at first.

193. The French philosopher Voltaire was greatly respected. Voltaire spent almost a year imprisoned in the Bastille.

a. The French philosopher Voltaire was greatly respected, so he spent almost a year imprisoned in the Bastille.

b. The French philosopher Voltaire was greatly respected with almost a year imprisoned in the Bastille.

c. The French philosopher Voltaire was greatly respected, or he spent almost a year imprisoned in the Bastille.

d. The French philosopher Voltaire was greatly respected, yet he spent almost a year imprisoned in the Bastille.

194. I must buy some new shoes to wear to the prom. My date, Donnie, will be upset if I wear my flip-flops.

   a. Unless my date, Donnie, will be upset if I wear my flip-flops, I must buy some new shoes to wear to the prom.

   b. I must buy some new shoes to wear to the prom, and my date, Donnie, will be upset if I wear my flip-flops.

   c. I must buy some new shoes to wear to the prom, for my date, Donnie, will be upset if I wear my flip-flops.

   d. My date, Donnie, will be upset if I wear my flip-flops while I must buy some new shoes to wear to the prom.

195. The rules of statistics say that it is possible for all the air in a room to move to one corner. This is extremely unlikely.

   a. The rules of statistics say that it is possible for all the air in a room to move to one corner, or this is extremely unlikely.

   b. The rules of statistics say that it is possible for all the air in a room to move to one corner, but this is extremely unlikely.

   c. This is extremely unlikely in that the rules of statistics say that it is possible for all the air in a room to move to one corner.

   d. For all the air in a room to move to one corner, this is extremely unlikely, according to the rules of statistics saying that it is possible.

196. I must buy my dog a new license. If I don't, I will have to pay a fine.

   a. I must buy my dog a new license, and I will have to pay a fine.

   b. I must buy my dog a new license; I will have to pay a fine.

   c. Unless I buy my dog a new license, I will have to pay a fine.

   d. I will have to pay a fine since I must buy my dog a new license.

197. Bats are not rodents. Bats bear a surface resemblance to a winged mouse.

   a. Bats are not rodents, although they do bear a resemblance to a winged mouse.

   b. Bats are not rodents that they bear a surface resemblance to a winged mouse.

   c. Bats are not rodents, when they bear a surface resemblance to a winged mouse.

   d. Bats are not rodents, if they bear a surface resemblance to a winged mouse.

198. Art is not only found in the museum or concert hall. Art can be found in the expressive behavior of ordinary people, as well.

   a. Art can be found not only in the museum or concert hall, and it can be found in the expressive behavior of ordinary people, as well.

   b. In the museum or concert hall, art can be found not only there and in the expressive behavior of ordinary people, as well.

   c. Although in the expressive behavior of ordinary people, as well, art can be found not only in the museum or concert hall.

   d. Art can be found not only in the museum or concert hall, but in the expressive behavior of ordinary people, as well.

199. In lucid dreams, the dreamer knows she is dreaming. It gives her a sense of unlimited freedom.

    a. In lucid dreams, the dreamer knows she is dreaming, although it gives her a sense of unlimited freedom.

    b. In lucid dreams, the dreamer knows she is dreaming, while it gives her a sense of unlimited freedom.

    c. In lucid dreams, the dreamer knows she is dreaming, where it gives her a sense of unlimited freedom.

    d. In lucid dreams, the dreamer knows she is dreaming, which gives her a sense of unlimited freedom.

200. She never responded to the invitation we sent. We assumed she wasn't coming.

    a. She never responded to the invitation we sent; however we assumed she wasn't coming.

    b. While we assumed she wasn't coming, she never responded to the invitation we sent.

    c. She never responded to the invitation we sent, whether we assumed she wasn't coming.

    d. Because she never responded to the invitation we sent, we assumed she wasn't coming.

201. Elizabeth is an athletic woman. Elizabeth cannot swim or ride a bike.

    a. Elizabeth cannot swim or ride a bike, while she is an athletic woman.

    b. Elizabeth cannot swim or ride a bike and is an athletic woman.

    c. Although Elizabeth cannot swim or ride a bike, she is an athletic woman.

    d. Being an athletic woman, Elizabeth cannot swim or ride a bike.

202. This neighborhood is called "baby central." Almost every family within a three-block radius has a child under the age of one.

    a. Almost every family within a three-block radius has a child under the age of one, while this neighborhood is called "baby central."

    b. Almost every family within a three-block radius has a child under the age of one, but this neighborhood is called "baby central."

    c. Almost every family within a three-block radius has a child under the age of one; therefore, this neighborhood is called "baby central."

    d. This neighborhood is called "baby central:" meanwhile, almost every family within a three-block radius has a child under the age of one.

203. The new shopping mall has 200 stores. The new shopping mall doesn't have a pet shop.

    a. The new shopping mall has 200 stores; however, it doesn't have a pet shop.

    b. Instead of a pet shop, the new shopping mall has 200 stores.

    c. With 200 stores, the new shopping mall doesn't have a pet shop.

    d. The new shopping mall has 200 stores, and it doesn't have a pet shop.

204. Eugene has a difficult personality. Eugene is unreliable.

    a. Eugene has a difficult personality, and furthermore, he's unreliable.

    b. Eugene has a difficult personality, although he is unreliable.

    c. While he is unreliable, Eugene has a difficult personality.

    d. Being unreliable, Eugene has a difficult personality.

205. We never eat candy or ice cream. We do drink soda.

   a. We never eat candy or ice cream, but we do drink soda.

   b. Because we never eat candy or ice cream, we drink soda.

   c. We never eat candy or ice cream, so we do drink soda.

   d. We never eat candy or ice cream and drink soda.

206. She loves celebrating her birthday. She always has a big party.

   a. She loves celebrating her birthday, to where she always has a big party.

   b. Although she loves celebrating her birthday, she always has a big party.

   c. She always has a big party, meanwhile she loves celebrating her birthday.

   d. She loves celebrating her birthday, so she always has a big party.

207. Insomnia is not usually a physical problem. It can affect one's physical health.

   a. Insomnia is not usually a physical problem; therefore, it can affect one's physical health.

   b. Insomnia is not usually a physical problem, yet it can affect one's physical health.

   c. Insomnia not usually a physical problem can affect one's physical health.

   d. Insomnia is not usually a physical problem, so it can affect one's physical health.

208. True narcolepsy is the sudden and irresistible onset of sleep during waking hours. True narcolepsy is extremely dangerous.

   a. While true narcolepsy is the sudden and irresistible onset of sleep during waking hours and is extremely dangerous.

   b. The sudden and irresistible onset of sleep during waking hours, which is true narcolepsy but extremely dangerous.

   c. True narcolepsy is the sudden and irresistible onset of sleep during waking hours, yet narcolepsy is extremely dangerous.

   d. True narcolepsy is the sudden and irresistible onset of sleep during waking hours, and it is extremely dangerous.

209. There has been much interest in dreams throughout the ages. The empirical, scientific study of dreams is relatively new.

   a. Despite much interest in dreams throughout the ages, the empirical, scientific study of dreams being relatively new.

   b. There has been much interest in dreams throughout the ages, yet the empirical, scientific study of dreams is relatively new.

   c. While much interest in dreams throughout the ages, although the empirical, scientific study of dreams is relatively new.

   d. There has been much interest in dreams throughout the ages, for the empirical, scientific study of dreams is relatively new.

Replace the underlined portion with the alternative that best completes the sentence. If the sentence is correct as is, choose **a**.

210. I look forward to welcoming you and having the opportunity to show you around our office.
a. correct as is
b. I will look forward to our welcome and having
c. As I look forward to welcoming you and to have
d. I look forward to welcoming you and have
e. Looking forward to welcoming you and hoping to have

211. For a wide variety of different reasons, more and more people are making the choice to vacation close to home.
a. correct as is
b. For a variety of many reasons, much more people
c. For a number of reasons, more people
d. More people, for various different reasons,
e. Lots of people, for many numerous reasons

212. The likelihood that she will decide to take the job is great, she is never completely predictable.
a. correct as is
b. Although the likelihood
c. Since the likelihood
d. In fact, the likelihood
e. Knowing that the likelihood

213. Most of a human tooth is made up of a substance known as dentin, which is located directly below the enamel.
a. correct as is
b. dentin, and which is located
c. dentin but located
d. dentin, which it is located
e. dentin, that its location is

214. Jackson Pollock, a twentieth-century American painter, is well known and renowned for creating abstract paintings by dripping paint on canvas.
a. correct as is
b. an American painter who lived and painted in the twentieth century, is well known for the creation of
c. renowned and prominent, was known as a twentieth-century American painter for creating
d. he is an American painter famous and renowned for creating
e. a twentieth-century American painter, is famous for creating

215. Having missed class several times, this was the cause of our poor grades.
a. correct as is
b. After missing class several times, our poor grades were anticipated.
c. Because we missed class several times, we received poor grades.
d. We received poor grades missing class several times.
e. Receiving poor grades, we missed class several times.

216. Because of the need for accuracy, <u>all employ-ees must diligently review their work at the end of every day.</u>
  a. correct as is
  b. all employees who work here must be dili-gent and careful to review their work at the end of every day.
  c. employees must be diligently reviewing and checking their work at the end of every day.
  d. workers and employees must diligently review their work at the end of every day.
  e. all employees must diligently review and assess their work daily, every day.

217. <u>Beside his expertise in gardening,</u> Malcolm is also an accomplished carpenter.
  a. correct as is
  b. Beside gardening,
  c. In addition also to his accomplished carpentry,
  d. Besides his expertise in gardening,
  e. Beside his gardening,

218. Baseball is a sport that is <u>popular in the United States like Japan.</u>
  a. correct as is
  b. as well popular in Japan as it is in the United States.
  c. just as popular in the United States than in Japan.
  d. popular in the United States as well as in Japan.
  e. popular as well as in both Japan and the United States.

219. I decided to paint the kitchen <u>yellow, and after I had painted, my husband</u> informed me that he'd rather it be blue.
  a. correct as is
  b. yellow, and after I had painted my husband
  c. yellow and after I had painted, my husband
  d. yellow; and, after I had painted my husband
  e. yellow and after I had painted my husband

220. <u>Yelling after it as the taxi drove away, leaving Austin and me standing helplessly on the sidewalk.</u>
  a. correct as is
  b. While yelling after it and watching the taxi drive away, which left Austin and me stand-ing helplessly on the sidewalk.
  c. Left helplessly standing on the sidewalk after Austin and me yelled after the taxi and watched as it drove away.
  d. As we yelled after it, the taxi drove away, leaving Austin and me standing helplessly on the sidewalk.
  e. After having yelled after it, the taxi driving off and leaving Austin and me on the side-walk, watching helplessly.

221. When making a chocolate torte, <u>only the best ingredients should be used.</u>
  a. correct as is
  b. you should use only the best ingredients.
  c. the best ingredients only should be used.
  d. one should have used only the best ingredients.
  e. using only the best ingredients is essential.

222. With her book *Coming of Age in Samoa*, anthropologist Margaret Mead emphasized the role of culture, <u>rather than biology, in shaping human behavior.</u>
- **a.** correct as is
- **b.** rather than biology with shaping human behavior.
- **c.** somewhat better than biology to shape human behavior.
- **d.** in shaping human behavior, and not biology.
- **e.** in shaping human behavior over biology.

223. <u>This was the fifth of the five speeches the mayor gave during this the month of May.</u>
- **a.** correct as is
- **b.** Of the five speeches the mayor gave during May, this was the fifth one.
- **c.** Thus far during the month of May, the mayor gave five speeches and this was the fifth.
- **d.** This fifth speech of the mayor's given during the month of May was one of five speeches.
- **e.** This was the fifth speech the mayor has given during the month of May.

224. An American poet of the nineteenth century, <u>Walt Whitman's collection of poems, *Leaves of Grass*,</u> celebrates nature and individualism.
- **a.** correct as is
- **b.** *Leaves of Grass*, a collection of poems by Walt Whitman,
- **c.** a collection of poems, *Leaves of Grass*, by Walt Whitman,
- **d.** Walt Whitman published poems, collected as *Leaves of Grass*, that
- **e.** Walt Whitman published a collection of poems entitled *Leaves of Grass*, that

225. We loved our trip to the <u>desert where you could see</u> the tall cactus, the blooming flowers, and the little desert animals.
- **a.** correct as is
- **b.** desert; you could see
- **c.** desert; where we saw
- **d.** desert; we saw
- **e.** desert in that you saw

226. <u>Opposite in what many financial analysts had predicted,</u> the stock market rose by 22 points this month.
- **a.** correct as is
- **b.** Contrary to the predictions of many financial analysts,
- **c.** As against the predictions of many financial analysts,
- **d.** Contrasting of many financial analysts' predictions,
- **e.** Contrary with what many financial analysts predicted,

227. A standardized extract made from the leaves of the ginkgo biloba tree <u>is proving to be effective in treating</u> mild to moderate Alzheimer's disease.
- **a.** correct as is
- **b.** has shown its proof of effectiveness with treating
- **c.** may have proven effective treatment for
- **d.** is effectively proving in treating
- **e.** have given a proven effectiveness in the treatment of

228. The citizens' action committee has accused the city council members <u>with being careless with the spending of</u> the taxpayers' money.

   a. correct as is
   b. as to carelessness in the spending of
   c. of carelessness in the spending of
   d. of careless spending to
   e. with spending carelessly of

229. Aspirin was known exclusively <u>as a painkiller until the time when cardiologists began prescribing it as a preventive for</u> heart attacks.

   a. correct as is
   b. to be a painkiller since when cardiologists prescribed it to be a prevention for
   c. as a way to kill and stop pain until cardiologists began to prescribe it as a method for the prevention of
   d. as a painkiller until cardiologists began prescribing it as a preventive for
   e. to be a painkiller up to when cardiologists prescribed its preventive for

230. The news reporter who <u>had been covering the story suddenly became ill, and I was called</u> to take her place.

   a. correct as is
   b. was covering the story suddenly becomes ill, and they called me
   c. is covering the story suddenly becomes ill, and I was called
   d. would have been covering the story suddenly became ill, and I am called
   e. covers the story, suddenly became ill, and they called me

231. <u>Donald Trump, the son of a real estate developer, he</u> has built a billion-dollar empire.

   a. correct as is
   b. Donald Trump, being the son of a real estate developer,
   c. While he was the son of a real estate developer, Donald Trump
   d. The son of a real estate developer, Donald Trump
   e. Donald Trump, the son of a real estate developer, and he

232. The troposphere is the lowest layer of Earth's <u>atmosphere, it extends</u> from ground level to an altitude of seven to ten miles.

   a. correct as is
   b. atmosphere of which it extends
   c. atmosphere. Extending
   d. atmosphere, and extending
   e. atmosphere; it extends

233. <u>Along with your membership to our health club and</u> two months of free personal training.

   a. correct as is
   b. Along with your membership to our health club you receive
   c. With your membership to our health club,
   d. In addition to your membership to our health club being
   e. Added to your membership to our health club,

234. <u>Our contention is that a body of common knowledge shared by</u> literate Americans of the twenty-first century and that this knowledge can be defined.
a. correct as is
b. To contend that a body of common knowledge is shared by
c. We contend that we share a body of common knowledge in
d. That a common body of knowledge is shared is our contention with
e. It is our contention that a body of common knowledge is shared by

235. <u>Whether they earn</u> a BS degree, chemical engineers are almost guaranteed a job.
a. correct as is
b. If they earn
c. If earning
d. To earn
e. Since earning

Choose the sentence that is incorrectly written or unclear. If all sentences are correct, choose answer **d.**

236. a. We asked him to pick us up in the morning.
b. Mrs. Jacobs needed a ride to the airport.
c. The car racing up the street.
d. no mistakes

237. a. Our neighbors went on vacation, going to the Grand Canyon.
b. There are yellow and red tulips in my garden.
c. We invited Molly to our house for dinner.
d. no mistakes

238. a. We are planning to build a new fence in our backyard.
b. Where is the new diner that everyone is talking about?
c. There's nothing I can do to help.
d. no mistakes

239. a. Make sure the door is locked.
b. I love pumpkin pie Pearl does too.
c. Yes, I will bring the dessert.
d. no mistakes

240. a. After he left, I went straight to bed.
b. For the first time, I understood what she was talking about.
c. We visited the town where my father grew up last summer.
d. no mistakes

241. a. Kate was allergic to all dairy products.
b. Which of the Beatles' songs is your favorite?
c. The company newsletter explained the new vacation policy.
d. no mistakes

242. a. They went to the park and flew a kite.
b. "Don't tell me what to do," she shouted.
c. Liam loves the warm weather, unless he knows it won't last much longer.
d. no mistakes

243. a. Bring your umbrella tomorrow it's supposed to rain.
b. The dancers' costumes were being delivered on Saturday.
c. Would you consider bringing me as your guest?
d. no mistakes

244. **a.** Marlene likes my apple crisp better than Aunt Kate's.

b. The people in the auditorium, whether they were seated or standing.

c. I registered for a class in West Indian literature.

d. no mistakes

245. **a.** The free passes were given to Lena and me.

b. Where's my purple umbrella?

c. After midnight, the light on the front porch goes off.

d. no mistakes

246. **a.** Katya and I were in the same pottery class.

b. The weather was nicer today than it was yesterday.

c. The grapes cost more than the melon does.

d. no mistakes

247. **a.** His jacket is just like mine.

b. Talia went to yoga class, and that she forgot her mat.

c. Indira visits her relatives frequently.

d. no mistakes

Choose the sentence that expresses the idea most clearly.

248. **a.** For three weeks, the Merryville fire chief received taunting calls from an arsonist, who would not say where he intended to set the next fire.

b. The Merryville fire chief received taunting calls from an arsonist, but he would not say where he intended to set the next fire, for three weeks.

c. He would not say where he intended to set the next fire, but for three weeks the Merryville fire chief received taunting calls from an arsonist.

d. The Merryville fire chief received taunting calls from an arsonist for three weeks, not saying where he intended to set the next fire.

249. **a.** There is no true relationship between ethics and the law.

b. Ethics and the law having no true relationship.

c. Between ethics and the law, no true relationship.

d. Ethics and the law is no true relationship.

250. **a.** Some people say jury duty is a nuisance that just takes up their precious time and that we don't get paid enough.

b. Some people say jury duty is a nuisance that just takes up your precious time and that one doesn't get paid enough.

c. Some people say jury duty is a nuisance that just takes up precious time and that doesn't pay enough.

d. Some people say jury duty is a nuisance that just takes up our precious time and that they don't get paid enough.

251. **a.** A sharpshooter for many years, a pea could be shot off a person's shoulder from 70 yards away by Miles Johnson.

b. A sharpshooter for many years, Miles Johnson could shoot a pea off a person's shoulder from 70 yards away.

c. A sharpshooter for many years, from 70 yards away off a person's shoulder Miles Johnson could have shot a pea.

d. A sharpshooter for many years, Miles Johnson could shoot from 70 yards away off a person's shoulder a pea.

252. **a.** By the time they are in the third or fourth grade, the eyes of most children in the United States are tested.

b. Most children by the time they are in the United States have their eyes tested in the third or fourth grade.

c. Most children in the United States have their eyes tested by the time they are in the third or fourth grade.

d. In the United States by the time of third or fourth grade, there is testing of the eyes of most children.

▶ Sentence Completion and Vocabulary Building

A sentence is both the opportunity and the limit of thought—what we have to think with, and what we have to think in.

—Wendell Berry

Sentence completion exercises help you increase your vocabulary by introducing key vocabulary words within the context of a sentence. Since repeated exposure to a word is the best way to increase your vocabulary, it is a good idea to supplement the exercises in this section by reading texts that will increase your exposure to new words. Some valuable vocabulary-building resources include the following:

- magazines such as *Scholastic Junior* and *Smithsonian*
- encyclopedias
- scientific articles
- comic books (surprisingly enough, many comic books use complex high-level vocabulary words!)
- an electronic dictionary with phonetic spell correction and audio pronunciation of words

When you stumble across a strange and unfamiliar word, you can usually figure out its meaning by using your detective skills to make an educated guess. Since all of the words in a sentence are interrelated, drawing on **context** to determine a word's meaning is especially useful when encountering **homonyms**, which are words with more than one meaning, such as *well*, and **homophones**, which are words pronounced alike but different in meaning and spelling, such as *beat* and *beet*. The word *well* in the sentence "Are you feeling well today?" has a vastly different meaning from the word *well* as used in the sentence "The man drew a bucket of water from the well in his backyard." Readers can draw a conclusion about its meaning by noting how the word *well* fits into the context of the sentence.

Word Bite: *Context*

Context is the meaning and positioning of neighboring words and phrases, which can help define an unfamiliar word.

When you are working on sentence completion exercises, it's important to understand that there are four main types of sentence completions: restatement, contrast, comparison, and cause and effect. By recognizing the key phrases associated with these four types, you can use logic and the process of elimination to select the most appropriate answer.

Restatement sentences repeat an idea that has already been stated. The following clue phrases can be used to identify a restatement sentence: *in other words*, *in fact*, *namely*, and *that is*. Some sentences focus on examining the differences between one or more people, places, or things. Sentences focusing on differences use words that **contrast** one item with another: *however*, *despite*, and *but*. Sentences focusing on **comparisons** use words or phrases that point out what is similar: *similarly*, *and*, *just as*, and *likewise*. To identify **cause and effect** sentence completions, look for words that highlight a cause and the consequences or end result (effect). Whenever there is a cause, an effect is sure to follow, so search for clue words such as *consequently*, *because*, *as a result*, and *due to*.

Get a Grip on Vocabulary

To Err Is Human, but to Misspell or Mispronounce Words Is Just Plain Unnecessary

- *Accept* and *except* are commonly confused. Use *accept* (verb) when you mean to agree or receive and *except* (preposition) when you mean with the exclusion of.
- *A lot* is always written as two separate words. There are no exceptions!
- *It's* and *its* are often confused. *It's* is a contraction for the words *it is* or *it has*. If you mean *it is* or *it has*, then you may use the contraction *it's*. *Its* is a possessive pronoun.
- Verboten! *Anyway* should never be pronounced as *anyways*. *Anyway* does not have, and never has had, an *-s* ending.
- *Mischievous* is a squirrelly word that is often mispronounced. It should always be pronounced using three syllables, not four syllables. Say "mis-chie-vous," not "mis-chie-vi-ous."
- President George W. Bush is infamous for mispronouncing the word *nuclear*. Don't say "nu-cu-lar." The proper pronunciation is "nu-cle-ar."

Get a Grip on the Root of the Problem

If a vocabulary word has stumped you, try to figure out its meaning by using your knowledge of common root words, suffixes, and prefixes. A **root word** is the base word from which other words are formed, much as the roots of a tree provide the base from which the trunk, branches, and leaves grow. Meanings change when an affix is attached either to the front (**prefix**) or the end (**suffix**) of a root word. For example, the suffix -*or* is usually used in words related to people (*professor, collector, inspector*), while the suffix -*able* is attached to words communicating an ability (*capable, viable*). When you are in doubt about a word's meaning, dig deeply into its roots!

▶ Practice Questions

253. Phillip's _____ tone endeared him to his comical friends, but irritated his serious father.
    a. aloof
    b. jesting
    c. grave
    d. earnest
    e. conservative

254. Brian's pale Irish skin was _____ to burn if he spent too much time in the sun.
    a. prone
    b. urbane
    c. eminent
    d. erect
    e. daunted

255. Over the years, the Wilsons slowly _____ upon the Jacksons' property, moving the stone markers that divided their lots farther and farther onto the Jacksons' land.
    a. encroached
    b. jettisoned
    c. conjoined
    d. repudiated
    e. teemed

256. His suit of armor made the knight _____ to his enemy's attack, and he was able to escape safely to his castle.
    a. vulnerable
    b. churlish
    c. invulnerable
    d. static
    e. imprudent

257. Choosing a small, fuel-efficient car is a(n) _____ purchase for a recent college graduate.
    a. corrupt
    b. tedious
    c. unhallowed
    d. sardonic
    e. judicious

258. With all of the recent negative events in her life, she felt _____ forces must be at work.
   a. resurgent
   b. premature
   c. malignant
   d. punctilious
   e. antecedent

259. The _____ rumors did a great deal of damage, even though they turned out to be false.
   a. bemused
   b. prosaic
   c. apocryphal
   d. ebullient
   e. tantamount

260. Racha's glance was a _____ invitation to speak later in private about events of the meeting.
   a. trecherous
   b. scintillating
   c. tactful
   d. tacit
   e. taboo

261. She reached the _____ of her career with her fourth novel, which won the Pulitzer Prize.
   a. harbinger
   b. apogee
   c. metamorphosis
   d. dictum
   e. synthesis

262. The governor-elect was hounded by a group of _____ lobbyists and others hoping to gain favor with her administration.
   a. facetious
   b. abstruse
   c. magnanimous
   d. fawning
   e. saccharine

263. The busy, _____ fabric of the clown's tie matched his oversized jacket, which was equally atrocious.
   a. mottled
   b. bleak
   c. credible
   d. malleable
   e. communicable

264. Kendrick's talent _____ under the tutelage of Anya Kowalonek, who as a young woman had been the most accomplished pianist in her native Lithuania.
   a. bantered
   b. touted
   c. flourished
   d. embellished
   e. colluded

265. The children were _____ by the seemingly nonsensical clues until Kinan pointed out that the messages were in code.
   a. censured
   b. striated
   c. feigned
   d. prevaricated
   e. flummoxed

266. As the _____ in *Romeo and Juliet*, Romeo is a hero able to capture the audience's sympathy by continually professing his love for Juliet.
a. protagonist
b. enigma
c. facade
d. activist
e. catechist

267. I have always admired Seymour's _____; I've never seen him rattled by anything.
a. aplomb
b. confluence
c. propriety
d. compunction
e. nostalgia

268. The soldiers received a military _____ to inspect all their vehicles before traveling.
a. allotment
b. dominion
c. affectation
d. calculation
e. mandate

269. The curious crowd gathered to watch the irate customer _____ about the poor service he received in the restaurant.
a. antiquate
b. trivialize
c. rant
d. placate
e. fetter

270. Ron didn't know the rules of rugby, but he could tell by the crowd's reaction that it was a critical _____ in the game.
a. acclamation
b. conviction
c. juncture
d. enigma
e. revelation

271. The _____ sound of the radiator as it released steam became an increasingly annoying distraction.
a. sibilant
b. scintillating
c. diverting
d. sinuous
e. scurrilous

272. In such a small office setting, the office manager found he had _____ responsibilities that required knowledge in a variety of different areas.
a. heedless
b. complementary
c. mutual
d. manifold
e. correlative

273. David's _____ entrance on stage disrupted the scene and caused the actors to flub their lines.
a. untimely
b. precise
c. lithe
d. fortuitous
e. tensile

274. The settlers found an ideal location with plenty of _____ land for farming and a mountain stream for fresh water and irrigation.
  a. candid
  b. provincial
  c. arable
  d. timid
  e. quaint

275. The _____ seventh-grader towered over the other players on his basketball team.
  a. gangling
  b. studious
  c. mimetic
  d. abject
  e. reserved

276. Carson was at first flattered by the _____ of his new colleagues, but he soon realized that their admiration rested chiefly on his connections, not his accomplishments.
  a. reprisal
  b. adulation
  c. bulwark
  d. rapport
  e. retinue

277. Searching frantically to find the hidden jewels, the thieves proceeded to _____ the entire house.
  a. justify
  b. darken
  c. amplify
  d. ransack
  e. glorify

278. The police officer _____ the crowd to step back from the fire so that no one would get hurt.
  a. undulated
  b. enjoined
  c. stagnated
  d. permeated
  e. delineated

279. Through _____, the chef created a creamy sauce by combining brown sugar, butter, and cinnamon in a pan and cooking them over medium-high heat.
  a. impasse
  b. obscurity
  c. decadence
  d. diversion
  e. liquefaction

280. Harvey was discouraged that his visa application was _____ due to his six convictions.
  a. lethargic
  b. immeasurable
  c. nullified
  d. segregated
  e. aggravated

281. The rebel spies were charged with _____ and put on trial.
  a. sedition
  b. attrition
  c. interaction
  d. reiteration
  e. perdition

282. Keith was _____ in his giving to friends and charities throughout the year, not just during the holidays.
a. munificent
b. portly
c. amphibious
d. guileful
e. forensic

283. Although I'd asked a simple "yes" or "no" question, Irfan's reply was _____, and I didn't know how to interpret it.
a. prodigal
b. irate
c. equivocal
d. voracious
e. harrowing

284. The high-profile company CEO was given an _____ for speaking at the monthly meeting of the area business leaders' society.
a. expiation
b. honorarium
c. inoculation
d. interpretation
e. inquisition

285. Zachary was doomed to a miserable life, for no matter how much he had, he always _____ the possessions of others.
a. protracted
b. exalted
c. engendered
d. coveted
e. filibustered

286. Sheila's grueling hike included passing through numerous _____.
a. terrariums
b. neoprene
c. jurisdictions
d. ravines
e. belfries

287. The college professor was known on campus as a(n) _____ character—bland but harmless and noble in his ideals.
a. staid
b. stagnant
c. auspicious
d. sterile
e. dogmatic

288. The toy store's extensive inventory offered a _____ of toys from baby items to video games for teenagers.
a. manifold
b. lexicon
c. burrow
d. gamut
e. motif

289. Only a small number of people in the audience laughed at the comic's _____ sense of humor, while the rest found him to be too sarcastic.
a. consequential
b. avaricious
c. venturous
d. dauntless
e. mordant

290. Dogs growl and show their teeth in an attempt to _____ the animal or person they perceive as a threat.
- **a.** bolster
- **b.** waylay
- **c.** cow
- **d.** exacerbate
- **e.** appease

291. In biology class, Sabine observed the arthropod's _____, its barely discernible movement in the tank.
- **a.** parody
- **b.** prescience
- **c.** torpor
- **d.** insight
- **e.** vigor

292. The battalion's _____ was a well-fortified structure near the enemy lines.
- **a.** labyrinth
- **b.** summary
- **c.** villa
- **d.** vinculum
- **e.** garrison

293. Walking through the _____ forest in spring was a welcome escape from the cold, gray winter we had spent in the city.
- **a.** pliant
- **b.** verdant
- **c.** factious
- **d.** bland
- **e.** innocuous

294. Meredith used the _____ to steer the horse and keep him in line.
- **a.** jolt
- **b.** bristle
- **c.** chine
- **d.** quirt
- **e.** hearth

295. Oliver was unable to _____ himself from the difficulties he had caused by forging the documents.
- **a.** reprove
- **b.** pique
- **c.** oust
- **d.** extricate
- **e.** broach

296. The _____ of our expedition was still so far away that I felt we would never get there.
- **a.** nadir
- **b.** terminus
- **c.** speculation
- **d.** apex
- **e.** dungeon

297. If he expected to _____ as a doctor, Lou knew he would have to study hard in medical school and work long hours to gain experience and skill.
- **a.** perpetrate
- **b.** palliate
- **c.** palpitate
- **d.** prosper
- **e.** mediate

298. Doc Wilson grew up in Florida and was not prepared to face the _____ climate of the Alaskan winter.
a. freshwater
b. gelid
c. compendious
d. subsidiary
e. improvident

299. Marvin's _____ prevented him from finishing his work and was evidenced in his large phone bills.
a. loquacity
b. heroism
c. decadence
d. depreciation
e. rescission

300. The graph clearly showed the company reaching the _____ in profits during the 1980s when the economy was in a boom period.
a. narthex
b. gullet
c. gamut
d. quiescence
e. vertex

301. Victor Frankenstein's creature was a(n) _____, detested by everyone he met.
a. itinerant
b. anathema
c. cosmopolitan
d. mercenary
e. anomaly

302. Ariana was outstanding as the moderator; she handled the intensely heated debate with great _____, diplomatically and tactfully keeping the conversation fair and on track.
a. finesse
b. pretentiousness
c. prowess
d. succor
e. aversion

303. The class endured a loud and lengthy _____ by the teacher on the subject of submitting written work on time.
a. guile
b. polemic
c. bravado
d. tirade
e. heresy

304. Must we be subjected to your _____ complaints all day long?
a. tiresome
b. fearsome
c. awesome
d. gleesome
e. wholesome

305. The new political candidate refused to print _____ about her aggressive opponent, but that did not stop him from printing lies about her.
a. dispensation
b. assignation
c. rendition
d. libel
e. compunction

306. Awkwardly tall and prone to tripping over her own feet, Grace felt her name was truly a _____.
a. misnomer
b. preoccupation
c. universality
d. garrulity
e. benevolence

307. Although the villagers' lives were profoundly different from her own, Jing-Mae felt a deep _____ for the people when she served in the Peace Corps.
a. reparation
b. affinity
c. injunction
d. exigency
e. analogy

308. In the famous balcony scene, Romeo _____ Juliet's beauty in one of the most romantic soliloquies ever written.
a. sanctions
b. extols
c. peruses
d. beguiles
e. fetters

309. The surgeon placed a _____ on the femoral artery to bind it during the long and exhausting surgery.
a. ligature
b. doctrine
c. premise
d. synopsis
e. degeneration

310. By sheer _____ force, the men pushed the truck to the side of the road and out of danger.
a. virile
b. persnickety
c. meticulous
d. suave
e. contentious

311. To settle the dispute, the students elected a faculty member to serve as a(n) _____.
a. maverick
b. dystopia
c. arbiter
d. fiduciary
e. martyr

312. The _____ man with amnesia was unable to recognize where he was.
a. endogenous
b. euphoric
c. nonplussed
d. amicable
e. pliable

313. Justin's _____ solution to the problem revealed that he did not spend much time considering the consequences.
a. facile
b. obsolete
c. resilient
d. pristine
e. ardent

314. It is every American's _____ to live the life he or she chooses.
a. composite
b. eloquence
c. prerogative
d. allusion
e. demise

315. After the boisterous customers left the café without tipping, Carlos _____ at them through the restaurant's front window.
a. interjected
b. jostled
c. glowered
d. emulated
e. skulked

316. Kinnel's reelection is being threatened by a growing _____ of disgruntled union members.
a. rogue
b. faction
c. pariah
d. guise
e. anathema

317. The peasants passed their weary days in much _____ and little comfort.
a. pertinence
b. renown
c. travail
d. exile
e. repose

318. Lyasia is a _____ of the clarinet; she has performed solos with many orchestras and bands around the world.
a. neophyte
b. novice
c. virtuoso
d. termagant
e. plethora

319. The concert audience was frustrated by the poor _____ of the sounds coming from the speakers.
a. modulation
b. recrimination
c. terminus
d. dissidence
e. assertion

320. With an _____ blow of the whistle, the meddling parent interrupted the game to reiterate the rules of the tournament.
a. industrious
b. illustrious
c. eloquent
d. officious
e. enviable

321. The candidate's inappropriately sexist remark was met with a _____ of denunciations from the angry crowd.
a. bastion
b. fusillade
c. mélange
d. dichotomy
e. solecism

322. The _____ employee decided to complain publicly about the unacceptable working conditions.
a. discreet
b. prudent
c. precarious
d. malcontent
e. stupendous

323. The judge dismissed the extraneous evidence because it was not _____ to the trial.
a. pertinent
b. pretentious
c. synonymous
d. abject
e. inalienable

324. The _____ nature of the song is supposed to be reminiscent of shepherds calling to their flocks at night.
a. vocative
b. endemic
c. surreptitious
d. preternatural
e. inane

325. The _____ child caused great difficulties for her parents and teachers, because she refused to correct her bad behavior even in the face of punishment.
a. adorable
b. sincere
c. incorrigible
d. lamentable
e. demure

326. The castaway's hut was _____ by the natives curious to see who was the intruder upon their island.
a. beset
b. surmised
c. precluded
d. garnered
e. lauded

327. The defense attorney's choice of words _____ that there were other possible versions of the crime, but the jury was unconvinced.
a. pervaded
b. insinuated
c. discounted
d. imposed
e. ensconced

328. Ted's enthusiasm for becoming a professional drummer _____ when he realized he would have to practice several hours a day.
a. waxed
b. waned
c. deranged
d. flouted
e. preempted

329. Some would say Muzak is a(n) _____ form of music, a kind of background noise designed to be heard but not listened to.
a. arable
b. degenerate
c. volatile
d. pivotal
e. exemplary

330. The teacher was dismissed for the _____ act of helping his students cheat on the exam.
a. steadfast
b. meritorious
c. unconscionable
d. pristine
e. fortuitous

331. The reformed criminal could not forget his guilty past; he was in a living state of _____.

a. perdition
b. tact
c. composure
d. principle
e. veracity

332. The _____ yoga instructor waited patiently for her students to find the proper pose, which she performed with ease.
a. unabashed
b. lissome
c. cosmopolitan
d. sneering
e. disparaging

333. Because it had been worn and washed so often, Linus's favorite T-shirt was tattered and _____ with holes.
a. salvaged
b. circulated
c. riddled
d. emulated
e. congregated

334. Eels swim using a rapid _____ motion that propels them through the water.
a. dissipating
b. undulating
c. eradicating
d. objurgating
e. irritating

335. Sick and tired of her boring job, Cecilia began to _____ what it would be like to quit.
a. ponder
b. disengage
c. negate
d. relinquish
e. alleviate

336. The way my father likes to _____ with any salesperson to see if he can bargain for a lower price is embarrassing.
a. striate
b. variegate
c. capitulate
d. teem
e. wrangle

337. The _____ construction crew built large buildings all over the East Coast, wherever the demand for qualified workers took them.
a. laconic
b. irresolute
c. itinerant
d. parietal
e. peremptory

338. The CEO's large expense accounts proved she was a(n) _____ spender with the company's money.
   a. injurious
   b. ineffectual
   c. liberal
   d. malignant
   e. insolvent

339. The young, thin boy surprised his wrestling opponent with his _____ strength.
   a. fraudulent
   b. wiry
   c. frolicsome
   d. pretentious
   e. endemic

340. When Arnold's grandmother began to complain about the excruciating pain in her knees and legs, she was referred to a(n) _____ specialist for a diagnosis.
   a. optical
   b. oral
   c. archeological
   d. osteopathic
   e. psychological

341. Charlie's _____ behavior made it clear that he had been highly educated in matters of etiquette.
   a. decorous
   b. surreptitious
   c. erratic
   d. caustic
   e. irksome

342. Given his _____ nature, it was appropriate that he decided to be a trial lawyer after law school.
   a. lackluster
   b. engrossed
   c. penitent
   d. litigious
   e. obsolete

343. Sanji went abroad as a(n) _____ young man; when he returned two years later, he seemed like an experienced man of the world.
   a. sardonic
   b. egalitarian
   c. reticent
   d. callow
   e. loquacious

344. The protesters were concerned that the proposed legislation would have a(n) _____ effect on the state's nature preserves.
   a. scintillating
   b. deleterious
   c. insipid
   d. punctilious
   e. parsimonious

345. Not swayed by his student's _____ flattery, the professor told him that his grade would not be changed.
   a. forlorn
   b. striated
   c. undulating
   d. unctuous
   e. frowsy

346. Tonya found Isaac's public declarations of his love for her _____ and embarrassing.
a. necrotic
b. intriguing
c. witless
d. malodorous
e. pliant

347. The kitten was _____ when it noticed the menacing dog entering the yard.
a. servile
b. diligent
c. scornful
d. pavid
e. optimistic

348. According to pirate lore, a terrible _____ would follow whoever opened the treasure chest.
a. precursor
b. precession
c. rendition
d. insurgence
e. malediction

349. When we were renovating the old house, we found a(n) _____ of $10 and $20 bills hidden inside the old laundry chute.
a. odyssey
b. matrix
c. lament
d. fodder
e. cache

350. The workers attempted to _____ the supervisor's authority by negotiating terms with the clients themselves.
a. contradict
b. instigate
c. resonate
d. placate
e. undermine

351. The student failed his research paper because he chose to _____ material from a another author's work.
a. authorize
b. stimulate
c. overrule
d. plagiarize
e. meditate

352. The _____ old cowboy had a complexion that spoke of many years in the desert sun, rounding up wild horses.
a. secular
b. suave
c. turgid
d. wizened
e. truant

353. The swimmer's back injury _____ his prospects for a gold medal at the world championship competition.
a. compelled
b. advanced
c. jeopardized
d. maintained
e. expounded

354. Lynette had to learn the _____ of the insurance profession before she felt comfortable describing products to her clients.
  a. lexicon
  b. classicism
  c. juncture
  d. cessation
  e. asperity

355. Marta had to pay off her _____ to the credit card company before she could get a mortgage.
  a. stipend
  b. liability
  c. remuneration
  d. concession
  e. consolidation

356. With Justine's _____ nature and passion for art, she would make an excellent tour guide for the museum.
  a. volatile
  b. congenial
  c. servile
  d. fledgling
  e. trite

357. The employee's claim of being out with the flu did not seem very _____, because he returned from sick leave with a deep tan.
  a. inattentive
  b. inarticulate
  c. tactful
  d. plausible
  e. vulnerable

358. The con man used his _____ to convince the elderly woman to sign over her life savings to him.
  a. estuary
  b. melee
  c. flagrancy
  d. malleability
  e. wile

359. Sunlight shining through a window was an obvious _____ in the nearly every one of the artist's works.
  a. disjunction
  b. hindrance
  c. repugnance
  d. motif
  e. variance

360. I like listening to Wesley go on about politics and social issues; his opinions are _____ with my own beliefs.
  a. latent
  b. explicit
  c. consonant
  d. ensconced
  e. rife

361. Most people will find the film silly and childish in its humor; the most _____ viewers will find it downright crass and offensive.
  a. servile
  b. petulant
  c. fastidious
  d. arcane
  e. boisterous

362. The goal of any company is to have its product name become _____ and be constantly at the forefront of the consumer's mind.
   a. garrulous
   b. unctuous
   c. tremulous
   d. ubiquitous
   e. portentous

363. During the holiday season, the _____ theme is "Peace on Earth, goodwill toward all."
   a. mitigated
   b. arrogant
   c. controversial
   d. prevalent
   e. prestigious

364. Our cottage by the sea offers many days of relaxation with warm sunshine and soothing _____.
   a. zephyrs
   b. dervishes
   c. stanchions
   d. ebbs
   e. torques

365. When Melinda arrived in the impoverished city, she was immediately _____ by bands of children begging for food.
   a. bedraggled
   b. accosted
   c. infiltrated
   d. rebuked
   e. exacerbated

366. According to the terms of the agreement, if Nicole defaulted on her loan, she would have to _____ her house and car, both of which would become property of the bank.
   a. usurp
   b. evince
   c. debut
   d. forfeit
   e. stigmatize

367. The food at the buffet table was a _____ array of delights that even the most disciplined dieter would find difficult to resist.
   a. tempestuous
   b. tantamount
   c. truculent
   d. temporal
   e. tantalizing

368. After fighting the five-alarm fire, the _____ firefighter could not relax enough to unwind and get some rest.
   a. amicable
   b. treacherous
   c. pliable
   d. durable
   e. overwrought

369. The firefighter was _____ in the news for his heroic rescue of a child from a burning house.
   a. mandated
   b. inferred
   c. reconstituted
   d. augmented
   e. lauded

370. The villagers locked their doors when they heard about the pirates who were _____ unprotected villages along the island's coastline.
a. reforming
b. marauding
c. reclaiming
d. conceding
e. recapitulating

371. I could tell by Angelica's _____ tone that she was still very angry with me.
a. ingratiating
b. adjacent
c. oblique
d. acerbic
e. eloquent

372. After years of living at a(n) _____ pace, Paola decided it was time to slow down and learn how to relax.
a. frenetic
b. pedestrian
c. pretentious
d. colloquial
e. insipid

373. Living on several acres of land dotted with oak and maple trees makes autumn leaf-raking a(n) _____ task.
a. fatuous
b. toilsome
c. tardy
d. obsequious
e. fawning

374. It would take many hours of cleaning and repairing for the young family to transform the _____ into a clean and comfortable little cottage.
a. territory
b. manor
c. hovel
d. demesne
e. hacienda

375. It was once believed that alchemists could _____ common metals to gold.
a. transmute
b. commute
c. execute
d. repute
e. denote

376. The close-up of the actor drinking the popular brand of cola in the movie was a(n) _____ display of commercialism.
a. dispassionate
b. languid
c. apathetic
d. gratuitous
e. unpunctual

377. This summer's movies are _____ for audiences of escape-the-heat mindless entertainment; not one film offers a substantive or even plausible plot.
a. privation
b. dulcet
c. jargon
d. fodder
e. germane

378. The dictator used propaganda and intimidation to _____ the revolution.
    a. prelude
    b. intimate
    c. congregate
    d. irradiate
    e. quell

379. Simona's _____ with her money caught up with her when she didn't have the resources to buy a badly needed new car.
    a. miserliness
    b. thriftiness
    c. wantonness
    d. intuition
    e. predilection

380. The architect designed the ceiling using wood _____ that would remain uncovered, creating a rustic ambience in the living room.
    a. pediments
    b. joists
    c. mullions
    d. banisters
    e. abutments

▶ Resources

Other than conditioning your skills through these practice tests, you can use dictionaries, the Internet, and vocabulary-building games as tools to help maximize your vocabulary power. Here are a few resources you might want to refer to in conjunction with these lessons:

Print Resources

American Heritage Dictionaries Editors. *100 Words Almost Everyone Confuses & Misuses* (Boston: Houghton Mifflin, 2004).

American Heritage Dictionaries Editors. *100 Words Every High School Freshman Should Know* (Boston: Houghton Mifflin, 2004).

Burchers, Sam, Max, and Bryan. *Vocabulary Cartoons*, 2nd ed. (Punta Gorda, FL: New Monic Books, 1997).

Roget's Thesaurus of English Words and Phrases (New York: Penguin, 2002).

Internet Reference Sites

Fake Out!—a fun definition guessing game to hone vocabulary skills (www.eduplace.com/dictionary/)

Visual Thesaurus (www.visualthesaurus.com)

Yahoo! Education—a website featuring free sample SAT tests and useful reference guides (http://education.yahoo.com)

Vocabulary- and Grammar-Building Word Games

Angaramania! vocabulary-building word game

Nymble learning name-finder game with emphasis on synonyms, antonyms, and homonyms

Squeeze Phrase word recognition game

Word Sweep dictionary word game

► Practice Questions

381. When the house on the corner burned down, the entire neighborhood _____ together to help to the victims reestablish their lives.
   a. rallied
   b. recited
   c. skulked
   d. disintegrated
   e. expedited

382. The massage therapist's _____ fingers quickly eased the tension in Blanche's back.
   a. deft
   b. furtive
   c. listless
   d. tentative
   e. blithe

383. As she walked through the halls of her old grade school, Madeline became _____, remembering her old friends and teachers.
   a. prolific
   b. nostalgic
   c. credulous
   d. precocious
   e. ambitious

384. Ignacio's pain was so _____ that he called 911.
   a. remiss
   b. rapacious
   c. genteel
   d. resolute
   e. acute

385. The captain _____ the cargo to keep his ship afloat.
   a. rebuked
   b. listed
   c. disunited
   d. flanked
   e. jettisoned

386. The teacher tried to _____ her class off their dependence on the number lines pasted to the tops of their desks.
   a. wane
   b. wax
   c. whet
   d. wean
   e. wield

387. Ricky is a _____ of the local coffee shop; you can find him there just about every morning.
   a. diva
   b. relic
   c. denizen
   d. maverick
   e. pariah

388. Having never left the landlocked Midwest his entire life, Albert found that swimming in the ocean was quite a(n) _____.
   a. familiarity
   b. extrovert
   c. instinct
   d. novelty
   e. tabernacle

389. The rowdy crowd at the rock concert
_____ Herve, and he spilled his soda
on his pants.
  a. jettisoned
  b. harrowed
  c. jostled
  d. lauded
  e. superceded

390. Blinded by _____, Nicholas
accepted the job offer with the highest pay but
the least possibility of making him happy.
  a. ennui
  b. heresy
  c. infamy
  d. avarice
  e. temperance

391. We knew Jana had _____ motives
for running for class president: She wanted the
nearby parking space that came with the
office.
  a. anterior
  b. interior
  c. inferior
  d. posterior
  e. ulterior

392. The villainous gang's hideout was a den of
_____ that no one would dare to
enter.
  a. innocence
  b. habitants
  c. iniquity
  d. accolades
  e. innovation

393. Although it was so ridiculous that no one
believed it to be true, the reporter's
_____ still cost the governor his
reelection.
  a. hegemony
  b. sedition
  c. malaise
  d. compendium
  e. calumny

394. People on the street stopped to
_____ over the artist's rendition of
the Eiffel Tower, amazed by his ability to
capture the detail.
  a. bedazzle
  b. innovate
  c. rave
  d. counteract
  e. objectify

395. The veteran lieutenant was not happy with his
_____ rank behind the two
inexperienced men.
  a. tertiary
  b. silly
  c. unctuous
  d. superior
  e. fastened

396. The prime minister was admired by all, a(n)
_____ even in an environment of
corruption and disdain.
  a. admonishment
  b. alleviation
  c. nonpareil
  d. prototype
  e. profanation

397. The queen's _____ fell ill during his journey and was unable to negotiate on her behalf when he arrived at the economic summit.
- **a.** penury
- **c.** emissary
- **b.** miscreant
- **d.** denizen
- **e.** zealot

398. Tai was _____ by a series of setbacks that nearly made him miss his deadline.
- **a.** ensconced
- **b.** relegated
- **c.** beleaguered
- **d.** solicited
- **e.** winnowed

399. Patsy was shocked to discover how much higher her IQ was than the _____.
- **a.** norm
- **b.** stimulation
- **c.** prudence
- **d.** solitude
- **e.** derivative

400. Although she appeared confident, once she began her speech, the valedictorian's _____ voice indicated her nervousness.
- **a.** supercilious
- **b.** resonant
- **c.** tenuous
- **d.** placating
- **e.** tremulous

401. A charming painting of a pleasant _____ landscape hung above Vitaly's fireplace, in marked contrast to the noise and lights of the bustling city outside his window.
- **a.** nascent
- **b.** histrionic
- **c.** bucolic
- **d.** indigenous
- **e.** ersatz

402. Since his parents had little money, Peter was _____ to his uncle for paying for his college education.
- **a.** alleged
- **b.** provided
- **c.** obliged
- **d.** demented
- **e.** fortified

403. With great _____, we stepped gingerly onto the planks of the dilapidated bridge that spanned a rocky stream 20 feet below.
- **a.** trepidation
- **b.** instigation
- **c.** perdition
- **d.** refraction
- **e.** endowment

404. The paper was _____ so that it could be easily removed from the bound notebook.
- **a.** voracious
- **b.** infectious
- **c.** fickle
- **d.** perforated
- **e.** fluent

405. Jayne's paintings were not minimalist, but they were _____, using only the most elemental and essential elements.
a. elliptical
b. truculent
c. pernicious
d. perfunctory
e. abstemious

406. Wendell's prolonged illness was the _____ that ignited his interest in science and led to his illustrious career in medical research.
a. hyperbole
b. catalyst
c. penchant
d. insolence
e. caveat

407. After stopping to admire the _____ in the front yard, the young woman continued on with her gardening duties.
a. paradigm
b. compost
c. clutter
d. oleander
e. patagium

408. In a(n) _____ expression of pleasure, the infant clapped her hands and squealed with joy.
a. overt
b. obligatory
c. illusive
d. peremptory
e. turbulent

409. The play's _____ debut was not a good sign for the struggling producer.
a. unsubstantial
b. inauspicious
c. copious
d. disembodied
e. immaterial

410. At one time, it was in _____ for women to wear gloves and hats whenever they were out in public.
a. gore
b. gauge
c. vogue
d. brawn
e. vain

411. To ensure that Brenda wouldn't know where we were going for her birthday, I took the most _____ route I could think of.
a. ardent
b. craven
c. enigmatic
d. circuitous
e. mercurial

412. The editorial was essentially a(n) _____ to the governor, praising her for enacting a series of environmental laws and for balancing the state budget for the first time in 20 years.
a. juggernaut
b. imprecation
c. cabal
d. oeuvre
e. encomium

413. Claude felt particularly _____ as he carried the large satchel filled with cash through the dark streets to the bank.
- **a.** inclusive
- **b.** vulnerable
- **c.** reclusive
- **d.** unwieldy
- **e.** torrential

414. Niall's _____ attitude toward the boss is embarrassing; he does nearly everything for him except scratch his nose!
- **a.** subservient
- **b.** subversive
- **c.** subtle
- **d.** sundry
- **e.** surly

415. Jeremy didn't want to appear _____, but his brothers simply could not convince him to change his mind.
- **a.** pitiful
- **b.** scrupulous
- **c.** harmonious
- **d.** obstinate
- **e.** unabated

416. Although it was supposed to be written for the general public, the report was so _____ that only those with inside knowledge of government workings could understand it.
- **a.** indigenous
- **b.** ebullient
- **c.** truculent
- **d.** pugnacious
- **e.** esoteric

417. Todd set up a rope to _____ the part of the exhibit that was off-limits.
- **a.** circumscribe
- **b.** laud
- **c.** efface
- **d.** undulate
- **e.** beguile

418. François fell into a groggy _____ after having suffered a high fever for several days.
- **a.** profundity
- **b.** sluggard
- **c.** verve
- **d.** stupor
- **e.** grovel

419. Blaine had a tendency to _____ certain details of his evenings out when he didn't want his parents to know where he had been.
- **a.** excel
- **b.** oscillate
- **c.** corroborate
- **d.** juxtapose
- **e.** omit

420. Someone who is in love may find the beloved's _____—often annoying to or disparaged by others—to be charming and endearing.
- **a.** foibles
- **b.** mendacity
- **c.** ennui
- **d.** aplomb
- **e.** penchants

421. Terreh was able to _____ the traffic jam by taking a series of one-way streets that led to the bridge.
a. staunch
b. diffuse
c. corroborate
d. circumvent
e. juxtapose

422. Moving all the heavy cinder blocks by hand from the driveway to the backyard seemed like a(n) _____ task.
a. precipitous
b. poignant
c. onerous
d. salient
e. gallant

423. Claudia's _____ face gave no clue to her hard, cold heart.
a. winsome
b. gruesome
c. fatuous
d. ironic
e. flaccid

424. She realized mortgage rates had declined and decided it was _____ to continue paying rent when she could now afford a monthly payment for her own home.
a. referable
b. relative
c. subsequent
d. episodic
e. inexpedient

425. As the city grew and stretched its borders, it began to feel the _____ problems of urban sprawl and overpopulation.
a. improvident
b. mendacious
c. ersatz
d. concomitant
e. surreptitious

426. Terrance, a dentist, _____ to be with the media, so he could see the concert for free.
a. facilitated
b. conjugated
c. purported
d. tended
e. placated

427. _____ on a lounge chair by the pool was the very tan owner of the estate, relaxing in the midday sunshine.
a. Trident
b. Renegade
c. Fraught
d. Renowned
e. Supine

428. Observing his sister's _____ behavior of riding without a helmet, Jorge ran to get his mother.
a. contemptuous
b. contented
c. fictitious
d. parlous
e. pensive

429. In an attempt to _____ the enemy, Braveheart rallied hundreds of fierce warriors.
a. alienate
b. scoff
c. obliterate
d. ostracize
e. minimize

430. The film was completed on schedule despite the _____ circumstances regarding the location and extreme weather conditions.
a. tenuous
b. imperial
c. cryptic
d. contrived
e. adverse

431. Many employers like to visit college campuses and _____ college seniors to work for their companies.
a. daunt
b. recruit
c. illuminate
d. dither
e. flout

432. The company officials felt the rising cost of health coverage was _____ enough to raise their employees' insurance premiums.
a. moratorium
b. justification
c. symbolism
d. disposition
e. habitude

433. The _____ of the sheriff's department ended at the county line.
a. prerequisite
b. emendation
c. alliteration
d. jurisdiction
e. respite

434. We could not describe the scene before us; it was filled with such _____ beauty.
a. inexorable
b. unutterable
c. uproarious
d. mnemonic
e. fretful

435. The subject matter was _____ because the mumbling professor spoke too quickly.
a. obscure
b. magnanimous
c. treacherous
d. vital
e. maximized

436. Arnie becomes so _____ when he talks about painting that it is hard not to be infected by his enthusiasm.
a. laconic
b. circuitous
c. impertinent
d. ardent
e. recalcitrant

437. Don't let Julie's enthusiasm fool you; she's just a _____, not a professional dancer.
- **a.** maverick
- **b.** denizen
- **c.** mercenary
- **d.** maven
- **e.** dilettante

438. Normally, Maya would not have made so many spelling mistakes in her essay; she is usually _____ about her spelling.
- **a.** sumptuous
- **b.** scurrilous
- **c.** ridiculous
- **d.** scrupulous
- **e.** fatuous

439. In the Roman myth, Artemis made a pilgrimage to the _____, hoping to learn the answer to her dilemma.
- **a.** denouement
- **b.** decorum
- **c.** oracle
- **d.** vizier
- **e.** pillar

440. Orson was truly a(n) _____: Towering over others at six feet nine inches, he was also one of the most influential and successful producers in the feature film industry.
- **a.** behemoth
- **b.** anathema
- **c.** demagogue
- **d.** viceroy
- **e.** charlatan

441. Brian was an _____ child; he was sent to the principal's office on numerous occasions for his rude classroom behavior.
- **a.** impeccable
- **b.** impertinent
- **c.** observant
- **d.** obscure
- **e.** adjuvant

442. We must _____ the information about the agenda changes immediately so that the conference attendees have time to adjust their schedules.
- **a.** burnish
- **b.** disseminate
- **c.** galvanize
- **d.** placate
- **e.** admonish

443. If you can adhere to the _____ rules of a military society, the Marines may be an excellent career choice.
- **a.** strident
- **b.** raucous
- **c.** stringent
- **d.** pedantic
- **e.** lurid

444. The natural _____ of the canyon cause it to be an everlasting source of new adventures and beauty.
- **a.** blandishments
- **b.** vicissitudes
- **c.** mores
- **d.** platitudes
- **e.** nebulas

445. A lifelong vegetarian, Xiomara
_____ when she learned that the
sauce she'd just eaten was made with chicken
broth.
- **a.** wavered
- **b.** blanched
- **c.** coalesced
- **d.** stagnated
- **e.** thwarted

446. At the beginning of the ceremony, the high
school band _____ the arrival of the
graduates by playing the alma mater loudly
and with enthusiasm.
- **a.** decried
- **b.** heralded
- **c.** permeated
- **d.** conjured
- **e.** thwarted

447. Although Sophie was afraid of heights, she
seemed to have no _____ about
driving over bridges.
- **a.** enormity
- **b.** qualms
- **c.** imminence
- **d.** resurrection
- **e.** severity

448. I will write a rough draft of the proposal, and
then you can edit it for any _____
material so that it is as convincing and concise
as possible.
- **a.** grandiose
- **b.** incontrovertible
- **c.** extraneous
- **d.** abysmal
- **e.** pensive

449. Minnie finally _____ to her sister's
constant barrage of questions and revealed the
identity of her new boyfriend.
- **a.** reiterated
- **b.** succumbed
- **c.** seceded
- **d.** reneged
- **e.** retaliated

450. The proposed design includes many
_____ features that are not
functional and can be eliminated to cut costs.
- **a.** jovial
- **b.** germane
- **c.** kinetic
- **d.** nonchalant
- **e.** extrinsic

451. Carly's _____ spending on shoes
and clothing caused her parents a great deal of
concern, because she was no longer saving
money for college.
- **a.** monotypic
- **b.** inconsistent
- **c.** perfunctory
- **d.** immoderate
- **e.** specious

452. The professor studied the _____
physics of ballet dancers and even published a
study on the topic of dancers and movement.
- **a.** creditable
- **b.** kinetic
- **c.** symbolic
- **d.** prevalent
- **e.** monotonous

453. Philbert's _____ manner fit in well with the atmosphere of the posh country club.
  a. untoward
  b. riotous
  c. mundane
  d. salacious
  e. urbane

454. There were several _____ buildings on the street, making it difficult for Margaret to determine which one was the dentist's office.
  a. nondescript
  b. transient
  c. impervious
  d. zealous
  e. impressionable

455. To _____ a congressional bill, the president must use his official seal on all documents.
  a. nullify
  b. patronize
  c. victimize
  d. ratify
  e. mollify

456. There is no way around it: Plagiarism is _____ to thievery.
  a. tantamount
  b. apathetic
  c. fatuous
  d. unscrupulous
  e. indecisive

457. For _____ deeds during her mission overseas, Tyesha was awarded the Congressional Medal of Honor.
  a. inept
  b. valorous
  c. erroneous
  d. malodorous
  e. benign

458. I am _____ of the problems that this solution will cause, but I still believe that this is the best possible course of action.
  a. innocuous
  b. cognizant
  c. precipitous
  d. reminiscent
  e. belligerent

459. The spectacular presentation by a rainforest adventurer _____ Simon with the desire to travel to South America to see the jungles for himself.
  a. disheartened
  b. inhibited
  c. imbued
  d. reconstituted
  e. abhorred

460. When the senator's popularity suffered in the polls, he _____ his proposal to raise taxes.
  a. recanted
  b. pulverized
  c. enveloped
  d. detracted
  e. extenuated

461. Because of the _____ of reliable information, Quentin's report was comprised mostly of speculation.
a. dearth
b. diatribe
c. myriad
d. juxtaposition
e. tirade

462. The pain medication Kristy received after surgery offered relief; however, the overwhelming feeling of _____ was an unexpected side effect, and she didn't like being groggy.
a. extortion
b. compellation
c. acquisition
d. affirmation
e. lethargy

463. The ski lodge had a window that looked out upon a beautiful mountain _____.
a. vista
b. melee
c. fray
d. foray
e. frieze

464. The palace's great hall was rich in history and splendor, the walls hung with _____ tapestries.
a. mellifluous
b. malleable
c. prudent
d. illusive
e. ornate

465. After weeks of heavy rains, the earth gave way; mud and trees _____ down the mountain, swallowing cars and houses in their path.
a. ascended
b. inculcated
c. aspersed
d. hurtled
e. entreated

466. Several weeks of extremely hot, dry weather _____ the land, so instead of rowing across a river, we walked across a cracked, parched riverbed.
a. oscillated
b. desiccated
c. subverted
d. coalesced
e. thwarted

467. The pitcher's _____ workout regimen was the most grueling of the entire team, and he never took a day off.
a. Spartan
b. spasmodic
c. exclusive
d. turgid
e. truculent

468. I was bored with the _____ conversation of my roommates and longed for some intellectual stimulation.
a. egregious
b. pronounced
c. vapid
d. intriguing
e. exonerating

469. Ned's fear was _____ as he watched the 60-foot waves approach his little boat.
- **a.** futile
- **b.** genteel
- **c.** innovative
- **d.** palpable
- **e.** detrimental

470. Although others were fooled by "Doctor" Winston's speech, Lily knew him for what he was: a(n) _____.
- **a.** panacea
- **b.** charlatan
- **c.** prevarication
- **d.** accolade
- **e.** prima donna

471. After the neighbor's loud music woke her up for the fifth night in a row, Brenda felt _____ to complain.
- **a.** impelled
- **b.** rebuked
- **c.** augmented
- **d.** implicated
- **e.** destined

472. Carter is writing a letter of recommendation that I can include in my _____ for prospective employers.
- **a.** denunciation
- **b.** panacea
- **c.** dossier
- **d.** incantation
- **e.** restitution

473. _____ laughter came from the upstairs apartment where Trang was having a graduation party.
- **a.** Scurrilous
- **b.** Deleterious
- **c.** Fatuous
- **d.** Uproarious
- **e.** Malicious

474. In the middle of his eloquent _____, the audience suddenly broke into applause.
- **a.** ovation
- **b.** oration
- **c.** inclination
- **d.** provocation
- **e.** illusion

475. I like the _____ style of these essays; they make complex issues accessible by presenting them in everyday language.
- **a.** colloquial
- **b.** obsolete
- **c.** pristine
- **d.** exacting
- **e.** furtive

476. A diamond ring is the _____ symbol of love and affection.
- **a.** precocious
- **b.** fugacious
- **c.** supplemental
- **d.** quintessential
- **e.** barbarous

477. Nothing will _____ my memory of the night we first met; the images are forever burned in my mind.
a. appease
b. undulate
c. inculcate
d. efface
e. truncate

478. The devastating drought forced the _____ tribes of the rainforest to leave their homes and venture into the modern world.
a. indigenous
b. puritanical
c. indigent
d. imminent
e. munificent

479. Jason's _____ approach to management included narrowing the salary gap between the CEOs and office workers.
a. stoic
b. apathetic
c. utilitarian
d. endemic
e. proactive

480. My parents always seem to worry and _____ more about money when tax season is approaching.
a. proximate
b. quibble
c. supplicate
d. dabble
e. alienate

481. Samantha had an _____ trust in her grandfather, who was an honorable man and kind to everyone he met.
a. implicit
b. insecure
c. irreverent
d. irresolute
e. astringent

482. Although I meant it as a compliment, Zander _____ my remark as an insult.
a. construed
b. eradicated
c. truncated
d. permeated
e. redacted

483. The sailor's _____ complexion bespoke his many sunny days at the lookout post.
a. swarthy
b. syncopated
c. pallid
d. wan
e. pasty

484. Tanya is a _____ person, trusted by all who know her.
a. porous
b. voracious
c. spurious
d. specious
e. veracious

485. After the third relative was hired to an upper-level position, several people quit the company, claiming that _____ caused a decline in employee morale.
a. carrion
b. explicitness
c. skepticism
d. devotion
e. nepotism

486. Genevieve's stunning debut performance at the city opera has earned her _____ from some of the city's toughest critics.
a. antipathy
b. insinuations
c. destitution
d. lamentations
e. accolades

487. The shaggy neon-pink couch was a(n) _____ in the conservative room decorated with earth tones.
a. incongruity
b. insinuation
c. temerity
d. reiteration
e. intonation

488. Harris tried to _____ his fear of flying when he boarded the plane, but he could not curb his anxiety.
a. accelerate
b. expound
c. maximize
d. employ
e. repress

489. Gabi found that whenever she was confused about an idea or issue, writing about it would help _____ her true feelings.
a. vacillate
b. elucidate
c. wheedle
d. deprecate
e. indoctrinate

490. After the powerful windstorm, Marie discovered a splintered and fallen tree limb had _____ the vinyl lining of her swimming pool.
a. extenuated
b. calculated
c. retaliated
d. lacerated
e. curtailed

491. Johnny's good behavior in class yesterday was _____ by his disruptive outbursts this morning.
a. abated
b. negated
c. reiterated
d. mandated
e. nominated

492. Jason and Joshua made _____ plans to meet in the cafeteria to study for the test, provided Jason's class ended on time.
a. beguiling
b. tenuous
c. assured
d. tentative
e. promotional

493. The professor's lectures were filled with excessive _____, lasting much longer than was necessary to convey his ideas.
   a. verbiage
   b. herbage
   c. maliciousness
   d. portent
   e. intrigue

494. Ming's blatant lie revealed that he suffered no _____ about being dishonest to his parents.
   a. compunction
   b. repudiation
   c. vindication
   d. evanescence
   e. veracity

495. Diane, always teasing, was known for her _____, but as a result, nobody knew when to take her seriously.
   a. jocularity
   b. servitude
   c. logic
   d. austerity
   e. inclemency

496. "Absolute power corrupts absolutely," said Haines, quoting Lord Acton. "There is no such thing as a(n) _____ who is not a corrupt and cruel ruler."
   a. imbroglio
   b. pedant
   c. despot
   d. agnostic
   e. archetype

497. During his _____ in office, the mayor made several controversial decisions about city planning.
   a. treatise
   b. integration
   c. teem
   d. flout
   e. tenure

498. Recovering from the tragedy, Helena found the _____ sunrise reassuring, as it gave her something to rely on each and every morning.
   a. hidden
   b. clairvoyant
   c. cognizant
   d. deft
   e. quotidian

499. Flaws in Claire's opponent's chess game showed him to be _____, and Claire knew her victory was assured.
   a. predatory
   b. indistinguishable
   c. ornery
   d. vincible
   e. resolute

500. The ad didn't mention a specific salary; it just said "compensation _____ with experience."
   a. compulsory
   b. manifest
   c. prolific
   d. commensurate
   e. precluded

501. The _____ she felt for shopping made it impossible for her to walk by a sale window without stopping.
a. providence
b. blunder
c. omission
d. repulsion
e. fervor

502. The owners of the bed-and-breakfast were extremely _____ to their guests, who enjoyed elegant meals, prompt service, and beautifully decorated rooms.
a. hospitable
b. hostile
c. remiss
d. gallant
e. indomitable

503. Homeless people often lead a(n) _____ lifestyle because they repeatedly get uprooted from the streets and alleys where they live.
a. aristocratic
b. platonic
c. analytic
d. nomadic
e. ballistic

504. Linda's _____ for picking the right stocks made her a very wealthy woman.
a. knack
b. reception
c. rendition
d. impropriety
e. concourse

505. Computers and word processing software have made the art of handwriting letters virtually _____.
a. barren
b. boisterous
c. obsolete
d. dignified
e. relevant

506. Marco has an irresistibly _____ manner that many young women find charming and attractive.
a. obstinate
b. staid
c. bland
d. supple
e. suave

507. Chantel kept the _____ of her beloved foremost in her mind as she traveled to countries far and wide in her quest to find him.
a. prelude
b. armistice
c. hirsute
d. presage
e. visage

508. The cozy beach cottage was only _____ for summer tenants, because it lacked the insulation to make a winter stay comfortable.
a. stagnant
b. erroneous
c. resilient
d. habitable
e. ineffective

509. The settlers decided to build their town at the _____ of two rivers; that settlement became the city of Pittsburgh.
   a. veneer
   b. lexicon
   c. hiatus
   d. tirade
   e. confluence

510. Furious that Lou had lied about his references, Noi _____ her decision to promote him to assistant manager.
   a. elevated
   b. incriminated
   c. complied
   d. rescinded
   e. fortified

511. To prove your theory, you need to design an experiment that will provide _____ evidence.
   a. perfunctory
   b. elusive
   c. noxious
   d. empirical
   e. lamentable

512. Rachel's mother was appalled by the amount of _____ humor on television during hours when young children were still awake.
   a. fraudulent
   b. senile
   c. proportional
   d. lascivious
   e. laborious

513. The scared boy on the roller coaster made sure his seatbelt was _____ across his body.
   a. slack
   b. taut
   c. trite
   d. striated
   e. curt

514. The female fox's _____ over her burrow indicates that she has just birthed her young.
   a. vendetta
   b. preening
   c. vigilance
   d. sepulcher
   e. rendezvous

515. After Ginger banged her head, she noticed that a large lump began to _____ from her forehead.
   a. invade
   b. provoke
   c. sustain
   d. obtrude
   e. elevate

516. The devoted fans paid _____ to the late singer by placing flowers on his memorial and by holding lighted votive candles.
   a. tariffs
   b. accouterment
   c. retrospection
   d. appraisement
   e. homage

517. Losing his entire business to the flood, Bill's only _____ was to file bankruptcy.
  a. dross
  b. enigma
  c. fervor
  d. imprecation
  e. recourse

518. The new evidence convinced the judge to overturn Martin's conviction and _____ him.
  a. appropriate
  b. truncate
  c. elucidate
  d. exonerate
  e. protract

519. Christopher hired a tree-trimming crew to cut the _____ branches of the pine tree that were scraping the side of his house.
  a. fastidious
  b. lateral
  c. nebulous
  d. abject
  e. recessive

520. We both knew our summer romance was _____, and we would just be memories in each other's minds by the winter.
  a. restorative
  b. tempting
  c. temporary
  d. understated
  e. indecisive

521. The dissatisfied workers spread their _____ attitudes among themselves until there was a danger of a full-scale rebellion against the owners of the factory.
  a. paradoxical
  b. monochromatic
  c. benign
  d. virulent
  e. portentous

522. The junkyard was littered with _____ objects, making it unsightly to the neighborhood behind it.
  a. otiose
  b. obtuse
  c. jovial
  d. decorative
  e. buoyant

523. Although Maya's _____ sensibilities are quite different from mine, I think she is a remarkable interior decorator and I recommend her highly.
  a. aesthetic
  b. dialectical
  c. reclusive
  d. synthetic
  e. mercurial

524. The meticulous art student applied her paint colors in subtle _____ in her artwork.
  a. limitations
  b. gradations
  c. moratoriums
  d. junctures
  e. tinctures

525. J.P. recalled running through the _____ of tall rows of cornstalks that dominated his grandfather's summer garden.
  a. terminals
  b. temperament
  c. labyrinth
  d. basin
  e. deference

526. Peter displayed an air of _____ when the officer asked him if he knew the speed limit.
  a. omniscience
  b. obstinacy
  c. nescience
  d. obstetrics
  e. platitude

527. I have tried for years to get close to my brother Rae, but he has always remained _____.
  a. cognizant
  b. assiduous
  c. vociferous
  d. aloof
  e. accommodating

528. In his later years, the once wildly successful gambler lost his fortune, and became a homeless _____ on the streets of Las Vegas.
  a. granger
  b. miser
  c. strategist
  d. vagabond
  e. speculator

529. _____ animals are able to survive easily in the wilderness because, for example, they can live on berries or insects.
  a. Omnipotent
  b. Omnivorous
  c. Luminous
  d. Lavish
  e. Precarious

530. Sally had planted the seeds in the greenhouse three weeks ago; they would begin to _____ any day now.
  a. germinate
  b. revolve
  c. tint
  d. ratify
  e. modulate

531. Julia's parents gave her one _____ regarding her new job: It could not interfere with her schoolwork.
  a. procession
  b. consensus
  c. manifestation
  d. provision
  e. reprieve

532. The critics agreed that despite enthusiastic efforts from the supporting cast, the star of the play gave a(n) _____ performance, ruining the chance of lucrative box office sales.
  a. infallible
  b. vigorous
  c. victorious
  d. felicitous
  e. lackluster

533. The tenor's _____ voice filled the concert hall.

- **a.** sinuous
- **b.** timid
- **c.** tenuous
- **d.** sonorous
- **e.** striated

534. After the fire, there were ashes in every _____ of the old farmhouse.

- **a.** belfry
- **b.** reprieve
- **c.** tangent
- **d.** orifice
- **e.** tribunal

535. Luanne experiences serious _____ whenever she climbs several flights of steep stairs.

- **a.** vertigo
- **b.** inebriation
- **c.** exoneration
- **d.** fallacy
- **e.** plethora

536. The _____ of the successful product idea was attributed to the extraordinarily creative company president.

- **a.** demise
- **b.** genesis
- **c.** symmetry
- **d.** repletion
- **e.** dominion

537. Once the company reached its _____ of hiring a hundred college graduates, it proceeded to recruit older, more experienced candidates.

- **a.** quota
- **b.** hybrid
- **c.** detriment
- **d.** fiasco
- **e.** malady

538. After her extended illness, Delia experienced a long period of _____ when she did not want to work, exercise, or clean.

- **a.** languor
- **b.** arrogance
- **c.** insolence
- **d.** forethought
- **e.** recompense

539. Floyd has a distinctive _____ to his voice that is easily recognizable over the phone.

- **a.** viscosity
- **b.** brawn
- **c.** timbre
- **d.** diadem
- **e.** ingenuity

540. The house was consumed in flames, and not a _____ of it remained after the fire.

- **a.** vestige
- **b.** visage
- **c.** vestibule
- **d.** vicissitude
- **e.** viceroy

541. David felt as if the family picnic would be a(n) _____ time to talk with his grandmother about her plans for the holidays.
   a. opportune
   b. disastrous
   c. unctuous
   d. trite
   e. surly

542. The children were _____ for eating the whole batch of cookies before dinner.
   a. indignant
   b. belittled
   c. chagrined
   d. eluded
   e. admonished

543. During his routine, the stand-up comic refused to be shaken by the heckler who _____ him every few minutes.
   a. ignored
   b. abetted
   c. enforced
   d. gibed
   e. cited

544. Going away for spring break was not in the _____ of possibility, since neither Helga nor Olga had any money.
   a. fascism
   b. fulcrum
   c. introversion
   d. realm
   e. nadir

545. Oscar _____ his sister not to tell their mother what he had done, for he knew his punishment would be severe.
   a. beguiled
   b. vied
   c. exhorted
   d. maligned
   e. corroborated

546. _____ were in order as James performed brilliantly onstage in his first role as an understudy.
   a. Pathos
   b. Ignominies
   c. Kudos
   d. Subsidies
   e. Statutes

547. The Boston Tea Party happened because the colonists believed the British tea taxes were _____ their rights.
   a. trespassing
   b. reviling
   c. sublimating
   d. transgressing
   e. entreating

548. The old bridge's steel _____ were rusty and in need of repair.
   a. piers
   b. campaniles
   c. manacles
   d. girders
   e. spindles

549. The budding flowers, warm breezes, and births of young animals suggest the much-welcomed _____ atmosphere in the country after a long, hard winter.
   a. venial
   b. menial
   c. venal
   d. vernal
   e. verbal

550. Because she had not exercised in five years, Margarita's attempt to jog five miles on her first day of cardio training was a little _____.
   a. pessimistic
   b. irrelevant
   c. trivial
   d. quixotic
   e. relieved

551. The legal internship program was developed under the _____ of the district attorney's office.
   a. bastion
   b. propensity
   c. aegis
   d. faction
   e. cacophony

552. Frank feels such _____ toward his ex–business partner that he cannot stand to be in the same room with him.
   a. iniquity
   b. collusion
   c. avarice
   d. pallor
   e. animosity

553. Ronaldo celebrated the gathering of his _____ on Thanksgiving Day and spoke with relatives he had not seen in a long time.
   a. commonwealth
   b. surrogates
   c. representatives
   d. kindred
   e. infidels

554. After sitting in the contentious board meeting for two hours, Allen's necktie began to feel like a _____ around his neck.
   a. decorum
   b. garland
   c. noose
   d. renegade
   e. monstrosity

555. Even though he hated to work on holidays and weekends, Trevor hoped that his paycheck would serve as _____ for the time spent away from his family.
   a. metamorphism
   b. restitution
   c. enunciation
   d. proclamation
   e. kismet

556. Amanda's parents were shocked by her _____ decision to quit her job without notice and move to Hollywood.
   a. conscientious
   b. affable
   c. placid
   d. languid
   e. impetuous

557. The catlike movements of the sneaky
_____ served him well when he
picked pockets among the tourists on the
crowded boardwalk.

- **a.** forerunner
- **b.** knave
- **c.** vigilante
- **d.** dignitary
- **e.** bureaucrat

558. The student's _____ language
offended many others in the class.

- **a.** obsequious
- **b.** studious
- **c.** scanty
- **d.** surreptitious
- **e.** scurrilous

559. In winter, the frost on a car's windshield can
be _____ to the driver.

- **a.** lurid
- **b.** obstructive
- **c.** cynical
- **d.** purified
- **e.** salvageable

560. The prom was a(n) _____ royal ball
with so many handsome young men and
beautiful young ladies dressed to the ultimate
informality.

- **a.** affable
- **b.** virtual
- **c.** corrosive
- **d.** deleterious
- **e.** inevitable

561. As the roller coaster inched up to its starting
point at the top of the hill, Helena could feel
her heart begin to _____.

- **a.** exfoliate
- **b.** dominate
- **c.** reattribute
- **d.** palpitate
- **e.** ventilate

562. Paul's _____ humor is sometimes
lost on those who take his comments too
literally.

- **a.** piquant
- **b.** wry
- **c.** florid
- **d.** placid
- **e.** negligible

563. Hearing her sister approach, Marie-Helene
attempted to appear _____ as she
quickly hid the birthday gift behind her back.

- **a.** flamboyant
- **b.** stoic
- **c.** pivotal
- **d.** crass
- **e.** nonchalant

564. The knight sought to _____ his
broadsword in such a menacing fashion as to
frighten his attacker away.

- **a.** warrant
- **b.** procure
- **c.** placate
- **d.** wield
- **e.** ensue

565. At the banquet, the disappearance of the woman's jeweled bracelet from her wrist appeared to be the _____ of an accomplished thief.
a. attrition
b. sledge
c. sleight
d. dismastment
e. regalia

566. Something went _____ in our experiment, and instead of creating a green odorless vapor, we ended up with a noxious red liquid that stank up the laboratory for days.
a. hoary
b. awry
c. listless
d. derogatory
e. dilatory

567. When the movie star slipped out the back door of the hotel, the paparazzi adroitly gathered their _____ and raced around the building to catch her.
a. pandemonium
b. tenor
c. paraphernalia
d. venue
e. propaganda

568. Since Shane won the lottery, he has been living a life of _____ luxury, buying whatever he desires and traveling around the world in his 100-foot yacht as he is waited on hand and foot by a bevy of butlers, cooks, and maids.
a. arrant
b. vitriolic
c. ribald
d. seditious
e. fatuous

569. Confronted by his mother, the _____ four-year-old could not lie about scribbling on his bedroom walls with purple and blue markers.
a. guileless
b. inauspicious
c. untarnished
d. indiscriminate
e. vexed

570. The artist attempted to _____ the painting by adding people dressed in bright colors in the foreground.
a. excoriate
b. amplify
c. eradicate
d. vivify
e. inculcate

571. The artist drew the picture with such _____ that it was possible to count every blade of grass that he painted.
a. blasphemy
b. philosophy
c. nicety
d. consensus
e. purveyance

572. The highly publicized nature of the trial caused the judge to _____ the jury in order to shield members from evidence that might sway their verdict.
a. quarantine
b. retract
c. sequester
d. integrate
e. assimilate

573. Jillian was _____ by the contradictory diagnoses she received and decided she needed a third opinion.
a. intimidated
b. effaced
c. girded
d. usurped
e. bemused

574. Because he was antsy from having eaten too much candy, little William was unable to _____ himself in a respectable manner during the ceremony.
a. garner
b. quell
c. surmise
d. comport
e. subjugate

575. The chemistry professor believed her students could do better on their exams by searching for their own answers, and encouraged the class to apply the _____ method to prepare.
a. punctilious
b. nonconformist
c. salubrious
d. heuristic
e. determinate

576. Bea was known for her loud and domineering personality and was considered a _____ by many who knew her.
a. banality
b. debutante
c. scapegoat
d. trifle
e. virago

577. Even though he was only in kindergarten, Joel was very _____ and could intuit when his teacher was not pleased with his behavior.
a. obtuse
b. oblivious
c. inept
d. perceptive
e. indolent

578. During his many years of hard work, Paul was promoted several times and began to rise through the bank's _____ of employees.
a. declassification
b. surplus
c. hierarchy
d. principality
e. dominion

579. The heat was absolutely _____, making everyone irritable, sweaty, and uncomfortable.
a. taciturn
b. salient
c. replete
d. prosaic
e. oppressive

580. The biology students were assigned the task of testing the _____, but did not have enough time to prove its validity.
- **a.** lexicon
- **b.** hypothesis
- **c.** motif
- **d.** platitude
- **e.** genesis

581. It had rained all afternoon, but the fans remained _____ that the baseball game would still be played.
- **a.** pessimistic
- **b.** sadistic
- **c.** optimistic
- **d.** domineering
- **e.** truant

582. If you have any special needs or requests, speak to Val; she's the one with the most _____ around here.
- **a.** synergy
- **b.** clout
- **c.** affinity
- **d.** guile
- **e.** infamy

583. Because Virgil had been _____ as a child, he had an extremely difficult time adjusting when he enrolled in the military academy.
- **a.** fettered
- **b.** intrepid
- **c.** coddled
- **d.** pallid
- **e.** odious

584. Far from being a _____, Bob gets up at dawn every morning to prepare for a long day at work, after which he attends classes in evening.
- **a.** moderator
- **b.** drone
- **c.** replica
- **d.** sycophant
- **e.** sluggard

585. The vulgarity used by the football fans at the stadium was _____ and eventually led to a penalty for the team.
- **a.** rakish
- **b.** quiescent
- **c.** sagacious
- **d.** reproachable
- **e.** mundane

586. After the debate, Karim _____ upon many of the campaign issues in a series of detailed editorials.
- **a.** expounded
- **b.** ebbed
- **c.** doffed
- **d.** temporized
- **e.** wrought

587. Since the judge hearing the case was related to one of the defendants, she felt she could not offer a truly _____ opinion.
- **a.** unbiased
- **b.** indifferent
- **c.** unilateral
- **d.** uninterested
- **e.** understated

588. Abdul found his ten-hour shifts at the paper clip factory repetitive and _____.
a. fatuous
b. nebulous
c. malleable
d. indelible
e. wearisome

589. Jonelle is a(n) _____ of the kind of student we seek: someone who is both academically strong and actively involved in the community.
a. paradox
b. exemplar
c. catalyst
d. mandate
e. harbinger

590. Tomas is a(n) _____ businessman who knows a good opportunity when he sees it.
a. insolent
b. astute
c. mercurial
d. indifferent
e. volatile

591. Sean would _____ whenever it became his turn to do the dishes.
a. premeditate
b. palter
c. reform
d. distend
e. ponder

592. The barnyard scene outside the 4-H tent made a charming _____ for visitors to the state fair.
a. melee
b. tabloid
c. tableau
d. rant
e. tangent

593. The jellyfish, known for its shimmering _____, is one of nature's most intriguing creatures.
a. resonance
b. opulence
c. didactics
d. omniscience
e. translucence

594. A decade after the _____, the members of the tribe began to drift home again, hoping to rebuild the community they had fled during the war.
a. kowtow
b. redaction
c. cloister
d. diaspora
e. chimera

595. After performing a(n) _____ of the cow, scientists determined that it did not have mad cow disease, and there was no need to notify the federal authorities.
a. extrapolation
b. autopsy
c. interment
d. elongation
e. vivisection

596. Charged with moral _____, the judge was called off the case even though he denied receiving bribes from the plaintiff's counsel.
   a. lassitude
   b. restitution
   c. turpitude
   d. torpor
   e. vicissitude

597. I knew from Inga's _____ reply that she was offended by my question.
   a. sinuous
   b. vivacious
   c. sinister
   d. garrulous
   e. brusque

598. The cult leader's _____ obeyed his every instruction.
   a. predecessors
   b. sycophants
   c. narcissists
   d. panderers
   e. elocutionists

599. The _____ wallpaper in his living room makes it difficult to find curtains and furniture that will be compatible with it.
   a. blunt
   b. fatuous
   c. verbose
   d. variegated
   e. meticulous

600. Homer's *Odyssey* was not translated into many people's _____ until after the invention of the printing press.
   a. caste
   b. epicure
   c. vernacular
   d. debutant
   e. nomenclature

601. *Don Quixote* describes the adventures of a(n) _____ knight who believes that windmills are giants and the barmaid Dulcinea is a princess.
   a. gregarious
   b. eloquent
   c. fickle
   d. errant
   e. steadfast

602. The _____ espionage plot was so sophisticated it was impossible to believe it was the work of teenage computer hackers.
   a. simple
   b. vaporized
   c. byzantine
   d. mystical
   e. fusty

▶ Answers

180. c. *Even though* is the most logical subordinating phrase, showing a contrast. The other choices are not only illogical but ungrammatical.

181. a. The word *despite* establishes a logical connection between the main and subordinate clauses. *Whereupon* and *so that* (choices **b** and **c**) make no sense. Choice **d** is both illogical and ungrammatical.

182. c. The subordinator *because* in choice **c** establishes the logical causal relationship between subordinate and main clause; choices **a** and **b** do not make sense. Choice **d** has faulty construction.

183. b. *Whereas* is the logical subordinator, establishing contrast. The other answer choices make no sense.

184. c. The subordinator *although* shows a logical contrasting relationship between subordinate and main clause. The other choices do not make sense.

185. b. The conjunction *so* establishes the correct causal relationship between the clauses. The other sentences do not point to a cause.

186. d. The subordinator *yet* establishes a contrasting relationship between the clauses. The other choices do not establish a logical relationship.

187. a. The subordinator *whereas* correctly establishes a contrast between subordinate and main clause. The other choices point to an illogical causal relationship.

188. c. Choice **a** contains a misplaced modifier. Choice **b** is a run-on sentence. Choice **d** establishes a faulty causal relationship between main and subordinate clauses. Choice **c** correctly states a simple fact.

189. c. The conjunction *but* sets the reader up for a contrast or opposite: *TV . . . passive . . . but computer game . . . active.*

190. b. The conjunction *so* indicates a causal relationship: *Socrates taught* [something obviously controversial], *so he was both . . . loved and . . . hated.* Choice **c** is incorrect because it has a misplaced modifier.

191. a. The conjunction *for* in this sentence means *because* and prepares the reader for a logical causal relationship. Choice **d** is a run-on sentence.

192. a. The conjunction *so* indicates that there is a causal relationship between the two clauses.

193. d. The conjunction *yet* prepares the reader for a contrast: *respected, yet . . . imprisoned.* Choice **b** is wrong because it is unclear.

194. c. In this sentence, the conjunction *for* means *because* and prepares the reader for a logical causal relationship.

195. b. The conjunction *but* sets the reader up for an opposite or contrast: *it is possible . . . but . . . unlikely.* Choices **c** and **d** make no sense.

196. c. The word *unless* sets up the causal relationship between the two clauses in the sentence. The other choices are illogical.

197. a. The subordinating conjunction *although* signals an impending contradiction. The other choices do not make sense.

198. d. The subordinator *but* contrasts the main clause and subordinate clause in a logical way. Choices **a**, **b**, and **c** do not make sense.

199. d. Choice **d** is the most economical of the choices and makes the most sense.

200. d. *Because* establishes the causal relationship between the woman not responding and our assumption that she would not attend.

201. c. The transitional word *although* correctly establishes a contrast between Elizabeth's athletic ability and her inability to swim or ride a bike.

202. c. The conjunctive adverb *therefore* establishes the causal relationship between the number of babies in the neighborhood and the neighborhood's nickname.

203. a. The transitional word *however* correctly establishes a contrast between the large number of stores in the shopping mall and the absence of a pet shop.

204. a. The transitional word *furthermore* correctly indicates the addition of one negative trait to another. Choice **d** is incorrect because not everyone who is unreliable has a difficult personality.

205. a. The conjunction *but* means on the contrary, and indicates that the negative in the first main clause will be followed by its opposite in the second: *never eat . . . but . . . do drink.*

206. d. The conjunction *so* correctly indicates the causality: The subject of the sentence always has a big party because she loves celebrating her birthday. Choice **a** indicates causality but is ungrammatical.

207. b. The conjunction *yet* prepares the reader for a contrast: *is not usually . . . yet it can.* Choice **c** is unclear.

208. d. The conjunction *and* in this sentence indicates *also.* Choice **a** is wrong because it is a sentence fragment. Choice **b** makes no sense; choice **c** prepares the reader for a contrast but fails to deliver.

209. b. The conjunction *yet* prepares the reader for a contrast: *much interest . . . throughout the ages, yet . . . scientific study . . . is . . . new.* Choices **a** and **c** are incomplete sentences.

210. a. The original sentence is the only one that has the same form (parallelism) between the verbs (*welcoming* and *having*).

211. c. This choice is the only one that does not contain repetition or wordiness. Choice **b** is grammatically incorrect.

212. b. This choice is correctly subordinated and is logical.

213. a. The original sentence is the only choice that does not have a faulty subordination. The first part of the sentence is an independent clause; the second part is a dependent clause that is correctly introduced by the relative pronoun *which.*

214. e. This is the only choice that does not contain repetition or wordiness. In the original sentence and in choices **c** and **d**, *well known, prominent, famous,* and *renowned* mean the same thing; in choice **b**, a painter obviously lived and painted.

215. c. This choice is constructed so that the sentence is logical and unambiguous. In the original sentence, the opening phrase *Having missed class several times* should be completed by a noun or pronoun that indicates who missed class.

216. **a.** The original sentence is the only choice that does not contain repetition or wordiness. In choice **b**, *diligent* and *careful* mean the same thing; in choice **c**, *reviewing* and *checking* mean the same thing; in choice **d**, *workers* and *employees* mean the same thing; and in choice **e**, *daily* and *every day* mean the same thing.

217. **d.** The word *beside* means at the side of; the word *besides* means other than or together with.

218. **d.** The comparison in this sentence between the United States and Japan requires *as well as*. Choice **d** does this while at the same time creating a clear and logical sentence.

219. **a.** Correct as is. A comma is needed before a coordinating conjunction and after a subordinating clause; choice **a** is the only one that does both.

220. **d.** In this complex sentence, choice **d** is the only choice that results in a complete sentence. The other choices are sentence fragments.

221. **b.** This is the only choice in which the sentence construction is clear and unambiguous. In the original sentence and in choice **c**, the sentence reads as though the ingredients were making the torte. In choice **e**, no one is making the torte. Choice **d** is incorrect because there is a shift in tense from present (*making*) to past perfect (*should have used*).

222. **a.** The original sentence makes a comparison between culture and biology that is logical and clear. Choice **b** is wrong because the use of the preposition *with* does not observe standard usage conventions. The phrase *somewhat better* in choice **c** makes no sense. Choices **d** and **e** result in an unclear comparison.

223. **e.** This is the only choice that does not contain excessive wordiness or a redundancy. In the original sentence, the phrase *the fifth of the five* is redundant. Choices **b**, **c**, and **d** also repeat *five* and *fifth*.

224. **e.** The opening phrase, *An American poet of the nineteenth century*, should modify a noun that identifies the poet. Only choice **e** does this. In the original sentence and in choices **b** and **c**, either *collection* or *Leaves of Grass* is illogically credited with being the poet. Choice **d** is incorrect because the subject of the resulting dependent clause, *poems*, does not agree with its verb, *celebrates*.

225. **d.** Choice **d** is correctly punctuated with a semicolon between two independent clauses, and there is no shift in person. The original sentence and choices **b** and **e** are incorrect because the sentence shifts from the first person (*we*) to the second person (*you*). Choice **c** uses a semicolon when no punctuation is necessary.

226. **b.** In this sentence, *contrary to*, which means opposite to or in conflict with, is used correctly. In the original sentence, *in* is inappropriately used with *opposite*. Similarly, choices **c**, **d**, and **e** do not use standard phrasing.

227. **a.** The sentence is correct as is. Choices **b** and **e** are wordy, while choices **c** and **d** are awkward.

228. **c.** The original sentence and choices **b** and **e** are awkward and wordy. Choice **d** is unclear and ambiguous; the use of the preposition *to* distorts the meaning of the sentence.

229. **d.** This choice is clear, logical, and unambiguous and does not use extraneous words. In the original sentence, *until the time when* is redundant. Choice **b** is also redundant (*since when*) and uses extraneous words. The redundancy in choice **c** is *to kill and stop*. In choice **e**, the phrase *up to when* is awkward, and the word *its* has an unclear referent.

230. **a.** When constructing sentences, unnecessary shifts in verb tenses should be avoided. The original sentence is best because all three verbs in the sentence indicate that the action occurred in the past (*had been covering*, *became*, and *was called*). In choice **b**, there is a shift to the present (*becomes*). Choice **c** begins in the present (*is covering*, *becomes*), then shifts to the past (*called*). Choice **d** makes two tense shifts, and choice **e** shifts once, from present to past tense.

231. **d.** This is the only choice that is both grammatically and logically correct. The original sentence has a shift in construction; there are two subjects that mean the same thing (*Donald Trump* and *he*). Choice **b** has a modifier problem; the sentence implies that Donald Trump built a billion-dollar empire because he was the son of a real estate developer. Choice **c**, though constructed differently, results in the same faulty logic. Choice **e** creates faulty subordination.

232. **e.** The correct punctuation between two independent clauses is a semicolon. The original sentence is wrong because it creates a comma splice. Choice **c** creates a sentence fragment. Choices **b** and **d** create faulty subordination.

233. **b.** This is the correct choice because it is the only one that is a complete sentence.

234. **e.** This is the correct choice because the sentence is complete, logical, and unambiguous.

235. **b.** This is the only choice that is logical and unambiguous.

236. **c.** This is a sentence fragment.

237. **a.** The comma and the word *going* needs to be deleted.

238. **d.** There are no errors.

239. **b.** This is a run-on sentence.

240. **c.** The modifier *last summer* is misplaced. A modifier should be nearest to the subject or action that it modifies; in this case, that action is *visited*, not *grew up*. The sentence should read: *Last summer, we visited the town where my father grew up.*

241. **d.** There are no errors.

242. **c.** The word *unless* does not logically connect the independent clauses. The sentence needs a word that indicates contrast, because what Liam loves and what Liam can expect are two opposite things; the coordinating conjunction *but* should replace *unless*.

243. **a.** This is a run-on sentence.

244. **b.** This is a sentence fragment.

245. **d.** There are no errors.

246. **d.** There are no errors.

247. **b.** The word *that* is unnecessary; two independent clauses use a comma and a coordinating conjunction.

248. a. The other choices are unclear because they are awkwardly constructed, obscuring who intends to set the fire.

249. a. Choices **b** and **c** are sentence fragments. Choice **d** represents confused sentence structure as well as lack of agreement between subject and verb.

250. c. The other choices contain unnecessary shifts in person: from *people* to *their* and *we* in choice **a**, to *your* and *one* in choice **b**, and to *our* and *they* in choice **d**.

251. b. This is the only choice that does not have a misplaced modifier. Because Miles Johnson is the sharpshooter, his name should be placed immediately after the introductory phrase—which rules out choices **a** and **c**. Choice **d** is awkwardly constructed and unclear.

252. c. This is the only choice that is clear and logical. Choice **a** reads as though the eyes are in the third or fourth grade. Choices **b** and **d** are unclear.

253. b. *Jesting* (adj.) means characterized by making jests; joking; playful.

254. a. *Prone* (adj.) means having a tendency or inclination to something.

255. a. To *encroach* (v.) means to gradually or stealthily take the rights or possessions of another; to advance beyond proper or formal limits; trespass.

256. c. *Invulnerable* (adj.) means incapable of being damaged or wounded; unassailable or invincible.

257. e. *Judicious* (adj.) means being wise or prudent; showing good judgment; sensible.

258. c. *Malignant* (adj.) means disposed to cause distress or inflict suffering intentionally; inclining to produce death or injury.

259. c. *Apocryphal* (adj.) means of questionable authenticity or doubtful authority; fictitious, false.

260. d. *Tacit* (adj.) means unspoken yet understood.

261. b. *Apogee* (n.) means the highest or farthest point, culmination; the point in its orbit where a satellite is at the greatest distance from the body it is orbiting.

262. d. *Fawning* (adj.) means attempting to win favor or attention by excessive flattery, ingratiating displays of affection, or servile compliance; obsequious.

263. a. *Mottled* (adj.) means blotched or spotted with different colors or shades.

264. c. To *flourish* (v.) is (of artists) to be in a state of high productivity, excellence, or influence; to grow luxuriously, thrive; to fare well, prosper, increase in wealth, honor, comfort or whatever is desirable; to make bold, sweeping movements.

265. e. To *flummox* (v.) is to confuse, perplex, bewilder.

266. a. A *protagonist* (n.) is the main character in a drama.

267. a. *Aplomb* (n.) is self-assurance, composure, poise, especially under strain.

268. e. *Mandate* (n.) is a command or authoritative instruction; an authorization.

269. c. To *rant* (v.) means to speak loudly, vehemently, or violently.

270. c. *Juncture* (n.) is a point of time, especially one that is significant.

271. a. *Sibilant* (adj.) means characterized by a hissing sound.

272. d. *Manifold* (adj.) means many and varied; of many kinds; multiple.

273. a. *Untimely* (adj.) means happening before the proper time.

274. **c.** *Arable* (adj.) means suitable for cultivation; fit for plowing and farming productively.

275. **a.** *Gangling* (adj.) means awkward, lanky, or unusually tall and thin.

276. **b.** *Adulation* (n.) means strong or excessive admiration or praise; fawning flattery.

277. **d.** To *ransack* (v.) means to thoroughly search, to plunder, pillage.

278. **b.** To *enjoin* (v.) means to issue an order or command; to direct or impose with authority.

279. **e.** *Liquefaction* (n.) is the process of liquefying a solid or making a liquid.

280. **c.** To *nullify* (v.) means to make invalid or nonexistent.

281. **a.** *Sedition* (n.) means resistance, insurrection; conduct directed against public order and the tranquility of the state.

282. **a.** *Munificent* (adj.) means extremely generous or liberal in giving; lavish.

283. **c.** *Equivocal* (adj.) means open to two or more interpretations, ambiguous and often intended to mislead; open to question, uncertain.

284. **b.** *Honorarium* (n.) is payment or reward for services for which payment is not usually required.

285. **d.** To *covet* (v.) is to wish or long for; to feel immoderate desire for that which belongs to another.

286. **d.** A *ravine* (n.) is a deep, narrow canyon.

287. **a.** *Staid* (adj.) means of a steady and sober character; prudently reserved and colorless.

288. **d.** A *gamut* (n.) is an entire range or a whole series.

289. **e.** *Mordant* (adj.) means bitingly sarcastic or harshly caustic.

290. **c.** To *cow* (v.) is to intimidate; to frighten with threats or a show of force.

291. **c.** *Torpor* (n.) means extreme sluggishness; lethargy or apathy; dullness.

292. **e.** A *garrison* (n.) is a fort or outpost where troops are stationed; any military post.

293. **b.** *Verdant* (adj.) means green with vegetation.

294. **d.** A *quirt* (n.) is a riding whip with a short handle and braided rawhide lash.

295. **d.** To *extricate* (v.) is to disengage from an entanglement or difficulty.

296. **b.** The *terminus* (n.) is the final point or goal; the final stop on a transportation line.

297. **d.** To *prosper* (v.) means to be successful.

298. **b.** *Gelid* (adj.) means icy or extremely cold; possessing a cold or unfriendly manner.

299. **a.** *Loquacity* (n.) is talkativeness; the state of continual talking.

300. **e.** *Vertex* (n.) means the highest point of anything; the apex or summit.

301. **b.** An *anathema* (n.) is one who is detested or shunned; one who is cursed or damned; a curse or vehement denunciation; a formal ban, curse, or excommunication.

302. **a.** *Finesse* (n.) is the subtle, skillful handling of a situation; diplomacy; tact; refined or delicate performance or execution.

303. **d.** A *tirade* (n.) is a long and blusterous speech given especially when the speaker is denouncing someone or something.

304. **a.** *Tiresome* (adj.) means causing to be weary.

305. **d.** *Libel* (n.) is defamatory writing; misrepresentative publication (writing, pictures, signs) that damages a person's reputation.

306. **a.** *Misnomer* (n.) is a misnaming of a person or place; a wrong or unsuitable name.

307. **b.** An *affinity* (n.) is a natural attraction or liking; a feeling of kinship, connection, or closeness; similarity; relationship by marriage.

308. b. To *extol* (v.) means to praise highly, exalt, glorify.

309. a. A *ligature* (n.) is something that ties or binds up, such as a bandage, wire, or cord.

310. a. *Virile* (adj.) means having masculine strength; vigorous or energetic.

311. c. An *arbiter* (n.) is one selected or appointed to judge or decide a disputed issue, an arbitrator; someone with the power to settle matters at will.

312. c. *Nonplussed* (adj.) means greatly perplexed, filled with bewilderment.

313. a. *Facile* (adj.) means arrived at or achieved with little difficulty or effort, thus lacking depth, superficial; performing or speaking effectively with effortless ease and fluency, adroit, eloquent.

314. c. *Prerogative* (n.) means an exclusive or special right or privilege.

315. c. To *glower* (v.) means to stare angrily or sullenly, to look intently with anger or dislike.

316. b. A *faction* (n.) is a group or clique within a larger group, usually a minority, acting in unison in opposition to the larger group; internal dissension or conflict within an organization, nation, or other group.

317. c. *Travail* (n.) means hard or agonizing labor.

318. c. *Virtuoso* (n.) means a master in the technique of some particular fine art.

319. a. *Modulation* (n.) is regulation by or adjustment to a certain measure, such as in music or radio waves.

320. d. *Officious* (adj.) means marked by excessive eagerness in offering unwanted services or advice to others; unofficial.

321. b. A *fusillade* (n.) is a barrage; a rapid discharge of firearms, for example, simultaneously or in rapid succession.

322. d. *Malcontent* (adj.) means one who is dissatisfied, uneasy, or discontented; a rebel.

323. a. *Pertinent* (adj.) means applicable, related to the subject matter at hand.

324. a. *Vocative* (adj.) means pertaining to the act of calling.

325. c. *Incorrigible* (adj.) means bad to the point of being beyond correction; uncontrollable; impervious to change.

326. a. To *beset* (v.) means to surround on all sides; to annoy or harass persistently; to decorate with jewels.

327. b. To *insinuate* (v.) is to hint or suggest; to intimate.

328. b. To *wane* (v.) means to diminish in intensity or size.

329. b. *Degenerate* (adj.) means having declined in quality or value, reduced from a former or original state, degraded.

330. c. *Unconscionable* (adj.) means not restrained by conscience; unscrupulous.

331. a. *Perdition* (n.) in its most modern use means eternal damnation or a hell.

332. b. *Lissome* (adj.) means lithe or lithesome, usually related to the body; moving or bending easily; limber.

333. c. To *riddle* (v.) means to pierce in many locations.

334. b. *Undulating* (adj.) means characterized by a wavelike motion.

335. a. To *ponder* (v.) is to weigh carefully in the mind.

336. e. To *wrangle* (v.) means to dispute, bicker, create an argument.

337. c. *Itinerant* (adj.) means traveling from one place to another, usually on a planned course; working in one place for a short while before moving on to another place to work; wandering.

338. **c.** *Liberal* (adj.) means characterized by generosity or a willingness to give freely in large amounts; untraditional or broad-minded in beliefs.

339. **b.** *Wiry* (adj.) means thin, but tough and sinewy.

340. **d.** *Osteopathic* (adj.) refers to a system of medicine pertaining to the bone and skeletal system.

341. **a.** *Decorous* (adj.) means characterized by good taste in manners and conduct, exhibiting propriety or decorum; proper.

342. **d.** *Litigious* (adj.) means inclined to disagree or dispute, especially in lawsuits; argumentative.

343. **d.** *Callow* (adj.) means lacking maturity or experience; immature, naïve.

344. **b.** *Deleterious* (adj.) means having a harmful or adverse effect; destructive, hurtful, noxious.

345. **d.** *Unctuous* (adj.) means characterized by insincere earnestness; oily or fatty in appearance.

346. **c.** *Witless* (adj.) means foolish, indiscreet, or silly.

347. **d.** *Pavid* (adj.) means timid or fearful.

348. **e.** *Malediction* (n.) is a curse or a proclaiming of a curse against someone; an imprecation.

349. **e.** A *cache* (n.) is a hiding place for storing or concealing provisions or valuables; a secret store of valuables or money, a stash.

350. **e.** To *undermine* (v.) means to subvert in an underhanded way.

351. **d.** To *plagiarize* (v.) is to steal thoughts or words in literary composition.

352. **d.** *Wizened* (adj.) means withered or dry, especially with age.

353. **c.** *Jeopardize* (v.) means to put in jeopardy or at risk; to expose to a hazard or danger.

354. **a.** *Lexicon* (n.) is the vocabulary used in a language, profession, class, or subject.

355. **b.** *Liability* (n.) is a debt or obligation; something for which one is liable.

356. **b.** *Congenial* (adj.) means having a friendly or pleasant disposition, sociable; having similar tastes, habits, or temperament; suitable to one's needs or nature.

357. **d.** *Plausible* (adj.) means apparently worthy of belief or praise.

358. **e.** *Wile* (n.) means an act or a means of cunning deception.

359. **d.** *Motif* (n.) is a recurrent theme or form in an artistic or literary work.

360. **c.** *Consonant* (adj.) means in agreement or accord, harmonious; having similar sounds.

361. **c.** *Fastidious* (adj.) means paying careful attention to detail, meticulous; difficult to please, exacting; extremely sensitive, squeamish, especially in regard to matters of cleanliness or propriety.

362. **d.** *Ubiquitous* (adj.) means being present everywhere.

363. **d.** *Prevalent* (adj.) means widespread or widely accepted; predominant or extensive.

364. **a.** A *zephyr* is a soft, gentle breeze; a breeze that blows from the west.

365. **b.** To *accost* (v.) means to approach and speak to someone, usually in a bold and aggressive manner as with a demand.

366. **d.** To *forfeit* (v.) means to be deprived of or lose the right to by the act of a crime, offense, fault, breach, or error.

367. **e.** *Tantalizing* (adj.) means tempting, attractive, often via the senses.

368. **e.** *Overwrought* (adj.) means labored to excess; anxious, agitated.

369. e. To *laud* (v.) is to praise, honor, or glorify.

370. b. To *maraud* (v.) is to rove and raid in quest of plunder.

371. d. *Acerbic* (adj.) means sharp or biting in tone, character, or expression; sour or bitter in taste.

372. a. *Frenetic* (adj.) means wildly excited or agitated, frenzied, frantic.

373. b. *Toilsome* (adj.) means laborious or involving hard work.

374. c. A *hovel* (n.) is a small, crude house; a filthy or disorganized hut or shed.

375. a. To *transmute* (v.) means to change in nature, substance, or form.

376. d. *Gratuitous* (adj.) means unjustified or unnecessary; of no cost.

377. d. *Fodder* (n.) is a consumable, often inferior resource or item, high in demand and usually abundant in supply.

378. e. To *quell* (v.) means to cease or suppress.

379. c. *Wantonness* (n.) means recklessness.

380. b. *Joist* (n.) is a small, horizontal beam that supports a ceiling or floor, usually made of wood, reinforced concrete, or steel.

381. a. To *rally* (v.) means to come together for a common purpose or as a means of support; to recover or rebound.

382. a. *Deft* (adj.) means quick and skillful in movement, adroit.

383. b. *Nostalgic* (adj.) is sentimentally yearning for a point in the past.

384. e. *Acute* (adj.) means extremely sharp or intense; keenly perceptive or discerning; of great importance or consequence, crucial; also, having a sharp tip or point.

385. e. To *jettison* (v.) is to toss goods overboard to lighten the load of a ship or aircraft to improve stability; to toss off (a burden).

386. d. To *wean* (v.) means to detach someone from that to which he or she is accustomed or devoted.

387. c. A *denizen* (n.) is one who frequents a particular place; one who lives in a particular place, an inhabitant.

388. d. A *novelty* (n.) is a new or unusual thing or occurrence.

389. c. To *jostle* (v.) is to push or shove roughly against; to drive with pushing; to disturb or bump.

390. d. *Avarice* (n.) means an excessive or insatiable desire for material wealth; inordinate greed.

391. e. *Ulterior* (adj.) means lying beyond or outside what is openly shown or said.

392. c. *Iniquity* (n.) is wickedness or overwhelming injustice.

393. e. *Calumny* (n.) means a false statement or accusation uttered maliciously to harm another's reputation; slander.

394. e. To *objectify* (v.) to treat a living being as an object or, to transform an abstract idea or concept into a more concrete and objective reality so that others can understand and relate to it.

395. a. *Tertiary* (adj.) ranking third in order of importance, position, or value.

396. c. A *nonpareil* (n.) is a person or thing of peerless excellence.

397. c. An *emissary* (n.) is an agent sent on a mission to represent the interests of someone else.

398. c. To *beleaguer* (v.) is to harass, beset, besiege.

399. a. A *norm* (n.) is an average standard, pattern, or type.

400. e. *Tremulous* (adj.) means characterized by trembling or unsteadiness.

401. c. *Bucolic* (adj.) means of or characteristic of country life or people, rustic, especially in an idealized sense; of or characteristic of shepherds or herdsmen, pastoral.

402. c. *Obliged* (v.) means to be indebted.

403. a. *Trepidation* (n.) means nervous uncertainty.

404. d. *Perforated* (adj.) means with a line of holes to facilitate separation; pierced with a pointed instrument.

405. a. *Elliptical* (adj.) means characterized by extreme economy of words or style; of, relating to, or having the shape of an ellipsis.

406. b. A *catalyst* (n.) is something that precipitates or causes a process or event; (in chemistry) a substance that initiates or accelerates a chemical reaction without itself being affected in the process.

407. d. An *oleander* (n.) is a beautiful but poisonous evergreen shrub.

408. a. *Overt* (adj.) means apparent, obvious.

409. b. *Inauspicious* (adj.) means not favorable or unfortunate; not promising success.

410. c. *Vogue* (n.) means the prevalent way or fashion.

411. d. *Circuitous* (adj.) means having or taking a roundabout, lengthy, or indirect course.

412. e. *Encomium* (n.) means a formal expression of praise, a glowing tribute.

413. b. *Vulnerable* (adj.) means assailable; capable of receiving injuries; open to attack.

414. a. *Subservient* (adj.) means following another's requests in a servantlike manner far below what is called for.

415. d. *Obstinate* (adj.) means stubborn.

416. e. *Esoteric* (adj.) means designed for, confined to, or understandable by only a restricted number of people, an enlightened inner circle.

417. a. To *circumscribe* (v.) is to draw a line around, encircle; to restrict or confine; to determine the limits of, define.

418. d. *Stupor* (n.) means profound lethargy, such as one might experience after being very ill.

419. e. To *omit* (v.) is to leave out; to neglect, disregard.

420. a. A *foible* (n.) is a minor weakness or character flaw; a distinctive behavior or attribute peculiar to an individual.

421. d. To *circumvent* (v.) is to go around, bypass; to get around or avoid through cleverness or artful maneuvering; to surround, enclose, entrap.

422. c. *Onerous* (adj.) is burdensome or troublesome.

423. a. *Winsome* (adj.) means attractive, often because of childlike charm and innocence.

424. e. *Inexpedient* (adj.) means not expedient; not suitable or fit for the purpose; not tending to promote a proposed object.

425. d. *Concomitant* (adj.) means occurring or existing concurrently; accompanying, attendant.

426. c. To *purport* (v.) means to give false appearance of being.

427. e. *Supine* (adj.) means lying on the back.

428. d. *Parlous* (adj.) means dangerous, risky, or extreme.

429. c. To *obliterate* (v.) means to blot out or destroy.

430. e. *Adverse* (adj.) means unfavorable acting against or contrary to; or opposed or opposing.

431. b. To *recruit* (v.) means to seek to induct or enroll; to enlist.

432. b. *Justification* (n.) is an explanation or reason that justifies or shows something to be necessary.

433. d. *Jurisdiction* (n.) is authority or power; sphere of power or authority.

434. b. *Unutterable* (adj.) means inexpressible.

435. a. *Obscure* (adj.) means not clearly expressed or easily understood; not easily seen or distinguished.

436. d. *Ardent* (adj.) means characterized by intense emotion or enthusiasm, passionate, fervent; glowing or burning like fire.

437. e. A *dilettante* (n.) is an amateur, one who dabbles in an art or field of knowledge for amusement; a lover of fine arts, a connoisseur.

438. d. *Scrupulous* (adj.) means extremely careful, cautious in action for fear of doing wrong.

439. c. An *oracle* (n.) is a person of great knowledge; the place where answers are given, as in a sanctuary.

440. a. A *behemoth* (n.) is a giant; something or someone who is enormous in size, power, or importance.

441. b. *Impertinent* (adj.) means improperly bold; rude; lacking good manners.

442. b. To *disseminate* (v.) means to scatter widely, diffuse, spread abroad.

443. c. *Stringent* (adj.) means rigid, strict, or exacting.

444. b. *Vicissitudes* (n.) means a change, especially a complete change, of condition or circumstances.

445. b. To *blanch* (v.) means to turn pale, as if in fear; to take the color from, whiten.

446. b. To *herald* (v.) is to proclaim or announce; to foreshadow.

447. b. A *qualm* (n.) is a sudden or disturbing feeling.

448. c. *Extraneous* (adj.) means not vital or essential; not pertinent or relevant; coming from the outside or an outside source.

449. b. To *succumb* (v.) means to give in, cease to resist.

450. e. *Extrinsic* (adj.) means not forming an essential part of a thing, extraneous; originating from the outside, external.

451. d. *Immoderate* (adj.) means excessive or extreme; exceeding reasonable limits.

452. b. *Kinetic* (adj.) means pertaining to motion or caused by motion.

453. e. *Urbane* (adj.) means characterized by refined manners; elegant or sophisticated.

454. a. *Nondescript* (adj.) means lacking any distinctive characteristics.

455. d. To *ratify* (v.) means to make valid.

456. a. *Tantamount* (adj.) means equal to; having equal or equivalent value in terms of seriousness.

457. b. *Valorous* (adj.) means courageous, valiant.

458. b. *Cognizant* (adj.) means fully knowledgeable or informed, conscious, aware.

459. c. To *imbue* (v.) is to inspire or pervade with ideas or feelings; to saturate with color; to permeate.

460. a. To *recant* (v.) means to renounce formally; to withdraw a former belief as erroneous.

461. a. *Dearth* (n.) means a severe shortage or scarce supply, especially of food; a lack of, an insufficient quantity.

462. e. *Lethargy* (n.) is the state of drowsiness or sluggish inactivity.

463. a. *Vista* (n.) means a view or prospect.

464. e. *Ornate* (adj.) means richly and artistically finished or stylized.

465. d. To *hurtle* (v.) is to rush with great speed; to move violently with great noise; to fling forcefully.

466. b. To *desiccate* (v.) means to dry out thoroughly, to become dry; to make dry, dull, or lifeless.

467. a. *Spartan* (adj.) means rigorously severe (from the Greek city-state Sparta, known for its austere and rigid lifestyle); marked by strict self-discipline; characteristically simple or frugal.

468. c. *Vapid* (adj.) means dull; lacking life, spirit, or substance; tedious.

469. d. *Palpable* (adj.) means tangible, noticeable; easily perceived and detected.

470. b. A *charlatan* (n.) is someone who makes elaborate, fraudulent claims to having certain skills or knowledge; a quack, imposter, fraud.

471. a. To *impel* (v.) is to motivate; push or drive forward; propel.

472. c. A *dossier* (n.) is a collection of papers giving detailed information about a particular person or subject.

473. d. *Uproarious* (adj.) means noisy.

474. b. An *oration* (n.) is a formal speech for a special occasion.

475. a. *Colloquial* (adj.) means characteristic of informal spoken language or conversation; conversational.

476. d. *Quintessential* (adj.) is the best and purest part of a thing; the most typical example of a thing.

477. d. To *efface* (v.) means to rub out, erase; to cause to dim or make indistinct; to make or conduct oneself inconspicuously.

478. a. *Indigenous* (adj.) means originating or being native to a specific region or country; also inherent or natural.

479. c. *Utilitarian* (adj.) means related to the ethical doctrine that actions are right because they are useful or beneficial to the greatest number of people.

480. b. To *quibble* (v.) means to find fault or criticize for petty reasons.

481. a. *Implicit* (adj.) means unquestioning or trusting without doubt; understood rather than directly stated; implied.

482. a. To *construe* (v.) is to interpret or understand; to make sense of, explain the meaning of.

483. a. *Swarthy* (adj.) means having a dark hue, especially a dark or sunburned complexion.

484. e. *Veracious* (adj.) means truthful, honest; habitually disposed to speak the truth.

485. e. *Nepotism* (n.) is favoritism for kin when conferring jobs, offices, or privileges.

486. e. An *accolade* (n.) is an award or special acknowledgment signifying approval or distinction.

487. a. *Incongruity* (n.) is the quality of being inappropriate or unbecoming; not consistent in character.

488. e. To *repress* (v.) means to keep under control or restrain; to curb or subdue.

489. b. To *elucidate* (v.) means to make clear or manifest; to free from confusion or ambiguity.

490. d. To *lacerate* (v.) is to rip, tear, or mangle.

491. b. To *negate* (*v.*) means to nullify, invalidate, or deny.

492. d. *Tentative* (adj.) means provisional or uncertain; not fixed or set.

493. a. *Verbiage* (n.) means the use of many words without necessity.

494. a. *Compunction* (n.) means a feeling of uneasiness or regret caused by a sense of guilt; remorse; a pang of conscience at the thought or act of committing a misdeed.

495. a. *Jocularity* (n.) is the state of being jocular, which is characterized by joking or jesting.

496. c. A *despot* (n.) is someone who rules with absolute power; a dictator or tyrant.

497. e. *Tenure* (n.) means the term during which a thing is held; often used in connection with career positions.

498. e. *Quotidian* (adj.) means occurring or returning daily.

499. d. *Vincible* (adj.) means conquerable, capable of being defeated or subdued.

500. d. *Commensurate* (adj.) means corresponding in size, degree, or extent; proportionate.

501. e. *Fervor* (n.) means a feeling of passion or zeal.

502. a. *Hospitable* (adj.) means treating guests kindly and generously; being agreeable, receptive, or of an open mind.

503. d. *Nomadic* (adj.) means roaming from place to place or wandering.

504. a. *Knack* (n.) is a natural talent; a clever way of doing something.

505. c. *Obsolete* (adj.) means antiquated, disused; discarded.

506. e. *Suave* (adj.) means having a smooth and pleasant manner.

507. e. *Visage* (n.) means the face, countenance, or look of a person.

508. d. *Habitable* (adj.) means acceptable for inhabiting.

509. e. *Confluence* (n.) means a flowing or coming together; a gathering or meeting together at a point or juncture; a place where two things come together, the point of juncture.

510. d. *Rescinded* (v.) means revoked.

511. d. *Empirical* (adj.) means relying on, derived from, or verifiable by; experimental or observational rather than theoretical.

512. d. *Lascivious* (adj.) means lewd, lustful, or wanton.

513. b. *Taut* (adj.) means stretched tight.

514. c. *Vigilance* (n.) means alert and intent mental watchfulness in guarding against danger.

515. d. To *obtrude* (v.) means to stick out, push forward.

516. e. *Homage* (n.) is respect paid publicly; reverence rendered; deference.

517. e. *Recourse* (n.) means a last option or way out.

518. d. To *exonerate* (v.) means to free from blame or guilt, absolve; to release from a responsibility or obligation, discharge.

519. b. *Lateral* (adj.) means pertaining to or extending from the side.

520. c. *Temporary* (adj.) means enduring for a short time; transitory.

521. d. *Virulent* (adj.) means exceedingly noxious, deleterious, malicious, or hateful.

522. a. *Otiose* (adj.) means needless, functionless; unemployed or useless.

523. a. *Aesthetic* (adj.) means concerning or characterized by an appreciation of beauty or good taste; characterized by a heightened sensitivity to beauty; artistic.

524. b. *Gradation* (n.) is the changing of a color, shade, or tint to another by gradual degrees; the process of bringing to another grade in a series; a stage or degree in such a series.

525. c. *Labyrinth* (n.) is a maze of paths or a complicated system of pathways in which it is challenging to find the exit; something extremely complex in structure or character.

526. c. *Nescience* (n.) is ignorance, or the absence of knowledge.

527. d. *Aloof* (adj.) means physically or emotionally distant; reserved, remote.

528. d. A *vagabond* (n.) is a wanderer; a person who does not have a permanent home.

529. b. *Omnivorous* (adj.) means feeding on both animal and vegetable substances; having an insatiable appetite for anything.

530. a. To *germinate* (v.) means to begin to grow or sprout; to cause to come into existence or develop.

531. d. A *provision* (n.) is a stipulation or qualification; a stock of supplies.

532. e. *Lackluster* (adj.) means lacking liveliness or brightness; dull.

533. d. *Sonorous* (adj.) means producing sound that is impressive or grand in effect.

534. d. An *orifice* (n.) is an opening, a hole; a perforation; a mouth or hole through which something may pass.

535. a. *Vertigo* (n.) is dizziness often caused by experiencing heights.

536. b. *Genesis* (n.) is the origin, beginning, or foundation; the act of forming something new; the first event in a series of events.

537. a. A *quota* (n.) is an assigned proportional share.

538. a. *Languor* (n.) is a lack of energy or interest; a feeling of being without spirit; sluggishness.

539. c. *Timbre* (n.) is the quality of a tone, as distinguished from intensity and pitch.

540. a. *Vestige* (n.) means a visible trace, mark, or impression, of something absent, lost, or gone.

541. a. *Opportune* (adj.) means well timed or convenient.

542. e. To *admonish* (v.) means to reprove kindly but seriously; to warn or counsel; to instruct or remind, as of a forgotten responsibility.

543. d. To *gibe* (v.) means to taunt or jeer; to utter a taunting or sarcastic remark.

544. d. A *realm* (n.) is a knowledge domain in which one is interested; a kingdom or domain.

545. c. To *exhort* (v.) means to urge strongly with a stirring argument, appeal, or advice; to make an urgent appeal.

546. c. *Kudos* (n.) are complimentary remarks; expressions of praise.

547. d. To *transgress* (v.) means to go beyond the limit or bounds of; usually in connection with a law.

548. d. A *girder* (n.) is a large horizontal beam, made of wood, steel, or concrete, to support weight or span an opening.

549. d. *Vernal* (adj.) means belonging to or suggestive of the spring.

550. d. *Quixotic* (adj.) means idealistic without regard for practicality.

551. c. *Aegis* (n.) means sponsorship or patronage; guidance or direction; protection.

552. e. *Animosity* (n.) means bitter, open hostility or enmity; energetic dislike.

553. d. *Kindred* (n.) is a group of people related to each other by birth or marriage.

554. c. A *noose* (n.) is a loop with a slipknot that tightens when pulled.

555. b. *Restitution* (n.) is a restoration of what is lost or taken away, especially unjustly.

556. **e.** *Impetuous* (adj.) means impulsive or passionate; characterized by sudden emotion or energy.

557. **b.** *Knave* (n.) is a dishonest, deceitful, or unreliable person.

558. **e.** *Scurrilous* (adj.) means grossly indecent or vulgar; offensive.

559. **b.** *Obstructive* (adj.) means blocking, hindering, obscuring.

560. **b.** *Virtual* (adj.) means being in essence or effect, but not in actual fact.

561. **d.** To *palpitate* (v.) is to flutter or move with slight throbs.

562. **b.** *Wry* (adj.) means ironic, cynical, or sardonic.

563. **e.** *Nonchalant* (adj.) means casual, indifferent.

564. **d.** To *wield* (v.) means to use, control, or manage, as a weapon or instrument, especially with full command.

565. **c.** A *sleight* (n.) means a trick or feat so deftly done that the manner of performance escapes observation.

566. **b.** *Awry* (adj.) means off-course, amiss; turned or twisted toward one side, askew; not functioning properly.

567. **c.** *Paraphernalia* (n.) means miscellaneous articles needed for particular professions, information, or operation; personal belongings.

568. **a.** *Arrant* (adj.) means complete, absolute, utter.

569. **a.** *Guileless* (adj.) means to be without guile; straightforward; honest; frank.

570. **d.** To *vivify* (v.) means to give or bring life to; to animate.

571. **c.** *Nicety* (n.) means precision, accuracy; a subtle distinction or detail; the state of being nice.

572. **c.** To *sequester* (v.) means to separate, segregate, seclude; cause to withdraw or retire, as with juries.

573. **e.** *Bemused* (adj.) means deeply absorbed in thought; bewildered or perplexed by conflicting situations or statements.

574. **d.** To *comport* (v.) means to conduct or behave (oneself) in a certain manner; to agree, accord, or harmonize.

575. **d.** *Heuristic* (adj.) means stimulating further investigation; encouraging learning through discoveries made by a student.

576. **e.** *Virago* (n.) means a bold, impudent, turbulent woman.

577. **d.** *Perceptive* (adj.) means having the ability to understand and be sensitive to.

578. **c.** *Hierarchy* (n.) is a series or system of people or things that are graded or ranked; groups of persons with various levels of authority.

579. **e.** *Oppressive* (adj.) means unreasonably burdensome; heavy.

580. **b.** *Hypothesis* (n.) is a proposition, believed to be probable, which is adopted to explain certain facts and which can be further tested.

581. **c.** *Optimistic* (adj.) means taking the most hopeful view; feeling that everything in nature is for the best.

582. **b.** *Clout* (n.) means influence, pull, or sway; power or muscle; a strike or blow, especially with the fist.

583. **c.** To *coddle* (v.) means to treat with excessive indulgence or tenderness, to baby or pamper. It also means to cook in water just below the boiling point.

584. **e.** A *sluggard* (n.) is a person who is habitually lazy or idle.

585. **d.** *Reproachable* (adj.) means needing rebuke or censure.

586. **a.** To *expound* (v.) means to explain in detail, elaborate; to give a detailed statement or account of.

587. **a.** *Unbiased* (adj.) means completely impartial to, as in judgment.

588. **e.** *Wearisome* (adj.) means fatiguing or tiresome.

589. **b.** An *exemplar* (n.) is one who is worthy of imitation, a model or ideal; a typical or representative example.

590. **b.** *Astute* (adj.) means having or showing intelligence and shrewdness; keen, discerning.

591. **b.** To *palter* (v.) is to act insincerely; to haggle; to play tricks; equivocate.

592. **c.** A *tableau* (n.) is an arrangement of inanimate figures representing a scene from real life.

593. **e.** *Translucence* (n.) means the property or state of allowing the passage of light.

594. **d.** A *diaspora* (n.) is a dispersion of people from their original homeland, or the community formed by such a people; the dispersion of an originally homogeneous group or entity, such as a language or culture.

595. **b.** *Autopsy* (n.) means the dissection of an animal, particularly for scientific research.

596. **c.** *Turpitude* (n.) means depravity; any action that violates accepted standards.

597. **e.** *Brusque* (adj.) means abrupt, curt, or blunt in a discourteous manner.

598. **b.** A *sycophant* (n.) is a servile flatterer, especially of those in authority or influence.

599. **d.** *Variegated* (adj.) means marked with different shades or colors.

600. **c.** *Vernacular* (n.) means the language of one's country.

601. **d.** *Errant* (adj.) means wandering, roving, especially in search of adventure; straying beyond the established course or limits.

602. **c.** *Byzantine* (adj.) means highly complicated, intricate, or involved; characterized by elaborate scheming and intrigue, devious; of or relating to or characteristic of the Byzantine Empire or ancient Byzantium, especially its architectural style; of or relating to the Eastern Orthodox Church.

5 ▶ Building Paragraphs from the Ground Up

ARE YOU ACCUSTOMED TO WRITING the mandatory five-paragraph essay? Would it surprise you to discover that an essay can run five pages or longer in length? Because most essays contain paragraphs that are a few sentences in length, it would also probably surprise some students to learn that the English rule book provides free rein to writers when it comes to paragraph length!

A paragraph can technically consist of only one word, or it can take up an entire page. Although there aren't any rules regarding paragraph length, there are some basic components of a well-written paragraph that you should keep in mind as you construct your paragraphs.

All paragraphs require a **topic sentence** that introduces the main idea. This sentence is much broader in scope than the detailed sentences that form the **body** of each paragraph. Ideally, every single paragraph should contain a final **concluding statement** to reinforce the key ideas.

When deciding about how to write about your topic, you must first decide who your **audience** is, and the **purpose** of your essay. Choose your introductory topic sentence carefully, because once you introduce a topic you are obligated to describe, explain, define, categorize, compare and contrast, provide examples for, and further elaborate on the topic that you've introduced. Your job as a writer is to inform your reader by using specific detail, factual evidence, and enough supporting information to effectively communicate all of your ideas to your readers.

The best way to narrow down a broad general topic is to use a controlling idea. Here is an example of how you can use a controlling idea to frame and guide the focus of your entire essay:

Broad topic: music
Narrow topic: rock music
Controlling idea: the top ten rock musicians of the 1960s

Get a Grip on an English Teacher's Worst Nightmare

Unless instructed to do so, avoid writing expository phrases, such as: "*I am going to write about* smoking and the reasons teenagers should quit smoking" or "*And now I'm going to write about* how I pulled a rabbit out of my hat during our school's magic contest." "Show, don't tell" is a writing adage that is as true today as it ever was.

Get a Grip on Why the Dictionary is so Important

EVOO, a term coined by celebrity chef Rachel Ray, has earned a place in the *Oxford American College Dictionary*. Rachel Ray invented the acronym EVOO to refer to extra-virgin olive oil. This is an excellent example of why the English language hasn't faded into extinction. It continues to grow and expand to suit the needs of the people who use it as new words are born and antiquated words retire. So . . . if you ever stumble across a word that you don't recognize—it might be because the word is a newbie!

▶ Practice Questions

For each of the following paragraphs, choose the topic sentence that best fits the rest of the paragraph.

603. _____. Residents have been directed to use the new plastic bins as their primary recycling containers. These new containers will make picking up recyclables faster and easier.
   a. The city has distributed standardized recycling containers to all households.
   b. Recycling has become a way of life for most people.
   c. While most Americans recycle, they also use more resources than residents of other countries.
   d. Even small cities have begun recycling to pick up used glass, plastic, and paper.

604. _____. No search of a person's home or personal effects may be conducted without a written search warrant. This means that a judge must justify a search before it can be conducted.

   a. There is an old saying that a person's home is his or her castle.

   b. Much of the U.S. legal system was based on the old British system.

   c. The Fourth Amendment to the Constitution protects citizens against unreasonable searches.

   d. _Personal effects_ is a term that refers to the belongings of a person.

605. _____. You must imitate as closely as possible the parents' methods of feeding. First, hold the beak open using thumb and forefinger. Then, introduce food into the beak with tweezers or an eyedropper.

   a. Recently, I read an article about baby birds.

   b. Hand-rearing wounded or orphaned baby birds requires skill.

   c. Baby birds are very special creatures, and they are also very small.

   d. I have been told that you should not touch a baby bird that has fallen out of its nest.

606. _____. All waves, though, have common characteristics that govern their height. The height of a wave is determined by its speed, the distance it travels, and the length of time the wind blows.

   a. Currents, unlike waves, are caused by steady winds or temperature fluctuations.

   b. Tsunamis used to be called tidal waves.

   c. Ocean waves can vary from tiny ripples to powerful, raging swells.

   d. A breaker is when a wave gets top-heavy and tips over.

607. _____. When people respect the law too much, they will follow it blindly. They will say, "The majority has decided on this law and therefore I must obey it." They will not stop to consider whether the law is fair.

   a. Some people say there is too little respect for the law, but I say there is too much respect for it.

   b. Sometimes, a judge will decide that a law is unfair.

   c. I believe that the majority of the people in this country do not understand what it means to have respect for other people.

   d. Most of the laws passed at the end of the twentieth century are fair laws.

608. _____. Gary was a very distinguished-looking man with a touch of gray at the temples. Even in his early fifties, he was still the one to turn heads. Gary checked his mirror often and felt great delight with what he saw. In fact, he considered his good looks to be his second most important asset in the world. The first was money. He was lucky in this area, too, having been born into a wealthy family. He loved the power his wealth had given him. He could buy whatever he desired, be that people, places, or things.

   a. Gary's gray hair was his worst characteristic.

   b. Conceit was the beginning and the end of Gary's character—conceit of person and situation.

   c. Gary felt blessed to be wealthy and the joy consumed his every thought.

   d. The only objects of Gary's respect were others who held positions in society.

609. The term *spices* is a pleasant one, whether it connotes fine French cuisine or a down-home, cinnamon-flavored apple pie. _____. Individuals have traveled the world seeking exotic spices for profit and, in searching, have changed the course of history. Indeed, to gain control of lands harboring new spices, nations have actually gone to war.

a. The taste and aroma of spices are the main elements that make food such a source of fascination and pleasure.

b. The term might equally bring to mind Indian curry made thousands of miles away and those delicious barbecued ribs sold down on the corner.

c. It is exciting to find a good cookbook and experiment with spices from other lands— indeed, it is one way to travel around the globe!

d. The history of spices, however, is another matter altogether, often exciting, at times filled with danger and intrigue.

610. _____. Although these mechanical alarms are fairly recent, the idea of a security system is not new. The oldest alarm system was probably a few strategically placed dogs that discouraged intruders with a loud warning bark.

a. Anyone who lives in a large, modern city has heard the familiar sound of electronic security alarms.

b. Everyone knows that a large, barking dog will scare away strangers, even the mail carrier.

c. Why spend money on an alarm system when you can get the same service from an animal?

d. Without a good alarm system, your place of business could be vandalized.

611. _____. According to scholars, these patterns almost certainly represent the labyrinth that held the Minotaur, a monster with the head of a bull and the body of a man. Legend has it that in ancient times King Minos built the labyrinth in order to imprison the Minotaur, which loved to dine on human flesh.

a. Patterned corridors are commonplace in many architectural structures.

b. In the palace at Knossos, on the isle of Crete, there is a corridor leading to the outside that is decorated with coils and spiral patterns.

c. Archeologists contend that patterns on the walls and corridors of ancient architectural structures are usually meaningful.

d. Scholars who have studied the palace at Knossos, on the isle of Crete, are at a loss to explain the meaning of the coils and spirals on its corridor walls.

612. _____. It is important to take special precautions to keep these medications in a secure place, where a child cannot get to them. Every item in the medicine cabinet should be labeled clearly. Even if you believe the medicine cabinet is too high for a child to reach, it should be locked at all times.

a. Many families have small children.

b. Many medications are extremely dangerous if swallowed.

c. If your child accidentally swallows a medicine, rush him or her to the hospital right away!

d. New, life-saving medicines are being approved by the Food and Drug Administration every day.

613. _____. It is true that Ernest Hemingway went to war to gather material for his stories, and F. Scott Fitzgerald lived a life of dissolution that destroyed him. However, Emily Brontë seldom ventured outside her father's tiny country rectory, yet she wrote _Wuthering Heights_, a tale of passionate love and intense hatred, and one of the greatest works in the English language.

   a. It is not necessary for a writer to endanger his or her life in order to have something to write about.

   b. There are many ways for gifted writers to collect material for their stories and novels.

   c. Ernest Hemingway, F. Scott Fitzgerald, and Emily Brontë are all known for the passion with which their work is imbued.

   d. Hemingway and Fitzgerald are well known for their reckless lifestyles, which nevertheless gave rise to some of the finest works in the English language.

614. _____. Hearsay that depends on the statement's truthfulness is inadmissible because the witness does not appear in court and swear an oath to tell the truth. This means that his or her demeanor when making the statement is not visible to the jury, the accuracy of the statement cannot be tested under cross-examination, and to introduce it would be to deprive the accused of the constitutional right to confront the accuser.

   a. Hearsay evidence is not acceptable in a criminal trial because the witness cannot be cross-examined.

   b. Hearsay evidence in a trial is inadmissible because there is too great a chance that it will be false.

   c. The definition of hearsay evidence is the "secondhand reporting of a statement" and is sometimes allowable.

   d. Hearsay evidence, which is the secondhand reporting of a statement, is allowed in court only when the truth of the statement is irrelevant.

615. _____. One type of tickler system is the index-card file with 12 large dividers, one for each month, and 31 small dividers, one for each day. Whenever secretaries need to schedule a reminder, they jot it down on a card and place it behind the appropriate divider. Each morning, they review the reminders for that particular day.

a. As busy secretaries, we cannot expect to remember all the details of our daily responsibilities without some help.

b. At the beginning of the day, good secretaries review and organize the tasks they must attend to during that day.

c. The word _tickler_ perfectly describes the organizational system to which it refers.

d. All secretaries need a good reminder system, sometimes known as a "tickler" system because it tickles the memory.

616. _____. Space shuttle astronauts, because they spend only about a week in space, undergo minimal wasting of bone and muscle. But when longer stays in microgravity or zero gravity are contemplated, as in the international space station or a proposed two-year round-trip voyage to Mars, these problems are of particular concern because they could become acute. Fortunately, studies show that muscle atrophy can be kept largely at bay with appropriate exercise; however, bone loss caused by reduced gravity unfortunately cannot.

a. Space flight, especially if it is prolonged, can be hazardous to the health of the astronauts.

b. The tissues of human beings are ill-prepared for the stresses placed upon them by space flight.

c. In space flight, astronauts must deal with two vexing physiological foes—muscle atrophy and bone loss.

d. Travel on the space shuttle does less damage to an astronaut's bones and muscles than an extended stay on a space station.

617. _____. Rather, asthma is now understood to be a chronic inflammatory disorder of the airways—that is, inflammation makes the airways chronically sensitive. When these hyper-responsive airways are irritated, air flow is limited, and attacks of coughing, wheezing, chest tightness, and difficulty breathing occur.

a. No longer is asthma considered a condition with isolated, acute episodes of bronchospasm.

b. The true nature of asthma has only recently been understood.

c. Since the true character of asthma is now understood, there is more hope for a cure than there was in earlier times.

d. No age is exempt from asthma, although it occurs most often in childhood and early adulthood.

618. _____. Many experts, including those in the American Diabetes Association, recommend that 50 to 60% of daily calories of patients suffering from non-insulin-dependent diabetes (NIDD) come from carbohydrates, 12 to 20% from protein, and no more than 30% from fat. Foods that are rich in carbohydrates, like breads, cereals, fruits, and vegetables, break down into glucose during digestion, causing blood glucose to rise. Additionally, studies have shown that cooked foods raise blood glucose higher than raw, unpeeled foods.

a. In 1986, a National Institutes of Health panel gave broad recommendations as to the type of diet that is best for non-insulin-dependent diabetics.

b. It is extremely important for certain medical patients to watch what they eat.

c. A good cookbook is the best friend a non-insulin-dependent diabetes (NIDD) patient can have!

d. Non-insulin-dependent diabetes patients can lead long, healthy lives if only they pay attention to their diets.

Choose the alternative that best develops the topic sentence given.

619. Indoor pollution sources that release gases or particles into the air are the primary cause of indoor air-quality problems in homes.

   a. Inadequate ventilation can increase indoor pollutant levels by not bringing in enough outdoor air to dilute emissions from indoor sources.

   b. Some physicians believe that the dangers of so-called environmental allergens are greatly exaggerated.

   c. Although there are more potential pollution sources today than ever before, environmental activists are working hard to make our world a safer place.

   d. I'll choose a good, old-fashioned log cabin any day to the kind of squeaky-clean, hermetically sealed modern condos you find in the big American cities.

620. Because of the cost of medical care these days, many Americans self-diagnose and self-medicate.

   a. Because of the abundance of over-the-counter medications that exist, this can be a bewildering task.

   b. Today, much of the work doctors used to do is done by medical assistants, who are even allowed to write prescriptions.

   c. With so many prescriptions written by doctors each day, there is always the chance of dangerous drug interactions.

   d. Medical care today is routinely done by specialists, who are apt to be less personally involved than the old-style family doctor.

621. Because of technological advances, much communication between companies and businesses is now conducted via e-mail, and office workers must face that fact.

   a. Every day, the U.S. Postal Service is subjected to a huge deluge of junk mail.

   b. Checking e-mail every morning is as important a task for a secretary as sorting and opening the boss's paper mail.

   c. It is hard to believe that a century ago, the mail was delivered on horseback.

   d. Unsolicited commercial e-mails, also known as spam, not only are annoying, but in large quantities can clog e-mail systems.

622. There are many good reasons to eat organic food. It tastes great. It is grown and handled according to strict guidelines to ensure that it is safe and pesticide-free. And organic farming respects the balance demanded of a healthy ecosystem.

   a. Many restaurants and supermarkets now carry organic products.

   b. Health-food stores are popping up all over the country.

   c. An organic lifestyle is good for you, and for our world.

   d. Ten years ago, it was much more difficult to find organic food in traditional supermarkets.

623. This contract will confirm our agreement in connection with your services as freelance writer for the work entitled *Why Kangaroos Can't Fly*.
a. The title, although rather silly, accurately sums up the tone and style of the book.
b. You agree to assist us in preparation of the book by developing content for it, based on your zoo-keeping experience.
c. It is important to have a legal contract before turning your written work over to a publishing company.
d. This book will make an important contribution to kangaroo lore around the world.

624. America's fascination with reality television is a topic of much discussion. Many think that people tune in simply to keep up-to-date with the latest popular culture trends.
a. Whether you love it or hate it, reality television is definitely here to stay.
b. Every season brings several new reality television shows. However, not every one of them succeeds.
c. Reality television has no redeeming qualities whatsoever. Critics find it shallow, sensationalistic, and mindless.
d. Ordinary people might also see themselves in these reality television personalities, leading to a sense of exhilaration as they watch their television counterparts achieve celebrity status and win big prizes.

625. Before we learn how to truly love someone else, we must learn how to love the face in the mirror.
a. Don't be shy about meeting members of the opposite sex.
b. No one can really love you the way you can love yourself.
c. Love is not something that lasts unless one is very lucky.
d. Learning to accept ourselves for what we are will teach us how to accept another person.

626. During colonial times in America, juries were encouraged to ask questions of the parties in the courtroom.
a. The jurors were, in fact, expected to investigate the facts of the case themselves. If jurors conducted an investigation today, we would throw out the case.
b. Many states are experimenting with new ways to get more people to serve on juries. All eligible voters can be called to serve.
c. There are usually two attorneys: a prosecutor and a defense attorney. This sometimes makes the courtroom lively.
d. There were 13 colonies. Each colony at first had its own legal system.

627. Landscapers do not recommend rosebushes for homeowners who have shade-filled gardens and who don't spend a great deal of time maintaining outdoor plants.

   a. Bugs called aphids can destroy roses. However, you can get rid of them by spraying with a solution of water and dish soap.

   b. Gardening can be quite time-consuming. Most gardeners spend hours in their gardens each week.

   c. When these conditions are present, a better choice would be hostas. They are extremely hardy and easy-to-grow shade plants with attractive foliage.

   d. Landscapers can be hired on a weekly or monthly basis to care for lawns and gardens. They can also be hired for a one-time consultation or for a specific lawn or garden project.

628. Ginkgo biloba extract is the most commonly prescribed plant remedy in the world.

   a. There are many plant remedies, including the ones that can be purchased in health-food stores. Not all plant remedies have been approved.

   b. It is a highly refined compound produced from the leaves of the ginkgo tree. Many people take ginkgo to treat conditions such as headaches, asthma, and hearing loss.

   c. Ginkgo has also been widely prescribed in Europe. It has been approved by the German government for the treatment of memory loss.

   d. A 1977 study with ginkgo was conducted with 20 patients. These patients ranged in age from 62 to 85.

629. Life on Earth is ancient and, even at its first appearance, unimaginably complex.

   a. Scientists place its beginnings at some 3,000 million years ago. This was when the first molecule floated up out of the ooze with the unique ability to replicate itself.

   b. The most complex life form is, of course, the mammal. The most complex mammal is us.

   c. It is unknown exactly where life started. It is unknown exactly where the first molecule was "born."

   d. Darwin's theory of evolution was an attempt to explain what essentially remains a great mystery. His theory, of course, has been discounted by some people.

For each of the following paragraphs, choose the sentence that does NOT belong.

630. (1) The cassowary, a solitary, meat-eating creature that makes its home deep in the jungles of New Guinea, hardly seems like a bird at all. (2) It is enormous, weighing up to 190 pounds. (3) Its plumage is more like hair than feathers; its song is a deep, menacing rumble; and it has lost the capability of flight. (4) Human beings have long been fascinated by birds, particularly by their ability to fly.

   a. sentence 1

   b. sentence 2

   c. sentence 3

   d. sentence 4

631. (1) Ratatouille is a dish that has grown in popularity over the past few years. (2) It features eggplant, zucchini, tomato, peppers, and garlic, chopped, mixed together, and cooked slowly over low heat. (3) Zucchini is a summer squash and has a smooth, dark green skin. (4) As the vegetables cook slowly, they make their own broth, which may be extended with a little tomato paste.
a. sentence 1
b. sentence 2
c. sentence 3
d. sentence 4

632. (1) An odd behavior associated with sleep and dreaming is somnambulism, commonly known as sleepwalking. (2) Sleepwalkers suffer from a malfunction in a brain mechanism that monitors the transition from REM to non-REM sleep. (3) REM sleep is vitally important to psychological well-being. (4) Sleepwalking episodes diminish with age and usually cause no serious harm—the worst thing that could happen would be a fall down the stairs.
a. sentence 1
b. sentence 2
c. sentence 3
d. sentence 4

633. (1) Lyme disease is sometimes called the "great imitator" because its many symptoms mimic those of other illnesses. (2) When treated, this disease usually presents few or no lingering effects. (3) Left untreated, it can be extremely debilitating and sometimes fatal. (4) One should be very careful when returning from a trek in the woods to check for deer ticks.
a. sentence 1
b. sentence 2
c. sentence 3
d. sentence 4

634. (1) The harp is a musical instrument that has an upright triangular frame. (2) Its strings are positioned perpendicular to the sounding board. (3) Harps are found in Africa, Europe, North and South America, and a few parts of Asia. (4) Its beautiful sound, which is capable of stirring great emotion, might bring tears to your eyes.
a. sentence 1
b. sentence 2
c. sentence 3
d. sentence 4

635. (1) In the summer, the northern hemisphere is slanted toward the sun, making the days longer and warmer than in winter. (2) Many religions make use of the solstices in their rites. (3) The first day of summer is called *summer solstice* and is also the longest day of the year. (4) However, June 21 marks the beginning of winter in the southern hemisphere, when that hemisphere is tilted away from the sun.
a. sentence 1
b. sentence 2
c. sentence 3
d. sentence 4

636. (1) People are quick to blame the meteorologist if it rains on their parade! (2) The American Meteorological Society defines a meteorologist as a person "who uses scientific principles to explain, understand, observe, or forecast the earth's atmospheric phenomena and/or how the atmosphere affects the earth and life on the planet." (3) Many meteorologists have degrees in physics, chemistry, and other fields. (4) Their work often involves teaching, weather forecasting, atmospheric research, and other kinds of applied meteorology.

a. sentence 1
b. sentence 2
c. sentence 3
d. sentence 4

637. (1) The park was empty, except for a child who stood just on the other side of the fence, a little girl about seven years old, thin and pale, with dark eyes and dark hair—cut short and ragged. (2) The statistics on neglected children in our country probably fall short of the actual numbers. (3) The child wore no coat, only a brown cotton skirt that was too big for her—pinned at the waist with a safety pin—and a soiled, long-sleeved yellow blouse with rhinestone buttons. (4) Her fingernails were dirty and broken, the tips of her fingers bluish with cold.

a. sentence 1
b. sentence 2
c. sentence 3
d. sentence 4

638. (1) Ghosts can be either benevolent or malevolent. (2) As someone once said, "I don't believe in ghosts, but I'm afraid of them." (3) They can be comic and comfortable, like the old sea captain in *The Ghost and Mrs. Muir*, or horrific beyond belief, like the ghosts of the revelers at the party in the Overlook Hotel in Stephen King's *The Shining*. (4) They can emerge from the afterlife to teach us lessons, like old Marley in *A Christmas Carol*, or come back moaning to be avenged, like the ghost in *Hamlet*.

a. sentence 1
b. sentence 2
c. sentence 3
d. sentence 4

639. (1) Most criminals do not suffer from antisocial personality disorder; however, nearly all persons with this disorder have been in trouble with the law. (2) Sometimes labeled "sociopaths," they are a grim problem for society. (3) Their crimes range from con games to murder, and they are set apart by what appears to be a complete lack of conscience. (4) There is a long-standing debate among psychiatrists whether hardened criminals can ever truly be rehabilitated.

a. sentence 1
b. sentence 2
c. sentence 3
d. sentence 4

640. (1) Jessie Street is sometimes called the Australian Eleanor Roosevelt. (2) Eleanor Roosevelt was one of the most admired and revered women in history. (3) Like Roosevelt, Street lived a life of privilege, but at the same time devoted her efforts to working for the rights of the disenfranchised laborers, women, refugees, and Aborigines. (4) In addition, she gained international fame when she was the only woman on the Australian delegation to the conference that founded the United Nations—just as Eleanor Roosevelt was for the United States.
  a. sentence 1
  b. sentence 2
  c. sentence 3
  d. sentence 4

641. (1) Joining a health club allows you to exercise even when the weather is bad. (2) If you're a fitness walker, there is no need for a commute to a health club. (3) Your neighborhood can be your health club. (4) You don't need a lot of fancy equipment to get a good workout, either; all you need is a well-designed pair of athletic shoes.
  a. sentence 1
  b. sentence 2
  c. sentence 3
  d. sentence 4

642. (1) Members of your office staff may have talents and abilities that you are not aware of. (2) As supervisor, it is your job to identify and encourage this potential talent. (3) Employee incentive programs are becoming increasingly common. (4) When a new project is under way, you should brainstorm with your staff to draw out their ideas and suggestions, rather than just assuming that each member is only capable of performing a very rigid role.
  a. sentence 1
  b. sentence 2
  c. sentence 3
  d. sentence 4

643. (1) Firefighters must learn the proper procedures for responding to residential carbon monoxide (CO) emergencies. (2) Upon arriving at the scene of the alarm, personnel shall put on protective clothing and then bring an operational, calibrated CO meter onto the premises. (3) CO poisoning can be lethal, both to firefighters and to ordinary citizens. (4) Occupants of the premises shall then be examined, and if they are experiencing CO poisoning symptoms—headaches, nausea, confusion, dizziness, and other flulike symptoms—an Emergency Medical Services (EMS) crew shall be sent immediately to evacuate and administer oxygen to the occupants.
  a. sentence 1
  b. sentence 2
  c. sentence 3
  d. sentence 4

For each of the following groups of numbered sentences, choose the sentence order that would result in the best paragraph.

644. (1) Figures have the power to mislead people. (2) Mathematics tells us about economic trends, patterns of disease, and the growth of populations. (3) Math is good at exposing the truth, but it can also perpetuate misunderstandings and untruths.
- **a.** 1, 2, 3
- **b.** 2, 3, 1
- **c.** 3, 1, 2
- **d.** 3, 2, 1

645. (1) The reason for so many injuries and fatalities is that a vehicle can generate heat of up to 1,500° F. (2) Firefighters know that the dangers of motor-vehicle fires are too often overlooked. (3) In the United States, one out of five fires involves motor vehicles, resulting each year in 600 deaths, 2,600 civilian injuries, and 1,200 injuries to firefighters.
- **a.** 1, 2, 3
- **b.** 1, 3, 2
- **c.** 2, 3, 1
- **d.** 3, 2, 1

646. (1) There is no harm in putting a special treat in your child's lunchbox from time to time. (2) Usually, healthy snacks are defined as foods with low sugar and fat content. (3) Some examples include carrot and celery sticks, granola bars, yogurt drinks, and string cheese. (4) However, in general, it is a much better idea to provide healthy snacks.
- **a.** 2, 4, 1, 3
- **b.** 1, 4, 2, 3
- **c.** 1, 2, 3, 4
- **d.** 3, 1, 2, 4

647. (1) Additionally, once a year, the association hosts a block party with food, music, and games. (2) The association organizes neighborhood watch teams and liaises with the police department on issues of crime and safety. (3) The main goal of the neighborhood association is to help make the community a safer place.
- **a.** 1, 2, 3
- **b.** 3, 2, 1
- **c.** 2, 3, 1
- **d.** 3, 1, 2

648. (1) Leaving us behind in a bitter cloud of exhaust, the bus would cough and jolt down the narrow main street of Crossland. (2) Then, even before the bus got moving, she'd look away, ahead toward her real life. (3) But I could always imagine the way it would be once it got out on the open highway, gathered speed, and took Grandma back to a life as exotic to me as the deserts of Egypt. (4) When Grandma's visit was over, we'd take her down to the Greyhound station, watch her hand her ticket to the uniformed driver, disappear inside, and reappear to wave good-bye— her expression obscured by the bus's grimy window.
- **a.** 4, 2, 1, 3
- **b.** 4, 1, 3, 2
- **c.** 1, 3, 4, 2
- **d.** 1, 2, 3, 4

649. (1) The Fifth Amendment of the U.S. Constitution guarantees citizens freedom from double jeopardy in criminal proceedings. (2) It also means a person cannot be tried for a crime for which he or she has already been convicted; that is to say, a person convicted by a state court cannot be tried for the same offense in, for example, federal court. (3) Finally, a person cannot be punished more than once for the same crime. (4) This means that a person cannot be tried for a crime for which he or she has already been acquitted.
a. 1, 4, 2, 3
b. 1, 2, 4, 3
c. 3, 2, 1, 4
d. 3, 4, 2, 1

650. (1) If these new policies are any indication, employees will have much less freedom than they did before. (2) The handbook also states that employees must give at least three weeks' notice before taking a personal day. (3) The new employee handbook states that anyone who is out sick for more than three days must provide a doctor's note.
a. 2, 3, 1
b. 3, 1, 2
c. 3, 2, 1
d. 1, 3, 2

651. (1) Every spring the softball field became his favorite destination, and he had taken his son, Arnie, there when he was small to teach him how to pitch. (2) He walked home, as usual, through the park and, as usual, passed by the softball field. (3) This memory made him feel sad and guilty. (4) Arnie hadn't been in the least interested in softball, and so after two or three lessons, he had given up the idea.
a. 2, 1, 4, 3
b. 3, 2, 1, 4
c. 4, 3, 1, 2
d. 2, 3, 4, 1

652. (1) If there are expenses incurred, complete report form 103; if there was damage to equipment, complete form 107. (2) If form 107 and form 103 are required, complete form 122 also. (3) Log on to the computer and go to the directory that contains the report forms. (4) As an employee, you must complete all paperwork following a fire.
a. 3, 2, 1, 4
b. 1, 3, 4, 2
c. 2, 1, 4, 3
d. 4, 3, 1, 2

653. (1) In some areas, the salt is combined with calcium chloride, which is more effective in below-zero temperatures and which melts ice better. (2) After a snow- or icefall, city streets are treated with ordinary rock salt. (3) This combination of salt and calcium chloride is also less damaging to foliage along the roadways.
a. 2, 1, 3
b. 1, 3, 2
c. 3, 2, 1
d. 2, 3, 1

654. (1) Yet the human brain is the most mysterious and complex object on Earth. (2) It has created poetry and music, planned and executed horrific wars, and devised intricate scientific theories. (3) It thinks and dreams, plots and schemes, and easily holds more information than all the libraries on Earth. (4) It weighs less than three pounds and is hardly more interesting to look at than an overly ripe cauliflower.

 a. 1, 3, 4, 2
 b. 2, 1, 4, 3
 c. 3, 1, 2, 4
 d. 4, 1, 2, 3

655. (1) Before you begin to compose a business letter, sit down and think about your purpose in writing the letter. (2) Do you want to request information, order a product, register a complaint, or apply for something? (3) Always keep your objective in mind. (4) Do some brainstorming and gather information before you begin writing.

 a. 4, 3, 2, 1
 b. 2, 4, 3, 1
 c. 1, 2, 4, 3
 d. 3, 2, 1, 4

656. (1) The idea communicated may even be purely whimsical, in which case the artist might start out with symbols developed from a bird's tracks or a child's toy. (2) Native American art often incorporates a language of abstract visual symbols. (3) The artist gives a poetic message to the viewer, communicating the beauty of an idea through religious symbols or by reproducing a design from nature—such as rain on leaves or sunshine on water.

 a. 3, 1, 2
 b. 2, 3, 1
 c. 2, 1, 3
 d. 1, 3, 2

Answer questions 657–659 on the basis of the following passage.

(1) Greyhound racing is the sixth most popular spectator sport in the United States. (2) Over the past decade, a growing number of racers have been adopted to live out retirement as household pets, once there racing careers are over.

(3) Many people hesitate to adopt a retired racing greyhound because they think only very old dogs are available. (4) People also worry that the greyhound will be more nervous and active than other breeds and will need a large space to run. (5) _____. (6) In fact, racing greyhounds are put up for adoption at a young age; even champion racers, who have the longest careers, work only until they are about three and a half years old. (7) Since greyhounds usually live to be 12 to 15 years old, their retirement is much longer than their racing careers. (8) Far from being nervous dogs, greyhounds have naturally sweet, mild

dispositions, and, while they love to run, they are sprinters rather than distance runners and are sufficiently exercised with a few laps around a fenced-in backyard every day.

(9) Greyhounds do not make good watchdogs, but they are very good with children, get along well with other dogs (and usually cats as well), and are very affectionate and loyal. (10) A retired racing greyhound is a wonderful pet for almost anyone.

657. Which sentence, if inserted in the blank labeled 5, would best help to focus the writer's argument in the second paragraph?
a. Even so, greyhounds are placid dogs.
b. These worries are based on false impressions and are easily dispelled.
c. Retired greyhounds do not need race tracks to keep in shape.
d. However, retired greyhounds are too old to need much exercise.

658. Which of the following changes is needed in the first paragraph?
a. Sentence 1: Change *growing* to *increasing*.
b. Sentence 2: Change *there* to *their*.
c. Sentence 1: Change *is* to *was*.
d. Sentence 2: Change *have been adopted* to *have adopted*.

659. Which of the following sentences, if added between sentences 9 and 10 of the third paragraph, would be most consistent with the writer's purpose, tone, and intended audience?
a. Former racing dogs make up approximately 0.36% of all dogs owned as domestic pets in the United States.
b. Despite the fact that greyhounds make excellent domestic pets, there is still a large number of former racers that have not been adopted.
c. Good-natured and tolerant dogs, greyhounds speedily settle into any household, large or small; they are equally at ease in an apartment or a private home.
d. It is imperative that people overcome the common myths they harbor about greyhounds that are preventing them from adopting these gentle dogs.

Answer questions 660–662 on the basis of the following paragraphs.

(1) Following an overwhelmingly enthusiastic response, the school administration has decided to expand the Community Mural Painting Program—now a part of two high school curriculums—to the middle school level. (2) A pilot program conducted in the school district last year was a successful initiative for students and for the community.

(3) Money to fund the program came from a national grant designed to promote community involvement as well as art appreciation among teenagers. (4) A committee that consists of art teachers, social studies teachers, and school social workers oversees the program.

(5) Studies have shown that young people who have been exposed to similar programs are much less prone to apathy. (6) The same studies state that these programs promote a sense of purpose that serves young people well both inside and outside the academic setting. (7) When the students were interviewed by the program committee. (8) In addition, the community attitude toward teenagers is improved also.

(9) It is projected that this year more than 150 students will be involved and that more than 20 murals will be painted.

660. Which sentence in the third paragraph is a nonstandard sentence?
   a. sentence 5
   b. sentence 6
   c. sentence 7
   d. sentence 8

661. Which of the following changes should be made to sentence 8 of the passage?
   a. Remove the word *also*.
   b. Change *community* to *communities*.
   c. Change *teenagers* to *teenagers'*.
   d. Change *toward* to *according to*.

662. Which of the following sentences, if inserted after sentence 2 of the passage, would best develop the ideas in the first paragraph?
   a. The program could benefit other districts as well.
   b. One particularly beautiful mural was painted on a playground wall on the east side of town.
   c. Fifty high school students were involved, and they spent five weeks painting ten murals throughout the community in locations that were in great need of some attention.
   d. The school district is interested in trying other pilot programs in addition the Mural Painting Program.

Answer questions 663–665 on the basis of the following passage.

(1) Although eating right is an important part of good health, most experts agree that being physically active is also a key element in living a longer and healthier life. (2) The benefits of physical activity include improved self-esteem, a lowered risk of heart disease and colon cancer, stronger bones, muscles, and joints, and enhanced flexibility. (3) Physical activity, in addition to its many other rewards will also help manage weight gain.

(4) One of the simplest and most effective ways to increase physical activity are walking; walking requires no special equipment and no particular location, and it can be easily incorporated into even the busiest lives. (5) Add ten minutes or ten blocks to your usual dog-walking routine. (6) Park several blocks away from your destination and walk briskly the rest of the way. (7) Walk up or down the

soccer or softball field while watching your kids play. (**8**) Find a walking buddy who will take a long walk with you once or twice a week. (**9**) You'll be less likely to skip the walk if someone is counting on you to be there.

(**10**) _____. (**11**) Before long, it will become a normal part of your daily routine and you'll hardly notice the extra effort. (**12**) In addition, the increased energy and overall sense of well-being you'll experience will inspire you to walk even more.

663. Which of the following revisions is necessary in sentence 4 of the passage?
   a. One of the simplest and most effective ways to increase physical activity are walking; walking requires no special equipment and no particular location and it can be easily incorporated into even the busiest lives.
   b. One of the simplest and most effective ways to increase physical activity is walking; walking requires no special equipment and no particular location, and it can be easily incorporated into even the busiest lives.
   c. One of the simplest and most effective ways to enhance physical activity are walking; walking requires no special equipment and no particular location, and it can be easily incorporated into even the busiest lives.
   d. One of the simplest and most effective ways to increase physical activity are walking; only walking requires no special equipment and no particular location, and it can be easily incorporated into even the busiest lives.

664. Which of the following sentences, if inserted in the blank line numbered sentence 10, would be most consistent with the development and grammar of the paragraph?
   a. People will benefit from putting on your walking shoes and pounding the pavement.
   b. So jog, bicycle, and walk as much as you can.
   c. While people will benefit from increased physical activity, it cannot replace the necessity of your eating right.
   d. So put on your walking shoes and start pounding the pavement.

665. Which of the following changes is needed in the passage?
   a. sentence 3: Insert comma after *rewards*.
   b. sentence 1: Replace *most* with *more*.
   c. sentence 5: Insert a comma after *minutes*.
   d. sentence 2: Insert a colon after *activity*.

Answer questions 666 and 667 on the basis of the following passage.

(**1**) Police officers must read suspects their Miranda rights upon taking them into custody. (**2**) When suspects who are merely being questioned <u>incriminate</u> themselves, they might later claim to have been in custody and seek to have the case dismissed on the grounds of not having been <u>appraised</u> of their Miranda rights. (**3**) In such cases, a judge must make a determination as to whether a reasonable person would have believed himself to have been in custody, based on certain <u>criteria</u>. (**4**) Officers must be aware of these criteria and take care not to give suspects grounds for later claiming they believed themselves to be in custody. (**5**) The judge must <u>ascertain</u> whether the suspect was questioned in a threatening manner (threatening could mean that the suspect was seated while both officers remained standing) and whether the suspect was aware that he or she was free to leave at any time.

666. Which of the underlined words in the paragraph should be replaced by a more appropriate, accurate word?
a. incriminate
b. appraised
c. criteria
d. ascertain

667. Which of the following changes would make the sequence of ideas in the paragraph clearer?
a. Place sentence 5 after sentence 1.
b. Reverse sentences 3 and 5.
c. Reverse the order of sentences 4 and 5.
d. Delete sentence 2.

Answer questions 668 and 669 on the basis of the following passage.

(1) Snowboarding, often described as a snow sport that combines skateboarding and surfing, is an increasingly common winter sport throughout the world. (2) Snowboarding involves strapping a board to one's feet and sliding down snow-covered mountains. (3) In addition to the snowboard, a snowboarder's equipment consists of special boots that attach to the board.

(4) Some find snowboarding more difficult to learn than skiing however, others consider it easier, requiring the mastery of one board as opposed to two skis and two poles. (5) All agree, though, that once the sport is mastered, it is exciting, stimulating, and fun. (6) Those who excel in the sport may even find himself bound for the Olympics since snowboarding became medal-eligible in 1998.

668. Which of the following parts of the passage is a nonstandard sentence?
a. sentence 1
b. sentence 3
c. sentence 4
d. sentence 6

669. Which of the following changes is needed in the passage?
a. Sentence 1: Change *combines* to *combine*.
b. Sentence 2: Change *snow-covered* to *snow covered*.
c. Sentence 5: Change *agree* to *agreed*.
d. Sentence 6: Change *himself* to *themselves*.

Answer questions 670 and 671 on the basis of the following passage.

(1) An ecosystem is a group of animals and plants living in a specific region and interacting with one another and with their physical environment. (2) Ecosystems include physical and chemical components, such as soils, water, and nutrients that support the organisms living there. (3) These organisms may range from large animals to microscopic bacteria. (4) Ecosystems also can be thought of as the interactions among all organisms in a given habitat; for instance, one species may serve as food for another. (5) People are part of the ecosystems where they live and work. (6) Environmental Groups are forming in many communities. (7) Human activities can harm or destroy local ecosystems unless actions such as land development for housing or businesses are carefully planned to conserve and sustain the ecology of the area. (8) An important part of ecosystem management involves finding ways to protect and enhance economic and social well-being while protecting local ecosystems.

670. Which of the following numbered parts is least relevant to the main idea of the paragraph?
a. sentence 1
b. sentence 6
c. sentence 7
d. sentence 8

671. Which of the following changes is needed in the passage?
a. Sentence 5: Place a comma after *live*.
b. Sentence 2: Remove the comma after *water*.
c. Sentence 6: Use a lowercase *g* for the word *Group*.
d. Sentence 8: Change *involves* to *involved*.

Answer questions 672–674 on the basis of the following paragraphs.

(1) By using tiny probes as neural prostheses, scientists may be able to restore nerve function in quadriplegics, make the blind see, or the deaf hear. (2) Thanks to advanced techniques, an implanted probe can stimulate individual neurons electrically or chemically and then record responses. (3) Preliminary results suggest that the microprobe telemetry systems can be permanently implanted and replace damaged or missing nerves.

(4) The tissue-compatible microprobes represent an advance over the typically aluminum wire electrodes used in studies of the cortex and other brain structures. (5) Previously, researchers data were accumulated using traditional electrodes, but there is a question of how much damage they cause to the nervous system. (6) Microprobes, because they are slightly thinner than a human hair, cause minimal damage and disruption of neurons when inserted into the brain because of their diminutive width.

(7) In addition to recording nervous system impulses, the microprobes have minuscule channels that open the way for delivery of drugs, cellular growth factors, neurotransmitters, and other neuroactive compounds to a single neuron or to groups of neurons. (8) The probes usually have up to four channels, each with its own recording/stimulating electrode.

672. Which of the following changes is needed in the passage?
a. Sentence 8: Change *its* to *it's*.
b. Sentence 6: Change *their* to *its*.
c. Sentence 6: Change *than* to *then*.
d. Sentence 5: Change *researchers* to *researchers'*.

673. Which of the following includes a nonstandard use of an adverb?
a. sentence 2
b. sentence 4
c. sentence 6
d. sentence 8

674. Which of the following numbered sentences should be revised to reduce unnecessary repetition?
a. sentence 2
b. sentence 5
c. sentence 6
d. sentence 8

Answer questions 675–677 on the basis of the following passage.

(1) Loud noises on trains not only irritate passengers but also create unsafe situations. (2) They are prohibited by law and by agency policy. (3) Therefore, conductors follow these procedures:

(4) A passenger-created disturbance is by playing excessively loud music or creating loud noises in some other manner. (5) In the event a passenger creates a disturbance, the conductor will politely ask the passenger to turn off the music or stop making the loud noise. (6) If the passenger refuses to comply, the conductor will tell the passenger that he or she is in violation of the law and train policy and will have to leave the train if he or she will not comply to the request. (7) If police assistance is requested, the conductor will stay at the location from which the call to the Command Center was placed or the silent alarm used. (8) Conductors will wait there until the police arrive, will allow passengers to get off the train at this point, and no passengers are allowed back on until the situation is resolved.

675. Which of the following is a nonstandard sentence?
   a. sentence 3
   b. sentence 4
   c. sentence 6
   d. sentence 7

676. Which of the following sentences is the best revision of sentence 8 in the passage?
   a. Conductors will wait there until the police arrive, will allow passengers off the train at this point, and no passengers will be allowed on until the situation is resolved.
   b. Conductors will wait there until the police arrive, will allow passengers off the train at this point, and, until the situation is resolved, no passengers are allowed on.
   c. Conductors will wait there until the police arrive, will allow passengers off the train at this point, and will not allow passengers on until the situation is resolved.
   d. Conductors will wait there until the police arrive, will allow passengers off the train at this point, and no passengers are allowed on until the situation is resolved.

677. Which of the following numbered sentences contains a nonstandard use of a preposition?
   a. sentence 2
   b. sentence 6
   c. sentence 7
   d. sentence 8

Answer questions 678–680 on the basis of the following passage.

(1) In her lecture "Keeping Your Heart Healthy," Dr. Miranda Woodhouse challenged Americans to join her in the fight to reduce the risks of heart disease. (2) Her plan includes four basic strategies meant to increase public awareness and prevent heart disease. (3) Eating a healthy diet that contains nine full servings of fruits and vegetables each day can help lower cholesterol levels. (4) More fruits and vegetables means less dairy and meat, which, in turn, means less

cholesterol-boosting saturated fat. (**5**) Do not smoke. (**6**) Cigarette smoking which increases the risk of heart disease and when it is combined with other factors, the risk is even greater. (**7**) Smoking increases blood pressure, increases the tendency for blood to clot, decreases good cholesterol, and decreases tolerance for exercise. (**8**) Be aware of your blood pressure and cholesterol levels at all times. (**9**) Because their are often no symptoms, many people don't even know that they have high blood pressure. (**10**) This is extremely dangerous, because uncontrolled high blood pressure can lead to heart attack, kidney failure, and stroke. (**11**) Finally, relax and be happy. (**12**) Studies show that being constantly angry and depressed can increase your risk of heart disease, so take a deep breath, smile, and focus on the positive things in life.

678. Which of the following is a nonstandard sentence?
 a. sentence 3
 b. sentence 6
 c. sentence 2
 d. sentence 10

679. Which of the following sentences, if inserted between sentences 2 and 3 of the passage, would best focus the purpose of the writer?
 a. While the guidelines will help those who are free of heart disease, they will not help those who have already experienced a heart attack.
 b. Extending the life of American citizens will make our country's life expectancy rates the highest in the world.
 c. The following is a brief outline of each of the four strategies.
 d. Getting people to stop smoking is the most important element of Dr. Woodhouse's program.

680. Which one of the following changes needs to be made to the passage?
 a. Sentence 2: Change *includes* to *is inclusive of*.
 b. Sentence 3: Change *Eating* to *To eat*.
 c. Sentence 9: Change *their* to *there*.
 d. Sentence 12: Change *show* to *shown*.

Answer questions 681–684 on the basis of the following passage.

(**1**) Artist Mary Cassatt was born in Allegheny City, Pennsylvania, in 1844. (**2**) Because her family valued education and believed that traveling was a wonderful way to learn. (**3**) Before she was ten years old, she'd visited London, Paris, and Rome.

(**4**) Although her family supported education, they were not at all supportive of her desire to be a professional artist, but that didn't stop her from studying art both in the United States and abroad. (**5**) A contemporary of artists including Camille Pissarro and Edgar Degas. Cassatt was an active member of the school of painting known as impressionism. (**6**) However, in later years, her painting evolved and she abandoned the impressionist approach; for a simpler, more straightforward style.

(**7**) Cassatt never married or had children, but her best known <u>painting's</u> depict breathtaking, yet ordinary scenes of mothers and children. (**8**) Cassatt died in 1926 at the age of 82, leaving a large and inspired body of work and an example to women everywhere to break through traditional roles and follow their dreams.

681. Which one of the following changes needs to be made to the passage?

   a. Sentence 3: Change *Before* to *Because.*

   b. Sentence 4: Insert a comma after *Although.*

   c. Sentence 5: Insert a comma after *Degas.*

   d. Sentence 7: Change *breathtaking* to *breathtakingly.*

682. Which one of the following numbered parts is a nonstandard sentence?

   a. sentence 1

   b. sentence 2

   c. sentence 3

   d. sentence 8

683. Which of the following is a nonstandard sentence?

   a. sentence 3

   b. sentence 4

   c. sentence 6

   d. sentence 8

684. Which of the following should be used in place of the underlined word in sentence 7 of the last paragraph?

   a. painting

   b. paintings

   c. paintings'

   d. artwork's

Answer questions 685–687 on the basis of the following passage.

(1) If you have little time to care for your garden, be sure to select hardy plants, such as phlox, comfrey, and peonies. (2) These will, with only a little care, keep the garden brilliant with color all through the growing season. (3) Sturdy sunflowers and hardy species of roses are also good selections. (4) As a thrifty gardener, you should leave part of the garden free for the planting of herbs such as lavender, sage, thyme, and parsley.

(5) If you have a moderate amount of time, growing vegetables and a garden culture of pears, apples, quinces, and other small fruits can be an interesting occupation, which amply rewards the care languished on it. (6) Even a small vegetable and fruit garden may yield radishes, celery, beans, and strawberries that will be delicious on the family table. (7) _____. (8) When planting seeds for the vegetable garden, you should be sure that they receive the proper amount of moisture, that they are sown at the right season to receive the right degree of heat, and that the seed is placed near enough to the surface to allow the young plant to reach the light easily.

685. Which of the following editorial changes would best help to clarify the ideas in the first paragraph?

   a. Omit the phrase *with only a little care* from sentence 2.

   b. Reverse the order of sentences 2 and 3.

   c. Add a sentence after sentence 4 explaining why saving room for herbs is a sign of thrift in a gardener.

   d. Add a sentence about the ease of growing roses after sentence 3.

686. Which of the following sentences, if inserted in the blank line numbered 7, would be most consistent with the writer's development of ideas in the second paragraph?

   a. When and how you plant is important to producing a good yield from your garden.

   b. Very few gardening tasks are more fascinating than growing fruit trees.

   c. Of course, if you have saved room for an herb garden, you will be able to make the yield of your garden even more tasty by cooking with your own herbs.

   d. Growing a productive fruit garden may take some specialized and time-consuming research into proper grafting techniques.

687. Which one of the following changes needs to be made in the passage?

   a. Sentence 2: Change *through* to *threw*.

   b. Sentence 5: Change *languished* to *lavished*.

   c. Sentence 8: Change *sown* to *sewn*.

   d. Sentence 8: Change *surface* to *surfeit*.

Answer questions 688–690 on the basis of the following passage.

(1) Augustus Saint-Gaudens was born March 1, 1848, in Dublin, Ireland, to Bernard Saint-Gaudens, a French shoemaker, and Mary McGuinness, his Irish wife. (2) Six months later, the family immigrated to New York City, where Augustus grew up. (3) Upon completion of school at age 13, he expressed strong interest in art as a career so his father apprenticed him to a cameo cutter. (4) While working days at his cameo lathe, Augustus also took art classes at the Cooper Union and the National Academy of Design.

   (5) At 19, his apprenticeship completed, Augustus traveled to Paris where he studied under Francois Jouffry at the renown Ecole des Beaux-Arts. (6) In 1870, he left Paris for Rome, where for the next five years, he <u>studies</u> classical art and architecture, and worked on his first commissions. (7) In 1876, he received his first major commission—a monument to Civil War Admiral David Glasgow Farragut. (8) Unveiled in New York's Madison Square in 1881, the monument was a tremendous success; its combination of realism and allegory was a departure from previous American sculpture. (9) Saint-Gaudens' fame grew, and other commissions were quickly forthcoming.

688. Which of the following numbered sentences requires a comma to separate two independent clauses?

   a. sentence 1

   b. sentence 3

   c. sentence 7

   d. sentence 9

689. Which of the following words should replace the underlined word in sentence 6?

   a. studied

   b. will study

   c. had been studying

   d. would have studied

690. Which one of the following changes needs to be made to the passage?

   a. Sentence 2: Change *where* to *when*.

   b. Sentence 5: Change *renown* to *renowned*.

   c. Sentence 8: Change *its* to *it's*.

   d. Sentence 3: Change *expressed* to *impressed*.

Answer questions 691–693 on the basis of the following passage.

(1) Everglades National Park is the largest remaining subtropical wilderness in the continental United States. (2) It's home to abundant wildlife; including alligators, crocodiles, manatees, and Florida panthers. (3) The climate of the Everglades are mild and pleasant from December through April, though rare cold fronts may create near-freezing conditions. (4) Summers are hot and humid; in summer, the temperatures often soar to around 90° and the humidity climbs to over 90%. (5) Afternoon thunderstorms are common, and mosquitoes are abundant. (6) If you visit the Everglades, wear comfortable sportswear in winter; loose-fitting, long-sleeved shirts and pants, and insect repellent are recommended in the summer.

(7) Walking and canoe trails, boat tours, and tram tours are excellent for viewing wildlife, including alligators and a multitude of tropical and temperate birds. (8) Camping, whether in the back country or at established campgrounds, offers the opportunity to enjoy what the park offers firsthand. (9) Year-round, ranger-led activities may help you to enjoy your visit even more; such activities are offered throughout the park in all seasons.

691. Which of the following numbered sentences contains a nonstandard use of a semicolon?
a. sentence 6
b. sentence 2
c. sentence 9
d. sentence 4

692. Which of the following numbered sentences needs to be revised to reduce unnecessary repetition?
a. sentence 4
b. sentence 6
c. sentence 9
d. sentence 8

693. Which of the following changes is needed in the passage?
a. Sentence 2: Change *it's* to *its*.
b. Sentence 3: Change *are* to *is*.
c. Sentence 6: Remove the comma after *Everglades*.
d. Sentence 8: Remove the comma after *campgrounds*.

Answer questions 694 and 695 on the basis of the following passage.

(1) Choosing a doctor is an important decision; here are some things you can do to make the best choice. (2) The single most important thing is to interview the doctors you are considering. (3) Ask questions about the practice, office hours, and how quick he or she responds to phone calls. (4) Pay attention to the doctor's communication skills and how comfortable you are with them. (5) The second thing you should do is to check the doctor's credentials. (6) One way to do this is to ask your healthcare insurance company how they checked the doctor's credentials before accepting him or her into their network. (7) The cost of healthcare insurance is quite high and many families have difficulty affording it. (8) Finally, spend a little time talking with the receptionist. (9) Keep in mind that this is the person you'll come into contact with every time you call or come into the office. (10) If he or she is pleasant and efficient, it will certainly make your overall experience better.

694. Which of the following numbered parts is least relevant to the paragraph?
   a. sentence 2
   b. sentence 3
   c. sentence 7
   d. sentence 9

695. Which of the following changes needs to be made to the passage?
   a. Sentence 3: Change *quick* to *quickly.*
   b. Sentence 10: Change *better* to *more better.*
   c. Sentence 6: Change *accepting* to *accepted.*
   d. Sentence 10: Change *efficient* to *efficiently.*

Answer questions 696–698 on the basis of the following passage.

(1) Being able to type good is no longer a requirement limited to secretaries and novelists; thanks to the computer, anyone who wants to enter the working world needs to be <u>accustomed</u> to a keyboard. (2) Just knowing your way around a keyboard does not mean that you can use one efficiently, though; while you may have progressed beyond the hunt-and-peck method, you may never have learned to type quickly and accurately. (3) Doing so is a skill that will not only ensure that you pass a typing <u>proficiency</u> exam, but one that is essential if you want to advance your career in any number of fields. (4) This chapter <u>assures</u> that you are familiar enough with a standard keyboard to be able to use it without looking at the keys, which is the first step in learning to type, and that you are aware of the proper <u>fingering</u>. (5) The following information will help you increase your speed and accuracy and to do our best when being tested on timed writing passages.

696. Which of the following numbered sentences contains a nonstandard use of a modifier?
   a. sentence 1
   b. sentence 2
   c. sentence 3
   d. sentence 5

697. Which of the following words, underlined in the passage, is misused in its context?
   a. assures
   b. proficiency
   c. fingering
   d. accustomed

698. Which one of the following changes needs to be made in the passage?
   a. Sentence 3: Remove the comma after *exam.*
   b. Sentence 4: Insert a colon after *that.*
   c. Sentence 1: Change *needs* to *needed.*
   d. Sentence 5: Change *our best* to *your best.*

Answer questions 699–701 on the basis of the following passage.

(1) O'Connell Street is the main thoroughfare of Dublin City. (2) Although it is not a particularly long street Dubliners will tell the visitor proudly that it is the widest street in all of Europe. (3) This claim usually meets with protests, especially from French tourists who claim the Champs Elysees of Paris as Europe's widest street. (4) But the witty Dubliner will not <u>ensign</u> bragging rights easily and will trump the French visitor with a fine distinction: The Champs Elysees is the widest boulevard, but O'Connell is the widest street.

(5) Divided by several important monuments running the length of its center, the street is named for Daniel O'Connell, an Irish patriot. (6) An impressive monument to

him towers over the entrance of lower O'Connell Street and overlooking the Liffey River. (7) O'Connell stands on a sturdy column high above the unhurried crowds of shoppers, businesspeople, and students; he is surrounded by four serene angels seated at the corners of the monument's base.

699. Which of the following words should replace the underlined word in sentence 4 of the passage?
   a. require
   b. relinquish
   c. acquire
   d. assign

700. Which of the following changes needs to be made to the second paragraph of the passage?
   a. Sentence 7: Replace the semicolon with a comma.
   b. Sentence 5: Change *Irish* to *irish*.
   c. Sentence 5: Change *running* to *run*.
   d. Sentence 6: Change *overlooking* to *overlooks*.

701. Which of the following changes needs to be made to the first paragraph of the passage?
   a. Sentence 2: Insert a comma after *that*.
   b. Sentence 3: Replace the comma after *protests* with a semicolon.
   c. Sentence 4: Remove the colon after *distinction*.
   d. Sentence 2: Insert a comma after *street*.

Answer questions 702–704 on the basis of the following passage.

(1) Mrs. Lake arriving 20 minutes early surprised and irritated Nicholas, although the moment for saying so slipped past too quickly for him to snatch its opportunity.

(2) She was a thin woman of medium height, not much older than he—in her middle forties he judged—dressed in a red-and-white, polka-dot dress and open-toed red shoes with extremely high heels. (3) Her short brown hair was crimped in waves, which gave a incongruous, quaint, old-fashioned effect. (4) She had a pointed nose. (5) Her eyes, set rather shallow, were light brown and inquisitive.

(6) "Dr. Markley?" she asked. (7) Nicholas nodded, and the woman walked in past him, proceeding with little mincing steps to the center of the living room, where she stood with her back turned, looking around. (8) "My my," she said. (9) "This is a nice house. (10) Do you live here all alone?"

702. Which of the following changes should be made in sentence 3?
   a. Change *was* to *is*.
   b. Change *gave* to *gives*.
   c. Change *a* to *an*.
   d. Change *effect* to *affect*.

703. Which of the following numbered parts contains a nonstandard use of a modifier?
   a. sentence 7
   b. sentence 5
   c. sentence 3
   d. sentence 2

704. Which one of the following changes needs to be made to sentence 1?
   a. Insert a comma after *early*.
   b. Change *too* to *two*.
   c. Change *Lake* to *Lake's*.
   a. Change *its* to *it's*.

Answer questions 705 and 706 on the basis of the following passage.

(1) Understand that your boss has problems, too. (2) This is easy to forget. (3) When someone has authority over you, it's hard to remember that they're just human. (4) Your boss may have children at home who misbehave, dogs or cats or parakeets that need to go to the vet, deadlines to meet, and/or bosses of his or her own (sometimes even bad ones) overseeing his or her work. (5) If your boss is occasionally unreasonable, try to keep in mind that it might have nothing to do with you. (6) He or she may be having a bad day for reasons no one else knows. (7) Of course, if such behavior becomes consistently abusive, you'll have to do something about it—confront the problem or even quit. (8) But were all entitled to occasional mood swings.

705. Which of the following numbered sentences contains a nonstandard use of a pronoun?
   a. sentence 3
   b. sentence 4
   c. sentence 7
   d. sentence 8

706. Which of the following changes needs to be made to the passage?
   a. Sentence 5: Change *unreasonable* to *unreasonably*.
   b. Sentence 7: Change the dash to a semicolon.
   c. Sentence 8: Change *were* to *we're*.
   d. Sentence 4: Change *deadlines* to *a deadline*.

Answer questions 707 and 708 on the basis of the following passage.

(1) Beginning next month, City Transit will institute the Stop Here Program, who will be in effect every night from 10:00 P.M. until 4:00 A.M. (2) The program will allow drivers to stop the bus wherever a passenger wishes, as long as they deem it is safe to stop there. (3) This program will reduce the amount of walking that passengers will have to do after dark. (4) Passengers may request a stop anywhere along the bus route by pulling the bell cord a block ahead. (5) During the first two months of the program, when anyone attempts to flag down a bus anywhere but at a designated stop, the bus driver should proceed to the next stop and wait for the person to board the bus. (6) Then the driver should give the passenger a brochure that explains the Stop Here Program.

707. Which of the following editorial changes in the passage would best help to clarify the information the paragraph intends to convey?

a. Add a sentence between sentences 4 and 5 explaining that while the Stop Here Program allows passengers to leave the bus at almost any point, passengers may board only at designated stops.

b. Delete sentence 6.

c. Add a sentence between sentences 5 and 6 explaining the safety advantages for passengers of flagging down buses at night.

d. Reverse the order of sentences 4 and 5.

708. Which of the following numbered sentences contains a nonstandard use of a pronoun?

a. sentence 1

b. sentence 2

c. sentence 3

d. sentence 5

Answer questions 709 and 710 on the basis of the following passage.

(1) Last October, a disastrous wildfire swept across portions of Charlesburg. (2) Five residents were killed, 320 homes destroyed, and 19,500 acres burned. (3) A public safety task force was formed to review emergency procedures.

(4) The task force findings were as follows. (5) The water supply in the residential areas was insufficient, some hydrants could not even be opened. (6) The task force recommended a review of hydrant inspection policy.

(7) The fire companies that responded had difficulty locating specific sites. (8) Most companies came from other areas and were not familiar with Miller Point. (9) The available maps were outdated and did not reflect recent housing developments.

(10) Evacuation procedures were inadequate. (11) Residents reported being given conflicting and/or confusing information. (12) Some residents of the Hilltop Estates subdivision ignored mandatory evacuation orders, yet others were praised for their cooperation.

709. Which of the following is a nonstandard sentence?

a. sentence 7

b. sentence 5

c. sentence 3

d. sentence 12

710. Which one of the following changes needs to be made to the passage?

a. Sentence 12: Change *were* to *we're*.

b. Sentence 12: Insert a comma after *others*.

c. Sentence 2: Remove the comma after *killed*.

d. Sentence 4: Replace the semicolon with a colon.

Answer questions 711–713 on the basis of the following passage.

(1) In 1519, Hernando cortez led his army of Spanish Conquistadors into Mexico. (2) Equipped with horses, shining armor, and the most advanced weapons of the sixteenth century, he fought his way from the flat coastal area into the mountainous highlands. (3) Cortez was looking for gold, and he were sure that Indian groups in Mexico had mined large amounts of the precious metal. (4) First, he conquered the groups, and then seized their precious gold using very organized methods.

711. Which of the underlined words in the passage could be replaced with a more precise verb?
a. was looking
b. equipped
c. conquered
d. seized

712. Which of the following sentences uses the verb incorrectly?
a. sentence 1
b. sentence 2
c. sentence 3
d. sentence 4

713. Which of the following changes needs to be made to the passage?
a. Sentence 1: Capitalize the *c* in *Cortez*.
b. Sentence 2: Delete the comma after *horses*.
c. Sentence 3: Insert a comma after *groups*.
d. Sentence 4: Place a semicolon after *groups*.

Answer questions 714 and 715 on the basis of the following passage.

(1) Charles Darwin was born in 1809 at Shrewsbury England. (2) He was a biologist whose famous theory of evolution is important to philosophy for the effects it has had about the nature of man. (3) After many years of careful study, Darwin attempted to show that higher species had come into existence as a result of the gradual transformation of lower species, and that the process of transformation could be explained through the selective effect of the natural environment upon organisms. (4) He concluded that the principles of *natural selection* and *survival of the fittest* govern all life. (5) Darwin's explanation of these principles is that because of the food supply problem, the young born to any species compete for survival. (6) Those young that survive to produce the next generation tend to embody favorable natural changes which are then passed on by heredity. (7) His major work that contained these theories is *On the Origin of Species*, written in 1859. Many religious opponents condemned this work.

714. Which of the following corrections should be made in punctuation?
a. Sentence 1: Insert a comma after *Shrewsbury*.
b. Sentence 2: Insert quotation marks around *nature of man*.
c. Sentence 3: Delete the comma after *study*.
d. Sentence 4: Insert a comma before *and*.

715. In sentence 7, *On the Origin of Species* is italicized because it is
a. a short story.
b. the title of a book.
c. the name of the author.
d. copyrighted.

Answer questions 716 and 717 on the basis of the following passage.

(1) Theodore Roosevelt <u>were</u> born with asthma and poor eyesight. (2) Yet this sickly child later won fame as a political leader, Rough Rider, and hero of the common people. (3) To conquer his handicaps, Teddy trained in a gym and became a lightweight boxer at Harvard. (4) Out West, he hunted buffalo and ran a cattle ranch. (5) He was a civil service reformer in the east and also a police commissioner. (6) He became President McKinley's Assistant Secretary of the Navy during the Spanish-American War. (7) Also, he led a charge of cavalry Rough Riders up San Juan Hill in Cuba.

(8) After achieving fame, he became governor of New York and went on to become the Vice President and then President of the United States.

716. Which of the following sentences represents the best revision of sentence 5?
 a. Back East he became a civil service reformer and police commissioner.
 b. A civil service reformer and police commissioner was part of his job in the East.
 c. A civil service reformer and police commissioner were parts of his job in the East.
 d. His jobs of civil service reformer and police commissioner were his jobs in the East.

717. Which of the following should be used in place of the underlined verb in sentence 1 of the passage?
 a. will be
 b. are
 c. is
 d. was

Answer questions 718–720 on the basis of the following passage.

(1) Cuttlefish are very intriguing little animals. (2) The cuttlefish resembles a rather large squid and is, like the octopus, a member of the order of cephalopods. (3) Although they are not considered the most highly evolved of the cephalopods, cuttlefish are extremely intelligent. (4) _____. (5) While observing them, it is hard to tell who is doing the watching, you or the cuttlefish. (6) Since the eye of the cuttlefish is very similar in structure to the human eye, cuttlefish can give you the impression that you are looking into the eyes of a wizard who has metamorphosed himself into a squid with very human eyes.

(7) Cuttlefish are also highly mobile and fast creatures. (8) They come equipped with a small jet located just below the tentacles that can expel water to help them move. (9) For navigation, ribbons of flexible fin on each side of the body allow cuttlefish to hoover, move, stop, and start.

718. Which of the following sentences, if inserted into the blank numbered 4, would be most consistent with the paragraph's development and tone?
 a. Curious and friendly, cuttlefish tend, in the wild, to hover near a diver so they can get a good look, and in captivity, when a researcher slips a hand into the tanks, cuttlefish tend to grasp it with their tentacles in a hearty but gentle handshake.
 b. The cuttlefish can be cooked and eaten like its less tender relatives the squid and octopus, but must still be tenderized before cooking in order not to be exceedingly chewy.
 c. Cuttlefish are hunted as food not only by many sea creatures, but also by people; they are delicious when properly cooked.
 d. Cuttlefish do not have an exoskeleton; instead their skin is covered with chromataphors.

719. Which of the following numbered sentences should be revised to reduce its unnecessary repetition?
 a. sentence 2
 b. sentence 5
 c. sentence 6
 d. sentence 9

720. Which of the following changes should be made in the final sentence?
- **a.** Change *For* to *If*.
- **b.** Change *allow* to *allot*.
- **c.** Change *each* to *both*.
- **d.** Change *hoover* to *hover*.

Answer questions 721–723 on the basis of the following passage.

(1) As soon as she sat down on the airplane, Rachel almost began to regret telling the travel agent that she wanted an exotic and romantic vacation; after sifting through a stack of brochures, the agent and her decided the most exotic vacation she could afford was a week in Rio. (2) As the plane hurtled toward Rio de Janeiro, she read the information on Carnival that was in the pocket of the seat in front of hers. (3) The very definition made her shiver: "from the Latin car-navale, meaning a farewell to the flesh." (4) She was searching for excitement, but had no intention of bidding her skin good-bye. (5) "Carnival," the brochure informed her, originated in Europe in the Middle Ages and served as a break from the requirements of daily life and society. (6) Most of all, it allowed the hardworking and desperately poor serfs the opportunity to ridicule their wealthy and normally humorless masters." (7) Rachel, a middle manager in a computer firm, wasn't entirely sure whether she was a serf or a master. (8) Should she be making fun, or would others be mocking her? (9) She was strangely relieved when the plane landed, as though her fate were decided.

721. Which of the following changes needs to be made to the passage?
- **a.** Sentence 2: Insert *the* before *Carnival*.
- **b.** Sentence 3: Italicize *carnavale*.
- **c.** Sentence 6: Italicize *serfs*.
- **d.** Sentence 9: Change *were* to *was*.

722. Which of the following numbered sentences contains a nonstandard use of a pronoun?
- **a.** sentence 1
- **b.** sentence 5
- **c.** sentence 7
- **d.** sentence 8

723. Which of the following changes needs to be made to sentence 5 of the passage?
- **a.** Insert quotation marks before *originated*.
- **b.** Remove the comma after *her*.
- **c.** Remove the quotation marks after *Carnival*.
- **d.** Insert quotation marks after *society*.

Answer questions 724–726 on the basis of the following passage.

(1) A metaphor is a poetic device that deals with comparison; compares similar qualities of two dissimilar objects. (2) With a simple metaphor, one object becomes the other: *Love is a rose.* (3) Although this doesn't sound like a particularly rich image, a metaphor can communicate so much about a particular image that poets utilize them more than any other type of figurative language. (4) The reason for this is that a poet composes poetry to express emotional experiences. (5) Succinctly, what the poet imagines love to be may or may not be our perception of love. (6) Therefore, the poet's job is to enable us to *experience* it and feel it the same way. (7) You should be able to nod in agreement and say, "Yes, that's it! (8) I understand precisely where this guy is coming from."

724. The tone of this passage is very formal; the last sentence is not. Which of the following would be more consistent with the tone of the passage?

  a. This guy is right on.

  b. I can relate to the poet's experience.

  c. I know this feeling.

  d. This poem gets right to the point.

725. Which of the following numbered sentences contains a nonstandard use of a pronoun?

  a. sentence 3

  b. sentence 5

  c. sentence 6

  d. sentence 7

726. Which of the following adverbs should replace the underline word in sentence 5 of the passage?

  a. Consequently

  b. Normally

  c. Occasionally

  d. Originally

727. Which of the endings to the following sentence would be the best concluding sentence for this passage?

The most serious damage done by light pollution is to our

  a. artistic appreciation.

  b. sense of physical well-being.

  c. spiritual selves.

  d. cultural advancement.

728. Which of the following changes needs to be made to sentence 4 of the passage?

  a. Change *we* to *you.*

  b. Change *my* to *our.*

  c. Change *we* to *I.*

  d. Change *my* to *his.*

729. Which of the following numbered parts contains a nonstandard sentence?

  a. sentence 1

  b. sentence 2

  c. sentence 3

  d. sentence 4

Answer questions 727–729 on the basis of the following passage.

(1) Light pollution a growing problem worldwide. (2) Like other forms of pollution, light pollution degrades the quality of the environment. (3) Where once it was possible to look up at the night sky and see thousands of twinkling stars in the inky blackness, one now sees little more than the yellow glare of urban sky glow. (4) When we lose the ability to connect visually with the vastness of the universe by looking up at the night sky, we lose our connection with something profoundly important to the human spirit, my sense of wonder.

Answer questions 730–732 on the basis of the following passage.

(1) Typically people think of genius, whether it manifests in Mozart composing symphonies at age five or Einstein's discovery of relativity, as having quality not just of the divine, but also of the eccentric. (2) People see genius as a good abnormality; moreover, they think of genius as a completely unpredictable abnormality. (3) Until recently, psychologists regarded the quirks of genius as too erratic to describe intelligibly; however, Anna Findley's groundbreaking study uncovers predictable patterns in the biographies of geniuses. (4) Despite the regularity of these

patterns, they could still support the common belief that there is a kind of supernatural intervention in the lives of unusually talented men and women. (**5**) _____. (**6**) For example, Findley shows that all geniuses experience three intensely productive periods in their lives, one of which always occurs shortly before their deaths; this is true whether the genius lives to age 19 or 90.

730. Which of the following sentences, if inserted in the blank numbered 5, would best focus the main idea of the passage?
   a. These patterns are normal in the lives of all geniuses.
   b. Eerily, the patterns themselves seem to be determined by predestination rather than mundane habit.
   c. No matter how much scientific evidence the general public is presented with, people still like to think of genius as unexplainable.
   d. Since people think of genius as a good abnormality, they do not really care what causes it.

731. Which of the following changes needs to be made to the passage?
   a. Sentence 1: Change _Mozart_ to _Mozart's_.
   b. Sentence 3: Change _too_ to _to_.
   c. Sentence 4: Change _there_ to _their_.
   d. Sentence 6: Change _geniuses_ to _geniuses'_.

732. Which of the following numbered sentences contains a nonstandard use of a pronoun?
   a. sentence 2
   b. sentence 3
   c. sentence 4
   d. sentence 6

Answer questions 733–735 on the basis of the following passage.

(**1**) The English-language premiere of Samuel Beckett's play _Waiting for Godot_ took place in London in August 1955. (**2**) _Godot_ is an avant-garde play with only five characters (not including Mr. Godot, who never arrives) and a minimal setting—one rock and one bare tree. (**3**) The play has two acts, the second act repeating what little action occurs in the first with few changes: the tree, for instance, acquires one leaf. (**4**) Famously, the critic Vivian Mercer has described Godot as "a play in which nothing happens twice." (**5**) Opening night critics and playgoers, greeted the play with bafflement and derision. (**6**) Beckett's play managed to free the theater from the grasp of detailed naturalism. (**7**) The line "Nothing happens, nobody comes, nobody goes. It's awful" was met by a loud rejoinder of "Hear! Hear!" from an audience member. (**8**) Despite the bad notices, director Peter Hall believed so passionately in the play that his fervor convinced the backers to refrain from closing the play at least until the Sunday reviews were published. (**9**) Harold Hobson's review in _The Sunday Times_ managed to save the play, for Hobson had the vision to recognize the play for what history has proven it to be—a revolutionary moment in theater.

733. Which of the following editorial changes should be made in order to improve the focus and flow of the passage?
   a. Reverse the order of sentences 6 and 7.
   b. Sentence 3: Remove the clause _the tree, for instance, acquires one leaf._
   c. Remove sentence 9.
   d. Remove sentence 6.

734. Which of the following changes needs to be made to the passage?
  a. Sentence 2: Italicize "Mr. Godot."
  b. Sentence 2: Do not italicize "Godot."
  c. Sentence 4: Italicize "Godot."
  d. Sentence 9: Do not italicize "The Sunday Times."

735. From which of the following numbered sentences should a comma be removed?
  a. sentence 3
  b. sentence 4
  c. sentence 5
  d. sentence 9

Answer questions 736–737 on the basis of the following passage.

(1) The Woodstock Music and Art Fair—better known to its participants and to history simply as "Woodstock"—should have been a colossal failure. (2) Just a month prior to its August 15, 1969, opening the fair's organizers were informed by the council of Wallkill, New York, that permission to hold the festival was withdrawn. (3) Amazingly, not only was a new site found, but word got out to the public of the fair's new location. (4) At the new site, fences that were supposed to facilitate ticket collection never materialized, all attempts at gathering tickets were abandoned. (5) Crowd estimates of 30,000 kept rising; by the end of the three days, some estimated the crowd at 500,000. (6) And then, on opening night, it began to rain. (7) Off and on, throughout all three days, huge summer storms rolled over the gathering. (8) In spite of these problems, most people think of Woodstock not only as a fond memory but as the defining moment for an entire generation.

736. In which of the following numbered sentences should a comma be inserted?
  a. sentence 1
  b. sentence 2
  c. sentence 3
  d. sentence 4

737. Which of the following sentences is a run-on?
  a. sentence 1
  b. sentence 2
  c. sentence 3
  d. sentence 4

Answer questions 738–740 on the basis of the following passage.

(1) Whether or not you can accomplish a specific goal or meet a specific deadline depends first on how much time you need to get the job done. (2) What should you do when the demands of the job precede the time you have available. (3) The best approach is to correctly divide the project into smaller pieces. (4) Different goals will have to be divided in different ways, but one seemingly unrealistic goal can often be accomplished by working on several smaller, more reasonable goals.

738. Which of the following sentences has an error in the verb infinitive?
  a. sentence 1
  b. sentence 2
  c. sentence 3
  d. sentence 4

739. Which of the following words should replace the underlined word in sentence 2 of the passage?
   a. exceed
   b. succeed
   c. supercede
   d. proceed

740. Which of the following sentences in the passage needs a question mark?
   a. sentence 1
   b. sentence 2
   c. sentence 3
   d. sentence 4

Answer questions 741 and 742 on the basis of the following passage.

(1) The Competitive Civil Service system is designed to give candidates fair and equal treatment and ensure that federal applicants are hired based on objective criteria. (2) Hiring has to be based solely on a candidate's knowledge, skills, and abilities (which you'll sometimes see abbreviated as KSA), and not on external factors such as race, religion, gender, and so on. (3) Whereas employers in the private sector can hire employees for subjective reasons, federal employers must be able to justify his decision with objective evidence that the candidate is qualified.

741. Which of the following sentences lacks parallelism?
   a. sentence 1
   b. sentence 2
   c. sentence 3
   d. sentences 2 and 3

742. Which of the following sentences has an error in pronoun agreement?
   a. sentence 1
   b. sentence 2
   c. sentence 3
   d. sentences 2 and 3

Answer questions 743 and 744 on the basis of the following passage.

(1) A light rain was falling. (2) He drove home by his usual route. (3) It was a drive he had taken a thousand times; still, he did not know why, as he passed the park near their home, he should so suddenly and vividly picture the small pond that lay at the center of it. (4) In winter, this pond was frozen over, and he had taken his daughter Abigail there when she was small and tried to teach her how to skate. (5) She hadn't been able to catch on, and so after two or three lessons Abigail and him had given up the idea. (6) Now there came into his mind an image of such clarity it caused him to draw in his breath sharply; an image of Abigail gliding toward him on her new Christmas skates, going much faster than she should have been.

743. Which of the following changes needs to be made to the passage?
   a. Sentence 3: Change the semicolon to a comma.
   b. Sentence 4: Remove the word *and*.
   c. Sentence 5: Change the comma to a semicolon.
   d. Sentence 6: Change the semicolon to a colon.

744. Which of the following changes needs to be made to the passage?
    a. Sentence 3: Replace *their* with *there*.
    b. Sentence 4: Remove the comma after *over*.
    c. Sentence 5: Change *him* to *he*.
    d. Sentence 6: Replace *Christmas* with *Christmas'*.

Answer questions 745–747 on the basis of the following passage.

(1) For years, Mount Desert Island, particularly its major settlement, Bar Harbor, afforded summer homes for the wealthy. (2) Finally, though, Bar Harbor has become a burgeoning arts community as well. (3) But, the best part of the island is the unspoiled forest land known as Acadia National Park. (4) Because the island sits on the boundary line between the temperate and subarctic zones the island supports the flora and fauna of both zones as well as beach, inland, and alpine plants. (5) Lies in a major bird migration lane and is a resting spot for many birds. (6) The establishment of Acadia National Park in 1916 means that this natural monument will be preserved and that it will be available to all people, not just the wealthy. (7) Visitors to Acadia may receive nature instruction from the park naturalists as well as enjoy camping, hiking, cycling, and boating. (8) Or they may choose to spend time at the archeological museum learning about the Stone Age inhabitants of the island.

745. Which of the following sentences is a sentence fragment?
    a. sentence 2
    b. sentence 3
    c. sentence 4
    d. sentence 5

746. Which of the following adverbs should replace the words *Finally, though* in sentence 2?
    a. Suddenly
    b. Concurrently
    c. Simultaneously
    d. Recently

747. Which of the following changes needs to be made to sentence 4?
    a. Insert a comma after the word *zones*.
    b. Delete the word *Because* at the beginning of the sentence.
    c. Delete the comma after the word *inland*.
    d. Add a question mark at the end of the sentence.

Answer questions 748 and 749 on the basis of the following passage.

(1) A smoke detector should be placed on each floor level of a home and outside each sleeping area. (2) A good site for a detector would be a hallway that runs between living spaces and bedrooms.

(3) Because of the "dead" air space that might be missed by turbulent hot air bouncing around above a fire, smoke detectors should be installed either at the ceiling at least four inches from the nearest wall, or high on a wall at least four, but no further than 12, inches from the ceiling. (4) Detectors should not be mounted near windows, exterior doors, or other places where drafts might direct the smoke away from the unit. (5) Also, it should not be placed in kitchens and garages, where cooking and gas fumes are likely to set off false alarms.

748. Which of the following numbered sentences contains a nonstandard use of a preposition?
   a. sentence 1
   b. sentence 3
   c. sentence 4
   d. sentence 5

749. In which of the following numbered sentences should a pronoun be replaced with a different pronoun?
   a. sentence 1
   b. sentence 3
   c. sentence 4
   d. sentence 5

Answer questions 750–752 on the basis of the following passage.

(1) Heat exhaustion, generally characterized by clammy skin, fatigue, nausea, dizziness, profuse perspiration, and sometimes fainting, resulting from an inadequate intake of water and the loss of fluids. (2) First aid treatment for this condition includes having the victim lie down; raising the feet 8 to 12 inches; applying cool, wet cloths to the skin; and giving the victim sips of salt water (1 teaspoon per glass, half a glass every 15 minutes) over the period of an hour. (3) _____.

   (4) Heatstroke is much more serious; it is an immediate life-threatening condition. (5) The characteristics of heatstroke are a high body temperature (which may reach 106° F or more); a rapid pulse; hot, dry skin; and a blocked sweating mechanism. (6) Victims of this condition may be unconscious, and first aid measures should be directed at cooling the body quickly. (7) Heatstroke often occurs among poor people in urban areas. (8) The victim should be placed in a tub of cold water

or repeatedly sponged with cool water until his or her temperature is lowered sufficiently. (9) Fans or air conditioners will also help with the cooling process. (10) Care should be taken, however, not to chill the victim too much once his or her temperature is below 102° F.

750. Which of the following sentences, if inserted into the blank numbered 3 in the passage, would best aid the transition of thought between the first and second paragraphs?
   a. Heat exhaustion is a relatively unusual condition in northern climates.
   b. The typical victims of heatstroke are the poor and elderly who cannot afford air conditioning even on the hottest days of summer.
   c. Heat exhaustion is never fatal, although it can cause damage to internal organs if it strikes an elderly victim.
   d. Air-conditioning units, electric fans, and cool baths can lower the numbers of people who suffer heatstroke each year in the United States.

751. Which of the following numbered sentences draws attention away from the main idea of the second paragraph of the passage?
   a. sentence 6
   b. sentence 7
   c. sentence 8
   d. sentence 10

752. Which of the following numbered parts contains a nonstandard sentence?
   a. sentence 1
   b. sentence 3
   c. sentence 5
   d. sentence 8

Answer questions 753 and 754 on the basis of the following passage.

(1) Glaciers consist of fallen snow that compresses over many years into large, thickened ice masses. (2) Most of the world's glacial ice is found in Antarctica and Greenland glaciers are found on nearly every continent, even Africa. (3) At present, 10% of land area is covered with glaciers. (4) Glacial ice often appears blue because ice absorbs all other colors but reflects blue. (5) Almost 90% of an iceberg is below water; only about 10% shows above water. (6) What makes glaciers unique is their ability to move? (7) Due to sheer mass, glaciers flow like very slow rivers. (8) Some glaciers are as small as football fields, while others grow to be over a hundred kilometers long.

753. Which of the following sentences is a run-on sentence?
   a. sentence 1
   b. sentence 2
   c. sentence 3
   d. sentence 4

754. Which of the following sentences contains an error in punctuation?
   a. sentence 3
   b. sentence 4
   c. sentence 5
   d. sentence 6

Answer question 755 on the basis of the following short description.

(1) Herbert was enjoying the cool, bright fall afternoon. (2) Walking down the street, red and yellow leaves crunched satisfyingly under his new school shoes.

755. Which of the following is the best revision of the description?
   a. Herbert was enjoying the cool bright fall afternoon. Walking down the street red and yellow leaves crunched satisfyingly under his new school shoes.
   b. Herbert was enjoying the cool, bright fall afternoon. He was walking down the street, red and yellow leaves crunched satisfyingly under his new school shoes.
   c. Herbert was enjoying the cool, bright fall afternoon. Walking down the street, he crunched red and yellow leaves satisfyingly under his new school shoes.
   d. Herbert was enjoying the cool, bright fall afternoon. Walking down the street, red and yellow leaves were crunched satisfyingly under his new school shoes.

Answer questions 756–758 on the basis of the following passage.

(1) The building in which Howard Davis was to teach his undergraduate evening course, Interpretation of Poetry, was Renwick Hall, the General Sciences Building. (2) Markham Hall, which housed the English Department offices and classrooms, was to be closed all summer for renovation.

(3) Howard's classroom was in the basement. (4) The shadowy corridor that led back to it was lined with glass cases containing exhibits whose titles read, *Small Mammals of North America*, *Birds of the Central United States*, and *Reptiles of the Desert Southwest*. (5) The dusty specimens perched on little stands; their tiny claws gripped the smooth wood nervously. (6) A typewritten card, yellow with age, bearing the name of its genus

and species. (7) The classroom itself was outfit-ted with a stainless steel sink, and behind the lectern loomed a dark-wood cabinet through whose glass doors one could see rows of jars, each holding what appeared to be an animal embryo floating in a murky liquid. (8) The classroom <u>wreaked</u> of formaldehyde.

756. Which of the following sentences, if inserted between sentences 6 and 7, would best fit the author's pattern of development in the second paragraph of the passage?
   a. Howard would be teaching Byron, Shelley, and Keats this term.
   b. In the display case opposite Howard's class-room, a pocket gopher reared up on its hind legs, staring glassy-eyed into the open doorway.
   c. Although Markham was at least 25 years younger than Renwick, the administration had chosen to renovate it rather than the aging, crumbling science building.
   d. Genus and species are taxonomic categories.

757. Which of the following numbered sentences is a nonstandard sentence?
   a. sentence 1
   b. sentence 2
   c. sentence 6
   d. sentence 7

758. Which of the underlined words in the second paragraph needs to be replaced with its homophone?
   a. led
   b. read
   c. their
   d. wreaked

▶ **Answers**

603. a. This is the best choice, because it is the only one that refers to recycling containers, which is the main focus of this paragraph. The other choices are statements about recycling in general.

604. c. This choice refers to *unreasonable searches*, which is the main focus of this paragraph. Choice **a** can be ruled out because this idea is not developed by the other two sentences. Choices **b** and **d** do not relate to the topic of unreasonable searches.

605. b. This choice clearly fits with the main focus of the paragraph, which is the skill that is needed to hand-rear orphaned baby birds. Choice **a** is too vague to be a topic sentence. Choices **c** and **d** introduce other topics.

606. c. The main focus of the paragraph is the height of a wave. This is the only choice that introduces that topic.

607. a. The paragraph expresses the writer's opin-ion about respect for the law. Choices **b** and **d** can be ruled out because they are irrele-vant to the main topic. Choice **c** can also be eliminated because it discusses respect for other people, not respect for the law.

608. b. Choice **b** addresses both of Gary's vanities: his person and his situation. Choice **a** deals only with Gary's vanity of person. Choice **c** deals only with his vanity of position. Choice **d** is not supported in the passage.

609. **d.** *Changed the course of history* and *gone to war* imply that the subject of the paragraph is history; these phrases also connote danger and intrigue.

610. **a.** This is the only choice that is in keeping with the main focus of the paragraph. Although dogs are mentioned in the paragraph, choices **b** and **c** can be ruled out because the other two sentences do not logically follow either choice.

611. **b.** This choice focuses the paragraph by speaking of a particular patterned corridor, as is described in the rest of the paragraph. Choices **a** and **c** only speak of patterned corridors in general. Choice **d** is contradicted in the passage.

612. **b.** This choice is most relevant to the rest of the paragraph, which is about protecting children from swallowing dangerous medications. Choices **a** and **d** do not mention danger; choice **c** does not mention protection and is also written in a different style than the rest of the paragraph.

613. **a.** This sentence contrasts writers who endanger their lives in order to have something to write about with those who do not. The rest of the paragraph illustrates this statement. Choice **b** is too broad. Choices **c** and **d** contain elements not expressed in the passage.

614. **d.** This choice specifically defines the kind of hearsay evidence that is admissible in a trial and would be logically followed by a definition of the kind of hearsay evidence that is inadmissible. It works better as a topic sentence than choice **c**, which is more general. Choices **a** and **b** are too limited.

615. **d.** Choice **d** is the only sentence that focuses on both the tickler and its usefulness to secretaries, and therefore is relevant to all the other sentences in the paragraph. Choices **a** and **b** are too general to effectively focus the paragraph; choice **c** is too narrow.

616. **c.** This choice focuses most sharply on the main topic of the paragraph—muscle atrophy and bone loss. Choices **a** and **b** are too broad to guide the reader to the focus of the paragraph. Choice **d** is too limited.

617. **a.** The word *rather* indicates a contrast to whatever came before. Choice **a** is the only sentence that guides the reader to the contrast between the old definition of asthma and the new. Choices **b** and **c** are less precisely related to the new understanding of asthma. Choice **d** is not related at all.

618. **a.** Choice **a** is more specific than the other choices and more sharply focused toward the entire paragraph. Choices **b** and **d** are more vague and general, and choice **c** is written in a slightly different, more upbeat style.

619. **a.** Choice **a** expands on the topic sentence. Choices **b** and **c** do not relate directly to indoor pollution. The style of choice **d** is more informal than that of the topic sentence.

620. **a.** Choice **a** relates directly to self-medication. The other choices do not.

621. **b.** Choice **b** elaborates on the topic sentence. Choices **a** and **c** are not related to it. Choice **d** is wrong because although it is true, and it is e-mail related, it is not related to the topic sentence, which focuses on the effect that e-mail has on office workers.

622. c. Choice **c** expands on the list of good reasons to eat organic food. The other choices are simply neutral facts.

623. b. The topic sentence is obviously from a contract and speaks of an agreement. Choice **b** goes on to explain, in the language of a contract, what that agreement is and so is more closely related to the topic sentence than the other choices.

624. d. This is the only choice that logically follows the topic: It provides a possible reason why Americans are fascinated with reality television. The other choices do not follow the topic sentence.

625. d. Only this choice deals with learning how to accept oneself and then relate that acceptance to another person. Choices **a** and **c** are both irrelevant to the topic sentence. Choice **b** states the opposite of the topic sentence.

626. a. This is clearly the only choice that logically follows the statement about juries in colonial times. Choices **b** and **c** can be ruled out because they do not refer back to colonial times. Choice **d** refers to colonial times but not to juries.

627. c. This choice develops the topic sentence by providing information about what a landscaper would recommend under these conditions. Choices **a**, **b**, and **d** veer away from the topic.

628. b. This is the only choice that develops the topic sentence. Choice **a** does not even mention ginkgo. Choice **c** is redundant because Europe is part of the world. Choice **d**, by referring to an old study, veers completely away from the topic.

629. a. This is the best choice because it directly follows the information that the earth is ancient and complex. Choice **b** changes the topic to mammals. Choice **c** also strays from the topic sentence. Choice **d** changes the topic to Darwin.

630. d. The passage is about the cassowary bird, not about human beings. Sentence 4 is irrelevant to the topic.

631. c. The focus of the paragraph is ratatouille, not zucchini.

632. c. This is the only sentence that does not mention sleepwalking, which is the subject of the passage.

633. d. Although there is a connection between Lyme disease and deer ticks, this connection is not made in the paragraph.

634. d. The first three sentences are written in an objective, professional tone. The tone of Sentence 4 is much more personal and subjective, so even though it says something about a harp, it is quite out of character in this paragraph.

635. b. This is the only sentence that mentions religion or any human activity at all. The other sentences define the solstices in lay science terms.

636. a. The other three sentences objectively discuss the role and qualifications of a meteorologist. Sentence 1 tells us what people think of weather forecasters. Its tone is also much more casual than the rest of the paragraph.

637. b. This choice has the objective tone of a textbook and is a general statement. The other choices describe a particular child and are written in a fictional style.

638. b. Choices **a**, **c**, and **d** list specific characteristics of the two different types of ghosts, benevolent (good) and malevolent (bad). Choice **b** is just an ironic observation on the general subject of ghosts.

639. d. Choices **a**, **b**, and **c** deal with the characteristics of sociopaths. Choice **d** simply talks about criminals, most of whom are distinguished from sociopaths in the very first sentence.

640. b. This choice has Eleanor Roosevelt as its focus. The other choices focus on Jessie Street.

641. a. Choice **a** addresses the benefits of being able to exercise even if the weather is bad. The remainder of the paragraph focuses on the benefits of exercising without fancy equipment or health clubs.

642. c. The paragraph as a whole deals with making the most of a staff's talents. It is also written directly to the supervisor. The word *you* is used in every sentence except choice **c**. Not only does choice **c** use a different tone and voice, but it also discusses a program that is designed to reward employees and veers away from the main topic.

643. c. This choice is a general statement about carbon monoxide poisoning. The other choices all relate to a firefighter's specific duties in dealing with victims of CO poisoning.

644. d. This is the correct chronological order of the events described in the paragraph.

645. c. Sentence 2 gives an overview of what the paragraph is about. Sentence 3 gives specific reasons why sentence 2 is correct. Sentence 1 gives the reason why sentence 3 is correct.

646. b. Sentence 1 provides a statement about adding a treat to a child's lunchbox periodically and gives no indication, by its tone or its wording, that it is based on any other sentence. Sentence 4 tells us that in spite of the truth in that statement, it is best, as a general rule, to provide healthy snacks and it uses the word *however,* which indicates that it is responding to another idea that we've already heard. Sentence 2, with the word *usually,* gives a definition of what is considered a healthy snack. Sentence 3 goes on to provide specific examples of healthy snacks.

647. b. Sentence 3 is the topic sentence and states the main goal of the neighborhood association. Sentence 2 goes on to cite specific tasks that help the association achieve that goal. Sentence 1, with the word *additionally,* tells us that there is one more thing the association does, even though it is a less frequent and less primary responsibility.

648. a. In this choice, the order is chronological. In sentence 4, they take Grandma to the Greyhound station. In sentence 2, the bus has not yet moved away from the station. In sentence 1, the bus jolts away but is still in town. In sentence 3, the bus (at least in the narrator's mind) is out on the open highway.

649. a. Sentence 1 is the topic sentence. Sentence 4 defines the term *double jeopardy* used in sentence 1; sentence 2 gives another definition, signaled by *also;* sentence 3 begins with the word *finally* and gives the last definition.

650. c. Sentence 3 is clearly the lead sentence, as it tells us something about the new employee handbook and is in no way based on information provided in the other two sentences. Sentence 2 uses the word *also* to indicate that it is telling us something else about the handbook, something that adds to a fact we've already been told. Sentence 1, which is making a generalization about the new policies, is based on information we already know from sentences 3 and 2. Because of this, it can only follow these sentences and not precede them.

651. a. Sentence 2 sets the stage—this is a memory. After that, the order is chronological: In sentence 1, the man tries to teach his son how to pitch. In sentence 4, the boy wasn't interested, so he gave up. Sentence 3 logically follows—the memory of giving up makes him feel sad and guilty.

652. d. Sentence 4 sets the reader up to expect a discussion of a procedure, the writing of reports of a fire. Sentence 3 tells how you can find the right report forms. Sentence 1 leads logically into sentence 2.

653. a. Sentence 2 is the topic sentence. Sentence 1 provides reasons for the procedure described in the topic sentence. Sentence 3 gives further definition as a conclusion.

654. d. The word *Yet* at the beginning of sentence 1 is a clue that this is not the beginning sentence. Sentences 4 and 1 are the only ones that logically follow each other, so the other choices can be ruled out.

655. c. Sentence 1 is the topic sentence and states the general situation. Sentence 2 poses a question about the situation in the topic sentence. Sentence 4 offers the response. Sentence 3 concludes the paragraph as it gives a reminder about the original goal.

656. b. Sentence 2 is the topic sentence, introducing the subject. Sentence 3 expands the topic, and sentence 1 gives more definition to the Native American art form.

657. b. The second paragraph contradicts the misconceptions potential adopters of racing greyhounds might have about the breed. Choice **b** states that certain popular beliefs about greyhounds are erroneous and acts as a transition to the facts that follow in the paragraph. Choice **a** does not focus on contradicting the misinformation; also, the phrase *even so* appears to agree with the misconceptions rather than contradict them. Choice **c** does not focus on the argument; instead, it repeats information given in the previous sentence. Choice **d**, rather than supporting the main purpose of the paragraph—which is to dispel myths about racing greyhounds—actually contradicts information in sentences 6 and 7.

658. b. The possessive pronoun *their* is correct.

659. **c.** This choice is the best because it retains the writer's informal, reassuring tone and because the information in it furthers the purpose of this paragraph—the suitability of greyhounds as household pets. This response also is clearly directed at a general audience of householders. Choice **a** is incorrect because the information does not keep with the topic of the paragraph; also, the tone set by the inclusion of a precise statistic is too formal. Choice **b** retains the informal tone of the selection, but it provides information that is not suitable to the purpose of this paragraph. The tone in choice **d** is argumentative, which defeats the author's purpose of trying to reassure the reader.

660. **c.** This question tests the ability to recognize a sentence fragment. Although choice **c** does include a subject and a verb, it is a dependent clause because it begins with the adverb *when*. Choices **a**, **b**, and **d** are all standard sentences.

661. **a.** This question assesses the ability to recognize redundancy in a sentence. Choice **a** removes the redundancy of sentence 8 by taking out the word *also*, which repeats the meaning of the introductory phrase *in addition to*. Choice **b** involves changing a singular noun to a plural and choice **c** changes a plural to a plural possessive noun, which would make the sentence grammatically incorrect. Choice **d** would change the meaning of the sentence incorrectly. The attitude of the community toward young people is being reported, not what young people have reported about the community attitude.

662. **c.** Choice **c** provides a fact that supports and expands upon the information given in the previous sentences. The first two sentences tell us about the program's success and the plans for expanding it. The third sentence would build on these ideas by providing detailed information about the results of the program and who was involved. Choice **a** changes the subject of this paragraph. This paragraph is about the program in a specific school district, and choice **a** makes a comment about other school districts, which may be true, but which is not related to the topic of this particular paragraph. Choice **b** adds a detail about the program, but it is a single detail as opposed to a conclusive, summarizing sentence that gives us a clear idea of the program specifics. Choice **d**, which mentions the possibility of other pilot programs, again changes the subject and veers away from the main topic of this paragraph, which is the Mural Painting Program within this particular school district.

663. **b.** This question assesses the ability to recognize the correct agreement of subject and verb. Choice **b** is correct because it uses the third-person singular of the verb *to be*, *is*, which agrees in number and in person with the subject *one*. Choice **a** is wrong because it does not correct the subject-verb agreement problem; instead, it removes an optional comma between *location* and *and*. Choice **c** is incorrect because it does not correct the agreement error; instead, it makes an unnecessary change in vocabulary from *increase* to *enhance*. Choice **d** is incorrect because it does not correct the agreement problem; instead, it creates an error by misplacing the modifier *only* directly after the semicolon.

664. d. This question tests the ability to recognize the logical connection of ideas in a paragraph and to recognize grammatical consistency. Choice **d** gives a general piece of advice (start walking), which is followed by two sentences that point to things that will result from following this advice. Choice **a** is incorrect because although it does give a general piece of advice that would make sense at the beginning of this paragraph, it contains an error in the pronoun-antecedent agreement (using the pronoun *your*, which disagrees in person with the antecedent *people*). Choice **b** is incorrect because it includes other forms of physical activity (jogging, bicycling) that are off the topic (walking) and are irrelevant to the development and order of ideas in the passage. Choice **c** is incorrect because it contains the same pronoun-antecedent agreement problem as choice **a**, and the sentence does not respect the order of ideas in the passage; it returns, to information and ideas that are more appropriate to the first paragraph.

665. a. Choice **a** is correct because a comma after the word *rewards* in sentence 3 closes off the parenthetical phrase between the subject, *physical activity*, and the predicate, *will*. Choice **b** is incorrect because it introduces an incomplete comparison into sentence 1. Choice **c** is incorrect because it inserts an unnecessary comma into sentence 5. Choice **d** is incorrect because it adds a misplaced colon to sentence 2.

666. b. The word *appraised*, meaning *judged*, does not make sense in the context; the correct word for the context is *apprised*, meaning *informed*. In choices **a**, **c**, and **d**, the words *incriminate*, *criteria*, and *ascertain* are all used correctly in context.

667. c. The information in sentence 5 continues the description of what judges must ascertain about such cases, which began in sentence 3. Skipping next to the responsibilities of officers and back to judges, as happens in the passage as it stands, is confusing. Choices **a** and **b** introduce examples before the passage states what the examples are supposed to show. Choice **d** is incorrect because deleting sentence 2 removes the statement from which all the paragraph's examples and information follow.

668. c. Sentence 4 is a run-on sentence; the conjunctive adverb *however* requires the use of either a colon or a semicolon before it in order to link two sentences. The other choices are standard sentences.

669. d. This choice provides the plural reflexive pronoun *themselves*, which agrees in number and person with the subject, *those*. Choice **a** is incorrect because it provides the verb *combine*, which does not agree in person or in number with the subject, *snowboarding*. Choice **b** is incorrect because it removes a hyphen necessary to the creation of a compound adjective. Choice **c** is incorrect because it changes the verb to the past tense, which does not agree with the present tense used throughout the paragraph.

670. b. The topic of the paragraph is about the ecology of an area; it does not specifically address environmental organizations.

671. c. Since *groups* is not a proper noun, it should not be capitalized. Choices **a**, **b**, and **d** are gramatically incorrect.

672. d. This question calls on the ability to identify standard usage of the possessive. Choice **d** is correct because the word *researchers* is actually a possessive noun, so an apostrophe must be added. Choice **a** substitutes a misused homonym for the word given. Choice **b** contains a faulty pronoun-antecedent—the *microprobes* have a diminutive width, not the brain.

673. b. In sentence 4, the adverb *typically* is misused as an adjective to modify the noun *wire*. The other choices do not contain nonstandard uses of modifiers.

674. c. The phrases *because they [microprobes] are slightly thinner than a human hair* and *because of their [microprobes'] diminutive width* contain the same information.

675. b. The predicate does not match the subject grammatically, which is necessary when using the verb *is*: *A passenger-created disturbance* doesn't match *by playing . . . or creating.*

676. c. This choice makes use of parallel structure because the list of the conductors' obligations are all expressed in the same subject-verb grammatical form: *Conductors will wait, will allow, will not allow.* In choices **a**, **b**, and **d**, the parallelism of the list is thrown off by the last item in the list, which changes the subject of its verb from operators to passengers.

677. b. Sentence 6 contains a nonstandard use of a preposition. The standard idiom is *comply with* rather than *comply to.* Choices **a**, **c**, and **d** do not contain nonstandard uses of prepositions.

678. b. Sentence 6 is a sentence fragment; it is a dependent clause. Choices **a**, **c**, and **d** all refer to standard sentences.

679. c. The main purpose of this paragraph is strictly informational, to outline Dr. Miranda Woodhouse's plan to reduce the risks of heart disease, and choice **c** focuses the reader's attention on the four strategies that Dr. Woodhouse proposes as part of this plan. Choice **a** contains seemingly contradictory information that is in no way implied or stated in the paragraph. Choice **b** focuses on the life expectancy rates of American citizens, and while lowering heart disease may boost life expectancy rates, this paragraph does not deal with that at all. It focuses exclusively on Dr. Woodhouse's plan for preventing heart disease. Choice **d** makes an argumentative claim about one part of Dr. Woodhouse's plan, which is out of place in a paragraph that seeks only to outline the basic strategies.

680. c. The possessive pronoun *their* is used erroneously in sentence 9. *There* is the word that should be used.

681. c. A comma is necessary after the first part of the sentence, which is an introductory phrase. Choice **a** is incorrect because visiting London, Paris, and Rome was not dependent on her being ten years old, so the word *because* wouldn't make sense. In choice **b**, a comma after *Although* would make the sentence grammatically incorrect. Choice **d** is incorrect because the word *breathtaking* is describing a noun (*scenes*) and requires an adjective, not an adverb. *Breathtakingly* is an adverb.

682. b. Sentence 2 is a sentence fragment. Choices **a**, **c**, and **d** all contain standard sentences.

683. c. The semicolon in sentence 6 must be followed by an independent clause, and here it is followed by a dependent clause. Choices **a**, **b**, and **d** all contain standard sentences.

684. b. The underlined word in sentence 7 needs to be made into a plural noun. Choice **a** is incorrect because it is a singular noun, which makes for incorrect subject-verb agreement. Choices **c** and **d** are incorrect because they are possessive.

685. c. The first paragraph mentions that saving room for herbs such as lavender, sage, thyme, and parsley is a characteristic of a thrifty gardener, but fails to explain why it is a sign of thrift. Choice **a** is incorrect because it removes information that is vital to explaining why the plants mentioned in sentence 1 are appropriate to a gardener who has little time. Choice **b** is incorrect because reversing the order of the sentences moves the demonstrative pronoun *these* in sentence 2 too far away from its antecedent. Choice **d** is incorrect because the passage does not indicate that growing roses is easy in general; rather, it suggests particular types of roses (hardy species) as appropriate to a garden that requires little time for maintenance.

686. a. This sentence creates a transition between the idea of harvesting food from a garden and the proper way of planting in order to achieve a good yield of food. Choice **b** is redundant, repeating information already stated in sentence 5. Choice **c** contains information that is on the subject matter of the first paragraph and is, thus, off-topic in the second. Choice **d** is off-topic and does not match the main idea of the paragraph; it mentions time-consuming work in a paragraph on the subject of gardening that takes a moderate amount of time.

687. b. The word *lavished* should be substituted for *languished*, which makes no sense in the context.

688. b. Sentence 3 requires a comma before the coordinate conjunction *so*. Choice **d** is incorrect because it already shows a comma separating the two independent clauses. Choices **a** and **c** each contain only one independent clause.

689. a. This answer is in the simple past tense, which is the tense used throughout the paragraph. Choices **b**, **c**, and **d** are incorrect because they suggest tenses inconsistent with the tense of the rest of the paragraph.

690. b. The context requires that the noun *renown* be replaced by the adjective *renowned*. Choice **a** is incorrect because the change to *when* makes no sense in the context; it would imply that Augustus grew up before immigrating. Choice **c** incorrectly inserts the contraction of pronoun *it* and verb *is* in a context where the possessive pronoun *its* is required. Choice **d** is incorrect because it introduces a diction error into the sentence.

691. b. The semicolon in sentence 2 is used incorrectly to introduce a list. In choices **a**, **c**, and **d**, the semicolon correctly separates two independent clauses.

692. c. The expressions *year-round* and *in all seasons* repeat the same idea. Choices **a**, **b**, and **d** are incorrect because none of these sentences contain unnecessary repetition. Sentence 4 may seem to, at first; however, the words *hot* and *humid* are described in more interesting and specific terms in the second part of the sentence.

693. b. The subject of sentence 3 is climate and therefore requires the third-person singular form of the verb to be—*is*. Choice **c** is incorrect because the comma is correctly placed after an introductory phrase. Choice **a** incorrectly inserts the possessive pronoun *its* in a context where the contraction of subject and verb *it is* is required. Choice **d** is incorrect because the comma is necessary to close off the interruptive phrase, *whether in the back country or at established campgrounds*, between the subject and verb.

694. c. Sentence 7 provides information about the high cost of healthcare insurance but doesn't give information about the main topic of this passage, which is how to choose a doctor. Choices **a**, **b**, and **d** all do provide information about, and guidelines for, choosing a doctor.

695. a. An adverb is required here because the word is being used to add information to a verb (*responds*). The correct form of the word is *quickly*. Choice **b** is incorrect because the term *more better* is grammatically incorrect. Choice **c** is incorrect because in the context of this sentence, using the past tense, *accepted*, is not appropriate. Choice **d** is incorrect because the sentence requires an adjective here, not an adverb.

696. a. In sentence 1, the adjective *good* is misused as an adverb; it needs to be replaced by the adverb *well*.

697. a. In sentence 4, the verb *assure*, a transitive verb meaing to make certain, is nonsensical in the context; it should be replaced by the verb *assume*, to suppose or take for granted. Choices **b**, **c**, and **d** are incorrect because all these words are used properly in their context.

698. d. The paragraph consistently uses the pronoun *you*; therefore, the inconsistent use of *our* should be replaced by *your*. Choice **a** is incorrect because the comma is necessary before the coordinate conjunction *but*. Choice **b** is incorrect because insertion of a colon would incorrectly divide a phrase. Choice **c** is incorrect because it would introduce an error of tense shift into the paragraph.

699. b. The context requires a word meaning to surrender or yield, so choice **b** is correct. The other choices are incorrect because each has the wrong meaning for the context of the sentence.

700. d. To make the pair of verbs in the sentence parallel, *overlooking* should be changed to *overlooks* to match the form of the verb *towers*. Choice **a** is incorrect because the change would convert sentence 7 into a run-on sentence. Choice **b** is incorrect because *Irish*, as the name of a people, must be capitalized. Choice **c** is incorrect because the word *running* is functioning as an adjective here; the verb *run* would make nonsense of the sentence.

701. d. A comma is required after an introductory dependent clause. Choice **a** would introduce a comma fault, separating a verb from its object. Choice **b** is incorrect because the semicolon would have to be followed by a complete sentence, which is not the case. Choice **c** is incorrect because removing the colon would create a run-on sentence.

702. c. Choices **a** and **b** would cause an unwarranted shift in tense from past (in which most of the passage is written) to present. Choice **d** would change the correctly written noun, *effect*, to an incorrect verb form. (*Affect* is a verb, except when used as a noun to denote a person's emotional expression, or lack thereof, as in: *He has a joyless affect.*)

703. b. The adjective *shallow* in sentence 5 actually modifies the verb *set*; therefore, the adjective should be revised to be the adverb *shallowly*. Choices **a**, **c**, and **d** are incorrect because none of them contain a nonstandard use of a modifier.

704. c. The proper noun *Lake* must be made possessive because it is followed by the gerund *arriving*. Choice **a** is incorrect because it introduces a comma fault into the sentence. Choices **b** and **d** introduce errors in diction into the sentence.

705. a. The antecedent of the pronoun *they* in this sentence is *someone*. Since *someone* is singular, the corrected subject pronoun should be *he or she*.

706. c. The sentence requires the contraction *we're*, short for *we are*. It is all right to use a contraction, because the writer uses contractions elsewhere in the passage. Choice **a** is incorrect because it introduces an error in modifier. Choice **b** is incorrect because a semicolon must be followed, here, by a full sentence. Choice **d** is incorrect because the singular *a deadline* would disrupt the parallelism of the list, the other elements of which are plural.

707. a. Another sentence is needed to add the information that the program is only for passengers leaving the bus, not for those boarding it. This information is implied in the paragraph but not directly stated; without the direct statement, the paragraph is confusing, and the reader must read between the lines to get the information. Choice **b** is incorrect because it removes an important instruction to drivers, rather than clarifying the paragraph's point. Choice **c** is incorrect because it adds information that contradicts the point the paragraph is making. Choice **d** is incorrect because it would place intervening material between the ideas of what the program is and how it operates; it would disorder the sequence of ideas.

708. a. The subjective pronoun *who* is incorrectly used to refer to the Stop Here Program; the pronoun *which* would be a better choice.

709. b. Sentence 5 contains two sentences linked only by a comma; a semicolon is required. Choices **a**, **c**, and **d** are all standard sentences.

710. d. In sentence 4, a semicolon is used incorrectly to introduce a list; it should be replaced by a colon. Choice **a** is incorrect because this sentence would not make sense if the contraction *we're*, which means *we are*, replaced the verb *were*. Choice **b** is incorrect because it would introduce a comma fault between the subject *others* and the verb *were*. Choice **c** is incorrect because the comma is needed to separate items in a list.

711. a. This paragraph is written with powerful verbs. *Was looking* is passive and has little impact in the passage. Choices **b**, **c**, and **d** use the active voice.

712. c. Sentence 3 says *he were sure. He* is singular and takes the verb *was*. Choices **a**, **b**, and **d** are incorrect because all verbs are used correctly.

713. a. *Cortez* is a proper noun and should begin with a capital letter. Choices **b**, **c**, and **d** would make the sentences grammatically incorrect.

714. a. Commas are used to separate city from country. Choices **b**, **c**, and **d** would make the sentences gramatically incorrect.

715. b. Titles of books are always underlined or italicized. Short stories (choice **a**) are punctuated with quotation marks. Authors' names (choice **c**) are not italicized. Copyrights do not need italics (choice **d**).

716. a. Choice **a** is written in the tone and style reflected in the passage. Choices **b**, **c**, and **d** are awkward versions of the same details.

717. d. The verb needs to be singular to agree with the singular subject of the sentence, *Theodore Roosevelt*. Choices **a**, **b**, and **c** are incorrect because they introduce a shift from the past tense of the rest of the passage.

718. a. The subject of this paragraph is the appearance and observation of cuttlefish. Choice **a** is about observing cuttlefish in the wild and in the laboratory. Choices **b** and **c** stray from the topic of the paragraph. Choice **d**, while having something to do with the appearance of cuttlefish, is written in jargon that is too technical to match the tone of the rest of the passage.

719. c. The double mention in sentence 6 of the human-like eyes of the cuttlefish is unnecessarily repetitious.

720. d. The correct choice is *hover*, because to *hoover* is a chiefly British phrase meaning to use a vacuum cleaner. *For* (meaning to indicate the purpose of the action) is the correct preposition for this sentence, so choice **a** is the incorrect choice. Choice **b** is incorrect because *allow* is the right word (*allot*, meaning to apportion, would not make sense). Choice **c** is incorrect, because it would make the sentence ungrammatical with regard to number.

721. b. The word *carnavale* is a foreign word; therefore, it must be italicized. Choice **c** is incorrect because there is no reason to italicize the word *serfs*, an ordinary noun, in the passage. Choice **a** is incorrect because the definite article is not needed before the word *Carnival* used as a proper noun. Choice **d** is incorrect because the verb *were* is used correctly here, in the subjunctive mood.

722. a. The objective pronoun *her* is misused in sentence 1 as a subject pronoun; it needs to be replaced with the pronoun *she*.

723. a. Quotation marks need to be inserted before the quotation is resumed after the interrupting phrase, *the brochure informed her.* Choice **b** is incorrect because the comma is required to set off the interrupting phrase from the quotation. Choice **c** is incorrect because the close quotation marks are necessary before the interrupting phrase. Choice **d** is incorrect because the quotation is not finished; it goes on for another sentence.

724. b. This statement maintains the formal tone established by the rest of the passage. Choices **a**, **c**, and **d** are still too informal.

725. d. In sentence 7, the pronoun *you* needs to be changed to *we* to agree in number and person to the antecedents used earlier in the passage. Choices **a**, **b**, and **c** are incorrect because none of these sentences contain a nonstandard use of a pronoun.

726. a. *Consequently* means *as a result of.* The adverbs listed in choices **b**, **c**, and **d** do not address this sequence.

727. c. Choice **c** reflects the sentiments in the last sentence of the passage. Choices **a**, **b**, and **d** do not state such a profound effect.

728. b. The pronoun *my* needs to be changed to *our* to agree in number and person with the pronoun *we*. Choices **a**, **c**, and **d** fail to correct the pronoun-antecedent agreement problem.

729. a. Sentence 1 is a fragment and needs a verb to make it a complete sentence. The sentences in choices **b**, **c**, and **d** are complete.

730. **b.** The main idea of this paragraph is that, while genius has a recognizable pattern, the patterns are extraordinary. Choice **b** directly states that the patterns have the eerie quality of fate. Choice **a** does not focus ideas, but rather repeats material already stated. Choice **c** focuses attention on the side idea of the popular opinions about genius. Choice **d** contains material that is irrelevant to the main idea and argument of the passage.

731. **a.** The possessive *Mozart's* is required before the gerund *composing*. Choice **b** is incorrect because *too*, meaning excessively, is required in this context, not the preposition *to*. Choice **c** is incorrect because *there*, not the possessive pronoun *their*, is required in this context. Choice **d** is incorrect because the possessive form does not make sense in this context.

732. **c.** Sentence 4 contains an error in pronoun-antecedent agreement; the pronoun *they* must be changed to *it* in order to agree in number and person with its antecedent, *regularity*. Choices **a**, **b**, and **d** are incorrect because they contain standard uses of pronouns.

733. **d.** Sentence 6 is a statement about the effect of the play in theater history in general; however, this statement is placed in the midst of a description of the reception of the opening of the play. The paragraph ends with a statement about the play's effect on theater history, so sentence 6 should either be moved to the end of the paragraph or be removed. Because there is no choice to move sentence 6 to the end of the paragraph, choice **d** is the correct answer. Choice **a** is incorrect because it still leaves sentence 6 in a position where its meaning is out of place. Choice **b** is incorrect because removing the phrase has little effect on the paragraph; it merely removes a concrete detail. Choice **c** is incorrect because removing sentence 9 excises the conclusion that the previous sentence has promised; it is necessary to the development of the paragraph.

734. **c.** The names of works that can be published on their own should be italicized, even if only part of the title (in this case *Godot*) is used to designate the work; therefore, choice **b** is incorrect. Choice **a** is incorrect because Mr. Godot names a character, not the play. Choice **d** is incorrect because the titles of newspapers must be italicized.

735. **c.** The comma in sentence 5 separates the subject, *critics and playgoers*, from its verb, *greeted*.

736. **b.** Inserting a comma in sentence 2, after the word *opening* separates the introductory phrase from the rest of the sentence. The sentences in choices **a**, **c**, and **d** are correct as they are written.

737. d. The two independent clauses in sentence 2 need a conjunction in order for the sentence to be gramatically correct. The sentences choices **a**, **b**, and **c** are correctly written.

738. c. *To correctly divide* is a split infinitive. The infinitive is *to divide*. Choices **a**, **b**, and **d** do not make this kind of error.

739. a. The context requires a verb that means *to extend beyond*, not *to come before*. The words in the other choices do not have this meaning.

740. b. Sentence 2 is the only interrogatory sentence in the passage. Because it asks a question, it needs a question mark as punctuation.

741. a. Since the sentence states that the *system is designed to give*, then it needs *to ensure* as well. Choices **b**, **c**, and **d** are correct as written.

742. c. The pronoun *his* should be replaced with *their* in order to agree with *federal employers*. There are no errors in pronoun agreement in choice **a**, **b**, or **d**.

743. d. A semicolon should separate two complete sentences (independent clauses); the second half of sentence 6 is not a complete sentence but a restatement of a portion of the first half. This makes a colon appropriate. Choices **a** and **b** would create run-on sentences. Choice **c** would incorrectly separate two independent clauses joined by a conjunction (*and*) with a semicolon.

744. c. The pronoun is one of the subjects of the sentence, and so it should be changed from the objective form *him* to the subjective form *he*. Choice **a** is incorrect because *their*, meaning belonging to them, is correct in this context. Choice **b** is incorrect because the comma is necessary before the conjunction. Choice **d** is incorrect because the possessive form is not suitable in this context.

745. d. Sentence 5 is the only sentence fragment in this passage. It needs a subject in order to express a complete thought.

746. d. *Recently* is the best contrast to *Finally, though* in sentence 2. Choices **a**, **b**, and **c** indicate time lapses that would not necessarily take place in the context of the passage.

747. a. The comma is needed to set off the introductory clause from the independent clause. Making the changes stated in choices **b**, **c**, or **d** would create a nonstandard sentence.

748. b. The phrase *at the ceiling* should be replaced with *on the ceiling*.

749. d. The pronoun *it* should be changed to *they* to agree in number and person with the antecedent, *detectors*.

750. c. The paragraphs are related in that they both talk about the physical effects of extreme heat on people and the treatment of these conditions, but the main subject of each paragraph details a different condition resulting from extreme heat. The second paragraph begins by mentioning that heatstroke is much more serious than the condition mentioned in paragraph 1, heat exhaustion. Choice **c** best aids the transition by ending the first paragraph with an explanation of the most serious effects of heat exhaustion, thereby paving the way for the contrasting description of the far more serious condition, heatstroke. Choice **a** is off-topic; choices **b** and **d** are both about heatstroke, so they belong in the second paragraph, not the first.

751. b. The main idea of this paragraph is a description of the symptoms and treatment of heatstroke. The information in sentence 7 about the most common victims of heat stroke is least relevant to the topic of the paragraph. The other choices, by contrast, all discuss either symptoms or treatment.

752. a. Sentence 1 is a sentence fragment; it contains no main verb.

753. b. Sentence 2 expresses two complete thoughts as one. To correct this sentence, a comma should be added after *Greenland*, followed by the conjunction *but* introducing the independent clause.

754. d. Even though it may look like a question, sentence 6 is not an interrogatory sentence. It should not be punctuated with a question mark.

755. c. This choice adds the subject *he* in the second sentence, eliminating the dangling modifier *walking down the street.* Otherwise, the sentence reads as if the leaves are walking down the street. All other choices ignore the problem of the dangling modifier and add grammatical mistakes to the sentences.

756. b. This paragraph's purpose is descriptive; it describes the classroom and the corridor outside it. Choice **b** is correct because the information in the sentence adds to the description of the corridor. Choice **a** is incorrect because it adds information that describes the course Howard is to teach, which is not the subject of this paragraph. Choice **c** is incorrect because it adds information about the two buildings mentioned in the first paragraph; therefore, it rightfully belongs in the first paragraph, not the second. Choice **d** is incorrect because it adds information irrelevant to the paragraph.

757. c. Sentence 6 is a dependent clause with no independent clause to attach itself to; therefore, it is a sentence fragment.

758. d. The word *wreaked* should be replaced in this context by its homophone *reeked.* The words in choices **a**, **b**, and **c** are all used correctly in their context.

6 ▶ Acing the Essay

Never be afraid to sit awhile and think.
—Lorraine Hansberry

THIS SECTION PROVIDES 24 essay writing practice exercises. Before you begin your essay practice, read over the Essay Scoring Criteria to familiarize yourself with the components of a high-scoring level 6 essay and the weaknesses associated with a poorly written essay that has scored only at level 1. You will also find sample essays in the Answers section. When you are studying a model essay, reflect on the following questions: What makes this essay so appealing or unappealing? How does the author use language? How does the author organize his or her essay? How does the author introduce the topic? What are this essay's strengths? What are this essay's weaknesses?

One of the most difficult challenges that a writer faces is the task of writing an interesting and relevant lead sentence during a timed writing session or test. The **lead sentence** sets the tone and framework for the remainder of the essay, so it's important to start on the right footing. Here are some suggestions for crafting an enticing lead sentence:

- Pose a provocative question. → *Would you sell your right to vote for a million dollars?*
- Introduce relevant statistics. → *A recent survey of high school seniors revealed a 30% increase in the number of students participating in volunteer work programs.*

- State a specific problem. → *Shockingly, the incidence of autism has dramatically doubled in the past ten years.*
- Introduce the story with a vivid narrative. → *I could hear the children's laughter emanating from the gymnasium as I marked English papers in the eerily silent sun-dappled classroom.*
- Start with an enticing quotation. → *Henry James wrote, "It takes a great deal of history to produce a little literature."*
- Introduce relevant dialogue. → *When my father said, "You're going to have to decide about college," I knew that I was about to make one of the most important decisions in my life.*
- Arouse the reader's curiosity with a surprising or unusual statement. → *During my childhood, I had a wide variety of pets: five cats, rabbits, a hen, and a squirrel named Riley.*
- Use an interesting case history. → *John D. lived in foster homes during the first five years of his life. He had been placed in his first foster home after his teenage mother realized that she could not afford to raise him.*
- Use hyperboles to shock and surprise the reader. → *I'm not saying that her diamond engagement ring was gaudy, but the reflection from the ice on her finger made the lights on the Empire State Building appear dim in comparison.*
- Kick off with an interesting definition. → *The pro-nature green moniker "tree hugger" is no longer relegated to granola-munching counterculture hippie environmentalists.*

Supporting paragraphs are similar to the middle cars of a train, because they move your essay further along with each additional paragraph. The **concluding paragraph** in an essay is similar to the train station where the passengers disembark.

Your readers' journey ends at the last sentence of your concluding paragraph. You'll want to be certain that you've helped your readers reach their final destination by providing a concluding paragraph that synthesizes and reinforces your main idea. Reflect on the following questions before writing your concluding paragraph:

- What main idea or ideas should your readers have grasped? What have they learned?
- Are there any final thoughts for your readers to reflect on?
- If you have been discussing a problem, can you offer a solution?
- Are you plagiarizing your own words by using similar words and ideas from your introductory paragraph? Ask yourself: Has my idea grown and developed as I've moved along, or is it still as raw and undeveloped as when I began discussing it?

Get a Grip Writing Tip

The Five Ws and H

Journalists have always relied on the "five Ws and H" formula to ensure that they provide the essential information that a reader needs to fully comprehend a news story: Who? What? Where? When? Why? How? Use this formula to be sure that you cover the basics when writing an essay.

▶ Resource List of Essay Models

Reading lots of good essays will lead to writing lots of good essays!

Cart, Michael, Marc Aronson, and Marianne Carus, eds. *911: The Book of Help* (Chicago: Cricket Books/Marcato, 2002). This is an anthology of memorable essays and short stories inspired by September 11, 2001.

Fulghum, Robert. *It Was on Fire When I Lay Down on It* (New York: Random House, 1989). These down-to-earth, lighthearted, and spirited personal essays teach valuable life lessons.

Gaskins, Pearl Fuyo, ed. *What Are You?* (New York: Henry Holt, 1999). These essays written by mixed-raced young people (ages 14 to 26) discuss issues such as relationships, racism, personal identity conflict, cultural issues, and more.

Get a Grip Writing Tip

A Title by Any Other Name Can Be Just Plain Boring

Don't feel as if you have to create a title as soon as you begin writing. If you're not very good at writing titles and lead sentences, start by writing your ending first and don't write your title until after you've completed your essay. Titles are important, because they entice the reader and provide a significant clue about the content of your essay. First impressions are crucial, so take the time to brainstorm interesting titles that will set the tone and draw the reader in.

▶ Essay Scoring Criteria

Use the following scoring guide to score each of your essays. Better yet, have someone else read your essay and use the scoring guide to help you see how well you have done. Sample essays for the first six essay topics follow this scoring guide.

A **"6" essay** is a highly effective response to the assignment; a few minor errors are allowed. It has the following additional characteristics:

- good organization and overall coherence
- clear explanation and/or illustration of main ideas
- variety of sentence syntax
- facility in language usage
- general freedom from mechanical mistakes and errors in word usage and sentence structure

A **"5" essay** shows competence in responding to the assigned topic but may have minor errors. It has the following additional characteristics:

- competent organization and general coherence
- fairly clear explanation and/or illustration of main ideas
- some variety of sentence syntax
- facility in language usage
- general freedom from mechanical errors and errors in word usage and sentence structure

A **"4" essay** displays competence in response to the assignment. It has the following additional characteristics:

- adequate organization and development
- explanation and illustration of some key ideas
- adequate language usage
- some mechanical but inconsistent errors and mistakes in usage or sentence structure

A **"3" essay** shows some competence but is plainly flawed. Additionally, it has the following characteristics:

- inadequate organization or incomplete development
- inadequate explanation or illustration of main ideas
- a pattern of mechanical mistakes or errors in usage and sentence structure

A **"2" essay** shows limited competence and is severely flawed. Additionally, it has the following characteristics:

- poor organization and general lack of development
- little or no supporting detail
- serious mechanical errors and mistakes in usage, sentence structure, and word choice

A **"1" essay** shows a fundamental lack of writing skill. Additionally, it has the following characteristics:

- practically nonexistent organization and general incoherence
- severe and widespread writing errors

A **"0" essay** does not address the topic assigned.

▶ Practice Questions

Make sure that your essays are well organized and that you support each central argument with concrete examples. Allow about 30 minutes for each essay.

759. In a review of Don DeLillo's novel *White Noise*, Jayne Anne Phillips writes that the characters are people "sleepwalking through a world where 'Coke is It!' and the TV is always on." On the other hand, television is said by some to have brought the world to people who would not have seen much of it otherwise. It has made possible a global village.

Write an essay in which you express your opinion of the effect of television on individuals or on nations. Include specific details from personal experience to back up your assertions.

760. Bob Maynard has said, "Problems are opportunities in disguise."

Write an essay describing a time in your life when a problem became an opportunity. How did you transform the situation? Explain what you did to turn the problem into an opportunity, and explain how others can benefit from your experience.

When you write an essay under testing conditions, you should plan on using about the first one-fourth to one-third of the time you are allotted just for planning. Jot down notes about what you want to say about the topic, and then find a good way to organize your ideas.

761. In his play, *The Admirable Crighton,* J.M. Barrie wrote, "Courage is the thing. All goes if courage goes."

Write an essay about a time in your life when you had the courage to do something or face something difficult, or when you feel you fell short. What did you learn from the experience?

762. Some people say that writing can't be taught. Educators debate the subject every day, while the teachers in the trenches keep trying.

Write an essay in which you take a position about the matter. You may discuss any kind of writing, from basic composition to fiction. Be sure to back up your opinion with concrete examples and specific details.

The most important step in writing an essay is to read the topic carefully. Make sure you understand the question. If you have a choice of topics, choose the one you understand fully.

763. Dorothy Fosdick once said, "Fear is a basic emotion, part of our native equipment, and like all normal emotions has a positive function to perform. Comforting formulas for getting rid of anxiety may be just the wrong thing. Books about *peace of mind* can be bad medicine. To be afraid when one should be afraid is good sense."

Write an essay in which you express your agreement or disagreement with Fosdick's assertion. Support your opinion with specific examples.

764. In the past several years, many state governments have permitted gambling by actually sponsoring lotteries, to increase state revenues and keep taxes down. Proponents of gambling praise the huge revenues gambling generates. Opponents counter that gambling hurts those who can least afford it, and increased availability of gamblers leads to an increase in the number of gamblers who need treatment.

Write an essay in which you take a position on the issue of state-sponsored gambling. Be sure to support your view with logical arguments and specific examples.

Take just 30 minutes to plan and write your essay. This is good practice for writing under timed conditions, as you have to do in a test.

765. The Western view of human rights promotes individual rights. The Eastern view argues that the good of the whole country or people is more important than the rights of individuals.

Write an essay in which you take a position on this debate. The Western view would be that individuals always have the right to express their opinions. The Eastern view would hold that individual expression must sometimes be fettered in order to promote harmony in a given society. Be sure to support your discussion with specific examples and logical arguments.

766. Barbara Tuchman once noted, "Every successful revolution puts on in time the robe of the tyrant it has deposed."

Write an essay in which you either agree or disagree with her observation. Support your opinion with specific examples.

When planning your essay, use an outline, a brainstorming list, a topic map, or any other method that works for you to jot down your ideas and organize them logically.

767. Gossip is fun, but if it is malicious, it can be hurtful.

Have you ever been the victim of gossip? Have you ever passed on gossip that you later found was untrue? How do you think the victim of malicious gossip should react or respond? What advice would you give to such a victim?

768. In 1997, scientists in Scotland successfully cloned a sheep. This event added to the debate over human cloning. Proponents of a ban on human cloning are concerned about issues such as genetic selection. Opponents of a ban point out that cloning could lead to significant medical advances.

Write an essay in which you take a position on the issue of human cloning. Be sure to support your view with logical arguments and specific examples.

When you write, make sure the first paragraph of your essay includes a thesis statement, a sentence that states the main idea of your essay.

769. Law enforcement agencies use a tool called profiling in certain situations. Profiling is the practice of outlining the looks and behavior of the type of person who is more likely than others to commit a particular crime. For example, if a person buys an airline ticket with cash, travels with no luggage, and returns the same day, that individual fits the profile for a drug courier. Opponents of profiling argue that it has the potential to unfairly target citizens based on their appearance. Proponents argue that law enforcement must take such shortcuts in order to effectively fight crime.

Write an essay in which you take a position on this debate. Be sure to use logical reasoning and support your view with specific examples.

770. Is it ever all right to lie? Some people say that little white lies are acceptable to spare someone else's feelings. Other people believe it is never right to lie, that telling a few little lies leads to telling more and bigger lies.

Which position do you hold? Is it possible to never lie? Is it possible to tell just the right kind of lies? Use examples to illustrate your position.

There's no specific number of paragraphs you have to have in an essay, but it would be difficult to write a good essay on any topic in fewer than three paragraphs. Most good essays will have four to seven paragraphs.

771. The United States owes the United Nations several million dollars in back dues and other fees. Opponents of paying this debt point to an inefficient bureaucracy at the United Nations and the tendency of the United Nations to support positions that are not in the United States' best interests. Proponents of paying this debt highlight a growing tendency toward internationalism and the fact that the United States depends on the United Nations for support.

Write an essay outlining why the United States should pay its United Nations debt or why it should not. Support your position with examples and logical arguments.

772. As juvenile crime increases, so do the calls for stricter punishments for juvenile offenders. One suggestion is to lower the age at which a juvenile may be tried as an adult. Supporters of this view believe that young people are committing crimes at younger and younger ages, and the crimes they are committing are becoming more and more heinous. Opponents of this view point to the success of juvenile crime prevention programs, such as teen centers and midnight basketball.

Write an essay in which you either defend or criticize the suggestion that juvenile offenders should be charged as adults at younger ages. Include examples and logical reasoning to support your position.

The essays in this set and the next few contain more personal topics—ones that ask you to reflect on a specific event in your life or on your personality.

773. Phyllis Bottome has said, "There are two ways of meeting difficulties. You alter the difficulties or you alter yourself to meet them."

Write about a time in which you attempted to alter a difficult situation, or decided to alter yourself. Were you successful? Are you pleased with the choice you made? Whichever you chose to alter, would it have been easier to alter the other? Would it have been better?

774. Bella Lewitzky once said, "To move freely you must be deeply rooted."

Write an essay in which you first state what you interpret this statement to mean (there is no right or wrong interpretation), then (using your own interpretation) agree or disagree with it. Support your opinion with specific examples and logical reasoning.

Each body paragraph of your essay should have a topic sentence that forecasts the main idea of that paragraph. Make sure your topic sentences are connected to your thesis statement in order to write a unified essay.

775. Most people have faced a situation—perhaps in a class, in an organization, or just with a group of friends—in which they held a strong, but unpopular, opinion.

Write about a time when you were in this circumstance. Did you speak up? Did you keep quiet? Why do you think you made the choice you did?

776. Do you consider yourself adventurous, a risk taker?

Write about a time in which you contemplated an undertaking that others considered dangerous. Did you do it? Why? If you did not do it, why not? Do you have regrets? The danger involved need not have been physical, although it could have been.

It's always important to explain yourself fully. How will the reader understand the event you're describing if you don't "show all"? In both personal and persuasive writing, it's important to include lots of details, images, and explanations to support your main idea.

777. Nadine Stair said, "If I had my life to live over again, I'd dare to make more mistakes next time."

Write an essay in which you agree or disagree with this assessment, using your own life as a touchstone. Why do you agree or disagree? How might your life have been different if you had dared to make more mistakes?

778. In the 1960s and 1970s, women were demanding the right to attend previously all-male educational institutions. Having won that right, some women are now reconsidering. Citing studies that indicate girls perform better in all-girls schools than in coed schools, some women are calling for the establishment of single-sex educational institutions.

Write an essay in which you take a position on the issue of single-sex schools. Be sure to include specific examples and solid reasoning in your opinion.

Often the best way to organize a personal essay is chronologically, in time order. But you should still make sure you have a thesis statement that responds to the question, and that your whole essay is related to your thesis statement.

779. Susanne Curchod Necker said, "Worship your heroes from afar; contact withers them."

Do you agree? Write about a time when you made contact with a hero. Were you disappointed with the experience or not? Or perhaps someone once thought of you as a hero. Did that admirer feel the same way after getting close to you? Did closeness make the relationship better or worse?

780. Most of us have been in a situation, perhaps at work or at school, in which we felt we were being treated unfairly.

Write about a time when you were treated unfairly. How did you react? What did you do or say about the treatment? If you had it to do over again, would you do something differently?

Whether you're writing a personal essay or a persuasive one, make sure you stick to the topic you are given.

781. An old cliché says, "You can't fight city hall."

Do you believe this is true? What advice would you give someone who wanted to convince a city council that a stoplight should be installed at a particular corner? Perhaps you can write about a time in which you tried to change or enact a law, or perhaps a regulation at school or at work. Were you successful? Why or why not?

782. Advances in genetic testing now allow scientists to identify people whose genetic backgrounds make them greater risks for certain diseases. A genetic predisposition to a certain disease, however, is far from a guarantee that a patient will contract that disease. Environmental factors, such as diet, exercise, and smoking also play a role. Insurance companies want to have access to genetic information in order to help keep their costs down. Opponents feel that insurance companies will misuse such information, by unfairly denying people coverage.

Write an essay in which you take a position on providing genetic testing information to insurance companies. Be sure to support your argument with specific examples and logical reasoning.

▶ **Answers**

759.

Sample "6" Essay

Television has an important place in society for two reasons. First, it is a common denominator that can be used as a teaching tool for kids. Second, it bridges gaps between cultures. With a simple flick of the switch people can tune in and watch congressional meetings, travel down the Ganges, or see the Scottish highlands. They can learn about other cultures, cooking, or architecture. They can witness events half a world away as soon as they take place.

Because everyone in every classroom from kindergarten to college has been exposed to television, its programs can bring about lively discussions and a meeting of the minds. Television opens windows on the world that are unique. It helps students see more of the world than any generation before them

could see. Given the right focus in a classroom, it can be the start of a writing exercise or a debate. The skills learned in these kinds of exercises prepare students for more complicated tasks later on in life.

By watching engaging, educational television programming, people from all walks of life can learn about others. Understanding the habits, religions, and cultural traits of people from distant parts of the globe helps bring the world closer together. It makes people more tolerant of others and can only promote peace in a global village that becomes increasingly smaller every day we live. Its place in society is vital.

Sample "4" Essay

Many people say they don't watch television, and I say good for them! There is very little on TV today that is worth watching. And yet, for all that, it has an important place in society. I believe, for example, that it is an excellent teaching tool for kids who have had less than a sterling formal education in the lower grades. It's something they can relate to and something they will have in common with the other people in their class. It's something they have in common with the teacher, for that matter. And that is all-important.

Television opens a window on the world that is unique. It helps students to see more of the world than any generation before them has been able to see. With a simple flick of the switch they can look in and watch the goings-on in congress; or travel down the Ganges river or see the Scotish highlands. They can learn about other cultures, learn how to cook or build a house. They can witness events half a world away as soon as they take place.

Here is one advantage of television, as it can be used as a teaching tool. In classrooms today, especially in community colleges, for example, there are students from every strata of society, from many different social classes. Television is one thing they have in common and can bring about lively discussions and a meeting of the minds. Rich and poor alike, privileged or under privileged, all have looked through that tiny window and see wonders and horrors, current events and events long-past. And all can be used as fodder for lively class discussion, for making the subjects we're teaching come alive.

We might take pride in saying we never watch television, but we shouldn't be so quick to put it down—especially as it pertains to teaching. Television is one thing students have in common, and I think it was Winston Churchhill who said, "The only thing worse than democracy is any other form of government." I think the same can be said for television: "The only thing worse than television is no television." Sure, theres a lot on that's not worth watching, but theres also a lot that is. And to ignore it's influence is to ignore an excellent, if flawed, teaching tool.

Sample "3" Essay

I sometimes wish TV had never been invented. Especially for the younger generation, who get much of their information about the world in a distorted fashion from "the box." Of course it is entertaining after a hard day, but at the end what have you gained?

And the news gets distorted. We get our news from "a reliabel source" but who is that? Some gossip columnist in Washington or New York that has nothing to do with our real life. We get to see how rotten our politicions are and maybe thats a good thing because earlier in history they could cover it up. We get to watch them on TV and judge for ourself instead of taking someone else's word for it. So television can be a good thing if watched in moderation.

Another way TV corrups society is through advertizing. It tells us to buy, buy, buy. It gives us super models and sport's figures to tell you what to buy and where. It gives you movie stars advertizing even in a TV movie away from comercials, by holding a

can of Coke or other product. All of which subliminaly tells you to buy Coke. They say they even have messages flashed on the screen so on the commercial you will get up and go to the kitchen. I find myself bringing home products I never even use. The worse thing is the shows in which dificult life situatsions get solved in a half hour. You could never do it in real life but on TV it is easy. It gives us a erronous view of the world.

I think we should try to do away with it in our homes even if it is hard. After all, its your baby-sitter and advise-giver, and even your friend if you are lonely. But give it a week to be away from it and then watch intermitently. You're life will be better for it.

Sample "1" Essay

TV can be good or bad depending on how you look at it. It can be all you do if you are not careful. It can take you away from your kids if you use it as a baby sitter or when you come home from work that is all you do. Also you will never get the real story. You will never know if they are telling the truth or trying a snow job to sell you something.

I grew up with television like most peopel. It is a good thing if you try to learn from it. It probably will help in a class room discussion if the children all watch the same show. In grade school where I went we had current events and television had it's place.

One example is the news. We know if we are going to war the minute the president makes his decission. We can watch it all happening. We can know if there is a scandel in Washington. And the latest medical facts are on TV. So TV can be good in that aspect.

It can be bad to. For example the shows for teen agers. When I was a teen ager I liked them, all the music and the dancing. But now it is diferent. Drugs are spread through MTV because of the musicions who you can tell do them. And they are models for our kids.

But in some aspects TV is good and in some it is bad. I think spending time away from it will make you feel better. all the news is bad news. But you can get an education too if you just watch public TV. It is good in some aspects and bad in some.

760.
Sample "6" Essay

Life is full of problems, but the method we use to approach those problems often determines whether we're happy or miserable. Bob Maynard says, "Problems are opportunities in disguise." If we approach problems with Maynard's attitude, we can see that problems are really opportunities to learn about others and ourselves. They enable us to live happier and more fulfilling lives.

Maynard's quote applies to all kinds of problems. To share a personal story, I faced a problem just last week when the plumbing for our family's kitchen sink developed a serious leak. Water puddled all over our new kitchen floor, and to make matters worse, our landlord was out of town for the week. Since my family is large, we couldn't afford to wait for the landlord's return nor could we afford an expensive plumbing bill. Taking charge, I decided to learn how to fix it myself. The best place to start was at my local library. There, I found a great fix-it-yourself book, and in just a few hours, I had figured out the cause of the leak. Not only did I repair the leak, but I know now that I can rely on my own abilities to solve other everyday problems.

I think it's important to remember that no matter how big a problem is, it's still an opportunity. Whatever kind of situation we face, problems give us the chance to learn and grow, both physically and mentally. Problems challenge us and give us the chance to do things we've never done before, to learn things we never knew before. They teach us what we're capable of doing, and often they give us the chance to surprise ourselves.

Sample "4" Essay

Just the word *problem* can send some of us into a panic. But problems can be good things, too. Problems are situations that make us think and force us to be creative and resourceful. They can also teach us things we didn't know before.

For example, I had a problem in school a few years ago when I couldn't understand my math class. I started failing my quizzes and homework assignments. I wasn't sure what to do, so finally I went to the teacher and asked for help. She said she would arrange for me to be tutored by another student who was her best student. In return, though, I'd have to help that student around school. I wasn't sure what she meant by that until I met my tutor. She was handicapped.

My job was to help her carry her books from class to class. I'd never even spoken to someone in a wheelchair before and I was a little scared. But she turned out to be the nicest person I've ever spent time with. She helped me understand everything I need to know for math class and she taught me a lot about what it's like to be handicapped. I learned to appreciate everything that I have, and I also know that people with disabilities are special not because of what they can't do, but because of who they are.

So you see that wonderful things can come out of problems. You just have to remember to look for the positive things and not focus on the negative.

Sample "3" Essay

The word "problem" is a negative word but its just an opportunity as Mr. Bob Maynard has said. It can be teaching tool besides.

For example, I had a problem with my son last year when he wanted a bigger allowance. I said no and he had to earn it. He mowed the lawn and in the fall he raked leaves. In the winter he shovelled the walk. After that he apreciated it more.

Its not the problem but the sollution that matters. My son learning the value of work and earning money. (It taught me the value of money to when I had to give him a bigger allowance!) After that he could get what he wanted at Toys Are Us and not have to beg. Which was better for me too. Sometimes we forget that both children and there parents can learn a lot from problems and we can teach our children the value of over-coming trouble. Which is as important as keeping them out of trouble. As well we can teach them the value of money. That is one aspect of a problem that we manytimes forget.

So problems are a good teaching tool as well as a good way to let you're children learn, to look at the silver lining behind every cloud.

Sample "1" Essay

I agree with the quote that problems are opportunities in disguise. Sometimes problems are opportunities, too.

I have a lot of problems like anyone else does. Sometimes there very difficult and I don't no how to handle them. When I have a really big problem, I sometimes ask my parents or freinds for advise. Sometimes they help, sometimes they don't, then I have to figure out how to handle it myself.

One time I had a big problem. Where someone stole my wallet and I had to get to a job interview. But I had no money and no ID. This happen in school. So I went to the principles office and reported it. He called the man I was supposed to interview with. Who

rescheduled the interview for me. So I still had the opportunity to interview and I'm proud to say I got the job. In fact I'm still working there!

Problems can be opportunities if you just look at them that way. Instead of the other way around.

761.
Sample "6" Essay

Courage and cowardice seem like absolutes. We are often quick to label other people, or ourselves, as either "brave" or "timid," "courageous" or "cowardly." However, one bright afternoon on a river deep in the wilds of the Ozark mountains, I learned that these qualities are as changeable as mercury.

During a cross-country drive, my friend Nina and I decided to stop at a campsite in Missouri and spend the afternoon on a boat trip down Big Piney River, 14 miles through the wilderness. We rented a canoe and paddled happily off. Things were fine for the first seven or eight miles. We gazed at the overhanging bluffs, commented on the dogwoods in bloom, and marveled at the clarity of the water. Then, in approaching Devil's Elbow, a bend in the river, the current suddenly swept us in toward the bank, under the low-hanging branches of a weeping willow. The canoe tipped over, and I was pulled under. My foot caught for just a few seconds on the willow's submerged roots, and just as I surfaced, I saw the canoe sweeping out, upright again, but empty. Nina was frantically swimming after it.

Standing by cravenly, I knew I should help, but I was petrified. I let my friend brave the treacherous rapids and haul the canoe back onto the gravel bar by herself. But then came the scream, and Nina dashed back into the water. In the bottom of the canoe, a black and brown, checkerboard-patterned copperhead snake lay coiled. I don't know exactly why, but the inborn terror of snakes is something that has passed me by completely. I actually find them rather charming in a scaly sort of way, but Nina was still screaming. In a calm way that must have seemed smug, I said, "We're in its home, it's not in ours." And gently, I prodded it with the oar until it reared up, slithered over the side of the canoe, and raced away.

Later that night, in our cozy, safe motel room, we agreed that we each had cold chills thinking about what might have happened. Still, I learned something important from the ordeal. I know that, had we encountered only the rapids, I might have come away ashamed, labeling myself a coward, and had we encountered only the snake, Nina might have done the same. I also know that neither of us will ever again be quite so apt to brand another person as lacking courage, because we will always know that just around the corner may be the snake or the bend in the river, or the figure in the shadows, or something else as yet unanticipated, that will cause our own blood to freeze.

Sample "4" Essay

Courage can be shown in many ways and by many kinds of people. One does not have to be rich, or educated, or even an adult to show true courage.

For example, a very heartbreaking thing happened in our family. It turned out all right but at the time it almost made us lose our faith. However, it also taught us a lesson regarding courage. In spite of his father's and my repeated warnings, my son Matt went ice-fishing with some friends and fell through the ice into the frigid water beneath. He is prone to do things that are dangerous no matter how many times he's told. Fortunately there were grown-ups near and they were able to throw him a life line and pull him to safety. However, when they got him onto shore they discovered he was unconscious. There

were vital signs but they were weak, the paramedics pronounced him in grave danger.

He is his little sisters (Nans) hero. He is 16 and she is 13, just at the age where she admires everything he does. When they took him to the hospital she insisted on going that night to see him, and she insisted on staying with me there. My husband thought we should insist she go home, but it was Christmas vacation for her so there was no real reason. So we talked it over and she stayed. She stayed every night for the whole week just to be by Matt's side. And when he woke up she was there. Her smiling face the was first thing he saw.

In spite of the fact she was just a child and it was frightning for her to be there beside her brother she loves so much, and had to wonder, every day if he would die, she stayed. So courage has many faces.

Sample "3" Essay

Courage is not something we are born with. It is something that we have to learn.

For example when your children are growing up you should teach them courage. Teach them to face lifes challanges and not to show there fear. For instance my father. Some people would say he was harsh, but back then I didnt think of it that way. One time he took me camping and I had a tent of my own. I wanted to crawl in with him but he said there was nothing to be afriad of. And I went to sleep sooner than I would have expect. He taught me not to be afriad.

There are many reasons for courage. In a war a solder has to be couragous and a mother has to be no less couragous if she is rasing a child alone and has to make a living. So, in me it is totally alright to be afriad as long as you face your fear. I have been greatful to him ever since that night.

Sometimes parents know what is best for there kids even if at the time it seems like a harsh thing. I learned not to show my fear that night, which is an important point to courage. In everyday life it is important to learn how to be strong. If we dont learn from our parents, like I did from my father, then we have to learn it after we grow up. But it is better to learn it, as a child. I have never been as afriad as I was that night, and I learned a valuble lesson from it.

Sample "1" Essay

Courage is important in a battle and also ordinary life. In a war if your buddy depends on you and you let him down he might die. Courage is also important in daly life. If you have sicknes in the family or if you encounter a mugger on the street you will need all the courage you can get. There are many dangers in life that only courage will see you through.

Once, my apartment was burglerised and they stole a TV and micro-wave. I didnt have very much. They took some money to. I felt afraid when I walked in and saw things moved or gone. But I call the police and waited for them inside my apartment which was brave and also some might say stupid! But the police came and took my statement and also later caught the guy. Another time my girlfreind and I were in my apartment and we looked out the window and there was somebody suspisious out in front. It turned out to be a false alarm but she was scard and she said because I was calm it made her feel better. So courage was important to me, in my relatinship with my girlfeind.

So courage is importand not only in war but also in life.

762.
Sample "6" Essay

Writing, at least the kind of basic composition needed to be successful in school, can be taught. The most important factor in teaching a basic composition class, which usually has students who have been less than successful writers in the past, is a simple one. The student should be asked to write about something interesting in a context with a purpose beyond English class. In other words, the student should *want* to learn to write. For students who have fallen behind for one reason or another, it's difficult to see a writing class as anything but an exercise in plummeting self-esteem. Many students believe that writing well is a mystery only those with talent can understand, and that English class is just something to endure. The first thing to teach students is that writing has a purpose that pertains to their lives. The teacher must appeal to emotion as well as to intellect.

I believe the best approach is to ask students to keep a journal in two parts. In one part, grammar and style shouldn't matter, the way they have to matter in the formal assignments that come later in the course. In this part of the journal, the students should be asked to keep track of things they encounter during the day that interest them or cause them to be happy, sad, angry, or afraid. In the second part of the journal they should keep track of subjects that make them sit up and take notice. These can include things that happen in class or ideas that come to them when reading an assignment for class. These journal notes should whet the intellect and excite curiosity.

For teaching grammar, the teacher can present exercises in the context of a one-page essay or story because it gives writing a context. Too often in the early grades, students complete dry drill and skill exercises that take the fun out of writing. Diagramming sentences, identifying nouns and verbs, or labeling adjectives seems far removed from the skill of writing. Appealing to emotion, intellect, and curiosity will really succeed in engaging the whole student and awakening the urge to write.

Sample "4" Essay

I believe writing can be taught if we work hard enough at it as teachers. The important thing is to teach students that it can be enjoyable. Years of fearing writing lie behind a lot of students, and it's one of the biggest stumbling blocks. But it can be gotten over.

Having them break up into small groups is one way to teach writing to reluctant or ill-prepared students. Have the students discuss a topic they are all interested in—say a recent TV show or an event coming up at school, then plan a paper and come back and discuss the idea with the whole class. Your next step can be to have them actually write the paper, then get into their small groups again and criticize what theyve done.

Another way for students who don't like the small groups is one on one conferences. But dont just talk about grammar or sentence structure or paragraphing, talk about the content of his paper. I did a summer internship teaching in an innter city school, and I rememmber one young man. He hated small groups so we talked privately. He had written a paper on going to a city-sponsered camping trip and seeing white-tailed deer, which was his first time. He was excited about it, and I suggested he write a paper about his experience. He did and, except for some trouble with grammar, it was an A paper, full of active verbs and telling detail!

Finally, try to get your students to read. If you have to, drag them to the community library yourself. Not only will it help their writing, it will help them in

life. Only by getting them interested in the written word and by helping them to see that it matters in their everyday lives can you really reach them and set them on the path of good writing.

Yes. Writing can be taught if you are willing to take the time and do the hard work and maybe give a few extra hours. No student is hopeless. And writing is so important in today's world that its worth the extra effort.

Sample "3" Essay

I dont think writing can be taught neccesarily, although if the students are half-way motivated anything's possible. The first thing is get them interested in the subject and give them alot of writing to do in class. They may not do it if it is all outside class as many poorly prepared students hate homework. I know I did as a kid!

Writing does not come natural for most people especially in the poorer school districs. Unless they are lucky enough to have parents who read to them. That is another aspect of teaching how to write. Assign alot of reading. If you don't read you can't write, and that is lacking in alot of students backgrounds. If your students wont' read books tell them to read comic books if nothing else. Anything to get them to read.

The second thing is to have the student come in for a conference once a week. That is one way to see what is going on with them in school and at home. A lot of kids in the poorer schools have conflict at home and that is why they fail. So give them alot of praise because thats what they need.

Finaly don't give up. It can be done. Many people born into poverty go on to do great things. You can help and you never know who you will inspire and who will remember you as the best teacher they ever had.

Sample "1" Essay

You will be able to tell I am one of the peopel that never learned to write well. I wish I had but my personal experience as a struggeling writer will inspire my students, thats the most I can hope for. Writing can be taught, but you have to be ready to inspire the student. Give them assignments on subjets they like and keep after them to read. Take them to the public libary if they havnt been and introduce them to books.

If you cant write people will call you dumb or stupid which hurts you're self-estem. I know from experience.

The next thing is have them come in and talk to you. You never know what is going on in there lifes that is keeping them from studying and doing there best.

Maybe they have a mom that works all the time or a dad who has left the home. Be sure to teach the whole person. Also have them write about what is going on in there lives, not a dry subject like the drinking age. Have the student write about there personal experience and it will come out better. Writing can be taught if the student is motivated. So hang in there.

Grade Yourself

The previous sample essays show you how the essay scoring guide works. For topics 763–782, simply use the scoring rubric on pages 181–182 to evaluate your essays.

7 ▶ Writing Boot Camp

We learn something by doing it. There is no other way.

—John Holt

REGARDING THE DEVELOPMENT of writing skills, the Greek philosopher Epictetus offered wise advice: "If you would be a reader, read; if a writer, write." One of the best ways to develop your writing skills to their fullest potential is to write on a consistent basis—at least five days a week. Because it is almost impossible to guess which topics are going to appear on a writing test or assignment, the best way to prepare for writing challenges is to master the essentials of brainstorming, outlining, writing a lead sentence, and writing powerful concluding paragraphs. The plain truth is that skillful writers do well on writing assignments and essay writing exams. If you wish to do well on writing exams, concentrate your energy on becoming a better writer by reading and writing consistently and asking for helpful feedback and pointers from teachers and professional writing tutors.

To help you reach your writing goals, this chapter contains specific advice for three main forms of writing: persuasive, expository, and narrative writing. A fourth form, literary analysis, is covered in the next chapter. In each section are writing prompts, helpful sidebars, writing models with which to compare and contrast your writing, and a scoring rubric.

Because it is impossible to predict the subject matter that will be presented on an essay-writing assignment or standardized examination, the key to success is to hone your critical thinking skills through consistent immersion in reading and writing activities such as the ones that are presented in this book.

This chapter provides you with a complete writing tool kit to help you excel on writing assignments. Within each section you will find models providing top-, middle-, and low-scoring writing examples that will help you grasp the key components of a successful essay. Carefully studying these models will help you become more proficient in identifying your own weaknesses and strengths.

A scoring rubric for each specific type of essay is also included in each section. After you complete each essay writing exercise, use the rubric to score your essay to see if you have scored the optimum score of 6. If you find that the majority of your content, development, organizing, and language scores are level 4 or lower, it is advisable that you rewrite your essay with the goal of improving on your areas of weakness.

The following writing guidelines will help maximize your writing practice:

- Schedule sufficient time for writing practice—a half hour to an hour, never less.
- Commit to a weekly writing prompt practice session.
- **Freewriting** is an effective method of warming up and generating ideas, because you must write as rapidly as you can without stopping to edit or censor your writing. First, select a writing prompt that strikes your fancy. Then, set a minute timer for ten minutes. Start writing anything and everything that relates to the writing prompt's main idea.

- Don't stop or try to correct mistakes—just keep freewriting until the timer starts buzzing!
- When you have finished freewriting, read over your work. If you like particular phrases or passages that you've written, consider using them in your first formal draft.
- After you have warmed up, write a formal response by focusing on the purpose of your essay. Ask yourself if you are being asked to define, persuade, compare and contrast, classify, illustrate, or narrate. Then brainstorm related ideas about your topic and decide which ideas will best help to support you in achieving your purpose.
- As you respond to your writing prompts, keep your target audience firmly in mind. Who will be reading your work?
- What works well when you are communicating with your friends on YouTube does not work in the middle school or high school classroom. When you are writing a formal essay, as you will be doing during these writing practices, it's advisable to leave your profanity, slang, and instant messaging lingo such as LOL (Internet shorthand for "laughing out loud") or LAWL (slang for "laughing a whole lot") at the door!
- Important factors to reflect upon before writing are audience gender, ethnicity, educational level, and occupation, as well as the audience's present knowledge of the subject.
- Remember, the concluding paragraph is the place to reinforce all of the most important ideas that you've presented—it's not the place to address a new subtopic. Repeat and then reinforce your main idea.
- The final sentence is as important as the lead sentence, so spend time crafting a powerful final sentence condensing the most important thoughts on your subject.

- **Revise. Revise. Revise.** Do not skip this important and necessary step!
- **Proofread** to be sure that your spelling and grammar are immaculate.

Word Bite: *Revising*

Revising is the process of editing and reworking the first rough draft. The revision process focuses on shaping and refining content and may require one draft or more.

Word Bite: *Proofreading*

Proofreading is the final step of the revision process, focusing on correcting spelling and grammatical errors.

Revision Checklist

- Is your title appropriate and not generic or boring? Does it entice the reader?
- Is your lead sentence appropriate? Does it introduce the main idea and provide a firm foundation for the sentences that follow it?
- Are your paragraphs uniform? Do all of the sentences in each paragraph relate to the topic sentence? Do you use a variety of sentence lengths?
- Did you elaborate on general ideas by providing details such as descriptions, examples, and explanations?
- Have you identified and eliminated any clichés?
- Are there any sentences that need to be shifted to a more appropriate paragraph or eliminated entirely?
- Does every sentence contain a subject and a predicate?
- Are your word choices as appropriate and precise as they could be? Have you looked up any words about which you were uncertain?

- Do your thoughts flow smoothly throughout the paper?
- Does your conclusion provide a final summary or judgment, or make a future prediction?
- Did you proofread manually?
- Did you run your word processor's spell-checker to check for spelling and punctuation errors?
- Did you read your paper aloud or have a friend or relative read it aloud to check for stilted phrasing, sentence fragments, and run-on sentences?
- Do all of the sentences in your essay relate to your main idea and topic?

▶ Persuasive Writing

Persuasive writing is a form of writing that is typically used in essays, advertising copywriting, sales letters, and newspaper editorials. A well-constructed persuasive essay hinges on the writer's ability to think logically and construct a bullet-proof argument built on factual information. Persuading readers to accept your argument is not an easy task, because you must provide enough proof to convince your fiercest opponents that your opinion is correct. While it is true that many arguments are won by appealing to a reader's emotions, facts obtained from reputable sources are an essential element. Presenting incorrect, weak, or misleading information will sabotage your attempts to sway readers to your point of view.

Presenting relevant examples that support your opinion is a good way to argue your case. For example, if you are arguing that your school's sports program needs to raise funds to purchase new equipment, you might want to compare and contrast examples of your school's antiquated sports equipment with the newer sports equipment provided by similar high schools in your area. Because you are comparing schools that are serving the same student population, your argument makes sense. However, if you were to use the example of the equipment provided by a Beverly Hills private school, your argument for new sports equipment would appear frivolous and unrealistic, because the budget of a posh private school in Beverly Hills can not be realistically compared to the budget of an average public school.

Get a Grip Reference Tip

Avoiding Bogus Blogs and Other Faulty Sources

Here are some essay types and the reputable reference sources the writers should use to find information to support their positions.

- crime statistics for a persuasive essay on criminal justice: the FBI's Internet site (www.fbi.gov/ucr/ucr.htm), which provides an annual crime report
- federal budget statistics for a persuasive essay arguing against raising taxes (www.whitehouse/gov)
- statistics and facts about heart disease for a persuasive essay against fat-filled cafeteria lunch menus or an expository essay on heart disease: American Heart Association (AHA) (www.americanheart.org)
- information on U.S. trade in the Asia-Pacific region for a narrative essay on the explosion of imported goods from China and Japan: the East-West Center (www.eastwestcenter.org)

Guidelines for Persuasive Writing

- **Speak out!** It's almost impossible to sway readers if you are not firmly convinced about your own beliefs, so take a strong and definite position and then support your perspective to the fullest.
- **Do your homework:** Before you start writing, be certain that you are knowledgeable about your topic and that none of your research information is outdated or inaccurate.
- **Three is the key:** After you have researched your topic, select three key points to support your argument, and focus separate paragraphs on each of those ideas by providing examples, facts, statistics, anecdotes, and other relevant information to sway your reader.
- **Make a prediction:** When writing a persuasive essay, it helps to predict the counterargument that will occur when someone reads your essay. Always show respect for opposing arguments by crafting a graceful and professional counterargument.
- **Keep it clean:** Don't use profanity or insults to make your point. A sharp wit and a good argument are your best defenses.
- **Bring it on home:** Before signing off, be sure to restate the most important points about your topic, and leave the reader with something to think about.

Get a Grip Research Tip

Wikipedia Wipeout

The Internet reference site, Wikipedia, is a fine place to get a speedy overview of your subject, but many instructors will not accept information that has been obtained from Wikipedia. Always check with your instructor before using information from this source.

Rubric for Persuasive Writing

SCORE	6 FOR A GRADE AT THIS LEVEL, YOUR WRITING:	5 FOR A GRADE AT THIS LEVEL, YOUR WRITING:	4 FOR A GRADE AT THIS LEVEL, YOUR WRITING:	3 FOR A GRADE AT THIS LEVEL, YOUR WRITING:	2 FOR A GRADE AT THIS LEVEL, YOUR WRITING:	1 FOR A GRADE AT THIS LEVEL, YOUR WRITING:
Content: Your written response shows an understanding and interpretation of the writing prompt.	■ satisfies the requirements of the writing prompt in a creative and original manner. ■ uses a clear thesis statement. ■ proves the thesis with insightful examples and details.	■ provides a thoughtful analysis of the writing prompt. ■ provides a clear thesis statement. ■ offers good examples to confirm the thesis statement.	■ meets some of the requirements of the prompt. ■ includes some key elements that help explain the thesis.	■ offers a simple interpretation of the writing prompt. ■ lacks a thesis from which to base the essay.	■ meets few of the requirements of the writing prompt. ■ discusses very basic ideas. ■ makes few connections to help explain the thesis.	■ minimally addresses the writing prompt. ■ digresses, repeats, or dwells on insignificant details throughout.
Development: Your written response gives a clear and logical explanation of ideas, using supporting material.	■ builds and elaborates thoroughly. ■ uses examples precisely. ■ develops the topic in an interesting and imaginative way. ■ demonstrates coherence in the development of ideas.	■ develops the topic in an acceptable way. ■ uses relevant examples throughout the essay. ■ develops ideas clearly and consistently.	■ answers the question in an abbreviated manner. ■ gives brief examples to explain ideas. ■ develops ideas somewhat inconsistently.	■ shows weakness in the development of ideas and/or develops ideas without thorough explanation.	■ contains inaccurate, vague, or repetitive details. ■ has limited development of ideas.	■ shows a lack of development of ideas.
Organization: Your written response shows a coherent, orderly, well-reasoned approach.	■ sets up and maintains a clear focus. ■ establishes a logical, rational sequence of ideas with transitional words and sentences.	■ has an obvious plan of organization. ■ focuses on the thesis statement. ■ uses appropriate devices and transitions.	■ has a general focus. ■ obviously attempts organization. ■ exhibits a logical sequence of ideas.	■ does not show a logical sense of organization. ■ strays from the topic. ■ can be difficult to follow.	■ shows an attempt to create a focus. ■ digresses from the topic. ■ is disorganized.	■ is less organized than a level 2 response. ■ exhibits no organizational pattern or focus.
Language Use/ Conventions: Your written response shows a sense of audience by using effective vocabulary and varied sentence structure.	■ has vivid language, fluidity, and a sense of engagement and voice. ■ has sophisticated style of sentence structure, sentence variety, and vocabulary. ■ has essentially no errors.	■ has good control of mechanics. ■ contains some errors when using sophisticated language. ■ has a slightly lower quality of sentence structure and sentence variety. ■ shows errors when using sophisticated vocabulary only.	■ has a sense of audience. ■ uses simple sentences. ■ uses an appropriate level of vocabulary. ■ demonstrates partial control of mechanics. ■ exhibits some errors that do not interfere with comprehension.	■ uses vocabulary that is slightly below level. ■ has a vague sense of audience. ■ shows a beginner's control of the language. ■ has errors that begin to interfere with comprehension.	■ exhibits little control of the language. ■ has errors that make comprehension difficult.	■ shows minimal control of language skills. ■ may be illegible or unrecognizable as English.

A ZERO PAPER is:
- ■ totally unrelated to the topic.
- ■ filled with illegible and indecipherable words.
- ■ incoherent with illogical or garbled syntax.
- ■ blank.

Use the persuasive writing prompts to write an essay for numbers 783–797. Each prompt has a model essay and two lower-scoring essays in the answer section that you can use to compare and contrast your writing. You can also use the Rubric for Persuasive Writing, included in this chapter, to give you an idea of the way your essay may be graded. If you have trouble interpreting the scoring guide, see a teacher or professor for help.

▶ Practice Questions

783. Many parents give children a weekly or monthly allowance regardless of their behavior because they believe an allowance teaches children to be financially responsible. Other parents give children an allowance only as a reward for completing chores or when they have behaved properly. Explain what you think parents should do and why.

784. More and more farmers and food manufacturers are genetically modifying their crops to reduce susceptibility to disease, improve flavor, and reduce costs. Do you think genetically modifying foods is a good idea? Why or why not? Use specific reasons and examples to support your position.

785. A few decades ago, many families had half a dozen or more children. Nowadays, more and more families are choosing to have only one or two children. Are smaller families better than larger ones? Why or why not? State your position and support it with specific reasons and examples.

786. Good habits improve our physical, emotional, and/or financial health. Select one of your good habits and write an essay persuading readers to make that habit a part of their lives.

787. Is there a book that you feel should be required reading for everyone? Write an essay persuading your audience to read this book.

788. Some people think of the United States as a nation of "couch potatoes." Write an essay persuading readers to be more physically active.

789. Nowadays, the private life of a politician is hardly private. In your opinion, should we be so concerned with the private life of a politician or political candidate? State your position and support it with specific reasons and examples.

790. Today's top professional athletes often have salaries and bonuses in the tens of millions of dollars. Do you think these athletes deserve such high compensation? Why or why not? Explain your position and use specific reasons and examples.

791. Is reading fiction a waste of time? Why or why not? Explain your answer using specific reasons and examples to support your position.

792. Some people think that school cafeterias should be required to provide low-fat and/or vegetarian lunch options to accommodate the eating habits of all students. Do you agree or disagree? Explain your position and use specific reasons and examples as support.

793. Many people feel that the use of surveillance cameras in public places, such as parking lots, is a good idea that can help ensure our safety. Others worry that too many cameras violate our right to privacy and give law enforcement officials too much power. In your opinion, should we install more surveillance cameras in public places? Why or why not? Support your position with specific reasons and examples.

794. Alexander Smith said, "The great man is the man who does a thing for the first time." Do you agree with this definition of greatness? Why or why not?

795. Should people lease or buy new cars? Make a case for the option that you think is better. Use specific reasons and examples to support your position.

796. The inventor and statesman Benjamin Franklin said, "Money never made a man happy yet, nor will it. There is nothing in its nature to produce happiness." Do you agree with this statement? Why or why not? Use specific reasons and examples to support your position.

797. Some states have now made it illegal to drive while talking on a handheld cell phone. Do you think this is a good law that should be passed in other states as well? Why or why not? Explain your answer.

▶ Expository Writing

Expository writing is writing that explains a concept or idea. You will most often use this writing style when you are writing research papers, process essays, definition essays, and technical instruction manuals. An expository essay might explain the steps that are needed in order to achieve a particular goal, such as applying for a job, or it might teach a skill, such as how to perform an Internet search for health information. Some writers will include chronologically numbered steps containing specific details and explanations, while others accompany their explanations with photographs or illustrations of each specific step.

Guidelines for Expository Writing

- Before committing one word to paper, decide on your audience and purpose: Who will be reading your paper? What are you trying to accomplish?
- Present your ideas and explanations or directions in an organized, clear, and precise manner.
- Add specific details and several topic-relevant examples to help the reader better understand the general topic. Remember to smooth the transition from your general statement to your specific example by using transitional phrases such as "to illustrate" or "an example of," but try not to cram too many of these phrases into your paragraphs. Choose your examples carefully. Providing one or two excellent examples is better than cramming your paragraph with three or four weak examples.
- Focus on explaining one specific step or concept at a time.

Rubric for Expository Writing

SCORE	6 FOR A GRADE AT THIS LEVEL, YOUR WRITING:	5 FOR A GRADE AT THIS LEVEL, YOUR WRITING:	4 FOR A GRADE AT THIS LEVEL, YOUR WRITING:	3 FOR A GRADE AT THIS LEVEL, YOUR WRITING:	2 FOR A GRADE AT THIS LEVEL, YOUR WRITING:	1 FOR A GRADE AT THIS LEVEL, YOUR WRITING:
Content: Your written response shows an understanding and interpretation of the writing prompt.	■ satisfies the requirements of the writing prompt in a creative and original manner. ■ uses an obvious theme throughout.	■ provides a thoughtful analysis of the writing prompt. ■ uses a clear theme throughout.	■ meets some of the requirements of the writing prompt. ■ includes some key elements that help explain the thesis.	■ offers a simple interpretation of the writing prompt. ■ lacks a theme.	■ meets few of the requirements of the writing prompt. ■ discusses very basic ideas. ■ makes few connections to help explain the thesis.	■ minimally addresses the writing prompt. ■ digresses, repeats, or dwells on insignificant details throughout.
Development: Your written response gives a clear and logical explanation of ideas, using supporting material.	■ builds and elaborates ideas thoroughly. ■ uses examples precisely. ■ develops the topic in an interesting and imaginative way. ■ demonstrates coherence in the development of ideas.	■ develops the topic in an acceptable way. ■ uses relevant examples throughout the essay. ■ develops ideas clearly and consistently.	■ answers the question in an abbreviated manner. ■ gives brief examples to explain ideas. ■ develops ideas somewhat inconsistently.	■ shows weakness in development of ideas and/or develops ideas without thorough explanation.	■ contains inaccurate, vague, or repetitive details. ■ has limited development of ideas.	■ shows a lack of development of ideas.
Organization: Your written response shows a coherent, orderly, well-reasoned approach.	■ sets up and maintains a clear focus. ■ establishes a logical, rational sequence of ideas with transitional words and sentences.	■ has an obvious plan of organization. ■ focuses on the thesis statement. ■ uses appropriate devices and transitions.	■ has a general focus. ■ obviously attempts organization. ■ exhibits a logical sequence of ideas.	■ does not show a logical sense of organization. ■ strays from the topic. ■ can be difficult to follow.	■ shows an attempt to create a focus. ■ digresses from the topic. ■ is disorganized.	■ is less organized than a level 2 response. ■ exhibits no organizational pattern or focus.
Conventions/ Language Use: Your written response shows a sense of audience by using effective vocabulary and varied sentence structure.	■ has vivid language, fluidity, and a sense of engagement and voice. ■ has sophisticated style of sentence structure, sentence variety, and vocabulary. ■ has essentially no errors.	■ has good control of mechanics. ■ contains some errors when using sophisticated language. ■ has a slightly lower quality of sentence structure and sentence variety. ■ shows errors when using sophisticated vocabulary only.	■ has a sense of audience. ■ uses simple sentences. ■ uses an appropriate level of vocabulary. ■ demonstrates partial control of mechanics. ■ exhibits some errors that do not interfere with comprehension.	■ uses vocabulary that is slightly below level. ■ has a vague sense of audience. ■ shows a beginner's control of the language. ■ has errors that begin to interfere with comprehension.	■ exhibits little control of the language. ■ has errors that make comprehension difficult.	■ shows minimal control of language skills. ■ may be illegible or unrecognizable as English.

A ZERO PAPER is:
■ totally unrelated to the topic.
■ filled with illegible and indecipherable words.
■ incoherent with illogical or garbled syntax.
■ blank.

- Proofread for errors in grammar, punctuation, and sentence structure.
- Proofread to be certain that necessary information or steps have not been omitted.
- Read your essay aloud to be certain that the language sounds natural and not forced or stilted.

Get a Grip
Proofreading Tip

Three Ways of Looking at an Essay

First, run the **spell-checker** on your word processor after completing a first draft or revision.

Second, **proofread manually** by folding a piece of paper in half and placing the folded edge directly under each sentence so that you can focus your undivided attention on one sentence at a time.

Third, when you are done proofreading manually, check for stiff and unnatural language and unnecessary words or phrases by **reading your paper aloud**, or ask a friend or relative to read your paper to you.

Use the expository writing prompts to write an essay for numbers 798–812. Each prompt has a model essay and two lower-scoring essays in the answer section that you can use to compare and contrast your writing. You can also use the Rubric for Expository Writing, included in this chapter, to give you an idea of the way your essay may be graded. If you have trouble interpreting the scoring guide, see a teacher or professor for help.

▶ Practice Questions

798. Explain the problems, both personal and societal, that result from obesity.

799. Describe the purposes of the Internet. Include various viewpoints, including those of users and providers.

800. Describe various styles of shoes as well as reasons for their popularity.

801. Math is a required subject. Explain why it is so important.

802. Describe a major environmental problem and what you believe should be done about it.

803. Describe how communication has changed in the past 20 years.

804. Discuss the events in the life of your favorite author, sports figure, or performer. Explain how these events relate to the person's achievements.

805. Explain the causes and effects of not voting in elections.

Get a Grip
Writing Tip

Don't Hardly Never Use No Double Negatives! These Word Divas Need to Shine Alone!

Using two negative describing words in a single phrase is wrong, plain wrong. The following negative words refuse to share star billing with their equally negative peers, so use only one of these at a time: *no, not, none, nothing, never, hardly, scarcely.*

806. Explain how to have a winning baseball team.

807. Explain how to choose the right college.

808. Your new job requires that you move to a different city. Describe the steps you will take to prepare for this move.

809. Many people spend a great deal of time with animals. Write about the relationships that people have with animals.

810. Describe an especially memorable photo or picture.

811. Write a letter to a teacher requesting information about a poor grade.

812. You want to organize a family reunion. Describe the steps you will take to contact people and to organize the event.

▶ Narrative Writing

When you are writing a **narrative** essay, you are telling a story that has a main idea or theme. To make your story interesting and realistic, you must include descriptive detail that will help the reader to visualize and experience the story as it unfolds. Create specific detail by appealing to the reader's five senses: sight, smell, taste, touch, and hearing. For example, if you are writing about a picnic, you might want to jot down details about how the food looked and smelled, the weather, and background sounds.

Avoid attaching vague labels to people, places, and things. For example, a reader can more easily visualize "a robin wrestling with a wiggling worm in its beak" than just "a bird." Because birds come in all shapes and sizes, if you simply write "a bird," the reader is left to figure out exactly what kind of bird you are discussing and what it is doing. Besides, the alliteration produced by "wrestling with a wiggling worm" may make the story more inviting to the reader's ear.

When you are organizing your essay, you have to make a decision about the order in which you will present your major ideas and information. **Chronological order** is used to write about events in time sequence from the past to the present, whereas reverse chronological order moves from the present to the past. **Space order** shifts the reader's attention from one space to another—from left to right, from top to bottom, from above to below, and so on. Space order is ideal for writing descriptions of landscapes, homes, people, and events.

Order of importance is a great way to capture the reader's attention and build suspense. It can be a helpful way to organize a science or technology paper, because starting off slowly prepares the reader for more complex concepts and ideas.

Get a Grip on Transitional Expressions

Here are signal words that help writers make smooth transitions when writing about events that have occurred in particular time sequences:

after	afterward	before	during
earlier	finally	first	immediately
later	next	soon	then
upon	when	while	

Rubric for Narrative Writing

SCORE	6 FOR A GRADE AT THIS LEVEL, YOUR WRITING:	5 FOR A GRADE AT THIS LEVEL, YOUR WRITING:	4 FOR A GRADE AT THIS LEVEL, YOUR WRITING:	3 FOR A GRADE AT THIS LEVEL, YOUR WRITING:	2 FOR A GRADE AT THIS LEVEL, YOUR WRITING:	1 FOR A GRADE AT THIS LEVEL, YOUR WRITING:
Content: Your written response shows an understanding and interpretation of the writing prompt.	■ satisfies the requirements of the writing prompt in a creative and original manner. ■ uses an obvious theme throughout.	■ provides a thoughtful analysis of the writing prompt. ■ uses a clear theme throughout.	■ meets some of the requirements of the writing prompt. ■ includes some key elements that help explain the thesis.	■ offers a simple interpretation of the writing prompt. ■ lacks a theme.	■ meets few of the requirements of the writing prompt. ■ discusses very basic ideas. ■ makes few connections to help explain the thesis.	■ minimally addresses the writing prompt. ■ digresses, repeats, or dwells on insignificant details throughout.
Development: Your written response gives a clear and logical explanation of ideas, using supporting material.	■ builds and elaborates ideas thoroughly. ■ uses examples precisely. ■ develops the topic in an interesting and imaginative way. ■ demonstrates coherence in the development of ideas.	■ develops the topic in an acceptable way. ■ uses relevant examples throughout the essay. ■ develops ideas clearly and consistently.	■ answers the question in an abbreviated manner. ■ gives brief examples to explain ideas.	■ shows weakness in development of ideas and/or develops ideas without thorough explanation.	■ contains inaccurate, vague, or repetitive details. ■ has limited development of ideas.	■ shows a lack of development of ideas.
Organization: Your written response shows a coherent, orderly, well-reasoned approach.	■ sets up and maintains a clear focus. ■ establishes a logical, rational sequence of ideas with transitional words and sentences.	■ has an obvious plan of organization. ■ focuses on the thesis statement. ■ uses appropriate devices and transitions.	■ has a general focus. ■ has an obvious attempt at organization. ■ exhibits a logical sequence of ideas.	■ does not show a logical sense of organization. ■ strays from the topic. ■ can be difficult to follow.	■ shows an attempt to create a focus. ■ digresses from the topic. ■ is disorganized.	■ is less organized than a level 2 response. ■ exhibits no organizational pattern or focus.
Conventions/ Language Use: Your written response shows a sense of audience by using effective vocabulary and varied sentence structure.	■ has vivid language, fluidity, and a sense of engagement and voice. ■ has sophisticated style of sentence structure, sentence variety, and vocabulary. ■ has essentially no errors.	■ has good control of mechanics. ■ contains some errors when using sophisticated language. ■ has a slightly lower quality of sentence structure and sentence variety. ■ shows errors when using sophisticated vocabulary only.	■ has a sense of audience. ■ uses simple sentences. ■ uses an appropriate level of vocabulary. ■ demonstrates partial control of mechanics. ■ exhibits some errors that do not interfere with comprehension.	■ uses vocabulary that is slightly below level. ■ has a vague sense of audience. ■ shows a beginner's control of the language. ■ has errors that begin to interfere with comprehension.	■ exhibits little control of the language. ■ has errors that make comprehension difficult.	■ shows minimal control of language skills. ■ may be illegible or unrecognizable as English.

A ZERO PAPER is:
■ totally unrelated to the topic.
■ filled with illegible and indecipherable words.
■ incoherent with illogical or garbled syntax.
■ blank.

Stale Is Bad.
Fresh Is Good.

Proverbs are time-tested nuggets of wisdom that will never go stale, because they add color and insight to your writing. But proverbs are not the same as **clichés** or **trite expressions**, which have become stale and dull due to overuse. Does the cliché *cold, cruel world* sound familiar to you? Because they are so universally recognizable, clichés can sometimes be used effectively to communicate an idea, but it's usually best to use your own words and phrases instead of relying on tried-and-true but possibly overused expressions. If you are using an expression or figure of speech that has been circulated as much as a library edition of the original Harry Potter novel, you just want to rethink your choice and dispense with the cliché!

Use the narrative writing prompts to write an essay for numbers 813–825. Each prompt has a model essay and two lower-scoring essays in the answer section that you can use to compare and contrast your writing. You can also use the Rubric for Narrative Writing, included in this chapter, to give you an idea of the way your essay may be graded. If you have trouble interpreting the scoring guide, see a teacher or professor for help.

▶ Practice Questions

813. People often say, "Don't judge a book by its cover." Describe a time when you misjudged someone based on his or her appearance or when someone misjudged you.

814. It has been said that the truth is often stranger than fiction. Describe an experience you had that was so strange others might think you made it up.

815. We all have things that we are afraid of, and sometimes we find ourselves in situations that force us to face our deepest fears. Tell about a time when you had to face one of your greatest fears.

816. Moving can be a very exciting but also difficult time in one's life. Tell about a time you moved and how it affected you.

817. As the saying goes, "If at first you don't succeed, try, try again." Describe a time when you persisted until you achieved your goal.

818. Movies and literature often deal with the theme of counting your blessings. Tell about an experience that led you to appreciate someone or something you'd taken for granted.

819. We are often surprised, even awed, by the experiences of our ancestors. Describe a time when you learned something important about your family history.

820. Most of us remember exactly where we were and what we were doing when we received shocking or important news. Tell the story of what you were doing when you heard about an important event and how that news affected you.

821. Many things can interfere with our plans. Sometimes an illness prevents us from doing something we really want to do. Describe a time when you became ill and missed out on doing something you'd really been looking forward to.

822. Many of our fondest memories are associated with food. Describe a memorable experience that took place while preparing or eating food.

823. Try as we might to avoid them, accidents happen. Tell about a time when you were involved in an accident.

824. Describe an experience you had that would be considered a near miss or a brush with disaster.

825. We all need help from others from time to time. Tell about a time you helped someone in need.

▶ Answers

Scoring Explanations for Persuasive Writing Essays

A score of "**6**" indicates that your essay satisfies the requirements of the writing prompt in a creative and original manner, using an obvious theme and thesis throughout. Your essay provides a clear and logical explanation of your ideas and uses supporting material precisely. You thoroughly articulate your ideas in a coherent fashion, use precise examples, and develop the topic in an interesting manner. Your essay is orderly and well reasoned, with a clear focus, a logical sequence of ideas, and transitional words and sentences. The essay demonstrates a sense of audience by using effective vocabulary, varied sentence structure, and fluid, sophisticated language that is essentially without errors.

A score of "**4**" indicates that your essay meets some of the requirements of the writing prompt, including some key elements that help explain the thesis. Your essay may answer the question in an abbreviated manner, giving only brief examples and developing ideas somewhat inconsistently. You give the essay a general focus, make an obvious attempt at organization, and present your ideas in a logical sequence. The language of your essay indicates a general control of mechanics but has a slightly lower quality of sentence structure and variety than a sample 6 score. An essay of this type contains errors only when using sophisticated language.

A score of "**1**" indicates that your essay only minimally addresses the writing prompt, digressing, repeating, or dwelling on insignificant details throughout. An essay on this level shows a lack of development and exhibits no organizational pattern or focus. Your writing may be illegible or unrecognizable as English.

Model Persuasive Writing Essays

783. Many parents give children a weekly or monthly allowance regardless of their behavior because they believe an allowance teaches children to be financially responsible. Other parents give children an allowance only as a reward for completing chores or when they have behaved properly. Explain what you think parents should do and why.

Sample 6 Score

Starting when I was about eight years old, my parents gave me a list of chores that had to be completed each week. If I did my chores, I got an allowance, a bit of change that I could use as I pleased. If I didn't do my chores, I didn't get my allowance. There was no other punishment, but no other punishment was necessary. That dollar or two a week was all the incentive I needed to help out around the house. Whether it was the latest Barbie or a six-pack of Hubba Bubba chewing gum, there was always something I wanted to buy. My parents could always count on me doing my chores.

I think that giving children an allowance for doing chores is a smart parenting move, for it accomplishes four important goals: It helps ensure that important work gets done around the house; it teaches children that they need to do their part to make things run smoothly for the whole family; it rewards children in a realistic, practical way for good behavior; and it helps teach children how to handle money.

I know that some people consider money for chores a form of bribery, and others feel that children should just do their chores anyway, without the incentive of an allowance. They argue that giving kids money for doing chores undermines the lesson that they need to help the family and do their part. I can understand that point of view, and when parents give

their children too much money, it does undermine those lessons. But when the allowance is small, it is simply a modern version of the age-old practice of rewarding good behavior. Once children reach a certain age, money is an appropriate and effective reward that helps them learn how to be responsible and how to manage money. They get a sense of what things are worth and how much they have to save and spend to get what they want. And learning to save in order to purchase a desired item teaches them patience and helps children better understand the value of hard work.

Giving children money for doing chores is also a good introduction to the reality of the workplace. If they do the work, they get paid; if they don't do the work, they don't. Extra work can be rewarded with bonuses and extra praise; poor work may result in a pay cut or demotion.

It's important for parents to find the right amount to give. Too much money may make a child feel like hired help and will undermine the goal of teaching children to help simply because they are part of a family that must work together. On the other hand, too little money may make a child feel resentful, as if his or her work isn't worth anything to the household. What's an appropriate amount? It depends on the amount of chores the child is expected to do and the child's age. If your nine-year-old is only expected to clean his or her room, a dollar a week is probably plenty. If your 14-year-old is expected to keep his room clean, take out the trash, water the plants, and vacuum the house, then ten dollars a week is more appropriate.

Being paid for my chores helped me have a good attitude about housework, taught me how to save money and spend it wisely, and enabled me to appreciate the hard work my parents did around the house. I'm really grateful that this was the way my parents chose to handle chores in our household.

Sample 4 Score

Should parents pay children for doing chores is a good question. My parents paid me, and my brothers and sister. I never liked doing chores, but getting an allowance each week (if I did my chores) made it not so bad. In fact, sometimes I did extra (like reorganizing the pantry) to get some extra money for something I really wanted.

I think having my allowance depend on my doing chores made me understand what it's like to work. In the "Real World," you don't get paid if you don't do your work. That's how it was in our house.

I also learned that it's hard work to keep a house going, I learned to appreciate all the hard work my mom and dad use to do. In addition, I learned how to save money. I would set aside my allowance to save up for something I wanted, like a new CD player or outfit.

In my opinion, parents should give an allowance for doing chores, but it shouldn't be too much. Children should know that they need to help no matter what. Too much money I think would make him or her feel like their hired help or something. Contrarily, too little money can make him or her feel like their help isn't worth anything to his or her parents. So finding the right amount is important.

In conclusion, giving children an allowance for doing household chores is a good idea. Children learn to work for their money and save what they earn.

Sample 1 Score

Many children they do not behave in properly, they should be punish, no getting reward. They should no be allowance anything. Chores is hard, on the contrary, there to learn for helping that's important. For the family. All to do the parts.

For me, it was vacuuming and the dusting. Every week, for Saturday or else. Forgetting the al-lowance, there wasn't. Only to be punish for what not to do.

Children should listen, to their parents. Its very important.

784. More and more farmers and food manufacturers are genetically modifying their crops to reduce susceptibility to disease, improve flavor, and reduce costs. Do you think genetically modifying foods is a good idea? Why or why not? Use specific reasons and examples to support your position.

Sample 6 Score

A few decades ago, manipulating genes in people, plants, and animals was just science fiction. Today, it's a reality, and genetic modification may have many positive applications in the future, including the eradication of many hereditary diseases. But like most scientific and technological advances, the genetic modification of organisms for our food supply can be as dangerous as it is beneficial. Because of the potential dangers of this technology, I think genetically altering plants and animals in the food supply is a practice that should be very tightly controlled and carefully studied before it is an accepted and common practice. Unfortunately, it may already be too late for that.

Many people don't even realize that many of their foods are genetically modified organisms (GMOs). GMOs are already prevalent in supermarkets and grocery stores across the country, but manufacturers are not required to label foods as having been made from GMOs. As a result, millions of Americans purchase and eat GMOs every day without even knowing it. Yet we don't even know if GMOs are harmful to our health. We don't really know how GMOs may affect our bodies or our ecosystem. When we mess with DNA, we may be making changes that have all sorts of dangerous repercussions, including some that we may not even realize for several generations.

One of the main concerns about GMOs is the unpredictability of the behavior of altered genes and of the bacteria, plants, and animals that interact with the altered organism. For example, a crop of corn genetically modified to be less susceptible to a particular insect may take on other unwanted characteristics due to the change. It may, for example, become more susceptible to another disease, or it could develop a tougher skin on its kernels, or it could decrease the crop's ability to produce vitamin E.

More frightening is the domino effect of genetically modifying foods. Any change in an organism's DNA has the potential to affect not only the organism but also anything that feeds off of it, including us. How do we know how GMOs might affect us on a microscopic, genetic level? We don't know, and can't know, without years of studies that track all sorts of potential outcomes over several generations.

Another fear is that transferred genes may escape from one organism into another. For example, imagine that strain A of sweet peas was altered by adding a gene that would increase its sugar production. Through cross-pollination, this altered genetic code could enter other strains and slowly (or quickly) infect the entire subspecies. If the alteration was beneficial, this could be a good thing. But the altered gene might not act the same way in all varieties, and the change may not be a good thing in the first place, and/or it may have unintended consequences.

Genetically modifying foods is a practice that has been driven by the desire to make more food available more quickly and more cheaply than ever before. This attitude puts profit first and consumers and the environment last, and that is simply dangerous. The agribusiness needs to slow down and stop selling us GMOs until their safety is certain.

Sample 4 Score

In my opinion GMOs (genetically modified organisms) are a bad thing. Because we don't know enough about them, and they could be dangerous, we don't even know it. There needs to be more studies done before we know for sure its safe.

For example, modified genes could jump from one GMO to another GMO. Another problem is we don't know what other effects a genetic modification might have. If you change a plant to produce more sugar or something that might make its fruit sweeter it might ruin something else in the plant.

We eat GMOs even though it may not say so on the label. I'm worried because we don't know how those GMOs might affect our bodies. Who knows? Technically these are new foods that no human being has ever eaten before. It may be a small change but it's a change and it could be dangerous.

I think there should be a lot of studies to determine the safety of GMOs and I think any food that has GMO in it should have a big "GMO" label on it. We should know what we're eating and how it might affect us.

Sample 1 Score

Do I think genetically modifying foods is a good idea? No. My idea, its bad. Could be very dangerous. We don't no, its genes an noone ever did this kind of thing before. What could be the affects? You changing the plant from its foundation. What are the other changes it could be? This is scaring for me.

I like eating healthy food like soy. These make me feel like I'm putting good in my body. GMOS these make me feel like I'm putting bad in my body. I worry who is the mad scientist.

785. A few decades ago, many families had half a dozen or more children. Nowadays, more and more families are choosing to have only one or two children. Are smaller families better than larger ones? Why or why not? State your position and support it with specific reasons and examples.

Sample 6 Score

I grew up in a large family—I am the oldest of six—and I have many wonderful memories from my childhood. I am very close to most of my siblings and I treasure my relationships with them. But when I have my own family someday, it won't be as big as the one I grew up in. As much as my large family was full of love, and as much as I learned about sharing, giving, and patience, I think having too many kids puts too much pressure on the parents and the oldest children.

When I think back on my childhood, I remember playing with my siblings or grandparents. I don't remember spending a whole lot of time with my mother and father. They were always around, but they were always busy. Although they did their best to spend some quality time with each of us, there was just too much to do to keep our large family going. My mother was always cooking, cleaning, nursing, changing a diaper, shopping, or taking someone to baseball practice or a playdate. She was always tired.

My father, on the other hand, was always working. He needed overtime whenever he could get it, and weekends were always full of projects around the house. He had lots of helpers, of course, but there are only so many things kids can do. Even when we were able to get away for vacation, Mom and Dad couldn't really relax, because there were so many kids to look after.

Money was also a constant worry for my family. With so many children, our budget was always tight.

Back-to-school shopping was always a stressful time; we all wanted the latest fashions, but we could get only a few things. My younger siblings wore hand-me-downs as much as they could. We shopped at bargain stores and often got clothes that we didn't really like because they were on sale. Our house always needed repairs, and there was never enough money to keep up with them.

Another problem with large families is that the older siblings always end up being babysitters. Like it or not (and most of the time I didn't like it), I had to watch my younger brothers and sisters. At age six, I could change a diaper like a pro. I was getting my brothers and sisters dressed, giving them breakfast, and helping them get ready for bed. I learned a lot about sharing, self-sacrifice, and responsibility at an early age, and these are important character traits that I value highly and want to instill in my children. But I also want to give them a chance to be children. I don't want them to have so much responsibility at such an early age.

I don't want to give the impression that I didn't have a happy childhood. I most definitely did; I was loved as much as my parents could love me, and I had wonderful fun with my brothers and sisters. But I always wanted a little more time with Mom and Dad, and I often resented having so much responsibility. I wished my mom wasn't always so tired and my dad didn't have to work so much. Because I want to be there more for my kids, because I want them to be kids throughout their childhood, I plan to have a much smaller family.

Sample 4 Score

These days, more and more families have only a couple of kids, whereas, a few decades ago, families were much bigger, with sometimes as many as ten kids in the family. I grew up in one of those big families (we have six kids, and I am the oldest). I had a great childhood, but based on my experience and my family's, I would say that it's better to have a smaller family.

One reason I say this is because I was the oldest, and I sure did a lot of babysitting. My mom was always asking me to watch the kids while she went to the store or took one of the other kids somewhere. I don't blame her, if I had that many kids I sure would need a helper, too. But lots of times I felt like it wasn't fair and I didn't get to do things with my friends because I had to watch my brothers and sisters. I also had to change a lot of diapers, too—and I mean a lot!

I also think smaller families are better for another reason: because my mom and dad were always working and tired. I guess if you have a whole lot of money, then it isn't such a problem. However, we didn't, and my dad was always working, while my mom was always working around the house or running us around somewhere. I wished I could have spent more time with them, too.

I really love my family and especially both of my parents. I did have a great childhood, but I think a smaller family is easier and better, especially for the oldest child.

Sample 1 Score

Are smaller families better than larger ones? This is a big question. I have a large family. There are six kids. I am the oldest children. I have three brothers and two sisters. My youngest brother is ten years younger than me.

My mom, she has 11 brothers and sisters. My dad, he has ten brothers and sisters. They live far away from us. My parents, they had good childhood but for them all it was a lot of work.

786. Good habits improve our physical, emotional, and/or financial health. Select one of your good habits and write an essay persuading readers to make that habit a part of their lives.

Sample 6 Score

When I was 15, I wanted to get a job so I could buy a car when I turned 16. My father sat me down at the kitchen table and said, "Excellent. But you can get a job on only one condition: 10% of every paycheck must go into a savings account. And you cannot touch that money except in an emergency."

"But Dad," I argued, "if I have to put 10% away, how will I ever save enough money to buy a car?"

"You'll have enough," he replied. "And you'll soon see how important it is to set money aside for savings."

I didn't believe him at the time, and in fact I often resented having to put that 10% in a separate account. But two years later when the transmission on my car blew, I didn't have to fret about coming up with the money for repairs. I was able to cover the cost easily and was back on the road in no time. It was then that I began to see the wisdom of my father's rule, which I adopted as my own. This habit has helped to give me a secure financial life, and I urge you to make this practice part of your life.

Ten percent of each paycheck may sound like a lot, and if you're on a tight budget to begin with, you might be thinking, "I just can't afford to do it." In truth, you can't afford *not* to do it. You never know when you are going to need an extra $100 or $1,000; life is full of surprises, and lots of them are expensive. You can afford to do this. In fact, you can't afford *not* to do this.

As tight as your budget may be, it's important to get started right away. If you are absolutely scraping by with every last penny going to bills, then start with just 5%, but move up to 10% as soon as you can. If you earn $500 a week, for example, put $25 to $50 in your savings account each week. At first, this may mean clipping coupons, renting a movie instead of going to the theater, or pressing your own shirts instead of taking them to the cleaner. Think carefully about ways you can save just a few dollars—because just a few dollars from each paycheck are all it takes to build up a solid savings account.

The money you save will add up quickly. For example, if your annual salary is $40,000, each year you would put $4,000 into your savings account. That still leaves you with $36,000 to cover all of your expenses. After ten years, you will have saved $40,000, plus interest. And the more money in your account, the more interest you earn, the larger your emergency fund, and the more you can afford to relax later in your life.

Once you get in the habit of putting 10% of your money into savings, it won't feel like a sacrifice. The 90% that's left will be your working budget, and you won't even miss that 10%, because you won't be used to spending it. Yet you will know that it is there, ready for an emergency, helping to keep you financially secure. So take my father's advice, and mine: Put a piece of each paycheck into your savings. It's a habit that's worth every penny.

Sample 4 Score

When I was 15, my dad helped me start a good habit that I still keep to this day, that is saving 10% of every paycheck. Whenever I get paid, I put 10% of that check into a savings account. I don't touch that money except for an emergency or special purchase.

I'm really grateful to my dad for helping me start this habit, though I wasn't at the time, because I wanted to buy a car and I didn't know how I could save up enough money if I didn't put it all to-

wards the car, but he was right, I did save enough, and then I had money for repairs because I'd saved carefully.

The great thing about this habit is, once you're in it, you don't feel like there's any money missing. You use the 90% to figure out your budget, not the 100%. In just one year you can save a whole lot of money.

You're probably thinking, like I did, "I can't afford to put some of my money away, I need it all." However, you're wrong. You can afford it, and you'll be glad because you'll always have money for an emergency. So get started today!

Sample 1 Score

Good habits improve our physical, emotional, and/or financial health. I have many good habit. One, is, I saving money every month. Another, is, I excersize everyday. Also, I am eating healthy. I also do not never use the bad language.

I am pride of my good habits. What habits do you do that are good for you? Save money like me, also excersize all the time, and eat healthy. It will be wise to do.

787. Is there a book that you feel should be required reading for everyone? Write an essay persuading your audience to read this book.

Sample 6 Score

Most people know who Frankenstein is—or at least they think they do. Because of the way Mary Shelley's brilliant 1818 novel has been adapted to film, most Americans think that Frankenstein is a towering, scar-faced monster who brings terror wherever he goes. In Shelley's novel, however, the real monster is Victor Frankenstein, the scientist who is the monster's creator. In her story of how Victor Frankenstein creates the monster and what he does after the monster comes to life, Shelley conveys several timeless messages about the dangers of science, the dangers of isolation, and the importance of being a good parent. It is a novel that everyone should read.

In the story, Frankenstein, eager for glory, wants to discover the "elixir of life" so that he can have the power to bring the dead back to life. He wants to create a new race of superhuman beings and wants them to worship him like a god. He wants to unlock the secrets of nature and use that power for his own selfish goals. Shelley's novel warns us that we must be careful what we do with science—how we apply the knowledge we discover. For when Frankenstein does discover the "elixir of life," and when he does create a superhuman being, he creates a creature that is beyond his control. The creature is more powerful and more intelligent than Victor Frankenstein, and the creature engineers Frankenstein's demise.

Shelley's novel also warns us about the dangers of isolation. Frankenstein's creation is so revolting and dangerous in part because Frankenstein works completely alone. He becomes so absorbed with his project that he completely blocks out family and friends. He stops communicating with others and works secretly; he does not consult others about his project, partly because he knows that what he is doing is wrong, and partly because he wants all the glory. But because he does not work with others and because he loses touch with his community of family and friends, he also loses touch with his responsibility to other human beings. When the creature comes to life, Frankenstein runs away, abandoning his creation even though he knows the creature might harm others.

This abandonment brings us to the novel's third timeless message: the importance of being a good parent. Frankenstein creates a living being and then abandons him because he is an "ugly wretch." He totally ignores his responsibility to the creature, who is born as innocent as a child, even though he is the size of a giant. The creature is abhorred by everyone he meets, and because no one has ever shown him love, he learns to hate. And the person he comes to hate most is the father who abandoned him. Shelley's message is clear: you are responsible for what you create, and if you are a parent, you must love your child, whatever his or her appearance.

In our age of cloning and genetic engineering, of scattered communities and neighbors who don't know each other's names, of abandoned children and abusive parents, Shelley's book may have more importance than ever. It is also a powerful and suspense-filled tale. Will Frankenstein capture the creature? Will he create a bride for the monster? Will Walton, the ship captain who records Frankenstein's story, learn from Frankenstein's tale? Find out for yourself. Grab a copy of this amazing novel and enjoy.

Sample 4 Score

Frankenstein isn't who most people think he is, which is the monster. The *real* Frankenstein is the scientist who brings the monster to life. You'd know this if you read one of the greatest novels ever written, Mary Shelley's *Frankenstein*, a book that I think everyone should read. This book is great because its suspensefull and teaches some important lessons, these lessons are maybe even more important to day than they were in Shelly's time. (Which was the 1800s.)

One lesson is about how to use science. Dr. Frankenstein in the story discovers how to bring a dead person back to life. But everything goes wrong after the creature wakes up. What was supposed to be a great thing that would bring Frankenstein all kinds of glory and make him like a master creator instead brought him and lots of other people all kinds of terrible horror. I think Mary is telling us to be very careful how we use science.

She also is telling us in this story to stay close to others. Frankenstein makes the creature all by himself. While he's working on the monster; he doesn't talk to anyone, no one in the university knows what on earth he's up to, he's got a big secret. He's so obsessed and he forgets to think about what will happen once this giant creature comes to life. He doesn't think about being responsible to and for the creature. Because he worked alone he forgot about that.

The third lesson is that we need to be good parents. Frankenstein is like the creature's father and mother. He created him, and he needs to take care of him. But he doesn't, he just runs away. That's when his horror begins, and the creature's, too. The poor creature is hated by everyone and his life is really sad.

Read this excellent book!

Sample 1 Score

Every school has required reading that all the kids are required to read for school. There are lots of different books on this list, I read some of them, some of them are good but I dont like them all.

One book that hard to read but I liked it, was, Frankenstien. The story of the monster. Frankenstin makes this monster out of dead body parts. Then he makes the monster come to life, through some secret way he doesn't tell anybody about. Then he runs away and gets attacked and becomes a killer because everyone hates him. Frankenstine, is a really good story.

788. Some people think of the United States as a nation of "couch potatoes." Write an essay persuading readers to be more physically active.

Sample 6 Score

Is your favorite place in the home sitting on the couch in front of the television? Do you spend hours and hours there each day, surrounded by bags of chips and cans of soda? Do you panic when you can't find the remote control and think that you might actually have to get up off of the sofa to change the channel?

If you answered "yes" to any of these questions, you are not alone. In fact, you are one of the millions of Americans who are "couch potatoes": people who spend their days and nights "vegging out" in front of the "tube."

Well, spud, it's time to get up out of that armchair and get some exercise!

I know how seductive television can be. I know how easy it is to plop onto the sofa and lose yourself in the world of sports, reality shows, and good old make-believe. I know how mesmerizing MTV and other channels can be and how hard it can be to pull yourself away. But all that television spells disaster for your body, because it needs to be active to be healthy. And it's no good for your mental health or social life, either.

Think about what all that time in front of the television is doing to your body. Think about what all that sagging muscle and growing belly is doing to your life. Think about how your lack of energy affects you at work.

Now think about how different things would be if you spent some of that TV time getting exercise instead: You would feel better during the day. You would sleep better at night. You would have more energy. You would look better. You would have more confidence. You would be more creative. You would be healthier and happier. And you would not even miss the television.

What sort of exercise can you do? Anything! Go for a walk. Ride a bike. Jog. Lift weights. Take an aerobics class. Do yoga. Join a basketball or hockey league. Swim. Rollerblade. Grab a friend, a fellow couch potato, and exercise together.

You can start with just 15 minutes a day, two or three days a week, and build up slowly. Before you know it, your couch potato days will be over, and you will wonder how on Earth you ever spent so much time in front of the TV.

Sample 4 Score

Americans everywhere are "couch potatoes." These are people who just sit in front of the TV all day and night. They spend so much time on the couch they're almost becoming part of the couch. They don't ever want to get up to change the channel, so the remote control is like a part of their hand. Is that what you're like? Do you spend too much time in front of the TV? Well, it's time to stop being a couch potato. You need to take care of your body. It's time for you to get up and get some excercise.

If you lay around all day, think of how that's just not good for you. It's not healthy. You need to get excercise to be healthy. Physical activity at least three times a week will get you back in shape. It will help you have a healthy heart, better sleep, and less likely to get sick and diseases because your immune system will be stronger. Furthermore, you'll have more energy and just feel better. This is especially good for you at work. In addition, you'll be more confident because you will look better and fit into nicer clothes. When you feel better about yourself, you're happier.

Its easy to get excercise. You can do some jumping jacks or jog or play tennis. Even just walking to the store instead of driving can help. Maybe you could join a gym or a sports team, like a basketball team in your neighborhood. Or ask a friend whose also a couch potato to excercise with you. Its easier when you have someone to excercise with.

So do yourself a favor, stop spending so much time in front of the TV! You'll be proud when your days as a couch potato are over.

Sample 1 Score

For some people's thinking, there are to many "couch potatos", all across the American country. There are lying on there couchs all the time, doing nothing. Except watching the TV all the time. Whereas they not getting any excersizing, not anything at all. Theres so much to do, like jogging or walking or tennis instead.

The couch potatos, they should not be just on the couch, but also excersizing. Think about being this like a potato. Is not a good thing! Instead, to be like a lion or strong like a bull.

789. Nowadays, the private life of a politician is hardly private. In your opinion, should we be so concerned with the private life of a politician or political candidate? State your position and support it with specific reasons and examples.

Sample 6 Score

When you think of former president Bill Clinton, what's the first thing that comes to mind? Unfortunately, for many people, the first thing they think of is Monica Lewinsky. Like millions of people around the globe, I was horrified by how much the investigation delved into Mr. Clinton's private life. No one needed to know the sort of details that were revealed by Ken Starr's investigation. But while I don't want to know the details, I do believe we have a right to know what sort of lives our politicians are living. I believe their behavior in private is a reflection of their true values and how they will behave in office.

For example, if a politician lies to his or her spouse (I'm talking about big lies, like infidelity, not little white lies), that tells us something about his or her character. In my opinion, this person is not to be trusted. I wouldn't have faith that this politician would keep his or her word. True, the relationship between a husband and wife is very different from that between a politician and his or her constituents. But the politician's respect for that relationship and how he or she deals with any problems in that relationship reflect his or her level of integrity.

Similarly, if a politician (or political candidate) behaves in an illegal manner, that shows a disrespect for the law. A government official who employs an illegal alien as a nanny or housekeeper, for example, or pays a nanny or housekeeper under the table to avoid taxes is acting as if he or she is above the law—or demonstrating that he or she simply doesn't care about the law. This is not the kind of person I want in a public office.

On the other hand, if a politician leads a respectable, law-abiding life at home, we can expect a respectable, law-abiding performance in office. A politician who deals honestly with family, friends, and business associates is likely to deal honestly with his or her constituents as well. A politician who respects the law in all aspects of his or her private life is likely to respect the law while in office, too. A candidate who behaves in a cautious, reserved manner regarding his or her personal affairs is likely to bring a similar approach to the office.

I know that nobody is perfect and that every politician may have skeletons in the closet. I'm not talking about transgressions from the distant past. But I am concerned with a politician's recent past and current behavior. Is he or she honest or does he or she break promises? Does he or she behave recklessly or in a thoughtful and controlled manner? We cannot separate who we are personally from who we are professionally. That is why I believe the public has a right to know.

Sample 4 Score

Politicians live very public lives. If their big politicians (like the president, for example), they don't really have any privacy. Everybody knows everything they

do. This probably bothers some people, however, I actually think that is a very good thing. I think we need to know what politicians are really like. How they are at home (in private) tells us about how they will be in the office.

It's true that we are different at home and in the office. However, we're still the same person. In other words, we will pretty much act the same, on the same values and principals, whether we're at home or in the office. If we would steal or lie at home, we would probably steal or lie in the office. So, if a politician lies to his wife, for example, or to her business partners, then we can probably expect them to lie to the people who elected them.

On the contrary, if a politician lives an honest life and always obeys the law. We can probably expect them to behave honestly and lawfully when they are in office. Because like I started to say before, you can't separate home and work. We're the same person in both places.

So, in conclusion, it's a good idea to have knowledge about politician's private affairs. They probably don't like it and want things to be private. However, since they are our elected officials, they have to be public, unfortunately for them about almost everything.

Sample 1 Score

The politicians, they have privacy in there homes. For them too much is knowed about everything what they is doing. This is bad; for them. Whereas, knowing the public are a very good thing for us. If lying and stealing there, also here. Don't you agree? It is clear. If they are a liar at home, we will be lying to also. So therefore, in my opinion, "we should be so concerned with the private life of a politician or political candidate."

790. Today's top professional athletes often have salaries and bonuses in the tens of millions of dollars. Do you think these athletes deserve such high compensation? Why or why not? Explain your position and use specific reasons and examples.

Sample 6 Score

When he was at the height of his basketball career, Michael Jordan was making approximately $300,000 per game. That's more than most people make in a year; indeed, it's more than some people earn in a lifetime. Yes, Michael Jordan was a phenomenal basketball player. Yes, he was also a fantastic role model. But no, he did not deserve to earn such a ridiculously high salary. Jordan, like many other top professional athletes, was grossly overpaid.

Why do top athletes earn such inflated salaries? Because they bring big bucks into their cities and franchises. But what sort of service do they provide to society? Do they save lives? No. Do they improve the standard of living or promote positive social change? No. Do they help keep our streets safe or educate our kids? No. True, many of the top athletes are good role models for our children. But seven-figure salaries don't always mean model behavior. Take NBA star Latrell Spreewell, for example, who choked and threatened to kill his coach.

It is true that professional athletes work hard, and many have spent their lives pursuing their goals. It is also true that most professional athletes have a relatively short career span—a decade perhaps at the top of their game. Limited as their professional sporting career may be, they don't deserve such high salaries. After their professional sports careers are over, they can certainly pursue other careers and work regular jobs like the rest of us. Ending their stints as professional athletes doesn't mean they have to stop earning incomes. They just

have to earn incomes in a different way. Why should they be any different from the rest of us who may need to switch careers?

It is also true that professional athletes may be injured while on the job; their work is indeed physical, and especially in contact sports like football, injuries are bound to happen. But, like the rest of us, they have insurance, and in nearly all cases, their exorbitant salaries more than cover their medical costs. And theirs is not the only high-risk job. What about miners, construction workers, or firefighters? They are at risk for physical injury every day, too—injuries that could likewise end their careers. But they sure aren't earning millions of dollars a year.

It is also true that professional athletes may spend years and years practicing with farm teams for a fraction of the salary they receive once they make it to the top. But in every career path, we start off with lower wages and must pay our dues and work our way up. Besides, farm team salaries are not always so low.

We're a sports-crazy country, a nation of fanatic sports fans and celebrity worshippers. We're awed and entertained by the best of them—the Michael Jordans, the Alex Rodriguezes, the Emmitt Smiths. But as much as they may inspire and entertain us, professional athletes do not deserve such high salaries. Those millions could be much more wisely spent.

Sample 4 Score

Do athletes get paid too much? You bet. That's my opinion.

Professional athletes, what do they do with all that money? Imagine Michael Jordan earning $300,000 per game! Plus all his money from Nike and other advertising. I think that money can be put to much better use in this country.

Professional athletes should get good salaries, but not the millions like they get now. It's just too much. Their job isn't dangerous, except maybe for football or ice hockey where it's easy to get a bad injury. It's easy to get a bad injury in lots of other jobs, too, like construction, but they don't get millions of dollars. I guess, the difference is that nobody likes to watch construction workers. There's fun in the game and people like the competition, sports teams bring lots of money into a city's economy.

If professional athletes could guarantee they'd also be a good role model for kids, then maybe they could have such high salaries. Because they'd be doing something good for society since so many kids are watching. For now though, it's too much.

Sample 1 Score

Today the athleets so much money. Millions an millions of the dollars. They playing baseball, basketball; football, even for golf. This is the not of the dangerous sport, even less than many of the others.

The money, it's too much, giving mine opinon. For the teems and the citys its so much there's else to pay for with the money, like homelessness. This is the need to be changed.

791. Is reading fiction a waste of time? Why or why not? Explain your answer using specific reasons and examples to support your position.

Sample 6 Score

Remember the last book that captured your imagination, that transported you to another place and time? Remember a book that made you fall in love with its characters, made you feel their pain and joy? Remember a story that taught you an important lesson, that helped you better understand others, or that helped you make sense of the human condition? If so, then you can understand why the question "Is reading fiction a waste of time?" is such a silly question.

Fiction, unlike a user manual, a magazine article, or a newspaper editorial, probably won't offer you any practical knowledge that you can put to immediate use. It won't inform you of current events or give you advice on how to cultivate a better garden. It probably won't help you decide which candidate to vote for or which product to buy. But that certainly doesn't mean it's useless or impractical. Indeed, fiction serves three important functions for human beings: It helps us be more compassionate to others, it helps us better understand ourselves, and it cultivates our imaginations. It can also teach us about history, psychology, even biology and other sciences.

Compassion for others is rooted in understanding and acceptance, and a good story brings us into the inner world of its characters so that we can understand them. In Toni Morrison's novel *The Bluest Eye*, for example, Morrison peels away the layers of her characters' histories piece by piece like an onion until we see into their core and understand what drives them. They may still do awful things to each other, but she shows us why they do the things that they do, and we learn that we shouldn't judge others until we understand their pasts. Their stories are sad and painful, and we learn to love even the outcast Pecola. In fact, we learn that those outcasts are the ones who need our love the most.

Many stories and novels also help us better understand ourselves. Joseph Conrad's dark and powerful novel *Heart of Darkness* helps us see that all of us have a dark side, and that we need to acknowledge this dark side in order to control it. It makes us question just how civilized we are and indeed what it means to be civilized in the first place.

Good fiction also cultivates our imagination, which is more important to us than some might think. Without imagination, we live a sad, empty life.

Imagination is central to our emotional health and is a key factor in our level of intelligence. Facts are one thing; but facts can be of no real use unless coupled with imagination. Fiction can help us by keeping our imaginations fresh and active. In a story like Franz Kafka's "Metamorphosis," for example, we are asked to imagine that Gregor, the main character, wakes up one morning and has turned into a giant bug. Crazy? Perhaps. But once we accept this premise and imagine Gregor as a five-foot-long cockroach, we can feel his family's horror and imagine his agony as he finds himself trapped in his room and abandoned by those he loves.

Is reading fiction a waste of time? That's like asking if laughing is a waste of time. We don't need fiction to survive, but we do need it to be kinder, more understanding, and more creative human beings.

Sample 4 Score

Is reading fiction a waste of time? I am surprised by this question. I never thought of it as a waste of time. I understand that it is not practical like reading a "how-to" article or something like that. However, on the other hand, it is good for you. I think it helps you have a good imagination and be a better person.

I think fiction helps you be a better person because it helps you understand people. Lots of stories help you understand why people do what they do. For example, in *The Bluest Eye*, at the end of the story we understand why the people do the things that they do. We judge the characters right away but then we learn about them and maybe change our judgment. The book was written by Toni Morrison.

Second, I think fiction also helps you understand yourself. Some stories help us see that we all have a good side and a dark side within. Fiction can also help us have a good imagination, and this is important in helping us be creative. Being creative can

help you better solve problems and think of original things.

I love reading fiction, and I never think it is a waste of time. It may not be practical, like reading the newspaper, however it is a lot more fun and helps me be a better person.

Sample 1 Score

Is reading fiction a waste of time? is a question. How is the answer? Like you and me, wondering, is fun things a waste of time too, or only do the practical what you should? These be important questions. What the answer?

In my opinion, no way, Jose! It fun to read fiction stories. Its like imagenation, cool things.

So don't beleive it. Say who! Reading fiction ain't wasting time. In my opinion.

792. Some people think that school cafeterias should be required to provide low-fat and/or vegetarian lunch options to accommodate the eating habits of all students. Do you agree or disagree? Explain your position and use specific reasons and examples as support.

Sample 6 Score

It's a fact: There are students across the United States who are vegetarian and/or health conscious, and school cafeterias should be required to provide low-fat and/or vegetarian lunch options for them. Even more importantly, many teenagers' dietary decisions are based not only on health concerns but also on religious and/or moral issues. In this day and age, an individual's eating habits often reflect his or her identity. For these reasons, it's imperative that each school's cafeteria menu be as diverse as its student body.

Just by reading headlines in any of the major news magazines, it becomes clear that the United

States is a nation that needs to slim down. In every town and city, there is an abundance of fast-food restaurants that lure teenage customers with fast, inexpensive, and tasty food, but these foods are typically unhealthy. Unfortunately, school cafeterias, in an effort to provide food that is appetizing to young people, mimic fast-food menus, often serving items such as burgers and fries, pizza, hot dogs, and fried chicken. While these foods do provide some nutritional value, they are relatively high in fat, and many of them, namely burgers, hot dogs, and fried chicken, are clearly not designed for vegetarians.

Many of the lunch selections currently offered by most school cafeterias could be made vegetarian and/or more healthy with a few simple and inexpensive substitutions. Veggie burgers, for example, offered alongside beef burgers would give both vegetarians and the health conscious more options. A salad bar would also serve the dual purpose of providing both vegetarians and low-fat food eaters the opportunity for a satisfying meal. This is not to say that accommodating every desire or food preference is plausible, but students should have the right to be served foods that coincide with their life choices.

Sample 4 Score

In the United States there are many people who are vegetarian. In addition, there are people who choose to eat low-fat foods, either to lose weight or to stay healthy. Many of these people are students who eat lunch at their school cafeterias on a daily basis. Surprisingly though, school cafeterias are not required to provide low-fat nor vegetarian options for students.

Unfortunately, vegetarian options may be limited to the french fries (served with burgers) or pizza. While these are vegetarian (non-meat) options, they do not necesarily serve as low-fat foods. I think schools should have a wider variety of low-fat and/or

vegetarian options such as a salad bar, or perhaps even something with tofu.

While cafeterias can't meet all the demands of students, it is important to offer those commited to a healthy or vegetarian lifestyle the choice. Schools should create a menu that offers these options for all students.

Sample 1 Score

Lot's of people are overwait and even fat, and the other people are vegetaran who dont eat meat. The food at schools are bad enouf and then why should they hafe to have stuff that those people like. School's shoudl have good food and meat, but not fat food for everyone.

793. Many people feel that the use of surveillance cameras in public places, such as parking lots, is a good idea that can help ensure our safety. Others worry that too many cameras violate our right to privacy and give law enforcement officials too much power. In your opinion, should we install more surveillance cameras in public places? Why or why not? Support your position with specific reasons and examples.

Sample 6 Score

Not long ago, the nation was gripped by the horrifying news that a baby had been stolen from a car in a parking lot while her mother, who was returning a shopping cart, was just a few feet away. Thanks to the description of the kidnapper captured by surveillance cameras in the parking lot and broadcast over radios, television, and highway overpass signs, the kidnapper was quickly caught and the baby returned, unharmed, to her mother. Had it not been for those surveillance cameras, that mother would probably never have seen her baby girl again.

I can't think of a much better argument for the use of surveillance cameras in public places. That baby's life was saved by those parking lot cameras.

Many people worry about the use of surveillance cameras in public places such as parking lots, stores, parks, and roadways. They don't like the idea that they are being watched. They worry that the information captured on the surveillance tapes can somehow be used against them. But how? It seems to me that the only reason we should worry about being caught on surveillance cameras is if we are doing something wrong. If we are behaving lawfully in a public place, then why worry if it is captured on film?

Surveillance cameras can provide two immensely important services. One, they can help us find those who commit crimes, including thieves, kidnappers, vandals, and even murderers. Two, they can serve as a powerful deterrent to crime. A thief who plans to steal a car may think twice if he knows he will be caught on video. A woman who hopes to kidnap a child may abandon her plans if she knows she will be captured on film.

Surveillance cameras can also help us in less critical but nonetheless practical ways. In some towns in England, for example, radio deejays use information from surveillance cameras to announce the availability of parking spaces in crowded public parking lots. Problems of all shapes and sizes can also be noted and addressed through video surveillance. For example, imagine a video camera installed in a local town square. Reviewing the films, officials might realize that people who meet in the square move quickly into the shade of the one tree in the center of the square. This could move officials to plant more trees or provide tables with umbrellas so that people could meet and relax in the shade. Similarly, a video camera in a grocery store might reveal that aisle 7 is always overcrowded, prompting the manager to rearrange items to more evenly distribute shoppers.

Of course it's possible to have too much of a good thing, and if surveillance cameras cross the line and start being installed on private property—that is, in our offices and homes—then we will have the "Big Brother is watching" scenario opponents fear. If that were the case, I would be against surveillance cameras, too. But as long as surveillance cameras are limited to public places, they can help ensure our safety.

Sample 4 Score

Many public places now have surveillance cameras, the main reason being to ensure safety. I think this is a good idea, and that more places should have them.

Surveillance cameras are a good thing because they help keep us safe. If people know they might be on video then, they probably won't do something bad or against the law, like stealing. This is a big protection for us. It makes me feel safer, especially like in a parking lot in the night time. The other good thing about surveillance cameras, is that they can help us catch someone who does do something bad. For example, stealing a car in a parking lot. The camera can get a good picture of the thief and the police will have a good description of the person who stole the car. That makes it a lot easier to catch the thief.

I think surveillance cameras can also be used for other good things, like helping fix traffic jams in grocery stores. I mean if you can see that people are always crowding in one isle, for example.

I know that some people are upset about this kind of thing (being on film) and think that it's like "Big Brother is watching," or something. Also, some people just don't like being on cameras. However, if you're not doing anything wrong, it shouldn't matter. Their only for finding people who do things wrong. To me, I think that makes a lot of sense.

Sample 1 Score

In my opinion, should we install more surveillance cameras in public places? I think, "yes," is a good idea. Why or why not? In my opinion, it is for making ensured the safety in places such as parking lots. This is what our right to privacy can do and tell the law enforcement officials and government too.

794. Alexander Smith said, "The great man is the man who does a thing for the first time." Do you agree with this definition of greatness? Why or why not?

Sample 6 Score

Just as there are many definitions of success, there are also many definitions of greatness. Alexander Smith said that a great person is someone who does a thing for the first time. He's right, and the list of those great people is long and includes the likes of Neil Armstrong, Jackie Robinson, and Thomas Edison. But Smith's definition isn't broad enough to include many other people who I believe are also great. In my opinion, greatness can also be attained by doing something to improve the lives of others.

Mother Teresa is the first person to come to mind under this broadened definition. Mother Teresa, who received the Nobel Peace Prize in 1979, dedicated her life to helping the poor, the sick, and the hungry. She left her homeland of Yugoslavia to work with the impoverished people of India, where she selflessly served others for almost 70 years. She became a nun and founded the Missionaries of Charity sisterhood and the House for the Dying. She embraced those that many in society chose to disdain and ignore: the crippled and diseased, the homeless and helpless. She gave them food, shelter, medical care, and the compassion that so many others denied them. She was certainly not the first to dedicate her life to the care of others, but she was certainly a great woman.

Another great person who also won a Nobel Peace Prize was Dr. Albert Schweitzer, a German doctor who, like Mother Teresa, also selflessly served the poor and sick. Schweitzer dedicated himself to the people of Africa. There, he built a hospital and a leper colony, a refuge for those who had been rejected by society. Again, he was not the first to offer care and comfort for the sick and suffering. But he certainly was great.

Harriet Tubman is also clearly a great woman. She led hundreds of American slaves to freedom along the underground railroad, risking her life over and over again to bring her fellow slaves to freedom. She gave them the greatest gift one can offer: freedom to live a better way of life. She wasn't the first to escape, and she wasn't the first to go back for others. But she was the one who kept going back. She knew that each time she returned for another, she was risking her life. But like Mother Teresa and Dr. Schweitzer, Harriet Tubman was utterly dedicated to improving the lives of others.

Greatness comes in many forms, and we are lucky to have many examples of greatness upon which to model our lives. Some great people are those who were able to be the first to accomplish something marvelous. Others, like Mother Teresa, Albert Schweitzer, and Harriet Tubman, are great because they worked tirelessly to ease the suffering of their fellow human beings.

Sample 4 Score

According to Alexander Smith, "The great man is the man who does a thing for the first time." In my opinion, this is a good definition, but it is also too narrow. By that I mean that it is not broad enough to include lots of other people that I believe are great. There are many people who didn't necessarily do anything for the first time who have done great things.

One example was Mother Teresa. Another is Albert Schweitzer, and a third is Harriet Tubman.

Albert Schweitzer opened up a hospital and leper colony in Africa to take care of the sick and abandoned people who had no money or access to health care. This was a great thing. Without his hospital, people would die or suffer and be outcast by society.

Harriet Tubman is famous for being a woman who kept going back to the South to free slaves. She led them through the "underground railroad" and brought them to freedom. She wasn't the first to escape or help others escape, but she was great because she kept doing it and kept helping others.

Finally, Mother Teresa helped so many people. She went to India and opened up a place for the sick and the dying to be taken care of. She helped to feed and comfort hungry and sick people, thousands of them. She is what it means, to be compassionate towards others.

All three of these people and lots of others like them are great for what they did to help others.

Sample 1 Score

What does it mean, to be great. Alexander Smith say that "The great man is the man who does a thing for the first time." I know a lot of great men, the list can be long: George Washington, Robert Kennedy, Mother Teresa, Harriet Tubman, Beethoven, Jackie Robinson, Reggie Jackson (I like baseball), Martin Luther King, and etc. the list goes on and on.

To be great is not an easy thing. Having to do something for the first time, or doing something else that is great. You can be leading others or helping them. In fact not everyone who does this is great.

795. Should people lease or buy new cars? Make a case for the option that you think is better. Use specific reasons and examples to support your position.

Sample 6 Score

Planning to lease a car because you don't think you can afford to buy? Think again. Leasing can end up being just as expensive as buying—and you don't even get to keep the car. Even if you decide to buy the car at the end of your lease, you may end up paying considerably more money than if you'd decided to buy from the beginning.

Most people who are thinking about leasing are attracted to this option because they believe it will cost them less money. And they're right—it is cheaper, but only in the short term. For example, if you were to lease a new Subaru Forester, with $2,500 down, you might pay $250 per month for the car. If you were to buy the same car, with $2,500 down, you would pay closer to $350 per month. Over a three-year lease, that's $3,600—a big savings. But after your lease is over, you'll have to give the car back. If you want to keep driving, you'll either have to put another down payment on another lease, or, if you have the option to buy the car, you'll have to pay thousands of dollars to purchase the vehicle—dollars that won't be spread out in more manageable monthly payments.

Many people want to lease because they can then drive a nicer car than they might otherwise be able to afford. For example, if your monthly budget allowed you to spend $250 on your car, you might be able to lease a brand-new Ford Explorer. For the same price, you might have to buy an Explorer that was two or three years old with 50,000 miles, or buy a new but considerably less expensive make and model. A lease therefore allows you to drive in the latest models of more expensive cars. But when your lease is over, you will have to return that Explorer. Whatever car you can afford to buy, you get to keep it, and it will always have a resell or trade-in value if later on you want to upgrade to a newer car.

Furthermore, people who lease cars are often shocked by how much they must pay when the lease is over. Most leases limit you to a certain number of miles, and if you go over that allotment, you must pay for each mile. As a result, at the end of your lease, you may end up paying thousands of dollars in mileage fees. For example, if your lease covers you for 25,000 miles over three years, but you drive 40,000 miles, that's an extra 15,000 miles. At 11¢ per mile, that's $1,650 you'll have to pay. And you still won't have a car.

In addition, when you lease, you still have to pay for regular maintenance and repairs to the vehicle. Because you must return the car when your lease expires, you are paying to repair *someone else's* car. If you own the car, however, you would know that every dollar you spend maintaining or repairing the car is an investment in a real piece of property—your property, not someone else's.

By now, the benefits of buying over leasing should be clear. But if you're still not convinced, remember this fundamental fact: If you lease, when your lease is up, after you've made all of your monthly payments, paid for extra mileage, and paid for repairs, you *must give the car back.* It isn't yours to keep, no matter how much the lease cost you. Whatever make or model you can afford to buy, it is yours to keep after you make your payments. There's no giving it back, and that makes all the difference.

Sample 4 Score

When you need a car, you can lease, or buy it. A lot of people think leasing is better, than buying. I think it makes more sense to buy. It really actually costs less money in the long run.

With a lease you can pay less each month for a car. If you buy it you'd probably have to pay a lot more each month, like a hundred dollars more a month. But the good thing about buying is you get to keep the car. With a lease of course, you have to give the car back.

With a lease you also have to pay for the extra miles you put on the car. You are only allowed to put so many miles on the car and if you go over that, you have to pay for each mile. That can add up to thousands of dollars even though its only a few sense for each mile.

You will also need to pay for any repairs on the car just like you would if you owned it, which you don't, because you still have to give it back. When you owne the car, you still have to pay for repairs, but, it's your car. Leasing feels like throwing money away.

Sample 1 Score

Lot of people they buy car, so many others they leasing. Leasing mean pay money each month and then giving the car back. Leasing can be for one year or two even three or four. Most any car, you can lease it. Any car you can buy, too, new one or use one.

Leasing sometime you pay fewer monies because you don't keep the car. Buying sometime it cost more but you keep the car. Down paying can be a lot of money and hard to save.

Buying or leasing, is up to you. Which works for you.

796. The inventor and statesman Benjamin Franklin said, "Money never made a man happy yet, nor will it. There is nothing in its nature to produce happiness." Do you agree with this statement? Why or why not? Use specific reasons and examples to support your position.

Sample 6 Score

Benjamin Franklin is one of the greatest figures in American history, and I have a great deal of respect for this incredible inventor, politician, and writer. But I must respectfully disagree with his claim that "Money never made a man happy yet, nor will it. There is nothing in its nature to produce happiness." I agree that money in and of itself does not make a person happy; but I believe that money can help provide one thing that is essential to happiness: good health.

While money can do nothing to change our genetic makeup and our physiological predisposition to illness and disease, it can give us access to better healthcare throughout our lives. This begins with pre-natal care and childhood vaccinations. In impoverished third-world countries, infant mortality rates are three, four, even ten times higher than in the United States, and as many as one in four women still die in childbirth because they do not have access to modern medical care. Sadly, people who are too poor to afford vaccinations and routine healthcare for their children watch helplessly as many of those children succumb to illnesses and diseases that are rarely fatal here in the United States.

Money also enables us to afford better doctors and see specialists throughout our lives. If your child has difficulty hearing, for example, and you have insurance (which costs money) or cash, you can see a hearing specialist and pay for therapy. If you have migraines that make you miserable, you can see a headache specialist and afford medication and treatment. Having money also means being able to afford preventative measures, such as taking vitamins and getting regular check-ups. It means being able to afford products and services that can enhance our health, such as gym memberships, organic foods, and acupuncture.

Another important thing money can do is enable us to live in a healthy environment. Many of the world's poorest people live in dirty, dangerous places—unsanitary slums crawling with diseases and health hazards of all sorts. In a particularly poor area of the Bronx, for example, children had an abnormally high rate of asthma because their families couldn't afford to move away from the medical waste treatment plant that was poisoning the air.

Money can also help us be healthy by enabling us to afford proper heating and cooling measures. This includes being able to afford a warm winter coat and the opportunity to cool off at a pool or in the ocean. On a more basic level, it means being able to afford heat in the winter and air-conditioning in the summer. During heat waves, victims of heat-stroke are often those who are too poor to afford air-conditioning in their apartments. In extreme cold, the same is true: people who freeze to death or become gravely ill from the cold are often those who are unable to afford high heating bills.

Having money may not make people happy, but it sure goes a long way toward keeping them healthy. And as they say, if you haven't got your health, you haven't got anything.

Sample 4 Score

Benjamin Franklin once said that "Money never made a man happy yet, nor will it. There is nothing in its nature to produce happiness." I do not agree with this statement because money can buy access to good health care. In my opinion, good health is essential to happiness. Therefore, money can make you happy by keeping you healthy.

Money first of all can get you access to good doctors, even specialists if you need them. With money, you can afford all kinds of things, like tests that check for diseases and special treatments if you find something wrong. If your pregnant you can get good pre-natal care and have a good birth, while in poor countries lots of women die in childbirth and lots of babies die while their infants.

If you have money you can buy an air conditioner so it's not too hot in the summer and you can afford to have heat all winter. If you don't you might suffocate in the heat or freeze to death. You can also stay out of poor areas like slums which are unhealthy and dangerous to live in.

As they say, money can't buy you love, but I think it can buy you good health, and if you don't feel good, it's hard to be happy.

Sample 1 Score

Benjamin Franklin was a great inventer of America. He famous for inventing electricity. He also wrote a lot. One thing he said once was that "Money never made a man happy yet, nor will it. There is nothing in its nature to produce happiness." Do you agree or disagree with this statement? Every one has their opinion. Another question is what is happiness? I also like to be with my family and friends.

Some times I need money to spend with them, like to fly on a plane to see my brother in Colorado. It is as beautifol there as every one told me it was.

797. Some states have now made it illegal to drive while talking on a handheld cell phone. Do you think this is a good law that should be passed in other states as well? Why or why not? Explain your answer.

Sample 6 Score

No matter how careful a driver you may be, when you do something else while driving, whether it's drinking coffee, changing the radio station, looking at a map, or making a call on your cell phone, you endanger yourself and others because you are distracted from your driving. Even a fraction of a second of distraction is enough to cause an accident. While no state can make it illegal to drink coffee or switch stations while driving, all states can, and should,

make it illegal to drive while talking on a cellular phone.

In the past decade, as the popularity of cellular phones has risen, so have the number of accidents caused by people talking on their cell phones. Whether they were dialing a number, listening to a message, or simply in a heated conversation, they were momentarily distracted from the task of driving, and suddenly— crash! Fortunately, many of these accidents have been minor fender-benders. But all too many have been deadly accidents that could have been prevented by a stricter cell-phone use laws.

Cell phone proponents may argue that talking on a cell phone is no more dangerous than, for example, having a cup of coffee while on the road or talking to someone in the backseat. But unlike a cup of coffee, which you can put down between sips, you must keep the phone in your hand. That means that you have only one hand on the wheel while you're driving. That makes cell phones doubly dangerous: not only are you distracted by dialing or by the conversation; you are also driving one-handed, which means you are less in control. If you suddenly need both hands on the wheel to prevent an accident or to keep your car from sliding, the extra second it takes to get your hand back on the wheel can make the difference between an accident and an accident narrowly averted, between a serious injury and a minor one.

Cell phones are also dangerous because when you are busy talking, especially if you really have to concentrate on the matter you are discussing, your mind is not fully focused on the road, and this has a significant effect on your reaction time. You will be slower to make important driving decisions such as how soon to brake and when to switch lanes, and you will be less able to respond to situations on the road.

Many people use cell phones to report accidents and emergencies, to let loved ones know they'll be late, and to stay in touch when they're out of town. I'm not arguing that you shouldn't have a cell phone in your car. What I am saying is that you shouldn't be driving when you're talking on that phone. Until your state outlaws handheld cell phones in cars, pull over to the side of the road when you are ready to make a call. It may add a few extra minutes to your commute, but it just might save your life.

Sample 4 Score

Driving with a cell phone is dangerous, and it should be illegal. Its all ready illegal in some states, in my opinion it, should be illegal in all of them.

First of all, driving with a cell phone is dangerous because your distracted. Especially when you're dialing a number, then you're not even looking at the road. What if the cars in front of you suddenly stop?

You can also be distracted by the conversation you are having and lose focus from driving. This means that you may not be able to react quick enough to dangers on the road. Another problem is that with a cell phone, you don't have both hands on the wheel, and that's for the whole time you're talking. You can't make sharp turns and handle sudden curves with just one hand.

Lots of people think, oh, it's just one quick call, no problem. But even just a quick call makes you distracted, even just for a quick second. That's enough to cause an accident. So don't drive when you need to talk on your cell phone. Instead, be safe and pull over.

Sample 1 Score

In many states of the United States they make it again the law for talking while driving with cellular telephone. In my opinion, is this a good idea? I believe.

For to many accidents, are happening with the cellular telephone, the driver he don't see (what happens) ahead. This terrible for every one especial the

ones they getting hurt. Some accident really very terrible and, everyone going to the hospital. This should be the law.

Scoring Explanations for Expository Writing Essays

A score of "6" indicates that your essay satisfies the requirements of the writing prompt in a creative and original manner, using an obvious theme and thesis throughout. Your essay provides a clear and logical explanation and uses support material. Your ideas are articulated in a coherent fashion; there are precise examples; and the topic is developed in an interesting manner. Your essay is well reasoned, with a clear focus, a logical sequence of ideas, and transitional words and sentences. You demonstrate a sense of audience by using effective vocabulary, varied sentence structure, and fluid, sophisticated language that is essentially without errors.

A score of "4" indicates that your essay meets some of the requirements of the writing prompt, including some key elements that help explain the thesis. Your essay may answer the question in an abbreviated manner, giving only brief examples and developing ideas somewhat inconsistently. Your essay has a general focus, makes an obvious attempt at organization, and presents ideas in a logical sequence. The language of your essay indicates a general control of mechanics but has a slightly lower quality of sentence structure and variety than a sample 6 score. An essay of this type contains errors only when using sophisticated language.

A score of "1" indicates that the essay only minimally addresses the writing prompt, digressing, repeating, or dwelling on insignificant details throughout. The essay shows a lack of development and exhibits no organizational pattern or focus. Your writing may be illegible or unrecognizable as English.

Model Expository Writing Essays

798. Explain the problems, both personal and societal, that result from obesity.

Sample 6 Score

A single overweight person might not warrant much attention. But a nation whose population is increasingly obese is cause for concern. In the United States, 14% of children and teenagers are categorized as overweight. Why is this a serious problem instead of simply a matter of personal choice? What are the causes of this constantly increasing percentage of obese persons? What is to be done about this, and what organized steps should be taken to solve the problem?

Just as there are ripples from a stone thrown into the water, there are far-reaching and unending effects resulting from obesity. From a psychological perspective, most obese persons would prefer not to be overweight. Our society glorifies the ultrathin, so if you are obese you do not fit in with acceptable modes of appearance. We know that children are often cruel about taunting their heavy classmates. All too often we hear friends say, "I've got to lose weight before that trip," or "before the wedding." However, there are more objective measures of the negative results of obesity. Type 2 (adult onset) diabetes, an illness with serious consequences, including damage to the heart, damage to the eyes, and difficulty in healing infections, is attributed to obesity. Public health agencies are dealing with the continual rise in this type of diabetes. Asthma is also on the rise as a result of the obesity epidemic, as are sleep disorders such as sleep apnea. Recent research indicates a relationship between some types of cancer and obesity. Society pays the price when citizens are ill, are unable to work, and require constant medical care.

Questions arise: "What can be done about this?" "Who or what is to blame?" Discussing blame is a delicate problem. There are undoubtedly overweight individuals with inherited tendencies toward diabetes or heart disease, and there is evidence that a hormone that gives people a sense of fullness after eating may be lacking in some obese people. Yet, knowing that they are at risk would suggest that steps be taken to thwart the onset of the physical consequences of obesity.

Most authorities agree that diet is key. The avoidance of foods high in sugars, carbohydrates, and saturated fats is recommended by most physicians as a way to ward off obesity and its dire consequences. But this is difficult in our society where fast-food outlets are ubiquitous, where we are bombarded by advertising of unhealthy foods, and where we lead increasingly sedentary lives. Sugar-laden soft drinks are sold in schools, and profits from these sales are high. An elementary school in Los Angeles received $50,000 for allowing Coca-Cola to install its vending machines. This company and PepsiCo constitute the majority of the school soft drink market, and while they profit from the present sales, they are also building brand loyalty and creating future habitual soft drink consumers.

Lack of adequate exercise is a concomitant contributor to the rise in obesity. Children are often playing video games instead of engaging in sports. Adults watch television instead of exercising. People will drive around shopping centers to avoid walking a few extra steps. The quintessential "couch potato" device has just been invented. Now you can get a universal remote with which, from your comfortable couch, you can control not only your television, but your oven, lights, and, presumably, other things that we can only begin to imagine.

Society suffers when its population is increasingly unhealthy, has rising medical costs, notes absenteeism from work and school, and has social inequalities. This last result, social inequalities, reflects the assertion recently made by a school administrator that

50% of children in poorer school districts are obese. Experts seem to believe that obesity is a problem that can, with diligence and desire, be eliminated or at least mitigated with two simple changes in lifestyle—eating more healthily and getting more exercise.

Sample 4 Score

Obesity is a growing problem in this country. But I don't think obese people actually want to be overweight because being overweight makes you get sick more often. Doctors say obesity causes asma, diabetes, and even heart disease. If people understood the effects of obesity, they would probably try harder to lose weight because no one likes to get sick. Being sick makes kids miss school and adults miss work and often causes a lot of hospital bills. So, in the end, obesity hurts kids educations and their parent's jobs and is also incredibly expensive.

Lately, more and more kids are becoming obese. This is a real problem because teenagers shouldn't have to worry about their heart! They should be playing sports and having fun and getting an education. But when students have asma attacks, they can't breath, which means they can't go to class or take gym. So, having asma and missing school interferes with their education.

Obesity also causes diabetes, a really terrible disease that can make you blind. Of course, some people get diabetes because their parents have it not because they're obese. Heart disease is the number one cause of death in America and can also be caused by obesity. In a way, obesity is more than just being overweight, its like three diseases wrapped up in one. That's exactly why everyone needs to learn more about it, so we can stop it from getting out of hand.

Some people may be obese because they don't like to exercise. But they need to find a way to exer-cise because if you exercise every day, you will probably stay in shape. Then you won't have to pay expensive doctor bills or go to the hospital as often and everyone will be healthier, miss less school and work, and be better off.

Sample 1 Score

I think obesity is bad but not that bad. If you like sodas you want to have a soda and you may need a mashin. My best friend may be obese but so what if your nice. They try to make you do sports but what if you like tv and the soaps bettr. I don't think yul die if you eat fries and I like that food best so whats the big deel?

799. Describe the purposes of the Internet. Include various viewpoints, including those of users and providers.

Sample 6 Score

In today's world, the first place people turn to when there is a question to be answered, information to be located, or people to be contacted is often the Internet. Yes, the Internet may have supplanted the traditional encyclopedia as well as a number of other sources of service and information. We can make reservations, plan vacations, play interactive games, learn a language, listen to music or radio programs, read the newspaper, and find out about a medical condition without coming face-to-face with another person. There is no limit to the subject matter you can research on the Internet. Just go to a search engine such as Yahoo! or Google, type in a few keywords or a Web address, and presto, you will probably summon links to more sources than you could have imagined. The Internet allows you to remain at your computer and shop no matter what you wish to purchase. And if you are looking for a bargain or an unusual item, you can go to a popular auction site and either sell or buy.

If, however, you do wish to speak directly to a person, there are the chat rooms. On practically any given topic, groups of people converse with each other. They may be giving opinions about a perfect travel itinerary, a book, or even a political party. The most prevalent use of the Internet also involves directly writing to a person, and that is the sending of e-mail messages to friends and associates. It is possible to communicate instantly with anyone, anywhere, as long as there is an Internet connection. In a world where people frequently travel and families do not necessarily live in the same neighborhoods, e-mail is a means of making simple, inexpensive, immediate contact. Not only do we send verbal messages, but also now digital cameras take pictures that can be stored and then instantly transmitted on the Internet.

Unfortunately, there are individuals who subvert the opportunities offered by this technology. They are less than honest, disguise their identity, bilk people in financial scams, and entice unsuspecting people, including children, into giving them personal information. Caveats about these problems are currently being publicized so those Internet users will not be victimized.

Of course, the Internet providers, such as AOL, hope to make a profit, and there is usually a monthly fee for the hookup. To increase the profits, the providers sell advertising, which may pop up on the subscriber's screen and require the user to stop and respond, either positively or negatively, to the ads.

When you consider that, among other things, you can hear a concert, read a book, visit a museum and view its contents, visit the websites of numerous individuals and organizations, play a game with one or more people, and pay your bills, you will realize that the uses of the Internet are too vast for a short list. Most would agree that much has been added to people's lives by connecting them to the Internet, and that we probably cannot anticipate what new purposes will be explored in the future.

Sample 4 Score

The internet is very useful. You can send e-mail to your friends. They can write back to you. You can do this whenever you want. You can write to people you don't know. You can meet people through the internet. When someone goes to college you can write to them every day.

You can look things up. If you want to find out about something you can look it up. You don't have to go to the library. If you have to read a book you can find out about it and not read it. There are good games you can put in your computer. I like these games. I want to get more games. You can hear good music on the computer. I like to do this. I know how to download the music.

I like to buy stuff on the internet. My friends do this too. I can buy anything and just give a credit card number. I don't have to go the store.

There are many, many things you can do on the internet right from your computer.

Sample 1 Score

I have the internet. I do not use it a lot it takes to long to get things on it if you have to find it out. If you have a computer you shud have it then you can rite on it and music but who nose how the music I like noone els likes I like hard rock what about you.

If you have internet only 1 can use it so how do you no who it is and why fite. If you have a movie more than 1 are alowd not just 1. But the internet has good purposes.

800. Describe various styles of shoes as well as reasons for their popularity.

Sample 6 Score

Visit the shoe department of a large department store and you will undoubtedly see a variety of shoe styles on display. This suggests that the store is satisfying the customers' desire for an assortment of shoes.

Logically, shoes should protect and support the feet. An example of such a shoe is the sneaker. Originally an inexpensive canvas, rubber-soled version of a leather oxford (a shoe with laces), the sneaker has become increasing popular and has supplanted the oxford for regular everyday use for many students and some adults. Sneakers, like living things, have evolved and branched out. They are now mostly made of leather and have much cushioning to minimize stress on the wearer's joints. They have become specialized into separate sneakers for walking, running, tennis, and basketball. There are sneakers for aerobic classes, and for the eclectic exerciser, there are cross trainers. There is justification for their popularity, for they are comfortable and are engineered to properly support the foot during a particular activity. It has also become acceptable to wear sneakers with street clothes because they just plain feel good. An endorsement by a popular athlete spreads their appeal as well as increases their cost.

At the opposite end of the spectrum is a shoe style that is uncomfortable, harmful, and impractical. These adjectives describe the women's shoes with pointed toes and thin, high heels. Doctors say that the pointed toes cause deformities of the feet, and the three- to four-inch heels are unstable and can cause back problems. With so many negatives, why are these styles consistently popular? Wearers may admit that they are uncomfortable, but say that they are fashionable and that, in time, they get used to them. Historically, people follow fashion, and here again, advertising preys upon this need to keep up with the current trends.

A shoe that can be totally practical, simply fashionable, or a combination of both, is the boot. For cold or inclement weather, no footwear is as desirable as an insulated, rubber-soled boot. Boots are popular because they are practical, long lasting, and a desirable fashion accessory. But there are boots whose entire function is fashion. Yes, these boots have the same pointed toes and spiked heels as the shoes described earlier, but they are boots because the leather continues high on the leg.

Historically, shoe styles change, but there are some shoes that are comfortable as well as fashionable, like sandals and sneakers. And, there are those styles some would consider fashionable but harmful to the feet, or worse. If the choice were between comfort and fashion, many people would probably risk discomfort in order to be fashionable.

Sample 4 Score

Shoes are popular because they're necessary for doing almost anything. You need them to walk, play sports, and even to enter drug stores and restaurants. Without them, you'd have to sit at home all day. Shoes also protect your feet when your walking on a hot sidewalk or hiking in the woods. Nowadays, people even use shoes to make fashion statements. Some shoes are more expensive than ever just because they're so popular.

My favorite shoes are my sneakers. Everyone at school has sneakers because they're required for gym class. They're also popular outside of school because they come in so many colors and styles. I have a lot of friends at school but none of us has the exact same pair of sneakers. In high school, sneakers are a good way to express your personality, and on top of that they're really comfortable.

Sandals are also popular, especially in the summer, because they're also comfortable and don't hurt your feet. You can move your toes around when you where them and they don't make your feet sweat like sneakers sometimes do.

I also have new high heel boots with a 4 inch heel. They hurt my feet when I wear them for a long time, but I don't care because they look so cool. I think looking good is worth the pain. Besides, I only wear them on special ocasions. My mother thinks I'll end up ruining my feet, but you should see the heels she wears to work!

Sample 1 Score

I like shoe styles they are good. One time I went to buy shoes and my cuzin was there and we huged becuz we did not see each other for ever. We went to her house and watched tv. I need new sneakers. I like sneakers. They cost to much so I cant get them now. I want high heels my mother wears them and they kill her feet but I want them to. Everyone wants them.

801. Math is a required subject. Explain why it is so important.

Sample 6 Score

If you complain about the universality of math as a required subject, just try to spend one day without encountering some form of mathematics. From page numbers to prices to today's date, math puts things in order and enables us to compare quantitatively. Figuring how much time is required, how much of an ingredient must be measured, how much carpet to buy, all of these everyday experiences require familiarity with math. To survive financially you must use math to allocate your resources. If you want to invest in a business or in the stock market, you must know how to deal with the numbers. Understanding graphs and other analyses about the economy or politics or consumer confidence is enhanced by the applications of math. Mathematical applications in the study of science are essential. Tracking the or-

bits of planets and the locations of stars in the galaxy cannot be done without numerical comparisons. Every discipline, from archeology to zoology, benefits in some way from the use of mathematics.

Practical reasons for the need for mathematics are omnipresent, but there are other, perhaps more esoteric reasons for interest in this subject. The amazing coincidences found in numbers provide continual fascination. An example is the fact that the numbers in each product of the "9-times table" add up to nine: Nine times five equals 45, and four plus five equals nine; similarly, the numbers in the product of seven times nine also equal nine. Mathematicians are also especially fascinated with unique geometric relationships. An example is the fact that three pyramids of the same height will exactly fit into a prism of equal height.

A teacher of mathematics once told me, "Math is in everything," and some people say, "Mathematics is the something for which the world was written." These are reasons enough for requiring its study.

Sample 4 Score

Math is a required subject because it is important in school and in every day life. If you don't understand simple math, you'll never know if the cashier is giving you the right change or if your getting a good deal on a new car. Without math, shopping would be impossible. You wouldn't be able to figure out what you could afford. Some people think they don't need math but they do. You need math to know if its hot or cold outside or to know what pages you have to study for a particular test.

Math is also important because you need to use it in almost every other subject. Sometimes you need math in science to make a graph or to measure amounts for an experiment. There's no way you could pass science without math. I use math in history class to remember dates and in English class we use it to understand poetry. You can't even write a haiku without math because you wouldnt be able to count the number of syllables and lines.

In every day life, you need math to balance your checkbook and to know how much time you have before the movie starts. Without it, you'd never be on time, and your friends would hate you. Math is necessary even to make a simple phone call. When you think about it numbers are everywhere so it's important to understand them.

Sample 1 Score

We have to take math. I don't like it. It is stupid. We have to draw in the boxes on graf paper what is this art. I faled art anyway so why do it in math. I can use the kalkuate so I don't even need to study it where allowd to use the kalkuate and so I do not care if math is important.

802. Describe a major environmental problem and what you believe should be done about it.

Sample 6 Score

A major environmental problem, the magnitude of which we are just beginning to realize, is global warming. When people say that the winters aren't as cold as they used to be, or that there was definitely more snow in past years, they are correct. In addition to these personal testimonials, there is concrete visual evidence of global warming. Most noticeable is the depletion of the ice caps. In recent years, glaciers have been receding in greater amounts than in former years. One only has to visit a national park where this recession is marked with signs indicating where the glacier reached in a particular year. The visitor can see how much further away from a particular spot the ice is at the present moment.

When the ice caps, made of fresh water, melt, they change the salinity of the oceans, change the

currents, and change the conditions for survival for myriad species. Additionally, invasive species might move in, affecting the entire ecosystem. This has a domino effect, as all species are interdependent and survive according to predictable sources of food and living conditions. A specific example recently described on an environmental calendar told of the effect of global warming on polar bears. The bears cannot go out on the melted ice, which is how they get their food. This causes them to lose body fat and even to be unable to give birth to cubs.

Global warming causes flooding, and because the warming of the earth causes dryness, fires increase.

When speaking of the causes of global warming, some experts say that ice ages followed by warming have been cyclical throughout the eons and that there is not much that can be done about it. However, most scientists believe that the actions of humans have speeded up this process. They blame the increased burning of wood and fossil fuels—oil and coal—on an increasing population needing heat for warmth and cooking. More energy consumption places carbon dioxide and other pollutants in the atmosphere. Warm air trapped around the earth has been deemed the greenhouse effect.

While we cannot stop the naturally occurring climate changes, we can try to mitigate the rapid warming by reducing our use of fossil fuels. Much publicity has been given to the love that Americans have for sports utility vehicles, which burn an inordinate amount of fuel and are not required for the kind of ordinary driving done by most owners. There are numerous additional ways in which we can reduce our dependence on these fuels, ranging from insulating our homes to lowering the thermostat in winter and raising it when we use air-conditioning. Perhaps researchers can develop alternate sources of energy. A hybrid automobile uses gas initially and then automatically switches to electricity. Theoretically, this car will be able to run for 50 miles on one gallon of gasoline. Additionally, we can support the scientific study of the effects of global warming. Perhaps we can predict such things as where floods will occur or where crops will have difficulty surviving and take steps to overcome these problems.

One thing is certain: Global warming is a serious environmental problem with ramifications that affect almost every aspect of life.

Sample 4 Score

Global warming which means that it is getting warmer all over the globe, is a serious environmental problem. It is bad for the environment, nature, animals, and humans as well. Global warming causes a lot of glaciers to melt which then causes more floods and makes the ocean warmer which could hurt certain kinds of fish. Global warming also leads to more fires in general and increases the rate of cancer in humans, especially skin cancer.

In order to stop global warming, we should study the greenhouse effect. Because we use too much oil and gas and pollute the air on a regular basis, hot air can't escape the atmosphere. We need to use less oil and gas so the hot air can get out. People don't need to drive trucks and SUVs all the time because they use more gas and cause more air pollution. We also don't have to use air conditioning all the time. People need to remember that minivans and air conditioning are luxuries not neccessities.

If everyone agreed to change their habits, it would help the environment a lot. So, we should find out what needs to be done to solve this serious environmental problem and do whatever it takes.

Sample 1 Score

A environmental problem is called global warming. The globe is getting hot. I am not sure about this we had plenty of cold days and I like it hot in summr. How do

they no do they mesure all over the globe. 1 day it was so cold my hands froze and I got in trubel because I was not aloud out so I had no time to gebt gloves. I gess I don't like global warming if it gets to hot but maybe its only far away anwe don't need to wory about it hear.

803. Describe how communication has changed in the past 20 years.

Sample 6 Score

Who could have predicted 20 years ago that communication would change as radically as it has? Today, communication is instantaneous. No longer do we have to use a pen, pencil, or typewriter to write a letter. No longer do we have to use a postal service to mail it. No longer do we have to wait for a response that takes several days. Nor do we have to stay near a telephone or search for a public phone while traveling. Things have speeded up exponentially.

In the past 20 years, we have benefited from tremendous changes in telecommunication. The relatively simple change to portable phones enabled us to roam around the house while chatting, not limited by the length of the cord that attaches the receiver to the base of the telephone. Then came the beeper, allowing us to get a message when away from a telephone. Now, of course, there is the ubiquitous cell phone. Watch the crowds walking along a sidewalk, and you can't help noticing people purposefully striding along while talking on their cell phones.

What if we must write a message? We now have e-mail. We send these messages immediately after typing them on the computer keyboard and never have to go to the post office. No more "snail mail." Perhaps we have a written copy that must be sent but cannot be conveniently sent via the computer. Simply dial a phone number, push a few buttons, and send a fax. The copy is transmitted to the receiver at once. The ability to telecommute is almost like handing the copy to the recipient. What a difference 20 years has made. Just as most of us could not imagine the speed and ease of communication in the twenty-first century, we probably cannot anticipate the changes that will occur in the next 20 years. Perhaps we will be able to send instant messages simply by thinking about them, from one brain to the brain of the intended recipient.

Sample 4 Score

I believe communication has definitely changed in the last 20 years. It is much different. I can send e-mails to my friends every day. Even twice a day if I want. I could not do this a few years ago. It's great. So I think communication is much faster and I definitely think it is much easier if you have a computer. Every school and office has a computer.

I believe the best change is the cell phone. I have a cell phone that I carry everywhere I go. I can turn it off in the movie and it will vibrate (shake). Then I know I have a call and I can leave and answer it. I don't think it is right for you to bother someone with your cell phone.

I don't even need stamps to send cards. I can send them on the computer. All my friends have e-mail. And if they don't they don't get a card untill they do.

I can also send a FAX on the telephone if I have to send a copy right then.

These are the ways communication has changed in the last 20 years.

Sample 1 Score

Communication is talking. In some ways it has changed in the last 20 years. I think I can talk easily now because I cary around with my phone. It is pink and everyone likes it. Because I worked to earn it each month. You don't have to read the paper you

can watch tv if you want. Tv tells you about clothes and stuff that you care about. So communication is grate. Communication is also the computer which is all over. I hate to rite so I use my cell but I could if I felt like it. My mother uses it. So she says it is much better.

804. Discuss the events in the life of your favorite author, sports figure, or performer. Explain how these events relate to the person's achievements.

Sample 6 Score

Herman Melville was a nineteenth-century writer whose works foreshadowed themes that would become prevalent in the twentieth century. He wrote about his distaste for the oppression of underlings, of the need to accept different cultures and to appreciate the contributions of ordinary people. His novels probe into psychological reasons for characters' actions in a way that would be relevant today.

Born into a New York family that was prominent, although in constant debt, Melville was forced to end his formal schooling at the age of 12. He was nevertheless widely read and informed on numerous subjects, including, but not limited to, literature, art, science, biology, navigation, mythology, and geography. Thus, he was largely self-educated, as was Ishmael, the narrator of *Moby Dick*, Melville's most acclaimed novel. Ishmael said, "A whale ship was my Yale College and my Harvard."

Just as Ishmael's experiential education mirrored Melville's own informal schooling, so were many other aspects of his life reflected in his writings. Signing up as a cabin boy on a ship going to Liverpool, England, when he was 20, provided Melville with material for the novel *Redburn*. The novel was about a lonely 20-year-old orphan wandering around Liverpool and is thought to be the writer's most autobiographical work.

Motivated by the need to earn money, Melville signed up for a four-year voyage as a common seaman in spite of the fact that his family connections could have easily gotten him an officer's commission. Melville had a progressive view about equality that was unusual for his time. He believed in the dignity of all work, which was reflected in his sympathetic, even admiring, excruciatingly detailed descriptions of the jobs of the working people in his writings. He decried nationalistic prejudice and believed that all people are related. He wrote, "You cannot shed a drop of American blood without shedding blood of the whole world."

Among the first white men to explore the South Sea Islands, Melville was surely the first literary artist to do so. Unable to bear the inhumane treatment on this long voyage, he deserted in the Marquesas Islands. He was ill and fortunately was cared for by a kindly native family. A grown son in the family was covered with tattoos, and Melville learned that these people were cannibals who feasted on their enemies. In order to leave, he had to escape, finding refuge on an Australian ship. He deserted from this ship also, landing in Tahiti. These experiences provided material for the novel *Typee*, about the South Sea Islands; the novel *Omoo*, based on his experiences in Tahiti; and the novel *White Jacket*, which exposed the cruelty of navy flogging. The tattooed man who cared for Melville provided the prototype for Quequeg, one of the most memorable characters in literature.

Herman Melville also was a crew member of a whaling ship, where he learned the intricacies involved in the type of multiyear voyage that he used as the setting for *Moby Dick*. This novel, considered a literary masterpiece, provided a forum for Melville's ideas about the necessity for connectedness. The savage, Quequeg, and the sailor, Ishmael, were mutually supportive of this theme. In addition, Melville was a great believer in democracy and the benefits of diversity, and these beliefs were reflected in his descriptions of the crew on the whaling voyage. The ship was a metaphor for the world, with its crew coming from every known location and background, all being necessary for success. A monomaniacal captain, devoid of empathy, driven by his selfish aims, and unable to connect with others, could only lead to disaster.

Thus, Herman Melville's real-life experiences undoubtedly made possible his descriptive novels, but they would not have been possible without his independently drawn conclusions about the dignity of man and his place in the universe.

Sample 4 Score

Herman Melville was a 19th century American writer who wrote many famous books including *Moby Dick*. Like *Moby Dick*, most of his books where about topics that were of personal interest to him like ships and whaling. He spent a lot of time on ships and also knew a lot about whales. Melville led an exciting life and put a lot of that excitement into his books. Because his books were based on real life events and topics he knew alot about, the writing was incredibly detailed and vivid. When people read his books, even when people read them today, they feel as though they've been taken into another world. When you read Melville's books, you learn a lot about whales and foreign lands, but you also learn a lot about him as a person.

Moby Dick is a great book. After reading it, you can understand a lot more about Meville. The story is about a crazy man named Captain Ahab who wants to kill a great whale named Moby Dick. In the book, Melville really seems to care about his characters and makes it clear that all of the characters are equal in his eyes. Ahab's ship is supposed to be a symbol of the entire world and characters like Quequeg and Ishmael are simply every day people. Because Ahab is so selfish, he ends up destroying the entire ship. After realizing that, Melville wants us to know that selfish world leaders will also ruin the world if regular citizens like Ishmael and Quequeg aren't given any power. Melville was all for democracy which you can easily tell after reading this book.

Sample 1 Score

My clas had to read Moby dick. I learned about the author. He is Herman Melville and I like him he is brave he went on trips. I never went on many trips but I wuld. I wuld go to florida. He Herman never went there but he went other places and wrote about it. i don't think nobody in my class akshuly read it.

805. Explain the causes and effects of not voting in elections.

Sample 6 Score

Voting is the privilege for which wars have been fought, protests have been organized, and editorials have been written. "No taxation without representation" was a battle cry of the American Revolution. Women struggled for suffrage, as did all minorities. Eighteen-year-olds clamored for the right to vote, saying that if they were old enough to go to war, they should be allowed to vote. Yet Americans have a deplorable voting history.

Interviewing people about their voting habits is revealing. There are individuals who state, almost boastfully, that they have never voted. They somehow set themselves apart from the requirements of citizenship in a democracy. Many who avoid voting do so consciously. It is not as if they were ill or unavoidably detained on election day. Often they claim that their one vote doesn't matter. "What's one vote?" they ask. Perhaps one vote may not count in some elections, although there have been results determined by one or very few votes. In addition, the total of single votes that are not cast can add up to a signifi-

cant difference in a particular race. Some people blame the fact that they do not know enough about the issues for their absence from the voting booth. Others say that they avoid learning about the news because it is too depressing. In a democracy, we can express our opinions to our elected leaders, but more than half of us sometimes avoid choosing these people who make the policies that affect our lives.

One of the effects of this statistic is that politicians will cater to the groups that do vote in large numbers, giving more weight to their needs than to those of other groups or of the general population. Since so many do not vote, elected officials can, with impunity, promote policies that benefit the special interests that contribute financially to the election campaigns. Another effect of not voting is the free rein given to those in office to disregard the expressed opinions of constituents. For if you do not vote, why should the candidate worry about you?

It seems ironic that in this most democratic of societies, we abrogate the privilege for which so many have struggled. How many countries do not have a choice of candidates, yet their citizens are forced to participate in sham elections? In the United States we have choices. We can vote to fire an officeholder who does not live up to our expectations by choosing an opponent in the next election, and we are free to choose someone whose ideas appeal to us.

Perhaps a major reason for not voting is the failure to convey how precious and unique is the right to vote and how important is each and every vote. The major effect is that we are voluntarily giving up our rights as citizens to ascertain that our elected officials truly represent us. This is because we have not done our part in choosing them, so in effect, we are telling these officials that we don't care enough to bother to vote.

Sample 4 Score

Many people do not vote because they think its a hassle or that their vote won't make a difference. Some people say they don't care who wins, but everyone should care because government officials make decisions that effect all of us. People need to learn more about their own government. So many Americans think our government is made up of one person, the president! But there are so many other people involved and so many other elections to think about too.

Not having time to vote or not knowing who to vote for is no excuse for not voting at all. People should take the time to learn as much as they can about the people who are running and make an informed decision. If you don't vote then you'll never get what you want and you won't be able to complain when politicians make bad decisions.

But if you're smart and vote for whoever you feel is the best candidate, then if that person is elected, you can know that it's their responsibility to listen to you. Our government is supposed to be for the people and run by the people, so everyone should realize it is their right and also their responsbility to vote during every election.

Sample 1 Score

Most people don't vote I wouldn't my mother don't she says she has no time she is so bizy she works and how can she vote if she works. My brother says if you vote you can called to the juree and who need that his friend had it and it was boring and he culdve lost his job. If you care who wins you shud vote if you don't care don't.

806. Explain how to have a winning baseball team.

Sample 6 Score

Whether professional or amateur, a baseball team, like a fine meal, needs the right ingredients to create a winning result. Talented athletes are the first requirement. After that, astute coaching, which discerns and then develops the unique capabilities of the players, can be as important as the athletes themselves. Flexibility and the willingness to try different strategies are the hallmarks of winning coaches. All the talent in the world could be wasted without creative and shrewd coaching.

A player with the ability to sprint, needed both for infield defense and for speedy base running, can be invaluable. A fast runner can steal bases and get to first base with a carefully placed bunt.

Good pitching is essential for a winning baseball team. A pitcher who is "on" is the first line of defense in baseball. It is well known that the pitcher is often the poorest hitter, but it is the pitcher who keeps the opponents from scoring. The pitcher's teammates accept this and acknowledge that it is their job to score the runs. Here again, a good coach decides who is the optimum pitcher for today's game, and equally important, when to take a tired or poorly performing pitcher out of the game.

Recruiting strong and consistent batters will be a factor in creating a winning baseball team. Having a home run hitter with several players who can be counted on to get base hits and pinch hits is needed because the best pitching and the best fielding will be for naught if runs aren't scored.

Even with a plethora of natural ability, to become a winning baseball team, the players must continually practice, not only to maintain their skills, but also to improve them. In fact, a motivated player who practices diligently may eventually surpass those with superior natural ability that is not developed. Along with this desire to continually improve one's individual playing ability, there is the motivation to succeed because of loyalty to the group. This type of esprit de corps can make the difference between a merely good and a winning baseball team. Putting the team first, while striving to give one's all, puts the finishing touches on the recipe for a winning baseball team.

Sample 4 Score

A winning baseball team would need good hitters, fast runners, a skilled pitcher and catcher, and a knowledgable and patient coach. It would also need to have a group of players who got along without any jealousy or hostility and were capable of rooting for each other.

Good hitters and runners are important because you have to get alot of hits and runs to win. You can't win without scoring runs. Also, the runners need to be speedy, so they can get to the base before the ball gets there. You also have to have a skilled pitcher who can strike people out. The pitcher has to be good or else the other team will score more runs and you will lose. The catcher is important as well because if the catcher drops the ball when the pitcher throws it, that is an error.

Finally, you also need to have a good coach who can help the players improve and who knows when to put certain players in the game and when to take them out. The coach should keep the team running smoothly and solve any fights or disagreements.

Sample 1 Score

I don't want to be on a baseball teem but I want to win if I do. My brother did and he never got a hit and he wont even look at me so who cars about baseball. I think you need to be a athleet and take lessons. And I think the uniforms are ugly I don't look good in it and it is swetty. I will pick the best players if I have to play so I mite as well win right.

807. Explain how to choose the right college.

Sample 6 Score

One of the most important decisions young adults make is where to go to college. Your college education will affect the rest of your life, so you should weigh your options carefully. The perfect school may not exist, but I believe there are three factors that are integral to choosing the right college: location, size, and curriculum. You can narrow down your search based on these criteria.

First, you should consider location. Some questions you should ask yourself include: Do I prefer to live in a city, the suburbs, or a rural area? Do I want to live in a temperate or colder climate? Do I prefer to be near my family, or in another part of the country? The answers to these questions will help you make the best choice.

Second, you should consider size. Perhaps your high school experience will affect your choice of colleges. If you attended a small high school with a low teacher-student ratio, you may be accustomed to small class sizes and knowing your fellow students extremely well. On the other hand, if you attended a large high school, you may be used to new faces and larger classes. Would you prefer a school such as the University of California at Santa Barbara (UCSB) with 50,000 students, or a smaller school with fewer than 5,000 students? Remember, the attention you receive will be affected by the size of the student population.

Finally, in order to choose the right college, you should take the time to decide what you would like to study. Although most colleges offer a myriad of courses, some of them specialize in certain fields and subjects or offer a wider selection of classes. For example, if you are interested in studying the classics, did you know that the University of Texas has one of the best classics departments in the United States?

Choosing the right college will require some effort. After you have decided on the location, size, and curriculum you prefer, do some research. Learn about different colleges from your guidance counselor, the Internet, or from the colleges themselves.

As with any important decision, make sure your choice is an educated one.

Sample 4 Score

It's not easy to choose the right college. There are three things you should consider when applying and deciding on a college. These are: location, classes, and size.

First of all, you should decide where you want to go to school for four years. Decide if you want to be in a city or in a rural area, or if you want to be near to or far from your family. Then, if you know what you want to study, you should make sure that the college offers classes. There would be no need to go to a school that does not teach the Classics, if that's what you want to study. Finally, you should think about whether you want to go to a school with alot of students or not too many. For example, there are more than 50,000 students at UCSB, but maybe you prefer to go to a school with only 5,000.

When deciding on a college, take your time and consider all of these things. College is important for the rest of your life so choose wisely!

Sample 1 Score

Evryone shoold go to college because that educasion are good for You. Its right to go to college becaus you need it for work and job's and life too. The right colege for You is one You like alot when You are done with hi-scool.

808. Your new job requires that you move to a different city. Describe the steps you will take to prepare for this move.

Sample 6 Score

Although Americans move more than most people in the world, a move is acknowledged to be one of life's more stressful experiences. There are, however, steps that can be taken and preparations that can be made that will mitigate the inevitable strain.

If I were to move to a different city because of a job change, I would find a sponsor in the new location, preferably someone who could give me insight into the kind of situation I could expect in the workplace and about the cultural and other differences in the new community. Different cities may be diverse in many ways: in ideas about appropriate behavior, in social expectations, and even in emotional reactions. If the city had special sites or events to generate civic pride, I would like to investigate those. Or there may be popular gathering places such as parks or cafés. This knowledge would be helpful in getting to understand the attitudes of the residents and to become part of the community.

Spending time with a real estate agent would be a necessity, not only for finding a satisfactory residence, but also for gaining information about different neighborhoods, schools, libraries, and other community resources. In fact, it would be worthwhile to take the time to deliberately explore the community by walking or driving around.

My family members are interested in horses, sailing, and playing bridge. As a way to find out how we can pursue these interests and find people similarly inclined, we could visit stables, marinas, or social clubs. Striking up a conversation with people in these places and telling them that I am moving there shortly would create a more knowledgeable transition. In addition to picking the brains of people, there may be published material, such as maps and guidebooks, that could be informative. The same is true of Internet sites.

All this preparation cannot eliminate the probability that leaving my friends; seeing my belongings picked up, packed, and moved to a different city; and facing new routines and new surroundings will be somewhat traumatic. However, visualizing daily life in the new city can help make the move easier and the transition smoother.

Sample 4 Score

If I find out that I have to move to a different city I will try to make some plans. First of all I will have to find a house. I will get a real estate person and look at houses. I will find out how much they cost and if I can afford it. Then I will try to find a nice area. The schools should be good and near the house and the church to.

I like to play basketball and ride my bike and I will look around for places to play. Maybe I can meet some people who live there and make friends. Maybe they can show me around the place. I will try to meet someone who works at the new job. They can give me hints about how things are done there.

I will say goodbye to my friends and give them my new address. It will be sad to move, but also there will be good things coming up. At least I wont be going in cold. I will have a place to live that is nice and I know maybe a few people already. I think I am starting to know what it will be like in my new home.

Sample 1 Score

I have to move becuz my job it changed. I will go there to see what it is there. Is there a good house. I hate to pay for a house they always rip you off and the boss dosent car. I will find our if the boss is good or not like this 1 I hate now. What can you do you want a job rite. I wil sell my house and use it to by the new 1 and I would learn the name of the new city and how to rite it.

809. Many people spend a great deal of time with animals. Write about the relationships that people have with animals.

Sample 6 Score

Since they were first domesticated, people have had relationships with animals that have enhanced their lives. Probably animals that were trained to hunt and to retrieve prey were among the first to become valuable to their owners. Useful animals include those used for transportation, for hauling loads, and, in recent times, to assist handicapped people. The latter are usually dogs trained to guide the blind and to assist paraplegics. Although these animals have specific functions, it is probable that a special bond inevitably arises between them and the humans they serve, and this goes far beyond the dependency each has on the other.

Can a relationship with an animal improve a person's health? Many recent reports seem to suggest this possibility. Pets give us abundant and unconditional love. Always happy to see us, our pets allow us to be ourselves, to talk to them, and even to believe that they understand us. When we come home, we might feel reluctant to talk to ourselves, but it is perfectly all right to greet, chat, and interact with our dog, cat, bird, and even our fish. Some mental health workers are so insistent upon the beneficial influences of pets that they have an animal present during therapy sessions, claiming that this causes patients to be more relaxed and responsive. Studies have proven that relationships with animals reduce stress and actually can measurably lower blood pressure.

For people who are depressed or living alone, having a pet is not only therapeutic; it is a means of encouraging a healthier lifestyle. A pet owner must live according to a regular timetable so that the pet can be fed and cared for appropriately. For dog owners, there is an additional social benefit that accrues from having to go outdoors for a walk. Encountering other dog walkers often leads to further social interaction and, perhaps, friendship. For cat owners, there is the admiration for the cat's characteristic independence, which makes any affection from the cat so much more meaningful. Keeping the bird feeders filled gives a sense of satisfying the needs of creatures that, in turn, delight us with their beauty and their antics.

Other beneficial effects of relationships with animals continue to be discovered. A recent article suggests that kindness to people and animals may be interconnected. Role-playing that increases children's empathy for animals helps them not only psychologically, but also physically and socially. Another discovery shows that riding horses, for reasons not completely understood, has been shown to benefit autistic children. Pet owners can now volunteer to take their pets to hospitals and nursing homes, where residents seem to welcome them.

It is probable that continued research will shed additional light on what happens when people and animals form a bond. For the present, it is certain that almost anyone can benefit from the resulting security, understanding, fun, laughter, and love that come from having a pet.

Sample 4 Score

I enjoy my pets. I have a cat and a bird and I like to spend time with them. When no one is home I play with my cat, or I may try to hold my bird. When I have a pet I feel good and happy. Some people have horses for pets. They get to ride them and take care of them. Even if you have a cat and don't have to take it for a walk you have to feed it.

One of the good things about pets is it teaches you things. I learned that I have to take care of my pets. They need me to feed them every day. I think they look at me funny if I forget or if I am late. I no that little babies like to pet animals and that they like them. So there are relationship with animals for all ages. Old people like animals to. If they live alone they can have someone to talk to. Pets are like friends.

I no a blind man and he has a seeing dog and he goes all over with it. So he has a relationship with his dog. The dog helps him and he helps the dog by loving and taking care of it.

Relationships with animals are good for both people and animals.

Sample 1 Score

What are animals that have a relationship they are pets. I have a dog I hate to feed it and it shed but it wags its tale its kut. Wen I got the dog it was little and kut and now it isnt so kut because its to big. But I love it and he loves me not like my boyfreind who I don't have a relationship with. So I have a relationship with my pet it ushuly feel good.

810. Describe an especially memorable photo or picture.

Sample 6 Score

You might think a memorable picture would be in vivid color, have an appealing or inspirational theme, or be something you might want to display and look at every day. That is not the case with the picture that is most memorable to me. This picture is really a large mural, painted in 1937 by the Spanish artist Pablo Picasso to protest the bombing of a small village in northern Spain.

Surprisingly, there is no vivid red color to show the flowing blood. One must imagine this, for the mural is startlingly gray, black, and white. But there is no avoiding the horror of the images. The figures are not realistically drawn, but are cubist and abstract, and it is apparent that innocent civilians are being slaughtered. A mother screams with her mouth wide open, her head tipped back in heartrending anguish, as she holds her dead baby. A soldier lies dead on the ground, clutching his broken sword, and three other people are shown in shock and agony. Animals, including a tortured horse and a crying bird, are also portrayed as innocent victims of a massacre. Some symbols are open to interpretation. What is the meaning of the bull, which seems simply to be observing, or of the lightbulb emitting rays at the top of the mural? Does the bull symbolize brute force, and does the lightbulb signify that there is hope? Yet there is no doubt that the distorted, horrible images are intended to shock the viewer. This depiction of human grief is a profound statement of the cruelty and senselessness of war. Limiting the picture to black and white adds a funereal element to the shocking depiction of the catastrophe.

The memory of the picture cannot be erased; it is a metaphor for the senselessness and the horror of war. Whereas it was painted to protest atrocities in a long-ago war, it is as relevant today as the recollection of the horrors of September 11, 2001. Perhaps it should be shown to all those who contemplate starting a war. Would it be worth it to have another Guernica?

Sample 4 Score

The picture I remember is Guernica. It is by Picasso. It is not realist. The shapes don't look real but you know what they are in real life. It is in black and white. It is not in color like most pictures. But it really gets to you. It shows people getting killed or already killed. A baby is killed and a soldier is killed. The mother is screaming because her baby is dead. You won't forget that.

What this picture does is to make you know that war kills people and it is just awful. It kills people and it kills animals and even if you are not killed you will probly be screaming or crying. This picture could be for any war it doesn't matter. You remember it because it makes you upset and you wish there would never be a war. Then people wouldn't have to suffer. This picture is memorable because you remember how the people suffered and they probly didn't do anything.

Sample 1 Score

I remember a picture that is very big. It is Guernica. It is about people dieing and screaming and horses. I don't like it it dosent make sens. Who cared about a horse and why is it in black and white. I don't like black and white movies or pithcers. My sister had black and whites at her wedding and of cours I hated it. But I do remember it because everyone is yelling.

811. Write a letter to a teacher requesting information about a poor grade.

Sample 6 Score

Dear Ms. Jones:

Your class was one of the most informative I have ever taken, and I learned a tremendous amount in the relatively short time of one semester. Therefore, I felt obliged to write to you when I received the disappointing grade of C on my term paper.

Checking the criteria you provided and thoroughly discussed in class, I felt that I complied with each one in a superior manner, not just passably, as reflected in my grade. Four arguments in support of my thesis were stated and each was in turn discussed with several relevant examples given. You required only three arguments. Bibliographical citations were given in the exact format you demonstrated in class. As suggested, Internet sites were used in addition to first-person accounts and editorial material.

Although I spent an inordinate amount of time on this project, I felt it to be most worthwhile because it was a wonderful learning experience. When I saw the grade on the paper, I looked in vain for comments or suggestions. It would be helpful to me if I understood how you arrived at this grade. Would it be possible for us to arrange a meeting, during which time you could offer hints about what you felt was lacking in my work, and, perhaps, I could hope that you might reconsider and raise my grade.

Thank you for your kind consideration of this request.

Sincerely yours,

Your Student

Sample 4 Score

Dear Ms. Jones:

I was really upset at my grade. I don't think I am a C student. I tried hard and got some B's a few times. Don't you think I did everything on the checklist you gave us? I had the right number of examples and I tried to tell a little about the examples. There was only one where I couldn't get an example, but does that mean I get a C?

I worked hard on this and I think anyone would get a C even if they didn't work so hard. I never did such a long paper. I hope you noticed the good bibliography. I copied it just the way you showed it. And you didn't write any corrections so what was wrong with it?

Could you tell me what was wrong with it. I think I should get at least a B.

Sincerely yours,

Your Student

Sample 1 Score

Dear ms Jones,

Why do you pick on me im as good as anyone. Why do I get the lousy grad. I culdnt do that bibliography but I did do some examples. My friend was over and who had time she was having a big prolben with the famly. I tried to help her but it was no use. Anyway I wish yud be nice for wuns sins its over the class is and whats the big deel. Just give me a better grade I was only abset 8 tims.

Your friend,

A student

812. You want to organize a family reunion.

Describe the steps you will take to contact people and to organize the event.

Sample 6 Score

My family is united genetically but not by proximity. We live in far-flung locations, including three continents and both the northern and southern hemispheres. Some of us have kept in touch, while others might as well be considered MIA. It would seem close to impossible to organize a family reunion for such a peripatetic group. Yet, that is what I decided to attempt.

Initially I sent e-mails to all those I regularly heard from and requested any and all addresses of other relatives to be forwarded to me. South Africa was the farthest location and was the source of some previously unknown addresses. Internet searches yielded still more. How delighted I was that there seemed to be universal interest in the project. Several people volunteered to help. We generated a list and added to it as soon as we received further information.

Relatives were located in Alaska, Canada, and six states. Thus the first big hurdle was overcome: the list of potential invitees. Then, with solicited input from all concerned, it was decided to choose a location near New York, the original point of origin of the family.

It then became necessary to choose a site for the get-together and then to find accommodations for approximately 55 people ranging in age from under one year to 85. An all-suite hotel, which agreed to charge reduced rates if a minimum number of reservations were confirmed, was selected. The hotel agreed to hold rooms for us until two weeks prior to the weekend of the get-together. A list of nearby motels and bed-and-breakfasts was also compiled. We now had the who, where, and when, the latter being the last weekend in September when the weather was still moderate and travel not likely to be a problem. Why we were getting together seemed obvious. There was curiosity to catch up, and even to meet relatives known only by reputation.

Now we came to the question of how the weekend would be organized. Since most people would be arriving on Friday, that day was to be relaxed and unstructured. On Saturday, there would be games and an informal picnic lunch in a nearby county park, the permission for which was easily obtained. Saturday night would be the highlight, a catered dinner in a restaurant that could easily hold a group of this size. People had been asked to bring photos and anecdotes, and a list of speakers was generated. The youngest members would be introduced, and those traveling great distances would be recognized. The oldest members might wish to share their reminiscences. Sunday would again be an informal day, probably punctuated with hugs, the sharing of addresses, and promises to do this again. All of the activities would be recorded on videos and a digital camera so that they could easily be forwarded via e-mail.

Thus, the planning for a family reunion must begin well in advance of the date. Planners must seek out addresses of the relatives, and must settle on a location, a date, and, of course, a place to stay. These would vary according to the size and needs of the group. Some groups might prefer to simply chat informally, while others would appreciate planned activities. Once a family has done this, a second reunion would be much easier. The addresses are known, faces can be associated with names, and an evaluation of the previous schedule can be solicited. One caveat: have alternate plans in case of bad weather.

Sample 4 Score

The first step in planning a family reunion is having a family. Who is included? Do you invite the divorced ones? After you decide who to invite you should make up a list. Then you should call them, maybe getting someone to help as this is a big job.

The second step is to decide what to do. So you need to know exactly or pretty nearly how many are coming. So you have to pick a date that is good for everyone. Will it be just one day. Or two? You could play games and have people tell stories. It would be fun to hear about things the old people remember. Will you all get together or will it be by ages? You will have to decide. I think it is best to have all ages see each other and become friends if possible.

The third step is deciding where to get together. How about your house? Do you have room? Do you want the mess? If everyone brings something you will probly still have to get most of the stuff and have the most work anyway. I would do it one time and then have someone else take a turn.

So you now have everybody together for a family reunion. I hope it is fun. I hope it is not boring. I must tell you that some of my known relatives are boring but they are my relatives.

Sample 1 Score

I wanted to try to have a family reunion. My friend had it. What if someone couldn't get there. Well that's life. What if they didn't like the food—hot dogs and hamburgers—well we could ask people to bring something.

One thing I wanted was to see pitchers of my aunt's and uncles and my mom and dad when they were young. Its hard to believe that they were ever kids. Some of the family hates each other at least they don't speak to each other and sometims you cant menshun there names. So what, I can invite them. Acept maybe one dum cousin. But I will take pitchers to show my kids but I don't think I want any. Kids that is.

Scoring Explanations for Narrative Writing Essays

A score of **"6"** indicates that your essay satisfies the requirements of the writing prompt in a creative and original manner, using an obvious theme throughout. You thoroughly articulate your ideas in a coherent fashion, use precise examples, and develop the topic in an interesting manner. The narrative uses dialogue effectively, contains believable characters, and conveys vivid emotions and situations. The story itself is orderly, with a clear focus, a logical sequence of ideas, and transitional words and sentences. Your writing demonstrates a sense of audience by using effective vocabulary, varied sentence structure, and fluid, sophisticated language that is essentially without errors.

A score of **"4"** indicates that your essay meets some of the requirements of the writing prompt but develops ideas somewhat inconsistently. Your essay may answer the question in an abbreviated manner, using little dialogue and giving only brief examples to support the thesis. Your essay has a general focus, makes an obvious attempt at organization, and presents your ideas in a logical sequence. The language of your essay indicates a general control of mechanics but has a slightly lower quality of sentence structure and variety than a sample 6 score. An essay of this type contains errors only when using sophisticated language.

A score of **"1"** indicates that the essay only minimally addresses the writing prompt, digressing, repeating, or dwelling on insignificant details throughout. Your essay shows a lack of development and exhibits no organizational pattern or focus. Your writing may be illegible or unrecognizable as English.

Model Narrative Writing Essays

813. People often say, "Don't judge a book by its cover." Describe a time when you misjudged someone based on his or her appearance or when someone misjudged you.

Sample 6 Score

When Maria Mariella Panontin first showed up at our school, here's what I thought: *Look at that girl. She dresses like she's some exotic gypsy or something. Looks like a real high-maintenance kind of girl. Not my type; I'm not going to bother trying to get to know her.* So I didn't. Too late, I realized what a mistake I'd made.

Maria Mariella (she went by both names) was a foreign exchange student from Italy who was staying with a friend of mine, Joanne. Joanne and I weren't that close, but we hung out in the same general crowd, so when the extended clique got together, Maria Mariella was often part of the group. We were friendly to each other, but we never tried to become friends until Shanda's party.

I wasn't planning on going to Shanda's party because I had a big track meet the next day, but my friend Elaine convinced me to go for a little while. When I was saying good-bye, Joanne rushed up to me.

"Hey, Jenine, can you do me a really big favor? Maria Mariella needs to go home, but I want to stay. Would you mind dropping her off at my house?"

I didn't really want to, but it was on the way, and I would have looked like a real jerk if I said no, so I said, "Sure, no problem." Maria Mariella was right behind Joanne. I looked at her and said, "Let's go."

We hopped into my car. As I was pulling out of the driveway, I popped in a 10,000 Maniacs cassette and turned the sound up loud.

"I love this song!" Maria Mariella shouted over the music.

"Really?" Not even my American friends appreciated this band. "You like the 10,000 Maniacs?"

"I love them," she said with her heavy Italian accent.

After that, it seemed like Maria Mariella and I couldn't stop talking to one another and finding things in common. I loved that she was straightforward and honest, like me. She shared my taste in music and film. We both had crushes on the same movie stars. It felt like a friendship that was meant to be.

Then, just two weeks later, Maria Mariella threw a party at Joanne's house. It was a going-away party. Her mother had developed a serious illness, and Maria Mariella was going home to be with her. At that party, a group of us were playing Truth or Dare, one of our favorite games. It was Maria Mariella's turn.

"Truth!" she said.

"Name something you regret," our friend Denise demanded.

Maria Mariella pointed a long finger at me. "I wish I'd taken the time to get to know you sooner. I didn't think you were worth my time."

A sad smile came across my face. "I thought the same thing, Maria Mariella," I said. "That is something I'm always going to regret."

Sample 4 Score

They say you shouldn't judge a book by it's cover, but people often do. I learned my lesson about this in high school when I met Maria Mariella. I didn't think she was worth getting to know but I was very wrong. She turned out to be a great friend, but by the time I realized it she was gone.

Maria Mariella came to our school from Italy, she stayed with a friend of mine, Joanne. I saw Maria Mariella a lot at school and parties but I never really talked to her. Just from how she looked and dressed (like a gypsy), I didn't think I'd like her. Then one night Joanne asked me to take Maria Mariella home because I was leaving early and she wanted to leave early too. So I did, and I found out she loved the 10,000 Maniacs as much as I did, not even my best friend liked the same music. After that we started talking and hanging out, and we kept finding that we had all kinds of things in common. The more we talked, the more we liked each other.

Its a sad thing that our friendship was so short. Maria Mariella had to go back to Italy a few weeks later because her mother got sick. At her good-bye party, we were playing "Truth or Dare." It was our favorite game. When it was Maria Mariella's turn she said "truth." Denise asked her to tell the truth about something she regrets.

Maria Mariella said, "I wish I'd gotten to know you sooner, I didn't think you were worth my time." I said, me too, and that's something we both regret.

Sample 1 Score

One time I misjudeged someone based on their appearance and someone misjudged me also. In high school. We shouldn't not to judge other people because it is wrong, you must to get to know somebody first and then you can have an opinion on them what there like. When you judge some one first you can be a lot wrong in fact really wrong about what that person is to be like. For example, Maria Mariella, in high school. I didn't not liked her because I thought she looked stupid the way she dressing up all the time. Although she really was nice. It was too late.

Don't not judge a book by its cover, it can make you very sad.

814. It has been said that the truth is often stranger than fiction. Describe an experience you had that was so strange others might think you made it up.

Sample 6 Score

My friends still think I made this story up, even though they've never known me to be a liar. When it happened I couldn't believe it myself, but it's true. This really happened.

My best friend and I were working one summer as line chefs in the Marriott at the sprawling Tan-Tara Resort on the Lake of the Ozarks, Missouri. One Tuesday morning, as I walked through the kitchen to get to the time clock, half a dozen people said to me, "Uh-oh, man, the executive chef wants to see you." The executive chef? But I hadn't done anything wrong. What could he want? Why was I in trouble?

I clocked in and knocked on the executive chef's door. "Listen," he said angrily when I sat down, "I don't know what you guys did or how you did it, but you and your buddy Jim have off on Friday." Friday was our busiest night; no one gets off on Friday without a *very* good reason. "Just one thing," he said sternly as I got up to go. "Don't you guys tell anyone why you're not coming in. Understand?"

"Understand," I replied, but I had no idea what he was talking about. I had to find Jim as soon as possible and figure out what was going on. But every time I asked Jim about it, he simply said, "I'll tell you later. Just don't worry about it." No matter how much I begged, he wouldn't tell me what was going on and why we had the day off. By Thursday night, he still hadn't told me what was happening Friday. As we were watching TV in our apartment, he said, "Let's hit the sack early tonight. We're going to need lots of rest for tomorrow." Jim never went to bed early. What on Earth was going on?

In the morning, Jim woke me up (another anomaly) and told me to get a quick shower, put on my bathing suit, and pack a change of clothes. A few minutes later, a dark SUV with tinted windows pulled up in front of our building. "There's our ride," Jim said with a secretive smile. We walked out to the car, but I wasn't getting in without an explanation. So Jim shoved me in. Inside, I looked up, and there in the passenger seat was a famous Hollywood actor.

Now Jim had no choice but to explain. It turns out that a friend of a friend of Jim's knew the actor and knew that he wanted to get away for a totally private vacation between films. This friend said that he knew two guys at a large secluded lake in Missouri who would take care of him for the day. So the actor called the executive chef and asked for Jim and me to have the day off.

We all spent the day out on the lake waterskiing, fishing, eating, drinking, and telling stories. We did our best to treat him like just another guy spending the day with a couple of new friends. We didn't ask him anything about Hollywood or his latest high-profile romance; we just let him relax and be himself for a day without cameras or fans.

At the end of the day, as we pulled back in to the dock, he said, "Listen, guys, I had a really good time today. It was just what I needed. I appreciate it, man." He shook our hands. "One favor, though?" he asked. "Don't tell anybody about this. If people find out I'm here, I won't get any peace and quiet. I need some time alone."

"No problem," we said, and headed home. The next day, everyone kept asking what was so special that we had to have Friday off. The night was a disaster for the kitchen, and they were all upset that we hadn't been there. All we could say was, "Nothing, man, nothing. We were just hanging out." We had a great time, too, and we kept our promise.

Sample 4 Score

My friends still don't believe me when I tell them this story, but its true. I was working in a restaurant at a big lake resort, in Missouri, when my boss called me into his office. I thought I was in trouble. Instead, he told me that me and my roommate and best friend, Jim, had Friday off. Normally you have to beg and plead or have an emergency to have a Friday off, here I was getting the day off without even asking. I had no idea what was going on. He seems angry, too, and says, "don't you and your friend tell anybody why your not coming in Friday, understand"? I said yes, but I was clueless.

I kept asking my roommate about it but he decides not to tell me anything. "Just don't worry," he keeps saying, and it was starting to drive me crazy. For three days, he kept the secret. Then, Friday morning, he wakes me up early (I'm always the one up first, so I thought this was really weird) and tells me to get dressed. A few minutes later, a black SUV with dark windows pulls up, and he tells me to get in. No way, I say, but he pushes me in, and that's when I see whose in the car, a famous Hollywood actor.

"What is going on?" I demand so I finally get my explanation. A friend of a friend of Jim heard that the actor needed a vacation between movies, told him to go to this lake which is pretty private because its really big, you can hide away there if you want. He also gave him our names and said we would take care of him for the day if he wanted, so he called our boss and told him to give us the day off. We went out on the lake then and spent the day out on the boat.

It turns out that he was a really cool guy. It was hard to treat him like just another guy, but we did, because that was what he wanted. We didn't ask him about his movies or anything, actually he kept asking us questions about us. We all had a great time. At the end of the day, he thanks us and asks us not to tell anyone so that people don't chase him with cameras and stuff. We promised. It was so hard not to tell anyone what we did that day!

Sample 1 Score

Some people they make up storys all the time, you don't know when to beleive them if its true or not. Some time, the storys are super strange like it couldn't really of happened in the first place, then no body is going to beleive it. One time a story like that happen to me, when I met an actor, he was on vacation and asks my boss for me to have the day off. So me and my friend could hang out with him. But we're not aloud to tell any body any thing. That was so frustrating! For me.

This guy he was a really good actor, I seen him in a lot of films, I was like wow when I met him but I have to play it cool, like I don't care how famous he is. That was so hard. We hung out all day and he was a really nice guy to. He was glad noone else knows that he is there on the lake or else they all come after him with cameras and stuff and bother him a lot.

815. We all have things that we are afraid of, and sometimes we find ourselves in situations that force us to face our deepest fears. Tell about a time when you had to face one of your greatest fears.

Sample 6 Score

Every kid in the neighborhood knew the Robinson house and avoided it like a bowl of brussels sprouts. Mr. Robinson was a notorious crank, the house was always dark and creepy, and his dog was a terror—a mean, fang-toothed creature that looked like she would love to tear you apart.

The dog's name was Angel, but she scared the devil out of us. She was half pit bull, half Doberman pinscher. Mr. Robinson kept her out on the front lawn, chained to a thin pole stuck in the ground near his front door. It was a long chain, and when I walked past the house to the bus stop, Angel always bounded toward me, barking furiously. *One of these times that chain will break, I thought, and I'll be Angel's dinner.* When I got to the Robinson house, I always walked past it as quickly as I could. Sometimes I could see Mr. Robinson watching from the window, laughing.

Then it happened. We had gotten our report cards in school that day, and I was so proud of my marks and my teachers' comments that I just had to look at them again on my way home from the bus stop. I was so wrapped up in that report card that I didn't realize how close I was to Mr. Robinson's house, and Angel startled me when she started barking. I dropped my report card, and just then, a big gust of wind took the paper up into the air. It landed right smack in the middle of Mr. Robinson's lawn, about two feet away from Angel.

Angel, growling ferociously, was straining her chain, trying to get closer to me. I could see her long canines. I could even smell her from where I was standing. I think I was shaking. But I needed to get that report card back. My mom had to sign it. Besides, she had to see those fantastic grades.

I thought about yelling for Mr. Robinson, but I was just as afraid of him as of the dog. So I decided to see if maybe, just maybe, Angel would let me get close enough to get that piece of paper.

I remembered my uncle telling me that dogs can sense your fear, and that most dogs will be friendly if you approach them in the right manner. So I did my best not to look scared. I straightened up, softened my face, and walked slowly toward Angel. She kept barking and growling. Saliva was dripping from her chin. I closed my eyes and gulped. I was about six feet away from Angel, and I put my fist out in front of me for her to smell, saying, "Here, girl. Nice girl. Good girl," as calmly as I could. But she was barking so loudly and angrily that I'm sure she didn't hear a word.

Inside, I had never been more frightened. *This dog is going to tear me to pieces, I thought.* But I kept going, slowly. I had never earned such good marks before. I wasn't going to let a crazy old dog keep me from showing that report card to my parents.

I was about three steps away from Angel when the wind blew again, this time sending my report card just out of Angel's reach. I didn't have to confront that dog after all. It was a good thing, too—Mr. Robinson later told my folks that Angel surely would have bitten me badly. I realized that what I'd planned to do was dangerous and that I was simply being stubborn. But part of me was proud, because I was brave enough to try to get close to Angel.

Sample 4 Score

Growing up, a dog named Angel was one of my biggest fears. She was a vicious dog, half pit bull and half Doberman pincher. I had to walk past her house a lot, and every time I did, I walked as fast as I could. Sometimes I saw her owner, Mr. Robinson, watching out the window. He was as creepy as she was mean.

One day we got our report cards and I saw I'd gotten the best grades ever. I couldn't wait to show my parents. On my way home, passing the Robinsons house, I was looking at my report card again. I was just so proud. But then Angel started to bark, and that scared me. I dropped my report card, and some wind came along and blew it right next to Angel.

Angel was pulling on her chain and growling at me, scaring me to death. But, I had to get my report card back. What was I going to do? I decided to try to make friends with Angel. I know that if you hold your hand out to a dog and don't act scared they'll often be friendly to you because then they don't fell threatened. So, I slowly approached Angel trying not to look to scared. I thought she was going to attack me, but I kept going slowly towards her.

Luckily, just then the wind blew again. This time my report card blew towards me and far enough away from Angel that I could get it safely. I breathed a big sigh of relief and headed home. Later Mr. Robinson told my parents that Angel surely would have bitten me. It's a good thing I didn't get any closer. Still I'm proud that I got as close as I did.

Sample 1 Score

Dogs can be really scarey. In my neighborhood they're was a really scarey dog named "Angel." She was mean and always barking. Everyone was scared of her. We all thought her owner Mr. robinson was weird too and scarey. He was always peaking out of his windows and watching.

One day when I was coming home from school. My report card blue out of my hands next to Angel. I was really scared, more then ever. I got close and then the wind blue again, luckily for me. She just kept barking and growling all the time, too. I was sure her chain would brake.

816. Moving can be a very exciting but also difficult time in one's life. Tell about a time you moved and how it affected you.

Sample 6 Score

As the new kid in town, I was eager—okay, desperate —to make new friends, and fast. My dad had just accepted a promotion that required a transfer, and we had moved from Chicago to Oakland, California, just a few days before I was to begin the sixth grade. I hadn't even had a chance to get to know any of the kids in the neighborhood before school started.

After the first day of school, I could tell that Charlie Jenkins was the one who would make me or break me. He was a bully for sure, but he was so good-looking and charming that everyone seemed to like him. He was clearly the center of power in that classroom, and I knew I would have to win his approval. I just wasn't sure what I'd have to do to get it.

My answer came at the end of the third week of school, when Ms. Harcourt gave us our second writing assignment. We'd been reading and discussing fables, and now it was our turn to write our own. That afternoon, Charlie cornered me on the playground.

He teased me about being a new kid, yet he seemed interested in the fact that I was a good writer. Our teacher, Ms. Harcourt, had read aloud one of my poems in class just the day before, and obviously he was paying attention.

"Hey, new kid, hold on a second," he said, standing between the gate and me. "You seem to be pretty good with writing."

I admitted that I had a flair for writing, and at first I was flattered that he noticed. But, he had an ulterior motive.

"I'll tell you what," he said, moving closer, until his face was just a few inches from mine. "Why don't you just write an extra fable, one for you, one for me? Let me see what you can do."

So that was it. I was going to do Charlie's English homework for him. That was the price I was going to pay to be accepted.

Charlie didn't wait for an answer. "Bring a fable to school for me on Monday," he said. That would give him time to copy it over in his own handwriting to submit to Ms. Harcourt on Tuesday.

Over the weekend, I wrote two fables, both of them quite good, I thought, but one was definitely better than the other. On Monday morning, I met Charlie in the schoolyard as planned.

"Here's your fable," I said to Charlie, handing him a piece of paper. I gave Charlie the fable that I thought was inferior, keeping the better fable for myself, and turned to walk away.

He questioned me about the quality of the paper, read it quickly, and decided that it passed muster. Without saying thank you or goodbye, he swaggered off into the building.

A few days later, Ms. Harcourt returned our fables. I looked at my paper, expecting to see an A or A+, but my grade was an A–. Then I looked over at Charlie. He was holding his paper up high so I could see his grade: A+. I knew the fable I'd kept for myself was better. Perhaps Charlie's charm was factored into his grade.

Fortunately, I only had to do one more assignment for Charlie before he and his family abruptly moved to another town. Now Charlie was going to be the new kid in the classroom. I often wondered what he had to do there to be accepted.

Sample 4 Score

One of the hardest things about moving is trying to make new friends. When we moved to Oakland, I didn't have time to make any friends before school started. I was the "new" kid in the classroom. The most popular kid in the sixth grade was Charlie, and I had to make sure he liked me. I could tell right away you wouldn't want Charlie as your enemy.

After a couple weeks of school, we were given an assignment in English, we had to write our own fables. (We'd been studying fables in class). Charlie came up to me in the playground that day. He'd found out I was a good writer, and he said I better write an extra fable for him. If I wanted Charlie to like me, I was going to have to do his English homework for him. "Meet me here Monday before school starts, with my fable," he said.

So I wrote two fables that weekend. Both of them were good, but one was better than the other. That's the one I kept for myself. I gave the other one to Charlie, outside of school on Monday morning, just like he said. He made me stand there while he read it

to make sure it was good. He seemed to like it, and he let me go.

A few days later we get our fables back, and I couldn't believe it. Charlie got an A+ on his fable while I got an A–. I know my fable was better than his (which was really mine, of course). Maybe the teacher really liked Charlie. That's the only way I can explain it.

A few weeks later Charlie's family had to move, so I only had to do one more assignment for him. Now he had to be the new kid. I wonder how he handled it.

Sample 1 Score

Moving is a hard thing. It is often very difficult for family's. Especially children. I remember a time we moved. It affect me strongly. I had to do someone elses schoolwork. He ask me to do his assinment and I have to or else he wont like me and he is the most popular.

I do his homework for him and mine too. Then even though mine is better he gets an even better grade! This was not fare at all. I think the teacher had a big problem. Sometimes the popular kids are even poplar with teechers, they get better grades for nothing. This made me very angry.

I was very happy when he moved away then I didn't have to do any more work for him or worry if he likes me.

817. As the saying goes, "If at first you don't succeed, try, try again." Describe a time when you persisted until you achieved your goal.

Sample 6 Score

In seventh grade, I had a best friend who was an incredible athlete. I was pretty coordinated myself, but because I was so insecure, I never seemed to be any good at sports. I was so afraid of missing the ball that I would be sure to swing and miss, even if it was right over the plate. But Katie was my best friend, and if she joined a team, I did, too. Or at least I tried. Katie was a starter for the junior varsity field hockey team; I sat on the bench all season. Katie played regularly in JV basketball; I was cut during tryouts. I figured I was headed for a similar fate with lacrosse. But Katie was my best friend, so I signed up anyway.

Katie was a natural, and she picked up the new sport quickly. I, on the other hand, couldn't seem to hold the lacrosse stick comfortably. I caught one out of ten throws, if I was lucky, and my tosses were always way off their mark. I was clumsy and feeling clumsier, and I thought maybe it was time to give it up. But that would create an even wider gulf between Katie and me. Already she was spending more and more time with the girls who, like her, excelled at sports. I was beginning to be left behind.

Determined to stick it out and save our friendship, I begged my mom to take me to a sporting goods store and buy me an early birthday present: my own lacrosse stick and ball so I could practice at home. Katie was impressed with my stick, but I could tell that she thought it was a waste of money. She figured I would never get to use that stick in a game.

I was hurt by her reaction, and again I felt the distance between us. If I was going to keep Katie as a friend, I thought, I simply had to get the hang of this sport. It was my last chance. Somehow, someway, I had to learn how to throw and catch the ball in that net and be respectable on the playing field.

So I practiced, and I practiced, and I practiced some more. I often felt like there was no hope, and I broke two windows in the garage, but I kept at it.

Then, one day, just after the first official game of the season (during which I sat on the bench), something happened. I paired off with Suzie, who had become my partner since Katie had quickly proven to be too good to play with me. That day, when Suzie sent me her first throw, I caught it. When I threw the ball back to her, I hit her stick dead on. I caught her next throw, and the next. Something was happening. I was *getting* it. The stick was actually feeling good in my hands. The movements were becoming natural. I was catching and throwing the ball accurately.

I still don't know what exactly happened that day, but I will always be grateful for it. By the end of the season, I was starting for the JV team. I scored 12 goals that year, and the next year I was playing varsity. My success on the field gave me confidence that I desperately needed. Katie and I continued to drift apart, but Suzie turned out to be a great friend. She quit the team after the first year, but she came to every game to cheer me on.

Sample 4 Score

They say that if you don't succeed, try, try again until you do. When I was in Junior High School, I tried many sports because my best friend did. She was a great athlete; I was not. I sat on the bench all of field hockey season and I got cut during basketball tryouts, too. I stuck with it, though and finally made it on the lacrosse team.

My friend Katie picked up lacrosse right away, but I struggled. Even though she was my best friend I couldn't be partners with her during practice. Because she was so much better than me. I was afraid that if I didn't learn how to be good at lacrosse, our friendship would be over. She was spending more and more time with her sports friends, and I was feeling more and more left out.

I decided to do something to save our friendship. I went out and bought a lacrosse stick. After practice, I'd come home and practice. I practiced on weekends, too. I tried and tried and tried. Some days I felt like there wasn't any hope, but I kept trying.

Then one day, it happened. I was throwing and catching the ball with Suzie, my new partner. Suddenly, I caught the ball. I caught the next one she threw, too. My throws to her were accurate. From that day on, I got better and better. I had more confidence, too. I ended up playing a lot that season on the JV team and even scored 12 goals. Suzie quit the team, but she was my new friend, and she came to cheer me on. I'm really glad I kept trying.

Sample 1 Score

As the saying goes if at first you don't succeed try try again. This is good advise to everyone. I try and try and try until I get good at lacross.

This is a fun sport, I really enjoy it. You have to throw and catch the ball in a net. When I first start I was lousy at it. I couldnt catch or through the ball right. I was sitting on the bench all the time. My friend was really good at it. She even plays varsity her first year.

This friend shes looking for other friends who are like her good at sports not like me. She really hurt me a lot that way. However I make new friends like Suzie. She was my partner in practices. She stayed with me even when I learned how to play right.

818. Movies and literature often deal with the theme of counting your blessings. Tell about an experience that led you to appreciate someone or something you'd taken for granted.

Sample 6 Score

I often complained about our lack of wealth to my parents, who often replied that I had no idea what it means to be poor and that someday they'd show me what poverty was really like. I thought they were all talk, but one day, they proved me wrong—and showed me just how right they were.

Thehe images from that day still haunt me. My parents were very active in their church, and they had arranged to deliver clothing and food donations

to a church in a deeply impoverished area on the edge of the Appalachian Mountains, a four-hour drive from our home.

I'd seen pictures of poverty before, of course. But seeing a picture of a shack with seven malnourished children and actually walking into such a shack are two entirely different things. The pastor of the church took us into a few homes so we could deliver some of the items (a crib, a box of linens, canned goods) personally. I had never felt so uncomfortable before. These people had so little! Eight family members living in two rooms . . . no electricity or running water . . . no couches or microwaves or cable television . . . soon I began to realize just how lucky I was. True, I didn't have as much as my friends. But I had so much more than the people we visited that day. I felt greedy and guilty for having so many things.

When we got back home, I got on the Internet and found a soup kitchen not too far from our home. I've been volunteering there twice a week ever since. Two of my friends have joined me. Every time we go, we count our blessings.

Sample 4 Score

On one afternoon I'll never forget, my parents taught me to appreciate what I have. We lived in a very rich neighborhood but we ourselves were not rich, we were only middle class. Therefore I always felt like I was poor; compared to all my friends and their fancy houses and pools and cars. None of my friends had to work; but I had to work, to afford my car.

I guess my parents got tired, of me complaining, so one day they woke me up really early and took me on a long drive to a really poor neighborhood. I mean this place was really, really poor. I never saw such poverty before. The people, they lived in shacks, not houses. Everything was dirty, they had nothing like we have in our houses, most of them didn't even have running water or even electricity. And so many people living in such a little shack, with everyone on top of each other.

We went there to deliver some food and clothing donations to a church. The paster, he took us to some houses to deliver some of the food and clothes ourselves. Thus, I could see for myself how much I really had.

When I got back home, I found a soup kitchen I could go to help other people who really don't have anything, not even food to eat. They always remind me to count my blessings.

Sample 1 Score

I am told "to count your blessings" and appreciate someone or something that you'd taken for granted. Many movies and books are about this. I am sure you have seen some and read some. Like scary movies where people get killed can make us apreciate the blessing, we are still alive. Or a war movie, that were not fighting a war. When I went to a poor town once when I was in school I saw people even more poor than me. That made me sad, they live with so little. Compared to how much I have. All the time I felt poor since my friends, they were so rich.

819. We are often surprised, even awed, by the experiences of our ancestors. Describe a time when you learned something important about your family history.

Sample 6 Score

My dad wasn't the type to talk much about anything, and he was especially quiet about his past. There were a few things I knew: He'd come over from Hungary in 1956, after the Revolution. He'd fought with the rebels in Budapest. He was a toolmaker in Hungary, and he was a toolmaker here. He left behind his parents and 11 brothers and sisters, who still lived in the countryside. They exchanged letters once or twice a year. That was about all I knew.

The summer that I was 14, my dad received one of those letters. In it was the news that one of his brothers had died. Maybe it was the realization that he was so out of touch with his family. Maybe it was his own mortality he was facing. In any case, a few days after the letter came, he told me about his role in the Hungarian Revolution and his escape from Hungary.

The Hungarian Revolution began with a massive student protest on October 23, 1956, and ended just a few weeks later in November after the city was invaded by Soviet tanks and the rebellion crushed. My dad, just 22 years old, had decided to join the students who were protesting the Communist regime, and soon he was not just a protester but a soldier, and not just a soldier but an officer in the rebel army. "Wait a minute," he said, and he returned with a tattered copy of *Life* magazine's special issue devoted to the Hungarian Revolution. He flipped through the pages, showing me image after image of buildings demolished by bombs, rebels fighting on foot against tanks, bodies lying in the street. Then he found the picture he was looking for. "There," he said, pointing to a window in an abandoned, bullet-ridden building. "I was hiding in there, throwing Molotov cocktails at the Russian tanks."

It's a long and fascinating story, and I wanted to know all the details. How did he get involved? How did he escape? How close was he to being captured or killed? I had so many questions. But the question I wanted answered most was this: *Why did he fight?* At that age, I was just starting to find my footing in the swampy ground of ethics and moral stances. I was having a tough time figuring out what I believed in, and I wanted desperately to understand how someone could believe in something so strongly that he would be willing to die for it.

Why did he do it? There were a lot of reasons, he said. For one thing, the Communist regime was ruining the economy. As a toolmaker with several years of experience, he had a better salary than most, but still, he said, "I couldn't afford both clothes and food." If he respected the government, he would have been able to live with that. "But what I couldn't live with," he said, "was not being able to say what I wanted. The Communists, they had all kinds of restrictions on everything. You couldn't go to the next town without the proper permissions and papers. And you couldn't say anything, not *anything*, against the government, or else they'd put you in jail, or worse. They'd come and get you late at night and no one in your family would ever see you again." That's what happened to his best friend, Attila. He disappeared the night of September 22, and no one ever heard from him again.

My dad often complains about America. The politicians are crooks, criminals have too many rights, schools and parents aren't strict enough with children, and the taxes are "an abomination." But I don't need to remind him that at least in this country, he can complain as loudly as he pleases.

Sample 4 Score

The summer I was 14, I learned something about my dad. He never talked much and I didn't really know that much about him. After he found out about his brother dying back in Hungary, he must've felt like it was important for me to know more. He decided it was time to tell me about the Hungarian Revolution.

My dad was a toolmaker in Hungary. Because he didn't like the Communist government, he decided to join the protests led by students angry at the government. That's how the rebellion started. The communists wouldn't let anyone talk bad about the government, and the protesters were attacked. That started the fighting. He showed me pictures of the revolution with lots of destroyed buildings and people lying in the street. It was horrible. Because he was a little older than most of the students, my dad became an officer in the rebel army.

I wanted to know why he decided to fight. He told me that because of the communist government, he couldn't make enough money to buy food and clothes. He couldn't travel to another town without the right papers. The most important thing, though, was freedom of speech. He couldn't say what he wanted. He said that anyone who criticized the government would get taken away in the middle of the night and no one would see them again. That happened to his best friend. For my dad, that was the last straw.

My dad escaped with the other refugees, and he's been living in America ever since 1956. He complains about America a lot, especially the politicians. But he knows that here, no one is going to come and take him away for that.

Sample 1 Score

I was surprised by my dad when he told me about the Hungarian revelution he fought. I knew before that he fought but I didn't no anything else about it. It was a short war and the communists one. He was even an officer in the army. He didn't like to talk much so thats part of why I was so surprised.

One question I had, was, why did he fight. He said he didn't like the government and they'd take you away just for saying that. I can't imagine such a thing. I'd want to fight to. That's not the way it is here in America. This is a really grate country and I'm glad to live here.

820. Most of us remember exactly where we were and what we were doing when we received shocking or important news. Tell the story of what you were doing when you heard about an important event and how that news affected you.

Sample 6 Score

Every May the carnival came to town. It was the standard small-town fair: a ferris wheel, a fun house, a giant slide, and dozens of booths where you could buy greasy food and try to win cheap stuffed animals for your date.

That's where I was, with my date—sort of. We weren't actually in the fairgrounds. We were in his car in the parking lot, stealing some time together. I was 16, but I wasn't allowed to date, and I had the sort of father who just might come to the fair to check up on me to make sure I wasn't hanging out with any boys.

Keith had borrowed his mom's Buick Skylark, as usual. REO Speedwagon's "I Can't Fight This Feeling" was playing on the radio when Keith rather abruptly ended a kiss, interrupting what I thought had been a perfectly nice romantic moment.

"I have something to tell you," he said. He wouldn't look me in the eye. My heart dropped to the floor. *He's going to break up with me,* I thought in horror.

But that's not what happened. In fact, I never could have guessed at what Keith was about to tell me.

He took a deep breath and looked straight ahead at the windshield. "Your mom was married to someone else before she married your dad," he said softly. "You have an older brother. He lives in North Carolina."

I know what you're thinking, because it's exactly what I was wondering, too: *How on Earth did Keith know this?* He guessed what I was thinking, and said:

"My mom told me." Then, before I could ask, he added: "Edie told her." Edie was his mother's hairdresser.

Finding out that I had an older brother was a shock enough. To find out from my boyfriend, who found out from his mother, who found out from her hairdresser—that was just too much. I was too overwhelmed to respond.

After a few minutes of silence during which Keith held my hand, what Keith told me about how he found out began to make sense. Edie was the daughter of my dad's best friend, Samuel. Though our families were no longer close, when I was young, we spent a lot of time together. Edie and her older sister used to babysit my sister and me. It wouldn't be so unlikely for her to pick up a family secret or two.

Keith's mom had told him what Edie told her because she believed it was proof that I wasn't good enough to be his girlfriend. He wanted me to know about my brother, of course, but he also wanted me to know that he was going to have to cool it for a while until his mom got over it.

The next day, I told my mom that I knew about my brother. At first, she looked shocked; then she looked relieved, as if a tremendous burden had been lifted. She was glad I knew, although she was sorry about the way in which I'd found out. She gave me my brother's phone number and told me I could call whenever I was ready.

Today, my brother and I talk regularly, and he is one of my closest friends. One of these days, I have to thank Edie for being such a gossip.

Sample 4 Score

When the fair came to our town I went like I always did. There were rides and games. You could also buy lots of food. I enjoyed the fair, but this time I wasn't going on any rides. I was sitting with my boyfriend in his car in the parking lot.

I wasn't suppose to have a boyfriend. That's why we were hiding in his car. We were listening to music and talking and kissing. Suddenly Keith stopped.

He said he had something to tell me. I got really scared. Is he going to break up with me, I wondered?

That's what I thought was going to happen. But he surprised me even more.

"You have an older brother," Keith told me. I was shocked. He told me that my mother had been married before she met my dad. I never knew this, and I wondered how on earth Keith knew this if I didn't even know. I asked him, and he said, "My mom told me."

How on earth did his mom know, I demanded. It turns out her hairdresser, of all people told her. I was confused. But then I remember her hair dresser is Edie, who used to babysit us when we were little. Edie's dad and my dad were best friends a long time ago. Maybe that's how Edie found out. She must have heard them talking about it one time.

I was very upset that Keith knew something my parents hid from me. His mom told him because she wants him to break up with me. She was thinking our family is bad because of this. Plus he wanted me to know about my older brother. Well, the next morning I talked to my mom, and she gives me my brothers number. She says sorry for not telling me earlier, and now me and my brother we are very good friends. I am glad Edie liked to gossip.

Sample 1 Score

I am going to the fare like it always is coming to town and find out a secret about my brother from my boyfriend. We are in his car. Because I am not a loud to have boyfriends, so we hide there from my dad in case he is checking up on me. Then my boyfriend tells me his mom's hairdressing lady tells her about my brother and she tells him. I am all confuse, I say so he explain my brother is from my mom being married before she meets my dad. How, does he know. His mom tells him since her hairdressing lady tells her so he can break up with me.

I have to ask my mom right a way after this then she is gladly to know about it for me. Now I call my brother all the time, we are good friends.

821. Many things can interfere with our plans. Sometimes an illness prevents us from doing something we really want to do. Describe a time when you became ill and missed out on doing something you'd really been looking forward to.

Sample 6 Score

I'd been looking forward to my 12th birthday for months. We were going to have a party in school and a party at my house after school. My relatives from Ohio were coming, my mom was going to bake my favorite cake, and my brother and his friends were going to DJ. I spent weeks making up the playlist, though I might as well have just handed over my pile of Beach Boys albums, because just about every song I chose was a Beach Boys tune. I was the biggest Beach Boys fan on the East Coast.

The day before my birthday, however, I came down with the chicken pox. Everything for the next day was canceled, and I stayed home from school, itchy and cranky. I refused to get out of my pajamas or be civil to anyone. I just sat in my room, playing my Beach Boys albums and feeling miserable. The next day, my birthday, I was still itchy and cranky as can be, a total wretch. Until *he* called.

Just after lunch and my third "Three Stooges" episode, the phone rang. It was my dad telling me I had to believe his next statement. I rolled my eyes but agreed.

"In a few minutes, Brian Wilson is going to call you," he said.

"That's not funny, Dad," I replied.

He assured me that it would happen and hung up. He told me I had to believe him and to answer the phone when it rang.

Was he playing a joke on me? No, he couldn't be. My dad knew how much I loved the Beach Boys, and to play a joke of this sort would be too cruel. He *must be serious*, I thought, but I couldn't believe it.

"Okay," I said to myself as I placed the receiver down. *The* Brian Wilson was going to call me? I sat in a daze. Then, before I had a chance to digest what my father said, the phone rang. I thought it was my dad calling back to say he was just teasing. It wasn't.

At the other end of the line was none other than *the* Brian Wilson. I don't really remember what he said beyond that; once I realized it really was Brian Wilson, I went into a mild state of shock. He must have thought I was a terrible conversationalist because I could only say "yeah" or "no" to most of his questions. After a few minutes, he said good-bye. I hung up the phone, screamed, and cried.

Sample 4 Score

When I was about to turn 12, I came down with the chicken pox. That ruined all of my plans, we were going to have a party in school and a party at my house afterwards. I had all the music picked out that my brother was going to play (DJ) and my mom was making my favorite cake, but, everything got cancelled.

I was miserable as could be. My dad said he'd never seen me be crankier before in his life. I guess that's why he did what he did. He ended up giving me the best birthday present ever.

I think I must have been the biggest Beach Boys fan on the east coast of the United States. I had every record and knew every song. On my birthday, when I was home feeling blue, the phone rang. It was my dad, and he told me that "I have to believe him" and that Brian Wilson, THE Brian Wilson, was going to call me. I couldn't believe it.

"Are you kidding me," I asked my dad?

"No. Please believe me," he answered.

A minute later, the phone rang. "Hello, is Cassandra there," a familiar voice asked. It really was Brian Wilson! He wished me a "Happy Birthday" and told me, "Me and the boys are recording an album here in Indiana." We talked for a few minutes. Or, rather, he talked, and I stuttered, I was so excited and nervous I couldn't hardly say anything.

My dad told me that he managed to track the Beach Boys down and that Brian Wilson heard my story, that I was sick and a big fan on my birthday, and he agreed to call me. What a wonderful thing dad did for me. He made my birthday unforgettable.

Sample 1 Score

Many things can interfere with our plans. Sometime an illness prevents us from something we really want to do. One time I became ill and missed out on something I'd really been looking forward. We cancel my birthday party plan because I have the chicken pocks. I felt really sad. I was 12. I really love the beach boys music and suddenly when I am home crying Brian Wilson, he calls me. I cannot believe!! It was so important. I am so lucky for my dad to do such a thing.

822. Many of our fondest memories are associated with food. Describe a memorable experience that took place while preparing or eating food.

Sample 6 Score

Back when I was in junior high school, all students—boys as well as girls—were required to take home economics. In the fall, we sewed duffel bags and pillows shaped like animals. In the spring, we learned how to cook.

For our final cooking class project, we had to cook a dish at home and bring it to class. I knew right away what I was going to make: my Aunt Rosie's famous chocolate cake.

My Aunt Rosie made the best chocolate cake in the world. It was a recipe she had gotten from her grandmother, who swore her grandmother had personally made that chocolate cake for the Prince of Wales. When I started the cooking class, I had asked Aunt Rosie what made her chocolate cake so special. She told me the secret ingredient was coffee.

I had never tried to bake a cake from scratch before, and since the chocolate cake was Aunt Rosie's specialty, I thought for sure she would help me make it.

"But that would be cheating," she said as she handed me the recipe. "You go home and you make it yourself. Make sure you save a piece for me!" she hollered as I headed out the door.

At home, I got out my ingredients: eggs, butter, milk, sugar, fine powdered chocolate, cinnamon, baking powder, and coffee. The recipe looked easy enough, and I followed each step carefully. When I had mixed everything together, I carefully poured the batter into the pan. I put the cake into the oven, which I had preheated as directed, and set a timer for 50 minutes. When the buzzer went off, I stuck a toothpick into the middle of the cake to make sure it was done. It was perfect.

When the cake cooled, I opened up a can of Betty Crocker's chocolate frosting, spread a thick layer on top of the cake, and covered it with plastic wrap. It was a masterpiece, and I couldn't wait for my classmates to taste it.

The next morning, I carried my cake carefully to school. I passed out pieces to my classmates, beaming with pride. But when I saw the look on their faces, I knew something was terribly wrong. I took a bite and nearly burst into tears. No wonder they looked disgusted! Aunt Rosie's cake was never crunchy, and the crunchy things were bitter. The cake tasted aw-

ful. My heart sank as I watched Mrs. Wilson take a bite. She crunched, paused, crunched again, paused again, and looked at me thoughtfully.

"Sarah," she said gently, "does the recipe for this cake call for coffee?"

"Yes," I replied.

"Hmmm. I thought so."

When I questioned her about my mistake, she said, "You used coffee grounds. You were supposed to use *liquid* coffee," she said, and she laughed gently.

I was mortified. I vowed to correct my mistake and make a new cake for tomorrow.

This time, with a real cup of brewed coffee, I baked a cake that would have made Aunt Rosie proud.

Sample 4 Score

One of my most memorable school experiences had to do with food preparation. I was making a cake for my cooking class in junior high school, but things didn't turn out the way I'd planned.

We all had to make something at home for our final cooking project, and I wanted to make my Aunt Rosie's famous chocolate cake. She made the best chocolate cake in the world, all of my family and friends agreed. It was an easy enough recipe, I thought. What made it different—better than—most chocolate cakes was its secret ingredient, coffee.

When I had all of the ingredients out I started making the cake. I followed the recipe exactly, putting in three-quarters cup of coffee, just like the recipe called for. I put it in the oven at precisely 350 degrees and cooked it for exactly one hour. When I took it out of the oven, it looked beautiful. I covered it with some chocolate frosting and set it aside to take to school in the morning. I was so proud of it!

When I got to cooking class, however, I realized something was wrong. People made funny faces when they bit into the cake. So I tried it too, and it tasted awful. It was bitter and crunchy. Aunt Rosie's cake never tasted like this! What did I do wrong?

My teacher asked me if the recipe called for coffee. Yes, I told her. "You used coffee grounds, didn't you," she asked.

"Yes," I answered.

That was my mistake. I was supposed to use brewed coffee, not coffee grounds. Mrs. Wilson was really nice, though; she allowed me to make another cake for the next class and bring it in. That time, I did it right. My cake was delicious. It would have made Aunt Rosie proud!

Sample 1 Score

I like to cook. In school I even had a cooking class. We learn everything from measuring to whats different from frying and baking. The school was a nice kitchen for practicing. My friend Alisha was the best cook. She and her whole family cooked. In my family Aunt Rosie is the best cook. One time I baked a cake for class, and I messed it up bad and everyone in class though it was nasty tasting. I did it again the next time and it was delicious. Even Aunt Rosie think so.

823. Try as we might to avoid them, accidents happen. Tell about a time when you were involved in an accident.

Sample 6 Score

I was never one to believe in things like miracles or fate, but since my accident a few months ago, I look at things a little differently. Whether it was a miracle, or fate, or just plain luck, I'm still here to tell this story.

It was a Monday morning, just about 8:15. I was actually a little early for once and was glad I didn't have to race to work. It was my second week as a bank teller at Harrison Savings and Loan.

There had been some freezing rain earlier that morning, but the roads seemed clear as I pulled out

of the driveway. I turned left at the light, right at the Dunkin' Donuts, and then left again onto the on-ramp for Route 61. I sped up to merge with the southbound rush-hour traffic when suddenly I felt my car, a brand-new Durango, lose control. I'd hit a patch of ice.

What happened next probably lasted no more than 15 seconds, but if felt like hours. I spun around like a top, turning two full revolutions as I crossed the two southbound lanes. Then I hit the median strip and the car flipped over as it crossed into the northbound traffic. I skidded across the highway and the car stopped in the right-hand lane. There I was, upside-down and backwards, after crashing across four lanes, and somehow I was alive. Somehow I hadn't hit a single car.

But I had no time to appreciate that miracle, because when I looked out the shattered windshield, I saw an 18-wheeler bearing down on me at about 65 miles an hour. There was no time to get out of the car.

I screamed and braced myself for the impact. But instead of hearing the crunch of metal crashing into metal, I heard the screeching of brakes as the truck swerved around me, just in time to avoid a head-on collision. The truck skidded to a stop on the shoulder about a hundred feet away from me. Then the driver jumped out and ran over to see if I was okay.

That night at home, I eased my aching body into bed. But I was climbing into my own bed, in my own room, not in the hospital. Somehow, the only injuries I sustained were a few cuts on my face and hands, a bruised right shoulder, and two bruised calf muscles. My new car was totaled, but I didn't care. All that mattered was that I was alive.

Sample 4 Score

I was involved in a really terrible accident not long ago, and I'm very lucky to be alive. I was on my way to work at my new job when I hit a patch of ice as I was pulling onto a major highway. It's a miracle I didn't get seriously hurt.

When I hit the patch of ice, my car, my brand new Durango, that I was so proud of, lost control. I started spinning around like a top. I spun across the two north-bound lanes. Then my car hit the median strip and flipped over.

I thought, I ought to be dead already, but I wasn't. But it wasn't over yet. Now I went across the south bound lanes upsidedown. I stopped in the right hand lane and then I saw a big truck headed straight towards me.

Somehow, I don't know how, that truck managed to stop before it crashed into me. It swerved around me and saved my life. Then the driver got out to see if I was ok.

Luckily, I was OK. I only had just a few cuts and bruises and I bruised both of my calf muscles. My car was totaled, but, that didn't matter. I was just happy to be alive.

Sample 1 Score

One time I had bad accident. That almost got me killed. I hit a pach of ice. When I was go onto high way I spinned around a lot. Across all for lanes. First I hit the midean stripe that made my car flipped over. I was upside down thanking I was still a live. When a big truck was coming at me. There wasnt no time to got out. It was my brand new car that was totalled. I was ok after all that lucky for me my car wrecked but not me. The truck he stop on time and move around my car upsidedown still. He jump to see if I ok.

In hospital doctors say I ok. Just many number of bruises and cuts and some on my calfs and shoulder. I am ok all thogh my car it ruined.

824. Describe an experience you had that would be considered a near miss or a brush with disaster.

Sample 6 Score

I must have had a guardian angel that day.

I was six and had just learned how to ride a bicycle. My bike was a beauty: pink all over, with a stylish banana seat, iridescent fringes hanging off the handle bars, and a white woven basket with big, pink flowers on the front.

It was a Monday afternoon and I was alone, riding my bike in circles in the driveway. I was exalting in my freedom: no more training wheels, no more big brother or father pushing me from behind and holding me steady. Now I could start, stop, and ride all by myself, and I went around and around our circular driveway in complete bliss.

The sun shone on my face and made the black pavement hot, even though it was already late September. Emboldened by the warmth of the sun and the excitement of my success—eight laps around and I hadn't fallen yet—I decided it was time to leave the safety of the circle and ride down the steep hill that led to the road on which we lived: Route 309, a four-lane, heavily traveled highway. I warmed up with another two or three turns around the circle and then eased to my right and down the slope.

From the start of the circle to the edge of the highway, the driveway ran about 200 feet at an even 45 degrees. I began to pick up a lot of speed at 50 feet, more at 75, and by 100 feet I was flying. The road was getting closer; I could see the faces of the people driving by at 50, 60, 70 miles an hour. It was time to slow down, but I couldn't. I kept going faster, and faster, and I couldn't stop. In my panic, I forgot how to use the brakes.

In an instant I was out on the highway, a little pink streak that zoomed across all four lanes and somehow, some way, ended up on the other side, up on the Zeiglers' lawn, in one piece. In the seconds that it took me to cross the road, there had not been a single car. An instant later, they were back, and I had to wait several minutes before I slowly, shakily, walked my bike back across the street and up the driveway.

I never told anyone about what happened, and it was a long, long time before I ventured down that slope again. When I did, I used my brakes the whole way down. This time, I wasn't going to forget.

Sample 4 Score

I once had a brush with disaster and nearly got myself killed. I was six and just learned how to ride my bike by myself. I loved my bike. It was pink and had a banana seat and a basket in front.

On the day that this happened, I was riding around in our driveway. Our driveway was a long hill and then a big circle at the top. I was riding around in the circle.

It was the first time I was all alone on my bike. After a while because I didn't fall at all, I decided to go down the hill. I start down the slope and I realize I can't remember how to break. This of course is a problem because I start going faster and faster, any minute I will be out on the highway.

We lived on Route 309, a 4-lane highway that was always busy with cars. Suddenly I was zooming across that road. Somehow, I made it across all four lanes without getting hit by a car.

I don't know how I was so lucky, to not be hurt at all that day. Because a minute later, as soon as I was across, there were more cars on the road than I could count. Somehow, when I was going across, there just weren't any cars. Maybe I had a guardian angel watching over me.

Sample 1 Score

When I have just learned to ride a bike, I almost have a big accident. That almost gets me killed. My fa-vorite bike, I'm riding it around and around in the driveway. I like this bike so much. My aunt, she gived it to me as a present. For my birthday.

All of a suddenly I am starting going down the hill, I forgot how to stop, I am going across the road. There are four lanes and lots of cars. Somehow I don't get hit by nothing. I walk my bike back up the hill. I am thinking never to tell anyone. Boy I am so lucky!

825. We all need help from others from time to time. Tell about a time you helped someone in need.

Sample 6 Score

It was the hottest day of the summer, a record-breaking 102 degrees, hot and humid, sweltering even in the shade. I was driving back from visiting my older brother and his new baby. In the blistering heat, I could see the blacktop bubbling. I'd never been so grateful for air-conditioning before.

I cruised happily along County Route 2, which wound through the northern tip of the Sonoran Desert. Then I saw that a car had broken down up ahead. It was the first car I'd seen in about half an hour. In the distance, a few hundred feet ahead of the car, I saw a stooped figure walking with a gas can in his hands. There was nothing around for miles. There was no way this person was going to make it to the nearest town, which was a good 20 miles away, in this desert heat.

I'd always been told to stay away from strangers, but I thought if there ever was a time to do a good deed, this was it. Besides, as I neared the figure, I could tell that it was an elderly man, and I thought there was little chance he'd do me any harm. So I slowed down and pulled over. "Need a lift?" I asked.

Now that I could see him clearly, it was obvious the old man was already in trouble. He'd walked only a hundred yards or so, and he looked as if he was going to pass out any moment. "I'd be most grateful, young lady, if you could help me get to a gas station," he said slowly. "I seem to be out of petroleum."

"No problem," I replied. "I'm headed that way."

He climbed slowly into the car and I pulled back out onto the road. "Not a good day for car trouble, huh?" I asked.

"Indeed," he replied. I offered him a soda from the cooler I'd packed for my four-hour ride. He accepted it gratefully. He was silent for a few minutes while his body temperature normalized. We made a little small talk then, but just a little. He seemed to prefer the silence.

As we neared the gas station, I asked him if he would like a ride back to his car. "I don't have to be home until late this afternoon," I told him. "It's no trouble."

"I know it is quite out of your way," he replied. "But I would be most grateful." He paused. "And just where is home, young lady?"

"Elmwood," I replied. "By the way, my name is Emily. Emily Hampton."

"You're a very kind young lady, Emily Hampton. My name is Edward Gilliam."

Mr. Gilliam filled up his gas can and I drove him back to his car. We poured the gas into his tank, and I followed him back into town just to make sure he was okay. At the gas station, I beeped and waved and continued north toward home. Mr. Gilliam waved and nodded his thanks.

The next morning, the doorbell rang. My mom answered. "Emily!" she hollered. "Get down here!" I came down the stairs and saw a giant bouquet of flowers. They were stunning. A small note was attached:

"Dearest Emily, thank you for your incredible kindness yesterday. You just might have saved my life, and I am eternally grateful. You reminded an old man of how much beauty there is in this world. Yours, Edward Gilliam."

Sample 4 Score

I'd never picked up a hitchhiker or helped anyone along the highway before that day. But with that heat, how could I just drive by. It was the hottest day ever, I was driving through the desert when I passed a broken-down car. An old man was walking along the road carrying a gas can, I had to stop.

I asked him if he needed a ride. Which was a silly question—of course he did. It was over 100 degrees and the nearest town was more than 20 miles away. He'd die before he made it five miles in those conditions.

We didn't talk much; I think he was the quiet type. I offered him a soda and he drank it down like that. When we got to the nearest gas station, I asked him, if he wanted me to drive him back to his car? "It won't be any trouble," I told him. I didn't have to be home until the end of the day.

So we filled up his gas can and I drove him back. We talked a little more this time. He asked where I lived, and he told me he was on his way to visit his granddaughter. We filled up his tank and I followed him for a while to make sure he was ok. Then I drove the rest of the way home.

Next morning, the doorbell rang, there was a huge boquet of flowers for me. They were from Edward (that was his name). He was very grateful; he said "I saved his life yesterday" and that "I reminded him there was so much beauty in the world." I was so glad that I helped him.

Sample 1 Score

Everyone needs help sometime. One day I help an old man who car break down on the road in the hot hot dessert. He need a ride to get gas. He was so thankful he sends me a big giant bunch of flowers the next day.

Their was never such a hot day, he was crazy to try walking to get gas, the gas station was so far away. It was a dessert so their wasn't no shade or anything or places to rest awhile. He would have been in trouble for sure if I don't help. At the gas station I tell him I can take him back to his car, its not any problem because I have all day. His so thankful to me.

8 ▶ Literary Response Writing Prompts

THE LITERARY RESPONSE ESSAY demands an ability to examine the meaning of a literary text on multiple levels. In addition to explaining and summarizing the literal meaning of a story, you must also delve more deeply into concepts that are implied through the use of literary devices such as symbols, metaphor, and connotation. Before responding to any of the prompts in this chapter, you should read the scoring rubric carefully so that you understand what a successful literary response is.

One of the most common errors that students make when writing a literary essay is trying to cover too much material and too many ideas. Pay attention to the question that is being asked and then focus on writing responses that directly answer the question. When you are proofreading your final draft, check to be sure that every sentence supports your main idea. For example, if the question asks you to discuss a particular character's role as an evildoer, it would not be beneficial for you to write three entire pages detailing the story's setting unless you have a really compelling reason to do so—if, for example, the setting influenced his evildoing to a great extent.

Get a Grip on Style

Every writer has style. Just as Gucci designs differ from Baby Phat designs, it's also true that Mark Twain's writing style is different from J.D. Salinger's writing style. Each writer is unique in the way he or she constructs a sentence, uses description, or sets the overall tone. Set a goal to become more aware of the stylistic differences of the literature that you read. Eventually, you'll be so attuned to the nuances of each writer's individual style that you'll be able to identify a writer's work without even glimpsing the byline.

Before writing your literary responses to these prompts, it is suggested that you do the following:

- Use a timer to time each of your writing exercises. Keep a record of your response times and strive to decrease your average completion time over the weeks ahead.
- Read the question twice to make certain that you understand the question and the task that you have been given. Ask yourself these questions: What is the topic? What is the required method of response? Am I being asked to compare and contrast or am I being asked to identify and explain an important literary element? Or am I being asked to evaluate or illustrate a particular aspect of the story?
- Use scrap paper to brainstorm and compose a brief organizational outline.
- Narrow your response so that you don't include material that isn't essential to the required

response. When you are finished, look at the original question and ask yourself: Did I completely answer the question that was asked?

- Focus your attention on the key words in the question or text.
- Use examples from the text to support your statements, but be sure to retain your own voice when writing your response by not relying on excerpts from the text to develop your ideas.
- Be sure to proofread your response.

Get a Grip on Point of View

Most stories are written using either first-person or third-person point of view. The majority of academic reports are written using the **third-person** perspective, whereas personal essays, memoirs, writing journals, and reflection essays are written from the **first-person** perspective.

When the first-person point of view is used (*I*), the narrator lets his or her personal feelings and judgments color the perspective about people and events that have occurred. Therefore, you are getting only the narrator's limited and biased perspective. An example of this type of first-person narrative is *Miguel Street* by V.S. Naipaul.

She, *he*, and *it* are tip-offs that an author is telling the story from the distant and more objective third-person perspective. "The Story of an Hour" by Kate Chopin is written from a third-person perspective.

Rubric for Literary Response Writing

SCORE	6 FOR A GRADE AT THIS LEVEL, YOUR WRITING:	5 FOR A GRADE AT THIS LEVEL, YOUR WRITING:	4 FOR A GRADE AT THIS LEVEL, YOUR WRITING:	3 FOR A GRADE AT THIS LEVEL, YOUR WRITING:	2 FOR A GRADE AT THIS LEVEL, YOUR WRITING:	1 FOR A GRADE AT THIS LEVEL, YOUR WRITING:
Content: Your written response shows an understanding and interpretation of the writing prompt.	■ satisfies the requirements of the writing prompt in a creative and original manner. ■ establishes a controlling idea that reveals an understanding of the text. ■ uses a clear thesis statement. ■ proves the thesis with insightful examples and details.	■ provides a thoughtful analysis of the writing prompt. ■ establishes a controlling idea that reveals an understanding of the text. ■ provides a clear thesis statement. ■ offers good examples to confirm the thesis statement.	■ meets some of the requirements of the writing prompt. ■ establishes a controlling idea that shows a basic understanding of the text. ■ includes some key elements that help explain the thesis.	■ offers a simple interpretation of the writing prompt. ■ makes an attempt to establish a controlling idea, but it is weak. ■ makes superficial connections between the controlling idea and the text.	■ meets few of the requirements of the writing prompt. ■ reveals an incomplete understanding of the text. ■ fails to establish a controlling idea. ■ gives no examples to help explain the thesis.	■ minimally addresses the writing prompt. ■ reveals a minimal understanding of the text. ■ makes no connection to the text, to the ideas in the text, or to literary elements in the text.
Development: Your written response gives a clear and logical explanation of ideas, using supporting material.	■ builds and elaborates thoroughly. ■ uses examples precisely. ■ develops the topic in an interesting and imaginative way. ■ demonstrates coherence in the development of ideas.	■ develops the topic in an acceptable way. ■ uses relevant examples throughout the essay. ■ develops ideas clearly and consistently.	■ responds to some ideas more completely than others. ■ uses some specific and relevant evidence from the text.	■ shows weakness in the development of ideas and/or develops ideas without thorough explanation.	■ contains inaccurate, vague, or repetitive details. ■ has limited development of ideas.	■ shows a lack of development of ideas.
Organization: Your written response shows a coherent, orderly, well-reasoned approach.	■ sets up and maintains a clear focus based on the controlling idea. ■ establishes a logical, rational sequence of ideas with transitional words and sentences.	■ maintains focus on the controlling idea. ■ has an obvious plan of organization. ■ uses appropriate devices and transitions.	■ has a general focus. ■ obviously attempts organization but lacks consistency.	■ does not show a logical sense of organization. ■ strays from the topic. ■ can be difficult to follow.	■ suggests some organization but lacks focus.	■ exhibits no organizational pattern or focus.
Language Use/ Conventions: Your written response shows a sense of audience by using effective vocabulary and varied sentence structure.	■ has vivid language, fluidity, and a sense of engagement and voice. ■ has sophisticated style of sentence structure, sentence variety, and vocabulary. ■ has essentially no errors.	■ has good control of mechanics. ■ contains some errors when using sophisticated language. ■ has a slightly lower quality of sentence structure and sentence variety. ■ shows errors when using sophisticated vocabulary only.	■ has a sense of audience. ■ uses simple sentences. ■ uses an appropriate level of vocabulary. ■ demonstrates partial control of mechanics. ■ exhibits some errors that do not interfere with comprehension.	■ uses vocabulary that is slightly below level. ■ has a vague sense of audience. ■ shows a beginner's control of the language. ■ has errors that begin to interfere with comprehension.	■ exhibits little control of the language. ■ has errors that make comprehension difficult.	■ shows minimal control of language skills. ■ may be illegible or unrecognizable as English.

A ZERO PAPER is:
■ totally unrelated to the topic.
■ filled with illegible and indecipherable words.
■ incoherent with illogical or garbled syntax.
■ blank.

Use the literary response prompts to write an essay for numbers 826–902. Each of the first 14 prompts has a model essay and two lower-scoring essays in the answer section that you can use to compare and contrast your writing. You can also use the Rubric for Literary Response Writing, included in this chapter, to give you an idea of the way your essay may be graded. If you have trouble interpreting the scoring guide, see a teacher or professor for help.

▶ Practice Questions

826. Tone is the mood or feeling the author intends the reader to experience. Using a specific piece of literature, explain how tone enhances the work.

827. In the novel *Lord of the Flies*, by William Golding, a group of boys are stranded on a remote island to fend for themselves. Compare/contrast this novel to the popular television show *Survivor*. Use specific details in your answer.

828. Using a specific literary work, explain how a novel might influence change in society.

829. The theme of a literary piece is the central idea or message that it delivers. Cite a specific literary work and discuss the theme.

830. Compare/contrast the fear of terrorism and the concern with safety issues in present-day society with George Orwell's novel *1984*.

831. Personification is the technique wherein a nonhuman character is given human thoughts, feelings, and dialogue. Illustrate how this technique is used in a favorite novel or short story.

832. Many times in Shakespeare's plays, the setting changes from rural or pastoral to urban. Compare and contrast these settings. Explain the reason for the shift of scenery, using support from specific plays.

833. A type of conflict is called character versus him- or herself. This is also referred to as internal conflict, because the character must face self-inflicted fears and problems. Write about this type of conflict, using a piece of literature that you have read.

834. Discuss a piece of literature in which the author is also the narrator. Describe the way he or she uses actual events from his or her life in his or her writing.

835. The coming of age theme is very popular in literature. This theme refers to a preadolescent boy or girl going through many difficult, life-altering experiences in order to reach young adulthood. Using a novel you are familiar with, discuss this theme. Be sure to use supporting details and evidence in your essay.

836. Discuss how the reader might sympathize with the main character in Christopher Marlowe's *Dr. Faustus*, even though he sells his soul to the Devil.

837. Discuss a hero in a literary piece that you have read.

838. Write a literary analysis of a Robert Frost poem. Include theme and symbolism in your discussion.

839. Compare the society of *The Scarlet Letter* to our society today. Compare and contrast how Hester Prynne would have been treated today with how she was treated in the novel.

840. A struggle between two or more opposing forces in a work is called conflict. Cite a piece of literature and explain the conflict embodied in the work.

841. Walt Whitman uses second-person narration—a technique not often used by writers—in his poem "Crossing Brooklyn Ferry." In second-person narration, the narrator speaks directly to you. Discuss another work that uses second-person narration. Give examples from the work.

842. The setting of a novel is where the action takes place. Explain how the setting complements the story in a novel you have read.

843. The climax of a work is when all of the events come to a breaking point. Using a piece of literature that you know, explain the events that lead to the climax, what happens in the climactic scene, and how the story changes after the climax.

844. Third-person point of view is when the narrator has no part in the action. He or she is simply telling the story using the words *he*, *she*, or *they*. A story would be very different if it were told from the first-person (using the pronoun *I*) point of view. Using a novel written in the third person, discuss how it would be a very different story if it were told in the first person.

845. List ten sensory images for each of the four seasons—winter, spring, summer, and fall. Then, write a brief explanation of why you chose those specific images.

846. Narrative poetry tells a story and doesn't necessarily rhyme. Often, narrative poems are written about historical events. Name three historical events that could be considered worthy of a narrative poem. Describe the key elements from each historical event.

847. Describe a character from literature that you would trade places with, and explain why.

848. Imagine that you could become an omniscient character in a literary piece and change the plot somehow. Describe the piece of literature in which the character belongs, and tell how that character would alter the plot. Use details from the literary piece that you have chosen.

849. Explain the popularity of science fiction writing. Use a work from this genre to explain its appeal.

850. Using a work of literature you have read, describe the hero or heroine and his or her characteristics.

851. The protagonist in a story is usually the do-gooder, or the character that most readers emphathize with. Identify a piece of literature where the author wants us to empathize with the antagonist, or evildoer. Explain by using details from that work.

852. In drama, when a character speaks his or her innermost thoughts, it is called a monologue. Explain your favorite monologue from a dramatic piece and tell how this monologue affects the plot.

853. Explain the appeal of war literature. Use a piece of literature from this genre to describe its allure.

854. Foreshadowing is when the author gives hints to the reader about what is going to take place later in the work. Using a piece of literature that you are familiar with, explain how the author uses foreshadowing and how the use of foreshadowing adds to the plot.

855. Novels such as John Steinbeck's *The Winter of Our Discontent* and Ernest Hemingway's *For Whom the Bell Tolls* take their titles from lines in works by William Shakespeare and John Donne. Write an essay explaining and interpreting the significance of one of these titles and how it captures the theme of the book.

856. Discuss a character in literature that you loathed. Explain the techniques the author used that caused you to feel this way.

857. In William Faulkner's *Barn Burning*, a young boy must decide whether to turn his father in for breaking the law or to stay loyal to his family. Write about a situation in real life that is similar to this one.

858. Conflict, in a work of literature, is the struggle between opposing characters or opposing forces. One type of conflict is character versus character. Explain this type of conflict using a piece of literature that you have read.

859. Another type of conflict is called character versus nature. Using a piece of literature that you are familiar with, explain how the author uses this type of conflict.

860. Oral tradition is a form of storytelling that is passed on from generation to generation. It has often been said that an original story could be altered from when it was first told to when it was first written. Give examples of how this could happen using evidence from a story you know in the oral tradition.

861. Explain the items you would want to place in a time capsule.

862. Flashback is a technique whereby past events are recalled while telling a story in the present. Discuss this technique as it is used in a piece of literature that you have read and tell why this is the best way to tell the story.

863. Discuss your favorite character from Greek mythology. Be sure to include details and elements from the myth as you describe this character.

864. Repetition is a technique used by a poet to create sound or to emphasize a subject in a poem. Discuss how and why this technique is used in a poem that you know.

865. Discuss whether a piece of literature has ever predicted actual events. Using a work that you are familiar with, discuss this topic using specific details.

866. Ralph Waldo Emerson once wrote in one of his essays that he thought it amusing when a man could wear an expensive wristwatch, but could not tell time by looking at the position of the sun in the sky. Explain what he is saying about modern people and society.

867. Often, in literature, a character is viewed as an outsider or a loner. Using a piece of literature that you are familiar with, discuss such a character. Be sure to describe this character's attitudes toward himself or herself, and how he or she deals with the isolation that comes with these two labels.

868. Discuss a character from literature who seems to be present only for comic relief. Explain how this character adds to or detracts from the work.

869. Death has been symbolized many different ways in prose and poetry. Using either of these genres, discuss the symbols that authors use when they write about death. Describe the impact of these symbols.

870. Often, an author will give the reader more information than the characters have. Using a piece of literature that you are familiar with, speculate on the reasons an author would use this method.

871. Sometimes an author will write dialogue that illustrates a person's intelligence, speech pattern, or locality. Discuss a piece of literature in which this happens. Also discuss whether this technique helps or hinders your reading.

872. Discuss a piece of literature that uses the theme of personal survival.

873. Frequently, popular novels are adapted into motion pictures. Discuss a novel that you have read and that has been made into a motion picture. Compare/contrast the plot, setting, and characterization in both mediums.

874. Shakespeare's tragedy *Romeo and Juliet* is a powerful drama about young love and familial conflict. Compare this play to another piece of literature that you have read and that embodies the same themes.

875. Discuss the themes of two fairy tales that you know. Tell how these themes benefit young children.

876. Imagery is the use of descriptive details that appeal to the reader's senses. Using a literary piece that you are familiar with, discuss how the author's use of imagery enhances your reading experience.

877. Compare how a social studies textbook and historical fiction are similar yet different. Explain which medium you would choose in order to learn more about a historical period.

878. Each culture has its own unique literature. Discuss the literary contributions made by one particular culture. Cite a least three major works to illustrate your point.

879. Music and poetry have many similarities. Discuss the connection using specific examples from both musical and poetic works.

880. In the beginning of a novel, an author may present a character one way, but by the end of the novel, this same character may behave differently. Through characterization, we can learn to understand people. Using a piece of literature that you have read, discuss the ways in which the author uses characterization to present personality.

881. Explore the theme of social breakdown or anarchy, using a piece of literature that you have read.

882. Explore the theme of personal degeneration and abandoning morals, using a piece of literature that you have read.

883. Discuss the theme of social injustice, using a piece of literature that you have read.

884. Discuss a piece of literature in which the setting switches between the past and the present.

885. Discuss a literary trilogy wherein the reader must read the succession of novels to understand the plot.

886. Discuss a specific literary work that focuses on adolescent main characters.

887. Discuss how faith is symbolized in a piece of literature that you have read.

888. A burlesque, such as Oscar Wilde's *The Importance of Being Earnest*, is a literary piece that explores a serious subject in a trivial manner or a trivial subject in a serious manner. Choose a literary work that fits this description and explain why it should be classified as a burlesque.

889. Discuss a piece of literature that uses an object of worth, such as a sword, as its focus. Discuss the symbolic purpose of this object.

890. Discuss the imagery from a Civil War period novel that you have read.

891. Using a piece of literature that you are familiar with, discuss the theme of unrequited love.

892. Discuss why only men and boys performed in Shakespeare's dramatic works at the Globe Theater.

893. Using a piece of literature that you are familiar with, discuss how one character influences other characters to change.

894. Discuss a piece of literature that utilizes spirits or ghosts.

895. Discuss a character from literature who embodies a dark mood.

896. Discuss your favorite historical poem, its theme, and the historical events on which the poem is based.

897. Discuss the use of metaphor, imagery, and word play in Lewis Carroll's *Alice in Wonderland.*

898. Discuss an immigrant's point of view in America, using a piece of literature that you have read.

899. Discuss the theme of greed in a piece of literature that you have read.

900. Discuss a prominent leader in our society and his or her literary influences. Discuss what these literary influences reveal about that leader.

901. Discuss a piece of literature from the Industrial Revolution and its treatment of issues like child labor, working conditions, and social classes.

902. Often in literature, a character has ironic experiences that can be humorous or fateful. Discuss how this technique is used in a piece of literature that you have read.

▶ Answers

Scoring Explanations for Literary Response Essays

A score of "6" indicates that your essay satisfies the requirements of the writing prompt in a creative and original manner, using an obvious theme and thesis throughout. The essay provides a clear and logical explanation of your ideas, using specific support material, including direct quotations from the literary work. You thoroughly articulate your ideas in a coherent fashion, analyze and interpret specific literary elements and concepts, and avoid simple plot summary. The essay is orderly and well reasoned, with a clear focus, a logical sequence of ideas, and transitional words and sentences. The essay demonstrates a sense of audience by using effective vocabulary, varied sentence structure, and fluid, sophisticated language that is essentially without errors.

A score of "4" indicates that your essay meets some of the requirements of the writing prompt, including some key elements that help explain the thesis. The essay may answer the question in an abbreviated manner or rely heavily on plot summary, giving only brief or general examples and developing ideas somewhat inconsistently. Literary elements and concepts may be only minimally addressed. You give the essay a general focus, make an obvious attempt at organization, and present your ideas in a logical sequence. The language of the essay indicates a general control of mechanics but has a slightly lower quality of sentence structure and variety than a sample 6 score. An essay of this type contains errors only when using sophisticated language.

A score of "1" indicates that your essay only minimally addresses the writing prompt, digressing, repeating, or dwelling on insignificant details throughout. The essay shows a lack of development and exhibits no organizational pattern or focus. Your writing may be illegible or unrecognizable as English.

Model Literary Response Essays

826. Tone is the mood or feeling the author intends the reader to experience. Using a specific piece of literature, explain how tone enhances the work.

Sample 6 Score

Writers for TV sitcoms or movies are fortunate. Visuals often convey tone much more conveniently than words. Writers have to be very skillful in word choice in order to evoke emotions. While I began to explore Edgar Allan Poe's works, I was intrigued with the way Poe carefully chose language and with the way it evoked a very certain mood or tone.

In Poe's "The Tell-Tale Heart," I was amazed with the way the main character could grow to hate someone's physical appearance so much so that he could stare at him for hours on end. The plot of this story revolves around a young man who rents a room from an elderly man in a large, dark mansion. This is how Poe begins to create the tone or mood. If the setting were in a house with a white picket fence in Pleasantville, the setting might not be as effective for suspense or horror. However, Poe begins to masterfully build suspense in "The Tell-Tale Heart." For example, the deranged tenant slowly opens the elderly man's bedroom door at night and stares at his glass eye for hours in a seething rage. He does this numerous times, to where the reader begins to understand that this

man is far from normal. His obsession leads him to commit a horrible crime.

The rage this man feels about the eye finally comes to a point wherein he attacks the man and suffocates him in his bed. Afterwards, he dismembers his corpse and hides the pieces under the floorboards. By now, the reader is in complete disbelief and awe at such a heinous, unprovoked attack, but we must continue reading. The tone becomes very eerie, and will soon turn suspenseful.

Finally, the police investigate the home after a neighbor reports hearing screams coming from the house. The deranged man invites the police in, and invites them to sit with him in the room where the corpse lies. Poe now adds to the tone with more suspense and a feeling of anxiety as to whether the man will confess to the murder. While speaking with the police, the man begins to hear a faint heartbeat that continues to grow in volume. However, he is the only one who hears it. The man has attempted to cunningly fool the police officers while sitting over the corpse, only to now mentally break down from the noise inside his mind to the point that he confesses. The torture this man evokes on himself adds tremendously to the tone of the story.

Just as Poe creates an eerie, intense, and twisted tone to his fiction, authors can lead their readers to feel certain emotions through their writing.

Sample 4 Score

Tone can be called the way an author makes you feel while reading their work. I personally have been frightened, brought to tears, extremely angry, and have laughed out loud simply by the way an author creates the tone of a story. This is also very similar to what an audience experiences while watching a film.

I recall one work I read by Edgar Allen Poe called The Telltale Heart, which has a bizarre, twisted tone.

Initially, I thought this story was simply about a man who takes in a stranger. However, the tone of the story became strange when the tenant stares at his landlord while he sleeps. Poe leads us into the mind of a madman. I was on the edge of my seat as the police were asking questions of the man. The tone of the story, or the mood, was both frightening and suspenseful.

I enjoy reading all types of books because many times the tone is different. I especially like Poe's stories because I now know how he used tone in his twisted tales.

Sample 1 Score

Tone is like when the writer makes you feel good when you read books. I like to read a lot. In this essay I will tell you about tone.

I like many books that have tone. If you don't have tone, then sometimes I don't like to read these kinds. I like to read books about animuls, cars, and misteries. I really like misteries because you try an figure out what happens.

In this essay I have told you about tone.

827. In the novel *Lord of the Flies*, by William Golding, a group of boys are stranded on a remote island to fend for themselves. Compare/contrast this novel to the popular television show *Survivor*. Use specific details in your answer.

Sample 6 Score

William Golding's novel *Lord of the Flies* explores many themes, such as the dark side of human nature, allegiances, and how these boys mirror larger society. I feel as if the producers of the popular television show *Survivor* used this novel as the framework of their show. Golding's novel and the show have many similarities.

When the show *Survivor* premiered, I immediately thought of the novel *Lord of the Flies*. The novel is about a group of schoolboys who are shipwrecked on a deserted island. The boys attempt to create a "civilization," but ultimately transform into mere savages. This is an important novel for the psychological study Golding presents. One can't help but draw parallels to adult society. There is a true need for structure and control in any society, but the means of that control makes this novel all the more interesting.

One of the boys, Jack, is power-hungry and represents dictatorship. Some of the other boys, such as Simon and Piggy, try to do what is safe and conservative. The character of Ralph is symbolic of democracy and fairness. Throughout the novel, the boys engage in a power struggle and end up destroying one another. Golding's use of symbolism forces the reader to see characters and situations as larger ideas. The boys realize that they must create some type of order.

Similar to the television show *Survivor*, the boys hold council meetings, use objects as symbols of strength, and use fire as a symbol of hope. I remember watching the show and observing a contestant who won a physical contest against the other players. This person was given a pillow to use, whereas the other contestants had nothing. The pillow symbolized power, as did the conch in the novel. Also, whenever the show's council met on Sunday nights, they all brought their torches. When someone was voted off the island (seen as a liability or risk to the welfare of the group), that person's torch was extinguished, thus eliminating hope. Alliances were formed, and these alliances pitted the contestants against each other. Ultimately, the winner was the most cunning player who could convince the other members to follow. This is exactly the situation that occurred between Ralph and Jack in the novel.

William Golding's novel allows the reader to explore human nature and mankind. Often, we do not like to face the psychological aspects of our being. *Survivor* emulates the same underlying motives that form our nature.

Sample 4 Score

In William Goldings *The Lord of the Flies*, I can draw many parallels between the group of boys in the story and the basis for the television show "Survivor".

In "Survivor", contestants are forced to live together on a deserted island for a prolonged period of time. The rules are to form alliances and not to be deceived by the other players. This is similar to what happens in the novel *The Lord of the Flies*. A group of shipwrecked boys must form a society in order to have structure. Jack and Ralph are the two leaders with totally different ways of order. One wants to be a dictator and the other wants to be democratic.

Another similarity between the novel and the show is that they place importance on objects. In the book, the conch is symbolic of power. On the show, if someone wins a race or something, they get a prize and the others don't have anything! Also, both use fire as a lifeline. In the show, when you are voted off the island, you must put out your torch. And both the show and novel have tribal meetings.

I think the show "Survivor" and *The Lord of the Flies* tell about human nature and how societies are formed.

Sample 1 Score

I like survivor on tv and it reminds me of that book about the boys who were the lords of the flies. In the book, boys have to come together to live on an island which is like castaway. In survivor they are put on an iland to survive too. I think the show is cool and the boys in the book destroy everyone!

That is my essay on the survivor show and lord of the flies

828. Using a specific literary work, explain how a novel might influence change in society.

Sample 6 Score

Have you ever read a story that ultimately changed the way in which you thought about the world?

So often we form our opinions and lifestyles from our families and what we observe around us. Could it be possible that a novel might change people's thinking? After reading Harper Lee's *To Kill a Mockingbird*, I realized for the first time how complex racism was, and the necessity for societal change.

I have always been aware of cultural and racial differences in others. I was raised to accept people for their differences and judge people solely on their character. However, I wasn't aware of the problems encountered by black people in the Deep South during the 1940s. In her novel, Lee makes it apparent that the color of skin was a determinant of social stature, no matter your character.

I felt that having a first person narrator, with the story told from the perspective of a young girl in the South, was a brilliant way to tell this story. Scout is at the age where she is only beginning to understand how society handles diversity and cultural differences. A black man, Tom Robinson, is accused of raping a white woman, even though none of the evidence points to him. Scout's father, Atticus Finch, is a well-respected, highly moral lawyer who is defending Tom. Even though Atticus finds evidence contrary to the accusations, he has no hope of winning this trial. Scout fights a boy in her class who calls Tom a racial slur. Scout now begins to come to terms with her assumptions about people.

An interesting point is made in this novel. While the white people of this small town in Alabama discuss the horrors of Hitler persecuting Jewish people, Scout wonders how the same people could not understand that the white people of her town were doing the same to the blacks. This sends a powerful message to the reader through such a vivid analogy.

This novel elicits the reader to think about race relations and social bigotry. There are decent, moral black characters in this novel who are doomed because of their skin color. However, Lee portrays low-class white families, such as Bob's, as being undeserving of respect but able to enjoy a much higher social stature than the blacks. When Tom Robinson is killed escaping from prison, the town barely takes notice.

Through Lee's novel, society is faced with the vulgarities of race and social class, along with the racism of this Southern town. Her message that neither race nor class but rather actions define someone's character leaves the reader with important social issues to be re-examined.

Sample 4 Score

In Harper Lee's novel *To Kill a Mockingbird*, many racial issues are brought into the story for the reader to think about. I think Lee does a nice job of bringing these issues to light.

Atticus Finch, a white lawyer, defending Tom Robinson, a black man accused of raping a white woman, sees that he has no chance of winning this case in this small Southern town, set in the 1940's. Finch's daughter, Scout, tells the story. I liked how Lee used Scout to tell the story, because it was from a child's point of view. Scout must face prejudiced people in the novel who make fun of her father for taking this case, even though her father is respected.

Many things in the novel make the reader feel horrible for the treatment of black people in this town. None of the evidence points to Tom, and even when he is shot at the end of the novel, no one seems to even care.

I really believe because of this book, that many people's ideas about race have been changed. I think that people should be treated with respect no matter the color of their skin.

Sample 1 Score

In this essay, I will write about how a book can change peeple's mind. If you ever read To Kill A Mockingbird, you would see why. A small girl tells this stiory and a black man is being in court because people think he rapped a wehite woman. The reader no's this isn't true, but the town in the south don't believe him. When I read this I was sad because of the way people get picked on. This is my essay on changing society. Thank you.

829. The theme of a literary piece is the central idea or message that it delivers. Cite a specific literary work and discuss the theme.

Sample 6 Score

Theme is the underlying message an author presents to his or her audience. Many times the theme of a work is apparent. Often we ask ourselves upon completing a novel, "What did that character learn at the end?" We base our judgment of characters on our cultural beliefs and emotions we experience in our lives. In Herman Hesse's *Siddartha*, the theme seems apparent—fulfillment in life through spiritual peace.

The main character, Siddartha, takes the reader on his life's journey to find truth and meaning in life. He decides to leave home with his childhood friend, Govinda. The setting of this story is India, with the social caste system as the motivation for his journey. Siddartha realizes that he yearns for more knowledge and understanding, far more that his father can provide him with. He seeks spiritual fulfillment and wisdom. Even though this story is set in India, the theme is universal. Just as many of us decide to go on to college to learn more about the world and ourselves, Siddartha does the same.

At different stages of his journey he acquires wisdom, learns as much as he can, and forges on to new experiences. Siddartha is not unlike a person today in our culture. Many of us challenge ourselves with new ideas and experiences. Sometimes we fail, and other times we succeed. However, what unifies us is the desire to explore the unknown. The trade-off is we may discover we are much happier after taking those risks than if we had never ventured out. This is the theme in *Siddartha*. It is the message that is universal. In fact, there is a very popular book out now about moving cheese, which is a metaphor for the same theme as in *Siddartha*: moving out of our comfort zones into a new, unfamiliar arena, hoping to find what it is we are looking for.

Siddartha goes through both pleasant and unpleasant experiences in this novel. At one point, he acquires incredible wealth and has every material possession he could ever dream of. However, at this point in his life, he contemplates suicide! He has become so gluttonous that he sickens himself. He realizes material possessions cannot bring him peace. From this scene, the theme of attaining spiritual peace is strengthened. How many times have we come across people with enormous wealth, but little peace and fulfillment in their lives?

Siddartha is a great novel and its theme is apparent. The quest for spiritual peace, wisdom, and self-understanding is unpredictable, but attainable through the trials of life and what it has to offer.

Sample 4 Score

The theme of a literary work is the main idea, or message that we understand. Many times the theme is not stated directly, but the reader can usually figure it out. One particular novel I enjoyed reading was Siddartha by Herman Hesse. In this novel, a young man begins his life's journey towards spirituality and understanding. This is a common theme in literature.

While Siddartha is still a young man, he asks his father to explain certain things to him about life and religion. His father doesn't have all the answers for him, so Siddartha decides to leave home and try to find the answers for himself. He brings along his friend Govinda. This book takes place in India; that is the reason for the unfamiliar names. Siddartha and his friend encounter many new people and experiences.

Towards the end of his journey, Siddartha has discovered many things about himself. He realizes that possessions cannot make him happy. He becomes aware that true happiness and peace are found inside.

This theme is very common in literature. I think this is true because people everywhere go through what Siddartha did sometime in their life.

Sample 1 Score

Theme is where you can tell what a writer is thinking about. I think that sometimes writers like to fool with people and guess real hard to see if they can understand.

In Siddartha, a book about a boy who tries to see about life, I think the theme is about a boy in India who likes to go on trips and helps people.

That is my essay about theme. I hope you liked this essay.

830. Compare/contrast the fear of terrorism and the concern with safety issues in present-day society with George Orwell's novel *1984*.

Sample 6 Score

The events of September 11, 2001, shattered our belief that we as Americans are immune to terrorism and its proponents. Our society has taken for granted security and free will. However, new measures have been taken in public arenas to bolster our safety. With this heightened security comes the forfeiture of some civil liberties that George Orwell wrote about in his novel *1984*.

In his novel, Orwell was writing from the perspective of a nation that recently endured a world war. Orwell wrote his novel in 1948, and simply reversed the last two digits in the year to explore what the world might be like in the future. In this world that Orwell writes about, the government has surveillance in every imaginable public space. There is

also a law enforcement collaborative called the "thought police." In this society, no one could have anti-governmental sentiment, whether vocalized or internalized. If you violated this law, "Big Brother" took you away. This government (Big Brother) supposedly gave the citizens what they needed in order to survive. In this cold, mundane society, there was always a camera somewhere watching you. I think it is appropriate to assume that this society was under Communist rule, and Orwell was indeed frightening his readers with the thought of such a threat. This threat was very significant at the time this novel was written. Orwell was conveying the themes of manipulation of the truth and loss of identity. In our present-day society, there are many parallels to Orwell's novel.

Since September 11, 2001, our government has taken steps in order to tighten security and minimize terrorist attacks. By the same token, members of our society must forfeit certain civil liberties. For example, if you travel by air now, you must arrive extremely early before departure, your belongings are scrutinized more closely, and you may have to be patted down or asked to remove your shoes. These actions seem to be intrusive, but most people will accept them to ensure safety.

Furthermore, it is becoming commonplace to find video cameras in many public arenas. Many airports, stores, and offices install cameras for surveillance. Technology has produced cameras that are so small, they can be installed in a shirt or jacket button. Many parents install cameras in their homes to monitor activity if they must leave and hire a sitter. Many police vehicles are equipped with video recorders so that the tape might yield evidence in court. There are even popular television shows that air actual surveillance tapes. This is eerily reminiscent of what occurs in Orwell's *1984*.

Although we have no thought police, nor do we live under totalitarian rule, our society has definitely surrendered its privacy in order to protect its freedom. Orwell seemed to understand how technology can influence society and its freedoms.

Sample 4 Score

George Orwell seems to understand how our society can become disconnected from one another.

I believe since the terrorist attacks, that our sense of security has been compromised. We now have surveillance in almost every aspect of life.

In Orwell's 1984, the society he writes about is very similar to what I have learned about Communism. In this society, there is a dictator and his officials. No one in this society can think for themselves or think anything anti-government. If you do, then the "thought police" will come and get you. Also, there are cameras everywhere in the city. This is similar to what our society is going through now.

Since the terror attacks, our government leaders have asked us to be on alert and to endure tighter restrictions while in public places. For example, you may have to take off your shoes in the airport now, since a terrorist was caught on a plane trying to light a fuse in his sneaker that contained explosives.

Also, if you go to a store like 7-11 or Macy's, you can always find a camera looking at you. I personally feel frightened when I see a camera everywhere, but it just might be helpful to catch people who break the law.

I don't believe that our society will become like Orwell's society in 1984, but I do feel that camera surveillance and checkpoints are very similar to the plot in his novel.

Sample 1 Score

In 1984, people have no privacy because the powers to be want to know what they think and how they act. This reminds me of what happens today. I went in to a store and tried to buy some snacks. A man behind the counter started to scream at me because he thought he saw me stealing something.

Also, my dad flies, and he says that is hard now because all the people check everything you have and they pat you down like in the movies. I don't think this is fair and it reminds me of Orwells story.

831. Personification is the technique wherein a nonhuman character is given human thoughts, feelings, and dialogue. Illustrate how this technique is used in a favorite novel or short story.

Sample 6 Score

Personification is a clever technique wherein nonhuman characters are given human characteristics. Using this technique, the reader is able to understand how an animal feels, or what a tree is thinking, or even the most intimate thoughts of an old pair of sneakers! Rudyard Kipling's "Rikki-Tikki-Tavi" is one of my favorite short stories. In it, all of the animals are personified, which is crucial because the protagonist is a mongoose.

Rikki-Tikki-Tavi is a small mongoose who nearly drowns after a flood sweeps him away from his home. A boy named Teddy finds the mongoose, and he and his mother nurse the animal back to health. Rikki never converses in English with his human family; however, he does interact with the other animals in the garden, speaking in English. I find this technique to be helpful in formulating the plot. For example, a mongoose's natural enemy is the cobra. Kipling uses these two enemies in the wild and makes them the protagonist and antagonist of the short story.

Throughout the story, Rikki-Tikki finds himself battling adversaries in the garden in an effort to save Teddy's family.

This story follows the archetype of the battle between good and evil. If we look closely at the plot, biblical themes are apparent. Snakes in the garden may remind some of the biblical story of Adam and Eve. Without personification in this biblical story, Eve might not have been tempted if the serpent hadn't had the ability to speak. Although Rikki-Tikki cannot converse with the humans in the story, the reader is able to understand his character and his thoughts. For example, before he battles Nag, the male antagonist serpent, he is cautious and a bit nervous. However, he won't show his fear to his enemy. Only the reader understands Rikki's character from this point of view.

Rudyard Kipling was clever enough to observe what occurs in nature, blending it with personification and creating a timeless story of good versus evil.

Sample 4 Score

Personification is the technique where the author gives non-human characters human thoughts, speech, and feelings. I like how this is used in Rudyard Kipling's Rikki-Tikki-Tavi.

Without personification, the main character, who is a mongoose, would not be able to express his feelings. The story would need a narrator, like the kind you see on television's Wild Discovery. Some of those documentaries show animals in the wild, while a narrator tells the audience why the animals behave certain ways. With personification, a non-fictional event can be fictionalized.

For example, a mongoose's natural enemy in the wild is the cobra. In Rikki-Tikki-Tavi, the mongoose is the hero, while the cobra is the villain. Both animals have conversations with other animals and the reader can see what they are thinking about. Rikki-Tikki is nervous to fight the cobras, but doesn't show

it when he starts to battle. I like how the author lets the story unfold through personification.

Although Rikki can't talk with his human family, he behaves like a family pet. When the cobras plot to kill the family, Rikki defends them by killing the snakes. This story follows the common theme of good versus evil. Without personification, the story would not be so enjoyable.

Sample 1 Score

Personification sounds like person, and that is what it means. When a writer gives something words and feelings, it is called personification. In this essay, I will tell you about personification.

Rikki-Tikki is a animul who can talk and have conersashuns with other animuls. He fights snakes and wins! When I read this story I like how animus can talk because then I can see how they feel and stuff.

This is my essay on animuls and talking.

832. Many times in Shakespeare's plays, the setting changes from rural or pastoral to urban. Compare and contrast these settings. Explain the reason for the shift of scenery, using support from specific plays.

Sample 6 Score

Many times in Shakespeare's works, the setting changes from a city to a pastoral venue. Although change in setting is expected, there is an underlying reason why Shakespeare chooses these specific areas. In his play A *Midsummer Night's Dream*, the setting changes from the city of Athens to a forest near the city. The characters behave very differently in each setting.

The play deals with marriages, love, family, and nonconformity. The Duke of Athens is about to be married to a woman whom he recently defeated in war. Another element of the plot deals with a young woman whose father is demanding she marry a man she is not in love with. The woman decides to run away to the forest with the man she does love. There are two distinct settings here, and I believe Shakespeare was mirroring human nature in the change of scenery. Often someone when faced with a pressing problem or decision will retreat to a quiet place to meditate, or might go out with friends in order to find release from the issue or problem. Similarly in this play, the forest is viewed as a place of nonreality, or a dream world. Fairies and supernatural beings inhabit the forest. This is a place of refuge that is in contrast to the conformity of the city. There are, however, similarities in both settings.

Just as the Duke of Athens is marrying Hippolyta, there is King Oberon and his queen in the forest. Both couples are learning about the trials of love. There are colorful characters in both venues who keep the audience entertained also. One such character who lives in the forest is Puck. Puck is a fairy-type character who plays tricks on the characters and ultimately tries to teach them lessons throughout the play. One of the more famous lines from Shakespeare is found in this work when Puck states, "Oh what fools these mortals be." There are lessons to be learned in both the city and the forest, but the forest is more of a dream world or an escape from reality.

Shakespeare cleverly changes the setting in this play to expose human folly and lends keen insight into human nature.

Sample 4 Score

The change in setting in Shakespeare's *A Midsummer Night's Dream* is used to show contrast between a world of conformity and court life with a dream type world. Shakespeare does this to highlight human nature.

In this play, there are two different worlds. One is the city of Athens where the Duke is about to be married. The city has its strict rules and conformity. One part of the plot deals with a woman who doesn't want to marry the man her father wants her to. She decides to run away to the forest with the man she loves. The forest is now seen as an escape from reality. In the forest, there are fairies and other supernatural beings. People also do this in real life. If someone is sad, they may go down to the beach to think or just to be alone.

There is a similarity in both worlds though. There is the Duke of Athens in the city, and there is King Oberon in the forest. They both are involved with their marriages and try to help others with their problems.

I think Shakespeare does a great job using the city and the forest in this play to show two sides of human nature.

Sample 1 Score

In this essay I will talk about shakespeare's play a midsummer night's dream and how this play uses the setting. The setting is the place where things happened. I think the woods and the city are good places for this play. One place is nice, but full of fairies and weird stuff. The city is more like real life and has real people. this is the difference of the setting in the play.

833. A type of conflict is called character versus him- or herself. This is also referred to as internal conflict, because the character must face self-inflicted fears and problems. Write about this type of conflict, using a piece of literature that you have read.

Sample 6 Score

In many literary works there is a central conflict. Conflict can occur in many ways. There is character versus another character, character versus an outside force like nature, and internal conflict, where characters must battle themselves mentally and emotionally. Often these types of conflicts can occur simultaneously in a literary work. I have chosen to discuss my favorite type of conflict in one of my favorite plays by Shakespeare, *Hamlet*.

Internal conflict is the most intricate of all the types of conflict. We may read about characters who must physically defend themselves against other characters. Also, there are many characters who have to brave the elements and survive in life-threatening situations. For example, Ishmael, the narrator and sole survivor in Herman Melville's *Moby Dick*, tells the story of the giant white whale. But the most intense is internal conflict. In Shakespeare's *Hamlet*, a young prince must battle his conscience.

Hamlet, the main character, has recently lost his father. While he is still mourning, his mother marries his father's brother, Claudius. However, Hamlet's father's ghost appears to him and shows him the foul play that surrounded his death. Hamlet learns that his uncle actually murdered his father! This is where internal conflict is most present. In one of the most famous Shakespearian lines, Hamlet ponders, "To be, or not to be. . . ." Hamlet must now decide whether to take action and avenge his father's death or to remain passive. This decision weighs so heavily on his conscience that others notice a drastic change in his behavior. Hamlet must decide if being passive is the equivalent of being a coward. Eventually, Hamlet decides to avenge his father's murder, and this play comes to a tragic end.

I believe that internal conflict works ideally in literature. Of course, Shakespeare presents Hamlet's internal conflict through soliloquy, and this was performed onstage, but when you are able to read what a person is struggling through, you can more closely relate to the character. Internal conflict conjures up the fears that many of us have in everyday life. Hopefully, ours are not as tragic as Hamlet's were!

Sample 4 Score

Conflict is what makes literature interesting to read. If there were no problems, then the reader might become bored. One type of conflict is called internal conflict. This type occurs when a character is battling their conscience. One such character that experiences this is Hamlet from one of Shakespeare's most famous plays.

In *Hamlet*, the main character (by the same name), has just lost his father in a war. His father was the king of Denmark, and Hamlet is prince. Hamlet is visited by his father's ghost and shown that his death was murder by Hamlet's own uncle! This puts Hamlet in a really bad spot. Now he must decide whether to seek revenge for his father's death or do nothing. Why would he do nothing? Well, his uncle is marrying his mother now. Hamlet has the toughest time trying to decide whether to seek revenge. The famous quote "To be or not to be . . ." shows his internal conflict.

Hamlet does seek revenge, but I like how Shakespeare shows what a character is thinking and what goes on in their minds. Internal conflict adds interest for audiences.

Sample 1 Score

In this essay I will talk about what is internal conflict. In many works of writers, a person has thoughts that lead them to make choices. You can tell what that person is thinking by reading. Hamlet had one where he did not like his uncle and his dad was ded. Hamlet had to get even with his dads killers or do nothing. So Hamlet had a hard time trying to make up his mind.

I think that internal conflict is when you have a problem that needs to have solved.

834. Discuss a piece of literature in which the author is also the narrator. Describe the way he or she uses actual events from his or her life in his or her writing.

Sample 6 Score

In literature, there are varying points of view in relaying the events. If the narrator was actually part of the events, this is called first-person narration. When the narrator is merely telling a story, but was not part of the events, this is third-person narration. At times, a reader might be thankful that the narrator is only telling a story as the events unfold, especially if the main characters are in some sort of danger. I personally enjoy first-person narration because you are allowed into the mind of the main character. This was especially enjoyable while reading J.D. Salinger's *Catcher in the Rye*.

The main character, Holden Caulfield, is the narrator as well. He is a very complex character who doesn't seem to fit in socially. Salinger creates the world from Holden's point of view. Although Holden seems apathetic toward many things in his life such as his schoolwork and friends, he is a deeply sensitive character marred by his view of the world. For example, in the beginning of the novel, Holden questions why his roommates are so popular and can converse so well, especially with members of the opposite sex. His insecurities are revealed so that the reader can explore his character and perhaps identify with him. If Salinger had written this as a third-person narration, the reader might not understand Holden's character as well.

Even though Holden Caulfield is a tragic character, and many of his actions are not the most beneficial, Salinger allows us to identify with Holden's insecurities and private feelings.

Sample 4 Score

When the author is involved in the action in a book, it is called first person narration. This is my favorite type of narration because you can understand what goes on in a character's mind. A good example is J.D. Salinger's *Catcher in the Rye*.

The story is told from the viewpoint of the main character, Holden Caufield. He is a very shy, withdrawn young man who is also sensitive. He sometimes wonders if he is like other people, and he is trying to find himself. I think many readers can identify with Holden from time to time. I think everyone feels insecure at one time or another.

I think that Salinger chooses the narrator for this novel well. If this was written any other way, we might not sympathize with the main character as much.

Sample 1 Score

I think 1st person narrator is a nice way to tell a story. In this essay you will hear about this narrator.

In cather in the Rye, I forget the author, the story is told by the main character, Hulden. His is a boy who is afraid of everything! I can feel the way he did sometimes.

This is why I like the narrator person one.

835. The coming of age theme is very popular in literature. This theme refers to a preadolescent boy or girl going through many difficult, life-altering experiences in order to reach young adulthood. Using a novel you are familiar with, discuss this theme. Be sure to use supporting details and evidence in your essay.

Sample 6 Score

The "coming of age" theme is a common one, where an adolescent boy or girl is faced with decisions that ultimately lead them into adulthood. *Barn Burning*, by William Faulkner, embodies this theme with messages of family loyalty and morality.

The story is set in the South, roughly 30 years after the Civil War. The main character who comes of age is Sarty Snopes, a preadolescent whose father, Ab Snopes, is a poor sharecropper frustrated by the post–Civil War aristocracy. Sarty's father is a very destructive, immoral character. In the South at this time, a person who wanted to deliver the most potent form of revenge against a neighbor would have someone burn down the neighbor's barn. This crude assault makes perfect sense considering the main income-providing activity was agriculture and livestock. If people lost their barn where these things were stored, their lives would ultimately be ruined. Ab and his son drift from place to place, and Ab makes money as a hired hit for barns. His son is deeply troubled by his father's destructiveness, but follows along out of "blood," or the loyalty of family regardless of the activities.

Throughout the novel, Sarty is faced with internal conflict. He knows that his father is doing something highly illegal and immoral; however, he wishes to remain loyal to family. Faulkner explores this coming of age theme with real depth and conviction, as the boy struggles with his conscience.

The climax of this novel comes when the boy and his father are taken in by a warm, friendly man who provides the two with meals, lodging, and conversation. Sarty takes a genuine liking to the man; however, he knows that his father plans to burn the man's barn down. Although he tries to convince his father not to commit this heinous act, Ab takes the boy in the middle of the night toward the barn. Sarty makes the hardest decision of his life and warns the man. In the closing scene, a gunshot is heard and the reader can assume that the father has been caught and killed. Sarty has crossed the threshold of preadolescence and has deceived "blood" in order to preserve his morality.

William Faulkner's *Barn Burning* is a remarkable story of coming of age, where a boy must make the ultimate decision and thus becomes a man.

Sample 4 Score

Barn Burning, by William Faulkner, is a great story that has the theme coming of age. In this story, a young boy must decide whether to follow his father in committing unlawful acts, or listen to his own conscience.

Barn Burning takes place in the South, after the Civil War. The boy, Sarty Snopes, and his father, Ab, travel from place to place, hired to burn down barns. Ab is a sharecropper who is angry at the society of the South. During this time, it was the worst thing you could do to someone, burning down their barn. This is where a person would make all of their money, so it was the ultimate slap in the face if you wanted revenge on someone. Sarty doesn't like what his dad does, but stays with him because it's his family duty. He is conflicted on whether to follow hi father or do what he knows is right.

Sarty and his dad are taken in by a man on a plantation and treated very nicely. Sarty begins to really like this man, however he knows that his father is planning to burn down his barn. Sarty is faced with turning in his father or being loyal. In the end, he turns his dad in and this is where he finally comes of age. I think this was a very powerful story.

Sample 1 Score

In this essay, I will tell you about to come to age in Barn Burning. This story was wen a man and his son burn barns, but the boy does not want to do it. He tries to think about what is right, but he wants to stick with blood. His family should not snitch. Barn burning was very bad in this time near the civil war, so The boy at the end turns in his father and becomes a man. That is my essay on barn Burning.

836. Discuss how the reader might sympathize with the main character in Christopher Marlowe's *Dr. Faustus*, even though he sells his soul to the Devil.

Sample 6 Score

The familiar adage about selling one's soul to the devil conjures up two distinct images—dabbling with the occult and being granted magical gifts. Although most people would not want to or dare to cross into such dangerous territory, Dr. John Faustus, the renowned scholar in this Elizabethan tragedy, could not resist.

Christopher Marlowe, author of *Dr. Faustus*, created a complex character in the play of the same name. This character is tragic, foolish, ambitious, intelligent, and to be pitied. For all the good and bad traits he has, the audience cannot help but share in Faustus' regret at the end of the play.

Faustus has mastered many disciplines and is a well-known scholar. However, he yearns for more knowledge beyond the realm of what is offered. Faustus summons the occult and encounters a demon named Mephistopheles, a servant to Lucifer. Faustus makes an offer to give his soul to the devil in exchange for 24 years of magic. Mephistopheles tries to dissuade Faustus from such a fate, but Faustus persists until the deal has been made. Once this occurs, Faustus is ready to satisfy his ambitions.

At this point in the play, the audience—although apprehensive about Faustus' choice—is just as curious as he was about magic and infinite knowledge. Faustus wants to learn the secrets of the universe. He also wants a wife. Basically, he desires the things that most humans desire, and this is where Marlowe captures the audience's empathy. We know that what Faustus has done is immoral and tragic, but we want to share in this display of power as he entertains courts by summoning historical spirits. The audience has pity for Faustus when he has bouts with his conscience. For example, at one point he prays desperately to God for forgiveness, but the audience realizes that no matter how desperately or how much he pleads, the devil will make sure the contract is honored. What is particularly powerful at the end of the play is the torment and desperation Faustus experiences as he fights the clock and tries to hold back time. But, the hours and minutes close in on his fate. Colleagues find his body the next day, and the audience realizes that he has been dragged down to hell.

Although the audience can blame Faustus for summoning the occult and bringing this tragedy on himself, Marlowe creates such a complex character that he is to be pitied for his choices.

Sample 4 Score

Christopher Marlowe creates a character that can be both loathed for his attitude, but also pitied for his choices in Dr. Faustus.

In this play, a young doctor with a lot of knowledge desires more from his studies. He realizes he can't get this knowledge from earth, so he summons the help of the devil. The devil's servant, Mephistopheles, tries to convince Faustus that this is something he should not play around with. Faustus is persistent, so the deal with the devil is finally sealed in blood.

Faustus enjoys his newly found powers, such as bringing up spirits. He does however have bouts with his conscience about his choices. The audience feels pity for him because we would want his power, but we definitely don't want his fate. He tries to bargain and pray, but it is no use. The devil finally wins at the end, and we feel sorrowful for Faustus.

In conclusion, even though Faustus does something that he knows he shouldn't have, the audience still feels pity for him when he has to trade in his soul.

Sample 1 Score

The devil in the play Docter Faust plays a trick on him because he wants to be smarter. I think that Faust is a good man that does wrong.

In the play he has magic but this does not help the devil or make Faust a smart man. He must go to hell when this is done, so he feels sorry for hisself. The people who watch the play fell bad for him to. Oh, well, he made his choice in life and now he is doomd.

837. Discuss a hero in a literary piece that you have read.

Sample 6 Score

In her autobiographical novel *I Know Why the Caged Bird Sings*, Maya Angelou relates her story as a poor black girl living in racially segregated Stamps, Arkansas. As the story unfolds, she describes relationships with her family and members of the community, her love of reading, her feeling of inequality, the racial prejudice she suffers, and her experiences as a single mother. What makes Angelou heroic, I think, is her perseverance over a multitude of odds.

In the beginning of the novel, the reader learns that Angelou is living with her grandmother because her birth mother abandoned her. She has no direction or positive influence in her life until a woman introduces her to "her first white love"—William Shakespeare. Reading becomes an escape from her reality. In real life, Angelou weathered many hardships on her path to adulthood. What then makes her a hero?

The archetype of a hero usually involves hardship, struggle, and an arduous journey. When this hero reaches a certain breaking point or climactic scene, a turn of events usually brings about resolution, self-awareness, and peace. This is true in Angelou's book.

Throughout the novel, racial prejudice is an overriding factor in her life. Even though Angelou documents her struggles against prejudice, lack of a formal education, and personal failure, she comes full circle when her son is born. She embarks on a new self-awareness and peace. There is a heroic quality about a woman who has overcome so many odds.

Although Angelou is both author and subject, she embodies the spirit of a heroic character who ultimately prevailed against the odds.

Sample 4 Score

An hero in my opinion is the author Maya Angelou. Often people think of heroes as sports stars or world leaders, but Maya Angelou is a hero.

In Maya's book, *I know why the caged bird Sings*, Maya is really the main character. In fact, this is an autobiography of her life. In the book she goes through many hard times and has tough choices to make. The town she is from is in Arkansas, and it is a very racially divided town. Her grandmother is also raising her. One thing that Angelou loves to do is read. She meets a woman who shows her how to read, and well!

I think she is a hero because she survived being a victim. Angelou was treated poorly because of her race, she was raped by a relative, abandoned by her mother, and becomes a mother herself. Similar to a hero, she has to be brave and strong-willed.

I think Maya Angelou is a great person and a true hero.

Sample 1 Score

A hero is a person who is in comic books and things, but did you know something about Miya Angeloo?

She is a writer and she came from being very poor to becoming a success. In this essay I will talk abot angeloo.

Well, maya had problems because some poeple are rasist, but she made her problems beter and even rote about them. And I think she is very nice and brave i hope everyone reades about this strong hero.

838. Write a literary analysis of a Robert Frost poem. Include theme and symbolism in your discussion.

Sample 6 Score

Robert Frost's comforting, sad, and often poignant poetry is usually filled with metaphors and vivid imagery. Perhaps my favorite Frost poem is "Stopping by Woods on a Snowy Evening." The imagery creates a memorable portrait of the beauty and power of nature.

Near the beginning, the narrator is introduced as a working man, who has stopped to rest: "My little horse must think it queer / To stop without a farmhouse near." The narrator suggests that his days are mostly spent in labor, moving from place to place. On a whim, he stops riding to watch the "woods fill up with snow." During this brief moment, the narrator achieves spiritual transcendence and peace as he connects with nature.

Throughout the poem, the narrator's horse is a symbol of daily labor and the constant struggle of civilization. Taken from the wilds of nature, domesticated, and trained to obey orders, the horse no longer has any appreciation of nature. While the narrator relaxes in the woods, his horse "gives his harness bells a shake / To ask if there is some mistake." The irony here is that the man becomes even more connected to nature than the once-wild beast he rides.

It's important that this event takes place during "the darkest evening of the year," because the darkness allows the narrator to be hidden from the civilized and unnatural world he lives in every day. At the same time, the darkness of the evening is ironic because the narrator can't really see the beauty of the woods very clearly. In this way, Frost suggests that nature's beauty is more than just visual. It's spiritual, too. In the "lovely, dark, and deep" woods, the narrator is able to fully appreciate the beauty of nature without seeing it.

After his brief moment of peace, the narrator must return to the working world. The line, "And miles to go before I sleep" is repeated at the end to show how weary and tired the narrator has become. Here, the "miles" represent long spans of time. He has a long time to wait before he gets home that night, and he also has a long time to wait before he reaches the ultimate sleep of death. But in this poem, the idea of death isn't negative because when the narrator dies, he will finally be permanently reunited with the beauty of nature.

Sample 4 Score

Robert Frost's poem "Stopping By Woods On A Snowy Evening" can be interpreted as a man learning to appreciate nature.

The poem starts out as a man in a horse-drawn carriage stops to appreciate the serenity of a dark, snowy evening. Although this might seem to be a simple poem using imagery, Frost sends a message about the power of nature. The man seems to enjoy the woods even more than his horse, who was probably born in the woods. It's a dark evening but somehow the man can still appreciate the lovely forest.

At the end of the poem, Frost says that he can't stop to rest anymore because he has things to do. I thought this part was really sad because the man seemed so tired and didn't want to leave.

This poem has many symbolic elements in it and I enjoyed this very much.

Sample 1 Score

Roburt frost has made a poem about a snowy evening. In this essay I will explain about the message in the poem I have read.

The poem is about a man who goes into a cold forest and stops to watch snow. I like to snowboard in the winter, so I know what he is felling. Afterwards, frost says he cannot stop anymore because he has to go into town and help people. This is my intreputashun of his poem.

839. Compare the society of *The Scarlet Letter* to our society today. Compare and contrast how Hester Prynne would have been treated today with how she was treated in the novel.

Sample 6 Score

Hester Prynne, from Nathaniel Hawthorne's *The Scarlet Letter*, would not necessarily have fared much better today than in her own time. Some of the Puritanical influences in Salem, Massachusetts, at that time still exist in modern society. Public ridicule remains an integral part of our culture, infidelity is still deplored, and unfortunately, women are still often seen as the more guilty party of any extramarital affair.

In *The Scarlet Letter*, Reverend Dimmesdale is a spiritual leader of the community. However, he impregnates a young woman named Hester Prynne, who believes her husband has died at sea. As a result of their affair, Hester is forced to wear a scarlet "A" on her chest and stand in the midst of the town on a scaffold. Meanwhile, Dimmesdale keeps his distance and remains silent out of fear. In modern times, it would be hard to imagine anyone who has had an affair being forced to wear a red letter on his or her clothes for all to see, but, at the same time, public ridicule has become a part of modern culture as well. Celebrities are publicly ridiculed on the covers of tabloid magazines every day, and the details of their private lives are frequently broadcast on shows like Access Hollywood. In our society, extramarital affairs have become public knowledge. From celebrities to politicians, one way or another, affairs make news and sell papers.

Also, in the book, Hester Prynne is unfairly singled out as the guilty one as a result of Dimmesdale's silence. Even now, it is often the woman who is viewed as the immoral one with poor judgment. Although Dimmesdale finally delivers a powerful sermon toward the end of the novel, confessing to the affair before his congregation, he dies—rather conveniently—shortly after, thereby escaping any punishment or public ridicule. So, in the end, Hester Prynne may not have been treated much better in our times. For its portrayal of this timeless situation, *The Scarlet Letter* remains a viable novel.

Sample 4 Score

Our society views women the same as in Nathaniel Hawthorne's Scarlet Letter. It's very interesting how things change very little in such a wide span of time. Hester Prynne is brought in front of the town on a scaffold for having an affair and becoming pregnant. Her husband is assumed lost at sea, however the townspeople scorn her and exclude her from society. She is made to wear a letter A on her clothes for embarrassment. Although sometimes women who have affairs are treated badly, they don't ever have to wear scarlet letters anymore.

Reverend Dimmsdale is never really looked at badly, even though at the end he confesses. It's the same today. Usually, there is one person who is viewed as the bad guy, and one person who is innocent, even though both people are having the affair. It's the same sort of thing you read in the newspapers with celebrities and politicians, it seems someone is always having an affair. For all these reasons, I think that what happens in the book is mostly the same as what would happen in modern times.

Sample 1 Score

Hester in the scarlet letter was a women who had had an afair with an important man and she was made fun because of it. She had to where an A letter to show she was sorry. Everyne in the town didnt like her becase they think she did something very bad and they also were not mean to the man. I wouldnt treet poeple like that along time ago today or in the futur either.

Grade Yourself

The previous sample essays show you how the literary response scoring guide works. For topics 840–902, simply use the Rubric for Literary Response Writing on page 269 to evaluate your essays. You can also refer to the Essay Scoring Criteria section in Chapter 6 for more information.

9 ▶ Critical Reading

A writer lives in awe of words, for they can be cruel or kind, and they can change their meanings right in front of you. They pick up flavors and odors like butter in a refrigerator.

—John Steinbeck

REALISTICALLY SPEAKING, standardized tests are an important gauge of a student's academic achievement, and every student should strive to succeed on standardized tests such as the SAT, ACT, GRE, and school entrance exams. The best way to prepare for reading tests and for future reading challenges is to become a critical reader—the kind of active reader who reaches to find a deeper meaning beyond the literal. Active readers interpret a text by analyzing literary devices and by drawing conclusions based on facts and events presented in the text. A well-told fictional story is a joy to read, and active readers experience an even richer reading experience by exploring the meaning beyond the surface. Active readers analyze, scrutinize, and make judgments and connections regarding important elements such as plot, characterization, and the author's use of setting and literary devices. Armed with the ability to form inferences and draw logical conclusions, the experienced critical reader has little to fear when faced with a standardized test or entrance exam.

▶ Critical Reading Strategies

Here are strategies that will help you to become a more active and successful reader:

- Start by surveying the book's title, topic sentences, or photo captions for clues about the main idea. Ask yourself: What is the ongoing theme? Is there more than one theme? Is the theme stated in the title or in the body of the book? Is it implied? What is the author trying to achieve?

- When you stumble upon a word that is unfamiliar to you, use the context of the surrounding words to clue you in to its meaning. Read difficult paragraphs more than once to be certain that you have grasped the full meaning.

- Analyzing dialogue is an important method of understanding a character's personality and the manner in which he or she interacts with the other characters. Pay attention to what characters say to one another. Are they engaged in conflict? Dialogue also reveals important clues about a character's educational, regional, social, and economic background and his or her moral character.

- What is the author's tone? Is the story an optimistic or a pessimistic one? Does the author think that the world is a cruel, harsh place to live in, or does he or she have a positive worldview?

- Every story contains conflict woven into the plot, because without conflict there isn't usually much of a story. There can be more than one conflict going on, and the conflict can involve individuals, nature, and concepts (man versus nature, man versus man, man versus society). Ask yourself: What are the roots of the conflict? What are the consequences or effects of the conflict? Is the conflict ever resolved? If so, how?

- Setting details are important and should be analyzed. Historical, scientific, and technological events, climate, economic conditions, occupations, traditions, and religious and cultural customs are important setting details that impact a story and its characters. The racially charged Southern Depression-era setting in the Southern Gothic novel *To Kill a Mockingbird* by Harper Lee is an excellent example of the connection between setting and plot development. The science fiction genre often introduces technology in settings that are vastly different from the present-day world.

- When you are writing a response to a literary text, it is important that you incorporate quotations from the text to support your ideas. Unless you are asked to refer to outside sources, focus on extracting information from the text itself. Use specific quotations to support your analysis. However, don't let your use of quotations dominate the page or drown out your own voice and ideas.

► Literary Devices Crossword Puzzle

Across

4. a person, place, event, or thing that is used to communicate meaning beyond the literal

6. the emotional, historical, or traditional association with a particular word

7. the main idea and perspective in a fiction or nonfiction story or other form of writing, such as poetry or essays

8. a figure of speech in which two items are compared using the words *like* or *as*

10. the literal meaning of a word

12. the sensory descriptive detail that is used to created vivid images in the reader's mind

13. the time period and geographical location in which a story takes place

Down

1. a figure of speech in which the author suggests a similarity or connection between two things that are not alike

2. an overly dramatic exaggeration that is used to increase the impact of a statement

3. clue to future plot development

5. the author's general attitude or philosophy

9. the overall feeling created by the author's use of language, setting, sound, and other details—for example, joyful, mysterious, romantic

11. when an author applies human traits to a nonhuman

Word Bite: *Epithet*

An **epithet** is used to emphasize a special or distinctive characteristic of a geographical location, an individual, or a thing. For example, New York City is well-known as "the Big Apple" and New Orleans is often referred to by its epithet "the Big Easy."

Get a Grip on Citations

Your own voice and ideas should dominate your report. When citing outside sources, direct quotations and paraphrasing should be limited to approximately 20% of your final draft.

Idioms

Idioms are colorful expressions that add spice and color to the stories in which they appear. Since idioms are hard to figure out logically, the best way to understand what one of these expressions means is to look up its meaning in a reference book. Idioms come from local folklore, slang expressions, sports, proverbs, authors, and other sources.

Here are some common idioms and their meanings:

- ***It's going to the dogs.***—It's declining in quality or heading to ruination.
- ***Take it with a grain of salt.***—View it with a bit of skepticism.
- ***Birds of a feather flock together.***—People who are alike usually attract one another.
- ***Someone is mad as a wet hen.***—The person is expressing extreme anger, agitation, or distress.

▶ Practice Questions

Read the following passages and choose the best answer.

Questions 903–905 are based on the passage on the following page.

903. According to the passage, why did James Russell invent the CD?
   a. He was tired of turning over his records to hear both sides.
   b. He wanted to record more music on a new format.
   c. He wanted a purer, more durable sound than he could get from vinyl records.
   d. He was interested in getting patents.
   e. He wanted to work with lasers.

904. What would happen if the detector on a CD player malfunctioned?
   a. The spiral track would not be read properly.
   b. The pits and land would look like one unit.
   c. The changes in reflectivity would be absorbed back into the laser.
   d. The music would play backwards.
   e. The information read by the laser would not be converted into music.

The following selection is about the invention of the compact disc, and explains how it works.

(1) Compact discs (CDs), which may be found in over 25 million American homes, not to mention backpacks and automobiles, first entered popular culture in the 1980s. But their history goes back to the 1960s, when an inventor named James Russell decided to create an alterna-
(5) tive to his scratched and warped phonograph records—a system that could record, store, and replay music without ever wearing out.

The result was the compact disc. Made from 1.2 mm of polycarbonate plastic, the disc is coated with a much thinner aluminum layer that is then protected with a film of lacquer. The lacquer layer can be
(10) printed with a label. CDs are typically 120 mm in diameter, and can store about 74 minutes of music. There are also discs that can store 80, 90, 99, and 100 minutes of music, but they are not as compatible with various stereos and computers as the 74-minute size.

The information on a standard CD is contained on the polycar-
(15) bonate layer, as a single spiral track of pits, starting at the inside of the disc and circling its way to the outside. This information is read by shining light from a 780 nm wavelength semiconductor laser through the bottom of the polycarbonate layer. The light from the laser follows the spiral track of pits, and is then reflected off either the pit or the alu-
(20) minum layer. Because the CD is read through the bottom of the disc, each pit looks like a bump to the laser.

Information is read as the laser moves over the bumps (where no light will be reflected) and the areas that have no bumps, also known as land (where the laser light will be reflected off the aluminum). The
(25) changes in reflectivity are interpreted by a part of the compact disc player known as the detector. It is the job of the detector to convert the information collected by the laser into the music that was originally recorded onto the disc. This invention brought 22 patents to James Russell, who today says he working on an even better system for
(30) recording and playing back music.

905. Paragraph 3, lines 14–21, explains all of the
following EXCEPT
a. how the information on a CD is read.
b. why semiconductor lasers were invented.
c. where information is stored on a CD.
d. what pits and bumps are.
e. the purpose of the aluminum layer of a CD.

Questions 906–908 are based on the following passage.

This selection introduces the Computer Museum of America, and details an important item in its collection.

(1)   Wondering what to do with that old Atari home video game in the attic? It's on the wish list of the Computer Museum of America, in San Diego, California, which hopes you will donate it to their holdings. The Museum was founded in 1983 to amass and preserve historic

(5)   computer equipment such as calculators, card punches, and typewriters, and now owns one of the world's largest collections. In addition, it has archives of computer-related magazines, manuals, and books that are available to students, authors, researchers, and others for historical research.

(10)   One item currently on display is a 1920s comptometer, advertised as "The Machine Gun of the Office." The comptometer was first sneered at by accountants and bookkeepers, many of whom could add four columns of numbers in their heads. The new machine was the first that could do the work faster than humans. The comptometer

(15)   gained a large following, and its operation became a formal profession that required serious training. But by the 1970s, computers took over, and comptometers, and the job of operating them, became obsolete.

906. All of the following are probably part of the collection of the Computer Museum of America EXCEPT
a. adding machines.
b. old computers.
c. operation manuals for calculators.
d. card punch machines.
e. kitchen scales.

907. In line 12, the author used the words *sneered at* to show
a. a negative image of accountants.
b. what accountants and bookkeepers looked like.
c. the negative reaction to the comptometer.
d. the precursor of the comptometer operator.
e. how accountants and bookkeepers add.

908. What term paper topic could probably be researched at the Computer Museum of America?
a. Alexander Graham Bell's contributions to American society
b. IBM's contribution to the development of the modern computer
c. more than just paintings: the museums of California
d. the rise and fall of the comptometer operator
e. why video games are harmful to our nation's youth

Questions 909–916 are based on the following passage.

The following selection explains the origins and development of the modern shopping mall.

(1)   Today's shopping mall has as its antecedents historical marketplaces, such as Greek agoras, European piazzas, and Asian bazaars. The purpose of these sites, as with the shopping mall, is both economic and social. People go not only to buy and sell wares, but also to be seen,

(5)   catch up on news, and be part of the human drama. Both the marketplace and its descendant the mall might also contain restaurants, banks, theaters, and professional offices.

The mall is also the product of the creation of suburbs. Although villages outside of cities have existed since antiquity, it was the techno-

(10)   logical and transportation advances of the nineteenth century that gave rise to a conscious exodus of the population away from crowded, industrialized cities toward quieter, more rural towns. Since the suburbs typically have no centralized marketplace, shopping centers or malls were designed to fill the needs of the changing community, pro-

(15)   viding retail stores and services to an increasing suburban population.

The shopping mall differs from its ancient counterparts in a number of important ways. While piazzas and bazaars were open-air venues, the modern mall is usually enclosed. Since the suburbs are spread out geographically, shoppers drive to the mall, which means that park-

(20)   ing areas must be an integral part of a mall's design. Ancient market-places were often set up in public spaces, but shopping malls are designed, built, and maintained by a separate management firm as a unit. The first shopping mall was built by J.C. Nichols in 1922 near Kansas City, MO. The Country Club Plaza was designed to be an

(25)   automobile-centered plaza, as its patrons drove their own cars to it, rather than take mass transportation, as was often the case for city shoppers. It was constructed according to a unified plan, rather than as a random group of stores. Nichols' company owned and operated the mall, leasing space to a variety of tenants.

(30)   The first enclosed mall was the Galleria Vittoria Emanuele in Milan, Italy, in 1865–1877. Inspired by its design, Victor Gruen took the shopping and dining experience of the Galleria to a new level when he created the Southdale Center Mall in 1956. Located in a suburb of Minneapolis, it was intended to be a substitute for the traditional city center.

(35)   The 95-acre, two-level structure had a constant climate-controlled temperature of 72 degrees, and included shops, restaurants, a school, a post office, and a skating rink. Works of art, decorative lighting, fountains, tropical plants, and flowers were placed throughout the mall. Southdale afforded people the opportunity to experience the pleasures of urban

(40)   life while protected from the harsh Minnesota weather.

In the 1980s, giant megamalls were developed. While Canada has had the distinction of being home to the largest of the megamalls for

over 20 years, that honor will soon go to Dubai, where the Mall of
Arabia is being completed at a cost of over five billion U.S. dollars.
(45)   The 5.3-million-square-foot West Edmonton Mall in Alberta, Canada,
opened in 1981, with over 800 stores, 110 eating establishments, a
hotel, an amusement park, a miniature-golf course, a church, a zoo,
and a 438-foot-long lake. Often referred to as the "eighth wonder of
the world," the West Edmonton Mall is the number-one tourist
(50)   attraction in the area, and will soon be expanded to include more retail
space, including a facility for sports, trade shows, and conventions.

The largest enclosed megamall in the United States is the Mall of
America in Bloomington, MN, which employs over 12,000 people. It
has over 500 retail stores, an amusement park that includes an indoor
(55)   roller coaster, a walk-through aquarium, a college, and a wedding
chapel. The mall contributes over one billion dollars each year to the
economy of the state of Minnesota. Its owners have proposed numerous expansion projects, but have been hampered by safety concerns
due to the mall's proximity to an airport.

909. The statement that people went to marketplaces to *be part of the human drama* (line 5)
suggests that people
  a. prefer to shop anonymously.
  b. like to act on stage rather than shop.
  c. seem to be more emotional in groups.
  d. like to be in community, interacting with
  one another.
  e. prefer to be entertained rather than shop
  for necessities.

910. In line 1, *antecedents* most nearly means
  a. designers.
  b. planners.
  c. predecessors.
  d. role models.
  e. teachers.

911. All of the following questions can be explicitly
answered on the basis of the passage EXCEPT
  a. Who designed the Southdale Center Mall
  in Minnesota?
  b. Why was the Country Club Plaza
  automobile-centered?
  c. What are three examples of historical
  marketplaces?
  d. Where is the Galleria Vittoria Emanuele?
  e. What is the West Edmonton Mall often
  referred to as?

912. How was the Country Club Plaza different
from an urban shopping district?
  a. It consisted of many more stores.
  b. It was built by one company that leased
  space and oversaw operations.
  c. It was enclosed.
  d. It had both retail stores and restaurants,
  and offered areas for community programs.
  e. It was based on an Italian design.

913. According to the passage, how did Southdale expand the notion of the shopping mall?

a. It added an amusement park.

b. It was unheated.

c. It was the first to rise above two stories.

d. It was designed with more parking spaces than any previous shopping mall.

e. It was intended to be a substitute for the traditional city center.

914. According to paragraph 5, which is the only activity visitors to the West Edmonton Mall cannot enjoy?

a. staying in a hotel

b. gambling in a casino

c. visiting animals in a zoo

d. playing miniature golf

e. riding an amusement park ride

915. The statement in lines 38 to 40 that *Southdale afforded people the opportunity to experience the pleasures of urban life* means that

a. they could perform necessary and leisurely activities in one location.

b. they could have a greater variety of retailers to choose from.

c. they could see more artwork and botanicals than they would in a city.

d. they could be entertained as they would be in a city.

e. they could have taller buildings in their landscape.

916. What is NOT a probable reason for the proposed expansion of the Mall of America?

a. so it can contribute more to the economy of its state

b. to keep it closer in size to the other megamalls

c. so it can employ more people

d. to attract more tourists

e. to compete for visitors with the Mall of Arabia

Questions 917–924 are based on the passages on pages 302–304.

917. The author's tone in Passage 1, lines 1–7, may best be described as

a. satire concerning a man's journey through life.

b. cynicism about the reasons people go on reality TV shows.

c. humor regarding the content of reality TV.

d. irony about the maturation process.

e. sarcasm toward the television networks.

918. Based on the passages, which statement would both authors agree with?

a. Reality TV has had a long history.

b. *Big Brother* is about the desire for fame and money.

c. The popularity of reality TV is an indication of a decline in morals.

d. *Survivor* is the most successful reality TV show.

e. There is nothing wrong with reality TV.

Both of these passages were adapted from high school newspaper editorials concerning reality television.

Passage 1

(1)   There comes a time in every boy's life when he becomes a man. On this fateful day, he will be swept up and put on an island to compete for one million dollars. Then, this man will realize that money can't buy happiness. He will find his soul mate, as we all do, on national TV,

(5)   picking a woman out of a line of 20. By then it will be time for him to settle down, move to the suburbs, make friends with the neighbors, and then refurbish the neighbors' house.

Welcome to real life. That is, real life as the television networks see it.

(10)   Reality TV is flawed in many ways, but the most obvious is in its name. It purports to portray reality, but no "reality" show has succeeded in this endeavor. Instead, reality TV is an extension of fiction, and there are no writers who need to be paid. Television executives love it because it is so much cheaper to produce than any other type

(15)   of programming, and it's popular. But the truth is that there is little or no reality in reality TV.

Do you sing in the shower while dreaming of getting your own record deal? There are a couple of shows made just for you. Audition, and make the cut, so some British guy who has never sung a note can

(20)   rip you to pieces on live television. Or maybe you're lonely and fiscally challenged, and dream of walking down the aisle with a millionaire? Real marriage doesn't involve contestants who know each other for a couple of days. The people on these shows seem to be more interested in how they look on camera than in the character of the person they

(25)   might spend the rest of their life with. Let's hope that isn't reality.

There are also about a dozen decorating shows. In one case, two couples trade rooms and redecorate for each other. The catch is, interior designers help them. This is where the problem starts. Would either couple hire someone who thinks it's a great idea to swathe a

(30)   room in hundreds of yards of muslin, or to adhere five thousand plastic flowers as a mural in a bathroom? The crimes committed against defenseless walls are outrageous. When you add the fact that the couples are in front of cameras as well as the designers, and thus unable to react honestly to what is going on, you get a new level of "unreality."

(35)   Then there is the show that made the genre mainstream—*Survivor*, the show that pits men and women from all walks of life against each other for a million-dollar prize in the most successful of all the reality TV programs. What are record numbers of viewers tuning in to see? People who haven't showered or done their laundry in weeks are

(40)   shown scavenging for food and competing in ridiculous physical challenges. Where's the reality? From the looks of it, the contestants spend

most of their time, when not on a reality TV show, driving to the Burger Barn and getting exercise only when the remote goes missing.

(45)   So the television networks have used reality TV to replace the dramas and comedies that once filled their schedules, earning millions in advertising revenue. The lack of creativity, of producing something worth watching, is appalling. We are served up hundreds of hours of reality TV each week, so we can watch real people in very unreal situations, acting as little like themselves as possible. What's real about that?

Passage 2

(1)   Why does reality TV get such a bad rap? Editorials on the subject blame its popularity on everything from the degenerate morals of today's youth to our ever-decreasing attention spans. The truth is that reality-based programs have been around for decades. *Candid Camera*

(5)   first aired in 1948, a *Cops*-like show called *Wanted* was on CBS's lineup in the mid-1950s, and PBS aired a controversial 12-hour documentary filmed inside a family's home in 1973. But it was *Survivor*, which debuted on American TV in the summer of 2000, that spawned the immense popularity of the reality genre. There are now

(10)   more than 40 reality shows on the air, and, hinting that they are here to stay, the Academy of Television Arts and Sciences added "Best Reality Show" as an Emmy category in 2002.

          Why are these shows so popular today? Are they really a sign that our morals, and our minds, are on a decline? People have been tuning

(15)   in to reality TV for generations, so what makes today's shows any worse than their predecessors? Let's look at a number of current, popular shows to see what the fuss is about. MTV's *The Real World* has been on the air for over ten years. It places seven strangers in one house and tapes them as they live together for a few months. The show has been

(20)   a ratings home run for MTV, and tens of thousands of hopefuls audition each time they announce they are producing another show. Those who make the cut are attractive young singles not only looking for a good time, but also looking for fame, too. It's not uncommon for them to hire a show business agent before the taping starts.

(25)   Other reality shows take fame-seekers to the next level by having them compete against one another. *American Idol, Star Search*, and *Fame* showcase singers, actors, dancers, and model wannabes, and offer them a chance at professional success. Even those who don't win the big prize get national television exposure, and have a better chance

(30)   than they did before the show of becoming famous. *Survivor* offers another twist: Not only can you become an instant celebrity, but you have a chance to win a million dollars. The combination of fame and money has helped to make *Survivor* the most popular reality TV program of all time. But it's not alone in the format. *Big Brother* combines

(35)   the "group living together in a beautiful setting" concept of *The Real World* with a $500,000 prize, and *Fear Factor* pays $50,000 to the contestant who completes the most terrifying stunts.

Given television's long history of reality-based programming, why is there a problem now? Most reality TV centers on two common

(40)   motivators: fame and money. The shows have pulled waitresses, hairstylists, investment bankers, and counselors, to name a few, from obscurity to household names. These lucky few successfully parlayed their 15 minutes of fame into celebrity. Even if you are not interested in fame, you can probably understand the desire for lots of

(45)   money. Watching people eat large insects, jump off cliffs, and be filmed 24 hours a day for a huge financial reward makes for interesting viewing. What's wrong with people wanting to be rich and famous? Not much, and, if you don't like it, you can always change the channel.

919. The primary purpose of Passage 2 is to
   a. refute an argument.
   b. explore possible outcomes.
   c. give a brief history.
   d. explain how to get famous.
   e. show the need for change.

920. The two passages differ in that the author of Passage 1
   a. defends reality TV, while the author of Passage 2 does not.
   b. explains what he or she thinks is wrong with reality TV, while the author of Passage 2 does not.
   c. believes reality TV has many faults, while the author of Passage 2 thinks no one has a problem with it.
   d. blames reality TV for the lack of variety in programming, while the author of Passage 2 thinks it has improved variety.
   e. says reality TV is cheap to produce, while the author of Passage 2 disagrees.

921. In Passage 2, line 20, the phrase *ratings home run* means that
   a. a lot of people watch *The Real World*.
   b. *The Real World* beats baseball games in TV ratings.
   c. there are baseball players on *The Real World*.
   d. the Nielsen company likes *The Real World*.
   e. *The Real World* contestants play softball on the show.

922. Both passages illustrate the idea that
   a. people on reality TV shows become famous.
   b. Reality TV is all about getting rich.
   c. Reality TV is a good alternative to traditional programming.
   d. the producers of reality TV are getting rich.
   e. Reality TV is controversial.

923. *Swathe* in Passage 1, line 29 most nearly means

    a. to stitch.

    b. a combination of pleating and stapling.

    c. to cover.

    d. a way of making curtains.

    e. to cover the floor.

924. What does the author of Passage 1 find most troublesome about reality TV?

    a. It isn't original.

    b. It doesn't need writers to come up with scripts.

    c. It invades people's privacy.

    d. It doesn't accurately show reality.

    e. It shows how shallow people are.

Questions 925–931 are based on the following passage.

The following selection is adapted from a news story about a bill recently introduced in Congress.

(1)   In the past 30 years, Americans' consumption of restaurant and take-out food has doubled. The result, according to many health watchdog groups, is an increase in overweight and obesity. Almost 60 million Americans are obese, costing $117 billion each year in health

(5)   care and related costs. Members of Congress have decided they need to do something about the obesity epidemic. A bill was recently introduced in the House that would require restaurants with 20 or more locations to list the nutritional content of their food on their menus. A Senate version of the bill is expected in the near future.

(10)   Our legislators point to the trend of restaurants' marketing larger meals at attractive prices. People order these meals believing that they are getting a great value, but what they are also getting could be, in one meal, more than the daily recommended allowances of calories, fat, and sodium. The question is, would people stop "supersizing" or

(15)   make other healthier choices if they knew the nutritional content of the food they're ordering? Lawmakers think they would, and the gravity of the obesity problem has caused them to act to change menus.

    The Menu Education and Labeling (MEAL) Act would result in menus that look like the nutrition facts panels found on food in super-

(20)   markets. Those panels are required by the 1990 Nutrition Labeling and Education Act, which exempted restaurants. The new restaurant menus would list calories, fat, and sodium on printed menus, and calories on menu boards, for all items that are offered on a regular basis (daily specials don't apply). But isn't this simply asking restaurants to

(25)   state the obvious? Who isn't aware that an order of supersize fries isn't health food? Does anyone order a double cheeseburger thinking they're being virtuous?

    Studies have shown that it's not that simple. In one, registered dieticians couldn't come up with accurate estimates of the calories found in

(30)   certain fast foods. Who would have guessed that a milk shake, which

(35) sounds pretty healthy (it does contain milk, after all) has more calories than three McDonald's cheeseburgers? Or that one chain's chicken breast sandwich, another better-sounding alternative to a burger, contains more than half a day's calories and twice the recommended daily amount of sodium? Even a fast-food coffee drink, without a doughnut to go with it, has almost half the calories needed in a day.

The restaurant industry isn't happy about the new bill. Arguments against it include the fact that diet alone is not the reason for America's obesity epidemic. A lack of adequate exercise is also to blame. In addi-
(40) tion, many fast food chains already post nutritional information on their websites, or on posters located in their restaurants.

Those who favor the MEAL Act, and similar legislation, say in response that we must do all we can to help people maintain a healthy weight. While the importance of exercise is undeniable, the quantity
(45) and quality of what we eat must be changed. They believe that if we want consumers to make better choices when they eat out, nutritional information must be provided where they are selecting their food. Restaurant patrons are not likely to have memorized the calorie counts they may have looked up on the Internet, nor are they going to leave
(50) their tables, or a line, to check out a poster that might be on the opposite side of the restaurant.

925. The purpose of the passage is to
a. argue the restaurant industry's side of the debate.
b. explain why dieticians have trouble estimating the nutritional content of fast food.
c. help consumers make better choices when dining out.
d. explain one way legislators propose to deal with the obesity epidemic.
e. argue for the right of consumers to understand what they are ordering in fast food restaurants.

926. According to the passage, the larger meals now being offered in restaurants
a. cost less than smaller meals.
b. add an extra side dish not offered with smaller meals.
c. include a larger drink.
d. save consumers money.
e. contain too many calories, fat, and sodium.

927. In lines 16–17, the word *gravity* most nearly means
a. the force of attraction toward the earth.
b. a cemetery plot.
c. seriousness.
d. jealousy.
e. presumption of wrongdoing.

928. According to the passage, why is the restaurant industry against the new congressional bill?
a. They don't want any healthy items on their menus.
b. Because lack of adequate exercise is also responsible for the obesity epidemic.
c. They don't want to be sued if they incorrectly calculate the calories in their menu items.
d. They feel their industry is already overregulated.
e. Because people would stop coming to their establishments if they knew what was in the food.

929. Why is the chicken breast sandwich mentioned in paragraph 4?

 a. It is an example of a menu item that contains more fat than one would assume.
 b. It is the only healthy choice on some restaurants' menus.
 c. It has twice as much salt as the recommended daily allowance.
 d. It has as many calories as three McDonald's hamburgers.
 e. It is a typical selection in a Value Meal.

930. The passage explains that those in favor of the MEAL Act want nutritional information placed

 a. anywhere the consumer can make a menu selection.
 b. in print advertisements.
 c. on websites.
 d. on toll-free hotlines.
 e. on posters with print large enough to read from any position in the restaurant.

931. If the MEAL Act is passed, consumers would see

 a. menus that tell them how to select the healthiest complete meal.
 b. menus that look like nutritional labels on packaged food.
 c. restaurants with more extensive information on their websites.
 d. less television advertising of fast food restaurants.
 e. restaurants that serve healthier food choices.

Questions 932–935 are based on the following passage.

The following passage describes the medium of political cartoons as a graphic means of commenting on contemporary social or political issues.

(1)   A mainstay of American newspapers since the early nineteenth century, political cartoons use graphic art to comment on current events in a way that will inform, amuse, provoke, poke, and persuade readers. Cartoons take on the principal issues and leaders of the day, skewering

(5)   hypocritical or corrupt politicians and depicting the ridiculous, the ironic, or the serious nature of a major event in a single, deftly drawn image. Cartoons use few words, if any, to convey their message. Some use caricature, a technique in which a cartoonist exaggerates the features of well-known people to make fun of them. (Think of renderings

(10)   of Bill Clinton with a nose redder than Rudolph's and swollen out of proportion, or cartoons of George W. Bush's exaggerated pointy visage sporting a ten-gallon cowboy hat.)

   Because they have the ability to evoke an emotional response in readers, political cartoons can serve as a vehicle for swaying public

(15)   opinion and can contribute to reform. Thomas Nast (1840–1902), the

preeminent political cartoonist of the second half of the nineteenth century, demonstrated the power of his medium when he used his art to end the corrupt Boss Tweed Ring in New York City. His images, first drawn for Harper's Weekly, are still in currency today: Nast created

(20) the tiger as the symbol of Tammany Hall, the elephant for the Republican Party, and the donkey for the Democratic Party.

Created under tight deadlines for ephemeral, commercial formats like newspapers and magazines, cartoons still manage to have lasting influence. Although they tackle the principal issues and leaders of

(25) their day, they often provide a vivid historical picture for generations to come.

932. The author would most likely agree with which statement?

a. Political cartoons are a powerful means of influencing the public.

b. The more mean-spirited a political cartoon is, the more effective.

c. Political cartoonists must maintain their objectivity on controversial subjects.

d. Political cartoons cater to an elite class of intellectuals.

e. Because of their relevance to current affairs, political cartoons rarely serve as historical documents.

933. In describing the art of political cartooning in the first paragraph, the author's tone can be best described as

a. sober.

b. earnest.

c. critical.

d. impartial.

e. playful.

934. In line 14, *vehicle* most nearly means

a. automobile.

b. carrier.

c. tunnel.

d. outlet.

e. means.

935. The author cites Thomas Nast's depiction of an elephant for the Republican Party (lines 20–21) as an example of

a. an image that is no longer recognized by the public.

b. the saying "the pen is mightier than the sword."

c. art contributing to political reform.

d. a graphic image that became an enduring symbol.

e. the ephemeral nature of political cartooning.

Questions 936–943 are based on the following passage.

The following passage explores the role of Chinese Americans in the nineteenth-century westward expansion of the United States, specifically their influence on the development of California.

(1)　　While the Chinese, in particular those working as sailors, knew the west coast of North America before the Gold Rush, our story begins in 1850, as the documentation from the Gold Rush provides the starting point with which to build a more substantial narrative. Most Chinese immi-
(5)　　grants entered California through the port of San Francisco. From San Francisco and other ports, many sought their fortunes in other parts of California. The Chinese formed part of the diverse gathering of peoples from throughout the world who contributed to the economic and population explosion that characterized the early history of the state of Cal-
(10)　　ifornia. The Chinese who emigrated to the United States at this time were part of a larger exodus from southeast China searching for better economic opportunities and fleeing a situation of political corruption and decline. Most immigrants came from the Pearl River Delta in Guangdong (Canton) Province.

(15)　　　　Chinese immigrants proved to be productive and resourceful contributors to a multitude of industries and businesses. The initial group of Chinese argonauts sought their livelihood in the gold mines, calling California *Gam Saan*, Gold Mountain. For the mining industry, they built many of the flumes and roads, allowing for easier access and
(20)　　processing of the minerals being extracted. Chinese immigrants faced discrimination immediately upon arrival in California. In mining, they were forced to work older claims, or to work for others. In the 1850s, the United States Constitution reserved the right of naturalization for white immigrants to this country. Thus, Chinese immigrants lived at
(25)　　the whim of local governments, with some allowed to become naturalized citizens, but most not. Without this right, it was difficult to pursue livelihoods. For example, Chinese immigrants were unable to own land or file mining claims. Also in the 1850s, the California legislature passed a law taxing all foreign miners. Although stated in gen-
(30)　　eral terms, it was enforced chiefly against the Mexicans and the Chinese through 1870. This discrimination occurred in spite of the fact that the Chinese often contributed the crucial labor necessary to the mining enterprise.

　　　　Discriminatory legislation forced many Chinese out of the gold
(35)　　fields and into low-paying, menial, and often arduous jobs. In many cases, they took on the most dangerous and least desirable components of work available. They worked on reclaiming marshes in the Central Valley so that the land could become agriculturally productive. They built the stone bridges and fences, constructed roads, and
(40)　　excavated storage areas for the wine industry in Napa and Sonoma counties. The most impressive construction feat of Chinese Americans

was their work on the western section of the transcontinental railroad. Chinese-American workers laid much of the tracks for the Central Pacific Railroad through the foothills and over the high Sierra

(45)   Nevada, much of which involved hazardous work with explosives to tunnel through the hills. Their speed, dexterity, and outright perseverance, often in brutally cold temperatures and heavy snow through two record-breaking winters, is a testimony to their outstanding achievements and contributions to opening up the West.

936. The first paragraph (lines 1–14) of the passage serves what function in the development of the passage?
- **a.** provides an expert's opinion to support the author's thesis
- **b.** introduces the topic by describing general patterns
- **c.** compares common myths with historical facts
- **d.** draws a conclusion about the impact of Chinese immigration on the state of California
- **e.** condemns outdated concepts

937. Which of the following best describes the approach of the passage?
- **a.** theoretical analysis
- **b.** historical overview
- **c.** dramatic narrative
- **d.** personal assessment
- **e.** description through metaphor

938. Lines 15–20 portray Chinese immigrants as
- **a.** fortuitous.
- **b.** prideful.
- **c.** vigorous.
- **d.** effusive.
- **e.** revolutionary.

939. The author cites the United States Constitution (lines 23–24) in order to
- **a.** praise the liberties afforded by the Bill of Rights.
- **b.** show that the government valued the contributions of its immigrants.
- **c.** imply that all American citizens are equal under the law.
- **d.** emphasize the importance of a system of checks and balances.
- **e.** suggest that it did not protect Chinese immigrants from discrimination.

940. The word *enterprise* as it is used in line 33 most nearly means
- **a.** organization.
- **b.** corporation.
- **c.** industry.
- **d.** partnership.
- **e.** occupation.

941. According to the passage, which of the following is NOT a contribution made by Chinese immigrants?
- **a.** worked land so that it would yield more crops
- **b.** performed dangerous work with explosives
- **c.** built roads and bridges
- **d.** purchased older mining claims and mined them
- **e.** dug storage areas for California wine

942. In line 37, *reclaiming* most nearly means
   a. redeeming.
   b. protesting.
   c. objecting.
   d. approving.
   e. extolling.

943. The last sentence (lines 46–49) in the passage provides
   a. an example supporting the thesis of the passage.
   b. a comparison with other historical viewpoints.
   c. a theory explaining historical events.
   d. a summary of the passage.
   e. an argument refuting the position taken earlier in the passage.

Questions 944–951 are based on the following passage.

The following passage describes the Great Depression and the relief policies introduced under President Franklin Delano Roosevelt that aimed to mitigate the effects of the crisis.

(1)   The worst and longest economic crisis in the modern industrial world, the Great Depression in the United States, had devastating consequences for American society. At its deepest (1932–1933), more than 16 million people were unemployed, more than 5,000 banks had
(5)   closed, and over 85,000 businesses had failed. Millions of Americans lost their jobs, their savings, and even their homes. The homeless built shacks for temporary shelter—these emerging shantytowns were nicknamed "Hoovervilles," a bitter homage to President Herbert Hoover's failure to give government assistance to the jobless. Farmers
(10)   were hit especially hard. A severe drought coupled with the economic crisis ruined small farms throughout the Great Plains as productive farmland turned to dust and crop prices dropped by 50%. The effects of the American depression—severe unemployment rates and a sharp drop in the production and sales of goods—could also be felt abroad,
(15)   where many European nations were still struggling to recover from World War I.

    Although the stock market crash of 1929 marked the onset of the depression, it was not the only cause of it: deep underlying fissures already existed in the economy of America's Roaring Twenties. For
(20)   example, the tariff and war-debt policies after World War I contributed to the instability of the banking system. American banks made loans to European countries following World War I. However, the United States kept high tariffs on goods imported from other nations. These policies worked against one another: If other coun-
(25)   tries could not sell goods in the United States, they could not make enough money to pay back their loans or to buy American goods.

(30) And while the United States seemed to be enjoying a prosperous period in the 1920s, the wealth was not evenly distributed. Businesses made gains in productivity, but only one segment of the population—the wealthy—reaped large profits. Workers received only a small share of the wealth they helped produce. At the same time, Americans spent more than they earned. Advertising encouraged Americans to buy cars, radios, and household appliances instead of saving or purchasing only what they could afford. Easy credit policies allowed consumers to

(35) borrow money and accumulate debt. Investors also wildly speculated on the stock market, often borrowing money on credit to buy shares of a company. Stocks increased beyond their worth, but investors were willing to pay inflated prices because they believed stocks would continue to rise. This bubble burst in the fall of 1929, when investors lost

(40) confidence that stock prices would keep rising. As investors sold off stocks, the market spiraled downward. The stock market crash affected the economy in the same way that a stressful event can affect the human body, lowering its resistance to infection.

The ensuing depression led to the election of President Franklin D.

(45) Roosevelt in 1932. Roosevelt introduced relief measures that would revive the economy and bring needed relief to Americans who were suffering the effects of the depression. In his first hundred days in office, Roosevelt and Congress passed major legislation that saved banks from closing and regained public confidence. These measures,

(50) called the New Deal, included the Agricultural Adjustment Act, which paid farmers to slow their production in order to stabilize food prices; the Federal Deposit Insurance Corporation, which insured bank deposits in case a bank failed; and the Securities and Exchange Commission, which regulated the stock market. Although the New

(55) Deal offered relief, it did not end the depression. The economy sagged until the nation entered World War II. However, the New Deal changed the relationship between government and American citizens, by expanding the role of the central government in regulating the economy and creating social assistance programs.

944. The author's main point about the Great Depression is that

a. government policies had nothing to do with it.

b. the government immediately stepped in with assistance for the jobless and homeless.

c. underlying problems in the economy preceded it.

d. the New Deal policies introduced by Franklin D. Roosevelt ended it.

e. its effects were severe but not far-reaching.

945. The passage is best described as

a. an account of the causes and effects of a major event.

b. a statement supporting the value of federal social policies.

c. a condemnation of outdated beliefs.

d. a polite response to a controversial issue.

e. a comparison of economic conditions in the 1930s and those of today.

946. The author cites the emergence of
"*Hoovervilles*" (line 8) as an example of
a. federally sponsored housing programs.
b. the resilience of Americans who lost their
jobs, savings, and homes.
c. the government's unwillingness to assist
citizens in desperate circumstances.
d. a new paradigm of safety-net social programs introduced by the government.
e. the effectiveness of the Hoover administration in dealing with the crisis.

947. In line 10, *coupled* most nearly means
a. eloped.
b. allied.
c. centralized.
d. combined.
e. associated.

948. The term *policies* as it is used in line 24 most
nearly means
a. theories.
b. practices.
c. laws.
d. examples.
e. problems.

949. The passage suggests that the 1920s was a
decade that extolled
a. thrift.
b. prudence.
c. balance.
d. tranquility.
e. extravagance.

950. The example of the human body as a
metaphor for the economy (lines 41–43) suggests that
a. a stressful event like the stock market crash
of 1929 probably made a lot of people sick.
b. the crash weakened the economy's ability to
withstand other pressures.
c. the crash was an untreatable disease.
d. a single event caused the collapse of the
economy.
e. there is no way to diagnose the factors that
led to the depression.

951. The content of the last paragraph of the passage (lines 44–59) would most likely support
which of the following statements?
a. The New Deal policies were not radical
enough in challenging capitalism.
b. The economic policies of the New Deal
brought about a complete business recovery.
c. The Agricultural Adjustment Act paid
farmers to produce surplus crops.
d. The federal government became more
involved in caring for needy members of
society.
e. The New Deal measures went too far in
turning the country toward socialism.

Questions 952–961 are based on the following passage.

In 1804 President Thomas Jefferson sent Army officers Meriwether Lewis and William Clark on an expedition to explore the territory of the Louisiana Purchase and beyond and to look for a waterway that would connect the Atlantic and Pacific Oceans. This passage describes the collision of cultures that occurred between Native Americans and the representatives of the United States government.

(1) When Thomas Jefferson sent Lewis and Clark into the West, he patterned their mission on the methods of Enlightenment science: to observe, collect, document, and classify. Such strategies were already in place for the epic voyages made by explorers like Cook and Van-

(5) couver. Like their contemporaries, Lewis and Clark were more than representatives of European rationalism. They also represented a rising American empire, one built on aggressive territorial expansion and commercial gain.

But there was another view of the West: that of the native inhabi-

(10) tants of the land. Their understandings of landscapes, peoples, and resources formed both a contrast and a counterpoint to those of Jefferson's travelers. One of Lewis and Clark's missions was to open diplomatic relations between the United States and the Native American nations of the West. As Jefferson told Lewis, "it will now be proper

(15) you should inform those through whose country you will pass . . . that henceforth we become their fathers and friends." When Euro-Americans and Native Americans met, they used ancient diplomatic protocols that included formal language, ceremonial gifts, and displays of military power. But behind these symbols and rituals there were often

(20) very different ways of understanding power and authority. Such differences sometimes made communication across the cultural divide difficult and open to confusion and misunderstanding.

An important organizing principle in Euro-American society was hierarchy. Both soldiers and civilians had complex gradations of rank

(25) to define who gave orders and who obeyed. Kinship was important in the Euro-American world, but it was even more fundamental in tribal societies. Everyone's power and place depended on a complex network of real and symbolic relationships. When the two groups met—whether for trade or diplomacy—each tried to reshape the

(30) other in their own image. Lewis and Clark sought to impose their own notions of hierarchy on Native Americans by "making chiefs" with medals, printed certificates, and gifts. Native people tried to impose the obligations of kinship on the visitors by means of adoption ceremonies, shared names, and ritual gifts.

(35) The American republic began to issue peace medals during the first Washington administration, continuing a tradition established by the European nations. Lewis and Clark brought at least 89 medals in five sizes in order to designate five ranks of chief. In the

eyes of Americans, Native Americans who accepted such medals were
(40) also acknowledging American sovereignty as "children" of a new
"great father." And in a moment of imperial bravado, Lewis hung a
peace medal around the neck of a Piegan Blackfeet warrior killed by
the expedition in late July 1806. As Lewis later explained, he used a
peace medal as a way to let the Blackfeet know "who we were."

(45)   In tribal society, kinship was like a legal system—people depended
on relatives to protect them from crime, war, and misfortune. People
with no kin were outside of society and its rules. To adopt Lewis and
Clark into tribal society, the Plains Indians used a pipe ceremony. The
ritual of smoking and sharing the pipe was at the heart of much Native
(50) American diplomacy. With the pipe the captains accepted sacred obligations to share wealth, aid in war, and revenge injustice. At the end
of the ceremony, the pipe was presented to them so they would never
forget their obligations.

      Gift giving was an essential part of diplomacy. To Native Ameri-
(55) cans, gifts proved the giver's sincerity and honored the tribe. To Lewis
and Clark, some gifts advertised the technological superiority and others encouraged the Native Americans to adopt an agrarian lifestyle.
Like salesmen handing out free samples, Lewis and Clark packed bales
of manufactured goods to open diplomatic relations with Native
(60) American tribes. Jefferson advised Lewis to give out corn mills to
introduce the Native Americans to mechanized agriculture as part of
his plan to "civilize and instruct" them. Clark believed the mills were
"verry Thankfully recived," but by the next year the Mandan had
demolished theirs to use the metal for weapons.

952. The goals of the Lewis and Clark expedition include all of the following purposes EXCEPT to
a. expand scientific knowledge.
b. strengthen American claims to western territory.
c. overcome Native American resistance with military force.
d. introduce native inhabitants to the ways of Euro-American culture.
e. make peaceful contact with native inhabitants.

953. According to the passage, the United States government primarily viewed its role in relation to Native Americans as one of
a. creator.
b. master.
c. admirer.
d. collaborator.
e. agitator.

954. The word *protocols* as it is used in line 17 most nearly means
a. beliefs.
b. tenets.
c. codes.
d. tactics.
e. endeavors.

955. According to the passage, the distribution of peace medals exemplifies
   a. the American republic's attempt to forge a relationship of equals with native people.
   b. a cultural bridge connecting the Euro-Americans with Native American tribes.
   c. the explorers' respect for Native American sovereignty.
   d. the imposition of societal hierarchy on Native Americans.
   e. the acknowledgment of the power and authority of Native American chiefs.

956. The description of Lewis' actions in lines 41–43 is used to
   a. depict the expedition in a patriotic light.
   b. contradict commonly held views of imperialism.
   c. make an ironic statement about the meaning of the peace medals.
   d. give an explanation for the killing of a Piegan Blackfeet warrior.
   e. provide a balanced report of two opposing points of view.

957. The description of the pipe ceremony in lines 48–53 is used to illustrate
   a. the naïveté of the Plains Native Americans.
   b. cultural confusion.
   c. the superiority of the native inhabitants.
   d. how Plains Native Americans honored low-ranking members of society.
   e. the addictive properties of tobacco.

958. In line 47, *adopt* most nearly means
   a. advocate.
   b. nurture.
   c. promote.
   d. foster.
   e. accept.

959. The author uses the image of *salesmen handing out free samples* (line 58) in order to
   a. depict Lewis and Clark as entrepreneurs.
   b. illustrate the generosity Lewis and Clark showed the tribal people they met.
   c. suggest that Lewis and Clark hoped to personally profit from their travels.
   d. imply that everyone likes to get something for free.
   e. show the promotional intent behind the explorers' gift-giving.

960. The passage is developed primarily through
   a. the contrast of different abstract principles.
   b. quotations from one specific text.
   c. the analysis of one extended example.
   d. first-person narratives.
   e. recurring symbols.

961. The author's primary purpose in the passage is to
   a. describe Lewis and Clark's expedition into the West.
   b. show the clashing views of the Indian nations versus those of the American republic.
   c. explore the tribal system of kinship.
   d. make an argument supporting Jefferson's quest for scientific knowledge.
   e. criticize Lewis and Clark's use of peace medals to designate the rank of a chief.

Questions 962–972 are based on the following passages.

These passages concern themselves with the nineteenth-century arguments made for and against women's right to vote in the United States. Passage 1 is an excerpt from an address by Isabella Beecher Hooker before the International Council of Women in 1888. Passage 2 is an excerpt from an 1878 report from the Senate's Committee on Privileges and Elections in response to a proposed constitutional amendment that would give women the right to vote.

Passage 1

(1)   First let me speak of the constitution of the United States, and assert that there is not a line in it, nor a word, forbidding women to vote; but, properly interpreted, that is, interpreted by the Declaration of Independence, and by the assertions of the Fathers, it actually guarantees to

(5)   women the right to vote in all elections, both state and national. Listen to the preamble to the constitution, and the preamble you know, is the key to what follows; it is the concrete, general statement of the great principles which subsequent articles express in detail. The preamble says: "We, the People of the United States, in order to form a more per-

(10)   fect union, establish justice, insure domestic tranquility, provide for the common defense, promote the general welfare, and secure the blessings of liberty to ourselves and our posterity, do ordain and establish this Constitution for the United States of America."

   Commit this to memory, friends; learn it by heart as well as by head,

(15)   and I should have no need to argue the question before you of my right to vote. For women are "people" surely, and desire, as much as men, to say the least, to establish justice and to insure domestic tranquility; and, brothers, you will never insure domestic tranquility in the days to come unless you allow women to vote, who pay taxes and bear equally with

(20)   yourselves all the burdens of society; for they do not mean any longer to submit patiently and quietly to such injustice, and the sooner men understand this and graciously submit to become the political equals of their mothers, wives, and daughters—aye, of their grandmothers, for that is my category, instead of their political masters, as they now are,

(25)   the sooner will this precious domestic tranquility be insured. Women are surely "people," I said, and were when these words were written, and were as anxious as men to establish justice and promote the general welfare, and no one will have the hardihood to deny that our foremothers (have we not talked about our forefathers alone long

(30)   enough?) did their full share in the work of establishing justice, providing for the common defense, and promoting the general welfare in all those early days.

   The truth is, friends, that when liberties had to be gained by the sword and protected by the sword, men necessarily came to the front

(35)   and seemed to be the only creators and defenders of these liberties; hence all the way down women have been content to do their patriotic work silently and through men, who are the fighters by nature rather

(40) than themselves, until the present day; but now at last, when it is established that ballots instead of bullets are to rule the world . . . now, it is high time that women ceased to attempt to establish justice and promote the general welfare, and secure the blessings of liberty to themselves and their posterity, through the votes of men . . .

Passage 2

(1) This proposed amendment forbids the United States or any State to deny or abridge the right to vote on account of sex. If adopted, it will make several millions of female voters, totally inexperienced in political affairs, quite generally dependent upon the other sex, all incapable of

(5) performing military duty and without the power to enforce the laws which their numerical strength may enable them to make, and comparatively very few of whom wish to assume the irksome and responsible political duties which this measure thrusts upon them.

An experiment so novel, a change so great, should only be made

(10) slowly and in response to a general public demand, of the existence of which there is no evidence before your committee. Petitions from various parts of the country, containing by estimate about 30,000 names, have been presented to Congress asking for this legislation. They were procured through the efforts of woman-suffrage societies, thoroughly

(15) organized, with active and zealous managers. The ease with which signatures may be procured to any petition is well known. The small number of petitioners, when compared with that of the intelligent women in the country, is striking evidence that there exists among them no general desire to take up the heavy burden of governing, which so

(20) many men seek to evade. It would be unjust, unwise, and impolitic to impose that burden on the great mass of women throughout the country who do not wish for it, to gratify the comparatively few who do.

It has been strongly urged that without the right of suffrage women are and will be subjected to great oppression and injustice. But every

(25) one who has examined the subject at all knows that without female suffrage, legislation for years has improved and is still improving the condition of women. The disabilities imposed upon her by the common law have, one by one, been swept away until in most of the States she has the full right to her property and all, or nearly all the rights

(30) which can be granted without impairing or destroying the marriage relation. These changes have been wrought by the spirit of the age, and are not, generally at least, the result of any agitation by women in their own behalf.

Nor can women justly complain of any partiality in the adminis-

(35) tration of justice. They have the sympathy of judges and particularly of juries to an extent which would warrant loud complaint on the part of their adversaries of the sterner sex. Their appeals to legislatures against injustice are never unheeded, and there is no doubt that when

(40) any considerable part of the women of any State really wish for the right to vote it will be granted without the intervention of Congress.

Any State may grant the right of suffrage to women. Some of them have done so to a limited extent, and perhaps with good results. It is evident that in some States public opinion is much more strongly in favor of it than it is in others. Your committee regards it as unwise and

(45) inexpedient to enable three-fourths in number of the States, through an amendment to the National Constitution, to force woman suffrage upon the other fourth in which the public opinion of both sexes may be strongly adverse to such a change.

For these reasons, your committee reports back said resolution with

(50) a recommendation that it be indefinitely postponed.

962. The author of Passage 1 supports her argument by

a. providing information about the educational levels achieved by women.

b. sharing anecdotes about women who fought in the American Revolution.

c. referring to principles already accepted by her audience.

d. describing her personal experience as a citizen of the United States.

e. listing the states in the union that had granted women voting rights.

963. The phrase *learn it by heart as well as by head* in Passage 1, line 14 suggests

a. an emotional and intellectual response.

b. rote memorization.

c. learning from experience rather than books.

d. accepting an argument on faith.

e. presupposition of an outcome.

964. In line 27 of Passage 1, *anxious* most nearly means

a. irritable.

b. neurotic.

c. apprehensive.

d. hasty.

e. eager.

965. Lines 25–32 of Passage 1 portray American women as

a. rebellious.

b. ambitious.

c. patriotic.

d. uneducated.

e. vulnerable.

966. Which of the following best describes the author's strategy in Passage 2?

a. summarizing public perceptions of the issue

b. anticipating opposing viewpoints and then refuting them

c. relating an incident and describing its significance

d. persuading his audience through emotional appeal

e. providing evidence that supports both sides of the issue

967. As used in Passage 2, line 9, *novel* most nearly means
a. rare.
b. original.
c. untried.
d. brilliant.
e. intellectual.

968. In the third paragraph of Passage 2 (lines 23–33), the author characterizes the activists of the women's suffrage movement as
a. ardent.
b. courageous.
c. conformist.
d. modest.
e. genteel.

969. The author of Passage 2 cites the example of a woman's right to her property (lines 29 and 30) in order to
a. show that women are well represented by the legislature even if they cannot vote.
b. demonstrate that if women can be responsible for property, they can be responsible voters.
c. prove that unjust laws affect the condition of women.
d. support the belief that political change should happen quickly.
e. argue that political equality strengthens marriages.

970. Which aspect of the topic of women's voting rights is emphasized in Passage 2, but not in Passage 1?
a. the interpretation of the Constitution
b. the contributions of American women
c. the tax-paying status of women
d. how the judiciary treats women
e. how ready the country is to allow women the right to vote

971. The two authors would most likely agree with which statement?
a. Most women do not desire the right to vote.
b. Women are not meant to be soldiers.
c. Voting is more of a burden than a privilege.
d. American society is ready for female voters.
e. Men and women should be political equals.

972. The approaches of the two passages to the topic differ in that only Passage 1
a. describes an incident from the author's personal experience.
b. gives a point and argues its counterpoint.
c. cites several specific examples of laws that benefit women.
d. recommends an action to be taken.
e. There aren't any significant differences between Passage 1 and Passage 2.

Questions 973–976 are based on the following passage.

In this excerpt from Book One of his Nicomachean Ethics, *Aristotle expands his definitions of* good *and* happiness.

(1)   Good things are commonly divided into three classes: (1) external goods, (2) goods of the soul, and (3) goods of the body. Of these, we call the goods pertaining to the soul goods in the highest and fullest sense. But in speaking of "soul," we refer to our soul's actions and

(5)   activities. Thus, our definition [of good] tallies with this opinion which has been current for a long time and to which philosophers subscribe. We are also right in defining the end as consisting of actions and activities; for in this way the end is included among the goods of the soul and not among external goods.

(10)   Also the view that a happy man lives well and fares well fits in with our definition: for we have all but defined happiness as a kind of good life and well-being.

    Moreover, the characteristics which one looks for in happiness are all included in our definition. For some people think that happiness

(15)   is a virtue, others that it is practical wisdom, others that it is some kind of theoretical wisdom; others again believe it to be all or some of these accompanied by, or not devoid of, pleasure; and some people also include external prosperity in its definition.

973. According to the passage, the greatest goods are those that
  a. are theoretical.
  b. are spiritual.
  c. are intellectual.
  d. create happiness.
  e. create prosperity.

974. The word *tallies* in line 5 means
  a. keeps count.
  b. records.
  c. labels.
  d. corresponds.
  e. scores.

975. The author's definition of happiness in lines 11–12 is related to the definition of good in that
  a. living a good life will bring you happiness.
  b. happiness is the same as goodness.
  c. happiness is often sacrificed to attain the good.
  d. all things that create happiness are good things.
  e. happiness is a virtue.

976. In lines 13–18, the author's main purpose is to
  a. show that different people have different definitions of happiness.
  b. define virtue.
  c. prove that his definition of happiness is valid.
  d. explain the relationship between happiness and goodness.
  e. provide guidelines for good behavior.

Questions 977–984 are based on the following passage.

Written by John Henry Newman in 1852, the following passage presents Newman's idea of the purpose and benefits of a university education.

(1)   I have said that all branches of knowledge are connected together, because the subject-matter of knowledge is intimately united in itself. . . . Hence it is that the Sciences, into which our knowledge may be said to be cast, have multiple bearings on one another, and an inter-

(5)   nal sympathy, and admit, or rather demand, comparison and adjustment. They complete, correct, and balance each other. This consideration, if well-founded, must be taken into account, not only as regards the attainment of truth, which is their common end, but as regards the influence which they excise upon those whose education

(10)   consists in the study of them. I have already said, that to give undue prominence to one is to be unjust to another; to neglect or supersede these is to divert those from their proper object. It is to unsettle the boundary lines between science and science, to disturb their action, to destroy the harmony which binds them together. Such a proceed-

(15)   ing will have a corresponding effect when introduced into a place of education. There is no science but tells a different tale, when viewed as a portion of a whole, from what it is likely to suggest when taken by itself, without the safeguard, as I may call it, of others.

    Let me make use of an illustration. In the combination of colors,

(20)   very different effects are produced by a difference in their selection and juxtaposition; red, green, and white, change their shades, according to the contrast to which they are submitted. And, in like manner, the drift and meaning of a branch of knowledge varies with the company in which it is introduced to the student. If his reading is confined simply

(25)   to one subject, however such division of labor may favor the advancement of a particular pursuit, a point into which I do not here enter, certainly it has a tendency to contract his mind. If it is incorporated with others, it depends on those others as to the kind of influence that it exerts upon him. Thus the Classics, which in England are the

(30)   means of refining the taste, have in France subserved the spread of revolutionary and deistical doctrines. . . . In a like manner, I suppose, Arcesilas would not have handled logic as Aristotle, nor Aristotle have criticized poets as Plato; yet reasoning and poetry are subject to scientific rules.

(35)   It is a great point then to enlarge the range of studies which a University professes, even for the sake of the students; and, though they cannot pursue every subject which is open to them, they will be the gainers by living among those and under those who represent the whole circle. This I conceive to be the advantage of a seat of universal

(40)   learning, considered as a place of education. An assemblage of learned

men, zealous for their own sciences, and rivals of each other, are brought, by familiar intercourse and for the sake of intellectual peace, to adjust together the claims and relations of their respective subjects of investigation. They learn to respect, to consult, to aid each other.

(45)   Thus is created a pure and clear atmosphere of thought, which the student also breathes, though in his own case he only pursues a few sciences out of the multitude. He profits by an intellectual tradition, which is independent of particular teachers, which guides him in his choice of subjects, and duly interprets for him those which he chooses.

(50)   He apprehends the great outlines of knowledge, the principles on which it rests, the scale of its parts, its lights and its shades, its great points and its little, as he otherwise cannot apprehend them. Hence it is that his education is called "Liberal." A habit of mind is formed which lasts through life, of which the attributes are, freedom, equi-

(55)   tableness, calmness, moderation, and wisdom; or what in a former discourse I have ventured to call a philosophical habit. This then I would assign as the special fruit of the education furnished at a University, as contrasted with other places of teaching or modes of teaching. This is the main purpose of a University in its treatment of its students.

977. The main idea of the first paragraph (lines 1–18) is that

  a. each science should be studied independently.

  b. the sciences are interrelated.

  c. the boundary lines between each of the sciences should be clearer.

  d. some sciences are unduly given more emphasis than others at the university level.

  e. it is difficult to attain a proper balance among the sciences.

978. By *the Sciences* (line 3), the author means

  a. the physical sciences only.

  b. the social sciences only.

  c. the physical and social sciences.

  d. all branches of knowledge, including the physical and social sciences and the humanities.

  e. educational methodologies.

979. The word *excise* in line 9 most nearly means

  a. remove.

  b. cut.

  c. impose.

  d. arrange.

  e. compete.

980. By using the word *safeguard* in line 18, the author suggests that

  a. it is dangerous to limit one's education to one field or area of specialization.

  b. it is not safe to study the sciences.

  c. the more one knows, the safer one will feel.

  d. one should choose a second area of specialization as a backup in case the first does not work out.

  e. each science has its own specific safety guidelines.

981. The purpose of the second paragraph (lines 19–34) is to
   a. introduce a new idea.
   b. develop the idea presented in the previous paragraph.
   c. state the main idea of the passage.
   d. present an alternative point of view.
   e. compare and contrast different branches of knowledge.

982. The word *apprehends* as used in line 50 means
   a. understands.
   b. captures.
   c. fears.
   d. believes.
   e. contains.

983. Which of the following best describes the author's idea of a liberal education?
   a. in-depth specialization in one area.
   b. free education for all.
   c. a broad scope of knowledge in several disciplines.
   d. training for a scientific career.
   e. an emphasis on the arts rather than the sciences.

984. The author believes that a university should (1) have faculty representing a wide range of subjects and philosophies, (2) teach students how to see the relationships among ideas, (3) teach students to understand and respect other points of view, and (4) teach students liberal rather than conservative ideals.
   a. 1 and 2 only
   b. 1, 2, and 3
   c. 1 and 4
   d. 4 only
   e. all of the above

Questions 985–992 are based on the following passage.

The following passage tells of the mythological Greek god Prometheus.

(1)   Without a doubt, one of the most interesting mythological characters is the Greek god Prometheus. A complex character with an undying love for the human beings he created, Prometheus embodies a rich combination of often-contradictory characteristics, including loyalty

(5)   and defiance, trickery and trustworthiness. He shows resilience and resolve in his actions, yet weakness in his fondness for humankind.
       To reward Prometheus (whose name means "forethought") and his brother Epimetheus ("afterthought") for helping him defeat the Titans, Zeus, the great ruler of Olympian gods, gave the brothers the

(10)   task of creating beings to populate the land around Mount Olympus. Prometheus asked Epimetheus to give the creatures their various characteristics, such as cunning, swiftness, and flight. By the time he got

to man, however, there was nothing left to give. So Prometheus decided to make man in his image: he stood man upright like the gods
(15) and became the benefactor and protector of mankind.

Though Prometheus was particularly fond of his creation, Zeus didn't care for mankind and didn't want humans to have the divine gift of knowledge. But Prometheus took pity on mortal men and gave them knowledge of the arts and sciences, including the healing arts and
(20) agriculture.

Always seeking the best for his creation, one day Prometheus conspired to trick Zeus to give the best meat of an ox to men instead of to Zeus. He cut up the ox and hid the bones in layers of fat; then he hid the meat and innards inside the hide. When Prometheus presented
(25) the piles to Zeus, Zeus chose the pile that looked like fat and meat. He was enraged to find that it was nothing but bones.

To punish Prometheus for his deceit and his fondness for humans, Zeus forbade men fire—a symbol of creative power, life force, and divine knowledge. But Prometheus would not let his children be
(30) denied this greatest of gifts. He took a hollow reed, stole fire from Mount Olympus, and gave it to man. With this divine power, creativity, ingenuity, and culture flourished in the land of mortals.

Again Zeus punished man for Prometheus's transgression, this time by sending the first woman, Pandora, to Earth. Pandora brought with
(35) her a "gift" from Zeus: a jar filled with evils of every kind. Prometheus knew Zeus to be vengeful and warned Epimetheus not to accept any gifts from Zeus, but Epimetheus was too taken with Pandora's beauty and allowed her to stay. Eventually Pandora opened the jar she'd been forbidden to open, releasing all manner of evils, including Treachery,
(40) Sorrow, Villainy, Misfortune, and Plague. At the bottom of the jar was Hope, but Pandora closed the lid before Hope could escape.

Prometheus drew Zeus's greatest wrath when he refused to tell Zeus which of Zeus's sons would kill him and take over the throne. Believing he could torture Prometheus into revealing the secret, Zeus bound
(45) Prometheus to a rock where every day an eagle would come to tear at his flesh and eat his liver, which would regenerate each night. But Prometheus refused to reveal his knowledge of the future to Zeus and maintained his silence. Eventually, Prometheus was released by Heracles (also known as Hercules), the last mortal son of Zeus and
(50) the strongest of all mortals. Soon afterward, Prometheus received immortality from a dying centaur, to take his place forever among the great gods of Olympus.

985. The main idea of the first paragraph
(lines 1–6) is that Prometheus
   a. is disrespectful of authority.
   b. is the mythological creator of humans.
   c. has many admirable characteristics.
   d. should not have been so fond of humans.
   e. is a fascinating character because of his
   complexity.

986. The author's primary purpose in this passage
is to
   a. demonstrate the vengeful nature of Zeus.
   b. show how much Prometheus cared for
   humans.
   c. create in readers an interest in mythology.
   d. relate the story of Prometheus.
   e. prove that Prometheus, not Zeus, was the
   creator of man.

987. Based on this passage, it can be inferred that
Zeus disliked humans because
   a. Prometheus spent too much time with
   them.
   b. Prometheus cared for humans more than
   he did for Zeus.
   c. humans could not be trusted.
   d. humans did not respect Zeus.
   e. he did not create them.

988. Zeus becomes angry at Prometheus for all of
the following EXCEPT
   a. creating man.
   b. giving man fire.
   c. being excessively fond of humans.
   d. refusing to reveal which of his sons would
   kill him.
   e. tricking him into taking the undesirable
   part of an ox.

989. Based on the passage, the relationship between
Prometheus and humans can best be
described as that of
   a. parent and child.
   b. close friends.
   c. master and servant.
   d. bitter enemies.
   e. reluctant allies.

990. The word *transgression* as used in line 33
means
   a. villainy.
   b. trespass.
   c. irregularity.
   d. error.
   e. disobedience.

991. The fact that Zeus included Hope in Pandora's jar (lines 38–41) suggests that
a. Zeus really did love humans as much as Prometheus did.
b. while Zeus was a vengeful god, he did not wish humans to live in utter despair.
c. Zeus was just playing a trick on humans.
d. Zeus was trying to make amends with Prometheus.
e. Zeus wanted to drive Prometheus away from humans.

992. The content and style of this passage suggest that the intended audience
a. are experts on Greek mythology.
b. are religious officials.
c. is a general lay audience.
d. are family members and friends.
e. is a scholarly review board.

Questions 993–1001 are based on the following passage.

The following passage describes an influential group of nineteenth-century painters.

(1)   When one thinks of student-led rebellions and the changes they can create, one typically thinks of the struggles of the twentieth century, such as the Civil Rights movement or antiwar protests of the 1960s. But there have been less dramatic, though no less passionate, rebel-
(5)   lions led by young activists in previous centuries—rebellions that had lasting impact on the world around us. One such example is the Pre-Raphaelite Brotherhood.

In the mid-1800s, the art world in England was rattled by the initials PRB, which stood for Pre-Raphaelite Brotherhood. The PRB
(10)   was founded by William Holman Hunt, John Everett Millais, and Dante Gabriel Rossetti. These three burgeoning artists (the oldest of whom was 21) and their disdain for the artistic conventions of the time would have a dramatic influence on the art world for generations to come.

The PRB was formed in response to the brotherhood's belief that
(15)   the current popular art being produced in England was lacking in meaning and aesthetic honesty. During the era leading up to the PRB, the Royal Academy dominated British art. The Royal Academy advocated a style that was typically staid and relied heavily upon the use of dark amber and brown tones to depict overly idealized land-
(20)   scapes, carefully arranged family portraits and still lifes, and overly dramatic nature scenes such as boats caught in stormy seas. By contrast, the PRB believed that art should present subjects that, by their very nature, had greater meaning and more accurately depicted reality. The PRB was committed to bringing greater integrity to art and
(25)   even went so far as to publish *The Germ*, a journal that extolled the virtues of the PRB's aesthetic principles.

To develop subjects with greater meaning, the PRB initially turned to ancient myths and stories from the Bible. Many of the PRB's bib-

(30) lically themed paintings portrayed the religious figures as regular people. This departure from the convention of the time is notable in John Everett Millais's *Christ in the Home of His Parents*. In this painting, Jesus is portrayed as a young boy in his father's carpentry shop. Everyone in the painting, including Christ himself, looks like a common person of that time period, complete with dirty feet and hands. This realism—

(35) especially as it related to the Biblical figures—was not well received by many in the art world at the time. Later works done by fellow PRB members, and those inspired by them, utilized themes from poetry, literature, and medieval tales, often with the aim of highlighting the societal and moral challenges of the time.

(40) With the goal of bringing greater honesty to their work, the PRB ignored the convention of painting an imagined or remembered landscape or background. Instead, PRB members would hunt (sometimes for weeks) for locations to incorporate into their paintings and then paint them in exacting detail.

(45) One of the most distinctive aspects of PRB works—in contrast to both the works produced during the early nineteenth century and the art of today—is their dramatic use of color. By committing themselves to the accurate depiction of nature, the PRB members brought a freshness and drama to their work through the copious use of color. Further

(50) enhancing their work was a technique they used that involved applying the colored paint on top of wet white paint previously applied to their canvases. The effect was to make the colors even brighter and more dramatic. Even today, more than 150 years later, PRB paintings have a luminescence beyond those of other works from the same time

(55) period. It is believed that their paintings have this quality today because the white layer underneath the colored paint continues to add brightness and life to the paintings.

Originally founded by three upstart young men, the PRB had a tremendous influence on an entire generation of artists. William Mor-

(60) ris, Ford Maddox Brown, and Edward Burne-Jones are just a few of the significant artists of the time whose work was dramatically influenced by the PRB.

993. The word *upstart* in line 58 means
  a. well-regarded.
  b. conceited.
  c. beginning from an advanced position.
  d. suddenly raised to a high position.
  e. receiving numerous honors.

994. In the opening paragraph (lines 1–7), the author characterizes the PRB as all of the following EXCEPT
  a. young.
  b. revolutionary.
  c. rebellious.
  d. antiwar.
  e. passionate.

995. The word *burgeoning* in line 11 means
   a. bursting.
   b. developing.
   c. flourishing.
   d. expanding.
   e. prospering.

996. The PRB believed artists should do all of the following EXCEPT
   a. paint meaningful subjects.
   b. paint existing rather than imagined landscapes.
   c. use vibrant colors.
   d. choose subjects that address social issues.
   e. portray people and nature in an idealized manner.

997. According to the passage, the art world
   a. disliked the PRB's emphasis on realism.
   b. disdained the PRB's choice of subject matter.
   c. appreciated the PRB's attention to detail.
   d. embraced the PRB's style, especially their use of color.
   e. was offended by the PRB's attempts to change the Royal Academy's style.

998. The PRB's rebellion was rooted in
   a. a fascination with religious and mythological subjects.
   b. similar artistic rebellions in Europe.
   c. a belief that their peers' work lacked integrity.
   d. a distrust of realistic landscapes and poetic themes.
   e. a conflict over the use of color in painting.

999. According to the author, one of the most distinguishing features of PRB works is their
   a. surrealism.
   b. contrast to Royal Academy art.
   c. everyday subject matter.
   d. stoicism.
   e. vibrant colors.

1000. The author's main purpose in this passage is to
   a. describe the lives of the founders of the PRB.
   b. describe the artistic principles of the PRB.
   c. compare and contrast revolutions in art.
   d. describe the controversy created by the PRB.
   e. describe how the PRB influenced future artists.

1001. It can be inferred that members of the PRB
   a. were more socially conscious than members of the Royal Academy.
   b. were more educated than the members of the Royal Academy.
   c. were more popular than members of the Royal Academy.
   d. were bitter about being excluded from the Royal Academy.
   e. had a great deal of influence within the Royal Academy.

Questions 1002–1005 are based on the following passage.

The following passage is an excerpt from the National Institutes of Health that describes the effects and potential consequences of sleep deprivation.

(1) Experts say that if you feel drowsy during the day, even during boring activities, you haven't had enough sleep. If you routinely fall asleep within five minutes of lying down, you probably have severe sleep deprivation, possibly even a sleep disorder. *Microsleeps*, or very brief

(5) episodes of sleep in an otherwise awake person, are another mark of sleep deprivation. In many cases, people are not aware that they are experiencing microsleeps. The widespread practice of "burning the candle at both ends" in Western industrialized societies has created so much sleep deprivation that what is really abnormal sleepiness is now

(10) almost the norm.

Many studies make it clear that sleep deprivation is dangerous. Sleep-deprived people who are tested by using a driving simulator or by performing a hand-eye coordination task perform as badly as or worse than those who are intoxicated. Sleep deprivation also magni-

(15) fies alcohol's effects on the body, so a fatigued person who drinks will become much more impaired than someone who is well rested. Driver fatigue is responsible for an estimated 100,000 motor vehicle accidents and 1,500 deaths each year, according to the National Highway Traffic Safety Administration. Since drowsiness is the brain's last step

(20) before falling asleep, driving while drowsy can—and often does—lead to disaster. Caffeine and other stimulants cannot overcome the effects of severe sleep deprivation. The National Sleep Foundation says that if you have trouble keeping your eyes focused, if you can't stop yawning, or if you can't remember driving the past few miles, you are prob-

(25) ably too drowsy to drive safely.

1002. The passage suggests that falling asleep during a morning class

  a. means that the topic does not interest you.

  b. is a symptom of sleep deprivation.

  c. indicates that you should drink a caffeinated beverage at breakfast.

  d. means that you have a sleep disorder.

  e. requires a visit to the doctor.

1003. The image of *burning the candle at both ends* (lines 7–8) most nearly refers to

  a. an unrelenting schedule that affords little rest.

  b. an ardent desire to achieve.

  c. the unavoidable conflagration that occurs when two forces oppose each other.

  d. a latent period before a conflict or collapse.

  e. a state of extreme agitation.

1004. In line 16, the term *impaired* most nearly
means

   a. sentient.

   b. apprehensive.

   c. disturbed.

   d. blemished.

   e. hampered.

1005. The primary purpose of the passage is to

   a. offer preventive measures for sleep deprivation.

   b. explain why sleeplessness has become a common state in Western cultures.

   c. recommend the amount of sleep individuals need at different ages.

   d. alert readers to the signs and risks of not getting enough sleep.

   e. discuss the effects of alcohol on a sleep-deprived person.

Questions 1006–1009 refer to the following passage.

In the following passage, the author gives an account of the scientific discoveries made by Antoni van Leeuwenhoek in the seventeenth century.

(1)   The history of microbiology begins with a Dutch haberdasher named Antoni van Leeuwenhoek, a man of no formal scientific education. In the late 1600s, Leeuwenhoek, inspired by the magnifying lenses used by drapers to examine cloth, assembled some of the first microscopes.

(5)   He developed a technique for grinding and polishing tiny, convex lenses, some of which could magnify an object up to 270 times. After scraping some plaque from between his teeth and examining it under a lens, Leeuwenhoek found tiny squirming creatures, which he called "animalcules." His observations, which he reported to the Royal Soci-

(10)   ety of London, are among the first descriptions of living bacteria. Leeuwenhoek discovered an entire universe invisible to the naked eye. He found more animalcules—protozoa and bacteria—in samples of pond water, rainwater, and human saliva. He gave the first description of red corpuscles, observed plant tissue, examined muscle, and inves-

(15)   tigated the life cycle of insects.

    Nearly two hundred years later, Leeuwenhoek's discovery of microbes aided French chemist and biologist Louis Pasteur to develop his "germ theory of disease." This concept suggested that disease derives from tiny organisms attacking and weakening the body. The germ the-

(20)   ory later helped doctors to fight infectious diseases, including anthrax, diphtheria, polio, smallpox, tetanus, and typhoid. Leeuwenhoek did not foresee this legacy. In a 1716 letter, he described his contribution to science this way: "My work, which I've done for a long time, was not pursued in order to gain the praise I now enjoy, but chiefly from a craving

(25) after knowledge, which I notice resides in me more than in most other men. And therewithal, whenever I found out anything remarkable, I have thought it my duty to put down my discovery on paper, so that all ingenious people might be informed thereof."

1006. According to the passage, Leeuwenhoek would be best described as a
   a. bored haberdasher who stumbled upon scientific discovery.
   b. trained researcher with an interest in microbiology.
   c. proficient hobbyist who made microscopic lenses for entertainment.
   d. inquisitive amateur who made pioneer studies of microbes.
   e. talented scientist interested in finding a cure for disease.

1007. In line 3, *inspired* most nearly means
   a. introduced.
   b. invested.
   c. influenced.
   d. indulged.
   e. inclined.

1008. The quotation from Leeuwenhoek (lines 23–28) is used to illustrate
   a. the value he placed on sharing knowledge among scientists.
   b. that scientific discoveries often go unrecognized.
   c. that much important research is spurred by professional ambition.
   d. the serendipity of scientific progress.
   e. the importance of Leeuwenhoek's discoveries in fighting infectious diseases.

1009. The author's attitude toward Leeuwenhoek's contribution to medicine is one of
   a. ecstatic reverence.
   b. genuine admiration.
   c. tepid approval.
   d. courteous opposition.
   e. antagonistic incredulity.

Questions 1010–1013 are based on the following passage.

The following passage discusses the findings of several recent health surveys investigating the physical activity level of American adolescents.

(1) Almost 50% of American teens are not vigorously active on a regular basis, contributing to a trend of sluggishness among Americans of all ages, according the U.S. Centers for Disease Control (CDC). Adolescent female students are particularly inactive—29% are inactive
(5) compared with 15% of male students. Unfortunately, the sedentary habits of young couch potatoes often continue into adulthood. According to the Surgeon General's 1996 Report on Physical Activity and Health, Americans become increasingly less active with each year of age. Inactivity can be a serious health risk factor, setting the stage
(10) for obesity and associated chronic illnesses like heart disease and diabetes. The benefits of exercise include building bone, muscle, and joints; controlling weight; and preventing the development of high blood pressure.

Some studies suggest that physical activity may have other benefits
(15) as well. One CDC study found that high school students who take part in team sports or are physically active outside of school are less likely to engage in risky behaviors, like using drugs or smoking. Physical activity does not need to be strenuous to be beneficial. The CDC recommends moderate, daily physical activity for people of all ages, such
(20) as brisk walking for 30 minutes or 15–20 minutes of more intense exercise. A survey conducted by the National Association for Sport and Physical Education questioned teens about their attitudes toward exercise and about what it would take to get them moving. Teens chose friends (56%) as their most likely motivators for becoming more
(25) active, followed by parents (18%) and professional athletes (11%).

1010. The first paragraph (lines 1–13) of the passage serves all of the following purposes EXCEPT to

a. provide statistical information to support the claim that teenagers do not exercise enough.

b. list long-term health risks associated with lack of exercise.

c. express skepticism that teenagers can change their exercise habits.

d. show a correlation between inactive teenagers and inactive adults.

e. highlight some health benefits of exercise.

1011. In line 5, *sedentary* most nearly means

a. slothful.

b. apathetic.

c. stationary.

d. stabilized.

e. inflexible.

1012. Which of the following techniques is used in the last sentence of the passage (lines 23–25)?

a. explanation of terms

b. comparison of different arguments

c. contrast of opposing views

d. generalized statement

e. illustration by example

1013. The primary purpose of the passage is to

a. refute an argument.

b. make a prediction.

c. praise an outcome.

d. promote a change.

e. justify a conclusion.

Questions 1014–1022 are based on the following passages.

These two passages reflect two different views of the value of cosmetic plastic surgery. Passage 1 is an account by a physician who has practiced internal medicine (general medicine) for more than two decades and who has encountered numerous patients inquiring about cosmetic plastic surgery procedures. Passage 2 is written by a professional woman in her mid-forties who has considered cosmetic plastic surgery for herself.

Passage 1

(1) Elective and cosmetic plastic surgery is one of the fastest growing segments of healthcare, second only to geriatric care. As the baby boomers (those born between 1945 and 1965) reach their half-century mark, more Americans are seeking cosmetic procedures that mini-

(5) mize the visible signs of aging. The demand for self-improvement has increased as the job market has become more competitive and a high divorce rate spurs the search for new personal relationships. Increased discretionary wealth and a wider acceptance of cosmetic techniques have also contributed to the spike in cosmetic surgery.

(10) In the 1980s, I was just beginning as an internist, working in a private practice. Then in my late twenties, I felt pity for my patients who talked to me about a surgical fix for their wrinkles or other signs of aging. I felt that if they had a developed sense of self-esteem, they would not feel the need to surgically alter their appearance. I also felt

(15) a certain degree of envy for my cosmetic-surgeon colleagues, some of whom worked across the hall. To my "green" eye, they looked like slick salespeople reaping large financial rewards from others' insecurity and vanity. It was difficult for me to reconcile the fact that patients were willing to fork over thousands of dollars for cosmetic fixes, while

(20) primary care physicians struggled to keep their practices financially viable.

Since that time, my attitude has changed. Although cosmetic surgery sometimes produces negative outcomes—the media often highlights surgery disasters—for the most part, the health risk for cos-

(25) metic procedures is low and patient satisfaction is high. Often, people who have been hobbled by a poor self-image all of their lives walk

away from cosmetic surgery with confidence and the motivation to lead healthier lives. In addition, reconstructive surgery for burn and accident victims or those disfigured from disease restores self-esteem

(30) and well-being in a way that other therapies cannot. I believe it is time for members of the medical community to examine the benefits and results of cosmetic surgery without prejudice or jealousy.

Passage 2

(1) Beauty is only skin deep, or so goes the old adage. However, in a culture increasingly fixated on youthfulness and saturated with media images of ideal-looking men and women, cosmetic plastic surgery seems like the norm instead of the exception. Nearly 6.6 million

(5) Americans opted for cosmetic surgery in 2002, with women accounting for 85% of cosmetic-surgery patients, according to the American Society of Plastic Surgeons. Once the province of older women, cosmetic surgery is increasingly an option for 35- to 50-year-olds, who made up 45% of cosmetic-surgery patients in 2002.

(10) Coming of age in the 1970s, I grew up believing in the spirit of feminism, a ready warrior for equal rights for women in the home and workplace. I believed that women should be valued for who they are and what they do, and not for how they look. But as I approach my mid-forties, I look in the mirror and wonder about the reflection I see.

(15) Although I adhere to a healthy lifestyle, eat well, exercise regularly, and feel energetic, the reality is that I am beginning to look, well, middle-aged.

Because I am a successful professional, I have the means to afford elective surgery. And like Pandora's box, once I opened the door to anti-

(20) aging surgical possibilities, it seems almost impossible to close it again. In 2002, more than 1.1 million Americans had Botox injections— a procedure that erases wrinkles by paralyzing facial muscles. I find myself asking: Why not me? Is it time to jump on the bandwagon? In a competitive culture where looks count, is it almost *impractical*

(25) not to?

What stops me? Perhaps it is queasiness about the surgeon's scalpel. Risks accompany any kind of surgery. Perhaps I find the idea of paralyzing my facial muscles somewhat repellent and a betrayal of the emotions I have experienced—the joys and losses of a lifetime—that

(30) are written in those crow's-feet and worry lines. Perhaps it is my earlier feminist fervor and idealism—a remnant of my youth that I believe is worth preserving more than wrinkle-free skin.

1014. The word *adage* (Passage 2, line 1) most nearly means
- **a.** addition.
- **b.** rumor.
- **c.** saying.
- **d.** era.
- **e.** fib.

1015. The argument of Passage 1 would be most effectively strengthened by which of the following?
- **a.** information about making plastic surgery more affordable
- **b.** anecdotes about incompetent plastic surgeons
- **c.** facts to support the author's claim that health risks are low for cosmetic procedures
- **d.** a description of the author's personal experience with patients
- **e.** a description of the psychological benefits of improved body image

1016. In the second paragraph of Passage 1 (lines 10–21), how would the author characterize the motivation of cosmetic plastic surgeons?
- **a.** altruistic
- **b.** professional
- **c.** creative
- **d.** thrilling
- **e.** greedy

1017. Which audience is the author of Passage 1 most likely addressing?
- **a.** burn or accident victims
- **b.** women with poor body image
- **c.** plastic surgeons
- **d.** healthcare providers
- **e.** baby boomers

1018. In Passage 2, line 2 *saturated* most nearly means
- **a.** animated.
- **b.** decorated.
- **c.** gratified.
- **d.** permeated.
- **e.** tainted.

1019. The author of Passage 2 implies that feminists of the 1970s held which of the following beliefs?
- **a.** All women should have the right to safe, affordable cosmetic surgery.
- **b.** Looks should not be a factor in determining a person's worth.
- **c.** Cosmetic surgery is a beneficial tool in that it increases a woman's self-esteem.
- **d.** To be fair, men should be judged by their looks, too.
- **e.** Women should do whatever is necessary to compete in the job market.

1020. Which aspect of the cosmetic plastic surgery trend is emphasized in Passage 1, but not in Passage 2?
- **a.** professional envy among doctors
- **b.** nonsurgical techniques like Botox injections
- **c.** media's role in promoting plastic surgery
- **d.** surgical risks
- **e.** cost of procedures

1021. The two authors would most likely agree with which statement?

a. Cosmetic surgery takes away individuality.

b. Ideals of beauty are not culturally informed.

c. Plastic surgeons prey off of vulnerable patients.

d. American society is highly competitive.

e. The benefits of plastic surgery outweigh the risks.

1022. The approaches of the two passages to the topic are the similar in that they both use

a. first-person experiences.

b. second-person address to the reader.

c. references to other sources on the subject.

d. a summary of types of plastic surgery.

e. statistics on patient satisfaction.

Questions 1023–1032 are based on the following passage.

This passage describes the public's growing interest in alternative medicine practices in twenty-first-century United States.

(1)　　Once people wore garlic around their necks to ward off disease. Today, most Americans would scoff at the idea of wearing a necklace of garlic cloves to enhance their well-being. However, you might find a number of Americans willing to ingest capsules of pulverized garlic or other (5)　herbal supplements in the name of health.

　　　　Complementary and alternative medicine (CAM), which includes a range of practices outside of conventional medicine such as herbs, homeopathy, massage, yoga, and acupuncture, holds increasing appeal for Americans. In fact, according to one estimate, 42% of (10)　Americans have used alternative therapies. A Harvard Medical School survey found that young adults (those born between 1965 and 1979) are the most likely to use alternative treatments, whereas people born before 1945 are the least likely to use these therapies. Nonetheless, in all age groups, the use of unconventional healthcare practices has (15)　steadily increased since the 1950s, and the trend is likely to continue.

　　　　CAM has become a big business as Americans dip into their wallets to pay for alternative treatments. A 1997 American Medical Association study estimated that the public spent $21.2 billion for alternative medicine therapies in that year, more than half of which were out-(20)　of-pocket expenditures, meaning they were not covered by health insurance. Indeed, Americans made more out-of-pocket expenditures for alternative services than out-of-pocket payments for hospital stays in 1997. In addition, the number of total visits to alternative medicine providers (about 629 million) exceeded the tally of visits to (25)　primary care physicians (386 million) in that year.

　　　　However, the public has not abandoned conventional medicine for alternative healthcare. Most Americans seek out alternative therapies

(30) as a complement to their conventional healthcare, whereas only a small percentage of Americans rely primarily on alternative care. Why have so many patients turned to alternative therapies? Frustrated by the time constraints of managed care and alienated by conventional medicine's focus on technology, some feel that a holistic approach to healthcare better reflects their beliefs and values. Others seek therapies that will relieve symptoms associated with chronic disease, symp-

(35) toms that mainstream medicine cannot treat.

Some alternative therapies have crossed the line into mainstream medicine as scientific investigation has confirmed their safety and efficacy. For example, today physicians may prescribe acupuncture for pain management or to control the nausea associated with chemother-

(40) apy. Most U.S. medical schools teach courses in alternative therapies, and many health insurance companies offer some alternative medicine benefits. Yet, despite their gaining acceptance, the majority of alternative therapies have not been researched in controlled studies. New research efforts aim at testing alternative methods and providing the

(45) public with information about which are safe and effective and which are a waste of money, or possibly dangerous.

So what about those who swear by the health benefits of the "smelly rose," garlic?

Observational studies that track disease incidence in different pop-

(50) ulations suggest that garlic use in the diet may act as a cancer-fighting agent, particularly for prostate and stomach cancer. However, these findings have not been confirmed in clinical studies. And yes, reported side effects include garlic odor.

1023. The author's primary purpose in the passage is to

a. confirm the safety and effectiveness of alternative medicine approaches.

b. convey the excitement of crossing new medical frontiers.

c. describe the recent increase in the use of alternative therapies.

d. explore the variety of practices that fall into the category of alternative medicine.

e. criticize the use of alternative therapies that have not been scientifically tested.

1024. The author describes wearing garlic (line 1) as an example of

a. an arcane practice considered odd and superstitious today.

b. the ludicrous nature of complementary and alternative medicine.

c. a scientifically tested medical practice.

d. a socially unacceptable style of jewelry.

e. a safe and reliable means to prevent some forms of cancer.

1025. The word *conventional* as it is used in line 7 most nearly means
a. appropriate.
b. established.
c. formal.
d. moralistic.
e. reactionary.

1026. The author most likely uses the Harvard survey results (lines 10–13) to imply that
a. as people age they always become more conservative.
b. people born before 1945 view alternative therapies with disdain.
c. the survey did not question baby boomers (those born between 1945–1965) on the topic.
d. many young adults are open-minded to alternative therapies.
e. the use of alternative therapies will decline as those born between 1965 and 1979 age.

1027. The statistic comparing total visits to alternative medicine practitioners with those to primary care physicians (lines 23–25) is used to illustrate the
a. popularity of alternative medicine.
b. public's distrust of conventional healthcare.
c. accessibility of alternative medicine.
d. affordability of alternative therapies.
e. ineffectiveness of most primary care physicians.

1028. In line 28, *complement* most nearly means
a. tribute.
b. commendation.
c. replacement.
d. substitute.
e. addition.

1029. The information in lines 30–35 indicates that Americans believe that conventional healthcare
a. offers the best relief from the effects of chronic diseases.
b. should not use technology in treating illness.
c. combines caring for the body with caring for the spirit.
d. falls short of their expectations in some aspects.
e. needs a complete overhaul to become an effective system.

1030. The author suggests that *cross[ing] the line into mainstream medicine* (lines 36–37) involves
a. performing stringently controlled research on alternative therapies.
b. accepting the spiritual dimension of preventing and treating illness.
c. approving of any treatments that a patient is interested in trying.
d. recognizing the popularity of alternative therapies.
e. notifying your physician about herbs or alternative therapies you are using.

1031. In lines 49–54, the author refers to garlic use again in order to
  a. cite an example of the fraudulent claims of herbal supplements.
  b. suggest that claims about some herbs may be legitimate.
  c. mock people who take garlic capsules.
  d. offer a reason why some Americans are drawn to alternative health methods.
  e. argue that observational studies provide enough evidence.

1032. Which of the following best describes the approach of the passage?
  a. matter-of-fact narration
  b. historical analysis
  c. sarcastic criticism
  d. playful reporting
  e. impassioned argument

Questions 1033–1040 are based on the following passage.

In this excerpt from John Steinbeck's 1936 novel In Dubious Battle, *Mac and Doc Burton discuss "the cause" that leads hundreds of migratory farm workers to unite and strike against landowners.*

(1)   Mac spoke softly, for the night seemed to be listening. "You're a mystery to me, too, Doc."
       "Me? A mystery?"
       "Yes, you. You're not a Party man, but you work with us all the time;
(5)   you never get anything for it. I don't know whether you believe in what we're doing or not, you never say, you just work. I've been out with you before, and I'm not sure you believe in the cause at all."
       Dr. Burton laughed softly. "It would be hard to say. I could tell you some of the things I think; you might not like them. I'm pretty sure you
(10)   won't like them."
       "Well, let's hear them anyway."
       "Well, you say I don't believe in the cause. That's not like not believing in the moon. There've been communes before, and there will be again. But you people have an idea that if you can *establish* the thing, the
(15)   job'll be done. Nothing stops, Mac. If you were able to put an idea into effect tomorrow, it would start changing right away. Establish a commune, and the same gradual flux will continue."
       "Then you don't think the cause is good?"
       Burton sighed. "You see? We're going to pile up on that old rock
(20)   again. That's why I don't like to talk very often. Listen to me, Mac. My senses aren't above reproach, but they're all I have. I want to see the whole picture—as nearly as I can. I don't want to put on the blinders of 'good' and 'bad,' and limit my vision. If I used the term 'good' on a thing I'd lose my license to inspect it, because there might be bad in it. Don't
(25)   you see? I want to be able to look at the whole thing."
       Mac broke in heatedly, "How about social injustice? The profit system? You have to say they're bad."

Dr. Burton threw back his head and looked at the sky. "Mac," he said. "Look at the physiological injustice, the injustice of tetanus [. . .], the
(30) gangster methods of amoebic dysentery—that's my field."

"Revolution and communism will cure social injustice."

"Yes, and disinfection and prophylaxis will prevent others."

"It's different, though; men are doing one, and germs are doing the other."

(35) "I can't see much difference, Mac."

[. . .] "Why do you hang around with us if you aren't for us?"

"I want to see," Burton said. "When you cut your finger, and strepto-cocci get in the wound, there's a swelling and a soreness. That swelling is the fight your body puts up, the pain is the battle. You can't tell which
(40) one is going to win, but the wound is the first battleground. If the cells lose the first fight the streptococci invade, and the fight goes on up the arm. Mac, these little strikes are like the infection. Something has got into the men; a little fever has started and the lymphatic glands are shoot-ing in the reinforcements. I want to see, so I go to the seat of the wound."

(45) "You figure the strike is a wound?"

"Yes. Group-men are always getting some kind of infection. This seems to be a bad one. I want to see, Mac. I want to watch these group-men, for they seem to me to be a new individual, not at all like single men. A man in a group isn't himself at all, he's a cell in
(50) an organism that isn't like him any more than the cells in your body are like you. I want to watch the group, and see what it's like. Peo-ple have said, 'mobs are crazy, you can't tell what they'll do.' Why don't people look at mobs not as men, but as mobs? A mob nearly always seems to act reasonably, for a mob."

(55) "Well, what's this got to do with the cause?"

"It might be like this, Mac: When group-man wants to move, he makes a standard. 'God wills that we recapture the Holy Land'; or he says, 'We fight to make the world safe for democracy'; or he says, 'We will wipe out social injustice with communism.' But the group doesn't care about the
(60) Holy Land, or Democracy, or Communism. Maybe the group simply wants to move, to fight, and uses these words simply to reassure the brains of individual men. I say it might be like that, Mac."

"Not with the cause, it isn't," Mac cried.

1033. In lines 15–17, Doc Burton argues that
  a. even if the cause succeeds, it won't change anything.
  b. the cause is unstoppable.
  c. the supporters of the cause should establish a commune.
  d. the cause itself is always changing.
  e. change can only come about gradually.

1034. The *cause* the men refer to throughout the passage is
  a. democracy.
  b. communism.
  c. capitalism.
  d. insurgency.
  e. freedom.

1035. Doc Burton is best described as
   a. an objective observer.
   b. a representative of the government.
   c. a staunch supporter of the cause.
   d. a visionary leader.
   e. a reluctant participant.

1036. According to Doc Burton, the *strikes are like the infection* (line 42) because
   a. the strikes are life-threatening.
   b. many of the strikers are ill.
   c. the size of the group has swollen.
   d. the strikes are a reaction to an injury.
   e. the strikes are taking place on a battleground.

1037. By comparing *group-men* to a living organism (lines 48–50), Doc Burton
   a. reinforces his idea that individuals are lost in the larger whole.
   b. shows that group-men are constantly changing and growing.
   c. supports his assertion that the strikers are like an infection.
   d. explains why he is with the strikers.
   e. reflects his opinion that the strikes' success depends on unity within the group.

1038. According to Doc Burton, the main difference between *group-men* and the individual is that
   a. individuals can be controlled but groups cannot.
   b. individuals do not want to fight but groups do.
   c. individuals may believe in a cause but groups do not.
   d. groups are often crazy but individuals are not.
   e. people in groups can reassure one another.

1039. It can be inferred from this passage that Doc Burton believes the cause
   a. is just an excuse for fighting.
   b. is reasonable.
   c. will fail.
   d. will correct social injustice.
   e. will make America a more democratic place.

1040. Doc Burton repeats the word *might* in lines 56 and 62 because
   a. he doesn't believe Mac is sincere about the cause.
   b. he really wants Mac to consider the possibility that the group is blind to the cause.
   c. he is asking a rhetorical question.
   d. he doesn't want Mac to know the truth about the cause.
   e. he wants Mac to see that he isn't really serious in his criticism of the cause.

Questions 1041–1049 are based on the following passage.

This excerpt is from the final scene of George Bernard Shaw's 1916 play Pygmalion, *when Professor Higgins learns just how well he taught Liza.*

(1)   HIGGINS: If you're going to be a lady, you'll have to give up feeling neglected if the men you know don't spend half their time sniveling over you and the other half giving you black eyes. If you can't stand the coldness of my sort of life, and the strain of it, go back to

(5)   the gutter. Work 'til you are more a brute than a human being; and then cuddle and squabble and drink 'til you fall asleep. Oh, it's a fine life, the life of the gutter. It's real: it's warm: it's violent: you can feel it through the thickest skin: you can taste it and smell it without any training or any work. Not like Science and Literature and Classi-

(10)   cal Music and Philosophy and Art. You find me cold, unfeeling, self-ish, don't you? Very well: be off with you to the sort of people you like. Marry some sentimental hog or other with lots of money, and a thick pair of lips to kiss you with and a thick pair of boots to kick you with. If you can't appreciate what you've got, you'd better get

(15)   what you can appreciate.

LIZA (*desperate*): Oh, you are a cruel tyrant. I can't talk to you: you turn everything against me: I'm always in the wrong. But you know very well all the time that you're nothing but a bully. You know I can't go back to the gutter, as you call it, and that I have no real

(20)   friends in the world but you and the Colonel. You know well I couldn't bear to live with a low common man after you two; and it's wicked and cruel of you to insult me by pretending I could. You think I must go back to Wimpole Street because I have nowhere else to go but father's. But don't you be too sure that you have me

(25)   under your feet to be trampled on and talked down. I'll marry Freddy, I will, as soon as he's able to support me.

HIGGINS (*sitting down beside her*): Rubbish! You shall marry an ambassador. You shall marry the Governor-General of India or the Lord-Lieutenant of Ireland, or somebody who wants a deputy-

(30)   queen. I'm not going to have my masterpiece thrown away on Freddy.

LIZA: You think I like you to say that. But I haven't forgot what you said a minute ago; and I won't be coaxed round as if I was a baby or a puppy. If I can't have kindness, I'll have independence.

(35)   HIGGINS: Independence? That's middle class blasphemy. We are all dependent on one another, every soul of us on earth.

LIZA (*rising determinedly*): I'll let you see whether I'm dependent on you. If you can preach, I can teach. I'll go and be a teacher.

HIGGINS: What'll you teach, in heaven's name?

(40)   LIZA: What you taught me. I'll teach phonetics.

HIGGINS: Ha! ha! ha!

LIZA: I'll offer myself as an assistant to Professor Nepean.

HIGGINS (*rising in a fury*): What! That impostor! that humbug! that toadying ignoramus! Teach him my methods! my discoveries! You

(45)   take one step in his direction and I'll wring your neck. (*He lays hands on her.*) Do you hear?

LIZA (*defiantly resistant*): Wring away. What do I care? I knew you'd strike me some day. (*He lets her go, stamping with rage at having forgotten himself, and recoils so hastily that he stumbles back into his seat*

(50)   *on the ottoman.*) Aha! Now I know how to deal with you. What a fool I was not to think of it before! You can't take away the knowledge you gave me. You said I had a finer ear than you. And I can be civil and kind to people, which is more than you can. Aha! That's done you, Henry Higgins, it has. Now I don't care that (*snapping her fin-*

(55)   *gers*) for your bullying and your big talk. I'll advertise it in the papers that your duchess is only a flower girl that you taught, and that she'll teach anybody to be a duchess just the same in six months for a thousand guineas. Oh, when I think of myself crawling under your feet and being trampled on and called names, when all the

(60)   time I had only to lift up my finger to be as good as you, I could just kick myself.

1041. In lines 1–15, Higgins contrasts the *life of the gutter* with his *sort of life*, which is best described as

a. the life of an ambassador.

b. the life of the rich and famous.

c. the life of a tyrant.

d. the life of a scholar.

e. the life of the working class.

1042. Wimpole Street (line 23) is most likely

a. a fashionable area.

b. where Professor Nepean resides.

c. where Higgins teaches.

d. where Freddy lives.

e. where Liza grew up.

1043. Liza wants Higgins to

a. appreciate her work.

b. help her find a suitable husband.

c. marry her.

d. teach her everything he knows.

e. treat her with more respect.

1044. The word *common* in line 21 means

a. usual.

b. unrefined.

c. popular.

d. average.

e. shared by two or more.

1045. In lines 43–46, Higgins proves that
- **a.** he is a bully.
- **b.** Liza can't teach with Professor Nepean.
- **c.** Professor Nepean is a fake.
- **d.** he and Liza depend upon each other.
- **e.** he knows better than Liza.

1046. Higgins' use of the word *masterpiece* in line 30 implies that
- **a.** he is an artist.
- **b.** he thinks Liza is very beautiful.
- **c.** he thinks of Liza as his creation.
- **d.** he is in love with Liza.
- **e.** Liza is his servant.

1047. Which of the following best describes what Higgins has taught Liza?
- **a.** the history of the English language
- **b.** how to speak and act like someone from the upper class
- **c.** how to be independent of others
- **d.** how to understand literature and philosophy
- **e.** how to appreciate scholarly work

1048. In lines 37–61, the main reason Higgins is so upset is because
- **a.** Liza threatens to teach his methods to others.
- **b.** he realizes he has been a bad teacher.
- **c.** he realizes he is as abusive as someone from the gutter.
- **d.** he realizes he cannot control Liza.
- **e.** he realizes Liza does not love him anymore.

1049. The passage implies that Liza's most significant transformation in the play is from
- **a.** lower class to upper class.
- **b.** ignorant to educated.
- **c.** oppressed to empowered.
- **d.** single to married.
- **e.** cold to compassionate.

Questions 1050–1057 are based on the following passage.

In this excerpt from Charlotte Bronte's novel Jane Eyre, *the narrator decides to leave Lowood, the boarding school where she has lived for eight years.*

(1) Miss Temple, through all changes, had thus far continued superintendent of the seminary; to her instruction I owed the best part of my acquirements; her friendship and society had been my continual solace: she had stood me in the stead of mother, governess, and, latterly,
(5) companion. At this period she married, removed with her husband (a clergyman, an excellent man, almost worthy of such a wife) to a distant county, and consequently was lost to me.

  From the day she left I was no longer the same: with her was gone every settled feeling, every association that had made Lowood in some
(10) degree a home to me. I had imbibed from her something of her nature and much of her habits: more harmonious thoughts: what seemed better-regulated feelings had become inmates of my mind. I had given in allegiance to duty and order; I was quiet; I believed I was content: to

the eyes of others, usually even to my own, I appeared a disciplined and

(15) subdued character.

But destiny, in the shape of the Rev. Mr. Nasmyth, came between me and Miss Temple: I saw her in her traveling dress step into a post-chaise, shortly after the marriage ceremony; I watched the chaise mount the hill and disappear beyond its brow; and then retired to my own room,

(20) and there spent in solitude the greatest part of the half-holiday granted in honor of the occasion.

I walked about the chamber most of the time. I imagined myself only to be regretting my loss, and thinking how to repair it; but when my reflections concluded, and I looked up and found that the afternoon was

(25) gone, and evening far advanced, another discovery dawned on me, namely, that in the interval I had undergone a transforming process; that my mind had put off all it had borrowed of Miss Temple—or rather that she had taken with her the serene atmosphere I had been breathing in her vicinity—and that now I was left in my natural element, and

(30) beginning to feel the stirring of old emotions. It did not seem as if a prop were withdrawn, but rather as if a motive were gone; it was not the power to be tranquil which had failed me, but the reason for tranquility was no more. My world had for some years been in Lowood: my experience had been of its rules and systems; now I remembered that the real

(35) world was wide, and that a varied field of hopes and fears, of sensations and excitements, awaited those who had courage to go forth into its expanse, to seek real knowledge of life amidst its perils.

I went to my window, opened it, and looked out. There were the two wings of the building; there was the garden; there were the skirts of

(40) Lowood; there was the hilly horizon. My eye passed all other objects to rest on those most remote, the blue peaks: it was those I longed to surmount; all within their boundary of rock and heath seemed prison-ground, exile limits. I traced the white road winding round the base of one mountain, and vanishing in a gorge between two: how I longed to

(45) follow it further! I recalled the time when I had traveled that very road in a coach; I remembered descending that hill at twilight: an age seemed to have elapsed since the day which brought me first to Lowood, and I had never quitted it since. My vacations had all been spent at school: Mrs. Reed had never sent for me to Gateshead; neither she nor any of

(50) her family had ever been to visit me. I had had no communication by letter or message with the outer world: school-rules, school-duties, school-habits and notions, and voices, and faces, and phrases, and costumes, and preferences, and antipathies: such was what I knew of existence. And now I felt that it was not enough: I tired of the routine of

(55) eight years in one afternoon. I desired liberty; for liberty I gasped; for liberty I uttered a prayer; it seemed scattered on the wind then faintly blowing. I abandoned it and framed a humbler supplication; for change, stimulus: that petition, too, seemed swept off into vague space: "Then," I cried, half desperate, "grant me at least a new servitude!"

1050. Miss Temple was the narrator's
   a. teacher.
   b. friend.
   c. mother.
   d. teacher and friend.
   e. all of the above

1051. While Miss Temple was at Lowood, the narrator
   a. was calm and content.
   b. was often alone.
   c. had frequent disciplinary problems.
   d. longed to leave Lowood.
   e. felt as if she were in a prison.

1052. The word *inmates* in line 12 means
   a. captives.
   b. patients.
   c. prisoners.
   d. residents.
   e. convalescents.

1053. Mrs. Reed (line 49) is most likely
   a. the narrator's mother.
   b. the headmistress of Lowood.
   c. the narrator's former guardian.
   d. the narrator's friend.
   e. a fellow student at Lowood.

1054. It can be inferred from the passage that life at Lowood was
   a. very unconventional and modern.
   b. very structured and isolated.
   c. harsh and demeaning.
   d. liberal and carefree.
   e. urban and sophisticated.

1055. After Miss Temple's wedding, the narrator
   a. realizes she wants to experience the world.
   b. decides that she must get married.
   c. realizes she can never leave Lowood.
   d. decides to return to her family at Gateshead.
   e. determines to follow Miss Temple.

1056. The passage suggests that the narrator
   a. will soon return to Lowood.
   b. was sent to Lowood by mistake.
   c. is entirely dependent upon Miss Temple.
   d. has run away from Lowood before.
   e. is naturally curious and rebellious.

1057. In line 59, the narrator reduces her petition to simply *a new servitude* because she
   a. doesn't believe in prayer.
   b. is not in a free country.
   c. has been offered a position as a servant.
   d. knows so little of the real world.
   e. has been treated like a slave at Lowood.

Questions 1058–1065 are based on the following passage.

In this excerpt from Susan Glaspell's one-act play Trifles, *Mrs. Hale and Mrs. Peters make an important discovery in Mrs. Wright's home as their husbands try to determine who strangled Mr. Wright.*

(1)   MRS. PETERS: Well, I must get these things wrapped up. They may be through sooner than we think. (*Putting apron and other things together.*) I wonder where I can find a piece of paper, and string.

       MRS. HALE: In that cupboard, maybe.

(5)   MRS. PETERS (*looking in cupboard*): Why, here's a birdcage. (*Holds it up.*) Did she have a bird, Mrs. Hale?

       MRS. HALE: Why, I don't know whether she did or not—I've not been here for so long. There was a man around last year selling canaries cheap, but I don't know as she took one; maybe she did.

(10)   She used to sing real pretty herself.

       MRS. PETERS (*glancing around*): Seems funny to think of a bird here. But she must have had one, or why would she have a cage? I wonder what happened to it.

       MRS. HALE: I s'pose maybe the cat got it.

(15)   MRS. PETERS: No, she didn't have a cat. She's got that feeling some people have about cats—being afraid of them. My cat got in her room and she was real upset and asked me to take it out.

       MRS. HALE: My sister Bessie was like that. Queer, ain't it?

       MRS. PETERS (*examining the cage*): Why, look at this door. It's broke.

(20)   One hinge is pulled apart.

       MRS. HALE (*looking too*): Looks as if someone must have been rough with it.

       MRS. PETERS: Why, yes.

       (*She brings the cage forward and puts it on the table.*)

(25)   MRS. HALE: I wish if they're going to find any evidence they'd be about it. I don't like this place.

       MRS. PETERS: But I'm awful glad you came with me, Mrs. Hale. It would be lonesome for me sitting here alone.

       MRS. HALE: It would, wouldn't it? (*Dropping her sewing.*) But I tell

(30)   you what I do wish, Mrs. Peters. I wish I had come over sometimes when *she* was here. I—(*looking around the room*)—wish I had.

       MRS. PETERS: But of course you were awful busy, Mrs. Hale—your house and your children.

       MRS. HALE: I could've come. I stayed away because it weren't cheerful—

(35)   and that's why I ought to have come. I—I've never liked this place. Maybe because it's down in a hollow and you don't see the road. I dunno what it is but it's a lonesome place and always was. I wish I had come over to see Minnie Foster sometimes. I can see now—

(40)   (*Shakes her head.*)

MRS. PETERS: Well, you mustn't reproach yourself, Mrs. Hale. Somehow we just don't see how it is with other folks until—something comes up.

MRS. HALE: Not having children makes less work—but it makes a
(45) quiet house, and Wright out to work all day, and no company when he did come in. Did you know John Wright, Mrs. Peters?

MRS. PETERS: Not to know him; I've seen him in town. They say he was a good man.

MRS. HALE: Yes—good; he didn't drink, and kept his word as well as
(50) most, I guess, and paid his debts. But he was a hard man, Mrs. Peters. Just to pass the time of day with him—(*shivers*). Like a raw wind that gets to the bone. (*Pauses, her eye falling on the cage.*) I should think she would'a wanted a bird. But what do you suppose went with it?

MRS. PETERS: I don't know, unless it got sick and died.

(55) (*She reaches over and swings the broken door, swings it again. Both women watch it.*)

MRS. HALE: You weren't raised round here, were you? (MRS. PETERS *shakes her head.*) You didn't know—her?

MRS. PETERS: Not till they brought her yesterday.

(60) MRS. HALE: She—come to think of it, she was kind of like a bird herself—real sweet and pretty, but kind of timid and—fluttery. How—she—did—change. (*Silence; then as if struck by a happy thought and relieved to get back to everyday things.*) Tell you what, Mrs. Peters, why don't you take the quilt in with you? It might take up her mind.

(65) MRS. PETERS: Why, I think that's a real nice idea, Mrs. Hale. There couldn't possibly be any objection to it, could there? Now, just what would I take? I wonder if her patches are in here—and her things.

(*They look in the sewing basket.*)

MRS. HALE: Here's some red. I expect this has got sewing things in it.
(70) (*Brings out a fancy box.*) What a pretty box. Looks like something somebody would give you. Maybe her scissors are in here. (*Opens box. Suddenly puts her hand to her nose.*) Why—(MRS. PETERS *bends nearer, then turns her face away.*) There's something wrapped in this piece of silk.

(75) MRS. PETERS (*lifting the silk*): Why, this isn't her scissors.

MRS. HALE (*lifting the silk*): Oh, Mrs. Peters—it's—

(MRS. PETERS *bends closer.*)

MRS. PETERS: It's the bird.

MRS. HALE (*jumping up*): But, Mrs. Peters—look at it! Its neck! Look at
(80) its neck! It's all—to the other side.

MRS. PETERS: Somebody—wrung—its—neck.

(*Their eyes meet. A look of growing comprehension, of horror. Steps are heard outside. MRS. HALE slips box under quilt pieces, and sinks into her chair. Enter SHERIFF and COUNTY ATTORNEY HALE. MRS.*
(85) *PETERS rises.*)

1058. Based on the passage, the reader can conclude that
   a. Mrs. Peters and Mrs. Hale are old friends.
   b. Mrs. Peters and Mrs. Hale both know Mrs. Wright very well.
   c. Mrs. Peters and Mrs. Hale don't know each other very well.
   d. Neither Mrs. Peters nor Mrs. Hale likes Mrs. Wright.
   e. Neither Mrs. Peters nor Mrs. Hale has children.

1059. Mrs. Hale says she wishes she had come to Mrs. Wright's house (lines 30–31 and 37–39) because
   a. she realizes that Mrs. Wright must have been lonely.
   b. she enjoyed Mr. Wright's company.
   c. she always felt at home in the Wrights' house.
   d. she realizes how important it is to keep good relationships with one's neighbors.
   e. she had a lot in common with Mrs. Wright.

1060. According to Mrs. Hale, what sort of man was Mr. Wright?
   a. gentle and loving
   b. violent and abusive
   c. honest and dependable
   d. quiet and cold
   e. a strict disciplinarian

1061. In lines 60–62, Mrs. Hale suggests that Mrs. Wright
   a. had become even more like a bird than before.
   b. had grown bitter and unhappy over the years.
   c. was too shy to maintain an intimate friendship.
   d. must have taken excellent care of her bird.
   e. was always singing and flitting about.

1062. The phrase *take up her mind* in line 64 means
   a. worry her.
   b. make her angry.
   c. refresh her memory.
   d. keep her busy.
   e. make her think.

1063. It can be inferred that Mrs. Wright
   a. got the bird as a present for her husband.
   b. was forced into marrying Mr. Wright.
   c. loved the bird because it reminded her of how she used to be.
   d. had a pet bird as a little girl.
   e. fought often with Mr. Wright.

1064. When the women share a *look of growing comprehension, of horror* (line 82), they realize that
   a. Mrs. Wright killed the bird.
   b. Mr. Wright killed the bird, and Mrs. Wright killed him.
   c. they would get in trouble if the sheriff found out they were looking around in the kitchen.
   d. there's a secret message hidden in the quilt.
   e. they might be Mrs. Wright's next victims.

1065. The stage directions in lines 83–84 suggest that
   a. the women are mistaken in their conclusion.
   b. the women will tell the men what they found.
   c. the women will confront Mrs. Wright.
   d. the women will keep their discovery a secret.
   e. the men had been eavesdropping on the women.

Questions 1066–1072 are based on the following passages.

In Passage 1, an excerpt from Mary Shelley's Frankenstein, *Victor Frankenstein explains his motive for creating his creature. In Passage 2, an excerpt from H.G. Wells' 1896 novel* The Island of Dr. Moreau, *Dr. Moreau explains to the narrator why he has been performing experiments on animals to transform them into humans.*

Passage 1

(1)   I see by your eagerness, and the wonder and hope which your eyes express, my friend, that you expect to be informed of the secret with which I am acquainted; that cannot be: listen patiently until the end of my story, and you will easily perceive why I am reserved upon that

(5)   subject. I will not lead you on, unguarded and ardent as I then was, to your destruction and infallible misery. Learn from me, if not by my precepts, at least by my example, how dangerous is the acquirement of knowledge, and how much happier that man is who believes his native town to be the world, than he who aspires to become greater than his

(10)   nature will allow.
        When I found so astonishing a power placed within my hands, I hesitated a long time concerning the manner in which I should employ it. Although I possessed the capacity of bestowing animation, yet to prepare a frame for the reception of it, with all its intricacies of fibers,

(15)   muscles, and veins, still remained a work of inconceivable difficulty and labour. I doubted at first whether I should attempt the creation of a being like myself, or one of simpler organization; but my imagination was too much exalted by my first success to permit me to doubt of my ability to give life to an animal as complex and wonderful as

(20)   man. The materials at present within my command hardly appeared adequate to so arduous an undertaking; but I doubted not that I should ultimately succeed. I prepared myself for a multitude of reverses; my operations might be incessantly baffled, and at last my work be imperfect: yet, when I considered the improvement which every day takes

(25)   place in science and mechanics, I was encouraged to hope my present attempts would at least lay the foundations of future success. Nor could I consider the magnitude and complexity of my plan as any argument of its impracticability. It was with these feelings that I began the creation of my human being. As the minuteness of the parts

(30)   formed a great hindrance to my speed, I resolved, contrary to my first intention, to make the being of a gigantic stature; that is to say, about eight feet in height, and proportionably large. After having formed this determination, and having spent some months in successfully collecting and arranging my materials, I began.

(35)   No one can conceive the variety of feelings which bore me onwards, like a hurricane, in the first enthusiasm of success. Life and death appeared to me ideal bounds, which I should first break through, and pour a torrent of light into our dark world. A new species would bless

(40) me as its creator and source; many happy and excellent natures would owe their being to me. No father could claim the gratitude of his child so completely as I should deserve theirs. Pursuing these reflections, I thought, that if I could bestow animation upon lifeless matter, I might in process of time (although I now found it impossible) renew life where death had apparently devoted the body to corruption.

(45) These thoughts supported my spirits, while I pursued my undertaking with unremitting ardour. My cheek had grown pale with study, and my person had become emaciated with confinement. Sometimes, on the very brink of certainty, I failed; yet still I clung to the hope which the next day or the next hour might realize. One secret which (50) I alone possessed was the hope to which I had dedicated myself; and the moon gazed on my midnight labors, while, with unrelaxed and breathless eagerness, I pursued nature to her hiding-places. Who shall conceive the horrors of my secret toil, as I dabbled among the unhallowed damps of the grave, or tortured the living animal to animate the (55) lifeless clay? My limbs now tremble, and my eyes swim with the remembrance; but then a resistless, and almost frantic, impulse urged me forward; I seemed to have lost all soul or sensation but for this one pursuit.

Passage 2

(1) "Yes. These creatures you have seen are animals carven and wrought into new shapes. To that—to the study of the plasticity of living forms—my life has been devoted. I have studied for years, gaining in knowledge as I go. I see you look horrified, and yet I am telling you (5) nothing new. It all lay in the surface of practical anatomy years ago, but no one had the temerity to touch it. It's not simply the outward form of an animal I can change. The physiology, the chemical rhythm of the creature, may also be made to undergo an enduring modification, of which vaccination and other methods of inoculation with liv-(10) ing or dead matter are examples that will, no doubt, be familiar to you.

"A similar operation is the transfusion of blood, with which subject indeed I began. These are all familiar cases. Less so, and probably far more extensive, were the operations of those medieval practitioners who made dwarfs and beggar cripples and show-monsters; some vestiges of (15) whose art still remain in the preliminary manipulation of the young mountebank or contortionist. Victor Hugo gives an account of them in *L'Homme qui Rit*. . . . But perhaps my meaning grows plain now. You begin to see that it is a possible thing to transplant tissue from one part of an animal to another, or from one animal to another, to alter its (20) chemical reactions and methods of growth, to modify the articulations of its limbs, and indeed to change it in its most intimate structure?

"And yet this extraordinary branch of knowledge has never been sought as an end, and systematically, by modern investigators, until I

(25) took it up! Some such things have been hit upon in the last resort of surgery; most of the kindred evidence that will recur to your mind has been demonstrated, as it were, by accident—by tyrants, by criminals, by the breeders of horses and dogs, by all kinds of untrained clumsy-handed men working for their own immediate ends. I was the first man to take up this question armed with antiseptic surgery, and with (30) a really scientific knowledge of the laws of growth.

"Yet one would imagine it must have been practiced in secret before. Such creatures as Siamese Twins . . . . And in the vaults of the Inquisi-tion. No doubt their chief aim was artistic torture, but some, at least, of the inquisitors must have had a touch of scientific curiosity . . . ."

(35) "But," said I. "These things—these animals *talk!*"

He said that was so, and proceeded to point out that the possibili-ties of vivisection do not stop at a mere physical metamorphosis. A pig may be educated. The mental structure is even less determinate than the bodily. In our growing science of hypnotism we find the promise (40) of a possibility of replacing old inherent instincts by new suggestions, grafting upon or replacing the inherited fixed ideas. [. . .]

But I asked him why he had taken the human form as a model. There seemed to me then, and there still seems to me now, a strange wickedness in that choice.

(45) He confessed that he had chosen that form by chance.

"I might just as well have worked to form sheep into llamas, and llamas into sheep. I suppose there is something in the human form that appeals to the artistic turn of mind more powerfully than any ani-mal shape can. But I've not confined myself to man-making. Once or (50) twice . . . ." He was silent, for a minute perhaps. "These years! How they have slipped by! And here I have wasted a day saving your life, and am now wasting an hour explaining myself!"

"But," said I, "I still do not understand. Where is your justification for inflicting all this pain? The only thing that could excuse vivisection (55) to me would be some application—"

"Precisely," said he. "But you see I am differently constituted. We are on different platforms. You are a materialist."

"I am *not* a materialist," I began hotly.

"In my view—in my view. For it is just this question of pain that (60) parts us. So long as visible or audible pain turns you sick, so long as your own pain drives you, so long as pain underlies your propositions about sin, so long, I tell you, you are an animal, thinking a little less obscurely what an animal feels. This pain—"

I gave an impatient shrug at such sophistry.

(65) "Oh! But it is such a little thing. A mind truly open to what science has to teach must see that it is a little thing."

1066. In the first paragraph of Passage 1 (lines 1–10), Frankenstein reveals that the purpose of his tale is to
   a. entertain the reader.
   b. explain a scientific principle.
   c. teach a moral lesson.
   d. share the secret of his research.
   c. reveal his true nature.

1067. The word *baffled* in line 23 means
   a. hindered.
   b. confused.
   c. puzzled.
   d. eluded.
   e. regulated.

1068. During the creation process, Frankenstein could best be described as
   a. calm.
   b. horrified.
   c. evil.
   d. indifferent.
   e. obsessed.

1069. From Passage 2, it can be inferred that Dr. Moreau is what sort of scientist?
   a. artistic
   b. calculating and systematic
   c. careless, haphazard
   d. famous, renowned
   e. materialist

1070. *These things* that the narrator refers to in Passage 2, line 35, are
   a. Siamese twins.
   b. inquisitors.
   c. pigs.
   d. creatures Moreau created.
   e. tyrants and criminals.

1071. From the passage, it can be inferred that Dr. Moreau
   a. does not inflict pain upon animals when he experiments on them.
   b. has caused great pain to the creatures he has experimented on.
   c. is unable to experience physical pain.
   d. is searching for a way to eliminate physical pain.
   e. has learned to feel what an animal feels.

1072. Based on the information in the passages, Dr. Moreau is like Victor Frankenstein in that he also
   a. used dead bodies in his experiments.
   b. wanted his creations to worship him.
   c. made remarkable discoveries.
   d. kept his experiment a secret from everyone.
   e. had a specific justification for his pursuit of knowledge.

Questions 1073–1077 are based on the following passage.

The following passage describes the transition from the swing era to bebop in the history of jazz music.

(1)   Jazz, from its early roots in slave spirituals and the marching bands of
New Orleans, had developed into the predominant American musical
style by the 1930s. In this era, jazz musicians played a lush, orches-
trated style known as swing. Played in large ensembles, also called big
(5)   bands, swing filled the dance halls and nightclubs. Jazz, once considered risqué, was made more accessible to the masses with the vibrant,
swinging sounds of these big bands. Then came bebop. In the mid-
1940s, jazz musicians strayed from the swing style and developed a
more improvisational method of playing known as bebop. Jazz was
(10)   transformed from popular music to an elite art form.

Ṫhe soloists in the big bands improvised from the melody. The young
musicians who ushered in bebop, notably trumpeter Dizzy Gillespie and
saxophonist Charlie Parker, expanded on the improvisational elements
of the big bands. They played with advanced harmonies, changed chord
(15)   structures, and made chord substitutions. These young musicians got
their starts with the leading big bands of the day, but during World War
II—as older musicians were drafted and dance halls made cutbacks—
they started to play together in smaller groups.

These pared-down bands helped foster the bebop style. Rhythm is
(20)   the distinguishing feature of bebop, and in small groups the drums
became more prominent. Setting a driving beat, the drummer inter-
acted with the bass, piano, and the soloists, and together the musicians
created fast, complex melodies. Jazz aficionados flocked to such clubs as
Minton's Playhouse in Harlem to soak in the new style. For the young
(25)   musicians and their fans this was a thrilling turning point in jazz history.
However, for the majority of Americans, who just wanted some swinging music to dance to, the advent of bebop was the end of jazz as mainstream music.

1073. The swing style can be most accurately characterized as
   a. complex and inaccessible.
   b. appealing to an elite audience.
   c. lively and melodic.
   d. lacking in improvisation.
   e. played in small groups.

1074. According to the passage, in the 1940s you
would most likely find bebop being played
where?
   a. church
   b. a large concert hall
   c. music schools
   d. small clubs
   e. parades

1075. According to the passage, one of the most significant innovations of the bebop musicians was

a. to shun older musicians.

b. to emphasize rhythm.

c. to use melodic improvisation.

d. to play in small clubs.

e. to ban dancing.

1076. In the context of this passage, *aficionados* (line 23) can most accurately be described as

a. fans of bebop.

b. residents of Harlem.

c. innovative musicians.

d. awkward dancers.

e. fickle audience members.

1077. The main purpose of the passage is to

a. mourn the passing of an era.

b. condemn bebop for making jazz inaccessible.

c. explain the development of the bebop style.

d. celebrate the end of the conventional swing style of jazz.

e. instruct in the method of playing bebop.

Questions 1078–1083 are based on the following passage.

This passage details the rise and fall of the Seattle grunge-music sound in American pop culture of the 1990s.

(1)   The late 1980s found the landscape of popular music in America dominated by a distinctive style of rock and roll known as glam rock or hair metal—so called because of the overstyled hair, makeup, and wardrobes worn by the genre's ostentatious rockers. Bands like Poi-

(5)   son, White Snake, and Mötley Crüe popularized glam rock with their power ballads and flashy style, but the product had worn thin by the early 1990s. The mainstream public, tired of an act they perceived as symbolic of the superficial 1980s, was ready for something with a bit of substance.

(10)   In 1991, a Seattle-based band named Nirvana shocked the corporate music industry with the release of its debut single, "Smells Like Teen Spirit," which quickly became a huge hit all over the world. Nirvana's distorted, guitar-laden sound and thought-provoking lyrics were the antithesis of glam rock, and the youth of America were quick to pledge

(15)   their allegiance to the brand-new movement known as grunge.

     Grunge actually got its start in the Pacific Northwest during the mid 1980s, the offspring of the metal-guitar-driven rock of the 1970s and the hardcore, punk music of the early 1980s. Nirvana had simply brought into the mainstream a sound and culture that had gotten its

(20)   start years before with bands like Mudhoney, Soundgarden, and Green River. Grunge rockers derived their fashion sense from the youth cul-

ture of the Pacific Northwest: a melding of punk rock style and out-doors clothing like flannels, heavy boots, worn-out jeans, and cor-duroys. At the height of the movement's popularity, when other Seattle
(25) bands like Pearl Jam and Alice in Chains were all the rage, the trap-pings of grunge were working their way to the height of American fashion. Like the music, teenagers were fast to embrace the grunge fashion because it represented defiance against corporate America and shallow pop culture.

(30) Many assume that grunge got its name from the unkempt appear-ance of its musicians and their dirty, often distorted guitar sounds. However, rock writers and critics have used the word *grunge* since the 1970s. While no one can say for sure who was the first to characterize a Seattle band as "grunge," the most popular theory is that it originated
(35) with the lead singer of Mudhoney, Mark Arm. In a practical joke against a local music magazine, he placed advertisements all over Seat-tle for a band that did not exist. He then wrote a letter to the magazine complaining about the quality of the fake band's music. The magazine published his critique, one part of which stated, "I hate Mr. Epp and
(40) the Calculations! Pure grunge!"

The popularity of grunge music was ephemeral; by the mid to late 1990s its influence on American culture had all but disappeared, and most of its recognizable bands were nowhere to be seen on the charts. The heavy sound and themes of grunge were replaced on the radio
(45) waves by bands like 'N Sync, the Backstreet Boys, and the bubblegum pop of Britney Spears and Christina Aguilera.

There are many reasons why the Seattle sound faded out of the mainstream as quickly as it rocketed to prominence, but the most glaring reason lies at the defiant, anti-establishment heart of the
(50) grunge movement itself. It is very hard to buck the trend when you are the one setting it, and many of the grunge bands were never comfort-able with the celebrity that was thrust upon them. One the most suc-cessful Seattle groups of the 1990s, Pearl Jam, filmed only one music video, and refused to play large venues. Ultimately, the simple fact that
(55) many grunge bands were so against mainstream rock stardom even-tually took the movement back to where it started: underground. The American mainstream public, as quick as they were to hop onto the grunge bandwagon, were just as quick to hop off, and move on to something else.

1078. The author's description of glam rockers (lines 2–7) indicates that they

   a. cared more about the quality of their music than money.

   b. were mainly style over substance.

   c. were unassuming and humble.

   d. were songwriters first, and performers second.

   e. were innovators in rock and roll.

1079. The word *ostentatious* in line 4 most nearly means

   a. stubborn.

   b. youthful.

   c. showy.

   d. unadorned.

   e. popular.

1080. In lines 25–26, the phrase *the trappings of grunge* refers to

   a. the distorted sound of grunge music.

   b. what the grunge movement symbolized.

   c. the unattractiveness of grunge fashion.

   d. the clothing typical of the grunge movement.

   e. the popularity of grunge music.

1081. Which of the following is NOT associated with the grunge movement?

   a. Mr. Epps and the Calculations

   b. Pearl Jam

   c. Nirvana

   d. Green River

   e. White Snake

1082. Which of the following words best describes the relationship between grunge music and its mainstream popularity?

   a. solid

   b. contrary

   c. enduring

   d. acquiescent

   e. unprofitable

1083. In line 41, the word *ephemeral* most nearly means

   a. enduring.

   b. unbelievable.

   c. a fluke.

   d. fleeting.

   e. improbable.

Questions 1084–1092 are based on the following passages.

In Passage 1, the author describes the life and influence of blues guitarist Robert Johnson. In Passage 2, the author provides a brief history of the blues.

Passage 1

(1) There is little information available about the legendary blues guitarist Robert Johnson, and the information that is available is as much rumor as fact. What is indisputable, however, is Johnson's impact on the world of rock and roll. Some consider Johnson the father of mod-

(5) ern rock; his influence extends to artists from Muddy Waters to Led Zeppelin, from the Rolling Stones to the Allman Brothers Band. Eric Clapton, arguably the greatest living rock guitarist, has said that "Robert Johnson to me is the most important blues musician who

(10) ever lived. . . . I have never found anything more deeply soulful than Robert Johnson." While the impact of Johnson's music is evident, the genesis of his remarkable talent remains shrouded in mystery.

For Johnson, born in 1911 in Hazelhurst, Mississippi, music was a means of escape from working in the cotton fields. As a boy he worked on the farm that belonged to Noel Johnson—the man rumored to be (15) his father. He married young, at age 17, and lost his wife a year later in childbirth. That's when Johnson began traveling and playing the blues.

Initially Johnson played the harmonica. Later, he began playing the guitar, but apparently he was not very good. He wanted to learn, how-(20) ever, so he spent his time in blues bars watching the local blues legends Son House and Willie Brown. During their breaks, Johnson would go up on stage and play. House reportedly thought Johnson was so bad that he repeatedly told Johnson to get lost. Finally, one day, he did. For six months, Johnson mysteriously disappeared. No one knew what (25) happened to him.

When Johnson returned half a year later, he was suddenly a first-rate guitarist. He began drawing crowds everywhere he played. Johnson never revealed where he had been and what he had done in those six months that he was gone. People had difficulty understanding how (30) he had become so good in such a short time. Was it genius? Magic? Soon, rumors began circulating that he had made a deal with the devil. Legend has it that Johnson met the devil at midnight at a crossroads and sold his soul to the devil so he could play guitar.

Johnson recorded only 29 songs before his death in 1938, purport-(35) edly at the hands of a jealous husband. He was only 27 years old, yet he left an indelible mark on the music world. There are countless versions of "Walkin' Blues," and his song "Cross Road Blues" (later retitled "Crossroads") has been recorded by dozens of artists, with Cream's 1969 version of "Crossroads" being perhaps the best-known (40) Johnson remake. Again and again, contemporary artists return to Johnson, whose songs capture the very essence of the blues, transforming our pain and suffering with the healing magic of his guitar.

Passage 2

(1) There are more than 50 types of blues music, from the famous Chicago and Memphis blues to the less familiar juke joint and acoustic country blues. This rich variety comes as no surprise to those who recognize the blues as a fundamental American art form. (5) Indeed, in its resolution to name 2003 the Year of the Blues, the 107th U.S. Congress declared that the blues is "the most influential form of American roots music." In fact, the two most popular Amer-

ican musical forms—rock and roll and jazz—owe their genesis in large part (some would argue entirely) to the blues.

(10) The blues—a neologism attributed to the American writer Washington Irving (author of *The Legend of Sleepy Hollow*) in 1807—evolved from black American folk music. Its beginnings can be traced to songs sung in the fields and around slave quarters on Southern plantations, songs of pain and suffering, of injustice, of longing for a better life. A

(15) fundamental principle of the blues, however, is that the music be cathartic. Listening to the blues will drive the blues away; it is music that has the power to overcome sadness. Thus "the blues" is something of a misnomer, for the music is moving but not melancholy; it is, in fact, music born of hope, not despair.

(20) The blues began to take shape as a musical movement in the years after emancipation, around the turn of the century when blacks were technically free but still suffered from social and economic discrimination. Its poetic and musical forms were popularized by W.C. Handy just after the turn of the century. Handy, a classical guitarist

(25) who reportedly heard the blues for the first time in a Mississippi train station, was the first to officially compose and distribute blues music throughout the United States, although its popularity was chiefly among blacks in the South. The movement coalesced in the late 1920s and indeed became a national craze, with records by blues

(30) singers such as Bessie Smith selling in the millions.

The 1930s and 1940s saw a continued growth in the popularity of the blues as many blacks migrated north and the blues and jazz forms continued to develop, diversify, and influence each other. It was at this time that Son House, Willie Brown, and Robert Johnson

(35) played, while the next decade saw the emergence of the blues greats Muddy Waters, Willie Dixon, and Johnny Lee Hooker.

After rock and roll exploded on the music scene in the 1950s, many rock artists began covering blues songs, thus bringing the blues to a young white audience and giving it true national and international

(40) exposure. In the early 1960s, the Rolling Stones, Yardbirds, Cream, and others remade blues songs such as Robert Johnson's "Crossroads" and Big Joe Williams' "Baby Please Don't Go" to wide popularity. People all across America—black and white, young and old—listened to songs with lyrics that were intensely honest and personal, songs that told

(45) about any number of things that give us the blues: loneliness, betrayal, unrequited love, a run of bad luck, being out of work or away from home or broke or brokenhearted. It was a music perfectly suited for a nation on the brink of the Civil Rights movement—a kind of music that had the power to cross boundaries, to heal wounds, and to offer

(50) hope to a new generation of Americans.

1084. In Passage 1, the author's main goal is to
   a. solve the mystery of the genesis of Johnson's talent.
   b. provide a detailed description of Johnson's music and style.
   c. provide a brief overview of Johnson's life and influence.
   d. prove that Johnson should be recognized as the greatest blues musician who ever lived.
   e. explain how Johnson's music impacted the world of rock and roll.

1085. The information provided in the passage suggests that Johnson
   a. really did make a deal with the devil.
   b. was determined to become a great guitarist, whatever the cost.
   c. wasn't as talented as we have been led to believe.
   d. disappeared because he had a breakdown.
   e. owes his success to Son House and Willie Brown.

1086. The word *neologism* in Passage 2, line 10, means
   a. a new word or use of a word.
   b. a grassroots musical form.
   c. a fictional character or fictitious setting.
   d. the origin or source of something.
   e. the evolution of a person, place, or thing.

1087. In Passage 2, the sentence *People all across America—black and white, young and old—listened to songs with lyrics that were intensely honest and personal, songs that told about any number of things that give us the blues: loneliness, betrayal, unrequited love, a run of bad luck, being out of work or away from home or broke or brokenhearted* (lines 42–47), the author is
   a. defining blues music.
   b. identifying the origin of the blues.
   c. describing the lyrics of a famous blues song.
   d. explaining why blues remakes were so popular.
   e. making a connection between the blues and the Civil Rights movement.

1088. In the last paragraph of Passage 2 (lines 37–50), the author suggests that
   a. the blues should be recognized as a more important and complex musical form than rock and roll.
   b. the golden age of rock and roll owes much to the popularity of blues cover songs.
   c. music has always been a means for people to deal with intense emotions and difficulties.
   d. a shared interest in the blues may have helped blacks and whites better understand each other and ease racial tensions.
   e. the rock-and-roll versions of blues songs were better than the originals.

1089. Both authors would agree on all of the following points EXCEPT

a. listening to the blues is cathartic.

b. Robert Johnson is the best blues guitarist from the 1930s and 1940s.

c. the blues are an important part of American history.

d. "Crossroads" is one of the best-known blues songs.

e. blues music is deeply emotional.

1090. The passages differ in tone and style in that

a. Passage 1 is intended for a general audience while Passage 2 is intended for readers with a musical background.

b. Passage 1 is far more argumentative than Passage 2.

c. Passage 1 is often speculative while Passage 2 is factual and assertive.

d. Passage 1 is more formal than Passage 2, which is quite casual.

e. Passage 1 is straightforward while Passage 2 often digresses from the main point.

1091. Which of the following best describes the relationship between these two passages?

a. specific/general

b. argument/support

c. fiction/nonfiction

d. first/second

e. cause/effect

1092. Which of the following sentences from Passage 2 could most effectively be added to Passage 1?

a. *In fact, the two most popular American musical forms—rock and roll and jazz—owe their genesis in large part (some would argue entirely) to the blues. (lines 7–9)*

b. *A fundamental principle of the blues, however, is that the music be cathartic. (lines 14–16)*

c. *Thus "the blues" is something of a misnomer, for the music is moving but not melancholy; it is, in fact, music born of hope, not despair. (lines 17–19)*

d. *It was at this time that Son House, Willie Brown, and Robert Johnson played, while the next decade saw the emergence of the blues greats Muddy Waters, Willie Dixon, and Johnny Lee Hooker. (lines 33–36)*

e. *After rock and roll exploded on the music scene in the 1950s, many rock artists began covering blues songs, thus bringing the blues to a young white audience and giving it true national and international exposure. (lines 37–40)*

Questions 1093–1101 are based on the following passage.

This passage describes the formative experiences of the composer Wolfgang Amadeus Mozart.

(1)   The composer Wolfgang Amadeus Mozart's remarkable musical talent was apparent even before most children can sing a simple nursery rhyme. Wolfgang's older sister Maria Anna, whom the family called Nannerl, was learning the clavier, an early keyboard instrument,
(5)   when her three-year-old brother took an interest in playing. As Nannerl later recalled, Wolfgang "often spent much time at the clavier, picking out thirds, which he was always striking, and his pleasure showed that it sounded good." Their father Leopold, an assistant concertmaster at the Salzburg Court, recognized his children's unique
(10)   gifts and soon devoted himself to their musical education.

        Born in Salzburg, Austria, on January 27, 1756, Wolfgang was five when he learned his first musical composition—in less than half an hour. He quickly learned other pieces, and by age five had composed his first original work. Leopold settled on a plan to take Nannerl and
(15)   Wolfgang on tour to play before the European courts. Their first venture was to nearby Munich, where the children played for Maximillian III Joseph, elector of Bavaria. Leopold soon set his sights on the capital of the Hapsburg Empire, Vienna. On their way to Vienna, the family stopped in Linz, where Wolfgang gave his first public concert. By
(20)   this time, Wolfgang not only was a virtuoso harpsichord player but had also mastered the violin. The audience at Linz was stunned by the six-year-old, and word of his genius soon traveled to Vienna. In a much-anticipated concert, the children appeared at the Schönbrunn Palace on October 13, 1762. They utterly charmed the emperor and
(25)   empress.

        Following this success, Leopold was inundated with invitations for the children to play for a fee. Leopold seized the opportunity and booked as many concerts as possible at courts throughout Europe. After the children performed at the major court in a region, other
(30)   nobles competed to have the "miracle children of Salzburg" play private concerts in their homes. A concert could last three hours, and the children played at least two concerts a day. Today, Leopold might be considered the worst kind of stage parent, but at the time it was not uncommon for prodigies to make extensive concert tours. Even so, it
(35)   was an exhausting schedule for a child who was just past the age of needing an afternoon nap.

        Wolfgang fell ill on tour, and when the family returned to Salzburg on January 5, 1763, Wolfgang spent his first week at home in bed with acute rheumatoid arthritis. In June, Leopold accepted an invitation for
(40)   the children to play at Versailles, the lavish palace built by King Louis XIV of France. Wolfgang did not see his home in Salzburg for another

three years. When they weren't performing, the Mozart children were likely to be found bumping along the rutted roads in an unheated carriage. Wolfgang passed the long uncomfortable hours in the imaginary

(45) Kingdom of Back, of which he was king. He became so engrossed in the intricacies of his make-believe court that he persuaded a family servant to make a map showing all the cities, villages, and towns over which he reigned.

The king of Back was also busy composing. Wolfgang completed his

(50) first symphony at age nine and published his first sonatas that same year. Before the family returned to Salzburg, Wolfgang had played for, and amazed, the heads of the French and British royal families. He had also been plagued with numerous illnesses. Despite Wolfgang and Nannerl's arduous schedule and international renown, the family's

(55) finances were often strained. The pattern established in his childhood would be the template for the rest of his short life. Wolfgang Amadeus Mozart toiled constantly, was lauded for his genius, suffered from illness, and struggled financially, until he died at age 35. The remarkable child prodigy who more than fulfilled his potential was buried in an

(60) unmarked grave, as was the custom at the time, in a Vienna suburb.

1093. The primary purpose of the passage is to
a. illustrate the early career and formative experiences of a musical prodigy.
b. describe the classical music scene in the eighteenth century.
c. uncover the source of Wolfgang Amadeus Mozart's musical genius.
d. prove the importance of starting a musical instrument at an early age.
e. denounce Leopold Mozart for exploiting his children's talent.

1094. According to the passage, Wolfgang became interested in music because
a. his father thought it would be profitable.
b. he had a natural talent.
c. he saw his sister learning to play.
d. he came from a musical family.
e. he wanted to go on tour.

1095. What was the consequence of Wolfgang's first public appearance?
a. He charmed the emperor and empress of Hapsburg.
b. Leopold set his sights on Vienna.
c. Word of Wolfgang's genius spread to the capital.
d. He mastered the violin.
e. Invitations for the "miracle children" to play poured in.

1096. The author's attitude toward Leopold Mozart can best be characterized as
a. vehement condemnation.
b. mild disapproval.
c. glowing admiration.
d. incredulity.
e. veiled disgust.

1097. In line 40, the word *lavish* most nearly means
  a. wasteful.
  b. clean.
  c. extravagant.
  d. beautiful.
  e. glorious.

1098. The author uses the anecdote about Mozart's Kingdom of Back to illustrate
  a. Mozart's admiration for the composer Johann Sebastian Bach.
  b. the role imagination plays in musical composition.
  c. that Mozart was mentally unstable.
  d. that Mozart was an imaginative child.
  e. that Mozart's only friends were imaginary people and family servants.

1099. The author suggests that Mozart's adult life
  a. was ruined by repeated illness.
  b. was a disappointment after his brilliant childhood.
  c. was nothing but misery.
  d. ended in poverty and anonymity.
  e. followed the pattern of his childhood.

1100. In line 57, the word *lauded* most nearly means
  a. derided.
  b. praised.
  c. punished.
  d. compensated.
  e. coveted.

1101. Each of the following statements about Wolfgang Mozart is directly supported by the passage EXCEPT
  a. Mozart's father, Leopold, was instrumental in shaping his career.
  b. Wolfgang had a vivid imagination.
  c. Wolfgang's childhood was devoted to his musical career.
  d. Wolfgang's illnesses were the result of exhaustion.
  e. Maria Anna was a talented musician in her own right.

Questions 1102–1105 are based on the following passage.

This passage is adapted from an article by the environmental protection organization Greenpeace, regarding Finland's destruction of old-growth forests.

(1)   Time is running out for the old-growth forests of Finland. The vast majority of Finland's valuable old-growth forest is owned by the state and logged by the state-owned company Metsähallitus. Metsähallitus' logging practices include clear-cutting, logging in habitats of threat-
(5)   ened and vulnerable species, and logging in areas of special scenic or cultural value—including in areas that are critical for the reindeer herding of the indigenous Sami people.

Despite being involved in a dialogue process with two environmental organizations (the World Wildlife Fund and the Finnish
(10)   Association for Nature Conservation) to try to reach agreement regarding additional protection for old-growth forests, Metsähallitus is now logging sites that should be subject to negotiation.

In June 2003, Greenpeace and the Finnish Association for Nature Conservation (FANC) presented comprehensive maps of the old-
(15)   growth areas that should be subject to moratorium, pending discussion and additional protection, to all those involved in the dialogue process. Metsähallitus then announced a halt to new logging operations in these mapped areas. Sadly, the halt in logging was short lived. In August and September 2003 logging took place in at least six old-
(20)   growth forest areas in northern Finland.

It seems Metsähallitus wants to have its cake and eat it, too—friendly talks with environmental groups at the same time they keep logging critical habitat. To be blunt, their commitment to the dialogue process has proven untrustworthy. The new logging has been without con-
(25)   sensus from the dialogue process or proper consultation with the Sami reindeer herders. Now there's a risk the logging will expand to include other old-growth areas.

Greenpeace investigations have revealed a number of companies buying old-growth timber from Metsähallitus, but the great majority of
(30)   the timber goes to Finland's three international paper manufacturers, Stora Enso, UPM-Kymmene, and M-Real. Greenpeace recommends that companies ask for written guarantees that no material from any of the recently mapped old-growth areas is entering or will enter their supply chain, pending the switch to only timber that has been inde-
(35)   pendently certified to the standards of the Forest Stewardship Council in order to stop this risk to protected forests.

1102. According to the passage, which is NOT a logging practice engaged in by Metsähallitus?
   a. employing the clear-cutting method
   b. logging in the habitat of reindeer
   c. logging near scenic Finnish vistas
   d. logging within in the boundaries of the indigenous Sami
   e. logging in traditional Norwegian fjords

1103. As used in line 15, *moratorium* most nearly means
   a. an oral presentation.
   b. a bipartisan meeting.
   c. a cessation or stoppage.
   d. an increase in volume.
   e. an autopsy.

1104. The author's tone may best be classified as
   a. casual sarcasm.
   b. urgent warning.
   c. furtive anger.
   d. cool indifference.
   e. reckless panic.

1105. The primary purpose of this passage is to
   a. alert citizens that their forests may be in danger.
   b. expose the logging industry as bad for the environment.
   c. encourage consumers to boycott Finnish wood products.
   d. agitate for change in Finland's illicit logging practices.
   e. rally support for Greenpeace international causes.

Questions 1106–1110 are based on the following passage.

This passage describes the Great Barrier Reef and its inhabitants.

(1) Coral reefs are among the most diverse and productive ecosystems on Earth. Consisting of both living and nonliving components, this type of ecosystem is found in the warm, clear, shallow waters of tropical oceans worldwide. The functionality of the reefs ranges from provid-
(5) ing food and shelter to fish and other forms of marine life to protect-ing the shore from the ill effects of erosion and putrefaction. In fact, reefs actually create land in tropical areas by formulating islands and contributing mass to continental shorelines.
     Although coral looks like a plant, actually it is mainly comprised of
(10) the limestone skeleton of a tiny animal called a coral polyp. While corals are the main components of reef structures, they are not the only living participants. Coralline algae cement the myriad corals, and other miniature organisms such as tube worms and mollusks con-tribute skeletons to this dense and diverse structure. Together, these
(15) living creatures construct many different types of tropical reefs.

The Great Barrier Reef is the world's largest network of coral reefs, stretching 2,010 kilometers (1,250 miles) off Australia's northeastern coast. From microorganisms to whales, diverse life forms make their homes on the reef. Over 1,500 fish species, 4,000 mollusk species, 200

(20) bird species, 16 sea snake species, and six sea turtle species thrive in the reef's tropical waters. The reef is also a habitat for the endangered dugong (sea cow), moray eels, and sharks. In addition to teeming with animal life, the coral reef offers the viewer a spectrum of brilliant colors and intricate shapes, a virtual underwater garden.

(25) Although protected by the Australian government, the Great Barrier Reef faces environmental threats. Crown-of-thorns starfish feed on coral and can destroy large portions of reef. Pollution and rising water temperatures also threaten the delicate coral. But the most preventable of the hazards to the reef are tourists. Tourists have contributed to

(30) the destruction of the reef ecosystem by breaking off and removing pieces of coral to bring home as souvenirs. The government hopes that by informing tourists of the dangers of this seemingly harmless activity they will quash this creeping menace to the fragile reef.

1106. Which of the following statements does NOT describe the Great Barrier Reef?
- **a.** The Great Barrier reef is a colorful and active underwater structure.
- **b.** The Great Barrier Reef is a producer of small islands and landmasses.
- **c.** The Great Barrier Reef is threatened by vacationers.
- **d.** The Great Barrier Reef is the cause of much beachfront erosion in northeastern Australia.
- **e.** The Great Barrier Reef is home to endangered sea turtles.

1107. Based on information from the passage, 4,020 kilometers would be approximately how many miles?
- **a.** 402
- **b.** 1,250
- **c.** 1,500
- **d.** 2,010
- **e.** 2,500

1108. In line 6 of the passage, *putrefaction* most nearly means
- **a.** purification.
- **b.** decay.
- **c.** jettison.
- **d.** liquification.
- **e.** farming.

1109. The primary purpose of this passage is to
- **a.** inform the reader that coral reefs are a threatened, yet broadly functioning ecosystem.
- **b.** alert the reader to a premier vacation destination in the tropics.
- **c.** explain in detail how the Great Barrier Reef is constructed.
- **d.** recommend that tourists stop stealing coral off the Great Barrier Reef.
- **e.** dispel the argument that coral is a plant, not an animal.

1110. According to the passage, all of the following
are a threat to a coral reef EXCEPT
  a. tourists.
  b. pollution.
  c. erosion and putrefaction.
  d. rising water temperatures.
  e. crown-of-thorns starfish.

Questions 1111–1118 are based on the following two passages.

The following two passages tell of geometry's Divine Proportion, 1.618.

Passage 1

(1)   PHI, the Divine Proportion of 1.618, was described by the astronomer
Johannes Kepler as one of the "two great treasures of geometry." (The
other is the Pythagorean theorem.)

PHI is the ratio of any two sequential numbers in the Fibonacci
(5)   sequence. If you take the numbers 0 and 1, then create each subsequent number in the sequence by adding the previous two numbers,
you get the Fibonacci sequence. For example, 0, 1, 1, 2, 3, 5, 8, 13, 21,
34, 55, 89, 144. If you sum the squares of any series of Fibonacci numbers, they will equal the final Fibonacci number used in the series times
(10) the next Fibonacci number. This property results in the *Fibonacci
spiral* seen in everything from seashells to galaxies, and is written
mathematically as: $1^2 + 1^2 + 2^2 + 3^2 + 5^2 = 5 \times 8$.

Plants illustrate the Fibonacci series in the numbers of leaves, the
arrangement of leaves around the stem, and the positioning of leaves,
(15) sections, and seeds. A sunflower seed spiral illustrates this principle,
as the number of clockwise spirals is 55 and the number of counterclockwise spirals is 89; 89 divided by 55 = 1.618, the Divine Proportion. Pinecones and pineapples illustrate similar spirals of successive
Fibonacci numbers.

(20) PHI is also the ratio of five-sided symmetry. It can be proven by
using a basic geometrical figure, the pentagon. This five-sided figure
embodies PHI because PHI is the ratio of any diagonal to any side of
the pentagon—1.618.

Say you have a regular pentagon ABCDE with equal sides and equal
(25) angles. You may draw a diagonal as line AC connecting any two ver-
texes of the pentagon. You can then install a total of five such lines, and
they are all of equal length. Divide the length of a diagonal AC by the
length of a side AB, and you will have an accurate numerical value for
PHI—1.618. You can draw a second diagonal line, BD, inside the pen-
(30) tagon so that this new line crosses the first diagonal at point O. What

occurs is this: Each diagonal is divided into two parts, and each part is in PHI ratio (1.618) to the other, and to the whole diagonal—the PHI ratio recurs every time any diagonal is divided by another diagonal.

(35)   When you draw all five pentagon diagonals, they form a five-pointed star: a pentacle. Inside this star is a smaller, inverted pentagon. Each diagonal is crossed by two other diagonals, and each segment is in PHI ratio to the larger segments and to the whole. Also, the inverted inner pentagon is in PHI ratio to the initial outer pentagon. Thus, PHI is the ratio of five-sided symmetry.

(40)   Inscribe the pentacle star inside a pentagon and you have the pentagram, symbol of the ancient Greek School of Mathematics founded by Pythagoras—solid evidence that the ancient Mystery Schools knew about PHI and appreciated the Divine Proportion's multitude of uses to form our physical and biological worlds.

Passage 2

(1)   Langdon turned to face his sea of eager students. "Who can tell me what this number is?"

A long-legged math major in back raised his hand. "That's the number PHI." He pronounced it *fee*.

(5)   "Nice job, Stettner," Langdon said. "Everyone, meet PHI."

[. . .] "This number PHI," Langdon continued, "one-point-six-one-eight, is a very important number in art. [. . .] PHI is generally considered the most beautiful number in the universe."

[. . .] As Langdon loaded his slide projector, he explained that (10) the number PHI was derived from the Fibonacci sequence—a progression famous not only because the sum of adjacent terms equaled the next term, but because the *quotients* of adjacent terms possessed the astonishing property of approaching the number 1.618—PHI!

(15)   Despite PHI's seemingly mystical mathematical origins, Langdon explained, the truly mind-boggling aspect of PHI was its role as a fundamental building block in nature. Plants, animals, even human beings all possessed dimensional properties that adhered with eerie exactitude to the ratio of PHI to 1.

(20)   "PHI's ubiquity in nature," Langdon said, killing the lights, "clearly exceeds coincidence, and so the ancients assumed the number PHI must have been preordained by the Creator of the universe. Early scientists heralded one-point-six-one-eight as the *Divine Proportion*."

(25)   [. . .] Langdon advanced to the next slide—a close-up of a sunflower's seed head. "Sunflower seeds grow in opposing spirals. Can you guess the ratio of each rotation's diameter to the next?"

"PHI?" everyone said.

(30) "Bingo." Langdon began racing through slides now—spiraled pinecone petals, leaf arrangement on plant stalks, insect segmentation—all displaying astonishing obedience to the Divine Proportion.

"This is amazing!" someone cried out.

"Yeah," someone else said, "but what does it have to do with *art*?"

(35) [. . .] "Nobody understood better than Da Vinci the divine structure of the human body. [. . .] He was the first to show that the human body is literally made of building blocks whose proportional ratios *always* equal PHI."

Everyone in class gave him a dubious look.

(40) "Don't believe me?" [. . .] Try it. [. . .] Measure the distance from your shoulder to your fingertips, and then divide it by the distance from your elbow to your fingertips. PHI again. Another? Hip to floor divided by knee to floor. PHI again. Finger joints. Toes. Spinal divisions. PHI. PHI. PHI. My friends, each of you is a walking tribute to the Divine Proportion."

(45) [. . .] "In closing," Langdon said, walking to the chalkboard, "we return to *symbols*." He drew five intersecting lines that formed a five-pointed star. "This symbol is one of the most powerful images you will see this term. Formally known as a pentagram—or *pentacle*, as the ancients called it—the symbol is considered both divine and

(50) magical by many cultures. Can anyone tell me why that may be?"

Stettner, the math major, raised his hand. "Because if you draw a pentagram, the lines automatically divide themselves into segments according to the Divine Proportion."

Langdon gave the kid a proud nod. "Nice job. Yes, the ratios of line

(55) segments in a pentacle *all* equal PHI, making the symbol the *ultimate* expression of the Divine Proportion."

1111. The tone of Passage 2 may be described as
   a. fascinated discovery.
   b. blandly informative.
   c. passionate unfolding.
   d. droll and jaded.
   e. dry and scientific.

1112. According to both passages, which of the following are synonyms?
   a. pentagon and pentacle
   b. pinecones and sunflower seed spirals
   c. Divine Proportion and PHI
   d. Fibonacci sequence and Divine Proportion
   e. Fibonacci sequence and PHI

1113. In Passage 2, line 20, *ubiquity in nature* of PHI most nearly means its
   a. rareness in nature.
   b. accuracy in nature.
   c. commonality in nature.
   d. artificiality against nature.
   e. purity in an unnatural state.

1114. Both passages refer to the "mystical mathematical" side of PHI. Based on the two passages, which statement is NOT another aspect of PHI?
   a. PHI is a ratio found in nature.
   b. PHI is the area of a regular pentagon.
   c. PHI is one of nature's building blocks.
   d. PHI is derived from the Fibonacci sequence.
   e. PHI is a math formula.

1115. Which of the following techniques is used in Passage 1, lines 13–18 and Passage 2, lines 25–27?
   a. explanation of terms
   b. comparison of different arguments
   c. contrast of opposing views
   d. generalized statement
   e. illustration by example

1116. All of the following questions can be explicitly answered on the basis of the passage EXCEPT
   a. What is the ratio of the length of one's hip to floor divided by knee to floor?
   b. What is the precise mathematical ratio of PHI?
   c. What is the ratio of the distance from one's shoulder to fingertips divided by elbow to fingertips?
   d. What is the ratio of the distance from one's head to the floor divided by shoulder to the floor?
   e. What is the ratio of each sunflower seed spiral rotation's diameter to the next?

1117. According to both passages, the terms *ancient Mystery Schools* (Passage 1, lines 42–43), *early scientists* (Passage 2, line 24), and *ancients* (Passage 2, line 49) signify what about the Divine Proportion?
   a. Early scholars felt that the Divine Proportion was a magical number.
   b. Early scholars found no scientific basis for the Divine Proportion.
   c. Early mystery writers used the Divine Proportion.
   d. Early followers of Pythagoras favored the Pythagorean theorem over the Divine Proportion.
   e. Early followers of Kepler used the Divine Proportion in astronomy.

1118. Which of the following is NOT true of a regular pentagon?
   a. It is considered both divine and magical by many cultures.
   b. It is a geometric figure with five equal sides meeting at five equal angles.
   c. It is a geometric figure whereby PHI is the ratio of any diagonal to any side.
   d. If you draw an inverted inner pentagon inside a pentagon, it is in PHI ratio to the initial outer pentagon.
   e. A polygon having five sides and five interior angles is called a pentagon.

Questions 1119–1127 are based on the following passage.

The following passage describes the composition and nature of ivory.

(1)   Ivory skin, ivory teeth, Ivory Soap, Ivory Snow—we hear *ivory* used all the time to describe something fair and pure. But where does ivory come from, and what exactly is it? Is it natural or man-made? Is it a modifier meaning something pure and fair, or is it a specialized

(5)   and discrete substance?

Historically, the word *ivory* has been applied to the tusks of elephants. However, the chemical structure of the teeth and tusks of mammals is the same regardless of the species of origin, and the trade in certain teeth and tusks other than those of the elephant is well established and

(10)   widespread. Therefore, *ivory* can correctly be used to describe any mammalian tooth or tusk of commercial interest that is large enough to be carved or scrimshawed. Teeth and tusks have the same origins. Teeth are specialized structures adapted for food mastication. Tusks, which are extremely large teeth projecting beyond the lips, have

(15)   evolved from teeth and give certain species an evolutionary advantage that goes beyond chewing and breaking down food in digestible pieces. Furthermore, the tusk can be used to actually secure food through hunting, killing, and then breaking up large chunks of food into manageable bits.

(20)   The teeth of most mammals consist of a root as well as the tusk proper. Teeth and tusks have the same physical structures: pulp cavity, dentine, cementum, and enamel. The innermost area is the pulp cavity. The pulp cavity is an empty space within the tooth that conforms to the shape of the pulp. Odontoblastic cells line the pulp cavity and

(25)   are responsible for the production of dentine. Dentine, which is the main component of carved ivory objects, forms a layer of consistent thickness around the pulp cavity and comprises the bulk of the tooth and tusk. Dentine is a mineralized connective tissue with an organic matrix of collagenous proteins. The inorganic component of dentine

(30)   consists of dahllite. Dentine contains a microscopic structure called dentinal tubules which are micro-canals that radiate outward through the dentine from the pulp cavity to the exterior cementum border. These canals have different configurations in different ivories, and their diameter ranges between 0.8 and 2.2 microns. Their length is dic-

(35)   tated by the radius of the tusk. The three-dimensional configuration of the dentinal tubules is under genetic control and is therefore a characteristic unique to the order of the mammal.

Exterior to the dentine lies the cementum layer. Cementum forms a layer surrounding the dentine of tooth and tusk roots. Its main func-

(40)   tion is to adhere the tooth and tusk root to the mandibular and maxillary jawbones. Incremental lines are commonly seen in cementum.

Enamel, the hardest animal tissue, covers the surface of the tooth or tusk that receives the most wear, such as the tip or crown. Ameloblasts are responsible for the formation of enamel and are lost after (45) the enamel process is complete. Enamel exhibits a prismatic structure, with prisms that run perpendicular to the crown or tip. Enamel prism patterns can have both taxonomic and evolutionary significance.

Tooth and tusk ivory can be carved into an almost infinite variety of shapes and objects. A small sample of carved ivory objects includes (50) small statuary, netsukes, jewelry, flatware handles, furniture inlays, and piano keys. Additionally, warthog tusks, and teeth from sperm whales, killer whales, and hippopotamuses can also be scrimshawed or superficially carved while retaining their original shapes as morphologically recognizable objects.

(55) The identification of ivory and ivory substitutes is based on the physical and chemical class characteristics of these materials. A common approach to identification is to use the macroscopic and microscopic physical characteristics of ivory in combination with a simple chemical test using ultraviolet light.

1119. In line 5, what does the term *discrete* most nearly mean?
a. tactful
b. distinct
c. careful
d. prudent
e. judicious

1120. Which of the following titles is most appropriate for this passage?
a. Ivory: An Endangered Species
b. Elephants, Ivory, and Widespread Hunting in Africa
c. Ivory: Is It Organic or Inorganic?
d. Uncovering the Aspects of Natural Ivory
e. Scrimshaw: A Study of the Art of Ivory Carving

1121. The word *scrimshawed* in line 12 and line 53 most nearly means
a. floated.
b. waxed.
c. carved.
d. sunk.
e. buoyed.

1122. Which of the following choices is NOT part of the physical structure of teeth?
a. pulp cavity
b. dentine
c. cementum
d. tusk
e. enamel

1123. As used in line 13, what is the best synonym for *mastication*?

   a. digestion
   b. tasting
   c. biting
   d. chewing
   e. preparation

1124. Which sentence best describes *dentinal tubules*?

   a. Dentinal tubules are a layer surrounding the dentine of tooth and tusk roots.
   b. Dentinal tubules are micro-canals that radiate outward through the dentine from the pulp cavity to the exterior cementum border.
   c. Dentinal tubules are responsible for the formation of enamel and are lost after the enamel process is complete.
   d. Dentinal tubules cover the surface of the tooth or tusk that receives the most wear, such as the tip or crown.
   e. Dentinal tubules are extremely large teeth projecting beyond the lips that have evolved from teeth and give certain species an evolutionary advantage.

1125. According to the passage, all of the following are organic substances EXCEPT

   a. cementum.
   b. dentine.
   c. dahllite.
   d. ameloblasts.
   e. collagen.

1126. According to the passage, how can natural ivory be authenticated?

   a. by ultraviolet light
   b. by gamma rays
   c. by physical observation
   d. by osmosis
   e. by scrimshaw

1127. According to the passage, which statement is NOT true of enamel?

   a. It is an organic substance.
   b. It is the hardest of animal tissues.
   c. It should never be exposed to ultraviolet light.
   d. It structure is prismatic.
   e. It is formed with the aid of ameloblasts.

Questions 1128–1136 are based on the following passage.

This passage is about the process by which scientists prove theories, the scientific method.

(1)   The scientific method usually refers to either a series or a collection of processes that are considered characteristic of scientific investigation and of the acquisition of new scientific knowledge.
         The essential elements of the scientific method are:

(5)   *Observe:* Observe or read about a phenomenon.
         Hypothesize: Wonder about your observations, and invent a hypothesis, or a guess, that could explain the phenomenon or set of facts that you have observed.
         Test: Conduct tests to try out your hypothesis.
(10)   *Predict:* Use the logical consequences of your hypothesis to predict observations of new phenomena or results of new measurements.
         Experiment: Perform experiments to test the accuracy of these predictions.
(15)   *Conclude:* Accept or refute your hypothesis.
         Evaluate: Search for other possible explanations of the result until you can show with confidence that your guess was indeed the explanation.
         Formulate new hypothesis: as required.

(20)   This idealized process is often misinterpreted as applying to scientists individually rather than to the scientific enterprise as a whole. Science is a social activity, and one scientist's theory or proposal cannot become accepted unless it has been published, peer reviewed, criticized, and finally accepted by the scientific community.

(25)   **Observation**
         The scientific method begins with observation. Observation often demands careful *measurement*. It also requires the establishment of an *operational definition* of measurements and other concepts before the experiment begins.

(30)   **Hypothesis**
         To explain the observation, scientists use whatever they can (their own creativity, ideas from other fields, or even systematic guessing) to come up with possible explanations for the phenomenon under study. Deductive reasoning is the way in which predictions are used
(35)   to test a hypothesis.

Testing

In the twentieth century, philosopher Karl Popper introduced the idea that a hypothesis must be falsifiable; that is, it must be capable of being demonstrated wrong. A hypothesis must make specific predictions;
(40) these predictions can be tested with concrete measurements to support or refute the hypothesis. For instance, Albert Einstein's theory of general relativity makes a few specific predictions about the structure of space and flow of time, such as the prediction that light bends in a strong gravitational field, and the amount of bending depends in a pre-
(45) cise way on the strength of the gravitational field. Observations made of a 1919 solar eclipse supported this hypothesis against other possible hypotheses, such as Sir Isaac Newton's theory of gravity, which did not make such a prediction. British astronomers used the eclipse to prove Einstein's theory, and therefore eventually replaced Newton's
(50) theory.

Verification

Probably the most important aspect of scientific reasoning is verification. Verification is the process of determining whether the hypothesis is in accord with empirical evidence, and whether it will
(55) continue to be in accord with a more generally expanded body of evidence. Ideally, the experiments performed should be fully described so that anyone can reproduce them, and many scientists should independently verify every hypothesis. Results that can be obtained from experiments performed by many are termed *reproducible* and are given
(60) much greater weight in evaluating hypotheses than nonreproducible results.

Evaluation

Falsificationism argues that any hypothesis, no matter how respected or time-honored, must be discarded once it is contradicted by new
(65) reliable evidence. This is, of course, an oversimplification, since individual scientists inevitably hold on to their pet theories long after contrary evidence has been found. This is not always a bad thing. Any theory can be made to correspond to the facts, simply by making a few adjustments—called "auxiliary hypothesis"—so as to bring it into cor-
(70) respondence with the accepted observations. The choice of when to reject one theory and accept another is inevitably up to the individual scientist, rather than some methodical law.

Hence *all* scientific knowledge is always in a state of flux, for at any time new evidence could be presented that contradicts long-held
(75) hypotheses.

The experiments that reject a hypothesis should be performed by many different scientists to guard against bias, mistake, misunderstand-

(80) ing, and fraud. Scientific journals use a process of peer review, in which scientists submit their results to a panel of fellow scientists (who may or may not know the identity of the writer) for evaluation. Peer review may well have turned up problems and led to a closer examination of experimental evidence for many scientists. Much embarrassment, and wasted effort worldwide, has been avoided by objective peer review, in addition to continuing the use and proving the necessity of the scientific method.

1128. Which step in the process of scientific method do lines 63–72 speak of?
a. operational definition
b. verification
c. evaluation
d. phenomenon
e. hypothesizing

1129. What is the tone of this passage?
a. enigmatic
b. apathetic
c. abstruse
d. instructive
e. revealing

1130. In line 63, the word *falsificationism* most nearly means
a. validation.
b. qualification.
c. confirmation.
d. facilitation.
e. refutation.

1131. Which statement is NOT true?
a. Reproducible results can be obtained by experiments performed by a variety of scientists.
b. An auxiliary hypothesis can be made to correspond to the facts.
c. Einstein's theory of relativity makes space and time predictions.
d. Peer review is usually not a valuable tool for scientists.
e. Experiments are a necessary element in the scientific method.

1132. According to the passage, which is true of a hypothesis?
a. It is not a necessary process in the scientific method.
b. It cannot be discarded by a competing theory.
c. It is a guess.
d. It can make a broad and general prediction.
e. It is always considered auxiliary.

1133. What is the best title for this passage?
   a. The Theory of Relativity
   b. The Scientific Method: A Step-by-Step Process
   c. The Two Stages of Proving Theories
   d. How to Form a Hypotheses
   e. Evaluating Data with the Scientific Method

1134. What is meant by the term *operational definition* in line 28 of the passage?
   a. scientific law
   b. theory
   c. clear and practical definition
   d. scientific method
   e. hypothesis

1135. What do lines 36–50 of the passage indicate?
   a. The theory of general relativity is a hypothesis.
   b. Karl Popper proved the theory of relativity to be incorrect.
   c. Einstein was the father of the scientific method.
   d. Space and the flow of time theories are still in a state of flux.
   e. Sir Isaac Newton's theory of gravity disproved Einstein's theory.

1136. Which is NOT a step used in the process of scientific method?
   a. observation
   b. simplification
   c. evaluation
   d. verification
   e. hypothesis

Questions 1137–1141 are based on the following passage.

The following passage describes the Native American games that were predecessors to the modern sport of lacrosse.

(1)　　The roots of the modern-day sport of lacrosse are found in tribal stick-and-ball games developed and played by many native North American tribes dating back as early as the fifteenth century. The Native American names for these games reflected the bellicose nature of those early

(5)　　contests, many of which went far beyond friendly recreational competition. For example, the Algonquin called their game *baggattaway*, which meant "they bump hips." The Cherokee Nation and the Six Tribes of the Iroquois called their sport *tewaarathon*, which translated into "little brother of war." Rules and style of play differed from

(10)　　tribe to tribe and games could be played by as few as 15 to as many as 1,000 men and women at a time. These matches could last for three days, beginning at dawn each day and ending at sunset. The goals could be specific trees or rocks, and were a few hundred yards to a few miles apart. Despite these differences, the sole object of every game

(15) was the same: to score goals by any means necessary. Serious injuries caused by blows from the heavy wooden sticks used in the games were not uncommon, and often expected. Not surprisingly, the Native Americans considered these precursors to today's lacrosse excellent battle preparation for young warriors, and games were often used to

(20) settle disputes between tribes without resorting to full-blown warfare.

For the Six Tribes of the Iroquois, certain matches of *tewaarathon* held religious significance, as well. One of the most important gods the Iroquois worshipped was the Creator, Deganawidah. In Iroquois legend, the Creator united the Six Tribes into the one nation.

(25) *Tewaarathon* was played to please the Creator, and the competition was viewed as a re-creation of the Iroquois Creation Story, where supernatural forces of good and evil battled each other in an epic struggle.

1137. In line 4, *bellicose* most closely means
a. beautiful.
b. warlike.
c. peaceful.
d. family minded.
e. clumsy.

1138. The passage describes the early versions of lacrosse as
a. strictly regulated competitions.
b. intense games played against the Pilgrims.
c. serious and meaningful matches.
d. played only by the best athletes selected from each tribe.
e. friendly exhibitions.

1139. Which of the following titles would be the most appropriate for this passage?
a. Little Brother of War
b. Lacrosse: America's Most Violent Sport
c. The Origins of the Modern Lacrosse Stick
d. Deganawidah and the Six Tribes
e. Hockey: The Little Brother of Lacrosse

1140. In line 15, the author's use of the phrase *by any means necessary* emphasizes the
a. unpredictable nature of the game.
b. mild nature of the game.
c. violent nature of the game.
d. fact that both women and men participated in the games.
e. importance of scoring goals.

1141. The author's main purpose for writing this passage is to
a. illustrate the differences between the early games and today's lacrosse.
b. condemn the violent tactics often used by the Native American players.
c. show how ancient games influenced many games played today.
d. teach the reader about the Iroquois Creation Story.
e. describe the importance of these games in Native American culture.

Questions 1142–1150 are based on the following passage.

This passage details the life and career of Althea Gibson, an African-American pioneer in the sport of tennis.

(1)   Today, watching Venus and Serena Williams dominate the sport of women's tennis with their talent and flair, it is hard to imagine that just over 50 years ago African-American tennis players were barred from competing on the grandest stages of their sport. Jackie Robin-
(5)   son broke the color barrier in Major League Baseball in 1947, but the walls that kept African-Americans from playing professional sports did not come tumbling down overnight. Almost four years passed after Jackie Robinson's major league debut before a female African-American made a similar impact upon the sport of women's tennis.
(10)   That woman's name was Althea Gibson.

          Althea Gibson was born on a cotton farm on August 25, 1927, in Silver, South Carolina. The early stages of the Great Depression forced her sharecropper father to move the family from the bucolic Silver to the urban bustle of New York City when she was just three years old. As a
(15)   child growing up in the Harlem section of Manhattan, Althea found she had an affinity for athletics. Basketball and paddle tennis were her favorite sports, and she excelled at both. In fact, her talent at paddle tennis was so remarkable that in 1939 she won her age group at the New York City paddle tennis championships. Shortly after, a very good friend
(20)   of Althea's suggested that she try lawn tennis. She showed an incredible aptitude for the sport, and her play caught the attention of members of the predominantly African-American Harlem Cosmopolitan Tennis Club, who helped her raise money to become a member. At the age of 14, Althea took her first real tennis lesson at the club under the tutelage
(25)   of one-armed tennis coach Fred Johnson. She would never look back.

          A year later, in 1942, the major governing body for African-American tennis tournaments—the American Tennis Association (ATA)—sponsored the New York Girls Singles Championship at Althea's club. With her aggressive and dominating style of play, she won the title eas-
(30)   ily. It was her first of what was to be many victories, on and off the court.

          Althea dropped out of high school shortly after winning the New York Girls Singles Championship. She found the classes boring and wanted to concentrate on tennis. Her decision raised many eyebrows among members of the ATA, who had hoped that she would become
(35)   one of the sport's new stars. She was encouraged to leave New York City and move to Wilmington, NC, to live with the family of Hubert Eaton, a wealthy doctor who was active in the African-American tennis community. Dr. Eaton welcomed Althea into his family. He not only offered her guidance with her tennis career, but he also convinced her to finish
(40)   the remaining three years of high school. While living with the Eaton family in Wilmington, she would travel around the country to compete

in ATA tournaments. By the time she graduated in 1949, Althea had already won the first two of what would be ten consecutive ATA national titles. She was regarded by many as one of the most impressive young
(45) talents in the female game, but because of segregation she was not permitted to practice on any of the public courts in Wilmington. She was also yet to be invited to any of the major segregated tournaments.

By early 1950 Althea was making some headway. She was the first African-American to play in the national indoor tournament, where she
(50) finished second. Althea believed her two national championships and her strong showing at the indoor tournament were proof that she was one of female tennis's elite players. She and the ATA tried to lobby the United States Lawn Tennis Association (USLTA) for an invitation to the 1950 U.S. Nationals, but despite the ATA's efforts and Althea's obvious
(55) merit, the USLTA failed to extend her an invitation.

Not every member of the USLTA was pleased with the organization's decision. Former U.S. National and Wimbledon champion Alice Marble wrote a scathing editorial in the July 1950 issue of *American Lawn Tennis* magazine criticizing the USLTA's segregationist stance.
(60) Ms. Marble wrote, "The entrance of [African-Americans] into national tennis is as inevitable as it has proven in baseball, in football, or in boxing; there is no denying so much talent. . . . If Althea Gibson represents a challenge to the present crop of players, then it's only fair that they meet this challenge on the courts." The editorial caused a national
(65) uproar that quickly led the USLTA to finally extend Althea an invitation to play in the 1950 U.S. Nationals tournament. This invitation would open many doors for Althea, and the following year she was the first African-American to compete at Wimbledon.

It took a few years for Althea to adjust to the world-class level of play.
(70) She won her first major tournament in 1956 and would dominate the sport for the next five years, winning six doubles titles and a total of 11 Grand Slam events, including the U.S. Nationals and Wimbledon twice. Yet even at the height of her career as an international tennis champ, Althea was forced to endure discrimination. She was often refused hotel
(75) rooms and reservations at restaurants simply because of her skin color.

Althea once said that her extraordinary success was the product of being "game enough to take a lot of punishment along the way." The pioneering example set by Althea Gibson paved the way for future generations of African-American tennis players, and proved that beyond her
(80) tennis glory she was a true champion of the human spirit.

1142. What is the main purpose of the passage?

   a. to glimpse a piece of the past

   b. to glorify athletes

   c. to disparage segregation

   d. to teach the history of tennis

   e. to tell the story of Althea Gibson

1143. The word *bucolic* in line 13 most nearly means

   a. rural.

   b. urban.

   c. sickly.

   d. depressing.

   e. wealthy.

1144. All of the following questions can be answered based on information from the passage EXCEPT

   a. what factors influenced the USLTA to invite Althea Gibson to the U.S. Nationals?

   b. did Althea play in another ATA tournament after she was invited to the U.S. Nationals?

   c. why did Althea go to live with Dr. Eaton?

   d. to what specific types of discrimination was Althea subjected?

   e. how many times did Althea compete at Wimbledon?

1145. Which of the following best describes the USLTA's change of heart regarding Althea's invitation?

   a. buckling under the pressure of public opinion

   b. a calculated strike against segregation

   c. a sudden recognition of Althea's abilities

   d. a bold marketing strategy

   e. a desire to diversify the women's game

1146. The author uses Althea's quote about being *game enough* in line 77 to illustrate that

   a. Althea's career was plagued with injuries.

   b. the sport of tennis is more grueling than people realize.

   c. Althea believed the discrimination she faced served only to make her a stronger competitor.

   d. Althea was often fined for yelling at the referee.

   e. Althea believed talent was more important than mental toughness.

1147. Althea's achievements are best described as

   a. remarkable displays of talent and athleticism.

   b. groundbreaking triumphs in the face of adversity.

   c. important events that led to immediate civil rights reform.

   d. one woman's fight against the world.

   e. historically insignificant.

1148. Which statement best summarizes Alice Marble's quote in lines 60–64?

   a. Baseball, football, and boxing are more entertaining than tennis.

   b. Talent should dictate who could be a champion at a USLTA tournament, not race.

   c. There are players in the U.S. Nationals who do not deserve to be there.

   d. The USLTA should do away with invitations and make the tournament open to anybody.

   e. The ATA and USTLA should merge for the benefit of the sport.

1149. Why did Althea's friend suggest that she try lawn tennis?

    a. Lawn tennis is a more competitive game than paddle tennis.

    b. The friend preferred playing lawn tennis.

    c. There was more money to be made playing lawn tennis than paddle tennis.

    d. The friend thought Althea might enjoy playing lawn tennis, and excel at it.

    e. The friend was looking for a tennis partner.

1150. All of the following statements are supported by the passage EXCEPT

    a. Alice Marble was a white tennis player.

    b. Dr. Eaton's guidance helped Althea's career.

    c. Althea won the New York Girls Singles Championship when she 15.

    d. the public tennis courts in Wilmington were segregated.

    e. Althea Gibson won more Grand Slam titles than any other female tennis player.

Questions 1151–1159 are based on the following passage.

The following passage chronicles the 1919 Chicago White Sox baseball scandal.

(1) Professional baseball suffered during the two years the United States was involved in World War I. Many Americans who were preoccupied with the seriousness of the war raging overseas had little concern for the trivialities of a baseball game. After the war ended in 1918, many

(5) Americans wanted to put those dark years behind them and get back to the normal activities of a peaceful life. One of those activities was watching baseball. In the summer of 1918, ballparks that just one year earlier had been practically empty were now filled daily with the sights and sounds of America's favorite pastime. That year, the

(10) Cleveland Indians and New York Yankees were two of the strongest teams in baseball's American League, but one team stood head and shoulders above the rest: the Chicago White Sox.

    The Chicago White Sox, called the White Stockings until 1902, were owned by an ex-ballplayer named Charles Comiskey. Between

(15) the years 1900 and 1915 the White Sox had won the World Series only once, and Comiskey was determined to change that. In 1915, he purchased the contracts of three of the most promising stars in the league: outfielders "Shoeless" Joe Jackson and "Happy" Oscar Felsch, and second baseman Eddie Collins. Comiskey had to wait only two years for

(20) his plan to come to fruition; the 1917 White Sox, playing in a park named for their owner, won the World Series. Two years later they had the best record in all of baseball and were again on their way to the Series.

    Baseball players' salaries in that era were much different than the exorbitant paychecks of today's professional athletes. Often, ballplayers

(25) would have second careers in the off-season because of their mediocre

pay. To make matters worse, war-torn 1918 was such a horrible year for baseball attendance that many owners cut player salaries for the following season. However, it is said that in all of baseball there was no owner as parsimonious as Charles Comiskey. In 1917 he reportedly promised

(30)   every player on the White Sox a bonus if they won the American League Championship. After winning the championship, they returned to the clubhouse to receive their bonus—a bottle of inexpensive champagne. Unlike other owners, Comiskey also required the players to pay for the cleaning of their uniforms. The Sox had the best record in baseball, but

(35)   they were the worst paid, were the most discontented, and wore the dirtiest uniforms.

Comiskey's frugality did not sit well with the players. They were most upset with the fact that he did not raise salaries back to their 1918 levels, even though the ballpark attendance figures for 1919

(40)   were higher than any previous year. One player, Eddie Ciccotte, felt especially ill-treated by Comiskey. The owner promised the pitcher a bonus of $10,000 if he won 30 games, but after Ciccotte won his 29th game he was benched by Comiskey for the rest of the season.

(45)   Gamblers were such a common sight around the Chicago ballpark that Charles Comiskey had signs proclaiming "No Betting Allowed in This Park" posted conspicuously in the stands. The money with which these gamblers tempted the players was hard to refuse, and it was rumored that to supplement their income some of the lower-paid

(50)   athletes would offer inside tips to the bettors. But the gamblers' mingling with ballplayers wasn't solely confined to the White Sox. In 1920, allegations involving gambling among Chicago Cubs players brought to light a scandal that would shock Chicago and the rest of America: Eight members of the White Sox had thrown the 1919 World Series.

(55)   The exact facts regarding the scandal will never be known, but the most accepted theory is that just prior to the World Series, White Sox player Chick Gandil had approached a gambler by the name of Joseph Sullivan with a proposal that for $100,000 Gandil would make sure the Sox lost the Series. Gandil needed to recruit other players for the

(60)   plan to work. It was not hard for him to do—there were many underpaid players on the White Sox who were dissatisfied with the way Comiskey operated the team. Ultimately, the seven other players who allegedly were involved in the scheme were Eddie Ciccotte, Happy Felsch, Joe Jackson, Fred McMullin, Charles "Swede" Risberg, Buck

(65)   Weaver, and Claude Williams.

They were successful. The Chicago White Sox, heavily favored to beat an inferior Cincinnati Reds team, lost the nine-game World Series in eight games, due in most part to the inferior play of the eight conspiring players. When the scandal made headlines the following year,

(70) the press began to refer to them as the Black Sox, and the ignominious label would be used to describe them forever.

  When the eight players stood before an Illinois grand jury, it was determined that that there was not enough substantial evidence for any convictions, and the players were all eventually acquitted of any

(75) criminal wrongdoing. Interestingly enough, Charles Comiskey paid for the players' high-priced defense lawyers. Unfortunately for Comiskey, there was to be no similar reprieve from Major League Baseball: Every single one of the accused players was banned from the game for life. Comiskey's once-mighty team was decimated by the loss

(80) of its most talented players, and the 1921 White Sox finished the season in seventh place.

1151. According to the passage, who was the supposed ringleader of the Black Sox scandal?

 a. Charles Comiskey

 b. "Shoeless" Joe Jackson

 c. Eddie Ciccotte

 d. Eddie Collins

 e. Chick Gandil

1152. In line 29, the word *parsimonious* most nearly means

 a. generous.

 b. stingy.

 c. powerful.

 d. friendly.

 e. jovial.

1153. According to facts from the passage, what was the name of the White Sox ballpark?

 a. Chicago Park

 b. Comiskey Park

 c. Sullivan Stadium

 d. White Sox Park

 e. Sox Field

1154. In line 54, the word *thrown* refers to

 a. losing intentionally.

 b. pitching a baseball.

 c. projecting upon.

 d. dashing upon.

 e. abandoning something.

1155. According to the passage, how many World Series did the White Sox win between 1900 and 1919?

 a. none

 b. one

 c. two

 d. three

 e. four

1156. All of the following questions can be answered based on information from the passage EXCEPT

   a. who was the second baseman for the 1915 White Sox?

   b. did the White Sox play in the American League or the National League?

   c. what was the original name of the White Sox?

   d. how many games did Eddie Ciccotte pitch in 1918?

   e. why did many baseball owners lower player salaries for the 1919 season?

1157. In line 70, word *ignominious* most nearly means

   a. uneducated.

   b. dishonorable.

   c. exalted.

   d. worthy.

   e. unentertaining.

1158. The last paragraph of the passage suggests that Charles Comiskey

   a. thought the team was better off without the eight players.

   b. hoped all eight players would be convicted and sent to jail.

   c. wanted the players involved in the scandal to return to the team.

   d. was contemplating retirement.

   e. had a plan to get the White Sox back to the World Series.

1159. The passage as a whole suggests that

   a. The White Sox probably fixed the 1917 World Series, too.

   b. Charles Comiskey may have been partly to blame for his players' actions.

   c. ballplayers betting on games was a highly unusual occurrence.

   d. baseball never recovered after World War I.

   e. Charles Comiskey often bet against his own team.

Questions 1160–1170 are based on the following passages.

The following passages detail two very different perspectives of life aboard a ship in the age of sail. The first passage describes an English pleasure yacht in the early 1800s. The second passage recounts a young boy's impressions of the first time he set sail in a merchant vessel.

Passage 1

(1) Reader, have you ever been at Plymouth? If you have, your eye must have dwelt with ecstasy upon the beautiful property of the Earl of Mount Edgcumbe: if you have not been at Plymouth, the sooner that you go there the better. You will see ships building and ships in ordi-
(5) nary; and ships repairing and ships fitting; and hulks and convict ships, and the guard-ship; ships ready to sail and ships under sail; besides lighters, men-of-war's boats, dockyard-boats, bum-boats, and shore-boats. In short, there is a great deal to see at Plymouth besides the sea itself: but what I particularly wish now is, that you will stand at the bat-
(10) tery of Mount Edgcumbe and look into Barn Pool below you, and there you will see, lying at single anchor, a cutter; and you may also see, by her pendant and ensign, that she is a yacht.

You observe that this yacht is cutter-rigged, and that she sits grace-fully on the smooth water. She is just heaving up her anchor; her fore-
(15) sail is loose, all ready to cast her—in a few minutes she will be under way. You see that there are ladies sitting at the taffrail; and there are five haunches of venison hanging over the stern. Of all amusements, give me yachting. But we must go on board. The deck, you observe, is of narrow deal planks as white as snow; the guns are of polished brass;
(20) the bitts and binnacles of mahogany: she is painted with taste; and all the moldings are gilded. There is nothing wanting; and yet how clear and unencumbered are her decks! Let us go below.

There is the ladies' cabin: can anything be more tasteful or elegant? Is it not luxurious? And, although so small, does not its very confined
(25) space astonish you, when you view so many comforts so beautifully arranged? This is the dining-room, and where the gentlemen repair. And just peep into their state-rooms and bed-places. Here is the stew-ard's room and the buffet: the steward is squeezing lemons for the punch, and there is the champagne in ice; and by the side of the pail
(30) the long-corks are ranged up, all ready. Now, let us go forwards: here are, the men's berths, not confined as in a man-of-war. No! Luxury starts from abaft, and is not wholly lost, even at the fore-peak. This is the kitchen; is it not admirably arranged? And how delightful are the fumes of the turtle-soup! At sea we do meet with rough weather at
(35) times; but, for roughing it out, give me a *yacht*.

Passage 2

(1) My very first sea voyage was in a small merchant vessel out of New York called the *Alba*. I was only 12 years old at the time, and full of

dreams of boundless adventure upon the high seas. I was to serve as the ship's boy. I was given the post by my Uncle Joseph, the weath-
(5)   ered old captain of the *Alba* who uttered few words, choosing to speak more with his menacing gaze than with his mouth. The moment I stepped upon the bustling deck my Uncle Joseph set me straight about shipboard life. There were to be no special privileges afforded to me because of our relations. I was to live and mess in the 'tween
(10) decks with the other seamen, and because I was his nephew, I would probably have to work twice as hard as the others to prove my worth. From that point on I was to refer to my uncle as "Sir" or "Captain," and only speak to him when he addressed me. He then told me a bit about the *Alba*. I learned that she was a cutter, and all cutters were fore-and-
(15) aft rigged, and possessed only a single mast. After my brief lesson, he then sent me below deck to get myself situated.

What I found when I dismounted the ladder below was an entirely different world than the orderly brightness of the top deck. Here was a stuffy and dimly lit space barely tall enough for me to stand up
(20) straight in. It was the middle of July, and the heat was oppressive. There seemed to be no air at all, there certainly were no windows, and the stench that rose up from the bilge was so pungent it made me gag. From the shadows, a pair of eyes materialized. They belonged to a grimy boy no older than me.

(25) "Hello mate, you must be the new lubber just shipped aboard. I'm Nigel. Follow me, we're just in time for dinner."

My new friend led me into the tiny dining room where the crew messed. The men ate shoulder to shoulder on wooden tables bolted to the deck. The horrific smell of so many men crammed together was
(30) overpowering. We received our food from the ship's cook, a portly man in a filthy apron who, with the dirtiest hands I'd ever seen, ladled us out a sort of stew. We found two open spots at a mess table and sat down to eat. The stew was lukewarm and the mysterious meat in it was so tough I could barely chew it. I managed to swallow a few spoonfuls
(35) and pushed my dish aside.

With a smile that was graveyard of yellow sincerity, Nigel pushed the dish back to me and said, "I'd get used to the grub, mate. It ain't so bad. Besides, this is the freshest it'll be on the voyage."

After dinner, Nigel showed me our berth. It was a tiny lightless cub-
(40) byhole near the bow of the boat that was barely six feet long and only five feet high. There was a small area where I could stow my clothes, and at night we would string up our hammocks side by side with two other boys, both of whom were on duty at the moment.

That night when we were under way, the boat ran into a vicious
(45) Atlantic storm. The waves tossed the *Alba* around like it was a tiny raft. The ship made such noises; I was afraid it would simply break apart at

any moment. The seawater that crashed upon the deck leaked through the planks and dripped upon my head. It would have bothered me if I were not already horribly seasick. As I lay there miserably rocking

(50)   back and forth in my damp hammock, I asked myself, "What have I gotten myself into?"

1160. According to both passages, it is not uncommon for ships to
   a. meet rough seas.
   b. run out of fresh drinking water.
   c. not return home for quite a while.
   d. leak in heavy weather.
   e. have children onboard.

1161. In the last sentence of Passage 2, the narrator suggests that he
   a. may never recover from the seasickness.
   b. does not like Nigel.
   c. made a mistake taking the voyage aboard the *Alba*.
   d. should have eaten the stew.
   e. should have stayed in school.

1162. Which statement best summarizes the narrator's description of Plymouth in lines 3–8?
   a. The port at Plymouth is full of rowdy sailors.
   b. Plymouth is a dreary and overcrowded place.
   c. Plymouth is a deserted and overindustrialized area.
   d. There are many interest sights to behold at Plymouth.
   e. The British Royal Navy anchors at Plymouth.

1163. What do the yacht in Passage 1 and the *Alba* in Passage 2 have in common?
   a. They were both built in England.
   b. They both have only a single mast.
   c. They are both made of iron.
   d. They both have lifeboats.
   e. They are both fast.

1164. How do the yacht in Passage 1 and the *Alba* in Passage 2 differ?
   a. The yacht does not carry cargo.
   b. The yacht is much bigger than the *Alba*.
   c. There are no passengers aboard the *Alba*, only crew.
   d. The yacht is much more luxurious than the *Alba*.
   e. The yacht is much faster than the *Alba*.

1165. Why does the captain in Passage 2 (lines 13–14) demand that his nephew call him "Sir" or "Captain"?
   a. The captain wanted his nephew to understand who was in charge.
   b. The captain did not want any member of the crew to know the narrator was his nephew.
   c. The captain was afraid that if he showed affection to his nephew, he would lose his authority over the crew.
   d. The captain was not really the narrator's uncle.
   e. It was important that the crew understood that the boy was no more privileged than anyone else aboard.

1166. In Passage 1, line 26, the use of the word *repair* most nearly means

a. go.

b. fix things.

c. sit in pairs.

d. get dressed.

e. exercise.

1167. The narrator of Passage 1 most probably

a. is a seasoned sea captain.

b. is very wealthy.

c. is an experienced yachtsman.

d. suffers from seasickness.

e. was in the Royal Navy.

1168. In Passage 2, line 36, the narrator describes Nigel's smile as *a graveyard of yellow sincerity*. What figure of speech is the narrator employing?

a. onomatopoeia

b. simile

c. personification

d. alliteration

e. metaphor

1169. Together, these two passages illustrate the idea that

a. the reality of two seemingly similar situations can often be extremely different.

b. boating is a very dangerous pastime.

c. dreams sometimes fall very short of reality.

d. Plymouth is much nicer than New York.

e. hard work pays off in the end.

1170. The word *berth*, found in Passage 1, line 31, and Passage 2, line 39, most nearly means

a. a sailor's hometown.

b. the sleeping quarters aboard a boat.

c. the kitchen aboard a boat.

d. the bathroom aboard a boat.

e. the lower deck of a boat.

Questions 1171–1174 are based on the following passage.

The following passage examines the possibility that early humans used toothpicks.

(1)   Could good dental hygiene be man's earliest custom? The findings of paleontologist Leslea Hlusko suggest that 1.8 million years ago early hominids used grass stalks to clean their teeth. Many ancient hominid teeth unearthed in archaeological digs have curved grooves near the

(5)   gumline. Hlusko posited that these grooves were evidence of teeth cleaning by early man. However, critics pointed out that even though the use of toothpicks is still a common practice among modern man, similar grooves are not found on modern teeth.

      Hlusko, convinced that she was on the right track, experimented

(10)   with grass stalks to see if they might have been the cause of the grooves. Unlike the wood used for modern toothpicks, grass contains

(15) hard silica particles that are more abrasive than the soft fibers found in wood. A stalk of grass is also about the same width as the marks found on the ancient teeth. To prove her theory Dr. Hlusko took a baboon tooth and patiently rubbed a grass stalk against it for eight hours. As she suspected, the result was grooves similar to those found on the ancient hominid teeth. She repeated the experiment with a human tooth and found the same result.

(20) It seems that our early human ancestors may have used grass, which was easily found and ready to use, to floss between their teeth. As Hlusko suggests in the journal *Current Anthropology*, "Toothpicking with grass stalks probably represents the most persistent habit documented in human evolution."

1171. In line 5, the word *posited* most nearly means
  a. insisted.
  b. demanded.
  c. questioned.
  d. suggested.
  e. argued.

1172. Each of the following reasons is provided as evidence that early man used grass stalks as toothpicks EXCEPT the
  a. width of the grooves on ancient teeth.
  b. location of the grooves on ancient teeth.
  c. ready availability of grass.
  d. ongoing use of grass toothpicks.
  e. abrasive quality of grass.

1173. Dr. Hlusko's approach to determining the source of the grooves on ancient teeth can best be described as
  a. zealous.
  b. persistent.
  c. sullen.
  d. serendipitous.
  e. cautious.

1174. The passage suggests the theory that early man used grass stalks as toothpicks is
  a. a possibility.
  b. very probable.
  c. absolutely certain.
  d. fanciful.
  e. uncorroborated.

Questions 1175–1179 are based on the following passage.

The following passage analyzes data from the U.S. Census Bureau to draw conclusions about the economic well being of Americans in the years 1993 and 1994.

(1)   From year to year, the economic well-being of many Americans changes considerably, even though the median income of the population as a whole does not vary much in real terms from one year to the next. One measure of economic well-being is the income-to-

(5)   poverty ratio. This ratio measures a family's income compared to the poverty threshold (the income below which a family is considered to be in poverty) for that family. For example, the poverty threshold for a three-person family in 1994 was $11,817. A three-person family with an income of $20,000 would have an income-to-poverty ratio

(10)   of 1.69 $(\frac{\$20,000}{\$11,817})$.

Between 1993 and 1994 roughly three-quarters of the population saw their economic well-being fluctuate by 5% or more. Conversely, from year to year less than a quarter of Americans had stable incomes. In the 1990s, fewer people saw their incomes grow than in the 1980s,

(15)   and more people saw their incomes decline. Although the state of the economy is a notable factor in determining if incomes rise or fall, changes in personal circumstances are just as important. People had a good chance of seeing their incomes rise if they began to work full-time, the number of workers or adults in their house increased, they

(20)   married, or the number of children in the household decreased. Conversely, people could expect a decrease in their income if they ceased to be married or to work full-time.

Another factor that affected the direction of change in family income was the family's place on the economic ladder. The closer a

(25)   family was to poverty, the more likely they were to see their income rise, whereas 45% of families at the top of the economic ladder (those with income-to-poverty ratios of more than 4.0) experienced income decreases in 1994. While age, gender, and race play a significant role in determining one's place on the economic ladder, these factors are not

(30)   good predictors of a rise or fall in income. The only population for which one of these factors was significant was the elderly, whose incomes tended to be fairly stable.

1175. According to the passage, in general, income across the United States tends to
a. fluctuate wildly.
b. change incrementally.
c. increase slightly.
d. decrease steadily.
e. stay about the same.

1176. The first paragraph of the passage serves all the following purposes EXCEPT to
a. define the term *poverty threshold*.
b. explain income-to-poverty ratio.
c. provide an example of an income-to-poverty ratio.
d. state the author's thesis.
e. establish the subject of the passage.

1177. According to the passage, people's income in the 1990s was
a. likely to rise.
b. likely to fall.
c. greater than in the 1980s.
d. less than in the 1980s.
e. less likely to grow than in the 1980s.

1178. In the context of this passage, the phrase *the economic ladder* (lines 24, 26, and 29) most nearly means
a. the range of occupations.
b. the pecking order.
c. the capitalist social structure.
d. the caste system.
e. the range of incomes.

1179. The tone of this passage can best be described as
a. dry and neutral.
b. statistical.
c. unintentionally witty.
d. theoretical.
e. inflammatory.

Questions 1180–1188 are based on the following two passages.

Passage 1 describes the potlatch ceremony celebrated by native peoples of the Pacific Northwest. Passage 2 describes the kula ring, a ceremonial trading circle practiced among Trobriand Islanders in Papua New Guinea.

Passage 1

(1) Among traditional societies of the Pacific Northwest—including the Haidas, Kwakiuls, Makahs, Nootkas, Tlingits, and Tsimshians—the gift-giving ceremony called potlatch was a central feature of social life. The word *potlatch*, meaning "to give," comes from a Chinook trading
(5) language that was used all along the Pacific Coast. Each nation, or tribe, had its own particular word for the ceremony and each had different potlatch traditions. However, the function and basic features of the ceremony were universal among the tribes.

Each nation held potlatches to celebrate important life passages,
(10) such as birth, coming of age, marriage, and death. Potlatches were also

held to honor ancestors and to mark the passing of leadership. A potlatch, which could last four or more days, was usually held in the winter when the tribes were not engaged in gathering and storing food. Each potlatch included the formal display of the host family's crest and

(15) masks. The hosts performed ritual dances and provided feasts for their guests. However, the most important ritual was the lavish distribution of gifts to the guests. Some hosts might give away most or all of their accumulated wealth in one potlatch. The more a host gave away, the more status was accorded him. In turn, the guests, who had to accept

(20) the proffered gifts, were then expected to host their own potlatches and give away gifts of equal value.

Prior to contact with Europeans, gifts might include food, slaves, copper plates, and goat's hair blankets. After contact, the potlatch was fundamentally transformed by the influx of manufactured goods. As

(25) tribes garnered wealth in the fur trade, gifts came to include guns, woolen blankets, and other Western goods. Although potlatches had always been a means for individuals to win prestige, potlatches involving manufactured goods became a way for nobles to validate tenuous claims to leadership, sometimes through the destruction of property. It

(30) was this willful destruction of property that led Canadian authorities, and later the U.S. government, to ban potlatches in the late 1880s.

Despite the ban, the potlatch remained an important part of native Pacific Northwest culture. Giving wealth—not accumulating wealth, as is prized in Western culture—was a means of cementing leadership,

(35) affirming status, establishing and maintaining alliances, as well as ensuring the even distribution of food and goods. Agnes Alfred, an Indian from Albert Bay, explained the potlatch this way: "When one's heart is glad, he gives away gifts. . . . The potlatch was given to us to be our way of expressing joy."

Passage 2

(1) The inhabitants of the Trobriand Islands, an archipelago off the coast of Papua New Guinea in the South Pacific, are united by a ceremonial trading system called the kula ring. Kula traders sail to neighboring islands in large ocean-going canoes to offer either shell neck-

(5) laces or shell armbands. The necklaces, made of red shells called *bagi*, travel around the trading ring clockwise, and the armbands, made of white shells called *mwali*, travel counterclockwise.

Each man in the kula ring has two kula trading partners—one partner to whom he gives a necklace for an armband of equal value,

(10) although the exchanges are made on separate occasions, and one partner with whom he makes the reverse exchange. Each partner has one other partner with whom he trades, thus linking all the men around the kula ring. For example, if A trades with B and C, B trades with A and D, and C trades with A and E, and so on. A man may have only

(15) met his own specific kula partners, but he will know by reputation all the men in his kula ring. It can take anywhere from two to ten years for a particular object to complete a journey around the ring. The more times an object has made the trip around the ring, the more value it accrues. Particularly beautiful necklaces and armbands are also *(20)* prized. Some famous kula objects are known by special names and through elaborate stories. Objects also gain fame through ownership by powerful men, and, likewise, men can gain status by possessing particularly prized kula objects.

The exchange of these ceremonial items, which often accompanies *(25)* trade in more mundane wares, is enacted with a host of ritual activities. The visitors, who travel to receive kula from their hosts, are seen as aggressors. They are met with ritual hostility and must charm their hosts in order to receive the necklaces or armbands. The visitors take care to make themselves beautiful, because beauty conveys strength *(30)* and protects them from danger. The hosts, who are the "victims" of their visitors' charm and beauty, give the prized objects because they know that the next time it will be their turn to be the aggressor. Each man hopes that his charm and beauty will compel his trading partner to give him the most valuable kula object.

(35) The objects cannot be bought or sold. They have no value other than their ceremonial importance, and the voyages that the traders make to neighboring islands are hazardous, time-consuming, and expensive. Yet, a man's standing in the kula ring is his primary concern. This ceremonial exchange has numerous tangible benefits. It *(40)* establishes friendly relations through a far-flung chain of islands; it provides a means for the utilitarian exchange of necessary goods; and it reinforces the power of those individuals who win and maintain the most valuable kula items. Although the kula ring might mystify Western traders, this system, which has been in operation for hundreds of *(45)* years, is a highly effective means of unifying these distant islanders and creating a common bond among peoples who might otherwise view one another as hostile outsiders.

1180. According to Passage 1, *potlatch* is best defined as a

a. ceremony with rigid protocol to which all Pacific Northwest tribes adhere.

b. generic term for a gift-giving ceremony celebrated in the Pacific Northwest.

c. socialist ritual of the Pacific Northwest.

d. lavish feast celebrated in the Pacific Northwest.

e. wasteful ritual that was banned in the 1880s.

1181. According to Passage 1, the gift-giving central to the potlatch can best be characterized as

a. reciprocal.

b. wasteful.

c. selfless.

d. spendthrift.

e. commercialized.

1182. In Passage 1, the author's attitude toward the potlatch can best be described as
a. condescending.
b. antagonistic.
c. wistful.
d. respectful.
e. romantic.

1183. According to Passage 2, the men in a kula ring are
a. linked by mutual admiration.
b. hostile aggressors.
c. greedy.
d. motivated by vanity.
e. known to one another by reputation.

1184. In Passage 2, line 30, the word *victims* is in quotation marks because the
a. word might be unfamiliar to some readers.
b. author is implying that the hosts are self-pitying.
c. author is reinforcing the idea that the hosts are playing a prescribed role.
d. author wants to stress the brutal nature of the exchange.
e. author is taking care not to be condescending to the Trobriand culture.

1185. According to Passage 2, necklaces and armbands gain value through all the following means EXCEPT being
a. in circulation for a long time.
b. especially attractive.
c. owned by a powerful man.
d. made of special shells.
e. known by a special name.

1186. Gift-giving in the potlatch ceremony and the ritual exchange of the kula ring are both
a. a ritualized means of maintaining community ties.
b. dangerous and expensive endeavors.
c. a means of ascending to a position of leadership.
d. falling prey to Western culture.
e. peculiar rituals of a bygone era.

1187. Based on information presented in the two passages, both authors would be most likely to agree with which statement?
a. Traditional societies are more generous than Western societies.
b. The value of some endeavors cannot be measured in monetary terms.
c. It is better to give than to receive.
d. Westerners are only interested in money.
e. Traditional societies could benefit from better business sense.

1188. Which of the following titles would be most appropriate for both Passage 1 or Passage 2?
a. A Gift-Giving Ceremony
b. Ritual Exchange in Traditional Societies
c. Ceremonial Giving and Receiving in a Traditional Society
d. The Kindness of Strangers
e. Giving and Receiving in a Faraway Land

Questions 1189–1197 are based on the following passage.

The author of this passage, a professor of English literature at a major university, argues that affirmative action is a necessary part of the college admissions process.

(1)   When I began teaching at Big State U in the late 1960s, the students in my American literature survey were almost uniformly of European heritage, and most were from middle-class Protestant families. Attending college for these students was a lesson in homogeneity.

(5)   Although a number of students were involved in the Civil Rights movement and some even worked "down South" on voter registration, most students considered segregation to be a Southern problem, and many did not see the discrimination that was rampant on their own campus.

(10)   Since the 1960s there has been a sea change in university admissions. Key Supreme Court decisions and federal laws made equal opportunity the law of the land, and many institutions of higher learning adopted policies of affirmative action. The term *affirmative action* was first used in the 1960s to describe the active recruitment and pro-

(15)   motion of minority candidates both in the workplace and in colleges and universities. President Lyndon Johnson, speaking at Howard University in 1965, aptly explained the reasoning behind affirmative action. As he said, "You do not take a man who, for years, has been hobbled by chains and liberate him, bring him to the starting line in

(20)   a race and then say, 'You are free compete with all the others,' and still believe that you have been completely fair." Affirmative action programs in college admissions have been guided by the principle that it is not enough to simply remove barriers to social mobility; it is also necessary to encourage it for minority groups.

(25)   In recent years, affirmative action programs have come under public scrutiny, and some schools have been faced with charges of reverse discrimination. Preferential treatment of minority applicants is seen as discrimination against qualified applicants from the majority group. Despite widespread support for the elimination of prejudice,

(30)   most whites do not favor the preferential treatment of minority applicants, and affirmative action in college admissions has been abolished in several states. In my view, this trend is very dangerous not only for minority students but for all students. Thanks to a diversified student body, my classes today are much richer than when I began teaching in

(35)   the 1960s. For example, when I teach *A Light in August* by William Faulkner, as I do every fall, today there is likely to be a student in the class who has firsthand knowledge of the prejudice that is a central theme of the novel. This student's contribution to the class discussion of the novel is an invaluable part of all my students' education and a

(40)   boon to my experience as a teacher.

Some may argue that affirmative action had its place in the years following the Civil Rights movement, but that it is no longer necessary. To assume that all students are now on a level playing field is naive. Take for example the extracurricular activities, advanced placement

(45) classes, and internships that help certain applicants impress the admissions board: These are not available or economically feasible for many minority candidates. This is just one example of why affirmative action still has an important place on American campuses. When all things are equal, choosing the minority candidate not only gives minorities fair

(50) access to institutions of higher learning, but it ensures diversity on our campuses. Exposing all students to a broad spectrum of American society is a lesson that may be the one that best prepares them to participate in American society and succeed in the future.

1189. In line 4, the phrase *a lesson in homogeneity* can be most accurately described as
a. a slight against civil rights workers.
b. an ironic observation about the uniform character of the student body.
c. a comment on the poor quality of the education at Big State U.
d. a sarcastic comment about the authors' former students.
e. the author's' rueful view of his poor teaching skills.

1190. In line 10, the expression *sea change* means
a. increase.
b. storm.
c. decrease.
d. wave.
e. transformation.

1191. The author uses the quote from President Lyndon Johnson in lines 18–21 to
a. provide an example of discrimination in the past.
b. show how Howard University benefited from affirmative action policies.
c. make the passage more interesting.
d. explain the rationale for affirmative action.
e. prove that affirmative action has been effective at promoting diversity.

1192. According to the passage, the greatest danger of abolishing affirmative action in college admissions is
a. allowing reverse discrimination to take hold of college admissions.
b. creating a slippery slope of discrimination and prejudice.
c. losing the benefits of a diverse campus.
d. returning to the segregation of the past.
e. complicating the job of the college admissions board.

1193. From the information provided in the passage, one can conclude that the author
  a. has personally benefited from the effects of affirmative action.
  b. considers affirmative action a necessary evil.
  c. favors accepting poorly qualified candidates for the sake of diversity.
  d. despises the opponents of affirmative action.
  e. thinks that affirmative action will eventually be unnecessary.

1194. The word *feasible* in line 46 most nearly means
  a. advantageous.
  b. possible.
  c. attractive.
  d. probable.
  e. suitable.

1195. The tone of this passage can best be described as
  a. impassioned.
  b. impartial.
  c. reasonable.
  d. sarcastic.
  e. dispassionate.

1196. The author gives all the following reasons for continuing affirmative action in college admissions EXCEPT that it
  a. fosters diversity.
  b. provides fair access to higher education.
  c. is necessary to promote social mobility.
  d. exposes students to a broad spectrum of society.
  e. prepares students for the future.

1197. The argument for affirmative action in the workplace that most closely mirrors the author's reasoning about affirmative action in college admissions is
  a. it is the law of the land.
  b. diversity in the workplace better prepares a company to compete in the marketplace.
  c. a diverse workforce is more efficient.
  d. a less-qualified minority candidate is still a great asset to a company.
  e. it is the right thing to do.

Questions 1198–1200 are based on the following passage.

In this excerpt from Toni Morrison's 1970 novel The Bluest Eye, *Pauline tries to ease her loneliness by going to the movies.*

(1) One winter Pauline discovered she was pregnant. When she told Cholly, he surprised her by being pleased. [. . .] They eased back into a relationship more like the early days of their marriage, when he asked if she were tired or wanted him to bring her something from the
(5) store. In this state of ease, Pauline stopped doing day work and returned to her own housekeeping. But the loneliness in those two rooms had not gone away. When the winter sun hit the peeling green paint of the kitchen chairs, when the smoked hocks were boiling in the pot, when all she could hear was the truck delivering furniture down-
(10) stairs, she thought about back home, about how she had been all alone most of the time then too, but this lonesomeness was different. Then she stopped staring at the green chairs, at the delivery truck; she went to the movies instead. There in the dark her memory was refreshed, and she succumbed to her earlier dreams. Along with the idea of
(15) romantic love, she was introduced to another—physical beauty. Probably the most destructive ideas in the history of human thought. Both originated in envy, thrived in insecurity, and ended in disillusion.

1198. Pauline and Cholly live
   a. in a two-room apartment above a furniture store.
   b. in a delivery truck.
   c. next to a movie theater.
   d. with Pauline's family.
   e. in a housekeeper's quarters.

1199. Lines 1–5 suggest that just prior to Pauline's pregnancy, Cholly had
   a. loved Pauline dearly.
   b. begun to neglect Pauline.
   c. worked every day of the week.
   d. cared about Pauline's dreams.
   e. graduated from college.

1200. Pauline's loneliness is *different* from the loneliness she had felt *back home* (lines 10–11) because
   a. she's more bored than lonely.
   b. her family has abandoned her.
   c. she wants Cholly to be more romantic.
   d. she's a mother now.
   e. she shouldn't feel lonely with Cholly.

▶ Answers

Answer Key for Literary Devices Crossword

ACROSS	DOWN
5. symbol	1. metaphor
6. connotation	2. hyperbole
7. theme	3. foreshadowing
8. simile	4. tone
10. denotation	9. mood
12. imagery	11. personification
13. setting	

903. **c.** The answer may be found in lines 4 and 5, which state that Russell wanted an alternative to his scratched and warped phonograph records. You may infer that the problem with such records was their poor sound quality.

904. **e.** Lines 26–27 state that the detector's function is to convert data collected by the laser into music.

905. **b.** While the paragraph explains the function of semiconductor lasers in reading the information on CDs, it does not say anything about why they were invented.

906. **e.** Lines 5–7 mention calculators (adding machines), computers, card punches, and manuals. The only item not mentioned is kitchen scales.

907. **c.** A sneer is a facial expression that signals contempt or scorn. Accountants and bookkeepers didn't think the comptometer could perform their job faster than they could.

908. **b.** The Museum has a collection of computer-related magazines, manuals, and books (lines 7–8). They would not contain information on the inventor of the telephone (choice **a**), other museums in California (choice **c**), the profession of comptometer operation (choice **d**), or why video games are harmful (choice **e**). Since IBM played, and continues to play, an important role in the development of computers and computer-related technology, it could most likely be researched at the Museum.

909. **d.** Lines 4–5 explain that there was a social component to a trip to the marketplace. To be social means to be around others, suggesting that people sought out interaction with one another.

910. **c.** The prefix *ante-* means earlier, as does *pre-*. Additional context clues may be found in the first paragraph, which explains the similarities between historical marketplaces (those of long ago), and the malls of today, and in line 6, which states the mall is a descendant of the marketplace.

911. **a.** This information is not given in the passage.

912. **b.** The answer is in lines 27–29: *It was constructed according to a unified plan, rather than as a random group of stores. Nichols' company owned and operated the mall, leasing space to a variety of tenants.*

913. **e.** Lines 31–34 explain that Gruen took the shopping mall to the next level by intending it to take the place of a city center, with leisure and entertainment opportunities as well as shopping and dining.

914. **b.** All of the other choices are mentioned in lines 46–48.

915. a. Lines 36–38 list some of Southdale's offerings, such as shops, restaurants, a school, a post office, a skating rink, works of art, and fountains. These are also available in a city, and may be considered among the pleasures of urban life.

916. e. All of the other choices were mentioned in the last two paragraphs as positive impacts of megamalls. However, it is unlikely that a mall in Minnesota would be in direct competition for visitors with a mall located on the other side of the world.

917. c. The author does not have a bite to his argument, as required by satire, cynicism, and sarcasm. He is also not speaking to two audiences, one that gets it and one that doesn't, as with irony. He is simply trying to be funny, as in lines 1–3, which says that once a boy becomes a man, he will compete for cash on an island.

918. d. This is the only statement made by both authors (see Passage 1 lines 37–38, and Passage 2 lines 33–34). Don't be tricked by the choices that are true, such as **a**, **b**, and **e**. They need to be believed by both authors to be correct.

919. a. Passage 2 repeats a number of times its first question: Why does reality TV get such a bad rap? Lines 2 and 3 explain the argument further, saying its popularity is blamed on degenerate morals and a decreasing attention span. The first lines of paragraph 2 (13–16) again question the argument against reality TV, and the last paragraph repeats the questioning. There are no outcomes or any need for change mentioned. A brief history is given, and the subject of getting famous through exposure on reality TV is brought up, but neither is the primary purpose of the passage.

920. b. Passage 1 centers on a problem with reality TV, and while Passage 2 does mention some problems, they are not what he or she feels, but rather the opinion of *some people*. Choice **a** is incorrect because Passage 1 does not defend reality TV. Choice **c** is incorrect because the author of passage 2 acknowledges that some people have a problem with reality TV (lines 1–3 and 48–49). Choice **d** is incorrect because Passage 2 does not say anything about variety in TV programming. Choice **e** is wrong because Passage 2 doesn't mention the cost of producing TV shows.

921. a. The term *ratings* refers to how many people watch the show. A home run is the best possible kind of hit, so a *ratings home run* is a symbolic term meaning that many people watch the show. Choices **b**, **c**, and **e** reference ball games literally, but the author used the term figuratively, so those choices are incorrect. Nielsen is the company that gathers TV ratings, but high ratings have nothing to do with whether Nielsen likse a show.

922. e. Both passages show that there is a debate about reality TV. In Passage 1, the author is against it, but notes that it is popular (lines 10 and 37). The author of Passage 2 likes it, and also recognizes that it gets a *bad rap* (line 1). Although most of the other choices are factual, they do not appear in both passages, and are not illustrated by them.

923. c. The clue comes in Passage 1, which describes the swathing and flower gluing as crimes against defenseless walls. Swathing is therefore something done to a wall. The only choice that makes sense is **c**, to cover.

924. d. While there is evidence for the other choices, they are not the most troublesome. The author repeats in every paragraph the idea that reality TV isn't real.

925. d. First paragraph, where the theme is typically introduced, states, *Members of Congress have decided they need to do something about the obesity epidemic* (lines 5 and 6).

926. e. The answer is found in lines 12–14: *what they are also getting could be, in one meal, more than the daily recommended allowances of calories, fat, and sodium.*

927. c. Clues for this question are found in the first paragraph, in which the obesity problem is called an epidemic, and the staggering cost of the problem is mentioned.

928. b. Paragraph 5 states that the restaurant industry has responded to the bill by pointing out that *diet alone is not the reason for America's obesity epidemic. A lack of adequate exercise is also to blame.*

929. c. The answer is in lines 32–35: the chicken breast sandwich contains *twice the recommended daily amount of sodium.*

930. a. Paragraph 6 explains that those who support the MEAL Act believe *nutritional information must be provided where they are selecting their food* (lines 46 and 47).

931. b. The answer is in lines 18–20: *The Menu Education and Labeling (MEAL) Act would result in menus that look like the nutrition facts panels found on food in supermarkets.*

932. a. Lines 14–15 state that *political cartoons can serve as a vehicle for swaying public opinion and can contribute to reform.*

933. e. The consonance in the string of verbs *provoke, poke, and persuade* in line 3, as well as the verb choice *skewering* in line 4 expresses a playfulness of tone. The author's description of the cartoon images of Bill Clinton and George W. Bush (lines 9–12) also mirrors the playfulness of the art of caricature.

934. e. One meaning of *vehicle* is a way of carrying or transporting something. In this context, *vehicle* refers to a medium, or the means by which an idea is expressed.

935. d. The author cites Thomas Nast's symbols for Tammany Hall and the Democratic and Republican parties as examples of images that have entered the public consciousness and are *still in currency today* (line 19).

936. b. The first paragraph introduces the passage's thesis and gives an overview about who emigrated to California and why they came.

937. b. The passage provides a historical overview supported by facts and interpreted by the author. The author's opinion is evidenced in the last sentence of the passage (lines 48–49): *a testimony to their outstanding achievements and contributions.*

938. c. Line 15 states that the *Chinese immigrants proved to be productive and resourceful.* Lines 46 and 47 praises their *speed, dexterity, and outright perseverance.*

939. e. The passage states that at the time, the U.S. Constitution *reserved the right of naturalization for white immigrants,* excluding Chinese immigrants. Chinese immigrants could become citizens, depending on *the whim of local governments* (line 25).

940. c. *Enterprise* means an undertaking that is especially risky. It could also mean a unit of economic organization. In this instance, *industry* fits best within the context.

941. d. Chinese immigrants faced discriminatory laws that made them *unable to own land or file mining claims* (lines 27 and 28).

942. a. One meaning of *reclaim* is to rescue from an undesirable state, or to make something available for human use—this definition applies to the context. Another meaning is to reform or protest improper conduct.

943. a. The last sentence provides an example (Chinese immigrants performing hazardous railroad work in brutal conditions) that supports the general thesis of the passage—that Chinese immigrants made major *contributions to opening up the West* (line 49).

944. c. According to the passage, *deep underlying fissures already existed in the economy* (lines 18–19) and led to the Great Depression.

945. a. The passage is primarily an account that describes the causative factors (for example, tariff and war-debt policies, disproportionate wealth, and the accumulation of debt) that led to the Great Depression and its effects (for example, business failures, bank closings, homelessness, federal relief programs).

946. c. Lines 7–8 state that shantytowns were called "*Hoovervilles*" because citizens blamed their plight on the Hoover administration's refusal to offer assistance. Choice **b** may be true, but the passage does not directly support this claim.

947. d. In this context, *coupled* means to join for combined effect.

948. b. Although policies can refer to regulations or laws (choice **c**) or guiding principles or theories (choice **a**), in this context, *policy* refers to a course or method of action of a government or business intended to influence decisions or actions. Choice **b** is the only selection that implies action.

949. e. The passage describes the decade as one in which spending won out over prudent measures like saving (lines 31–32). The wild stock market speculation described in lines 35–37 is another example of the exuberant decade.

950. b. The analogy depicts the stock market crash of 1929 as a weakening agent to the economy (the way a stressful event may weaken the body's resistance to illness), not as the sole cause of the depression.

951. d. Lines 56–59 state that the New Deal expanded *the role of the central government in regulating the economy and creating social assistance programs.* Choices **b** and **c** are incorrect and choices **a** and **e** require an opinion; the author does not offer a viewpoint about the New Deal measures.

952. c. The Lewis and Clark expedition did not have a military goal and did not have any violent encounters except the one described in lines 41–43.

953. b. Jefferson and his representatives wanted Native Americans to acknowledge American sovereignty and to see themselves as children to his role as their "father."

954. c. One meaning of *protocol* is a code that demands strict adherence to etiquette.

955. d. The passage states that *Lewis and Clark sought to impose their own notions of hierarchy on Native Americans by "making chiefs" with medals, printed certificates, and gifts* (lines 30–32).

956. c. Placing a peace medal around the neck of a man killed by the expedition makes an ironic statement about the meaning of *peace.*

957. b. To the Plains Native Americans, the pipe ceremony meant that those who participated *accepted sacred obligations to share wealth, aid in war, and revenge injustice* (lines 50–51). The passage suggests that Lewis and Clark most likely did not understand the significance of the ceremony.

958. e. One meaning of *adopt* is to take by choice or accept into a relationship.

959. e. By giving manufactured goods to Native Americans, Lewis and Clark were promoting Euro-American culture. Jefferson hoped that these *free samples* would *introduce the Native Americans to mechanized agriculture as part of his plan to "civilize and instruct" them* (line 58).

960. a. The passage compares different abstract principles, or organizing principles, of Euro-American society versus those of tribal societies. For example, it explores the principles of hierarchy and kinship.

961. b. Choice **a** is too general to be the primary purpose of the passage, whereas choices **c** and **e** are too specific. Choice **d** is not supported by the passage.

962. c. Beecher Hooker invokes the Constitution (line 1) and recites the preamble (lines 9–13) in order to appeal to and persuade her audience.

963. a. Beecher Hooker plays on the two meanings suggested by the phrase *learn it by heart as well as by head.* She asks her audience to not only memorize the Constitution's preamble, but to use both emotion and intellect to understand its meaning.

964. e. One meaning of *anxious* is extreme uneasiness or dread. An alternative meaning applies to this context—that of ardently or earnestly wishing.

965. c. Passage 1 argues that the foremothers of the nation were patriotic and *did their full share* (line 30) of contributing to the early republic.

966. b. The passage anticipates the arguments of those in favor of women's right to vote and refutes them.

967. c. *Novel* means new and not resembling something known or used in the past. Choice **b,** original, could fit this definition, but its connotation is too positive for the context.

968. a. Passage 2 describes *woman-suffrage societies* as *thoroughly organized, with active and zealous managers* (lines 14–15). Choice **b,** *courageous,* is too positive for the context of the passage.

969. a. Passage 2 states that *every one . . . knows that without female suffrage, legislation for years has improved and is still improving the condition of women* (lines 24–27).

970. d. Passage 2 emphasizes how well women are served by judges in line 35. Passage 1 does not refer to this issue at all.

971. b. Passage 1 describes men as *fighters by nature* (line 37), but not women. Passage 2 describes women as *incapable of performing military duty* (lines 4–5).

972. e. There aren't any significant differences in the approaches cited in choices **a, b, c,** or **d.** Passage 1 and passage 2 demonstrate similar concepts.

973. b. Lines 3–4 state that the goods *pertaining to the soul* are called *goods in the highest and fullest sense.*

974. d. In line 5, Aristotle notes that the definition of good corresponds with the current opinion about the nature of the soul.

975. a. In the second paragraph, Aristotle states that *we have all but defined happiness as a kind of good life and well-being.* Thus, the definitions of happiness and goodness are intertwined; living a good life will bring happiness.

976. c. In the third paragraph, Aristotle lists several different ways that people define happiness to show that they all fit into the broad definition of *a kind of good life and well-being.*

977. b. In the first sentence, the author states that *the subject-matter of knowledge is intimately united* (line 2), while in the second sentence he adds *the Sciences . . . have multiple bearings on one another* (lines 3–4). In line 6 he states that the sciences *complete, correct, and balance each other.*

978. d. In the first sentence, the author states that *all branches of knowledge are connected together* (line 1). Then, in the second sentence, he writes *Hence it is that the Sciences, into which our knowledge may be said to be cast* (lines 3–4). Thus, Newman is using the term *the Sciences* to refer to all branches of knowledge.

979. c. The word *excise* here is used in an unusual way to mean *impose* or *put upon.* The main context clue is the word *influence,* which suggests a *giving to* rather than a taking away.

980. a. Throughout the first paragraph, the author emphasizes the interdependence of the branches of knowledge and warns against focusing on one branch to the neglect of others. He states that to *give undue prominence to one [area of study] is to be unjust to another; to neglect or supersede these is to divert those from their proper object* (lines 10–12). More important, he states that this action would serve *to unsettle the boundary lines between science and science, . . . to destroy the harmony which binds them together* (lines 12–14). Thus the knowledge received would be skewed; it *tells a different tale, when viewed as a portion of a whole* (lines 16–17).

981. b. The first sentence of the second paragraph shows that its purpose is to further develop the idea in the first by way of example. Newman writes, *Let me make use of an illustration* (line 19)—an illustration that further demonstrates how one's understanding of an idea changes in relation to the other ideas around it.

982. a. Here *apprehends* is used to mean *understands.* In this paragraph, the author describes what it is that university students would learn from their professors.

983. c. Throughout the passage, Newman argues that the branches of knowledge are interrelated and should be studied in combination and in relation to each other. He argues against focusing on one science or discipline, and he states that the university student *apprehends the great outlines of knowledge* (line 50), suggesting that he understands the broad issues in many subject areas.

984. b. At the beginning of the third paragraph, Newman states that *it is a great point then to enlarge the range of studies which a University professes* (lines 35–36) and that students would be best served *by living among those and under those who represent the whole circle* (lines 38–39) of knowledge. He argues that students will learn from the atmosphere created by their professors who *adjust together the claims and relations of their respective subjects* and who *learn to respect, to consult, to aid each other* (lines 43–45).

985. e. In the second sentence the author states that Prometheus is a *complex character*, and in this and the following sentence, the author lists several specific examples of the *rich combination of often-contradictory characteristics* of Prometheus.

986. d. The passage relates the key episodes in the life of Prometheus. This is the only idea broad enough and relevant enough to be the main idea of the passage.

987. b. Prometheus's actions show that he cared for humans more than he cared for Zeus. He gave man knowledge of the arts and sciences although Zeus wanted men to be kept in ignorance (lines 17–18); he tricked Zeus to give mankind the best meat from an ox (line 22); and he stole fire from Mount Olympus to give mortals the fire that Zeus had denied them (lines 28–31).

988. a. Zeus had given Prometheus and his brother the task of creating beings as a reward for their help in defeating the Titans (lines 7–10).

989. a. Prometheus helped create mortals and then became their *benefactor and protector* (line 15). He is thus most like a *parent* to humans.

990. e. The *transgression* refers back to the previous paragraph, which describes how Prometheus disobeyed Zeus and stole fire from Mount Olympus to give it to man.

991. b. The inclusion of Hope in the jar suggests that Zeus had some pity for mankind and that he wanted to send something to help humans battle the numerous evils he unleashed upon them.

992. c. The style is neither formal nor informal but an easygoing style in between to make the material easily understood and interesting to a lay audience. In addition, the passage does not take for granted that the reader knows basic information about mythology. For example, line 9 states that Zeus was *the great ruler of Olympian gods*.

993. d. The members of the PRB were young artists who suddenly found themselves leading a rebellion that had a *dramatic influence on the art world for generations to come* (lines 12–13). The concluding paragraph repeats this idea, stating that these three young men *had a tremendous influence on an entire generation of artists* (lines 58–59). Because *upstart* precedes *young*, we can infer that these men, like the leaders of other rebellions, were suddenly thrown into the spotlight, raised to a high (albeit controversial) position in the art world.

994. d. The author cites the PRB as an example of a rebellion led by *young activists* (line 5) and states that the PRB had *a dramatic influence on the art world* because of their *disdain for the artistic conventions of the time* (line 12). This suggests that their ideas about art were revolutionary, creating a significant and lasting change in the art world. That they were passionate about their beliefs is clear from the fact that they felt strongly enough to form an association and lead a rebellion.

995. b. Line 11 states that the oldest PRB member was only 21 years old, so it is clear that the members were young and still developing their skills as artists.

996. e. In the third paragraph (lines 14–26), the author states that the PRB believed their peers' art *was lacking in meaning and aesthetic honesty* because it often depicted *overly idealized landscapes, carefully arranged family portraits and still lifes, and overly dramatic nature scenes.* In contrast, the PRB believed in art that *more accurately depicted reality* and portray people, places, and things realistically instead of in an idealized way.

997. a. Lines 34–36 state that the PRB's *realism—especially as it related to the Biblical figures—was not well received by many in the art world at the time.*

998. c. Lines 14–16 state that the PRB *was formed in response to the brotherhood's belief that the current popular art being produced in England was lacking in meaning and aesthetic honesty.* In addition, line 24 states that the PRB was *committed to bringing greater integrity to art*, suggesting that their peers' work did not have integrity.

999. e. The topic sentence of the sixth paragraph states that *one of the most distinctive aspects of PRB works—in contrast to both the works produced during the early nineteenth century and the art of today—is their dramatic use of color* (lines 45–47).

1000. b. Throughout the passage, the author describes the principles of the PRB—why the group was formed (paragraphs 2 and 3) and how the group attempted to live up to its principles (paragraphs 4–6). There is little or no information offered about the other answer choices.

1001. a. In the third paragraph, the author states that the PRB rejected the style and subjects of the Royal Academy, seeking instead *subjects that, by their very nature, had greater meaning and more accurately depicted reality* (lines 22–23). In paragraph 4, the author describes how they chose their subjects and aimed to portray people more realistically, thus implying that the members of the PRB had a greater awareness of social issues. In addition, in lines 38–39, the author states that the PRB often chose themes *highlighting the societal and moral challenges of the time.*

1002. b. The passage states that daytime drowsiness, *even during boring activities* (lines 1–2), is a sign that a person is not getting enough sleep.

1003. a. This image connotes a state of working hard without adequate rest.

1004. e. The passage claims that lack of sleep *magnifies alcohol's effects on the body* (lines 14–15) implying that it hampers a person's ability to function.

1005. d. The first paragraph of this short passage deals with the symptoms of sleep deprivation, and the second paragraph discusses the dangers of not getting enough sleep. Choices **b** and **e** are too specific to be the passage's primary purpose. Choices **a** and **c** are not supported by the passage.

1006. d. Although he was *a man of no formal scientific education* (line 2), Leeuwenhoek demonstrated, in his own words, *a craving after knowledge, which I notice resides in me more than in most other men* (lines 24–26), who was the first to describe microorganisms. The phrase *stumbled upon* in choice **a** is too accidental to describe Leeuwenhoek's perseverance. The words *proficient* and *entertainment* in choice **c** do not accurately describe Leeuwenhoek's skill and drive depicted in the passage. Choices **b** and **e** are incorrect; Leeuwenhoek was not trained nor did he know that his discoveries would later help to cure disease.

1007. c. To *inspire* means to exert an animating or enlivening influence on. In the context of the passage, Leeuwenhoek's creation of microscope lenses were influenced by the lenses used by drapers.

1008. a. The quotation highlights the value Leeuwenhoek placed on sharing his discoveries with other scientists. He states that he *thought it my duty to put down my discovery on paper, so that all ingenious people might be informed thereof* (lines 27–28).

1009. b. The tone of the passage is positive. However, *ecstatic reverence* (choice **a**) is too positive and *tepid approval* (choice **c**) is not positive enough.

1010. c. Nowhere in the passage does the author speculate about whether teenagers can change their exercise habits.

1011. c. One meaning of *sedentary* is settled; another meaning is doing or requiring much sitting. *Stationary*, defined as fixed in a course or mode, is closest in meaning.

1012. e. The last sentence illustrates factors that motivate teenagers to exercise by using the results of a national survey to provide specific examples.

1013. d. The passage promotes change in teenagers' exercise habits by emphasizing the benefits of exercise, the moderate amount of exercise needed to achieve benefits, and some factors that may encourage teenagers to exercise.

1014. c. An *adage* is a word used to describe a common observation or saying, like *beauty is only skin deep* (Passage 2, line 1).

1015. c. The author states that *the health risk for cosmetic procedures is low* (Passage 1, lines 24–25) but does not give factual information to back this claim. The statement is important to the author's argument because he or she cites it as one of the reasons his or her attitude toward plastic surgery has changed.

1016. e. The author describes cosmetic plastic surgeons as *slick salespeople reaping large financial rewards from others' insecurity and vanity* (Passage 1, lines 17–18).

1017. d. The author of Passage 1 directly invokes the audience he or she hopes to reach in line 31: *members of the medical community.*

1018. d. One definition of *saturate* is to satisfy fully; another definition, which fits the context of the passage, is to fill completely with something that permeates or pervades.

1019. b. The author of Passage 2 claims that she grew up in *the spirit of feminism* (lines 10–11), and *believed that women should be valued for who they are and what they do, not for how they look* (lines 12–13). The author implies that this is a belief held by feminists of the 1970s.

1020. a. The author of Passage 1, a physician, discusses his or her professional jealousy in lines 14–21. The author of Passage 2 does not raise this issue.

1021. d. Passage 1 states that the demand for cosmetic surgery has increased in part *as the job market has become more competitive* (line 6). Passage 2 comments on *a competitive culture where looks count* (line 24).

1022. a. Both passages are first-person accounts that use personal experience to build an argument.

1023. c. Choice **d** is true, but too specific to be the author's primary purpose. Choice **e** can be eliminated because it is too negative, and choices **a** and **b** are too positive.

1024. a. The author contrasts the public's dismissal of the arcane practice of wearing garlic with its increasing acceptance of herbal remedies.

1025. b. In this context, *conventional* refers to the established system of Western medicine or biomedicine.

1026. d. Choice **a** is overly general and choice **b** is too negative to be inferred from the survey's findings. Choice **c** is incorrect—the author does not mention the baby boom age group, but that does not imply that the survey does not include it. The survey does not support the prediction in choice **e**.

1027. a. The statistic illustrates the popularity of alternative therapies without giving any specific information as to why.

1028. e. The author states that Americans are not replacing conventional healthcare but are adding to or supplementing it with alternative care.

1029. d. The shortcomings of conventional healthcare mentioned in lines 30–35 are the *time constraints of managed care* (line 31), *focus on technology* (line 32), and inability to *relieve symptoms associated with chronic disease* (line 34).

1030. a. The author states that once *scientific investigation has confirmed their safety and efficacy* (lines 37–38), alternative therapies may be accepted by the medical establishment.

1031. b. The author gives evidence of observational studies to show that garlic may be beneficial. Choice **d** is incorrect, however, because the author emphasizes that *these findings have not been confirmed in clinical studies* (lines 51–52).

1032. d. The passage does not offer a criticism or an argument about alternative healthcare, but rather reports on the phenomenon with some playfulness.

1033. d. In lines 15–17, Doc Burton emphasizes change. He tells Mac that *nothing stops* and that as soon as an idea (such as the cause) is put into effect, *it would start changing right away.* Then he specifically states that once a commune is established, the *same gradual flux will continue.* Thus, the cause itself is in flux and is always changing.

1034. b. The several references to communes suggest that the cause is communism, and this is made clear in line 31, when Mac says *Revolution and communism will cure social injustice.*

1035. a. In lines 21–25, Doc Burton describes his desire to *see the whole picture,* to *look at the whole thing.* He tells Mac he doesn't want to judge the cause as *good* or *bad* so that he doesn't limit his vision. Thus, he is best described as an objective observer.

1036. d. In the first part of his analogy, Doc Burton says that infections are a reaction to a wound—*the wound is the first battleground* (line 40). Without a wound, there is no place for the infection to fester. The strikes, then, are like the infection in that they are a reaction to a wound (social injustice).

1037. a. By comparing an individual in a group to a cell within the body (line 50), Doc Burton emphasizes the idea that the individual is really not an individual at all but rather part of a whole.

1038. c. In lines 59–62, Doc Burton argues that *the group doesn't care* about the cause it has created. *Maybe the group simply wants to move, to fight.* Individuals such as Mac, however, believe in a cause (or at least think they do).

1039. a. Doc Burton suggests that perhaps group-man *simply wants to move, to fight,* without needing a real cause—in fact, he states that the group may use the cause *simply to reassure the brains of individual men* (lines 61–62).

1040. b. Doc Burton knows how deeply Mac believes in the cause and knows that if he outright says the group doesn't really believe in the cause, Mac would not listen. Thus he says, "*It might be like this,*" emphasizing the possibility. Still Mac reacts hotly.

1041. d. As the introduction states, Higgins is a professor, and he contrasts the life of the gutter with *Science and Literature and Classical Music and Philosophy and Art* (lines 9–10). Thus, his life is best described as the life of a scholar.

1042. e. The answer to this question is found in Liza's statement in lines 22–24: *You think I must go back to Wimpole Street because I have nowhere else to go but father's.* This statement indicates that Wimpole Street is probably where Liza grew up.

1043. e. Liza's reply to Higgins suggests that she wants more respect. She criticizes him for always turning everything against her, bullying her, and insulting her. She tells him not to *be too sure that you have me under your feet to be trampled on and talked down* (lines 24–25). Clearly he does not treat her with respect, and as her actions in the rest of the excerpt reveal, she is determined to get it.

1044. b. Liza is from the *gutter,* but she can't go back there after being with Higgins and living the life of the scholar, a refined, educated, upper-class life. Thus the best definition of *common* here is unrefined.

1045. a. In these lines Higgins threatens Liza and *lays hands on her,* thus proving that he is a bully.

1046. c. Higgins refers to Liza as *my masterpiece*, indicating that he thinks of Liza as his creation—that he made her what she is today.

1047. b. The excerpt opens with Higgins telling Liza "*If you're going to be a lady*" and comparing her past—*the life of the gutter*—with her present—a cultured life of literature and art. We also know that Higgins taught Liza phonetics (line 40) and that Liza was once *only a flower girl* but is now a *duchess* (lines 55–56). Thus, we can conclude that Higgins taught Liza how to speak and act like someone from the upper class.

1048. d. Higgins realizes that Liza—with the knowledge that he gave her—now has the power to stand up to him, that she will not just let herself be *trampled on and called names* (line 59). He realizes that she has other options and she is indifferent to his *bullying and big talk* (line 55).

1049. c. Liza's final lines express her joy at realizing that she has the power to change her situation and that she is not Higgins' inferior but his equal; she can't believe that *all the time I had only to lift up my finger to be as good as you* (lines 59–60). She realizes that she can be an assistant to someone else, that she doesn't have to be dependent on Higgins.

1050. d. In the first few lines, the narrator states that Miss Temple was the *superintendent of the seminary* and that she received both *instruction* and *friendship* from Miss Temple, who was also like a mother to her: *she had stood me in the stead of mother.*

1051. a. The narrator states that with Miss Temple, *I had given in allegiance to duty and order; I was quiet; I believed I was content* (lines 12–13).

1052. d. The context here suggests existence or habitation, not captivity or illness.

1053. c. We can assume that the narrator would have liked to go home during vacations, but she spent all of her vacations at school because *Mrs. Reed had never sent for me to Gateshead* (line 49). Thus we can infer that Mrs. Reed was her guardian, the one who sent the narrator to Lowood in the first place.

1054. b. The narrator describes her experience with *school-rules* and *school-duties* (line 51) and how she *tired of the routine* (line 54) after Miss Temple left. She also contrasts Lowood with the *real world* of *hopes and fears, of sensations and excitements* (lines 34–35) and that the view from her window seemed a *prison-ground, exile limits* (lines 42–43). Thus, it can be inferred that Lowood is both a structured and isolated place.

1055. a. The narrator states in lines 26–27 that she had *undergone a transforming process* and that now she again felt *the stirring of old emotions* (line 30) and *remembered that the real world was wide* and *awaited those who had courage to go forth* (lines 36–37). She also looks at the road from Lowood and states *how [she] longed to follow it further!* More importantly, she repeats her desire for *liberty* and prays for *a new servitude*—something beyond Lowood.

1056. e. In lines 13–15, the narrator states that with Miss Temple at Lowood, she *believed* she was content, that *to the eyes of others, usually even to my own, I appeared a disciplined and subdued character*. This suggests that in her *natural element* (lines 29–30) she is not so disciplined or subdued. Her desire for freedom and to explore the world are also evident in this passage; she longs to follow the road that leads away from Lowood (line 46) and she is *half desperate* in her cry for something new, something beyond Lowood and the rules and systems she *tired of [. . .] in one afternoon* (line 56).

1057. d. Because Lowood had been the narrator's home for eight years and all she *knew of existence* was school rules, duties, habits, faces, and so on (lines 53–55)—because she had had *no communication . . . with the outer world* (lines 50–51), it is likely that she feels her initial prayers were unrealistic. At least a *new servitude* would provide some familiar territory, and it therefore seems more realistic and attainable than *liberty* or *change* (lines 55–57).

1058. c. The women refer to each other as "Mrs.," and their conversation reveals that they don't know much about each other. Mrs. Hale, for example, asks Mrs. Peters if she knew Mr. Wright (line 46) and if she were *raised round here* (line 57).

1059. a. Mrs. Peters says, *It would be lonesome for me sitting here alone* (lines 27–28). Mrs. Hale replies, *It would, wouldn't it?* and then expresses her wish that she'd come to see Mrs. Wright. She says that *it's a lonesome place and always was* in line 37 and then says *I can see now*—(lines 38–39), suggesting that she can understand now how Mrs. Wright must have felt.

1060. d. Mrs. Hale describes Mr. Wright as a *hard man* who was *like a raw wind that gets to the bone* (lines 51–52). Mrs. Wright's loneliness would be deepened by living with a man who was quiet and cold.

1061. b. The punctuation here—the dashes between each word—suggest that Mrs. Wright changed from the sweet, fluttery woman she was to a bitter, unhappy person over the years. The emphasis on her loneliness and the dead husband and bird add to this impression.

1062. d. The women decide to take the quilt to Mrs. Wright to keep her busy; it would give her something to do, something familiar and comforting.

1063. c. Because her house was so lonely, Mrs. Wright would have wanted the company of a pet—and a pet that shared some qualities with her (or with her younger self) would have been particularly appealing. She would have liked the bird's singing to ease the quiet in the house, and she also *used to sing real pretty herself* (line 10) and would have felt a real connection with the bird.

1064. b. The clues in the passage—the broken bird cage door, the dead bird lovingly wrapped in silk and put in a pretty box, the description of John Wright as a hard and cold man—suggest that he killed the bird and that Mrs. Wright in turn killed him for destroying her companion.

1065. d. The fact that Mrs. Hale *slips box under quilt pieces* suggests that she will not share her discovery with the men.

1066. c. Frankenstein says to his listener to, *learn from me . . . how dangerous is the acquirement of knowledge* (lines 6–8). He is telling his tale as a warning and does not want to lead his listener into the same kind of *destruction and infallible misery* (line 6).

1067. a. The context reveals that Frankenstein was prepared for *a multitude of reverses* or setbacks that would hinder his operations.

1068. e. Frankenstein describes himself as pursuing his *undertaking with unremitting ardour* and that his *cheek had grown pale with study, and [his] person had become emaciated with confinement* (lines 45–47). He also says that *a resistless, and almost frantic, impulse urged me forward; I seemed to have lost all soul or sensation but for this one pursuit* (lines 56–58). These are the marks of a man obsessed.

1069. b. Moreau states in lines 22–24 that *this extraordinary branch of knowledge has never been sought as an end . . . until I took it up!*, and in lines 28–30, he states that he *was the first man to take up this question armed with antiseptic surgery, and with a really scientific knowledge of the laws of growth.* This and the detail with which he explains the background of his investigations reveal that he is a calculating and systematic scientist. (Although he confesses that he chose the human form *by chance* (line 45), it is likely that Moreau did not just happen upon this choice but that he found the human form, as he later states, more appealing *to the artistic turn of mind . . . than any animal shape* (lines 48–49).

1070. d. Right after he says *these things*, the narrator says *these animals* to clarify that he is referring to the creatures that Moreau created. An additional context clue is provided by Moreau's response, in which he explains how animals may be *educated* so that they may talk.

1071. b. The narrator asks Moreau to justify *all this pain* (line 54), implying that he has inflicted great pain on the animals he has used in his experiments.

1072. c. Both men make remarkable discoveries in their fields; in the other aspects the men are different. Dr. Moreau uses live animals to change their form, and there is no evidence in the passage that he wants his creatures to worship him or that he has kept his experiment a secret (though these facts *are* evident in other passages in the book). Passage 2 also suggests that Moreau did not have a specific application or justification for his work; he responds to the narrator's request for a justification by philosophizing about pain.

1073. c. The passage describes swing as *vibrant* (line 6), a synonym for *lively*. It is also stated that soloists in big bands *improvised from the melody* (line 11), indicating that the music was melodic.

1074. d. In the 1940s, you would most likely hear bebop being played in clubs, such as *Minton's Playhouse in Harlem* (line 24).

1075. b. In lines 19–20, the author states that *rhythm is the distinguishing feature of bebop.*

1076. a. *Aficionado*, related to the word *affection*, means a devotee or fan. The meaning can be inferred from the sentence, which states that *aficionados flocked to such clubs . . . to soak in the new style*. The use of *fans* in line 25 is a direct reference to the aficionados of the previous sentence.

1077. c. The tone of the passage is neutral, so only the answer choices beginning with *explain* or *instruct* are possible choices. The passage does not explain how to play bebop music, so **c** is the best choice.

1078. b. Lines 2–7 describe how glam rock musicians were characterized by their flashy hair and makeup, and refers to their music as a *product*, as if it was something packaged to be sold. The choice that best describes a musician who puts outward appearance before the quality of his or her music is choice **b**, *style over substance*.

1079. c. *Ostentatious* is an adjective that is used to describe someone or something that is conspicuously vain or showy. There are numerous context clues to help you answer this question: Line 6 states that the glam rockers had a *flashy style*, and their music was *symbolic of the superficial 1980s* (line 8).

1080. d. *Trappings* usually refer to outward decoration of dress. If you did not know the definition of trappings, the prior sentence (lines 21–24) supplies the answer: *Grunge rockers derived their fashion sense from the youth culture of the Pacific Northwest: a melding of punk rock style and outdoors clothing. . . .* The author makes no judgment of the attractiveness of grunge fashion (choice **c**).

1081. e. Line 5 states that White Snake was a glam rock band and therefore not associated with the Seattle grunge scene. Don't be distracted by choice **a**; Mr. Epps and the Calculations may not have been a real band, but the name will nonetheless be forever associated with grunge music.

1082. b. The relationship between grunge music and its mainstream popularity is best described as *contrary*. The most obvious example of this is found in lines 50–51, when in describing the relationship, the author states *it is very hard to buck the trend when you are the one setting it*.

1083. d. *Ephemeral* is used to describe something that lasts only a short time, something that is fleeting. The context clue that best helps you to answer this question is found in lines 47–48, where the author states that grunge *faded out of the mainstream as quickly as it rocketed to prominence*.

1084. c. In Passage 1, the author provides a limited chronology of Johnson's life (paragraphs 2, 3, and 4) and briefly describes his influence on blues and rock and roll (paragraphs 1 and 5).

1085. b. In paragraph 3 of Passage 1, the author describes how Johnson was *not very good* at playing the guitar but that he *wanted to learn* and so *spent his time in blues bars watching the local blues legends* (lines 19–20). That he disappeared for some time and then returned as *a first-rate guitarist* (lines 24–27) also suggests Johnson's determination.

1086. a. In lines 10–12 of Passage 2, the author describes how the blues came to be called the blues—thus *neologism* means a new word or new meaning or use of a word.

1087. d. This sentence states that the blues remakes were enjoyed by all kinds of people—*black and white, young and old* (line 44)—and suggests why the songs were so popular by describing how the lyrics touched a common emotional chord in listeners, all of whom have had the blues from one or more of the sources listed in the sentence.

1088. d. The author states that the blues was *a music perfectly suited for a nation on the brink of the Civil Rights movement* because it was music that *had the power to cross boundaries, to heal wounds, and to offer hope to a new generation of Americans* (lines 47–50). The previous sentence states that the music was popular with both the *black and white, young and old* (line 43). Thus, the author suggests that this shared musical experience helped promote understanding across racial boundaries and thereby ease racial tensions.

1089. b. Robert Johnson died in 1938, before the 1940s. Also, neither author explicitly states that Robert Johnson is the best blues guitarist of his era, although this is implied by the author of Passage 1, who states that Johnson's *impact on the world of rock and roll* is *indisputable* (lines 3–4) and quotes Eric Clapton as saying Johnson is *the most important blues musician who ever lived* (lines 8–9). However, the author of Passage 2 simply lists Johnson in the same sentence as his mentors Son House and Willie Brown (line 34), without suggesting that any one of these artists was better than the others.

1090. c. Passage 1 states from the beginning that there is little information about Johnson and that the information that is available *is as much rumor as fact* (lines 2–3). There is also no definitive answer regarding how Johnson acquired his talent (paragraph 4), and the author uses the word *purportedly* in lines 34–35 to further emphasize the speculative nature of the narrative. Passage 2, on the other hand, provides many specific facts in the form of names and dates to present a text that is factual and assertive.

1091. a. Passage 1 describes the life and influence of one specific blues artist, while Passage 2 provides a general overview of the history of the blues.

1092. c. At the end of Passage 1, the author describes the reason so many artists record Johnson's songs: his *songs capture the very essence of the blues, transforming our pain and suffering with the healing magic of his guitar* (lines 41–42). This sentence proves the idea stated in Passage 2 that *"the blues" is something of a misnomer*. This is the only sentence from Passage 2 that fits the focus of Passage 1; the others concern the development or defining characteristics of the blues.

1093. a. The passage is a neutral narration of Mozart's childhood and the beginnings of his musical career. Choices **c**, **d**, and **e** can be eliminated because the author does not take a side or try to prove a point. Choice **b** is incorrect because the author does not make any generalizations about the classical music scene.

1094. c. The passage clearly states that Wolfgang took an interest in the clavier when his sister was learning the instrument.

1095. c. The passage states (line 18) that Wolfgang's first *public* appearance was at Linz and that after this concert word of his genius traveled to Vienna. The passage states earlier that Vienna was the capital of the Hapsburg Empire.

1096. b. The author's tone toward Leopold is mild—neither strongly approving nor disapproving. In a few places, however, the author conveys some disappointment, especially lines 34–36 in which she states that Leopold set an exhausting schedule for Wolfgang.

1097. c. *Lavish* means expended or produced in abundance. Both *wasteful* and *extravagant* are synonyms for *lavish*, but, because it is modifying *palace*, *extravagant* is the more logical choice.

1098. d. The author's language emphasizes Mozart's imagination. The phrase *engrossed in the intricacies of his make-believe court* suggests a child with a lively imagination. None of the other choices is directly supported by the text.

1099. e. The text directly states that *the pattern established in his childhood would be the template for the rest of his short life* (lines 55–56). Choice **d** could be misleading, as the text states that Mozart was buried in an unmarked grave. However, it also states that this was customary at the time, so one cannot infer that he died an anonymous pauper.

1100. b. *Lauded* means praised or blessed. The meaning of the word can be inferred from the structure of the paragraph. The paragraph begins by summing up Mozart's childhood, and then describes how the features of his childhood were mirrored in his adult life. In his childhood Mozart *played for, and amazed, the heads of the British and French royal families* and likewise as an adult he *was lauded for his genius*. From the structure, one can infer that to be lauded is something positive. Of the positive choices, *praised* makes more sense in the sentence than *coveted*.

1101. d. The author does not *directly* state that Mozart's illnesses were the result of exhaustion, but only implies this by describing Mozart's exhausting schedule and then stating that he became ill on tour. However, the connection is not explicitly stated.

1102. e. Answer choices **a–d** are all unauthorized logging practices performed by Metsähallitus in Finland. Choice **e** is incorrect because it refers to another country.

1103. c. Calling for a moratorium means to cease or stop an activity or concept. You can deduce this correct answer from the clue in line 17, *halt*.

1104. b. The author's tone can best be characterized as an urgent warning. The passage exposes an illegal logging practice that threatens to destroy forests in Finland. The author's genuine concern rules out choices **a** and **d**, and there is nothing in the passage to suggest that the author is either secretly angry, choice **c**, or in a state of panic, choice **e**.

1105. d. Though Greenpeace is clearly out to inform the reader of bad logging practices in Finland, it is not trying to rally support for the organization (choice **e**); rather, its goal is to promote awareness, and through awareness, change. Choice **a**'s suggestion that other forests are endangered is false, and choices **b** and **c** are not ideas put forth by the passage.

1106. d. The Great Barrier Reef does not cause erosion; it prevents it. All of the other choices are true and can be found in the passage.

1107. e. According to the passage, 2,010 kilometers is approximately 1,250 miles. So, twice as many kilometers (4,020) would be approximately twice as many miles (2,500).

1108. b. The phrase *ill effects of* that precedes *erosion and putrefaction* means that putrefaction is a negative consequence, as is erosion. The other choices are either neutral (**c**, **d**, and **e**) or positive (**a**).

1109. a. This statement encapsulates the entire passage, not just a part of it. Choices **c** and **e** are too specific to be correct. Choices **b** and **d** are not supported by the passage.

1110. c. *Erosion and putrefaction* (line 6) are the consequences to the shoreline if the coral reefs are neglected or destroyed.

1111. a. The tone is best described as one of fascinated discovery unfolding during a lecture. A clue to the tone is the use of exclamation points and the excited, choppy delivery of Langdon's information. Choices **b** and **e** may be considered as the tone of Passage 1. Choices **c** and **d** are not supported by the text.

1112. c. The mathematical ratio PHI is also known as the Divine Proportion. This is directly stated in lines 17–18 of Passage 1, and lines 23–24 of Passage 2.

1113. c. *Ubiquity* is used here to show that even though the concept of PHI in nature seems unusual or unique at first, it is actually a very common and predictable occurrence. The other choices are not supported by the passage.

1114. b. PHI is not the area of a regular pentagon. All other answers describe an aspect of PHI as found in the two passages.

1115. e. The subject of both paragraphs is Fibonacci spirals. Sunflower seeds, pinecones, and pineapples are mentioned as examples of the Fibonacci spiral.

1116. d. The answer for choices **a**, **b**, **c**, and **e** are all the same, according to Passage 2: 1.618. The ratio of head to floor divided by shoulder to floor (choice **d**) is not covered in the passage.

1117. a. Both passage refer to the fact that early or ancient scientists perceived the Divine Proportion to be a magical number. Choices **d** and **e** could be correct, but they are not supported by the passage. Choices **b** and **c** are false.

1118. a. This statement, while true, refers to the pentagram, not the pentagon. Choices **b**–**e** are all true statements about the pentagon.

1119. b. *Discrete* means *distinct*, and as used in the passage, it is paired with *specialized*, a context clue. Choices **a**, **c**, **d**, and **e** are all synonyms for the homophone, *discreet*.

1120. d. Choice **b** is not covered in the passage. Choices **a**, **c**, and **e**, while mentioned, are too specific to be viable titles. Choice **d** is broad-ranging enough to encompass the entire passage.

1121. c. *Scrimshawed* means carved, as in line 12. The word is often associated with whaling and seafaring, so answer choices **a**, **d**, and **e** are all distracters stemming from that confusion regarding context. Because scrimshaw and enamel are waxlike substances, a less careful reader may choose **b**.

1122. d. According to lines 21–23 of the passage, choices **a**, **b**, **c**, and **e** are all parts of the physical structure of teeth. Choice **d**, tusk, is not a component of teeth, but rather a type of tooth found in some mammals.

1123. d. From the context in lines 13–17, it can be deduced that *mastication* means the act of chewing, because tusks, evolved from teeth, are described in line 16 as able to go *beyond chewing*. Choices **a**, **b**, and **c** are distracters that might be chosen if not reading carefully. Choice **e**, preparation, is too vague.

1124. b. Lines 30–32 clearly state that dentinal tubules *are micro-canals that radiate outward through the dentine from the pulp cavity to the exterior cementum border.*

1125. c. In the passage, the substances in choices **a**, **b**, **d**, and **e** are all described as organic substances. Therefore, choice **c**, an inorganic substance (lines 29–30), is correct.

1126. a. Lines 55–58 identify how natural ivory can be authenticated.

1127. c. According to the fifth paragraph of the passage, enamel is the hardest animal tissue (animal tissue, by nature, is a living thing, and thus organic), ameloblasts help form it, and it has a prismatic structure (choices **a**, **b**, **d**, and **e**). Choice **c** is incorrect because lines 55–58 state that ivory is commonly tested via ultraviolet light, which would indicate exposure.

1128. c. Choice **c** is correct because these lines specifically speak to the evaluation process of the scientific method.

1129. d. The entire passage is instructive and about educating the reader.

1130. e. *Falsificationism* means to refute and prove wrong as supported in lines 38 and 63 of the passage.

1131. d. *Peer review* is proposed as a vital part of the scientific method, and it is directly supported as such by lines 78–83 in the passage. The other statements are all true.

1132. c. Lines 31–35 of the passage support this truth about hypotheses. The other statements about hypotheses are false.

1133. b. This is the best choice as it explains the overall point of the passage, which is a step-by-step process covering the scientific method. Choice **e** is close, but the entire passage is not about evaluating data. Choice **a** is incorrect because the theory of relativity is cited only as an example, not as a general topic. Likewise, choice **c** considers only a small part of the passage. Choice **d** is too specific.

1134. c. *Operational definition* can be defined as a clear and practical definition (lines 26–29).

1135. a. Choice **a** is supported by the passage. Choice **c** is not supported anywhere in the passage. Choices **b**, **d**, and **e** are all incorrect interpretations of information contained in the passage and are careless choices.

1136. b. All the other choices are indicated in the passage to be steps of the process of scientific method.

1137. b. *Bellicose* most closely means warlike. There are two major clues in this passage to help you answer this question. The first clue lies in the translation of the name *tewaarathon*, meaning "little brother of war." Another clue lies in lines 18–19, where the passage states that these games were *excellent battle preparation for young warriors.*

1138. c. The answer to this question can be found in lines 17–20, as well as in the entire second paragraph. The passage states that the games played by the Native Americans were often substitutes for war, and from time to time the games held religious and spiritual significance. Don't be fooled by choice **e**; the Native Americans may have played friendly exhibition matches, but this is not discussed anywhere in the passage.

1139. a. "Little Brother of War" is the best choice for the title of this passage because, in the first paragraph, the games are described as fierce and warlike. Choice **a** is also the name of the original Iroquois game, which was the subject of the entire second paragraph. The other choices do not fit because they are unsupported by the passage, or describe only a small portion of the passage.

1140. c. The answer can be found in the two sentences that follow the phrase. The sentences state that the games were often high-stakes substitutes for war, and it was not uncommon for players to suffer serious injuries at the hands (and sticks) of others. These statements describe the fierce nature of the games, and suggest that players would not hesitate to resort to violent tactics to score, *by any means necessary.* Choices **d** and **e** are true and mentioned in the passage, but they do not fit in context with the phrase.

1141. e. The author's primary purpose in writing this passage is to illustrate the importance of these games in Native American culture. The author does this by giving examples of the spiritual and peacekeeping significance of the games to the Native Americans. The passage does inform us that lacrosse evolved from these ancient games, but it does not specifically describe any aspect of modern lacrosse or any other sport; therefore, choices **a** and **c** are incorrect. Choices **b** and **d** are both mentioned by the author, but they are not the main subjects of the passage, and nowhere in the passage does the author condone or condemn the violence of the games.

1142. e. Glimpsing a piece of the past (choice **a**), glorifying athletes (choice **b**), disparaging segregation (choice **c**), and learning some tennis history (choice **d**) are all story elements that support the main purpose of the passage: To tell the story of Althea Gibson, the woman who broke the color barrier in professional tennis (choice **e**).

1143. a. The word *bucolic* is most often used to describe something typical of or relating to rural life. If you did not know what bucolic meant, there are contextual clues to help you. In lines 11–13, the passage tells us that Althea was born on a *cotton farm* and her father was a *sharecropper*. Also, in lines 13–14, the author contrasts the *bucolic Silver* with New York City's *urban bustle*.

1144. e. The passage states that Althea Gibson was a two-time Wimbledon champion. However, the passage does not offer the number of defeats, if any, she suffered at Wimbledon in her career.

1145. a. Althea's accomplishments in 1949 and 1950 should have earned her an invitation to the 1950 U.S. Nationals, but her efforts and the ATA's efforts to secure an invitation from the USTLA fell on deaf ears (lines 52–55). It was not until the national uproar spurred by Alice Marble's editorial (lines 57–64) that the USTLA, buckling under the weight of public pressure (choice **a**), relented and extended Althea an invitation to play.

1146. c. Althea was an extraordinarily gifted athlete, yet because of the color of her skin and the time in which she lived, her path to success from the very beginning was obstructed by segregation and discrimination. Althea was not allowed to practice on public tennis courts (lines 45–46), was barred from USLTA-sponsored events (line 55), and was refused hotel rooms and restaurant reservations (lines 74–75). Althea's ability to put these distractions aside and excel was a triumph of mental toughness, and the author uses the quote on line 80 to illustrate that fact.

1147. b. When looking at questions such as this one, it's important to think each choice through before hastily picking an answer. This question has two tough distracters: choices **c** and **d**. At first glance, choice **c** seems like a good pick, but the word *immediate* is what makes it incorrect. Althea Gibson's achievements were certainly victories for the Civil Rights movement, but in lines 6–7 it is stated that the color barrier *did not come tumbling down overnight*. Choice **d** is attractive, but Althea did not take on the world alone. The ATA and people like Dr. Eaton and Alice Marble all had a hand in guiding and assisting Althea on her pioneering path. Choice **e** is incorrect because Althea's historic achievements on and off the court were groundbreaking, and she accomplished it all in the face of adversity.

1148. b. Alice Marble believed that talent should decide who can be a champion, not race. Nowhere in her comments did Alice Marble say baseball, football, and boxing are more entertaining than tennis (choice **a**), or that there were undeserving players in the U.S. Nationals (choice **c**). Nor did she propose that the USLTA make the tournament open to anybody (choice **d**).

1149. d. Althea's friend probably suggested that Althea try lawn tennis because she was a champion paddle tennis player and enjoyed the sport very much (lines 16–19). The other choices either don't make sense or are not supported by facts from the passage.

1150. e. In lines 71–75, the passage states that Althea won a total of 11 Grand Slam titles in her career. However, nowhere in the passage does it state that those 11 titles were a record number for a female.

1151. e. The answer is found in line 57 of the passage. Chick Gandil first approached the gambler with his scheme, and then recruited the seven other players.

1152. b. *Parsimonious* is a word used to describe someone who is frugal to the point of stinginess. Comiskey's pay cuts (line 27), bonus of cheap champagne (line 32), refusal to launder uniforms (lines 33–34), and his benching of Eddie Ciccotte (lines 42–44) are all clues that should help you deduce the answer from the given choices.

1153. b. Answering this question involves a bit of deductive reasoning. Though the actual name of the ballpark is never given in the passage, lines 20–21 state that the 1917 White Sox won the World Series *playing in a park named for their owner.*

1154. a. As it is used in line 54, *thrown* means to have lost intentionally. The answer to this question is found in lines 58–59: *for $100,000 Gandil would make sure the Sox lost the Series.*

1155. c. Lines 14–16 state: *Between the years 1900 and 1915 the White Sox had won the World Series only once,* and then lines 20–21 tells us they won it again in 1917. Be careful not to mistakenly select choice **d**, three; the question asks for the number of World Series the Sox *won,* not the number of Series played.

1156. d. In lines 42–44, the author states that *after Ciccotte won his twenty-ninth game he was benched by Comiskey for the rest of the season.* Choice **d** asks for the number of games he *pitched.* It is stated that he pitched and won 29 games in 1919, but the passage doesn't mention the number of games he pitched in that he lost, if any, so you can't know for sure.

1157. b. *Ignominious* is a word used to describe something marked with shame or disgrace, something dishonorable. The *ignominious label* referred to in lines 70–71 is Black Sox—the nickname the Chicago press took to calling the scandalized and disgraced White Sox team.

1158. c. It is stated throughout the passage Comiskey was a frugal man, yet lines 75–76 say that he paid for the players' defense lawyers. Why? The answer to that and the biggest clue to answering this question lies in the last sentence of the passage: *Comiskey's once-mighty team was decimated by the loss of its most talented players, and the 1921 White Sox finished the season in seventh place.*

1159. b. Lines 45–50 state that gamblers would often target *the lower-paid athletes* and *the money with which these gamblers tempted the players was hard to refuse.* The passage tells that due to Charles Comiskey's stinginess with his players, *there were many underpaid players on the White Sox who were dissatisfied* (lines 60–61) and they *were the most discontented* team in baseball (line 35). These factors suggest that if Charles Comiskey had treated his players better, perhaps they might not have been so eager to betray him.

1160. a. In lines 34–35, the narrator of Passage 1 mentions *At sea we do meet with rough weather at times.* In Passage 2, lines 44–45, the boy recounts that his boat *ran into a vicious Atlantic storm. The waves tossed the Alba around like it was a tiny raft.* Choice **d** may seem like an attractive answer, but there is only evidence that the *Alba* leaks (line 47), not the yacht, and the question requires support from *both* passages.

1161. c. In the last sentence of Passage 2, the narrator questions his decision to take the voyage aboard the *Alba* by asking himself *What have I gotten myself into?* This self-doubt indicates that he believed his decision might have been a mistake. This choice best answers the question.

1162. d. In lines 2–3, the author of Passage 1 tells of *the beautiful property of the Earl of Mount Edgcumbe* and implores readers to visit Plymouth if they ever get the chance. He then goes on to describe the bustling harbor at Plymouth and finishes with: *there is a great deal to see at Plymouth besides the sea itself* (lines 8–9). In short, he describes all the interesting sights to behold at Plymouth. All the other choices either do not make sense or are not specifically supported by details from the text.

1163. b. In lines 11–12 of Passage 1, the narrator states that the yacht is a particular type of ship known as a cutter. In lines 14–15 of Passage 2, the Captain explains to his nephew that the *Alba* is cutter, as well. In that same conversation the nephew learns that all cutters share a similar trait: They possess *only a single mast* (line 15). Therefore, choice **b** is the correct answer.

1164. d. When answering this question, the key is to be sure to find the only choice that is supported by specific examples from the text. Nowhere in the text of Passage 1 does it state that the yacht carries cargo, but on the other hand it never mentions the fact that it does not. The same reasoning goes for choices **b**, **c**, and **e**. The yacht may be bigger and faster than the *Alba*, and the *Alba* may carry only crew, but these facts are never mentioned in the texts so we can't know for sure. That leaves only one possible answer: choice **d**. The yacht is most certainly more luxurious than the *Alba*, and this statement is backed by both narrators' descriptions of the their respective vessels.

1165. e. The captain knew it was important that the crew understood the boy was no more privileged than anyone else aboard the *Alba*. Evidence for this choice is found in the narrator's statement in lines 10–11: *because I was his nephew, I would probably have to work twice as hard as the others to prove my worth.* All the other choices do not make sense or are not backed by specific examples from the text.

1166. a. As used in Passage 1, line 26, the verb *repair* most closely means take themselves, or more simply, go. Today, repair is most commonly used as a verb that means to fix something (choice **b**). However, in the context of the sentence, this makes no sense. The easiest way to answer this question is to replace *repair* in the sentence with each the answer choices, and see which one fits best in context. By doing this, you should narrow down your choice to just one: choice **a**.

1167. c. The narrator's familiarity with yachts and the harbor at Plymouth (lines 1–12) in Passage 1 seems to indicate that he is an experienced yachtsman. He reveals his passion for yachting in lines 17–18, when he declares, *Of all amusements, give me yachting.* All the other answer choices either do not make sense or are not supported by specific examples from the text.

1168. e. Nigel probably had rotten or missing teeth. The narrator of Passage 2 chose to describe Nigel's smile as *a graveyard of yellow sincerity,* describing his yellow teeth as tombstones in a graveyard. When a writer uses a descriptive word or phrase in place of another to suggest a similarity between the two, this figure of speech is called a metaphor (choice **e**). If the boy had instead said, Nigel's smile was "*like a graveyard of yellow sincerity,*" it would have been a simile (choice **b**).

1169. a. Both passages are basically concerned with a similar situation—life aboard a cutter. The author of Passage 1 sets a pleasurable tone in the first paragraph by describing the idyllic scene at Plymouth and the anchored yacht. He later describes the yacht as *tasteful, elegant,* and *luxurious* (lines 23–24), and the smell of the food *delightful* (line 33). In stark contrast, the boy narrator in Passage 2 begins the passage by describing the menacing façade of his uncle and the immediate reality check the boy receives when he steps aboard (lines 6–9). His description of the heat and smell belowdecks (lines 20–22) and the horrible food (lines 33–35) effectively sets the dark and oppressive tone of the passage. Together, these two very different descriptions prove that the reality of two seemingly similar situations can often be extremely different (choice **a**).

1170. b. The word *berth,* when used as a noun, often refers to the sleeping quarters aboard a boat or a train. In lines 39–43 of Passage 2, the boy describes his berth as the place where *I* could *stow my clothes, and at night we would string up our hammocks.*

1171. d. To *posit* means to suggest. In this context, Hlusko suggests that grass stalks may have caused the grooves on early hominid teeth.

1172. d. The passage states that modern toothpicks are made of wood (line 11).

1173. b. Dr. Hlusko is described a being *convinced that she was on the right track* and *patiently* rubbing a baboon tooth with a grass stalk *for eight hours.* Both point to a persistent approach.

1174. b. In lines 19–20, the author states, *It seems that our early human ancestors may have used grass, which was easily found and ready to use, to floss between their teeth.* The use of *may* indicates that the author is not absolutely certain, but as the author does not suggest anything to contradict Dr. Hlusko's findings, we can conclude that the author finds her theory very probable.

1175. e. The passage clearly states that *the median income of the population as a whole does not vary much in real terms from one year to the next.* From this statement one can infer that, in general, income across the United States stays about the same.

1176. d. A thesis is an assertion, or theory, that the author intends to prove. The author of this passage is not making an assertion; rather, he or she is neutrally explaining information gathered in the U.S. Census.

1177. e. The passage clearly states that in the 1990s *fewer people saw their income grow than in the 1980s.* Choices **a** and **b** are incorrect because they do not include a comparison to the 1980s. Choices **c** and **d** are incorrect because the passage does not discuss *amount* of income, only change in income.

1178. e. The passage defines *top of the economic ladder* as families with high income-to-poverty ratios. From this, one can conclude that the economic ladder is the range of incomes from poverty to wealth.

1179. a. The tone is dry, in that the language is spare. The author does not use many adjectives, or any metaphors or other rhetorical flourishes. The author is neutral. Nowhere in the passage does he or she assert a point of view. Although the author uses statistics, the tone is not most accurately described as statistical.

1180. b. The passage clearly states that *potlatch* is a gift-giving ceremony. The author explains that *potlatch* is a generic word for the ceremony that comes from a shared trading language, while each nation has its own specific word for *potlatch.*

1181. a. The passage states that guests were expected to give a potlatch with gifts of equal value to what they received. This arrangement can best be described as reciprocal. The other choices are not supported by the passage.

1182. d. The author describes the ceremony in mostly neutral terms but in the last paragraph emphasizes the positive aspects of the tradition, which indicates a degree of respect.

1183. e. The passage explicitly states in lines 15–16 that a man *will know by reputation all the men in his kula ring.* None of the other choices is explicitly stated in the passage.

1184. c. The passage states in lines 26–27 that the visitors are *seen as aggressors* and are met with *ritual hostility.* This indicates that the visitors and hosts are playing the roles of aggressor and victims. The author uses quotes to indicate that the hosts are not really victims, but might call themselves the victims in the exchange.

1185. d. Lines 17–22 state the ways in which a kula object gains value; special shells are not mentioned.

1186. a. The final paragraph of each passage explicitly states the ways in which these ceremonies, or rituals, maintain community ties. None of the other choices is true for both passages.

1187. b. Both authors specifically discuss the non-monetary value of each ceremony. In Passage 1, lines 33–36, the author states, *Giving wealth—not accumulating wealth, as is prized in Western culture—was a means of cementing leadership, affirming status, . . .* In Passage 2, lines 35–39, the author states, *The objects . . . have no value,* and yet, *this ceremonial exchange has numerous tangible benefits.* None of the other choices is supported by the texts.

1188. c. Both potlatches and the kula ring involve giving and receiving, and both of the societies that participate in these rituals can be described as traditional. The tone of the title in choice **e** is more whimsical than the serious tone of each passage. Choice **b** is incorrect because neither article draws conclusions about traditional societies in general.

1189. b. The sentence preceding this phrase discusses the homogeneous, or uniform, makeup of the student body in the 1960s. The author is using the word *lesson* ironically in that a lack of diversity is not something on which many educators would pride themselves.

1190. e. A *sea change* is a transformation. This can be inferred from the next sentence, which states that colleges adopted policies of affirmative action. Affirmative action is a transformation in college admissions.

1191. d. The author clearly states in lines 16–18 that President Johnson *aptly explained the reasoning behind affirmative action.*

1192. c. After stating that he or she considers the trend of abolishing affirmative action to be very dangerous, the author explains how a diverse student body makes classes *much richer.*

1193. a. According to the author, one of the main benefits of affirmative action is diversity in the classroom, and he or she states that this diversity has been *a boon to my experience as a teacher* (line 40). So, affirmative action has personally benefited the author. None of the other choices is supported by the passage.

1194. b. *Feasible* can mean capable of being done (possible) or capable of being used (suitable). In this context, the author is suggesting that, for many minorities, extracurricular activities and the like are not economically possible, that is they are unaffordable.

1195. c. The author expresses an opinion about affirmative action in a moderate, or reasonable, tone. The passage is neither dispassionate nor passionate, in that it expresses some emotion but not much. The author is not impartial, as he or she is expressing an opinion.

1196. e. It is diversity, the result of affirmative action, not affirmative action itself, that prepares students for the future (lines 51–53).

1197. b. The author's main argument for affirmative action is that the student body benefits from diversity. The final point is that students who have been exposed to *a broad spectrum of American society* (lines 51–52) are better prepared for their futures. The idea that diversity benefits a company and makes it better prepared to compete in marketplace most closely mirrors this reasoning.

1198. a. Lines 6–7 reveal that there are two rooms, and lines 9–10 describe the truck *delivering furniture downstairs.*

1199. b. Lines 1–5 state that after Pauline became pregnant, Cholly had acted like the early days of their marriage when he would ask *if she were tired or wanted him to bring her something from the store.* This statement suggests that Cholly had not done that for a while, and therefore had begun to neglect Pauline.

1200. e. Although there is a *state of ease* (line 5) in the relationship between Pauline and Cholly, there is intense loneliness for Pauline. There may be less tension in this state of ease, but there does not appear to be more intimacy, because the loneliness prevails. We can infer that *back home* she was living with her family, not Cholly, and that Pauline would expect her husband to fulfill her need for companionship.

► Read More!

If you're looking for good books to read during your recommended half hour daily reading session, we've provided a sampling of books to help you get started. On the list is nonfiction, memoir, fiction, reference, folklore, short stories, and modern fantasy. Take your pick! If nothing on our list strikes your fancy, you can always opt to read newspaper editorials and essays, book reviews, magazine articles, plays, fables, computer manuals, puzzles, song lyrics, and comic books.

Enrichment Reading List

Adams, Richard. *Watership Down* (New York: Macmillan, 1974).

Amazon Shorts Classics: free digital downloads of classic works.

Anderson, Laurie Halse. *Speak* (New York: Farrar Straus Giroux, 1999).

Amory, Cleveland. *The Cat Who Came for Christmas* (Boston: Little, Brown, 1987).

Bonham, Frank. *Durango Street* (New York: Dutton, 1965).

Burland, Cottie. *North American Indian Mythology* (New York: P. Bedrick Books, 1985).

Crane, Stephen. *The Red Badge of Courage* (Various editions).

DailyLit: This website sends free serialized e-mail installments of classic books (www.dailylit.com).

D'Aulaire, Ingri, and Edgar Darin. *Norse Gods and Giants* (Garden City, NY: Doubleday, 1967).

Gibson, William. *The Miracle Worker* (New York: Bantam, 1964).

Lawrence, Jerome, and Robert E. Lee. *Inherit the Wind* (New York: Bantam, 1960).

Lipsyte, Robert. *The Contender* (New York: HarperTrophy, 1967).

Mazer, Anne, ed. *Working Days: Short Stories about Teenagers at Work* (New York: Persea Books, 1997).

Meyers, Susan. *Pearson, a Harbor Seal Pup* (New York: Dutton, 1980).

Na, An. *A Step from Heaven* (New York: Puffin, 2003).

Newton, Suzanne. *I Will Call It Georgie's Blues* (New York: Puffin, 1990).

Shakespeare, William. *Romeo and Juliet* (Various editions).

Sidford, Jennifer Karin. *Letters to a Girl: A Perennial Celebration of Growing Up Female* (N.p.: Three Sons Publishing, 2005).

Sleator, William. *House of Stairs* (New York: Dutton, 1974).

Strasser, Todd. *The Wave* (New York: Dell Laurel-Leaf, 1981).

Steinbeck, John. *Of Mice and Men* (Various editions).

Taylor, Mildred. *Roll of Thunder, Hear My Cry* (New York: Dial, 1976).

Terban, Marvin. *Scholastic Dictionary of Idioms* (New York: Scholastic Reference, 1998).

Twain, Mark. *Tom Sawyer* (Various editions).

Wells, H.G. *The Time Machine* (Various editions).

Yep, Laurence. *Dragon of the Lost Sea* (New York: HarperCollins, 1982).

Glossary

action verb a verb that expresses thought or activity.

active reader a reader who actively connects with what he or she reads.

adjective a part of speech that modifies a noun or pronoun. Adjectives answer *What kind? Which one? How much? How many?* about a noun.

adverb a part of speech that modifies a verb, an adjective, or other adverb. Adverbs answer *Where? When? How much? How many?* about the verb, adjective, or other adverb.

chronological order a structure of writing in which the author presents events in sequence, or the time order in which they happened.

clue phrase a group of words that gives a clue to the author's structure or point of view.

clue word a word that gives a clue to the author's structure or point of view.

colon (:) the punctuation mark that comes before a series, a lengthy quotation, or an example, or after the salutation in a business letter.

comma (,) the punctuation mark that separates words, phrases, clauses, and items in a series.

compare to look for ways things are alike.

complex sentence a sentence that is made up of an independent clause and a subordinate (dependent) clause.

compound-complex sentence a sentence that is made up of more than one independent clause and at least one subordinate clause.

compound sentence a sentence that contains at least two independent clauses with no subordinate (dependent) clauses.

compound subjects two or more subjects that share the same verb in a sentence.

compound word two or more separate words put together to create a new word. Compound words may be joined into one word or hyphenated.

conclusion the final paragraph in an essay, in which the writer restates the main idea, summarizes the main points, and closes with a value statement to bring effective closure to the essay.

conjunction a word that connects words or groups of words together.

connotation the suggested or implied meaning of a word.

contrast to look for how things are different.

dangling modifier a word or phrase that is meant to modify a specific part of the sentence, but has not been written next to that part, thus altering the meaning of the sentence.

demonstrative pronoun a word such as *this*, *that*, *these*, and *those* that is used to replace a specific noun in a sentence.

denotation the exact meaning of a word.

diction an element of writing style—the author's choice of words.

direct object the noun or pronoun that receives the action of the verb.

direct quotation the exact spoken or written words of a person, enclosed in quotation marks.

effect what happens as a result of something else.

emotional appeal an argument that appeals to the reader's emotions.

exclamation point (!) the punctuation mark that indicates strong emotion.

fact something that can be proven to be true.

figurative language words that do not have their literal meaning.

first person a point of view in which the narrator is a character in the story.

future tense a verb tense that implies that something hasn't happened yet, but will.

homonyms two distinct words with their own meanings but spelled and pronounced alike.

homophones two distinct words with their own meanings and spellings but pronounced alike.

hyphen (-) the punctuation mark that joins or separates numbers, letters, syllables, and words for specific purposes.

imperative sentence a sentence that expresses a request or command. The subject of any imperative sentence is always *you*, whether stated or understood.

implied main idea a main idea that is not explicitly stated.

indefinite pronoun a part of speech such as *no one*, *anyone*, *anybody*, or *somebody* that refers to a noun, but not a specific one.

independent clause a group of words that contains a subject and a predicate (verb) and can stand by itself as a sentence.

infinitive a verb written in the form of *to* plus the verb (e.g., *to walk*) that acts as a noun, an adjective, or an adverb in a sentence.

interjection a word or phrase that expresses strong emotion or feelings.

introduction the opening paragraph of an essay that draws the reader in and introduces the main idea and subtopics that will be explored.

literature a form of writing such as poems, novels, short stories, and plays.

logical appeal an argument that appeals to a reader's sense of reason.

main idea what a selection is mostly about.

misplaced modifier a word or phrase that is placed too far from the noun or verb it is modifying, thus altering or confusing the meaning of the sentence.

modifier a word that describes or clarifies another word. Adjectives modify nouns. Adverbs modify verbs, adjectives, and other adverbs.

noun a part of speech that names a person, place, or thing (including ideas and feelings).

object of a preposition (OOP) the noun or pronoun that follows a preposition, completing a prepositional phrase.

opinion   a belief.

order of importance   a text structure in which ideas are arranged based on how important they are.

parentheses [( )]   the punctuation marks that set off information that is not necessary to the surrounding sentence or words.

participle   a verb form that can be used as an adjective.

past tense   a verb tense that implies that something has already happened.

period (.)   the punctuation mark found at the end of a declarative sentence, an imperative sentence, and an indirect question, and in abbreviations.

personal pronoun   a part of speech such as *I, you, me, he, him, she, her, it, they, them,* and *we* that refers to the speaker, the person or thing being spoken about, or the person or thing being spoken to.

perspective   the point of view from which something is written.

phrase   a group of words that does not have a subject and a verb. Phrases can act like various parts of speech (noun, verb, adjective, adverb, or preposition).

point of view   the first-person, second-person, or third-person perspective from which something is written.

predicate   the action that the subject performs in a sentence; a verb plus any objects or modifiers.

preposition   a part of speech that shows the relationship of a noun or pronoun to another word in the sentence in terms of time and/or space.

prepositional phrase   a phrase beginning with a preposition and ending with a noun or pronoun (the object of the preposition).

present tense   a verb tense that implies action happening in the present or an action that happens constantly.

pronoun   a part of speech that takes the place of a noun.

proper noun   a specific noun that is capitalized.

punctuation   a set of special symbols that helps to convey to the reader the tone and pace of a writer's voice.

question mark (?)   the punctuation mark that appears at the end of an interrogatory sentence (a question).

quotation marks (" ")   the punctuation marks that indicate the exact words of a speaker or another writer or that convey irony in a writer's words.

run-on sentence   a sentence in which two or more complete sentences have been improperly punctuated and joined together.

second person   a point of view in which the reader is directly referred to as *you*.

semicolon (;)   the punctuation mark that joins two independent clauses that share a similar idea and are not already joined by a conjunction.

sentence   a group of words that has a subject and a predicate and expresses a complete thought.

sentence fragment   an incomplete thought that has been punctuated as a complete sentence.

sentence structure   an element of writing style—kinds of sentences an author uses.

simple sentence   an independent clause.

subject   topic, or what the text is about.

subject-verb agreement   the rule that the subject and verb of a sentence must agree in number and in person.

subordinate clause   a group of words that has a subject and a verb but cannot stand alone as a complete thought; also known as a *dependent clause.*

superlative   a comparative form of an adjective or adverb that implies the greatest degree when compared to something else. Superlatives typically end with the suffix *-est.*

theme the main message or messages that a piece of literature promotes. A story can have multiple themes.

thesis a statement in an essay that conveys the main idea or point.

third person a point of view in which the narrator is not a character in the story.

tone the perspective from which something is written, such as seriously or humorously.

topic the subject or main idea of an essay.

topic sentence a sentence that expresses the main idea of a passage.

verb a part of speech that expresses action or the condition (state of being) of the corresponding noun or pronoun. Verb tense can indicate the time of the action or condition.

NOTES

NOTES

NOTES

NOTES

NOTES

NOTES

NOTES

NOTES